Land of Blue Helmets

The publisher gratefully acknowledges the generous support of the Ahmanson Foundation Humanities Endowment Fund of the University of California Press Foundation.

Land of Blue Helmets

THE UNITED NATIONS AND
THE ARAB WORLD

EDITED BY

*Karim Makdisi and
Vijay Prashad*

UNIVERSITY OF CALIFORNIA PRESS

University of California Press, one of the most distinguished university presses in the United States, enriches lives around the world by advancing scholarship in the humanities, social sciences, and natural sciences. Its activities are supported by the UC Press Foundation and by philanthropic contributions from individuals and institutions. For more information, visit www.ucpress.edu.

University of California Press
Oakland, California

Library of Congress Cataloging-in-Publication Data

Names: Makdisi, Karim, 1970– editor. | Prashad, Vijay, editor.
Title: Land of blue helmets : the United Nations and the Arab world / edited by Karim Makdisi and Vijay Prashad.
Description: Oakland, California : University of California Press, [2017] | Includes bibliographical references and index.
Identifiers: LCCN 2016008400 | ISBN 9780520286931 (cloth : alk. paper) | ISBN 9780520286948 (pbk. : alk. paper) | ISBN 9780520961982 (ebook)
Subjects: LCSH: United Nations—Middle East—History.
Classification: LCC JZ4997.5.M54 L36 2017 | DDC 355.3/5709174927—dc23
LC record available at http://lccn.loc.gov/2016008400

Manufactured in the United States of America

25 24 23 22 21 20 19 18 17 16
10 9 8 7 6 5 4 3 2 1

CONTENTS

Acknowledgments ix

List of Abbreviations xi

Introduction 1
Karim Makdisi and Vijay Prashad

PART ONE
DIPLOMACY

1 · The Role of the UN Secretary-General:
A Historical Assessment 21
Andrew Gilmour

2 · Palestine, the Third World, and the UN as
Seen from a Special Commission 58
Lori Allen

3 · On Behalf of the United Nations: Serving as
Special Rapporteur of the Human Rights
Council for Palestinian Territories Occupied since 1967 74
Richard Falk

4 · The UN Statehood Bid: Palestine's Flirtation
with Multilateralism 95
Noura Erakat

5 · The Wrong Kind of Intervention in Syria 115
Aslı Bâli and Aziz Rana

PART TWO

ENFORCEMENT AND PEACEKEEPING

6 · Constructing Security Council Resolution 1701 in
Lebanon in the Shadow of the "War on Terror" 147
Karim Makdisi

7 · The UN Security Council and Ghosts of Iraq 170
Poorvi Chitalkar and David M. Malone

8 · Iraq: Twenty Years in the Shadow of Chapter VII 194
Coralie Pison Hindawi

9 · Libya: A UN Resolution and NATO's Failure to Protect 212
Jeff Bachman

10 · Peacekeeping and the Arab World: India's Rise and
Its Impact on UN Missions in Sudan 231
Zachariah Mampilly

PART THREE

HUMANITARIANISM AND REFUGEES

11 · The UN Human Rights Game and the Arab Region:
Playing Not to Lose 253
Fateh Azzam

12 · The Politics of the Sanctions on Iraq and the
UN Humanitarian Exception 278
Hans-Christof von Sponeck

13 · An Agency for the Palestinians? 301
Jalal Al Husseini

14 · Challenged but Steadfast: Nine Years with Palestinian
Refugees and the UN Relief and Works Agency 318
Filippo Grandi

15 · The UN High Commissioner for Refugees and the
Iraq Refugee Operation: Resettling Refugees, Shifting the
Middle East Humanitarian Landscape 335
Arafat Jamal

16 · The Syrian Refugee Crisis in the Middle East 359
Shaden Khallaf

17 · The Middle East: A Mandatory Return to
Humanitarian Action 372
Caroline Abu Sa'Da

PART FOUR
DEVELOPMENT

18 · The UN, the Economic and Social Commission for
West Asia, and Development in the Arab World 389
Omar Dahi

19 · The United Nations, Palestine, Liberation,
and Development 409
Raja Khalidi

20 · Peacebuilding in Palestine: Western Strategies in the
Context of Colonization 430
Mandy Turner

21 · The International Labour Organization and
Workers' Rights in the Arab Region:
The Need to Return to Basics 448
Walid Hamdan

22 · Peacekeeping, Development, and Counterinsurgency:
The United Nations Interim Force in Lebanon and
"Quick Impact Projects" 460
Susann Kassem

23 · The Protective Shields: Civil Society Organizations and
the UN in the Arab Region 481
Kinda Mohamadieh

List of Contributors 505
Index 511

ACKNOWLEDGMENTS

This book grew out of the United Nations in the Arab World research program directed by Karim Makdisi at the American University of Beirut's (AUB's) Issam Fares Institute for Public Policy and International Affairs (IFI). Thanks to the platform offered by IFI, the reputation of the AUB, and the dynamism of Beirut, scholars, students, affiliates, UN practitioners, diplomats and the general public mingled to explore and argue over the UN legacy and politics in the region.

We would like to acknowledge a number of people at IFI for their support. Rami Khouri—founding director of the IFI—facilitated the creation of the UN program, dug into his considerable networks, and ensured the uninterrupted funding of the program. Tarek Mitri, who succeeded Rami as IFI director as this book was taking off, shared his experience in, and knowledge of, the UN. Sarine Karajerjian's support in all administrative and financial aspects of the program was exemplary from the start. Dania Abbas, Rima Rassi, Rayan El-Amine, Nasser Yassin, Amir Richany, Zaki Boulos, Rabih Mahmassani, and Michael Huijer have all been of great assistance. Finally, and most importantly, we have relied on and benefited from the excellent UN in the Arab World program managers (and former AUB students) Muneira Hoballah, Susann Kassem, and Samar Ghanem, as well as a number of capable research assistants. They have been meticulous and stimulating colleagues.

For this book, special thanks and deep gratitude must go to Samar Ghanem. She often participated in the early brainstorming sessions with us, helped organize the book structure, read many of the chapters, and followed up diligently with the contributors.

Karim is grateful to Vijay, who first joined IFI's UN in the Arab World program as a senior fellow in 2014 and quickly worked his magic. Vijay's warm friendship, incredible enthusiasm, and infectious positivity have been invaluable. Karim thanks all the contributors, many of whom are colleagues and friends, for their fine essays, their valuable insights, and their goodwill during this long process. All my friends at the UN have shared their many experiences with me and sharpened my understanding of this "indispensable" institution, and I am grateful for that. To Filippo Grandi, thanks for spending your sabbatical year from the UN with us and for all the stimulating discussions and insights. To my dear friend Georges Nasr: you were taken much too early from your family and friends, and you are deeply missed. You exemplified all that is noble about service to the UN and all that is good in us. Tamerian and Dannoush, thanks for the support. Finally, Karim is very fortunate for the constant support of his parents Jean and Samir, his brothers Saree and Ussama, and above all his amazing wife Hala and daughters Layla and Iman. This is for them.

Vijay thanks Karim for bringing him along for the ride, introducing him to the world of the United Nations in the region, and helping him better understand the complexities of this institution. He is especially grateful to Rima Khalaf for her wise counsel. Nada al-Nashif, Walid Hamdan, Raja Khalidi, Rabi Bashour, Mustafa Said, and Omar Dahi played a central role in helping him find hope where none seemed possible. For Lisa, Zalia, and Rosa, again.

ABBREVIATIONS

3RP	Regional Refugee and Resilience Plan
ACTRAV	Bureau for Workers' Activities
AHDR	Arab Human Development Report
ANND	Arab NGO Network for Development
BDS	Boycott, Divestment, and Sanctions
BRICS	Brazil, Russia, India, China, and South Africa
BWIs	Bretton Woods Institutions
CAT	Convention against Torture
CEDAW	Convention on the Elimination of Discrimination against Women
CEDAW committee	Committee on the Elimination of Discrimination against Women
CIMIC	Civil Military Coordination
CPA	Coalition Provisional Authority
CRC	Convention on the Rights of the Child
CSOs	civil society organizations
DPKO	Department of Peacekeeping Operations
ESCWA	Economic and Social Commission for Western Asia
EU	European Union
FALD	Field Administration and Logistics Division
FSA	Free Syrian Army
GCC	Gulf Cooperation Council

HDI	Human Development Index
HRC	Human Rights Council
HRW	Human Rights Watch
IAEA	International Atomic Energy Agency
IBSA	India, Brazil, and South Africa
ICC	International Criminal Court
ICCPR	International Covenant on Civil and Political Rights
ICESCR	International Covenant on Economic, Social and Cultural Rights
ICPPED	International Convention for the Protection of All Persons from Enforced Disappearance
ICRC	International Committee of the Red Cross
ICRMW	International Convention on the Protection of the Rights of All Migrant Workers and Members of Their Families
IFIs	international financial institutions
IHL	international humanitarian law
ILO	International Labour Organization
IMF	International Monetary Fund
IS	Islamic State
ISIL	Islamic State of Iraq and the Levant
ISIS	Islamic State of Iraq and Syria
LAF	Lebanese Armed Forces
MDGs	Millennium Development Goals
MSF	Médecins sans Frontières/Doctors without Borders
NAM	Nonaligned Movement
NATO	North Atlantic Treaty Organization
NFZ	No-Fly Zone
NGO	nongovernmental organization
NIEO	New International Economic Order
OCHA	Office for the Coordination of Humanitarian Affairs

OFF	Oil-for-Food
OHCHR	Office of the High Commissioner for Human Rights
OIP	Office of the Iraq Program
OPCW	Organisation for the Prohibition of Chemical Weapons
OPEC	Organisation of the Petroleum Exporting Countries
OPT	Occupied Palestinian Territory
P3	The United States, the United Kingdom, and France
P5	Permanent Five: China, France, Russia, the United Kingdom, and the United States
PA	Palestinian Authority
PDP	Programme for the Development of the Palestinian National Economy
PEP	Paris Economic Protocol
PLO	Palestinian Liberation Organization
QIPs	Quick Impact Projects
R2P	Responsibility to Protect
SPLA	Sudan People's Liberation Army
SPLM	Sudan People's Liberation Movement
TCCs	Troop Contributing Countries
UAE	United Arab Emirates
UN	United Nations
UNAMI	United Nations Assistance Mission for Iraq
UNAMID	Joint African Union/UN Hybrid Operation in Darfur
UNCC	United Nations Compensation Commission
UNCCP	United Nations Conciliation Committee on Palestine
UNCTAD	United Nations Conference on Trade and Development

UNDP	United Nations Development Programme
UNEF	United Nations Emergency Force
UNESCO	United Nations Educational, Scientific and Cultural Organization
UNESOB	United Nations Economic and Social Office in Beirut
UNHCR	Office of the United Nations High Commissioner for Refugees
UNICEF	United Nations Children's Emergency Fund
UNIDO	United Nations Industrial Development Organization
UNIFIL	United Nations Interim Force in Lebanon
UNISFA	United Nations Interim Security Force for Abyei
UNMIS	United Nations Mission in Sudan
UNMISS	United Nations Mission in South Sudan
UNMOVIC	United Nations Monitoring, Verification and Inspections Commission
UNOHCI	United Nations Office of the Humanitarian Coordinator for Iraq
UNRWA	United Nations Relief and Works Agency for Palestine Refugees in the Near East
UNSCOM	United Nations Special Commission
UNSCOP	United Nations Special Committee on Palestine
UPR	Universal Periodic Review
USSR	Union of Soviet Socialist Republics
WFP	World Food Programme
WHO	World Health Organization
WMDs	Weapons of mass destruction

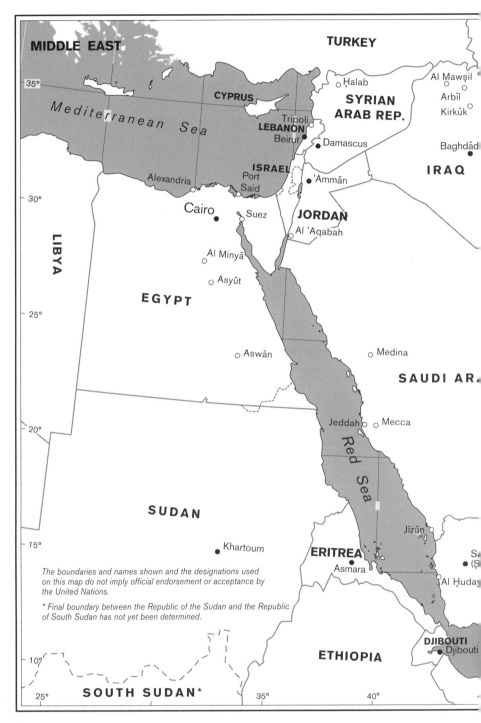

MAP I. Middle East, Map No. 4102 Rev.5, November 2011. Courtesy of the United Nations.

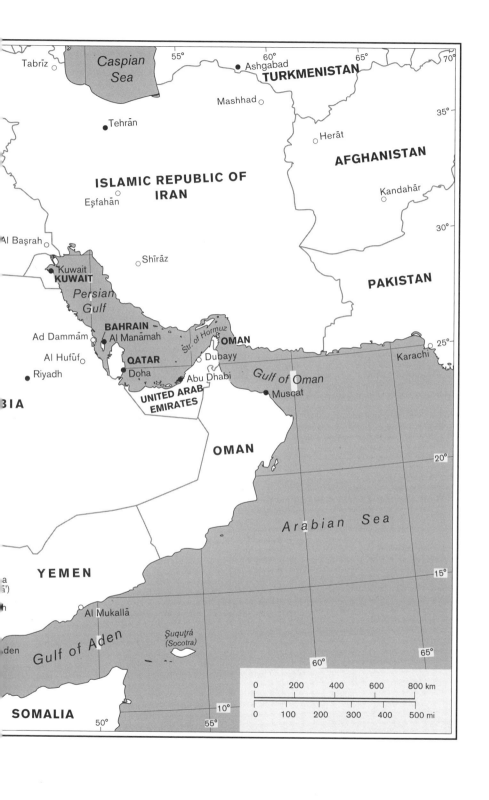

Introduction

Karim Makdisi and Vijay Prashad

SHAPED BY THE PALESTINE QUESTION

Born in 1945 in San Francisco, the United Nations cut its teeth in the Arab world. It hastened into action, unprepared, only two years after its creation when the British abandoned their obligations in Palestine under the League of Nations mandate. Pushed by the great powers that emerged dominant after World War II, a raw UN was asked to sort out what became its first mission and would remain its most enduring problem unresolved to this day. With a narrow majority, the UN General Assembly controversially partitioned Palestine over the vocal protests by the Arab and other states of the global South—then in a minority with the main decolonization period still around the corner.

Partition led to the first Arab-Israeli war in 1948 and the subsequent expulsion of hundreds of thousand of Palestinians from their homes. The declaration of the state of Israel, recognized immediately by the Soviet Union and the United States, put the various UN agencies in an impossible position. Palestinian refugees would need to be sheltered and taken care of until they would be—it was thought—permitted to return to their homes and an overall political solution was reached. As the Arab-Israeli conflict widened and Cold War lines hardened, the Security Council repeatedly failed in its primary objective of maintaining peace and security, leaving these fledgling UN agencies to mitigate the damage. This is where the UN remains today on the Palestine question, almost seven decades later.

Many of the early UN agencies were born of this conflict over Palestine, and many others yet would find themselves embroiled in it. Little that the UN did, or does, is not found in the narrow strip of land along the *mashriqi* (Levantine) coast, whether it be relief operations for the Palestinian refugees (the UN Relief and Works Agency [UNRWA]); observer missions and peace operations along the unsettled borders (the UN Truce Supervision Organization, the UN Emergency Force, the UN Disengagement Observer Force, the UN Interim Force in Lebanon [UNIFIL]); advisory opinions by the International Court of Justice (the "Construction of a Wall in the Occupied Palestinian Territory"); use of good offices by the secretary-general; fact-finding missions through the UN Human Rights Council; political negotiations and statehood bids at the UN General Assembly and Security Council; or participation in the post–Cold War "peace process" that was partially mediated by the UN, albeit through a distinctly ineffective role within the "Middle East Quartet."

The Palestine conflict introduced the idea of a political role for the special representative of the secretary-general (the Chinese official, Dr. Victor Hoo, whose role in 1946 effectively paved the way for what would become "peacemaking").[1] The struggle over Palestine produced the institutions of "peacekeeping" and of the "UN mediator" (with the appointment in 1948 of Count Folke Bernadotte, who, after his assassination in Jerusalem, was succeeded by the American Ralph Bunche, the first to receive a Nobel prize for such a role). "Peacekeeping" includes both the unarmed observer mission type (supervising the May 1948 truce) and the armed UN peacekeeping type (along the Egypt-Israel border following the Suez War of 1956). "Peacekeeping" was not mentioned in the UN Charter. For this reason, it required a special dispensation: the Dag Hammarskjöld peacekeeping doctrine with its core principles of consent of the parties, impartiality of the peacekeepers, and nonuse of force except in self-defense. Hammarskjöld's often-used term *Chapter Six and a Half* indicated that the phenomenon of peacekeeping would stand somewhere between peaceful resolution of disputes (Chapter VI of the UN Charter) and the use of force to restore peace and security (Chapter VII).

It is no wonder, therefore, that almost half the essays in this book cover the Palestine question, which has provided a mirror into the workings of the international community. UN special commissions came and went in Palestine, shows Lori Allen, but little moved in the way of an emancipatory politics. Reading the UN as a site where "the world" is imagined, Allen argues that it has been a venue both for making political claims and for offering hope. Ilana Feldman's work suggests that the creation of the very first UN peacekeeping force in 1956 along the Gaza-Israeli border represented a new way of thinking about international engagement in the cause of humanity and helped shape the basic principles of peacekeeping.[2]

Filippo Grandi and Jalal Al Husseini show us the contradictions between the UN's essential humanitarian role in advocating for Palestinians and its failure in the more political process of ensuring their self-determination. In his deeply personal essay, Grandi, the former commissioner-general of the UN agency tasked to manage Palestinian lives (UNRWA) and the current UN High Commissioner for Refugees, bears witness to the everyday struggles and resilience of refugees and explores why leading this agency is a "unique experience" and one of the UN's most challenging managerial tasks. For his part, Al Husseini offers insight into the interplay between humanitarian/developmental concerns of UNRWA and the political interests of the donors, host countries, and the refugees themselves. He suggests that this agency has become a site of contest among the different players and agendas.

The contemporary conflict around Palestine continues to draw the UN in and to expose the UN contradictions further as a site of conflict rather than a monolithic organization. Richard Falk's essay reflects on his role as special rapporteur on the situation of human rights in the Palestinian territories occupied in 1967, a position in the UN Human Rights Council. He details the controversies and pressures attached to this job and shows that the "UN" comprises different layers, agendas, and interests: while the secretary-general in New York, Falk says, permitted personal attacks against him, the leadership and professionals of the Office of the High Commissioner for Human Rights in Geneva strongly supported his efforts in what he calls the "legitimacy war." Noura Erakat's essay focuses on the latest Palestinian "statehood" bid at the UN starting in 2011, over fifty years after partition. She demonstrates that this bid marked the potential Palestinian leadership's return to the multilateral forum provided by the UN, a primary site of Palestinian advocacy until the start of the US-dominated "peace process" initiated at Oslo during the 1990s.

Part of the unresolved Palestinian conflict is of course the four-decade-long battle over southern Lebanon, where first Palestinian, then Lebanese resistance forces fought over land and narratives, culminating in the seminal 2006 Lebanon-Israel war that has produced a "balance of terror." Karim Makdisi's essay argues that the war on terror gave global meaning to this confrontation and to the construction of UN Security Council Resolution 1701, which authorized a more robust mandate to the long-standing peacekeeping mission in southern Lebanon (UNIFIL) that had largely gained, over two decades, the trust of the local population. He shows that Israel's failure to defeat Hizbullah in 2006 militarily resulted in Resolution 1701 comprising two contradictory narratives representing the battle for and against US domination, a battle that was transferred onto the Lebanese state. Susann Kassem's essay takes an ethnographic lens to zoom in at the practice of UNIFIL's post-2006 "Quick Impact Projects," small-scale and short-term development projects carried out with local municipalities. These projects, she argues, illustrate the mission's contradictions and its frequently thorny relations with the local population, who welcome the relief work but reject their underlying political objective of constructing a rival authority and influence to Hizbullah in southern Lebanon.

There is an increasing international acceptance that the US-led "peace process" for Palestine-Israel has failed. Violence is rife and occupation entrenched. Walid Khalidi has argued that no lasting reconciliation between Palestinians and Israelis is possible today without an acknowledgment of the deep historical context of the conflict. He warns that the dominant version of events in Israel and the West—that the UN partition plan was the start of the Palestinian problem, since Arabs rejected Israel—must be reconciled with the Palestinian narrative that the partition was a catastrophe (Nakba) that displaced enormous numbers of Palestinians from their homes.[3] In this sense, and with little hope of a political solution to the Palestine question in the near future, the UN has gradually moved toward nation building without national liberation. It is here that the keen analysis from Raja Khalidi and Mandy Turner come in, with both having looked carefully at the economic development of the Palestinian Authority and at the idea of peacebuilding.

Could Palestine, still under UN auspices, develop an economic agenda for the Palestinian people? Even the International Monetary Fund said in 2013 that the West Bank and Gaza Strip have a "dim" future unless "obstacles to economic growth" are removed through "a broad-based and sustained easing of Israeli restrictions, not linked to specific projects and underpinned by clear progress in the peace process."[4] The World Bank, as well, complained that development was not possible with checkpoints and other restrictions to movement.[5] Raja Khalidi's essay is premised on the kind of pessimism over conditions that even the International Monetary Fund and the World Bank recognize. For her part, Turner shows how the use of peacebuilding as a policy discourse and practice in the Palestinian territories has created what she terms a "zombie peace," an ambling corpse that "staggers on, refusing to die."

The Arab-Israeli wars dominated the UN's work in the region during the Cold War period (over 50 percent of peacekeeping missions worldwide were deployed there). In the post–Cold War era, there is no doubt that in Iraq, particularly after 1990, the UN faced its greatest challenge. The tragic great geopolitical game there ripped Iraq up over two wars (in 1990 and the 2003), a two-decade brutal UN sanctions regime, and a decade-long unremittingly bloody sectarian civil war. Indeed, no fewer than two new world orders were proclaimed at the UN in, or over, Iraq during this period. First President George H. W. Bush proclaimed the 1990 war to liberate Kuwait as the triumph of multilateralism embodied in the newfound activism of the UN Security Council, now equally liberated from Soviet checks and balances. Then President George W. Bush used Iraq as a main locus to prosecute the war on terror. Indeed one could add the more recent emergence of Islamic State of Iraq and Syria (ISIS) to the list of "international" problems that the wars in Iraq have produced.[6]

Before the UN resolutions to authorize the use of force against Iraq in 1990, the Security Council had used that authority only four times previously: once for the Korean War (1950), twice for the civil war in the Congo (1961), and once for the war in Rhodesia (1966). In the post–Cold War era, the West pushed the Council to use Chapter VII (use of force) resolutions with greater frequency. Iraq set the tone for the new era of use of force and sanctions. That is why some of the most powerful essays in this book are on the experience of the UN in Iraq. Poorvi Chitalkar and David Malone's essay speaks to the "Ghosts of Iraq," the lingering effects of the Security Council's engagement with Iraq over four decades. They show how this engagement has not only reflected wider patterns of international relations but also, crucially, *defined* them, and how learning from Iraq has changed the Council's approach to promoting international security.

Chitalkar and Malone's essay sets the tone for those that follow on the use-of-force resolutions (by Coralie Hindawi), on the sanctions regime (by Hans Christof von Sponeck, UN humanitarian coordinator for Iraq from 1990 to 2000), and on the refugees that then moved around the region in search of a provisional home (by Arafat Jamal, who served as the deputy head of mission for the main Iraq program of the UN High Commissioner for Refugees [UNHCR] in Jordan). Hindawi argues that rather than being reborn in Iraq after its demise during the Cold War (as was then loudly proclaimed), the UN collective security system was in fact buried again in Iraq as the Chapter VII regime became a trap from which Iraq had no chance to escape. Von Sponeck draws on his vast experience to vividly recount how the most comprehensive economic sanctions ever imposed by the United Nations (1990–2003) were implemented in "an iron-fist and an inhuman" way at the expense of the Iraqi civilians and traces how the humanitarian exception to these sanctions (via the innovative Oil-for-Food program) was overshadowed by powerful Western interests for regime change in Iraq. The UN was, in short, caught between geopolitical considerations and its humanitarian mission.

A seminal, traumatic moment for the UN in Iraq was on August 19, 2003, when a Kamaz truck settled near Baghdad's Canal Hotel, the UN headquarters since the 1990s. The truck bomb exploded and killed twenty-two people, including the UN special representative to Iraq, Sérgio Vieira de Mello. It was clear that the UN staff in the region had opposed an active UN mission in the country that was then under US occupation. The UN Secretariat had not been in favor of the 2003 invasion, and it did not want to be seen to be too close to what amounted to an illegal war and occupation. This was not to be. By the early 2000s, many UN agencies had little room to maneuver amid assertions in some quarters of the UN's irrelevancy in the war on terror era. However, Arafat Jamal argues forcefully that in the aftermath of the 2003 war's unprecedented, forced displacement of Iraqi refugees, UNHCR played a crucial (and unplanned) role in redefining the image of the UN by creating a space for international humanitarianism to take root in the region for the first time. The growing role for humanitarianism was, however, overwhelmed during the recent Syrian war as the extent of Syrian civilian displacement, and their voyages to settle somewhere safe, became epic.

It was the "ghost of Iraq" that lingered over the Syrian conflict during its first three years, making any effective UN action to resolve the war there impossible. But there was also the more recent ghost of the 2011 Libyan conflict—as Jeff Bachman shows. After Iraq, the West attempted to recover some of the legitimacy of humanitarian interventionism through the doctrine of Responsibility to Protect (R2P), accepted in principle by the UN member states in 2005 as part of the UN's mandate. R2P states that if civilians are threatened with serious harm in a conflict, and the state is unable or unwilling to protect them, then the international community has the responsibility to act. The test for R2P in the region came in Libya, where it was soon found, by member states such as China, India, and Russia, to have been misused.[7] Bachman argues that the intervention of the North Atlantic Treaty Organization (NATO) was predicated on an "ulterior motive exemption" that actually put civilians at greater risk and violated international law. The subsequent collapse of Libya into the morass of insecurity and violence has dented the idea of armed intervention as humanitarianism. After Iraq and Libya, it would be hard to get such a Chapter VII (use of force) resolution out of the UN Security Council.

In many of these recent wars that followed the Arab uprisings starting in 2010, the United Nations has become a convenient punching bag for all sides of the political spectrum. It is blamed if crises are not solved and if relief efforts fall short. In fact, as Richard Falk has shown elsewhere, the UN is always constrained by geopolitics, though it does serve as a site for struggle over legitimacy claims by warring factions.[8] Syria's intractable politics are placed squarely in the lap of the United Nations, as if the UN could itself cut through the Gordian Knot of geopolitical confusion and mendacity. In their essay, Aslı Bâli and Aziz Rana chart the politics that swirled around the UN as it sought to address the conflict's international security dimension, respond to the urgent humanitarian needs of the civilian population, and create a political framework for conflict resolution. Their essay cannot track the ongoing negotiations, but it does capture the essence. Clearly it is not the UN's fault that a political solution in Syria has not been found: the complexity of geopolitics, the regional dynamics set in motion in the aftermath of the US invasion of Iraq, the Arab Spring and the dangerous politics inside Syria have all played a part. Yet the UN is accused of being a failure. Such a view mystifies the UN and makes it appear far more powerful than it is.

The UN, however, has a more mundane and limited function than to fix all problems and solve all disputes. Bâli and Rana argue that unlike militarized intervention pursued contemporaneously by key states, only UN involvement retains the possibility or space for local and external parties to the Syrian conflict to negotiate a political settlement. The mediation attempts by UN envoys Kofi Annan, Lakhdar Brahimi, and Staffan de Mistura, for instance, tried to create space for Syria peace talks to proceed, and indeed some breakthroughs were reached in the Geneva meetings that brought together key international, regional, and local players in the conflict. Further possibilities were opened up when in September 2013, following a bilateral agreement between Russia and the United States, the Security Council authorized the Organization for the Prohibition of Chemical Weapons and the United Nations to establish a joint mission to eliminate Syria's declared

chemical weapons stockpile. Unprecedented international cooperation—
which involved complex land and maritime operations—and a willing Syrian
government seeking international legitimacy opened the way for the UN to
prove its worth when called upon. This "unique" mission, in the midst of a
civil war, achieved clear success by the summer of 2014. It did not, however,
have any impact on the larger political negotiations.[9] Those had to wait for the
2015 Russian intervention, which once again changed the geopolitics around
Syria and made space for UN involvement through the Russian-US entente.

POLITICS AROUND THE UNITED NATIONS

What is the United Nations? It is at least two different entities. The first and
most public face of the UN is the Security Council, which has come to stand
in as the executive of the UN body. It is made up of fifteen countries, five of
them permanent members (the P5: China, France, Russia, the United
Kingdom, and the United States) and the others elected by the UN General
Assembly for two-year terms. The P5 hold veto power over the decisions of
the Council, allowing any one of them to use their veto to scuttle a decision
not to their liking. The nonpermanent members are allocated on a fixed
regional basis: five for African and Asian States; two each for Latin American
and Western European (and other) States respectively; and one for Eastern
European States. By tradition, one of the seats allocated to Asia or Africa (on
a rotating basis) is held by an Arab state. The Security Council stands in for
the General Assembly, whose 193 members are able to pass resolutions that
try to set the tone for world opinion but that, in the post–Cold War period
in particular, are often ignored. The relationship between the Security
Council and the General Assembly is fraught, with the former seeing itself
as independently able to chart policy while the majority of the world's states
see the latter as the embodiment of a true democratic institution. The UN
General Assembly resolutions are unable to bind any discussion in the
Security Council, whose own resolutions can contravene those of the will of
the General Assembly, as the voting for the Palestine statehood bid in 2013
illustrated.

It is the task of the secretary-general to hold together the Security Council
and the General Assembly, the P5 and the rest of the planet. Andrew Gilmour
(who is currently director of the UN Secretary-General's Office for Political,
Peace-Keeping, Humanitarian and Human Rights) scans the history of the

secretary-generals and their work in the Arab world. As Gilmour explains, seven of the eight secretary-generals were confronted with Arab-Israeli wars, four faced Iraq, and every one of them had to deal with serious violence between Israel and some of its neighbors. We open the book with Gilmour's essay not only to provide a necessary historical sweep of the UN's work in the Arab world but also to show how the secretary-general has had to operate in the framework of international politics. Gilmour demonstrates that while secretary-generals do matter they have all too often been frustrated by (and scapegoated for) the unwillingness of the parties to resolve their problems and of other member states to play a constructive role in support of peace.

The second part of the UN is its myriad agencies, each set up to deal with the various crises of the modern age. Some of these agencies have histories that predate the UN itself. The International Labour Organization, for instance, was created in 1919 but was integrated into the UN system in 1946 to become the first specialized UN agency. Walid Hamdan shows how its work in the Arab world is constrained by regional politics—mainly the stranglehold of the Gulf countries over any discussion of labor reforms. Other agencies would follow: the UN Children's Emergency Fund (UNICEF), to advocate for the rights of children; the UN Educational, Scientific and Cultural Organization (UNESCO), to promote tolerance and respect for the world's cultures; and so on.

As the UN passed resolutions and drew up conventions, a wide range of specialized agencies developed to ameliorate the tragic conditions of modern life. These UN agencies provide relief and advocacy for refugees, move nuclear energy from war to peace, improve telecommunications around the world, provide development assistance, and many other functions. The range of work is impressive, although the outcomes tend to be more modest given the many challenges and limitations these agencies face, such as most obviously a dependency on funding from key states such as the United States. When the P5 do agree on an important task, such as eliminating Syria's chemical weapons, funding and political will become nonissues in the completion of the task. When they do not agree, there is paralysis. Zachariah Mampilly suggests another limitation, namely the uneven distribution of tasks in dangerous peacekeeping zones. In his essay on the peace operation in Sudan, Mampilly points to the alarming gap between peacekeeping contributor countries who provide troops (largely from the Third World) and the de facto peacekeeping policy makers (usually Western states). But anemic funds and uneven distribution of tasks result largely because of the contradictions among the P5, and between the P5 and the rest of the member states of the UN. It is, in the final analysis, the politics of the member states that has limited the potential of the United Nations as an institution.

POLITICAL ECONOMY OF THE UN

Over the past sixty years, the politics of the United Nations has depended upon the vicissitudes of global geopolitics. The historian Mark Mazower has traced the very idea of the UN to the British Empire's vision of world order embodied eventually through the creation of the League of Nations and then reborn in San Francisco in 1945.[10] Palestine's partition exemplified this order. In the throes of the Cold War, however, the animosity between the West and the East and the avenues for democracy in the United Nations system allowed the newly independent and assertive nations to insert their anti-imperial agenda into the interstices of the agencies and into the General Assembly.[11]

The Cold War between the United States and the USSR cooled the bonhomie of the early years in the UN. The USSR largely withdrew from the fray, taking the view that the West had already dominated the institutions. The main tussle in the UN in these early decades was, therefore, not between the United States and the USSR—which is what is almost always the assumption—but between the West and the Third World. There is no better testimony to this than the emergence of the Nonaligned Movement (1961), the UN Conference on Trade and Development (1964), and the Group of 77 (1964), the bloc of the South. These institutions—one of which was a UN specialized agency—would be the main sources of pressure on the West. The main arena of conflict was over the ideas of economic development, as represented by the General Assembly's *Declaration for the Establishment of a New International Economic Order* (1974), which was rejected by the Western bloc.

With the collapse of the USSR and the global debt crisis of the 1980s, the West seized power over the management of world affairs. Under the name of globalization, the West was able to push an ideological agenda in the various development agencies. The creation of the World Trade Organization and the marginalization of the UN Conference on Trade and Development illustrate this. By asserting itself through human rights interventionism, the West was able to bend the UN Security Council to its view of dangers in the world. The long conflict with Iraq from 1990 to the present highlights this. Political direction for the UN's work increasingly came from the Western capitals, with a UN bureaucracy often frustrated with the ideological nature of the demands on the agency. In the Arab world, the UN began to be seen increasingly as a hostile entity whose political, security, and development agendas represented Western interests. Even so, illustrating the UN's two worlds (Security Council and UN agencies), agencies such as UNICEF and UNESCO were fully accepted and continued to work as though they were part and parcel of local society.

Arab states, which had promised national development but held back, for the most part, on democracy, faced severe challenges in the 1980s. No longer could they subsidize food and provide employment in the state sector. Pressure from the Washington Consensus struck them hard. The national development agenda went by the wayside, as Omar Dahi shows. Weakened state policy on economic lines did not weaken the states themselves. Many became obdurate: much more harsh with repression, much less willing to consider alternatives. It is in this climate that the Arab Spring emerged, with a demand not only for greater political choices but also for economic justice. Here as well popular pressure played a role.

Human rights agencies and nonstate institutions began to make use of the UN—as Kinda Mohamadieh and Fateh Azzam show—to push the Arab regimes toward a more reasonable order. Azzam asserts that the Arab revolts starting in 2010 can be understood as a collective demand by citizens and civil society groups for a speedier implementation of a human rights–based approach in which the UN remains a crucially important forum to cajole Arab states. Mohamadieh suggests that Arab civil society groups have engaged with the UN in the region to conduct policy dialogue (otherwise denied them) with governments, hold them accountable, and advance alternative development narratives. In this sense, as in other cases illustrated in this book, the UN serves in a positive way as a site—otherwise absent—for national struggles and for legitimacy claims.

Still, broken politics on the world stage has made it extremely hard for the UN agencies to operate. Promises of funds come largely because of the gravity of the crises, but these funds are rarely delivered. Like Filippo Grandi's essay on UNRWA, Shaden Khallaf's essay on the Syrian refugee crisis shows us how the operations of the UN continue despite great financial challenges. She builds on her considerable experience with UNHCR to show how the extraordinary civilian suffering in Syria has engendered policy and funding challenges in formulating both emergency responses and longer-term developmental solutions that include host countries and communities as well. The UN has long-term commitments, which rely not only on long-term delivery of funds but on cooperation with member states—some of which might be implicated in the very problem that the UN seeks to address. Caroline Abu Sa'Da's critique of the UN from the standpoint of much more flexible agencies such as Doctors without Borders (MSF) should be taken very seriously but also seen in its context: MSF does not have the kinds of commitments that the UN must uphold in terms of long-term activity and working with member states. Perhaps the way to think of the UN and groups like MSF is that they do complementary work, not that one is more important than the other. Flexible and innovative approaches to acute crises are necessary, but so too are the more permanent linkages to member states to deal with chronic crises.

The contemporary history of the region is marked by political crises. The Palestine question and the Iraq war were catastrophes fueled by great-power intervention: their negative effects reverberate around the region. The breakdown of UN mediation efforts in Yemen, Libya, and Syria—and their descent into civil war fueled by regional powers such as Saudi Arabia and Iran—illustrate the crucial need for the Security Council, especially its P5, to fully understand the regional, national, and local milieu before attempting statebuilding exercises. Out of this chaos, nonstate players such as ISIS have carved out territory and power. War brings with it devastation: refugee crises, starvation, and social distress. Into the breach came the UN agencies. It was their task to make sure that the Arab world did not perish under the weight of its crises. The UN refugee agency worked to house and feed the Iraqi refugees, until of course host countries, such as Syria, became exporters of refugees themselves. Increasingly, Jordan and Lebanon became homes for refugees, first Palestinians and then Iraqis and Syrians. The UN's humanitarian relief soon became a substitute for the services of states in the region. Funding for this work has been inadequate. Money is easily raised for war but hard to obtain for the outcomes of war.

READINGS

The literature on the UN greatly expanded in the post–Cold War period in line with the complexity and reach of various UN missions and agencies. Indeed, the creation of the Academic Council on the United Nations System, and its prominent journal *Global Governance,* embodied this academic interest beyond individual institutes or case study analyses. However, there is remarkably very little *collective* work on the UN in the Arab world.

Perhaps more than any other project on the UN, Thomas G. Weiss and Rorden Wilkinson's coedited Global Institutions series for Routledge Press stands out as a comprehensive reference point for all matters of global governance, including the UN, with many dozens of volumes published over more than a decade. These cover, from a macro perspective, key international organizations, general concepts, and more in-depth knowledge in global governance. A small group of eminent scholars have worked over the years more specifically on a UN history project (a sixteen-volume project edited by Louis Emmerij, Richard Jolly, and Thomas Weiss for the University of Indiana Press), but this is mainly an institutional history of the UN rather than a history of UN engagement in this or that part of the world. Its titles are self-explanatory: *The Power of UN Ideas: Lessons from the First 60 Years* and *UN Voices: The Struggle for Development and Social Justice.*

Other prominent scholars have produced a growing number of general historical works (such as Mark Mazower's *No Enchanted Palace: The End of Empire and the Ideological Origins of the United Nations* or Stephen Schlesinger's *Act of Creation: The Founding of the United Nations*); dissection of seminal UN documents (such as William Durch et al.'s *The Brahimi Report and the Future of UN Peace Operations* or Gareth Evans's *The Responsibility to Protect: Ending Mass Atrocity Crimes Once and For All*); analyses of key UN agencies (such as Edward C. Luck's *The UN Security Council: Practice and Promise* and Alexander Betts et al.'s *The United Nations High Commissioner for Refugees (UNHCR): The Politics and Practice of Refugee Protection*); or textbooks (such as Thomas G. Weiss et al.'s *The United Nations and Changing World Politics,* Karen Mingst's *The United Nations in the 21st Century,* Sam Dawes and Thomas G. Weiss's *The Oxford Handbook on the United Nations,* or Alex Bellamy et al.'s *Understanding Peacekeeping*). Various UN practitioner biographies have also become more notable, including Kofi Annan's recent *Interventions: A Life in War and Peace* (co-written with Nader Moussavedeh), Brian Urquhart's *Ralph Bunche: An American Odyssey,* Marrack Goulding's *Peacemonger,* and Samantha Power's *Chasing the Flame: Sergio Vieira de Mello and the Fight to Save the World.*

UN books with a more regional focus have mainly been on Africa. Here there is an extensive literature. Adekeye Adebajo's edited volume *From Global Apartheid to Global Village: Africa and the United Nations* comprises thirty chapters on various aspects of the UN's work in Africa. Others have focused more particularly on peace operations in Africa, such as Adebajo's *UN Peacekeeping in Africa from the Suez Crisis to the Sudan Conflicts* and Wyss and Tardy's edited volume *Peacekeeping in Africa: The Evolving Security Architecture,* or on specific peace operations such as Funmi Olonisakin's *Peacekeeping in Sierra Leone: A History of UNAMSIL* and Severine Autesserre's *The Trouble with the Congo: Local Violence and the Failure of International Peacebuilding.* The genocide in Rwanda and violence in Darfur have been comprehensively covered in, among many other works, Michael Barnett's *Eyewitness to Genocide: The United Nations and Rwanda,* Romeo Dallaire's *Shake Hands with the Devil: The Failure of Humanity in Rwanda,* and Mahmoud Mamdani's *Saviours and Survivors: Darfur, Politics and the War on Terror.*

On the other hand, many scholars have built up a significant archive of writings on the UN's role in the Arab world. These include Ilana Feldman's *Governing Gaza: Bureaucracy, Authority and the Work of Rule, 1917–1967;* Lori Allen's *The Rise and Fall of Human Rights: Cynicism and Politics in Occupied Palestine;* Sari Hanafi et al.'s *UNRWA and Palestinian Refugees: From Relief and Works to Human Development;* Richard Falk's *The Costs of War: International Law, the UN, and World Order after Iraq;* Coralie Hindawi's *Vingt ans dans l'ombre du chapitre VII: Éclairage sur deux décennies de coercition à l'encontre de l'Iraq;* and David Malone's *The International Struggle over Iraq: Politics in the UN Security Council, 1980–2005.* Many of these authors are represented in this book. There have also been several case study books (such as Ramesh Thakur's *International Peacekeeping in Lebanon: United Nations Authority and Multinational Force*), biographies (including Emmanuel Erksine's *Mission with UNIFIL*), and of course essays on the region written for academic and policy forums by scholars prominent in UN studies.

We also have an enormous literature by practitioners, including UN staff, which is often buried in long reports or in UN resolutions that are read only by experts. Some UN reports, however, break out of these closed expert circles and become widely cited, from UN under-secretary-general Alvaro de Soto's leaked 2007 "End of Mission Report" that details his frustrations as UN special coordinator for the Middle East peace process, to the "Goldstone Report," which summed up the UN Human Rights Council's independent fact-finding mission into war crimes following Israel's 2009 war in Gaza; and the series of Arab Human Development Reports commissioned by the UN Development Programme that critiqued how the Arab world's knowledge deficits were holding back the region's "progress." Moreover, some key UN resolutions have themselves become considered as seminal in larger international political and legal terms, including the General Assembly's "Uniting for Peace" resolution—first used during the 1956 Suez war to bypass Security Council vetoes by France and the United Kingdom and establish the first peacekeeping mission, the UN Emergency Force; Security Council Resolution 242, which established the "land-for-peace" bargain in the aftermath of the 1967 Arab-Israeli war; and Security Council Resolution 1973, which resulted in the first military enforcement of the R2P doctrine during the 2011 NATO attacks on Libya.

There are also some useful memoirs by Arab diplomats who served in the UN that recount the logic and stories behind the role the UN played and the positions taken by Arab (and other) states at particular historical times, from Charles Malik's *Man in the Struggle for Peace* (1963) and Adnan Pachaghi's *Iraq's Voice at the United Nations, 1950–1969* to the more recent compilation by Lebanese ambassadors to the UN Ghassan Tueini and Nawaf Salam documenting their considerable experiences and Tarek Mitri's rich account of his experience as head of the UN mission in Libya. The UN's Oral History Archive has also become an important reference for practitioner voices from, and on, the region. In this regard, it seems clear that in a volume on the UN in the Arab world scholarly contributions must be supplemented by those of practitioners working in crucial moments of crisis in the region. Consequently, this book could not have been put together without the very important contributions of senior UN practitioners Andrew Gilmour, Hans Christof von Sponeck, Filippo Grandi, Fateh Azzam, Shaden Khallaf, Arafat Jamal, Raja Khalidi, Richard Falk, David Malone, and Walid Hamdan. They bring not only years of experience in the UN but also a keen analytical sense of the limitations of UN work. Indeed, their experiences and reflections clearly reveal that the UN is not just an institution but is made up of individuals whose work, often in struggle with others, matters.

Interest in the United Nations in the Arab world has grown exponentially as it has become apparent that the wars of the past decade and the war on terror in general have been quite good at generating instability but dangerously bad at setting the basis for peace. The UN has no magic bullet—indeed, it has been confronted with challenges that test its abilities. Public interest in the UN in the Arab region has not translated, however, into commensurate academic interest. Even in the region itself, and in Arabic, few in-depth academic works deal with the UN. Most of what is published in local Arabic journals or newspapers covers in more journalistic ways crucial moments of conflict: Iraq during the 2003 war, the Gaza wars and Palestine refugees, southern Lebanon, and more recently Syria. We hope very much that our book will spur more such work in both English and Arabic. Other research must follow, and more comprehensive attempts to capture the UN's role in the Arab world will be produced by our peers. In this regard, Riccardo Bocco and Nikolas Kosmatopolous's edited volume *Peace and Experts: Knowledge and the Politics of Peacemaking in the Middle East* (May 2016) uses ethnographic and historical approaches to argue that peacemaking by an array of institutions and actors working in the Arab world—including the UN—must be regarded primarily as a field of power, expert authority, and struggles for hegemony. Khouri, Makdisi, and Wählisch's 2016 volume *Interventions in Conflict: International Peacemaking in the Middle East* draws insights from renowned UN practitioners in the Middle East such as Lakhdar Brahimi, Filippo Grandi, and Jan Eliasson to contextualize and understand the obstacles and challenges in peacemaking in the region.

Our book is divided into four sections—Diplomacy; Enforcement and Peacekeeping; Humanitarianism and Refugees; and Development. We have chosen these themes as the most important elements of UN work in the region. In these sections, we have essays on several countries, from Iraq to Libya. We are aware of many gaps of emphasis and of coverage, but our aim has not been to take an encyclopedic approach. We have merely provided a window into the kind of work the UN does in the Arab world and the politics that frames this work. Our claim is that the UN is a constant feature in the Arab world and that the Arab world serves as a central location for the UN.

The critical approach taken by some of the authors in this book does not in any way take away from all the contributors' assumption—whether explicit or implicit—that the UN and its agencies are indispensable to the modern world order. What criticism does emerge, in fact, underscores this importance by exposing the gap between the core, noble objectives contained in the UN Charter and the all-too-often failure of member states (especially the more powerful ones) to pursue these goals when their political, security, financial, or economic interests are at stake. The UN staff, both in the Secretariat and in the field, navigate to the best of their abilities within this gap, while local citizens and movements in the Arab region and beyond cling to the promises contained in the Charter and make use of the UN as a site of struggle, even if they are otherwise disenchanted with the UN's role.

This book, finally, deals not only with the UN *in* the Arab world but also with the UN *as seen from* the Arab world. We think it important that the idea for this project was supported by and in the American University of Beirut's Issam Fares Institute for Public Policy and International Affairs, in a city (Beirut) that hosts the UN's regional commission (the Economic and Social Commission for Western Asia) and a vast array of UN agencies and key missions. It exemplifies the location of a dynamic interaction both between the local and the global and between the two levels of UN we have detailed in this volume. Thus we feel that this book adds to the general literature on the UN, and indeed connects UN studies with Middle East studies and studies in international affairs and global governance. Unlike other anthologies on the UN, moreover, this volume also draws considerably from voices located in and perspectives relevant to the Arab region, ones that even a quick glance at general books on the UN reveals are largely marginalized. This, we feel, makes this volume even more original and, we hope, useful.

NOTES

1. Manuel Frohlich, "The Special Representatives of the United Nations Secretary-General," in *Routledge Handbook of International Organization*, ed. Bob Reinalda (London: Routledge, 2013), 231–43.

2. Ilana Feldman, "Ad Hoc Humanity: Peacekeeping and the Limits of International Community in Gaza," *American Anthropologist* 112, no. 3 (2010): 416–29, and *Police Encounters: Security and Surveillance in Gaza under Egyptian Rule* (Stanford, CA: Stanford University Press, 2015).

3. Walid Khalidi, "Revisiting the UNGA Partition Resolution," *Journal of Palestine Studies* 27, no. 1 (Autumn 1997): 5–21; and Walid Khalidi, "The Hebrew Reconquista of Palestine," *Journal of Palestine Studies* 39, no. 1 (Autumn 2009): 24–42.

4. International Monetary Fund, "West Bank and Gaza: Staff Report Prepared for the September 2013 Meeing of the Ad Hoc Liaison Committee," September 11, 2013, 24, https://www.imf.org/external/country/WBG/RR/2013/091113.pdf.

5. World Bank, *Checkpoints and Barriers: Searching for Livelihoods in the West Bank and Gaza. Gender Dimensions of Economic Collapse* (Washington, DC: World Bank, 2010).

6. Vijay Prashad, *The Death of the Nation and the Future of the Arab Revolution* (Berkeley: University of California Press, 2016).

7. Vijay Prashad, "Syria, Libya and Security Council: An Interview with Hardeep Singh Puri, Permanent Representative of India to the United Nations," *Frontline,* PBS, March 10–23, 2012.

8. Richard Falk, "The UN in the Middle East, and the Arab Awakening," in *Interventions in Conflict: International Peacemaking in the Middle East,* ed. Rami G. Khouri, Karim Makdisi, and Martin Wählisch (New York: Palgrave Macmillan, 2016).

9. See Karim Makdisi and Coralie Hindawi, *Creative Diplomacy amidst a Brutal Conflict: Analyzing the OPCW-UN Joint Mission for the Elimination of the Syrian Chemical Weapons Program* (Beirut: Issam Fares Institute for Public Policy and International Affairs, 2016).

10. Mark Mazower, *No Enchanted Palace: The End of Empire and the Ideological Origins of the United Nations* (Princeton, NJ: Princeton University Press, 2009).

11. Vijay Prashad, *The Poorer Nations: A Possible History of the Global South* (New Delhi: LeftWord; New York: Verso, 2013); Branislav Gosovic, *The South Shaping the Global Future* (Bergen: Kolofon Press, 2014).

PART ONE

Diplomacy

———

ONE

The Role of the UN Secretary-General

A HISTORICAL ASSESSMENT

Andrew Gilmour

EVERY SECRETARY-GENERAL SINCE THE UNITED NATIONS' founding in 1945 has expended considerable energy on the Middle East. Most of the eight men who have held the position have also been significantly frustrated by—and at times unfairly scapegoated for—the unwillingness of the parties to resolve their problems and of other member states to play a truly constructive role in support of peace.

Seven of the eight were confronted with wars that pitted various Arab forces against Israel, four faced wars involving Iraq, and all had to deal with serious violence between Israel and one or more of its neighbors.[1] All eight tried to expand the UN's role in the region, and all were at times rebuffed by the parties and their backers for trying to do too much, while at the same time they were excoriated for not managing to do more. Each was simultaneously accused by some of being pro-Arab and by others of being pro-Israeli.

This chapter surveys the key activities undertaken by each secretary-general in the Middle East and draws some lessons and comparisons.

TRYGVE LIE (1945–53)

Exhausted by the Second World War and under growing pressure from both Arabs and Jews, as well as their outside backers, the British government—the mandatory power since a 1922 decision by the League of Nations—decided to withdraw from Palestine. In January 1947, the leader of the opposition, Winston Churchill, attacked the government: "It is said we must stay, because if we go there will be a civil war. I think it very likely, but is that a reason we should stay? The responsibility for stopping civil war in Palestine ought to be borne by the United Nations and not by this overburdened country." Unless the Americans came in to share the "bloodshed, odium, trouble and worry, we will lay our mandate at the feet of the United Nations."[2]

Thus dumped, Palestine became the first major challenge faced by the fledgling world organization. The Norwegian trade unionist who became the first secretary-general of the UN, Trygve Lie, immediately saw the need for an active involvement. As he later put it, if the great powers accepted that the situation in the Middle East could best be settled by leaving the forces concerned to fight it out among themselves, it was clear they would be tacitly admitting that the UN was "a useless instrument in attempting to preserve peace."[3]

Lie became deeply committed to the two-state solution known as the Partition Plan and urged member states to support it even though he was strongly criticized by Arab representatives. So committed did he become that he was outraged when the United States started to have second thoughts about this solution and flirted with the idea of a temporary trusteeship. He described this American reversal as a blow to the UN and stated, "It wounded me deeply."[4] He threatened to resign, though he was dissuaded from it, and in any case the United States reverted to the Partition Plan.

In 1949, Lie also worked behind the scenes to secure votes for Israel's admission to the UN—a policy at odds with that of his successors as secretary-general, who have almost invariably treated UN membership issues (in particular the highly contentious issue of Palestinian membership) as a matter for member states alone, rather than the Secretariat. For the rest of his term in office, and indeed his life, Lie considered the way Palestine was handled a great success for the UN and for himself personally.[5]

As predicted, the UN General Assembly vote for the partition of Palestine in November 1947 led to war, which intensified after Israel's declaration of independence in May 1948. The first UN mediator, Count Bernadotte, was an appointee of the Security Council (rather than the secretary-general, though he worked closely with Secretariat staff, especially Ralph Bunche). Bernadotte's first step was to arrange a truce, following which he put forward proposals for solving the conflict, including for Jerusalem to be declared an international city and for Arab refugees to be allowed to return home. In September 1948, he was assassinated by an extremist group that saw him as the main obstacle both to Israeli annexation of Jerusalem and to Jewish control of the whole of Palestine.[6]

Neither Bernadotte nor his successor, Ralph Bunche, regarded himself as being fully supported by Secretary-General Lie, whose refusal to visit the region did not engender their respect, and whom they viewed as partial to Israel.[7] The year 1949 saw the conclusion of the armistice talks in Rhodes between Israel, Egypt, Jordan, and Syria. The Israelis, with whom Bunche had argued the most, were especially generous in praising his role. A year later, he was awarded the Nobel Prize. Bunche wrote a letter turning it down, commenting that "peace-making at the UN is not done for prizes," but Secretary-General Lie persuaded him not to send it, since he felt the award should be seen as a tribute to the Secretariat as a whole.[8]

As the first to hold the position, Trygve Lie undoubtedly contributed to the development of the office of the UN secretary-general by his readiness to take an active position on the Palestine conflict. On the other hand, his own role in the issue has not generally received much praise—in contrast to two UN officials of the time who held lower positions. Bernadotte upset both Arabs and Israelis with his various compromise proposals and was assassinated.[9] Bunche had strongly disagreed with all the parties in the negotiations, but he still managed to piece together the complex armistice agreements that brought an end to hostilities and was awarded the Nobel Prize. In contrast, Lie, on two major questions—the Partition Plan and Israel's membership in the UN—actively campaigned in favor of Israel's position against that of the Arabs. He was able to do so because, on both points, he was aligned with the two superpowers, the United States and the USSR.[10] However, the UN's relevance in the Middle East during Lie's period derived less from the secretary-general and more from Bernadotte and Bunche.

DAG HAMMARSKJÖLD (1953–61)

The unknown and uncontroversial civil servant from Sweden who was chosen to succeed Lie in 1953, Dag Hammarskjöld, had a different conception of the value and values of the UN than his predecessor, though this was not immediately apparent. In 1956, responding to a Security Council request to involve himself in trying to restore adherence to the armistice between Israel and Egypt, he in effect invented the practice of shuttle diplomacy between Middle Eastern capitals.

Hammarskjöld developed an especially strong respect for and intellectual affinity with Israeli prime minister David Ben-Gurion. This did not stop him, however, from sending Ben-Gurion a fairly stinging letter over what he considered Israel's disproportionate military responses to provocations from

Egypt and Gaza. "You are convinced that acts of [Israeli] retaliation will stop further incidents. I am convinced they will lead to further incidents. . . . You believe that this way of creating respect for Israel will pave the way for sound co-existence with the Arab peoples. I believe that the policy may postpone indefinitely the time for such co-existence."[11]

In May 1956, Hammarskjöld wrote a private letter to the Swedish foreign minister in which he laid out his views with a frankness that secretaries-general have normally reserved for their postretirement memoirs. In it, he declared that the real situation in the Middle East was very different from what the world had been led to believe. His greatest concern was the Israeli attitude, which, "on the inside, is one of the harshest intransigence but, as presented by Israeli propaganda, one of a nation only wishing to live at peace with its neighbours, although continually harassed by them." Nasser, he stated, "has a very great patience but a lot of the guerilla mentality," whereas Ben-Gurion "is extremely impatient and believes it to be the height of moral-ity" to respond to incidents "by blunt, open strokes, not understanding the complete futility of such retaliation and its exceedingly dangerous psycho-logical consequences. Both have pushed self-righteousness to the point of honestly believing they always are right."[12] Hammarskjöld was convinced that neither of them had any plan to attack the other and that each wished to avoid war. In October, Hammarskjöld visited Ben-Gurion in the Negev but of course was not informed that Israel was planning a land, air, and sea war against Egypt, in collusion with Britain and France.

Like most world leaders, especially President Eisenhower, who declared his admiration for the way the UN secretary-general handled this crisis, Hammarskjöld was disgusted by the actions of the three aggressors and worked hard to reverse them. Had the Sinai and Suez invasion succeeded, he believed it would have been a "major catastrophe in which the death of the United Nations indeed might have been one of the less significant ele-ments."[13] Also like Eisenhower, he felt the occupation of the Suez Canal zone and the overthrow of Nasser had the potential to lead to a nuclear world war. Facing serious pressure from the US president, and with cover from the dip-lomatic effort spearheaded by the UN secretary-general and Lester Pearson of Canada that led to the deployment of the first-ever UN peacekeeping force (the United Nations Emergency Force), the British, French, and Israeli gov-ernments withdrew their forces from Egypt.[14]

Less than two years later, in the summer of 1958, the region was in crisis again, with conflict in Lebanon, a revolution in Iraq, and US and UK military interventions in Lebanon and Jordan respectively. Nasser's Egypt—at that point briefly linked with Syria in the "United Arab Republic"—was blamed by the West and its allies in the region for all of these. As in 1956, Hammarskjöld threw himself into trying to solve the problems, flying to Beirut and Cairo, setting in motion the establishment and later expansion of a UN Observation Group in Lebanon, fending off accusations of bias from all sides,[15] and appointing as a political presence on the ground a special representative in Amman with regional responsibilities (the first of scores of such representatives since then). Above all, Hammarskjöld provided the face-saving solution for the various parties that allowed the Americans to withdraw from Lebanon by November their fourteen thousand marines who had landed in July. Though publicly thanked by the United States for his role, he has rarely been credited for this achievement, one that was the result of his sustained and creative personal engagement with Cairo, Damascus, Beirut, Washington, London, Moscow, and others.[16]

Hammarskjöld was less successful when in June 1960 he was requested to recommend changes in the handling of the United Nations Relief and Works Agency for Palestine Refugees in the Near East (UNRWA) and the Palestinian refugees who had fled or been expelled from what became Israel in 1948—a task he embraced with some vigor. His report focused on how to reintegrate the refugee problem into the economic life of the region. While accepting that the long-term solution for the refugees was freedom of choice between repatriation to Palestine or compensation by Israel (in accordance with the General Assembly's decisions), he strongly believed that the Arab states should also do more in the short term to allow them employment— which he argued would be in the interests both of the states concerned and of the refugees themselves. To begin with, some Arab states showed interest. But after publication, to his disappointment, they rejected his emphasis on economic reintegration, presumably because they feared that it would come at the expense of pressure on Israel to allow repatriation.[17]

U THANT (1961–71)

The Middle East had led to some of Hammarskjöld's most successful interventions, thanks to his inspired creativity, personal magnetism, and determination. Following his death in a plane crash in Africa in 1961, he was succeeded by the Burmese diplomat U Thant, whose experience in the Middle East turned out to be very different. Indeed, that region brought about the absolute nadir in his fortunes, although the course he followed was probably almost identical to what Hammarskjöld would have done in the same circumstances.

In May 1967, as tensions between Egypt and Israel mounted, Cairo decided to demand the withdrawal of the United Nations Emergency Force (UNEF). Those forces were solely on the Egyptian side of the border, as Israel in 1956 (and again in 1967) had refused to consider their stationing on its territory. Egypt had the full legal right to demand their withdrawal, but the actual decision to do so was regarded as nothing short of suicidal by U Thant and his senior advisers, given the virtual inevitability of an Israeli military response.

Member states did very little to help the secretary-general. According to its rules, the General Assembly required a two-thirds majority to agree even to consider the issue, which was inconceivable given the widespread support for Egypt's sovereign right in this regard. Meanwhile, the Security Council could not consider the issue because—as a result of French and British vetoes in 1956—the decision to deploy UNEF in the first place had come from the General Assembly, meaning that a Security Council discussion was simply not possible. Some people advised U Thant to summon the Security Council under Article 99 of the Charter on the grounds that the situation posed a threat to international peace and security, but he refused to do that, as he knew it would descend into an East-West brawl and did not wish to pass the buck in that way.

As U Thant, Bunche, and Sir Brian Urquhart have all written, the key member states of the UN did very little to restrain either Egypt or Israel not only from taking the steps that led to the Six-Day War but also from subsequently engaging in the virulent scapegoating of the secretary-general—even though U Thant was in fact the only person who flew to Cairo in an effort to dissuade Nasser from his blockade of Israel. U Thant strongly protested that policy, warning Nasser that it would make an Israeli attack inevitable, and he did what he could to delay the UNEF withdrawal that he was obligated to carry out (indeed, the vast bulk of the force was still in place when Israel launched its attack). The result of the war was the immediate collapse of almost everything that had been achieved in the region by Bunche and Hammarskjöld. The armistice regime of 1949 lost much of its strength, and the pioneering experiment in peacekeeping ignominiously collapsed. For the UN organization as a whole, UNEF's withdrawal and the subsequent war are generally regarded as one of the biggest setbacks in its history.

After the war, Abba Eban, Israeli's ambassador to the UN, attacked the secretary-general in the General Assembly, asking what the use of a fire brigade was if it vanished from the scene as soon as the first smoke and flames appeared.[18] In the West, much of the reaction was the same—showing complete disregard of the realities that U Thant had to face as well as the fact that he, almost alone among the world's statesmen, had made strenuous efforts to stop the war. One American columnist accused U Thant of having "used his international prestige with the objectivity of a spurned lover and the dynamism of a noodle."[19] With the image of "U Thant's cowardice implanted in their minds," the Israelis' disdain for the UN increased, as did their disinclination to have more to do with it than they had to.[20]

A UN divided by the Cold War, with the two superpowers wishing to avoid a direct military confrontation, yet also encouraging—or at least not discouraging—their respective friends in the region with their mutual provocations, left U Thant to make the big decisions on his own.[21] Three years later, Nasser—insinuating that the UN had been in cahoots with Israel—put forward (with no evidence) the notion that U Thant and Bunche had deliberately enticed Egypt into occupying the Sinai, actually going so far as to say, "We fell into the trap set for us." He implied he had not really meant the UN force to withdraw (conveniently ignoring his belligerent speech to the Egyptian armed forces just before conflict erupted, in which he threatened that Egypt would treat the UN peacekeepers as a hostile force if they refused to withdraw from its territory).

Both Bunche and Urquhart have concluded that there was no alternative course that U Thant could have pursued. Egypt and its Arab allies had "grotesquely underestimated" Israel's capacity, and willingness, to react to a move that it perceived both as a threat to its security and as a "great historical opportunity." Nasser, in the heyday of the concept of the Arab Nation, was unshakable in his determination to "plunge over the precipice." From neither a legal nor a military point of view was U Thant in a position to challenge him. Urquhart concluded that the senior UN staff all labored under a crushing sense of failure and that U Thant suffered irreparable psychological damage as result of the debacle. U Thant could easily have convoked the Security Council to deal with the threat to the peace, thereby letting the blame fall on its members rather than himself. But he decided not to do so. In any case, such a tactic would not have prevented the disaster, but "The scapegoat would have escaped."[22]

On a happier note, but in geopolitical terms insignificant compared to the Six-Day War, was U Thant's handling of Bahrain, from which Britain was withdrawing in 1969 and which Iran was claiming as its fourteenth province. One year of intensive negotiations conducted in secrecy by Ralph Bunche led to a solution agreeable to all sides, including the Bahrainis, that was approved by the Security Council and that allowed Iran to give up its claim without loss of face. The Soviets complained that U Thant had exceeded his authority, but the episode is recognized as a classic example of genuinely preventive diplomacy: settling a dispute before it degenerated into conflict. U Thant himself believed it was the first time in the history of the UN that the parties to a dispute had entrusted it to the secretary-general's good offices by giving a prior pledge to accept without reservation the findings of the UN representative. He also believed that the perfect good-offices operation is one that nobody has heard of until it is successfully concluded. This was an important advance in the practices and standing of the secretary-general's good-offices function, and a welcome corrective to the otherwise thankless experiences U Thant had undergone elsewhere in the Middle East.[23]

KURT WALDHEIM (1971–82)

The former Austrian foreign minister, Kurt Waldheim, who became secretary-general in 1971, neither admired nor sought to emulate his predecessors. His conception of the office he held was very different, and at various times he argued against a morality-based approach, as well as suggestions that the secretary-general should be idealistic, humble, intellectual, or even activist.[24] One Israeli negotiator described Waldheim at a Middle East peace conference, "walking around like a head-waiter in a restaurant," greeting delegations at different tables, with the implication that he was grandly ceremonial but also servile and nonsubstantive.[25]

Waldheim's first visit to the Middle East was in August 1973. Given his wartime service in the German army (although the full grim and damaging details became public only after he left office), it was not surprising that the Israelis would regard him with some suspicion.[26] Though it was only two months before the "Yom Kippur War," the Israeli prime minister Golda Meir dismissed Waldheim's observation that the situation in the region was highly explosive, arguing instead that the Arabs were "getting used to" the status quo (i.e., Israel's retention of the territories captured from the Egyptians, Syrians, and Jordanians six years before) and that apparently there would be peace with them in just a few years.

Two weeks after war erupted on October 6, Waldheim called US secretary of state Kissinger to suggest that a UN peacekeeping force be placed between the Egyptian and Israeli forces. This was agreed to first by the Americans and then by the Security Council, and "blue helmets" were on the ground within twenty-four hours. But agreeing on the terms of reference for what was called UNEF II was harder, given differences between the Soviet Union and the West regarding the proper role of the secretary-general as opposed to the Security Council. Waldheim's report on the matter became the basis for future operations—the secretary-general would manage the force on a day-to-day basis, while the Security Council would keep overall political direction (on such crucial matters as withdrawal, the personal responsibility for which had been so damaging for U Thant with UNEF I).

The two superpowers agreed to hold a Middle East peace conference in December 1973 under UN auspices and convened by Waldheim (bringing Arabs and Israelis together officially for the first time since Rhodes in 1949). The following year, after weeks of shuttle diplomacy between Israel and Syria, Kissinger achieved agreement on a "UN Disengagement Observer Force" on the Golan Heights. The role of the secretary-general in politically bringing about that agreement, as opposed to implementing and supervising it, was very limited, however.[27]

This pattern was repeated in March 1978 when, in response to terrorist attacks, Israel launched a major incursion into southern Lebanon. Against the advice of Waldheim's key advisers, who were clear that conditions for peacekeeping were entirely lacking in the area, the United States and other Western powers pushed for the creation of the UN Interim Force in Lebanon (UNIFIL). The Israelis carried out part of their withdrawal from Lebanese territory in April, but then in June, instead of handing over the rest of the territory to UNIFIL, gave it to Major Saad Haddad, leader of a local Lebanese militia, and attacked the secretary-general in public. As Urquhart, Waldheim's key official on all matters relating to peace and security, later put it, "Much as I admire the talent of the Israelis for putting up a smokescreen of indignation to cover their own actions by loudly indicting others, this was too much." After all, they were handing over to Haddad, an Israeli proxy regarded by most Lebanese as a traitor, "and at the same time accusing us of all sorts of misdemeanours and demanding self-righteously that we mend our ways." Waldheim hit back in diplomatic but uncharacteristically strong terms.[28]

The situation in UNIFIL's area of operations remained tense, escalating again in July 1981. US negotiator Philip Habib played the key role in putting an end to the artillery barrages, but the secretary-general was also involved, since it was easier for Palestine Liberation Organization (PLO) leader Yasser Arafat to respond to Waldheim's call for a cease-fire than to Habib's. When the announcement was made that military action in both directions would cease, Israel declared this had been negotiated by the United States, whereas the PLO was able to claim it had been negotiated by the UN. Allowing ladders to be climbed down and peace to be restored without the loss of too much face for any party has always been one of the most important roles of the UN.

In September 1980, towards the end of Waldheim's second term (and while he was campaigning—unsuccessfully—for a third), Iraq invaded Iran. This led to eight years of carnage, but no government in the region or in the Security Council moved to stop it. Waldheim offered his good offices to both parties and brought the matter to the Security Council, although the result was a resolution that failed to condemn the Iraqi aggression and was rejected by Iran. Waldheim proceeded to appoint Olaf Palme, a former (and future) prime minister of Sweden, as his special representative. It was only under Waldheim's successor that any progress was made. But Waldheim can be credited with trying to end this terrible conflict at an early stage, despite the almost total lack of support from member states.

During his term of office, three important new peacekeeping operations were established (in Sinai, Golan, and southern Lebanon) that served to contain those conflicts and to reestablish international confidence in UN peacekeeping, which had been so seriously damaged in 1967. As a result, Waldheim's record in the Middle East was more positive than the current state of his overall reputation—resulting largely from his wartime service in the SS—would suggest.[29]

JAVIER PEREZ DE CUELLAR (1982–1991)

The cautious but consummately professional Peruvian diplomat who succeeded Waldheim, Javier Perez de Cuellar, provided another contrast in style—the hallmarks of which were consensus, discretion, and finesse. Like U Thant (and unlike, in radically different ways, Hammarskjöld, Waldheim, and Boutros Boutros-Ghali), he was considered highly self-effacing—to the extent that the US ambassador to the UN quipped that he would not create a splash if he fell out of a boat.[30]

Even by the standards of the Middle East, Perez de Cuellar's time in office coincided with many major developments, including the 1982 Israeli invasion of Lebanon, the first Palestinian intifada, efforts to start a Middle East peace process, the Iraqi invasion of Kuwait, the First Gulf War, and most of the Iran-Iraq War. In all these, the UN Secretariat played some role, but usually a heavily circumscribed one. Israel tended to make it clear that the secretary-general may have been preferable to the Security Council (let alone the other UN intergovernmental bodies), but, together with the United States, it ensured that the UN's involvement was marginal: for example, at the Madrid Peace Conference of 1991, the secretary-general's representative was placed so far in the back that he was even out of camera range.[31]

But in one area, the quiet and discreet role of the UN (a result of both the desire of some parties and also the personal style of Perez de Cuellar) paid handsome dividends. This concerned the release of several Western hostages held by groups in Lebanon, such as Hizbullah, in exchange for Lebanese detainees held by Israel, its proxy force in southern Lebanon, as well as economic inducements. It involved high-level exchanges between the secretary-general and presidents Bush and Rafsanjani, as well as countless dealings—including dangerous and secretive ones carried out by Perez de Cuellar's envoy Giandomenico Picco in Lebanon—with the Israelis, the Syrians, the Lebanese, and European powers. The whole episode, most of which took place in Perez de Cuellar's final year in office, was an undeniable success for the secretary-general and his particular brand of private, indeed secret, handling of diplomacy.

As secretary-general, Perez de Cuellar was almost invariably treated with respect. But many of his proposals on both the Lebanon and Palestine files gained little traction. Usually this was because of opposition from the United States and Israel, but he was also regularly frustrated by the Cold War paralysis of the Security Council at that time. For example, his proposal to put UN peacekeepers into Beirut in 1982 was blocked by the United States at Israeli behest; ironically, a year later (by which time the United States and Israelis were regretting that decision), it was the USSR that, at Syrian behest, blocked the deployment of UN observers for a Lebanese cease-fire that the United States and Israel wanted to promote.[32]

But while one of the parties worked to keep the UN out of Arab-Israeli issues, this was not the case with the Iran-Iraq War. Perez de Cuellar came to office conscious of the destructiveness of the conflict, its regional ramifications, and the UN's responsibility to try to end it. It was also clear to him that only he—and not the Security Council—was regarded as impartial by both sides. He worked away, quietly, for some years until the situation—both regionally (the parties were exhausted) and geopolitically (the Cold War was starting to thaw)—appeared riper for mediation. In 1987, he invited the five permanent members to meet him in private to discuss how to start a process that would lead to a negotiated settlement. Several months of secret negotiations gave rise to a Security Council resolution, and then a cease-fire a year later.

As one of his top officials described it, the secretary-general had taken the lead "cautiously and discreetly, in getting the five permanent members to face up to their responsibilities under the Charter and define the outlines of a settlement."[33] The underrated Perez de Cuellar himself believed that the UN as a whole, as well as the mediation potential of the secretary-general as an impartial UN organ, was strengthened by the Iran/Iraq experience and even that it marked the beginning of a "new era" in the UN's history.[34]

BOUTROS BOUTROS-GHALI (1992–96)

The "new era" did not last long. In terms of intellect, and also his stress on independence (from the great powers), there were aspects of Boutros Boutros-Ghali—Egypt's high-born and long-standing minister of state for foreign affairs—that recalled Hammarskjöld. The differences were more in personal style (with some of those great powers regarding him as arrogant) and in the international context, which was less tolerant of any manifestation of such independence by the UN than it had been in the 1950s. As US assistant secretary of state James Rubin, one of the architects of the US veto that prevented Boutros-Ghali's reelection, later put it, Boutros-Ghali had neglected one of the secretary-general's core duties: "smooth cooperation with the United States."[35]

Boutros-Ghali's stewardship of the UN was marked by three international crises outside the Middle East region: the breakup of Yugoslavia; the famine and anarchy of Somalia; and the genocide in Rwanda. Iraq was an ongoing issue, as was the Israel-Palestine track. This last was dominated by the Oslo agreement and some progress that derived from the peace process. Boutros-Ghali—from a prominent Coptic family in Egypt, with a Jewish wife, and one of the people most involved with Sadat's peace initiative with Israel—considered himself well placed to bring the UN more deeply into the peace process. He tried to work on what he considered a double crisis of confidence: to Israel, the UN was a "veritable war machine" made for condemning and undermining the Jewish state; to the Arab world, the UN was an organization "feudally dependent" on the United States in which pro-Arab resolutions in support of the Palestinian cause were never implemented. He informed the Israeli prime minister that, having contributed to the peace treaty between Israel and Egypt, he would now like to conclude a peace treaty between the UN and Israel.[36]

The new secretary-general believed that there was much in the UN record in the Middle East to deplore—including the withdrawal of peacekeepers in 1967, the UN refusal to accept the Egypt-Israel peace treaty, and the "Zionism is a form of racism" resolution of 1975 in the General Assembly. Boutros-Ghali moved the headquarters of UNRWA from Vienna to Gaza, appointed a UN coordinator for assistance to the Occupied Territory, and worked to increase aid elsewhere in the region.[37] But despite his intentions, and the mutual respect between Israeli prime minister Rabin and himself, UN relations with Israel did not improve. Instead, there arose a series of events that damaged relations between the secretary-general on the one hand and the United States and Israel on the other.

The first related to Israel's deportation, in December 1992, of four hundred Palestinian "fundamentalists" from the West Bank and Gaza to South Lebanon. Boutros-Ghali hoped to resolve the issue in the days remaining before the inauguration of President Clinton so that the latter would not come into office facing pressure to cast the first post–Cold War veto—a situation in which the United States would be blamed by the rest of the world for spoiling the new positive atmosphere in the Security Council "and, in turn, would blame the United Nations." Three UN missions in a month led to no positive response by the Israelis to ensure the immediate return of the deportees, which was unanimously demanded by the Security Council. Boutros-Ghali then reported on the matter (as he was requested to do by the Council), observing that this refusal "challenges the authority of the Security Council." The incoming Clinton administration was not appreciative, and the secretary-general was accused of being "confrontational."[38]

The second episode followed the massacre of twenty-nine Palestinian worshippers in Hebron by Baruch Goldstein in February 1994. Boutros-Ghali wrote to Prime Minister Rabin saying the UN was ready to help ease tensions, including with—should all parties agree—a UN presence in Hebron. This led to another negative reaction from the United States, and accusations that the secretary-general was anti-Semitic.[39]

The third—and worst—episode followed a large Israeli attack on South Lebanon in April 1996 aimed at Hizbullah, which had been targeting Israel. Many civilians had taken refuge in a UN compound in Qana, which was then hit by several Israeli artillery shells, leading to the death of one hundred civilians. Boutros-Ghali later wrote that this was "unprecedented. The armed forces of a UN member state had launched an attack on a UN peacekeeping post." Israel said the shelling was a mistake, but the UN military investigation concluded otherwise and the secretary-general reported to the Security Council accordingly. The reaction from both Israel and the United States was harsh, accusing the secretary-general of "pointing the finger" rather than "creating a climate of peace."

Boutros-Ghali later believed that the high level of outrage toward the course of action that he was morally bound to follow was connected to US and Israeli fears that it would damage the election campaign of Shimon Peres. Peres then lost, and Boutros-Ghali was blamed. The fact that the findings of the objective UN military report were published weeks before the Israeli election and months before both the US election and the vote on the secretary-general's reelection was unfortunate timing for Boutros-Ghali,[40] and Urquhart later acknowledged that it took "considerable moral courage" for him to act in the way he did.[41]

Undoubtedly acrimonious though these particular issues were, they are generally not considered to have been central to the US decision to undertake its major campaign to prevent a second term for Boutros-Ghali, the motivations for which, in a presidential election year, were primarily domestic. But few observers deny that there was considerable scapegoating of the secretary-general for the failure (primarily of the Western powers) to move faster and more decisively on the Bosnian war and for the death of US troops in Somalia. The whole affair ended in tremendous bitterness and resentment in many quarters. Revealingly, Boutros-Ghali provided his successor, Kofi Annan, with only one piece of advice: "Watch out for the question of Iraq. It will become very important."[42]

KOFI ANNAN (1997–2006)

Those words were prophetic. Problems relating to Iraq created a major crisis for the UN—and the secretary-general personally. But in Annan's first term, Iraq was an issue for which he was praised and that contributed to his award (jointly with the UN organization as a whole) of the Nobel Peace Prize in 2001.

The year 1998 saw one of Saddam Hussein's periodic episodes of brinkmanship when he continually obstructed the UN weapons inspections that had been imposed on the country as the price for its invasion of Kuwait in 1990 and its defeat by an international coalition the following year. Prospects of another war seemed increasingly likely when Annan decided to fly to Baghdad to make a last-ditch effort to secure a climb-down and avert conflict. Prior to departure he had worked painstakingly with the permanent members of the Security Council to see what he could offer—and threaten—Saddam Hussein. After a three-hour meeting with Hussein, he appeared with a memorandum of understanding whereby Iraq allowed the UN inspectors to resume operations. Although he returned to a rapturous welcome in New York, the triumph was short-lived; within a few months Hussein was reneging on the deal.

Like many of his predecessors, Annan began his term conscious that the office of the secretary-general had been "largely absent from every significant step of the modern peace process" in the Middle East. He attributed this political sidelining partly to the myriad resolutions passed by the General Assembly and the Commission on Human Rights harshly condemning Israel that demonstrated double standards and served usually only to convince the Israelis they would never get a fair hearing in those arenas. On the other hand, Annan felt that in the Security Council the United States wielded its veto "to protect the Israelis even from reasonable international scrutiny and pressure, paralyzing the Council on one of the world's central conflicts."

Annan was convinced—as he told the Security Council at the end of his tenure—that the Israeli-Palestinian conflict was "not simply one unresolved conflict among many": no other issue carried such a powerful symbolic and emotional charge affecting people far from the conflict and, indeed, the whole standing of the UN in international affairs. Soon after taking office, Annan made progress in changing perceptions in Israel with a speech in the Knesset by supporting Israel's quest for membership in a regional grouping of states (the "Western European and Others Group") at the UN, and through the appointment of a UN special coordinator, Terje Roed-Larsen, who had worked closely with Israeli—and Palestinian—officials during the Oslo negotiations.[43]

In 2000, Annan was quick to seize the opportunity presented by the decision of Israeli prime minister Ehud Barak to withdraw Israeli forces from southern Lebanon—an action Annan was convinced was in the common interests of Israel, Lebanon, and the UN. He told Barak that the withdrawal must be total, and the commitment must be in writing, if Israel was to receive UN certification that it was in full compliance with Security Council Resolution 425 (adopted after the 1978 invasion). This insistence helped Annan in his dealings with Lebanon, Syria, and Egypt, while he closely coordinated with Israel regarding what UN steps would follow which Israeli actions, until the withdrawal was carried out in May. Israel's complete pull-back to what became known as "the Blue Line," which corresponded to the UN assessment of what was the hitherto undemarcated border between Israel and Lebanon, was regarded as an important success for the UN and as being in the interests of almost all parties (except those Arabs who wanted the Israelis to remain in their Lebanese quagmire).[44]

Annan warned Barak that the Israeli withdrawal under military pressure from Hizbullah (like its later withdrawal from Gaza under pressure from Hamas) sent an unfortunate signal to those Palestinian moderates who were trying to secure a settlement with Israel through peaceful negotiations. Meanwhile the Oslo process was fraying, and then the collapse of the Camp David negotiations in summer 2000 led within two months to the second Palestinian intifada. Recognizing the disastrous effects of the tough Israeli response and escalating Palestinian violence, Annan did what he could to secure a UN role in international efforts to end the intifada. He was partially successful. At the Sharm el-Sheikh summit in November, convened by President Clinton, the UN was invited after having secured Arafat's attendance, prompting the European Union's high commissioner Javier Solana to tell Annan that this was the "first time" in the history of that part of the world that the UN secretary-general had been "allowed to play a role."[45]

Writing afterwards, Annan points to the irony that he was invited to the "peace table just as it was being upended," as the Clinton administration was replaced by the Bush administration. Annan played the key role in setting up the "Quartet," designed to keep the UN at the table by combining its universal legitimacy with the political power of the United States, the financial resources of the EU, and the regional prestige of Russia. The Quartet's "Roadmap" was intended to make clear that both terrorism and settlements had to be stopped and that the goal (missing from Oslo) was a two-state solution. But Annan left office four years later frustrated with what he, and most others, regarded as a lack of serious influence exercised on Israel by the

United States, and the consequent failure of the Quartet to insist on compliance with its own Roadmap.

Annan recognized that his decision to participate in the Quartet's isolation of the newly elected Hamas-led Palestinian Authority government in 2006 was one of the most controversial moves he ever took. It was a prime example of a dilemma routinely faced by secretaries-general. On the one hand, he needed to assert the primacy of the secretary-general's good-offices role, the UN's independence and prerogative to talk to all players in a given situation. On the other hand, he was far from optimistic that dialogue with Hamas would lead anywhere and felt that it carried the risk of excluding the UN from major constituencies in the United States and Israel. He thus went along with the US, EU, and Israeli position and was criticized in various quarters for doing so.[46]

Annan continued to play an active role on Lebanese issues, including events after the assassination of Prime Minister Hariri in 2005, the withdrawal of Syrian forces from the country, and efforts to bring about a prisoner swap with Israel. Most significant perhaps was his push for a cease-fire when in the summer of 2006 an attack by Hizbullah provoked a massive and sustained Israeli bombardment of Lebanon.

Annan never concealed his feelings about the long delays—caused mainly by the United States and the United Kingdom, though with behind-the-scenes support from some Arab governments—in getting Security Council agreement to insist on a cease-fire and a halt to the Israeli attack. "I would be remiss," he informed Council members, "if I did not tell you how profoundly disappointed I am that the Council did not reach this point much, much earlier. . . . [This] inability to act sooner has badly shaken the world's faith in its authority and integrity."[47] The Council left it to the secretary-general to finalize the actual cessation of hostilities with Israel and Lebanon. Despite Prime Minister Ehud Olmert's assurances to Annan, Israel went on the offensive in the final days, after the cease-fire had been agreed on—dropping hundreds of thousands of cluster munitions on Lebanon. But as Annan commented, "Misleading the Secretary-General was not an Israeli offence alone": after all, Syria's president Bashar al-Assad had assured him that Syria was giving no supplies to Hizbullah.[48]

The key element of Security Council Resolution 1701 was a beefed-up UNIFIL with a tougher mandate and better-equipped troops, as it had hitherto been perceived as too weak to counter Hizbullah's growing influence in southern Lebanon. Annan then worked hard to get European and other governments to commit eight thousand new troops, as well as to get Lebanon to deploy its army south of the Litani River in order to trigger Israel's withdrawal behind the Blue Line.

But despite all the tensions involving the Lebanese, the Israelis, and the Palestinians, it was Iraq that provoked the biggest crisis for the UN—as Annan struggled to steer a course between the United States and some of its allies on one hand and most of the rest of the international community on the other. It was not a happy position to be in, and the secretary-general was harshly assailed on all sides.

Annan believed that the question came down to two challenges that simply could not be met at the same time: first, the defiance by a brutal and predatory regime of its country's obligations under international law and the resolutions of the Security Council; and second, the decision of the "sole superpower to ignore the considered judgment of a majority of members of the international community to enter in a war that could not be justified under the Charter."[49]

Having not prevented war (his attempt of which led to criticism from those who wanted war, and his failure in which annoyed those who did not), Annan then positioned the UN to play a role in postinvasion Iraq. This was another controversial decision, objected to by those who felt the UN should keep its distance from the US-led occupation. But Annan felt it was neither realistic nor desirable for the UN to abstain from such a consequential set of issues, which would have had a further negative impact on perceptions of the UN's relevance as well as on the Iraqi people. As Mark Malloch-Brown, later Annan's deputy, put it, perhaps in an unconscious reference to Abba Eban's trenchant criticism of 1967, "If you're the fire brigade, you don't ask who started the fire and if this is a moral fire before you get started."[50]

What made Iraq such a problem for Annan's second term was a devastating combination of three sets of developments. The first was the bombing of the UN offices in Baghdad in August 2003 that led to the death of Annan's representative and friend, the charismatic Sergio Vieira de Mello, along with several others of the UN's "best and brightest." This was a major blow to Annan personally and the UN institutionally. The second came from the secretary-general's initial quiet opposition to the US war effort, culminating in his answer to questioning by a BBC reporter in 2004 that yes, he considered the Iraq war to be indeed "illegal." The fury that this admission created in conservative circles in the United States had a direct impact on the third set of difficulties. These related to the UN's Oil-for-Food humanitarian program in Iraq and allegations of corruption that also involved Annan's son.

The result was a vast assault on Annan's integrity and judgment, which soon extended to the entire UN. A large-scale investigation set up by Annan and headed by Paul Volcker followed, the conclusion of which was that the program was an overall success but that the UN and Annan were responsible for poor management, inadequate supervision, and lack of accountability. On the other hand, the overblown claims of systemwide UN corruption appearing in much of the American press were almost entirely dismissed.[51]

Taken together, these developments led to a temporary loss of morale on the part of Annan and questions about whether he would be able to complete his term of office. But he pulled through, and the United States pulled back. As he himself put it afterwards, although the "ideologues of the Bush administration who took their country and the world into a calamitous war wanted to see the UN shattered in the process," ultimately statesmanship on the part of the White House prevailed, and Washington "slowly realized the need for the organization to regain its indispensable role in international security." But it is hard to avoid the conclusion that, along with the 1967 war, this was one of the lowest points in the history of the UN and the office of the secretary-general.

BAN KI-MOON (2007–16)

The eighth (and current) secretary-general, Ban Ki-moon, who was foreign minister of the Republic of Korea, took office in 2007 and immediately found that that Middle East issues would rank among his major preoccupations.[52]

Instability in Lebanon was always a concern for Ban, who pushed the international community to generate funds for Lebanon's reconstruction following the widespread damage caused by the war of 2006. He also supported the efforts of the Special Tribunal to investigate Prime Minister Hariri's assassination, a historic attempt to end impunity that may turn out to be a precedent for elsewhere in the world. Ban continued the UN's push for the disarmament of Hizbullah, as well as the increased effectiveness of UNIFIL; and in 2013 he established an International Support Group to help the country cope with the ever-increasing fragility brought on by the Syrian civil war.

Like his predecessor, Ban reached out to Israel in various ways to try to reduce mistrust. For example, he repeatedly declared his understanding, as a

South Korean whose capital lies close to the border with the North, of how Israelis must feel living under constant threat of rocket attack. The Quartet met periodically, notwithstanding criticism about its effectiveness, as Ban and his envoys, Robert Serry and later Nickolay Mladenov, sought to support various US initiatives by Condoleeza Rice (Annapolis), Hillary Clinton (the Mitchell effort), and John Kerry. All the while, he continued to urge that final status parameters for an Israeli-Palestinian peace deal, launched through the Quartet and based in Security Council resolutions, were probably the only chance of getting parties with such deep distrust and asymmetrical bargaining power to negotiate a deal they could both live with.

By 2014, he was warning that the Kerry efforts seemed the last chance for a two-state solution, implying that, should they fail (a possibility he feared might happen as a result of Israel's continued settlement activity, which he said was "illegal under international law and runs totally counter to the pursuit of a two-state solution"), what would be left was a one-state possibility that both sides claimed they did not want.[53]

Ban paid particular attention to Gaza—which is not surprising given that major hostilities between Israel and Hamas and other Palestinian groups erupted there on three occasions during his first eight years in office. While retaining Annan's position on Hamas, the UN maintained some necessary contacts with the movement with a view to deescalating violence. Ban regularly condemned the firing of rockets from Gaza into southern Israel, and also the Israeli military response whenever he considered it disproportionate or excessive. He found the human suffering in Gaza deeply troubling and publicly urged Israel to "lift its harsh restrictions in order to ease the plight of civilians and bring an end to the closure. Keeping a large and dense population in unremitting poverty is in nobody's interest except that of the most extreme radicals in the region."[54] Ban used his trips to set up "deliverables," where he would press the Israelis to make some gesture to ease some aspect of the blockade.

When hostilities broke out in 2008, leading to the death of 1,300 Palestinians in Gaza and thirteen Israelis, Ban went to the region in an effort to stop the fighting. He soon concluded that it would be almost impossible for Israel and Hamas to agree to a simultaneous cease-fire. As he later put it, "The only way would be a unilateral ceasefire by Olmert, because the Israelis started this war and they should stop." He held three meetings with the Israeli prime minister and several telephone calls, after which Olmert issued his call for a unilateral cease-fire. The secretary-general then flew to Beirut,

Damascus (where he pressed President Assad to lean on the Hamas leadership), and Cairo. Ban recalled that within twelve hours of Olmert's announcement the Syrians were informing the secretary-general that, because of Assad's intervention, Hamas would also make an announcement, which they proceeded to do.[55]

In both 2012 and 2014, Ban again engaged in shuttle diplomacy—in close coordination with the United States—in an attempt to stop the fighting in Gaza, the victims of which were overwhelmingly Palestinian civilians. While fully accepting Israel's right to self-defense, he made clear in public statements, as well as in meetings with senior Israeli officials, his conviction that punishing the Gazan population so severely was a mistake on both ethical and pragmatic grounds. The Israelis and some of their supporters abroad vocally protested Ban's statements as the crisis went on, but Ban held his ground and continued to insist that the loss of lives and the destruction of Palestinian housing and infrastructure (especially a number of attacks on UN-run schools, where hundreds of civilians were taking refuge) were excessive.[56] He also continued to maintain that addressing the "root causes" of Palestinian desperation—in both Gaza and the West Bank—was a prerequisite for ending what he frustratedly called the build-destroy-build cycle, with the international community repeatedly called upon to pay for the reconstruction of the besieged Gaza Strip after each round of destruction.[57]

Early in 2016, as the situation in the West Bank seemed to deteriorate further and further, Ban informed the Security Council that Palestinian frustration was growing under the weight of occupation and the paralysis of the peace process. "Some have taken me to task for pointing out this indisputable truth. Yet, as oppressed peoples have demonstrated throughout the ages, it is human nature to react to occupation, which often serves as a potent incubator of hate and extremism."[58] The reaction from Israel was fast: within minutes Prime Minister Netanyahu accused him of providing a "tail-wind to terror." Ban became the subject of a campaign which maintained that the lone Palestinian attacks that were terrorizing Israeli civilians at the time were the product of incitement by the Palestinian Authority and had nothing to do with occupation. Strongly disagreeing, Ban then published an article in the *New York Times* where he made his position even clearer. He stated that no one could deny that the everyday reality of occupation provoked anger and despair, which were the major drivers of violence and undermined any hope of a two-state solution. He referred to the expanding illegal settlement construction and the demolition of Palestinian homes, with the result that

Palestinians were "losing hope over what seems a harsh, humiliating and endless occupation." Ban also called on the Palestinians to make political compromises to bring Gaza and the West Bank together, and to consistently denounce terrorism and take preventive action to end attacks on Israelis.[59]

In Iraq, following requests by the United States and others, Ban expanded the role of the UN Mission, which had never really recovered from the aftershocks of the Canal Hotel bombing. He authorized a greater political involvement from the UN special representative, including in the increasingly vexed relations between the central government in Baghdad, the Kurdistan Regional Government, and local Arab, Christian, Kurdish, and Turkmen communities. The issues concerned disputed areas, oil revenues, local power sharing, restitution of property, demographic shifts, and security arrangements. Following an extensive investigation and report by the UN Mission into the disputed areas, the secretary-general supported his team in efforts to negotiate confidence-building measures.

As political and security conditions deteriorated in Iraq, he increased his efforts to encourage a more inclusive Iraqi government in 2014. When Mosul fell to Islamic State of Iraq and the Levant (ISIL), Ban rapidly reached out to Prime Minister al-Maliki and Grand Ayatollah Sistani, and then visited them in Baghdad and Najaf respectively, in order to impress on them the paramount importance of combating ISIL, despite the atrocities ISIL was carrying out, in a way that respected human rights. Failure to do so, he told them, and the revenge killing of Sunni civilians by Shiite militias, would only serve as motivation for more recruitment to ISIL.

The secretary-general also worked over several years to improve Iraqi relations with Kuwait, addressing the concerns of the latter related to missing persons and property dating from the 1990 invasion by Iraq, and the removal of Iraq from consideration under Chapter VII of the UN Charter, which was largely accomplished by 2013. He pressed the Gulf states—especially King Abdallah of Saudi Arabia—to do more to integrate Iraq into the region. Indeed, by making several visits and staying in contact through phone calls, Ban established closer links to the leaders of the Gulf than any of his predecessors. This enabled him to call on them for important contributions to many causes where the UN was requesting resources—mainly for humanitarian efforts, but also to address terrorism and climate change.

Ban is regarded as having exercised most moral leadership during the Arab Spring. He was among the first world leaders to publicly call for President Mubarak of Egypt and Colonel Qaddafi of Libya to step down from office in

2011. This was despite opposition from China and Russia, two permanent members of the Security Council, to his stance on what they considered were "internal" affairs, just a few months before his reelection to a second term of office.[60] In January 2012, at a high-level conference on democracy in Beirut, Ban told Arab leaders that "the flame ignited in Tunisia will not be dimmed. . . . The old way is crumbling." He pointed out that the great changes began, not with a call for regime change, but with desire for dignity and an end to corruption. People "want jobs and justice, a fair share of political power. They want their human rights."[61] In Egypt, he repeatedly urged the new authorities (first under President Morsi, then under President al-Sisi) to respect human rights, and he criticized the harsh military and judicial crackdowns on demonstrators and journalists.

Before the Libyan regime finally collapsed, Ban instructed that plans be drawn up for a UN operation to support postrevolution statebuilding in Libya. Over the next five years, he called on the Western powers, as well as Libya's neighbors, to be more focused on the country, especially when it began to break down amid rival armed factions, serious human rights violations, competing parliaments, a vast source of illegal migration to Europe across the Mediterranean, and the growing presence of the "Islamic State" in the east.

The signing of the Libyan Peace Agreement in December 2015, after months of negotiations facilitated by the secretary-general and his representatives, was a critical step forward. These efforts continued through the first quarter of 2016, with Ban and UN special envoy Martin Kobler cajoling the parties and their respective backers abroad. When the Presidency Council was finally able to enter Tripoli on March 30, Ban then focused the UN's efforts on urging all Libyan political actors and public institutions to facilitate an immediate and peaceful handover of power.

In Yemen, Ban consistently worked to bolster the transition to democratic rule after the overthrow of President Saleh. The National Dialogue process, closely supported by the UN through Ban's envoy, Jamal Benomar, was an innovative attempt to bring Yemeni women, civil society, and previously excluded actors into the political and constitution-making process. But in late 2014, fighting in the country's north spiraled out of control, leading to the takeover of the capital, Sanaa, by Houthi forces backed by Saleh. Despite weeks of negotiations led by the UN, disputes over the draft constitution led to further conflict between President Hadi and the Houthis. Hadi fled Sanaa and requested a military intervention by Gulf countries in order to dislodge the Houthis and restore his government to power.

A massive Saudi-led military operation was launched in March 2015, with thousands of air strikes following (as well as casualties—one year later, well over six thousand Yemenis had been killed in the fighting, more than half of them civilians). Ban and his new envoy, Ismail Ould Cheikh Ahmed, rapidly pushed to convene peace talks to bring the country back to a peaceful political transition. Following unsuccessful talks in Geneva in June, the secretary-general continued to meet with Yemeni and regional leaders to urge a cessation of hostilities. Ban repeatedly pressed for the Saudi-led coalition in particular, as well as the Yemeni belligerents, to make far greater efforts to avoid civilian casualties and stop obstructing desperately needed humanitarian assistance to millions of affected civilians. A cease-fire was announced by Ban in December 2015 at a new round of talks in Biel, Switzerland. While this cessation of hostilities lasted only a few days, the secretary-general's envoy was able to announce a more robust cessation of hostilities and new talks in Kuwait in April 2016.

During Ban's second term, probably no issue affected him so profoundly as the continued fighting in Syria.[62] Shocked by the massive human rights abuses committed by the regime, as well as the uncompromising political stance of the parties, the secretary-general used strong language to convey his condemnation. In a speech to the General Assembly on June 7, 2012, he declared that for many months it had been "evident that President Assad and his Government have lost all legitimacy." He referred to specific acts of slaughter by government forces or allies and declared, "Any regime or leader that tolerates such killing of innocents has lost its fundamental humanity."[63] Peaceful protesters had bravely persisted in calling for dignity and freedom but often had been killed for doing so. The Syrian government, he continued, was not living up to its commitments under the plan endorsed by the Security Council two months before, and many elements of the opposition had also turned to arms.

As time went on, an increasingly radicalized opposition resorted to terrible acts of terrorism and murder, especially ISIL or Da'esh, and Ban strongly criticized their acts. But he continued to condemn the government's use of long-range missiles; "barrel bombs" dropped by helicopters; the imprisonment, torture, and disappearances of tens of thousands of civilians; and siege tactics that were causing severe hunger to two hundred thousand people by 2014. He insisted—despite protestations from Damascus—that terrorism was a consequence, not the cause, of the conflict in Syria.[64]

The problem of Syria was not just the brutality of the protagonists but also the actions of regional countries that fueled the fighting, and finally the paralysis of the Security Council, where three of the permanent members supported the opposition and two supported the government. Despite the secretary-general's successive appointment of some of the most qualified elder statesmen of the day—Kofi Annan, followed by Lakhdar Brahimi and later Staffan de Mistura—as the UN envoy on Syria, working either jointly or in close cooperation with the Arab League, the conflict had already been under way for a year when the issue finally came to the UN. It was therefore hugely difficult for the UN to overcome the internal, regional, and international divisions that kept the fighting going.

International conferences on Syria were convened in Geneva (2012) and Montreux (2014)—the first designed to secure regional and international commitment to a negotiated transition, and the second to launch Syrian talks to this end. These conferences underscored the convening power of the secretary-general and his senior envoys and could have opened paths for dialogue. However, amid the intransigence of the regime, the fragmentation of the opposition, and the continual pursuit by some regional powers of a military solution to the conflict, they had little impact on the extent of the fighting. The secretary-general, as well as Annan and Brahimi, believed that Iran should be invited to the two conferences, given its strong influence over the course of the war. Despite major pressures to the contrary, Ban decided to invite Iran to the 2014 conference but then felt let down when Iran did not live up to assurances to endorse the communiqué agreed on at the 2012 conference, and he declared that Iran's participation was not possible in these circumstances, despite the loss of face he had to endure as a result.

In 2014 and 2015, Ban strongly supported de Mistura's efforts to bring about a "freeze" in the fighting and positions in Aleppo—not, as he put it, to provide a substitute for a political dialogue (which neither side seemed to want) but to try to create space in which dialogue could be initiated. But UN efforts could not break the impasse created by the clear fact that both the Syrian government and the key backers of the opposition were more interested in fighting each other than in confronting the ISIL threat, let alone reaching a political compromise.

By February 2016, an international Syria support group (ISSG) of seventeen countries, cochaired by the United States and Russia, and including Iran and Saudi Arabia, sponsored a cessation of hostilities to move in parallel with a revitalized process of intra-Syrian negotiations on a political transition process. The cessation aimed at drastically reducing the level of violence throughout the country, while facilitating access of aid in particular to besieged areas. Meanwhile the Syrian parties were reconvened in proximity talks in Geneva to negotiate on governance and a new constitution, which was supposed to be followed by UN-supervised elections. As the cessation of hostilities threatened to unravel in April 2016, owing in large part to new Syrian government offensives especially around Aleppo, Ban did his utmost to keep the momentum going with continued public, telephone, and face-to-face diplomacy with the members of the ISSG. Following an especially gruesome aerial attack on a makeshift camp for displaced persons who had fled Aleppo near the Turkish border on May 5, 2016, he expressed his outrage over this apparent war crime and urged the Security Council to refer the situation in Syria to the International Criminal Court.

A major effort was made at the UN in 2013, with Ban playing a prominent role, to secure agreement on decommissioning Syria's chemical weapons arsenal, after conflicting allegations of who had been using them. Eliminating probably the largest—albeit previously undeclared, indeed denied—stocks of chemical weapons in the world was one of the most important and successful disarmament exercises to have been carried out for many years.

The secretary-general was personally instrumental in mobilizing funds for the immense UN humanitarian effort to alleviate the devastating effects of the conflict on the Syrian population and on neighboring countries. As the suffering increased in both extent and intensity, so that an ever-greater proportion of the Syrian population was in dire need of assistance, the humanitarian effort took up more of the secretary-general's energy. For four consecutive years, three in Kuwait and the last in London, the secretary-general cochaired donors' conferences to raise resources for life-saving support to millions of Syrian refugees and to the internally displaced.

During his last year in office (2016), a new problem unexpectedly erupted for Ban—one that probably qualifies as the single greatest crisis in relations between a UN secretary-general and an Arab government. Under Perez de Cuellar, the United Nations had in 1991 brokered a cease-fire between Morocco and the Western Sahara liberation movement known as the Polisario Front in exchange for a referendum on the territory's future. This led to the deployment of the UN Mission for the Referendum in Western Sahara (MINURSO), which had the double task of monitoring the cease-fire and making preparations for a referendum that, twenty-five years later, had not occurred.

During Ban's term, several problems with Morocco arose, almost invariably following the publication, each April, of the secretary-general's annual report to the Security Council on Western Sahara—to varying points of which Morocco took exception. The underlying point of contention derived from Morocco's claim of sovereignty over the massive territory (from which Spanish troops and administrators had departed in 1975). But that claim is not recognized by the International Court of Justice or the United Nations, whose membership continue to regard it as a "non-self-governing territory."

Never having done so before, Ban had for some time wished to visit Western Sahara, in particular the UN operation based there. In March 2016, prevented by Morocco from visiting Laayoune (the headquarters of MINURSO) in that part of Western Sahara under its control, he nevertheless proceeded with other parts of his regional tour, which included the Sahrawi refugee camps in southwest Algeria. Deeply moved by the desolation and hopelessness of the conditions of these refugees, as well as the outpouring of bitterness they exhibited toward the international community for having seemingly ignored their plight for decades, he referred in passing to their plight after "over forty years of occupation." The Moroccan government reacted with extreme vehemence to this remark and other alleged "slips" by the secretary-general (one of which was to mention the letter "R" in MINURSO's title, "Referendum"), which it claimed insulted the entire Moroccan people. Volleys of invective were leveled at the secretary-general and his advisers, and the Moroccan government expelled from Western Sahara the vast majority of the UN civilian staff who worked for MINURSO.

The secretary-general warned the Security Council that the removal of staff from the UN mission that the Council had established meant that the mission would soon not be able to function. This, he said, could lead to a "rupture of the cease-fire" and risk escalation into "full-scale war" (between Morocco on one side and the Polisario and Algeria on the other). Ban also pointedly told the members of the Security Council that should they fail to stand up for the UN mission that they themselves had established, then other governments around the world that hosted UN peacekeepers might also unilaterally decide to expel them.

Throughout this crisis with Morocco, which at least had the benefit of shining a spotlight once again on what had long been a forgotten and frozen conflict, Ban tried to keep the focus on what he called the "truly heart-wrenching human suffering" of the Western Saharans. He urged greater humanitarian assistance as well as considerably improved respect for their human rights.[65]

Overall, on the UN's approach to a whole range of questions involving the Arab world—the Palestinian conflict, Darfur and other Sudanese issues, the popular protests that marked the Arab Spring and their aftermath, the Syrian civil war, the Iraqi struggle with ISIL, and the plight of the Sahrawis—Ban consistently laid a greater stress on human rights than any of his predecessors had felt able or inclined to do.

SOME GENERAL OBSERVATIONS

The secretary-general of the United Nations has no financial or military power of his own. Any leverage he has must be based on his personal powers of diplomatic persuasion backed up by what limited authority is vested in him by the UN Charter or legislative bodies, combined with the universal moral legitimacy of the UN as a whole (a legitimacy that many Arabs as well as Israelis find questionable). One permanent challenge is to maintain a sufficient degree of cooperation with the key member states to be effective, while avoiding giving the impression that he is merely a "head-waiter" or a "letter-carrier."[66]

This chapter's survey reveals both common features and certain differences in how each secretary-general has handled the Middle East. The most obvious common feature is that this region dominated each one's attention during his time in office,[67] a result of the intensity of the problems there but also the wider international community's strategic interests and the UN's prior involvement in them.

Every secretary-general, understandably, has sought to make the UN more relevant to dispute resolution in the region. This was apparent from Trygve Lie's initial decision to involve the United Nations in the question of Palestine, including by being among the first to promote the "two-state solution" (at a time when the Jews and Israelis were keen on the idea and the Arabs were not—a position that later secretaries-general found was reversed during their own terms). Hammarskjöld introduced a number of practices that every one of his successors followed when dealing with the Middle East: the use of preventive diplomacy (prior to conflict), shuttle diplomacy (to bring conflict to an end), UN peacekeeping forces (placed between conflicting parties), and a UN political presence (to try to resolve the issues that led to the conflict in the first place). Perez de Cuellar, Annan, and Ban all worked hard to create new openings for the UN to make a more constructive contribution on a number of files relating to Palestine, Lebanon, and Iraq.[68]

Because of the nature of the job, all secretaries-general have been confronted with ethical dilemmas where the choice is often between the lesser of two evils. Partly as a result, the secretaries-general have been simultaneously criticized by all sides on Middle East questions. The present survey also highlights some of those instances when UN secretaries-general have been blamed by the warring parties themselves (or some in the wider international community) for either not preventing or not resolving the failures of the parties.

Most secretaries-general have made fairly dramatic dashes to the region in attempts either to prevent a war or to end one. Hammarskjöld, Thant, Waldheim, Perez de Cuellar, Annan, and Ban all made such trips. At least two (Thant in 1967 and Perez de Cuellar in 1991) knew that their chances of success were extremely small but considered that that they had an obligation, deriving from the office they held, to exert their moral authority and use every possible tactic in a last-ditch attempt to prevent a deeply damaging war. Every secretary-general has used envoys, often solely dedicated to the Middle Eastern task at hand, to work with the parties in the region, usually in a discreet manner.

For reasons of personality and the reigning state of geopolitical relations, secretaries-general have insisted on some of the key aspects of their office in a variety of ways. Impartiality is clearly something all secretaries-general have insisted on. Echoing Hammarskjöld, Annan said that impartiality must never mean neutrality in the face of evil, but rather strict and unbiased adherence to the principles of the Charter.[69]

The concept of independence goes a step beyond impartiality, as it implies not just an independent and impartial position on a given issue but independence of action and a conception of the role and legitimacy of the secretary-general as something distinct from (and implicitly much more than) that of a mere "secretariat" limited to servicing member states. Hammarskjöld and Boutros-Ghali were probably the two who were most insistent on the independence of the office. Indeed, Boutros-Ghali declared, "If one word above all is to characterize the role of the Secretary-General, it is independence";[70] the holder of that office had to never be seen as acting out of fear of, or in an attempt to curry favor with, one state. It is not a coincidence that those who most stressed their independence were also those who ended up having the most stupendous rows with key capitals (Hammarskjöld with Moscow, Boutros-Ghali with Washington). After Hammarskjöld, as one historian of the UN has put it, member states, although they could agree on little else, shared the view that they did not want a secretary-general to be allowed the capacity to curb their own freedom of action or the idea that the post had a genuinely supranational or moral standing.[71]

Perhaps inevitably, tensions have frequently arisen between the UN secretaries-general and the organization's most powerful member state on issues that the latter has often regarded as a major strategic concern. This is especially so given the strong alliance and sympathy that that member state (the United States) has with one of the key parties to the Middle East conflict (Israel) and the strength this gives the latter to withstand the views and pressures of the vast majority of other UN members, who are trying to push the secretary-general in the other direction. Such was less the case under Lie (whose sympathy mirrored that of the United States) or Hammarskjöld (given his and President Eisenhower's shared conviction that Israel and its allies, not Egypt, were to blame for the 1956 war). But from U Thant on, tensions with the United States have at times been evident—reaching a high point in the post–Cold War period, when US preponderance at the UN was at its most unquestioned, during the terms of Boutros-Ghali and Annan. Despite many differences of outlook on several key questions of style and substance, the memoirs of both those men have a common line on the manner in which US influence was exercised with them, not only on the Middle East but also on other issues.[72]

With the exceptions of Lie and Waldheim, other secretaries-general have—either explicitly or more guardedly—indicated that they believed their office has a moral component to it. Annan noted that he had more freedom of action than his predecessors, since the end of the Cold War had "transformed the moral promise of the role of the Secretary-General." It allowed him, he said, to place the UN at the service of the universal values of the Charter "without the constraints of ideology or particular interests."[73] However, he said this in 1998, five years before a divisive and what some termed an "ideological" war in Iraq and fourteen years before the UN Security Council demonstrated itself on Syria (and later Ukraine) to be as polarized as it had been during the Cold War.

Every secretary-general has condemned Arab acts of violence or terrorism against Israel and has unequivocally supported Israel's right to live within secure, recognized borders. Similarly every secretary-general has publicly condemned Israeli actions (responsive or preemptive) against Arab states or civilians when they have considered that excessive force was used or that these actions were in violation of international law. They have all expressed sympathy, in most cases repeatedly, for the predicament of the Palestinian people and have urged regional governments—mainly Israel, but also others—to adopt a less harsh attitude and to do more to alleviate their plight. But whatever the rights and wrongs—the humiliation and injustice of decades of occupation, the illegality of settlement building, terrorist attacks on civilians, the disproportionality of military actions—every UN secretary-general from Hammarskjöld on has also expressed frustration over what they have considered to be the counterproductive nature of Israeli policies when measured against that country's actual long-term interests.[74]

Since 1947, the Middle East—especially the question of Palestine—has played a defining role in the history of the United Nations. This applies both to the intergovernmental bodies and to the Secretariat, the organ headed by the secretary-general. Every secretary-general has made strenuous efforts to resolve conflicts in the Middle East, or at least to mitigate their more brutal effects. Testifying to the intractability of those issues, none (with the exception of Lie) have left office satisfied with the state of the region or their own record in managing to improve it. Most have been rebuked by one side or the other, or by public opinion, for either doing too much to bring the UN into these issues or not doing enough, and for either showing too much understanding for one side's position or not showing enough.

It has, after all, been demonstrated time and again that it is much easier to blame the United Nations and its most senior official for any perceived failures to bring peace than it is for the parties to show statesmanship themselves. It would be reassuring—though probably not realistic—to think that future secretaries-general may not have to encounter this same problem as they continue to grapple with the problems of the Middle East.

NOTES

1. The secretaries-general have been Trygve Lie (1945–53), Dag Hammarskjöld (1953–61), U Thant (1961–71), Kurt Waldheim (1971–82), Javier Perez de Cuellar (1982–91), Boutros Boutros-Ghali (1992–96), Kofi Annan (1997–2006), and Ban Ki-moon (2007, with his current term ending in 2016). The main wars between Arabs and Israelis have been in 1948, 1956, 1967, 1973, and 1982, as well as, though on a smaller scale, in 1978 and 2006 in Lebanon and in 2006, 2008–9, 2012, and 2014 in Gaza. The wars involving Iraq have been the Iran-Iraq War of 1980–88, the First Gulf War of 1991, and the Second Gulf War of 2003. Only Boutros-Ghali did not have a Middle East war during his watch (although up to 170 Lebanese were killed and five hundred thousand were temporarily displaced during Israeli attacks in 1996).

2. Quoted in Brian Urquhart, *Ralph Bunche: An American Life* (New York: Norton, 1993), 139–40.

3. Trygve Lie, *In the Cause of Peace: Seven Years with the United Nations* (New York: Macmillan, 1954), 76.

4. Quoted (in translation) in Ellen Jenny Ravndal, "Establishing the Norm of the Secretary-General as a Political Actor: The UN and the Palestine Problem, 1947–49," paper presented at the British International Studies Association conference, Birmingham, June 2013.

5. Ibid.

6. Urquhart, *Ralph Bunche*, 179. As Kati Marton put it in her book about the killing of Bernadotte, "So muted was the world body's reaction, so lacking in any real sanctions against the Jewish state for its failure to pursue the murderers of the United Nations' mediator, that for Israel 'world opinion' became an empty phrase." Kati Marton, *A Death in Jerusalem* (New York: Pantheon Books, 1994), 23.

7. Urquhart, *Ralph Bunche*, 196–97.

8. Ibid., 223, 231. Hammarskjöld later told Bunche that had he been secretary-general at the time, he would indeed have allowed Bunche to send the letter declining the prize.

9. The United Nations did not suffer a high-profile assassination of one of its leaders for fifty-six years, when Sergio Vieira de Mello was blown up, along with several of his colleagues, also in the Middle East, though in Baghdad. However, there is still much uncertainty over the death in a plane crash of Dag Hammarskjöld in 1961 and whether it was accidental or assassination.

10. In 1950, on Korea, his position was with one side and firmly against the other. In the end, faced with almost total noncooperation from the Soviet Union, he was compelled to resign.

11. Roger Lipsey, *Hammarskjöld: A Life* (Ann Arbor: University of Michigan Press, 2013), 13, 252. Years later, Ben-Gurion told Urquhart that Hammarskjöld was one of the best friends he had ever had. Each of Hammarskjöld's successors has made similar pronouncements regarding Israeli measures against Gaza.

12. Ibid., 263–64.

13. Ibid., 310.

14. Ibid., 297, 300; Brian Urquhart, *Hammarskjold* (New York: Knopf, 1972), chaps. 6 and 7.

15. Ben-Gurion wrote to Hammarskjöld accusing him of abandoning Lebanon to Egyptian-Syrian intrigues and asking, "Is not a Middle Eastern Munich in the making?" Hammarskjöld was lambasted in the Lebanese press, and at around the same time Hammarskjöld complained to the British foreign secretary about what he considered an officially inspired press campaign with "grotesque theories" that ever since Suez he had been considered "to be fooled by, if not a stooge of, Nasser." On the other side, Soviet and Arab nationalist officials and media continued to denounce him for his support of Western imperialism. Urquhart, *Hammarskjold*, 273–74.

16. Lipsey, *Hammarskjöld*, chap. 14; Urquhart, *Hammarskjold*, chaps. 6 and 7.

17. Urquhart, *Hammarskjold*, 300–301; Lipsey, *Hammarskjöld*, 372–73.

18. As Urquhart comments, "For the representative of a country that had refused to accommodate the 'fire-brigade' and had so dramatically initiated the actual fighting, this seemed self-serving indeed." The following day, U Thant responded to Eban in the General Assembly by pointing out that for ten years UNEF's effectiveness had been based on the cooperation of Egypt, whereas, in spite of the General Assembly's intention to have UNEF troops on both sides of the line, "Israel always and firmly refused to accept them on Israeli territory on the valid grounds of national sovereignty. There was, of course, national sovereignty on the other side of the line as well." Urquhart, *Ralph Bunche,* 413–14.

19. C. L. Sulzberger quoted in Urquhart, *Ralph Bunche,* 407. Urquhart also spells out in particular how strikingly little the two superpowers contributed to averting the crisis, which turned out to be a triumph for Israel and a disaster both for the Arab world (to a fairly large extent, but certainly not solely, self-inflicted) and for the UN.

20. Stanley Meisler, *United Nations: The First Fifty Years* (New York: Atlantic Monthly Press, 1997), 173–83. It was all a long way from the triumph of U Thant's early years, when President Kennedy declared that with his delicate handling of the Cuban missile crisis of 1963, "U Thant has put the whole world in his debt." After the 1967 war, the secretary-general allowed himself to become a convenient scapegoat for international inaction, accepting this unenviable role with as much Buddhist detachment as could be summoned. So wrote A. Walter Dorn in "U Thant: Buddhism in Action," in *The UN Secretary-General and Moral Authority: Ethics and Religion in International Leadership*, ed. Kent J. Kille (Washington, DC: Georgetown University Press, 2007), 177. See also Brian Urquhart, *A Life in Peace and War* (New York: Harper and Row, 1987), 215.

21. This was also the view of the force commander of UNEF, General Indar Jit Rikhye, *The Sinai Blunder: Withdrawal of the United Nations Emergency Force Leading to the Six-Day War of June 1967* (London: F. Cass, 1980).

22. Urquhart, *Life in Peace,* 215.

23. Urquhart, *Ralph Bunche*, chap. 31; U Thant, *A View from the UN* (London: David and Charles, 1977), 50.

24. For an important discussion of the contrast in the styles, principles, and values between Waldheim and other secretaries-general, see Manuel Frohlich, *Political Ethics and the United Nations* (London: Routledge, 2008), 199–201.

25. Simon Chesterman, introduction to *Secretary or General? The UN Secretary-General in World Politics*, ed. Simon Chesterman (Cambridge: Cambridge University Press, 2007), 2.

26. On that trip, he managed to offend both sides with small but (what were considered) inexcusable blunders: the Arabs by referring to Jerusalem as Israel's capital, and the Israelis by waving away the *kippa* that was offered when he visited Yad Vashem.

27. Urquhart, *Life in Peace,* 227–50; Meisler, *United Nations,* 198–99.

28. Urquhart, *Life in Peace,* 295 (for quotes) and chap. 22, "Lebanon 1978."

29. James Cockayne and David M. Malone, "Relations with the Security Council," in Chesterman, *Secretary or General?,* 70.

30. James Traub, "The Secretary-General's Political Space," in Chesterman, *Secretary or General?*, 189.

31. Javier Perez de Cuellar, *Pilgrimage for Peace: A Secretary-General's Memoir* (New York: St. Martin's Press, 1997), 80.

32. Ibid., 45.

33. Sir Marrack Goulding, "The UN Secretary-General," in *The UN Security Council: From the Cold War to the Twenty-First Century*, ed. David Malone (Boulder, CO: Lynne Rienner, 2004), 273.

34. Perez de Cuellar, *Pilgrimage for Peace*, 178.

35. In Cockayne and Malone, "Relations with the Security Council," 82. Other US diplomats have been even more explicit on this point. See Boutros Boutros-Ghali, *Unvanquished: A U.S.-U.N. Saga* (New York: Random House, 1999),291.

36. Boutros-Ghali, *Unvanquished*, 181.

37. Ibid., 205.

38. Ibid., 195–97.

39. Boutros-Ghali's remark to an ambassador that he had written to (Israeli prime minister) *Rabin* in Jerusalem but had instead gotten a reply from (US spokesman) *Rubin* in New York was attributed to anti-Semitism. Ibid., 204. Conversation between author and James Rubin, New York, 1994.

40. Authored by a Dutch general with a British deputy. Mortimer Zuckerman in *U.S. News and World Report* suggested that even making a report on the killing of civilians in a UN camp was tantamount to anti-Semitism on the secretary-general's part. Cited in Boutros-Ghali, *Unvanquished*, 263–64.

41. Whose overall assessment of Boutros-Ghali is far from uncritical. Brian Urquhart, "The Making of a Scapegoat," *New York Review of Books*, August 12, 1999.

42. Kofi Annan, *Interventions: A Life in War and Peace* (New York: Penguin Press, 2012), 319. Although the "Oil-for-Food" program for Iraq was to collapse during Annan's second term, it was a creation of the Boutros-Ghali tenure, with the direct involvement of the secretary-general himself. It took several years of especially frustrating negotiations to persuade Saddam Hussein, who seemed, to Boutros-Ghali, "to care nothing at all for the welfare of the poorest Iraqi people," to accept a closely monitored program that would allow Iraq to sell a certain amount of oil in exchange for food and medicines. Boutros-Ghali, *Unvanquished*, 208–10, 221, 258–61, 266–67.

43. Annan made repeated efforts to improve the UN's troubled relationship with Israel—in a way that sought to avoid compromising UN principles as much as possible. In December 2006, in his important last speech on the Middle East to the Security Council, he questioned the value of many of the UN's activities regarding Israel. "Some may feel satisfaction at repeatedly passing General Assembly resolutions or holding conferences that condemn Israel's behavior. But one should also ask whether such steps bring any tangible relief or benefit to the Palestinians. There have been decades of resolutions. There has been a proliferation of special committees, sessions, and Secretariat divisions and units. Has any of this had an effect on Israel's policies, other than to strengthen the belief in Israel, and among many of its sup-

porters, that this great organization is too one-sided to be allowed a significant role in the Middle East peace process?" See Eve Epstein, "Annan Made the Nations a Little Less United against Israel," *Jewish Daily Forward*, December 22, 2006.

44. Bruce D. Jones, "The Middle East Peace Process," in Malone, *UN Security Council*, 396–98. There was one area, a section of the village of Ghajar, from which the Israelis did not withdraw.

45. Annan, *Interventions*, 270. While not entirely accurate, it nevertheless illustrated the point.

46. Included in the "End of Mission Report" of Annan's personal envoy to the Quartet, Alvaro de Soto, May 2007. De Soto believed that the decision "effectively transformed the Quartet from a negotiation-promoting foursome ... into a body that was all-but imposing sanctions on a freely elected government of a people under occupation as well as setting unattainable preconditions for dialogue." But pressure on the UN was high. When in 2006 Annan was considering allowing midlevel UN officials to have contact with Hamas to discuss humanitarian issues, he was warned that the individuals concerned might lose their American visas. As Annan's deputy observed, "No wonder groups like Hamas have come to see the United Nations as an arm of their Western enemies," with major implications for the security of UN staff members. Quoted in Mark Malloch-Brown, *The Unfinished Global Revolution* (New York: Penguin, 2011), 75.

47. Annan, *Interventions*, 303.

48. Ibid., 305.

49. Ibid., 347–65.

50. Samantha Power, *Chasing the Flame: Sergio Vieira de Mello and the Fight to Save the World* (New York: Penguin, 2008), 368, 373.

51. Brian Urquhart, "The Evolution of the Secretary-General," in Chesterman, *Secretary or General?*, 29.

52. This chapter was finished in February 2015. Ban Ki-moon's term of office finishes at the end of 2016.

53. Ban Ki-moon, press statement, September 1, 2014, UN Secretariat website, www.un.org/sg/statements/index.asp?nid=7960.

54. Ban Ki-moon, remarks to the Human Rights Council, September 10, 2012, UN News Centre, www.un.org/apps/news/infocus/sgspeeches/statments_full .asp?statID=1643#.Vsajvza4mqQ.

55. Tom Plate, *Conversations with Ban Ki-moon: The Necessary Man of World Diplomacy* (Singapore: Marshall Cavendish, 2012), 134.

56. On July 30, 2014, he announced that another UN school sheltering thousands of Palestinian families had been attacked. "All available evidence points to Israeli artillery as the cause. Nothing is more shameful than attacking sleeping children. ... I condemn this attack in the strongest possible terms. It is outrageous. It is unjustifiable. And it demands accountability and justice." This and similar statements were criticized in some quarters but praised in others. An example of the latter was the *Independent*, which ran an editorial on August 4, 2014, saying that Ban's intervention was "crucial and commendable. For a man of his stature to raise

so openly the question of proportionality . . . was courageous. To refer to Sunday's attack . . . as a 'moral outrage and a criminal act,' while apparently pointing the finger at Israel, was remarkable. But the description was surely unarguable and his words appear to have emboldened the language of the US administration."

57. In his press remarks at the Gaza Reconstruction Conference on October 12, 2014, Ban stressed the need to "understand the level of frustration on the part of the international community, particularly donors. . . . Rebuild and destroy. This is already the third time. To put it simply, for a third grader student in Palestine . . . it is already the third war. Then what do you expect? As Secretary-General, I am also very much angry about this continuing violence. I have been urging that while we are ready to rebuild Gaza, it must be the last time." Ban Ki-moon, "Secretary-General's Press Encounter at Gaza Reconstruction Conference, Cairo, Egypt," October 12, 2014, www.un.org/sg/offthecuff/index.asp?nid=3678. Earlier that day, Ban had listed what he believed the "root causes" of the recent hostilities to be: "a restrictive occupation that has lasted almost half a century, the continued denial of Palestinian rights and the lack of tangible progress in peace negotiations." Ban Ki-moon, "Secretary-General's Remarks at the Cairo Conference on Palestine," October 12, 2014, www.un.org/sg/statements/index.asp?nid=8099.

58. Ban Ki-moon, "Secretary-General's Remarks to the Security Council on the Situation in the Middle East," January 26, 2016, www.un.org/sg/statements/index.asp?nid=9417.

59. Ban Ki-moon, "Don't Shoot the Messenger, Israel," *New York Times*, January 31, 2016.

60. "Egypt: Chinese, Russian Officials Question UN Secretary-General's Remarks," *Los Angeles Times*, February 4, 2011.

61. "Secretary-General's Keynote Address at High-Level Meeting on Reform and Transitions to Democracy," Beirut, January 15, 2012, UN Secretariat website, www.un.org/sg/STATEMENTS/index.asp?nid=5806.

62. When visiting the genocide site at Srebrenica in Bosnia in 2012, both deeply moved by what he was seeing and deeply frustrated by the divisions in the Security Council that seemed to prevent any agreed-upon action on Syria, he called on the international community to unite to prevent further bloodshed "because I do not want to see any of my successors in 20 years visiting Syria and apologizing for what we could have done to protect the civilians which we are not doing now." "UN's Ban Ki-moon Visits Srebrenica Graveyard," Associated Press, July 26, 2012.

63. Ban Ki-moon, "Secretary-General's Remarks to the General Assembly on the Situation in Syria," New York, June 7, 2012, UN Secretariat website, www.un.org/sg/statements/index.asp?nid=6109.

64. The Syrian position was not dissimilar to the Israeli position on this point. Diplomats from both countries maintained to the UN that terrorist acts should be condemned without qualification; as a result, the secretary-general was mistaken to insist on the need to address the "root causes" of terrorism (especially insofar as these were interpreted as being policies or tactics of either the Israeli or Syrian governments). The secretary-general did not change his position on either situation.

65. Ban Ki-moon, "Report of the Secretary-General on the Situation concerning Western Sahara," S/2016/355, April 19, 2016, http://reliefweb.int/report/western-sahara/report-secretary-general-situation-concerning-western-sahara-s2016355-enar.

66. Relatively mild terms of abuse used against Waldheim and Perez de Cuellar respectively (one by an Israeli, the other by an Iraqi). Boutros-Ghali—who earned the nickname "the Pharaoh"—had the opposite problem.

67. With the exception of Boutros-Ghali, who had to focus primarily on former Yugoslavia and African issues (including Somalia and Rwanda).

68. See, for example, Power, *Chasing the Flame*, 389.

69. The trouble for the UN (as Brian Urquhart put it) is that "failing a peaceful settlement, an impartial stance is often regarded partially by both sides." Brian Urquhart, "The United Nations in the Middle East: A 50-Year Retrospective," *Middle East Journal* 49, no. 4 (1995): 572–81.

70. Frohlich, *Political Ethics*, 205–11.

71. Traub, "Secretary-General's Political Space," 189.

72. Boutros-Ghali recounts how he once asked the US secretary of state and the UN ambassador if he could be allowed from time to time to differ publicly with US policy, as this would help the UN maintain its own integrity and dispel "the image among Member States that the UN is just the tool of the US." His words appeared to shock his guests, who apparently "looked at each other as though the fish I had served them was rotten. They did not speak" (*Unvanquished*, 198). Kofi Annan, similarly, observed about the then-secretary of state that "she had never quite understood that although the US had supported my candidacy for Secretary-General, I had to maintain an independent dedication to the principles of the Charter and be seen to be responsive to the wishes of all member states of the United Nations" (*Interventions*, 94).

73. Frohlich, *Political Ethics*, 211, cited in Ian Johnstone, "The Role of the UN Secretary-General: Power of Persuasion Based on Law," *Global Governance* 9 (2003): 441.

74. The words of several secretaries-general on this subject have been cited in this chapter, including Hammarskjöld, Annan, and Ban. To take one additional example, Perez de Cuellar expressed his "bewilderment and despair" that such intelligent leaders as Israel's should have been so "misguided" as to extend their "Operation Peace for Galilee" in 1982 into Beirut, thereby inflicting massive damage on Lebanon's capital, the Palestinians, and—ultimately—Israel itself.

TWO

Palestine, the Third World, and the UN as Seen from a Special Commission

Lori Allen

HISTORY OF PALESTINIAN COMMITMENT TO COMMISSIONS

As early as 1946, Arab political representatives advocating the Palestinian cause were announcing their loss of faith in investigative commissions as a means to the just resolution of the conflict. Muhammad Fādil al-Jamālī, the Iraqi delegate to the first General Assembly of the United Nations and principal founder of the Arab League, told the London Conference that Britain convened in 1946 to discuss the Palestine problem: "The Arabs have always expressed their grievances and raised their voice asking for their rights. What they are after is to reach a final settlement of their just cause. They are in despair. They have lost faith in Commissions and official statements, for, so far, they have shelved any decision which has been cognizant of their rights, while those decisions which favour the intruders have been carried out."[1] It was no wonder, this despair, given the frequency with which commissions had been dispatched to no salutary effect throughout the years of the British Mandate.[2]

A lack of faith in the integrity and neutrality of one of the first UN commissions, the UN Special Committee on Palestine (UNSCOP), led the Palestinian leadership to boycott it in 1947.[3] In contrast, the Zionists presented a thorough and well-organized lobby to UNSCOP. UNSCOP awarded them with a recommendation that mandatory Palestine be divided and that the Jews be given 62 percent of western Palestine, even though the Arabs outnumbered the Jews by almost two to one.

Since then, Palestinian engagement with UN commissions has been consistent and persistent. For decades Palestinians have been arguing their case in front of the "international community"—an imagined community most authoritatively embodied in the UN—in an attempt to secure their right to self-determination. Commissions summon their testimony, issue recommendations, sometimes prompt public and political debate, and release reports that usually are disregarded. From the UN's predecessor, the Permanent Mandates Commission of the League of Nations, to the UN Goldstone Commission that investigated the fighting in Gaza in 2009, and many commissions in between, Palestinians have demanded their collective and individual rights from the powers that be. But Israel's colonization of Palestine persists, and the violation of Palestinian rights continues. The United Nations, the source of many of those commissions, has posed little practical, effective hindrance to the Israeli occupation that is the root cause of those abuses. Yet Palestinians continue to engage with the UN, present their testimony when given the chance, and call for more investigative commissions.[4]

SYMBOLIC ASPECTS OF UN POLITICS

Although the early disastrous experience with boycotting UNSCOP may partially account for what we might call this "UN-compulsion," the impulse stems more fundamentally from the power of the UN as a symbolic realm. The UN is a site where "the world" is imagined and where humanitarian values are espoused. UNSCOP is a venue for the articulation of hopes in what the world, as embodied in the UN, can do. In summoning Palestinians to provide their testimony, asking them to state their case and provide proof of their abuses, members of the UN can confirm their Third World solidarities, their proud refusal of imperialism, and their support for universal human values. Crucially, the UN accommodates interactions that benefit—symbolically rather than immediately, practically, or politically—all those who choose to enter. For those who act as delegates, investigators, and arbiters, the issuers of declarations and passers of resolutions, the UN is a pulpit for the confirmation of values and a stage for the play of identity politics. For Palestinians, the UN has done more than offer a venue for making political claims. It has also provided hope. It encourages Palestinians to believe that "the world" will hear them. It presents a horizon of a peaceful future in which their freedom from subjection is assured. In giving Palestinians a forum in which to express their hope in that peaceful future, the UN also invites them to prove themselves reasonable political subjects.

Much critical analysis of the United Nations highlights the gap between the "quantitative accounting" of UN reporting and the subjective experiences of violence. The growing body of social science work on the UN regularly condemns the flattening effects of the UN's bureaucracy and its "technical approaches that focus on forms, procedures, and the organization of data into categories."[5] This work is laudable for drawing attention to the effects of bureaucratic forms and to the unequal power that characterizes the relationship of UN investigators and apparatchiks to victims of torture, the poor, and others who seek UN protection or recognition. But it is crucial that other dynamics, and other kinds of relationships, such as those that developed among Third World governments and peoples, also be recognized. It is only by appreciating these social, symbolic aspects of the politics of the UN that the apparently bureaucratic and ineffective form of UN commission activity and the superficial, repetitive content of UN reports and declarations can be understood. There is more going on than noble claims and realpolitik.

The foundations of the UN's symbolic role were laid in the UN's charter from the very beginning. It was not set up to enforce the moral values enshrined in its charter or the subsequently passed Universal Declaration of Human Rights. This was thanks to the United States in particular, which made sure that at the heart of the system there was a "basic inconsistency" between the UN's lofty goals and its practical capacity to realize them.[6] The praise of "eternal human values" and declarations of rights principles were only ever intended to be symbolic. Although justice, equality, and human rights are invoked throughout the articles of the UN Charter, presented as universal human values, they have been mostly mere rhetoric intended for idealistic Western activists and public opinion—those needing to be convinced of the legitimacy of this novel international institution.[7] The world's dominant states were willing to join the UN only because it had no real power, no authority to encroach on their sovereignty.[8] Human rights were incorporated into the Charter in an intentionally vague way. Rights principles were enshrined in formulations that would ensure their unenforceability and maintain Western state sovereignty.[9] The human rights principles that were incorporated in the UN Charter as "embellishment," as ornamental "preambular principles," provided the necessary symbolism and hopes—or smoke and mirrors—to sell the new system to the people.[10] The great powers intended the UN General Assembly in particular to be nothing more than a talking shop, a place, in the words of US president Roosevelt, for "small nations to blow off steam."[11]

Only little more than a decade later, however, those small nations, having grown in number and political clout as decolonization progressed, formed a significant bloc at the UN. The Bandung Conference of twenty-nine recently independent nations that met in Indonesia in 1955 created "the format for what would eventually become the Afro-Asian and then Afro-Asian-Latin American group in the United Nations."[12] By 1963 there were 34 African states in a membership of 113.[13] With the UN Declaration on Granting Independence to Colonial Countries and Peoples (1960), they had begun remolding the United Nations "to create institutional platforms for their Third World agenda."[14] Although it was a diverse group, opposition to imperialism and apartheid, and a shared understanding of colonialism from the perspective of its victims, formed the outlook that united them.[15] According to one somewhat idealistic rendering, the postcolonial states were also united in their belief "that they had directly benefited from the efforts of the United Nations and from the vision proclaimed by the UDHR [Universal Declaration of Human Rights]."[16]

More recent scholarship strikes a distinctly more cynical tone, dubious of the political significance of the Afro-Asian bloc and attentive to the changing significance of Third World human rights rhetoric.[17] The deployment of human rights language was often instrumental and was not so different from the rhetorical machineries of Western powers. This scholarship deems "shrewd political calculations" as much as postcolonial opposition to Western hegemony to be the beating heart of UN dynamics among Asian and African states too. As with most political behavior, it is likely that a mixture of motives and goals inspired the rhetoric and actions of the diplomatic members of Third World states, including a desire for colonialism's demise, a wish for greater human rights protections, and nation-state-specific projects and concerns. The human rights agenda also prompted "genuine optimism" in Third World diplomats. Their intention to pursue it was institutionalized in two special committees on decolonization and apartheid, which were created in the early 1960s and which gave voice to the group of new African states' "two main preoccupations."[18]

When Israel occupied the West Bank, the Gaza Strip, East Jerusalem, the Golan Heights, and the Sinai Peninsula in the summer of 1968, the UN's atmosphere was already distinctly inhospitable to such colonial incursions. During the 1968 General Assembly meeting, Palestine was the focus of two resolutions, along with several others dealing with the topics of colonialism, South Africa, apartheid, and racial discrimination.[19] Even the Security Council, which included the United States and United Kingdom as permanent members, unanimously issued Resolution 242, "emphasizing the inadmissibility of the acquisition of territory by war."[20]

ENTER THE "SPECIAL COMMITTEE"

Six months after the occupation began, the UN Special Committee to Investigate Israeli Practices Affecting the Human Rights of the Population of the Occupied Territories (hereafter "Special Committee") was established. The General Assembly announced this committee in Resolution 2443 (XXIII), entitled "Respect for and Implementation of Human Rights in Occupied Territories," which was adopted at its 1,748th plenary meeting in December 1968. The Special Committee's stated mission was to investigate violations and analyze the nature of the Israeli occupation.

Once the representatives of Ceylon, Yugoslavia, and Somalia were appointed to the Special Committee, they began their work in New York, one year after the General Assembly's decision to establish it. These countries had been supportive of the Palestinian cause, within the framework of the United Nations and beyond. Yugoslavia in particular, which had staked out a leading role for itself within the Nonaligned Movement, was supportive.[21] Sri Lanka, too, was sympathetic, a stance partly related to its tea trade with the Arab market and to the fact that Muslims in Sri Lanka were "closely identified with the Arab cause, and alienation of this minority was a political liability" that no Sri Lankan government could afford.[22] The position of solidarity deepened in 1970. With the opposition (United Front) leader Sirimavo Bandaranaike in power as the new prime minister, Sri Lanka's foreign policy had come more emphatically in line with the Nonaligned Movement, and strong ties were established with Yugoslavia.[23]

An impediment to the Special Committee's work, which it described as a "major obstacle," was the refusal of the government of Israel to cooperate with it.[24] Committee members have never been allowed to visit Israel or the Occupied Palestinian Territory. Despite this obstruction, the Special Committee forged ahead and decided to hear from witnesses who were in or could travel to neighboring countries, Geneva, or New York. In the committee's view, the urgency of the situation required the most immediate action:

"The paramount need, in the Special Committee's opinion, was to secure immediate alleviation of the conditions prevailing in the occupied territories and this could be achieved only if the primary evidence available was evaluated and the Special Committee's findings on it presented with the least possible delay."[25] Thus the committee placed ads in local newspapers that read: "Any person who has knowledge of practices affecting the human rights of the population of the territories occupied by Israel, who is prepared to testify before the Special Committee, either in open or private session, is requested to apply immediately to the Secretary of the Committee, giving name, address and brief summary of the information he is prepared to present."[26]

During its first round of investigations, which included forty-six meetings held in seven cities over a period of nearly three months, the three members of the Special Committee heard from 146 people. They collected reports, testimony, evidence, documents, and letters. They heard from those who had suffered torture in prison and could give accounts of witnessing the effects of torture on their fellow prisoners. They asked witnesses about their impressions, observations, and descriptions of "feelings of the population" and sense of the "atmosphere." They heard allegations of rape, summary execution, protracted curfews, collective punishment, prolonged administrative detention, and looting of shops and homes by Israeli soldiers. The Special Committee asked many witnesses about what seemed to be "deliberate policy" on the part of the Israeli authorities and concluded in their first report "that the occupying Power is pursuing a conscious and deliberate policy calculated to depopulate the occupied territories of their Arab inhabitants."[27] In its first report the Special Committee recommended "supervision by an independent authority," which would be "an arrangement whereby the Third and Fourth Geneva Conventions will be enforced."[28]

The Special Committee identified the root cause of rights violations to be the occupation as a whole. In its inaugural report, it recognized that the "ideal manner in which violations of human rights could cease would clearly be by the termination of the occupation itself."[29] And over a decade later the committee was still making this point, insisting that violations should not be examined and could not be understood without taking into account the structural context of the occupation.[30]

The Special Committee was the first UN commission to investigate the Israeli occupation. It challenged the fiction that Israel's was a moral army administering a "benign occupation."[31] During the first several years of the committee's work especially, its members were focused on gathering firsthand evidence of the occupation's effects. They regularly restrained witnesses when they ventured into the realm of hearsay, and they continuously sought proof of abuses that could be corroborated. A testy exchange between a witness and a committee member in the 1970s shows the juridical nature of the committee's early efforts and the emphasis the committee placed on finding credible evidence.

The witness began by discussing Israeli settlements in an area near the Golan Heights. After the witness described Israel's attempts to impose occupation law in the village, the inhabitants' refusal, and the Israelis' use of force against them, a committee member posed questions.

COMMITTEE MEMBER (CM): Who told you that?

WITNESS: One of my relatives.

CM: That's hearsay evidence. Can you tell me who the relative is, where, name, whether he can be traced?

WITNESS: No, definitely not.

CM: Then it is of no value as evidence. Everybody is investigated under duress and pressure and torture—that is a general statement. Yes, go on please.

The witness resumed his pre-prepared statement, proceeding to describe Israeli army harassment of inhabitants of an area in the northern Golan Heights. The committee member asked the witness, once again, how he knew these circumstances. The witness began to answer, "Through discussion with one of my . . ." The committee member interrupted him: "I must apologize, I am extremely sorry, but I just cannot keep recording hearsay evidence. Anybody can come and say anything. I have had plenty of stories of this nature. I could fill volumes with them but it's not proper evidence. . . . I'm sorry but I can't report to the UN that Mr. [Witness] came and said that he heard from somebody that such a thing is happening. That is useless—you must appreciate that we have a duty to perform and must perform it properly."

The witness began to respond, asking how else could "we otherwise get information about—." Once again, the chair interrupted, and although the transcripts offer no indication of the tone or tenor of the back and forth, one can imagine that a certain level of mutual frustration was evident.

CM: Don't question me . . .

WITNESS: I beg the Chairman to excuse me but—

CM: ... We daren't go before a tribunal and say that we heard this unless we can produce a person who has seen it. If you are not in a position to indicate who said it and if I am not in a position to interrogate that person, then the evidence is of no value to me. . . . But at the same time we cannot put evidence into our records unless it is evidence that will stand the usual test of credibility.[32]

The Special Committee's focus on obtaining reliable, firsthand witness testimony was strong in the early years of its work. Its members were not always, or even usually, so annoyed with their witnesses, however. In one meeting in the late 1980s, after a witness provided approximately one-and-a-half hours of articulate, organized testimony analyzing many aspects of the occupation, barely interrupted by committee questioning, the chair complimented the witness for "the thoroughness of the preparation of the material" that he presented.

The witness responded, humbly acknowledging that his presentation might not have been as complete as he would have liked. He went on to explain his motivations for appearing before the Special Committee and his expectations from it.

I should like to say that I am proud and happy to be here before you and to have testified. . . . Therefore I should like to thank you for having listened to my testimony, and with all my heart and with all sincerity I hope that this testimony will, through you, reach every honourable and free person in the entire world. I hope there will be more pressure in the end to put an end to the practices from which we suffer day to day. I hope that this meeting will yield a real ray of hope, to enable us together, we and you, the representatives of an official circle, to move towards a peaceful solution to our Palestinian cause, if you can bring pressure to bear on international public opinion, so that the Palestinian people will achieve its legitimate and just rights, so that the refugees may return and we may establish our independent state.[33]

Another witness during the early years of the committee's work said he came with the hope that, through the committee, his voice would "[reach] the United Nations and world conscience. . . . We are equally sure that the candid voice of truth which you have heard here and elsewhere will reach, through you, the General Assembly and the world forum to reveal and expose practices in violation of human rights in the occupied territories involving acts of systematic, cold-blooded torture, collective punishment, merciless reprisals and other atrocities."[34]

In these, as in many other speeches to the Special Committee, the witnesses nominate "the world" as their intended audience. Through their invocation "the world" comes into being, with the UN recognized as its legitimate representative. A mayor from the West Bank implored the Special Committee in the late 1970s: "I hope you will convey this truth to the whole world, so that the whole world will know that there is still a Palestinian people which is undergoing tremendous suffering."[35] This is a world figured in largely moral terms, and the UN as its embodiment is the forum for humanity's collective conscience—a worldly morality that must take account of the inhumane conditions of life under occupation. For one West Bank physician the committee provided "at least a ray of hope for us in the future of humanity."[36] Many of those who appeared before the Special Committee thanked and praised the UN for its work in upholding justice. As one witness who spoke before the committee in the early 1980s said: "I was convinced of the nobility and grandeur of your task ... because your task is a noble and humanitarian one, that of defending those who have no other means of defence at their disposal other than their faith and public opinion, the best part of it which is represented by organizations such as your own.... We hope that we will be able to eliminate racial discrimination and racism in order to build a better human society."[37]

Just as Palestinians called on "the world" to hear them, they also framed their plight as being one of universal human concern, a matter for, of, and representing world interest. The transnational dimension of Palestinian politics was strong in the 1970s, and the PLO saw and presented their struggle as being part of a broader Third World context of "global war against the forces of imperialism and neo-imperialism."[38] However, in the Special Committee testimony of witnesses from a variety of backgrounds, the crisis of Palestinians was described in terms resonant not only with Third World anti-imperialism but with humanity more generally. The Palestinian people were "an example of mankind," as one witness said.[39] The committee was held up as a body that worked "in the service of human rights" and "might make law known, to safeguard human values."[40] The Palestinian case as it was constituted by the Special Committee was universal, a case that should resonate with the values that were asserted by the UN and represented by it.

As time passed and the occupation continued, it became clear that the Special Committee could do little to see its recommendations made reality. While it continued to collect evidence from witnesses, it relied ever more on newspaper and human rights reports. And its investigations became, in some cases, less juridical and more ethnographic. During the first intifada, the Palestinian uprising against Israeli occupation that began in 1987, the Special Committee received testimony from injured Palestinians. In one meeting, most of the committee's interlocutors were paralyzed or partially disabled from being shot or beaten by Israeli forces. While one of the Special Committee members began the interviews with questions about the circumstances in which the injuries were received, another member pursued a line of questioning that had very little to do with gathering courtroom-style evidence or factual information about times and places of particular events.

Instead, the committee member evoked the personal, experiential dimensions of the intifada. Rather than pursuing the "credible, eye-witness" testimony that other committee members had sought, the questioner seems to have had a more emotional purpose, exhibiting as he did sympathy for the plight of these people as individuals and as members of a society under occupation. He repeatedly asked witnesses if they were optimistic about the prospects for peace. He ended most of his exchanges by asking each witness if he had hope in the future and whether he would be able to "forgive and forget" if peace was achieved. Most responded that they would.[41]

These questions gave Palestinians an opportunity to express their sense of grievance and to assert their nationalist aims and convictions. One respondent admitted that he was not optimistic in the short term but assured the Special Committee that Palestinians would not stop struggling until their rights were achieved. Others were hopeful that they would "regain the right to self-determination, the right to live like all other peoples in the world." Another stated: "I have great hopes. I know it is not easy to achieve all this, but with pressure on Israel exerted by the whole world, it may be possible to reach some solution."[42] In such testimony, the world is imagined as an entity out there with the power to change the status quo. With every invocation of "the world," these Palestinian witnesses pronounce the Special Committee, and the UN, to be the rightful conduit of global humanity's principles of equality and justice.

The inner workings of the Special Committee reveal a different side of Palestinian engagement with the UN, one that cannot be understood simply in terms of First World instrumentality or in terms of the relationship of a supplicant to a savior. As the witnesses' testimony shows, Palestinians did come to the UN in hopes that "the world" would hear their case, recognize their plight, maybe do something. But by the time of the Israeli occupation, the UN in its postcolonial Third World guise was also seeking a witness that would showcase the world organization's anticolonial, humanitarian, human rights values. By standing with the Palestinians, even if only symbolically, the Special Committee could perform its allegiance to universal, humanist values.

Issues regarding the stance or sympathies of the UN often get instrumentalized as people on different sides try to use the work and words of the UN polemically and politically. But what the preceding review of this special committee reveals is the heterogeneity of practices involved, the range of purposes that each person who talked with the committee, as member or witness, brought to the interaction. What has been consistent from the beginning is the Special Committee's insistence on understanding the occupation as the root cause of rights violations.[43] It has repeatedly reaffirmed "the fact that occupation itself constitutes a grave violation of the human rights of the Palestinian people in the occupied Palestinian territory."[44]

Most details of witnesses' stories—their assertions of optimism and their obliging natures, their willingness to forgive and forget the troubled conflict if peace were achieved—were never made public. Instead they were translated into lines in the Special Committee's annual report. In these repetitive documents the Special Committee pronounced its stance, strongly condemning Israeli policies and practices, such as the "killing and wounding of defenceless demonstrators," and the "breaking of bones and limbs of thousands of civilians."[45]

Over time, the Special Committee's yearly reports became a ritualized genuflection at the altar of international humanitarian and human rights law, a symbolic display of some part of the international community's recognition of the objectionable nature of the Israeli occupation. Year upon year, another layer of Special Committee reporting was laid atop the previous, including a regular rehearsal of the litany of previous UN resolutions on Palestine, the occupation, and the conflict with Israel. The introduction to the 1989 report recalled tens of prior UN resolutions condemning violent Israeli actions and calling upon that country to respect international humanitarian and human rights law:

> *Recalling* all its resolutions on the subject, in particular resolutions 32/91 B and C of 13 December 1977, 33/113 C of 18 December 1978, 34/90 A of 12 December 1979, 35/122 C of 11 December 1980, 36/147 C of 16 December

1981, ES-9/1 of 5 February 1982, 37/88 C of 10 December 1982, 38/79 D of 15 December 1983, 39/95 D of 14 December 1984, 40/161 D of 16 December 1985, 41/63 D of 3 December 1986, 42/160 D of 8 December 1987, 43/21 of 3 November 1988, 43/58 A of 6 December 1988 and 44/2 of 6 October 1989...

Recalling also the relevant Security Council resolutions in particular resolutions 605 (1987) of 22 December 1987, 607 (1988) of 5 January 1988, 608 (1988) of 14 January 1988, 636(1989) of 6 July 1989 and 641 (1989) of 30 August 1989...

Recalling further the relevant resolutions adopted by the Commission on Human Rights, in particular resolutions 1983/1 of 15 February 1983, 1984/1 of 20 February 1984, 1985/1 A and B and 1985/2 of 19 February 1985, 1986/1 A and B and 1982/3 of 20 February 1986, 1987/1, 1987/2 A and B and 1987/4 of 19 February 1987, 1988/1 A and B and 1988/2 of 15 February 1988 and 1988/3 of 22 February 1988, 1989/1 and 1989/2 of 17 February 1989 and 1989/19 of 6 March 1989, and by other United Nations organs concerned and the specialized agencies.[46]

Despite this chronicle of vague promises and unfulfilled expectations for justice, the Special Committee continues to stand as a concrete symbol representing a "world" that shares certain values, one that opposes colonization and occupation. As the testimony of many Palestinians show, the committee maintains, for some, a horizon of hope for a different future in which the broad international consensus that the Israeli occupation must end will be made reality. Through its recurring investigations and repetitive reports, the Special Committee enacts something like what anthropologists call a "ritual of intensification." Often conducted during times of crisis, such as after the death of a group member or a drought, intensification rituals like funerals and rain dances give people an opportunity to strengthen the relations between members and confirm their commitment to the group. The crisis in international law is evident in the impunity with which strong states and suprastates continuously act.[47] Violations of UN principles and human rights standards are legion. The Special Committee is enacted in the midst of a crisis of the UN and what it stands for. It performs an intensification ritual that gives Palestinians and those who stand in solidarity with them a forum for the enunciation of "eternal human values," to assert their membership in an international community that is united by certain values and ideas about justice. In so doing, the Special Committee has fostered a hope that there is an "international community" that cares about the Palestinians' predicament, and a false hope that it is doing something to defend them.

Acknowledgments: I would like to thank Ajantha Subramanian for her feedback on a draft of this chapter and James Eastwood for his research assistance. Conversations with Christopher Lee, Darryl Li, and Yezid Sayigh were also very helpful. I gratefully acknowledge the Arts and Humanities Research Council Early Career Fellowship that allowed me to conduct the research upon which this chapter is based. I also extend my sincere gratitude to His Excellency Dr. Palitha T.E. Kohona and to Susan Kurtas at the UN Legal Branch Library for facilitating this research. And thanks to Karim Makdisi and Vijay Prashad for bringing this important volume together.

1. Muhammad Fādil al-Jamālī, "Experiences in Arab Affairs, 1943–1958," n.d., http://users.physics.harvard.edu/~wilson/Fadhel.html#IRQANDPALESTINE.

2. Some of these commissions were the King-Crane Commission (1919), the Palin Commission (1920), the Haycraft Commission of Enquiry (1921), the Permanent Mandates Commission of the League of Nations (1923–48), the Shaw Commission (1929–30), the Hope-Simpson Commission (1930), the Peel Commission (1936), the Woodhead Commission (1938), and the Anglo-American Committee of Enquiry (1945–46).

3. Elad Ben-Dror, "The Success of the Zionist Strategy vis-à-vis UNSCOP," *Israel Affairs* 20, no. 1 (2014): 19–39.

4. Lori Allen, "Inquiring into International Commissions of Inquiry," Middle East Research and Information Project (MERIP), February 24, 2013, www.merip.org/inquiring-international-commissions-inquiry.

5. Sally Engle Merry and Susan Coutin, "Technologies of Truth in the Anthropology of Conflict," *American Ethnologist* 41, no. 1 (2014): 1–16; Tobias Kelly, "Politics of Shame: The Bureaucratisation of International Human Rights Monitoring," in *The Gloss of Harmony: The Politics of Policy Making in International Organizations,* ed. Birgit Muller (London: Pluto Press, 2012), 134–53.

6. Robert Normand and Sarah Zaidi, *Human Rights at the UN: The Political History of Universal Justice* (Bloomington: Indiana University Press, 2008), 136.

7. Mark Mazower, *Governing the World: The History of an Idea* (New York: Penguin Press, 2012), 196–97, 200, 212.

8. Mark Mazower, "The Strange Triumph of Human Rights, 1933–1950," *Historical Journal* 47, no. 2 (2004): 379–98.

9. Normand and Zaidi, *Human Rights,* 113–14, 131–35.

10. Samuel Moyn, *The Last Utopia: Human Rights in History* (Cambridge, MA: Harvard University Press, 2010), 61, 181, 183.

11. Normand and Zaidi, *Human Rights,* 110.

12. Vijay Prashad, *The Darker Nations: A Biography of the Short-Lived Third World* (New Delhi: LeftWorld Books, 2007), 56. Burke, however, contends that most who were at Bandung were not involved in human rights lobbying at the UN in later decades. Nevertheless, it was the Afro-Asian bloc that made antiracism and

anticolonialism central issues for the UN in the 1960s and 1970s. Roland Burke, *Decolonization and the Evolution of International Human Rights* (Philadelphia: University of Pennsylvania Press, 2010).

13. Normand and Zaidi, *Human Rights,* 292.

14. Prashad, *Darker Nations,* 14.

15. Dipesh Chakrabarty, "The Legacies of Bandung: Decolonization and the Politics of Culture," in *Making a World after Empire: The Bandung Moment and Its Political Afterlives,* ed. Christopher Lee (Athens: Ohio University Press, 2010), 51; Christopher Lee, introduction to Lee, *Making a World,* 10; Mark Mazower, *No Enchanted Palace: The End of Empire and the Ideological Origins of the United Nations* (Princeton, NJ: Princeton University Press, 2009), 152.

16. Paul Gordon Lauren, *The Evolution of International Human Rights: Visions Seen* (Philadelphia: University of Pennsylvania Press, 1998), 252.

17. According to Jan Eckel, for example, politicians and activists from the Third World brought initiatives to the UN "as a highly politicized, if largely symbolic, attempt to counter the global hegemony of First World states and to restructure the international state system." Jan Eckel, "Human Rights and Decolonization: New Perspectives and Open Questions," *Humanity* 1, no. 1 (2010): 113. Also see Reza Afshari, "On Historiography of Human Rights: Reflections on Paul Gordon Lauren's *The Evolution of International Human Rights: Visions Seen,*" *Human Rights Quarterly* 29 (2007): 1–67; Lee, *Making a World.* The UN's Third World contingent did express itself in a number of institutional frameworks. In 1964, for instance, the largest Third World coalition in the United Nations was established, the Group of 77, formed to coordinate developing countries in the United Nations and promote their collective economic interests. See "The Early Days of the Group of 77," *UN Chronicle* 51, no. 1 (May 2014), http://unchronicle.un.org/article/early-days-group-77/.

18. Eckel, "Human Rights and Decolonization," 120–21, 129; Burke, *Decolonization,* 69.

19. See UN General Assembly, "Resolutions Adopted by the General Assembly during Its Twenty-Third Session," December 1968, www.un.org/documents/ga/res/23/ares23.htm.

20. UN Security Council Resolution 242, S/RES/242, November 22, 1967, www.un.org/en/ga/search/view_doc.asp?symbol=S/RES/242%281967%29.

21. Ante Batovic, "Nonaligned Yugoslavia and the Relations with the Palestine Liberation Organisation," paper presented at the Eleventh Mediterranean Research Meeting at the European University Institute, Workshop 12, "Superpower Rivalry and the Third Way(s) in the Mediterranean," Florence, Italy, March 24–27, 2010, http://academiccommons.columbia.edu/catalog/ac:128788. Senegal was elected first chair of the UN Committee on the Exercise of the Inalienable Rights of the Palestinian People, which was founded in 1975 by Resolution 3376 of the UN General Assembly, and Yugoslavia was a member. Somalia was sometimes a member of this committee. See UN General Assembly Resolution 3376, A/RES/3376

(XXX), November 10, 1975, https://unispal.un.org/DPA/DPR/unispal.nsf/o/B5B4720B8192FDE3852560DE004F3C47.

22. Shelton U. Kodikara, *Foreign Policy of Sri Lanka: A Third World Perspective* (Delhi: Chanakya, 1982), 129.

23. H.S.S. Nissanka, *Sri Lanka's Foreign Policy: A Study in Non-alignment* (New Delhi: Vikas Publishing House, 1984).

24. UN General Assembly Special Committee to Investigate Israeli Practices Affecting the Human Rights of the Population of the Occupied Territories, "Report of the Special Committee to Investigate Israeli Practices Affecting the Human Rights of the Population of the Occupied Territories," A/8089, October 5, 1970, https://unispal.un.org/DPA/DPR/unispal.nsf/o/BC776349EAEE6F28852563E6005EDF08.

25. Ibid., see "Letter of Transmittal."

26. Ibid., see para. 19.

27. Ibid., see para. 67.

28. Ibid., see paras. 150–51.

29. Ibid., see para. 146.

30. UNGA Special Committee, "Report of the Special Committee to Investigate Israeli Practices Affecting the Human Rights of the Population of the Occupied Territories," A/34/631, November 13, 1979https://unispal.un.org/DPA/DPR/unispal.nsf/o/68B222A27C07C25F0525658C00691A57.

31. Neve Gordon, *Israel's Occupation* (Berkeley: University of California Press, 2008), 1; Edward Said, *The Question of Palestine* (1979; repr., New York: Vintage, 1992), 44.

32. UN records of testimony (reviewed with special permission of the committee chair on conditions of maintaining witnesses' anonymity).

33. UN records of testimony.

34. UN records of testimony.

35. UN records of testimony.

36. UN records of testimony.

37. UN records of testimony.

38. Paul Chamberlin, "The Struggle against Oppression Everywhere: The Global Politics of Palestinian Liberation," *Middle Eastern Studies* 47 (2011): 28.

39. UN records of testimony.

40. UN records of testimony.

41. UN records of testimony.

42. UN records of testimony.

43. UN General Assembly Special Committee, "Report of the Special Committee," A/8089, October 5, 1970, para. 146.

44. UN General Assembly Special Committee, "Report of the Special Committee," A/RES/44/48, December 8, 1989, www.un.org/documents/ga/res/44/a44r048.htm.

45. Ibid.

46. Ibid.

47. Jeffrey D. Sachs, "Ukraine and the Crisis of International Law," *Project Syndicate,* March 24, 2014, www.project-syndicate.org/commentary/jeffrey-d--sachs-sees-in-russia-s-annexation-of-crimea-the-return--with-us-complicity--of-great-power-politics?barrier=true. On the crisis in human rights, see Stephen Hopgood, *The End Times of Human Rights* (Ithaca, NY: Cornell University Press, 2013).

THREE

On Behalf of the United Nations

SERVING AS SPECIAL RAPPORTEUR OF THE HUMAN RIGHTS COUNCIL FOR PALESTINIAN TERRITORIES OCCUPIED SINCE 1967

Richard Falk

PRELIMINARY OBSERVATIONS

It is crucial to understand that acting within the United Nations in any capacity is colored by the political context, especially if the role and subject matter are perceived as having geopolitical relevance. The UN operates as a complex system of institutional actors that are loosely tied together by an administrative structure presided over by the UN secretary-general and headquartered in New York City. Its staff is a large bureaucracy that is organized in a hierarchical fashion, with a tendency to exhibit more responsiveness to political pressures at the higher levels of administrative responsibility. These pressures are exerted primarily by states, especially the five permanent members of the Security Council, and among these particularly the United States, to a lesser extent by private sector actors, and to a still lesser extent by civil society organizations.

Given this structure, it is hardly surprising that UN concerns about Israel and responses to Palestinian grievances are highly politicized within the organization. It is one of the sites of struggle between the generally pro-Palestinian consensus that prevails in the international community as a whole and the geopolitical center of gravity that continues to be the United States as usually reinforced by the governments of western Europe. This struggle has surfaced particularly at the UN Human Rights Council (HRC) in Geneva because it is one of the few institutional arenas within the UN in which non-Western priorities and viewpoints prevail, and none more so than in relation to the Israel/Palestine conflict. As a result of the limited capacity of the friends of Israel to control the agenda of the HRC because of the orientation of the membership, the focus of attack is on the institution itself. The HRC is accused by pro-Israeli nongovernmental organizations (NGOs) and by Israel and the US government, especially the US Congress, of being biased against Israel, as seen by its alleged practice of devoting disproportionate attention to Israeli violations of human rights as compared with countries that are alleged to be worse offenders whose behavior supposedly receives scant HRC attention. This criticism is connected to the argument that several governments guilty of severe violations of human rights are currently HRC members in good standing. During the presidency of George W. Bush this criticism grew so intense that the United States temporarily withdrew from membership in the HRC and did not resume participation until the Obama presidency. Renewed participation did not lessen American hostility to the HRC, accompanied by threats to withhold budgetary appropriations and the like. The entire UN, including the HRC, is sensitive to this kind of hostility from its most important member and tries to avoid provocations and to restore its good standing by adopting a posture of impartiality whenever possible.[1]

To circumvent some of these political difficulties, the HRC came up with the rather ingenious device of establishing special rapporteurs for a variety of human rights themes and, in a few instances, for particular states or conflict situations. These individuals are unpaid, are drawn from the ranks of civil society experts, enjoy independence from UN bureaucratic discipline, and are supposed to be selected on the basis of merit by a committee of ambassadors within the HRC. Because the special rapporteur on Palestine is the only truly independent voice available to the Palestinian people, it has been, especially in the last ten years, a valuable source of information and analysis relating to Israeli violations of human rights. To counter these adverse judgments, pro-Israeli NGOs, most notably UN Watch, have launched major attacks on the person of the special rapporteur and have done their best to divert attention from the message to the messenger.[2] It is against this background that I discuss the pros and cons of my experience as special rapporteur on Palestine from 2008 to 2014.

REFLECTIONS ON MY EXPERIENCE AS SPECIAL RAPPORTEUR FOR OCCUPIED PALESTINE

It came as a surprise to me when I was approached in early 2008 by NGOs in Geneva and by an official in the Office of the High Commissioner for

Human Rights (OHCHR) and asked whether I would accept the position of special rapporteur for Palestine if selected by the HRC. I was aware at the time that Israel was mounting a campaign to ensure that the selection of the next special rapporteur would be more sympathetic to their claims as occupier of Palestinian territories than John Dugard, a distinguished jurist from South Africa, who had served as special rapporteur for the prior seven years and whose reports were being widely cited as evidence of an Israeli pattern of disregard for its legal obligations under international humanitarian law.

It is likely also that Israel became more concerned during this period about the office of the special rapporteur and the increasing influence of its reports on international public opinion both via governments and by way of civil society organizations.[3] Dugard's reports, unlike those of the two special rapporteurs who preceded him, were comprehensive, factually grounded, and authoritative when it came to depicting Israeli occupation practices and their incompatibility with respect to international humanitarian law and international human rights standards. It was not credible to depict Dugard as biased or anti-Semitic, as in lawyerlike fashion he kept his distance from political undertakings relating to the conflict. Nevertheless, Israel and its infrastructure of NGO support mounted a personal attack on Dugard as biased in his reporting on Israeli violations of international humanitarian law and international human rights norms, and they campaigned hard to choose a less conscientious successor.

I mention this background partly to explain my surprise when I was informed in early 2008 that I had been selected as the new special rapporteur for Occupied Palestine.[4] I was only mildly surprised when the Israeli Foreign Ministry issued a statement at the time of my selection indicating that I would be denied entry to Israel and Palestine in my UN role because of my alleged bias. Some public figures also attacked the appointment, including the US ambassador to the UN at the time, John Bolton, who called me "a fruitcake" whose appointment clearly illustrated all that was wrong with the UN. I received a stream of hate mail, mainly e-mail, and some hostile media attention in the immediate aftermath of my appointment. The biggest evidence being used against me at the time was a rather obscure article I had published some years earlier in a Turkish English-language newspaper, *Daily Zaman,* that appeared with the admittedly provocative headline "Slouching toward a Palestinian Holocaust."[5] The article focused on the dire humanitarian situation in Gaza at the time, comparing the Israeli mentality of collective punishment exhibited toward the civilian population of Gaza with Nazi attitudes toward Jews as a persecuted group. My intention then was to warn readers of the cumulative ghastly consequences of a continuing oppressive administration of Gaza for the entrapped Palestinian civilian population. I wanted to challenge the prevailing international mood of apathy and the scandalous passivity of the international community and the UN in the face of Israel's unacceptable behavior. The central argument of the article was ignored by critics, and pro-Israeli anger focused on the supposed comparison of Israel and Nazi Germany, a comparison that I had not made and that did not reflect my views then or now.

Most of the criticism directed at me by professional Israeli apologists focused on my views toward other sensitive issues, generally pulled out of context and distorted. Particularly stressed in this regard was my association with David Ray Griffin, a distinguished philosopher of religion who became the leading 9/11 skeptic. In a foreword to the first of his eleven books devoted to 9/11 I praised Griffin as a celebrated and scrupulous scholar, primarily as a leader of the application of Whitehead's philosophy to process theology, a man who possessed the highest levels of academic credibility. I also indicated my belief that in his first 9/11 book Griffin raised a series of worrisome questions that cast heavy clouds of suspicion across the official account of the attacks. I continue to believe that the American people and the world deserved to have an authoritative process established that either removed these suspicions or confirmed them.[6] To this day, those that attack my role as critic of Israel falsely situate me in the ranks of "conspiracy theorists" as a partisan member of the denigrated "truther movement." Never having delved into evidence for and against a suspicious view, I consider myself agnostic as to whether the official version of the 9/11 attacks is essentially correct.

After a few weeks these criticisms subsided, and I began to discharge my responsibilities as special rapporteur as best I could. Because of the earlier official Israeli attack on my appointment I was worried that I might have trouble gaining entry to Jerusalem, the West Bank, and Gaza, but experienced administrators in Geneva assured me that it looked as though I would be treated as Dugard had been—no cooperation, but access allowed. They explained this optimistic assessment by saying that they had followed previous practice, submitting an itinerary of our proposed meetings and visits to the Israeli Mission in Geneva, without receiving any negative reaction and that they felt further reassured when visas were issued to my assistant and to an accompanying security officer of the OHCHR. On this basis, I felt that it was worth the effort to make the long trip from California to Israel in mid-December of 2008.

Clearly the OHCHR had misjudged the situation. On this occasion the government of Israel clearly wanted to teach the HRC a lesson by refusing entry to a special rapporteur that was selected despite their strongly voiced objections. At the Ben Gurion Airport, my assistants were let through immigration without questions raised, but when I handed the same official my passport along with the UN Travel Certificate, she excused herself while she checked with someone of higher authority. When she returned I was told to wait with a few others, mainly Palestinians, in a room set aside for problematic persons. After a few hours I was asked to come again to the window and was informed that I had been expelled from Israel by order of the Foreign Ministry and that I had to return to the place from which I had traveled. Israeli airports were administered by the Ministry of Interior, and their representative was unexpectedly friendly, even somewhat apologetic, indicating that Interior had no choice but to follow orders received from another government ministry. After another couple of hours during which my luggage and computer were searched and my cell phone was confiscated, I was taken in a van to a nearby detention center and placed in a filthy, overlit cell with five other "prisoners" who were being held for various nonpolitical reasons. On the following morning a guard escorted me directly to my seat on a plane bound for the United States while other passengers stared with worried looks as I took my seat, I suppose wondering quite reasonably what accounted for such "special treatment."

When the news story broke about my expulsion broke, the Israeli government lied about the incident.[7] A spokesperson for the Israeli Foreign Ministry told the media that I had been "warned" not to come when in fact I came only after it seemed as though I would be allowed entry in the same manner as Dugard. The *New York Times* published this Israeli version of the events without making any effort to talk with me, and when I requested a chance to give my side of the story I was politely refused. I mention this detail only to show how in a small incident of this sort the most trusted media outlets make no effort to get at the truth of the situation when Israel's reputation for veracity is at stake. From Israel's perspective my proposed visit was undoubtedly occurring at an awkward moment in the midst of an escalating security crisis. Ten days later, on December 28, 2008, Israel embarked on Operation Cast Lead, a massive air, land, and sea military operation in Gaza that continued for twenty-one days of brutal onslaught against a vulnerable and densely populated urban area where the people had no way of escaping the combat zone.[8]

My expulsion took place on a weekend, and my assistant unfortunately failed to convey an emergency alert to the OHCHR. There was no official protest by the UN in the aftermath of my expulsion, although I was told that back-channel efforts were later made at various subsequent times to secure my future entry. I never received any evidence of this, and there was never a change of heart on Israel's part. As the years passed I adapted to the situation, preparing my reports on the basis of available information and meetings in Cairo and Amman with Palestinians and others who could provide additional information and insights. In each report that I made over the six years I reported to the HRC, the brash leader of UN Watch, Hillel Neuer, would use his two minutes of time allotted to any accredited NGO that requests permission to speak during the so-called interactive dialogue to launch a vituperative attack on me personally with no reference whatsoever to the substance of my reports. Neuer generally repeated the same charges on each occasion, his allegations being mainly based on excerpts from my blog concerning controversial political issues unrelated to Israel-Palestine and of no relevance to my special rapporteur role or to the reports I had prepared.

UN Watch gained some traction in their ongoing campaign against my mandate by sending detailed letters containing these same discrediting allegations to prominent officials at the United Nations, as well as to officials at the US Mission and to the governments of such countries as Canada and Australia. What was most disturbing to me was the willingness of these officials, including the UN secretary-general on two occasions, to denounce my role as special rapporteur simply on the basis of the allegations by UN Watch, without making any independent effort to check on the accuracy or relevance of the defamatory attacks being disseminated. When I tried to get Secretary-General Ban Ki-moon to issue a clarifying statement, I was told in an apologetic tone by his chief aide that there had been a failure in the secretary-general's office to do "due diligence" and that the secretary-general was under pressure at the time from the US Congress to show that he was supportive of Israel in the midst of his campaign for reappointment. Others prominent critics of my role, such as the American ambassadors in New York Susan Rice and later Samantha Power, made harsh statements about my anti-Israeli bias as well as uncritically repeating the distorted presentations of my views on 9/11 and the Boston Marathon bombing.[9]

Perhaps what caused me the most trouble of all was a cartoon that I inadvertently included in a post on my blog that was critical of the International Criminal Court for issuing arrest warrants for the Libyan leader, Qaddafi, and two others close to him while the North Atlantic Treaty Organization (NATO) war of 2011 was being waged against Libya. I had included the cartoon in the body of the text because it showed the goddess of justice blindfolded while acting on America's behalf, seemingly oblivious to the discrimination associated her manner of discharging justice. What I did not see when posting, because the cartoon was extremely small and easy to overlook, was the presence in one corner of a tiny dog wearing an Israeli *kippa* while urinating on the pro-American goddess. I deciphered the objectionable contents of the cartoon only when I used a magnifying glass. I was initially attacked on my blog and actually missed the allusion at first because it was so unrelated to the subject of the post and certainly contrary to my intentions and had seemed underscore my criticism of the International Criminal Court. The cartoon was red meat for all those who wanted to demonstrate to the world that I was, in fact, a self-hating Jew and an unabashed anti-Semite. I removed the cartoon a few hours later as soon as I realized what was arousing the furor. The then high commissioner in Geneva, Navi Pillay, issued a statement of regret about the incident but felt reassured by my timely removal of the cartoon from the blog site. To this day, I am harassed by those that seek to deny me a venue for speaking by invoking the cartoon as proof of my hostility to Israel and Jews. The Wiesenthal Center in Los Angeles had the temerity to list me in 2013 as the third most dangerous anti-Semite in the world, exceeded in stature only by the supreme leader of Iran and the prime minister of Turkey.[10] In effect, enough mud was thrown in my direction to damage my professional reputation and make me "controversial" wherever I speak and regardless of topic.[11] Actually, my status as an "independent" appointee allowed UN and national officials to repeat the defamation charges while at the same time declaring their helplessness to have me dismissed.

This option was not available for liberal NGOs evidently fearful of arousing the ire of UN Watch and kindred groups. For instance, in direct and immediate response to a complaint by UN Watch, I was dumped from membership on the Santa Barbara Committee of Human Rights Watch (HRW) because of the convenient discovery *on the same day* of an obscure rule that disqualified membership in HRW organs in the event of any "conflict of interest." UN Watch publicized their success by accurately claiming to have caused my "dismissal" in response to their initiative, contending in their publicity that I was so anti-

Israeli as to be unacceptable even to HRW. I was disappointed although not surprised by the refusal of Ken Roth, its executive director, to be willing even to clarify in public HRW's reason for my removal from the committee despite my repeated requests that he do so. In effect, in a display of liberal opportunism Roth allowed defamatory charges leveled against me to appear as endorsed by HRW, presumably to avoid antagonizing UN Watch and irritating pro-Zionist funders and board members of his own organization.

My overall experience with the UN was decidedly mixed. There is little doubt that the secretary-general, despite having some prior friendly acquaintance with me, chose to attack me personally, reportedly as a means to curry favor with Israel and Washington. At the same time, Navi Pillay, the high commissioner for human rights, was consistently supportive, especially in our private meetings. She and others in the OHCHR hierarchy conveyed to me appreciation for my reports and diligence under fire and indicated their realization that I had been the target of unfair and irresponsible attacks. After some early unsatisfactory experiences with staff support, in my second term I had excellent help from diligent and highly intelligent professionals in Geneva.

THE ROLE AND OFFICE OF SPECIAL RAPPORTEUR

The special rapporteur position is a rather recent institutional innovation in UN practice and is currently limited in use to the HRC. The secretary-general and other organs of the UN use the term *special envoy* in a somewhat similar manner, although it is crafted in a more ad hoc manner. There are currently thirty-nine special rapporteurs, mostly devoted to thematic concerns, with a few focused on particular countries. The competitive procedure for selecting special rapporteurs has changed somewhat over the years to achieve greater transparency, objectivity, and the choice of more qualified candidates, although political connections and backroom pressures for and against play a role, especially in contested mandates. The current procedure relies on individuals being nominated by governments, NGOs, or international institutions and on applications for these positions made by individuals. All nominees and applicants are required to submit rather elaborate materials outlining their qualifications, a "motivation letter" explaining why they want the position, and reference letters from three persons capable of evaluating their abilities.

A preliminary short list is then prepared by staff at the OHCHR in Geneva. This list is submitted to a Consultative Group appointed by the president of the HRC that consists of five ambassadors of member countries, which reviews the qualifications of each candidate and conducts a phone interview with the three or four applicants whom it believes to be most the promising nominees for each special rapporteurship. The qualities that are supposed to guide the selection process are listed on the HRC website as "(a) expertise; (b) experience in the field of the mandate; (c) independence; (d) impartiality; (e) integrity; and (f) objectivity." On this basis the Consultative Group forwards its recommendations, rank-ordering the top one or two candidates, to the president of the Council, who normally goes along but occasionally exercises his or her authority to introduce or give priority to other candidates. As can be imagined, many pressures are brought to bear on the Consultative Group and the president in support of one or another candidate.

The final stage in the process is for the president to submit his slate of proposed appointments to a meeting of the forty-seven governments that constitute the membership of the HRC. The recommendations made by the president must be accepted by "consensus," which is interpreted to mean "unanimously" (that is, without a single negative vote; abstentions are ignored). The approval of the recommended slate usually goes forward without much friction. Special rapporteurs are initially chosen for a three-year term that is almost always renewed for an additional three years, with six years being the maximum allowed. Problems with this selection process are encountered in some cases because a region or country feels underrepresented and objects either to the process itself or to a particular person being proposed who turns out to be unacceptable to one or more governments. Such issues are usually resolved behind closed doors by various kinds of compromises and trade-offs, although occasionally controversies come into the open at public sessions of the HRC.

The position of special rapporteur has some unusual features in relation to UN employment. It is an unpaid position yet is quite widely sought after because of the visibility and prestige that have become associated with the post, and mainly because of the opportunity to influence the global policy discourse. The rapporteurs are not part of the UN civil service and are not subject to standard disciplinary procedures. They are considered fully independent and can be dismissed only if they are found to persist in carrying on activities outside the specifications of the mandate, although their work is subject to critical scrutiny within the OHCHR and is often sharply criticized, especially by governments, whether members to the HRC or not. By protocol, a country report is submitted to the government for comment prior to being disclosed to the public or put on the HRC website.

The duties of special rapporteurs vary somewhat but generally involve two overseas missions to their country or bearing on their theme. Comprehensive separate reports prepared by the rapporteurs are submitted annually to the HRC and to the General Assembly at an open session, accompanied by an oral summary and what is called in UN language "interactive dialogue," which is a misleading label. In fact, the format consists of an interminable series of short statements by governments (three minutes allowed) and even shorter ones by NGOs (two minutes allowed) that request an opportunity to speak, followed by a response by the special rapporteur that is supposed to take no more than ten minutes, a time constraint that usually makes it utterly impossible to offer considered responses to the array of questions and comments made by the various speakers.

This independence of a special rapporteur is often less than meets the eye. The OHCHR exercises continuing supervision by way of their various protocols of approval, whether it is a matter of editing texts, shaping the itineraries that are developed for missions, or giving governments a chance to object to reports or to edit public transmissions such as press releases before these are made public. Beyond this, most missions depend on receiving invitations from a relevant government. As of now, 108 governments have issued standing invitations, but for the others advance approval is required before a special rapporteur can visit a particular country, and these tend to be the governments that are most likely sensitive about having their policies and practices evaluated by an independent expert. The HRC has on several occasions confirmed the legal obligation of all states to cooperate with special rapporteurs and other designated UN experts in their discharge of official duties, but in practice the UN defers to the national sovereignty of governments, and the response of governments is decisive in determining whether a mission can be undertaken and what scope it can have.[12]

Although the experience and the quality of the work of the special rapporteurs vary greatly, it can be concluded that over the years this position has gained in influence and prominence. Given the complexity of global policy concerns, the special rapporteur as an expert without a nationalist or private sector axe to grind has increasingly been viewed by civil society, the media, and by many governments as a reliable and even authoritative source of useful information, helpful analysis, and prudent policy guidance. Degrees of effectiveness largely depend on the motivation, background, and ability of the individual rapporteur, as well as on the political sensitivity of the mandate. Also, human rights issues rise and fall over time with respect to the extent of interest exhibited and reflect wider geopolitical trends.

THE SPECIAL RAPPORTEUR FOR OCCUPIED PALESTINE

Against this background I now turn to consider some characteristics that distinguish the mandate established by the HRC and made applicable to Occupied Palestine.

In 1993 the Human Rights Commission, the UN body that preceded the HRC, established the mandate on Palestine in Resolution 1993/2A with the official name "Special Rapporteur on the Situation of Human Rights in the Palestinian Territories Occupied since 1967." In this chapter I use the simpler unofficial name of "Special Rapporteur for Occupied Palestine." This shorter version also acknowledges that the General Assembly by formal action on November 29, 2012, recognized Palestine as a nonmember state entitled to limited participation in UN activities.[13] Subsequent to the resolution, the UN has no longer perceived Palestine as constituted by "Occupied Territories" but has instead regarded it from a technical international law viewpoint as an "Occupied State." The shift from plural to singular in the designation should also be noted. Israel has pursued a politics of fragmentation since 1967, so the conception of the West Bank, East Jerusalem, and Gaza as essentially separate entities rather than as parts of a unified political community called Palestine has served its purposes.[14]

The implications of this shift in status are potentially important and are bitterly contested at present. Particularly significant and controversial is the legal capacity of Palestine to participate in various domains of international society as a sovereign state. Palestine, as represented by the Palestinian Authority, has become a party to the treaty establishing the International Criminal Court and on this basis is in a position to press charges against Israel, either in relation to the extensive settlement activity in the West Bank and East Jerusalem or in relation to excessive force, blockade, and crimes against humanity in Gaza.[15]

Unlike other mandates, this one was established to last "until the end of Israeli occupation." Because the initial mandate was limited to Palestinian territories, the Golan Heights of Syria are excluded from coverage although they were also occupied by Israel in the 1967 war. Critics of the mandate also complain that it discriminates against Israel because it does not extend its concerns about violations of human rights to wrongdoing by Palestinian governing authorities, the Palestinian Authority in the West Bank and Hamas since 2007 in Gaza. Israel further contends that it is no longer responsible as an occupying power in Gaza because of the implementation of its "disengagement" initiative in 2005, including the withdrawal of Israeli military forces and the removal of Israeli settlements and settlers. Israel's position has been rejected within the UN system, including the HRC, because of the effective control exercised by Israel over Gaza by way of entry and exit, airspace, and coastal waters. Israel also claims that Jerusalem is no longer occupied, as it was already annexed by Israel in 1967, and that the city is administered as a single unified entity. Again this position is rejected because of the overriding notion of occupation contained in Security Council Resolution 242 that territory cannot be legally acquired by force and because of its basic directive that Israel should withdraw from all Palestinian territories occupied in 1967, including those parts of Jerusalem previously under Jordanian administration. Finally, Israel claims that the West Bank is an instance of "disputed sovereignty" and thus is not occupied territory subject to international humanitarian law, a position rejected by a unanimous International Court of Justice in the advisory opinion on the separation war.[16]

Israel and its NGO supporters have generic objections to the mandate as singling Israel out for scrutiny and reflecting their contention that the HRC devotes disproportionate attention to Israel as compared to such other states as Syria and Iran that have bad human rights records. The response to this objection is by way of an appreciation that the Israeli/Palestinian conflict is unlike any other situation where a violent conflict persists for many years: the UN has been directly engaged with Palestine since its inception, and earlier during the period of the League of Nations when Palestine was administered as a British Mandate, which itself incorporated the colonialist gesture of endorsing the Zionist quest for a Jewish homeland contained in the 1917 Balfour Declaration.[17] Israel owes its own legitimacy as a state to the UN, which admitted the fledgling state to membership after the 1948 war. Further, the Palestinian ordeal can be traced back, in part, to its rejection of a partition proposal approved by the UN General Assembly in 1947.[18] Arguably the UN itself, by proposing such a territorial allocation without any prior ascertainment of the wishes of the people then living in Palestine, encroached upon Palestinian inalienable rights of self-determination. At every stage, the UN has been seen as vital to any kind of resolution of the conflict, and this is more pronounced than in relation to any other ongoing situation in the world. At the same time, the United States has acted in a supervisory role in relation to asymmetrical diplomatic efforts to resolve the conflict ever since the Oslo framework was agreed upon in 1993 and then solemnized by the handshake of Rabin and Arafat on the White House lawn.[19]

Israel also contends that the HRC as such is particularly biased and thus that all of its activities are tainted. It plays the anti-Semitic card, especially by way of pro-Israeli NGOs, mounting strong campaigns against those who occupy the position of special rapporteur. My predecessor John Dugard experienced such pressures, and it was certainly my experience from the moment my candidacy was proposed, continuing with intensifying fury until the end of my term.

Perhaps most revealing and disturbing in this regard, although not relating directly to the work of special rapporteurs, has been Israel's response to commissions of inquiry established to investigate their military operations in Gaza in 2008–9 and again in 2014. In both cases Israel, and the United States in a supporting role, used their leverage to oppose the establishment of the initiative, even though neither Israel nor the United States was a member of the HRC in 2009, and then exerted pressures behind the scenes to discourage individuals from taking on the assignment of leading such an effort. The experience of Richard Goldstone, who headed the earlier inquiry into the Cast Lead operation, is particularly illuminating. Goldstone, a former South African judge, was a respected international figure who had been the first prosecutor at the Hague Special Ad Hoc International Tribunal for the Former Yugoslavia, which had been set up by the UN Security Council, and held other important posts including chair of the Independent International Commission on Kosovo. More to the point, Goldstone was a lifelong Zionist with important existing ties to Israel, including membership on the Board of Hebrew University. The inquiry into Cast Lead had been preceded by several respected NGO reports, each of which had found Israel guilty of serious violations of international humanitarian law.[20] The actual report issued by the Goldstone Commission leaned over backward to address Israel's concerns and magnified the crimes of Hamas associated with firing indiscriminate rockets at Israeli civilian population centers, yet Goldstone and the report were vilified from the moment of publication.[21] The pressures mounted by Israel and Zionist groups led Goldstone to retract key portions of the report on his own initiative, without the agreement of the three other distinguished members, in a manner that suggests that he had been victimized by the backlash that occurred.

What makes these outcomes so distressing is that the breaches of international humanitarian law were blatant in relation to these large-scale attacks on Gaza, especially given the wider context of a sustained policy of collective punishment of the entire Gazan civilian population via a blockade in place since 2007 and by frequent violent intrusions.[22] Israel deftly plays the bias card, tied directly and indirectly to inhibiting allegations of anti-Semitism, to deflect attention from its wrongdoing under international law. These tactics involve defamatory attacks on individuals (Goldstone, William Schabas) and on the sponsoring institution itself. Their success in mitigating UN responses illustrates the subordination of international criminal law to geopolitical pressures in the setting of the Israel/Palestine conflict. It is notable that in other litmus tests of international morality, as posed by the struggles against colonialism or efforts to weaken the apartheid regime in South Africa, the UN has been more effective because such pressures, while also present, were weaker and more robustly opposed. One explanation of the difference is the presence in the United States of the Israeli lobby, which has caused the US government to give the highest priority to insulating Israel from censure and even criticism in callous disregard of the facts.[23] Another reinforcing explanation, of great importance in Europe, is inhibiting lingering memories of the Holocaust and of liberal democratic governments' failures to take action against Hitler's Germany until they were themselves victims of aggressive war.

WHAT WAS ACCOMPLISHED IN MY SIX YEARS AS SPECIAL RAPPORTEUR

In light of these frustrations and pressures I was often on the verge of resigning as special rapporteur during my first four years in the position. I kept recalling the words of my predecessor and friend John Dugard, "Remember, it is a thankless job." I resisted the urge to resign for several reasons: my steadfastness in the position appeared important to the Palestinian people with whom I had contact and seemed a soft echo of their own truly heroic *sumud;* I did not want to allow my irresponsible and nasty adversaries to have the pleasure or benefit of claiming to have forced my resignation by discrediting me; and I felt that the Palestinians deserved and needed an independent voice within the UN system and that the UN, for all of its shortcomings, has become a politically relevant arbiter of the legitimacy and illegitimacy of competing claims of right in conflicts that are brought to its attention.[24]

The most important of all my reasons for staying in the position was my belief that the exposure of Israel's flagrant violations of international law was making a positive contribution to the Palestinian struggle to uphold their rights, above all the right to self-determination. It may seem perverse to make such a claim given the two dominant realities that occurred during my six years as special rapporteur. The situation on the ground for Occupied Palestine steadily worsened from the perspective of the Palestinians—Israeli settlements accelerated their expansion beyond the point of no return; Israel proceeded with its effort to alter the ethnic character of Jerusalem so as to lend credibility to its insistence that the city should remain unified and part of Israel; and Palestinians trapped in Gaza endured a blockade during this period and suffered from three major Israeli military onslaughts in 2008–9, 2012, and 2014. During my years as a mandate holder there was diminished support for the Palestinian struggle in the Arab world, especially in the aftermath of the Egyptian coup of 2013 and in view of the new regional context in which Israeli and Saudi Arabian interests increasingly converged. This international situation was further reinforced by the unwavering support given by the United States to Israel, despite the 2009 failed initiative of the Obama presidency to push toward a more balanced diplomacy in the region, particularly with respect to the Palestinians.

April 2014 saw the collapse of direct negotiations between Israel and the Palestinian Authority that had been resumed in prior months at the strong urging of the American secretary of state, John Kerry, and in the face of obvious reluctance in both Ramallah and Tel Aviv. Finally, Netanyahu removed any reasonable doubts about this bleak assessment during the 2015 election campaign when he promised the Israeli electorate that no Palestinian state would be established so long as he was the leader of Israel.

This abandonment of negotiations was internationally interpreted as the end of any realistic prospect of achieving a two-state solution through the present framework of diplomacy, making it clear to almost all independent observers that the Oslo diplomatic framework was flawed from the start and incapable of producing a sustainable peace.[25] These international developments were further reinforced by the rightward drift of Israeli internal politics toward explicit advocacy of a unilateral "solution" that centered on incorporating all or most of the West Bank into Israel, with an accompanying effort to fix Israel's international borders to reflect this reality. There also became evident a growing Israeli support for transferring portions of the Arab minority to what remained of Palestine. The weakness of the Palestinian Authority in its role as representative of the Palestinian people was also part of the picture and was rendered more disabling by the inability of the Palestinian Authority and Hamas to reconcile their differences so as to present a credibly unified front in diplomatic settings.[26]

Against such a discouraging background, it may seem strange to claim that progress was achieved during my terms as special rapporteur. My underlying contention is that the core of the Palestinian struggle has shifted away from both armed resistance and international diplomacy, at least temporarily, and that it now centers on various coercive forms of nonviolent resistance that are bolstered by growing pro-Palestinian activism in global civil society, including within the United States and western Europe. In this regard, the BDS (Boycott, Divestment, and Sanctions) campaign is emblematic of a legitimacy war being waged on many fronts that the Palestinians are winning.[27] I believe that I was able to articulate this shift in the tactical and strategic nature of the Palestinian national movement that exerted some influence on the discourse surrounding the conflict that occurred within the UN system, especially within the HRC and General Assembly, as well as the media. Further along this line, by superseding the rhetoric of "occupation" and by viewing the Palestinian reality as one of "apartheid," "ethnic cleansing," "annexation," and "settler colonialism," I continued in my reports an effort begun by Dugard to use language that more accurately conveyed the true depth of the Palestinian ordeal than the formal euphemisms commonly relied upon in diplomatic discourse.

In this regard my semiannual reports highlighted and documented the critique of the severe encroachments on Palestinian rights and the futility of reliance on international diplomacy within the Oslo framework, the affirmation of civil society initiatives that were gaining persuasive weight, and the value of lending UN support to the BDS Campaign of global solidarity and such efforts as the Freedom Flotilla, a courageous multinational undertaking by activists to break the blockade of Gaza and respond to the humanitarian emergency created by the persistence of the Israeli blockade and related policies of harassment. In effect, in assessing the developments described above, I was able to formulate this new phase in the Palestinian struggle that included an appeal to the UN to be more active as a direct participant in the global solidarity movement. This took the specific form of encouraging governments to be more diligent in reminding corporations and financial institutions of their moral and legal obligation to avoid gaining commercial advantages from dealing with the unlawful Israeli settlements either by trade or by investment. The adoption of this narrow approach to corporate responsibility was chosen to achieve as broad a consensus as possible, especially in Europe. On a principled basis, there is a strong case for extending boycott and divestment reasoning to arms sales, whether as imports or exports. In several reports, specific corporations were mentioned as having such commercial arrangements.[28] My goal was to encourage the UN to realize that it must *act* as well as *speak* if it seeks to retain credibility and relevance with respect to the Palestinian struggle.[29] In this regard I made many efforts to familiarize the HRC and the third committee of the General Assembly with the appropriateness of the language of "legitimacy war" to describe the conflict and the current phase of the Palestinian struggle.

Conceptually, in my role as special rapporteur I was able to bring attention to the special conditions created by "prolonged occupation" that showed the inadequacy of existing international humanitarian law to uphold the basic human dignity of an occupied people living for decades under military administration without the protection of the rule of law. Such a lack of rights was further shown to be aggravated by Israel's persistent effort to make unlawful and irreversible changes in territory under its control, taking full advantage of their opportunity to do what international law prohibits—gain territory by force of arms and change the fundamental character of conditions in a society living under belligerent occupation—and, because of their geopolitical impunity, to suffer no adverse consequences.

I have reached several conclusions with respect to the role of a special rapporteur on Palestine in relation to the overall posture of the Palestinian conflict:

- The work of a special rapporteur will be scrutinized by pro-Israeli NGOs and civil society actors that seek to deflect attention from the message to the messenger, what I call "the politics of deflection." This process, which exposes the special rapporteur to unpleasant public pressure and is damaging to such a person's overall reputation, will be escalated to the degree that the work of the special rapporteur is perceived as having an impact.

- The nature of the UN role in relation to the conflict is shaped by geopolitical factors, especially the extent of effort made by the United States to ensure Israel impunity, including shielding Israel from criticism within the UN as much as possible. In general, the UN is a crucial player in legitimacy war settings, as it has a great influence on international public opinion and global discourse by the way in which it processes claims of right and wrong. The UN can also send a variety of signals to civil society. By encouraging greater corporate accountability in relation to Israeli settlements, the UN is also indirectly encouraging civil society initiatives that move in the same direction, such as the growing number of divestment initiatives being adopted and discussed at universities and by churches and labor unions. It is important to understand that the UN is *behaviorally* constrained by geopolitics yet *symbolically* able to act with sufficient independence to exert a constructive influence on political struggles of the sort that have gone on for so long between Israel and Palestine. This geopolitical setting is not stable, as recently illustrated by the very different effects of the Arab upheavals of 2011 and counterrevolutionary pushback that has restored authoritarian rule or produced chaos and extremism in the region during the last three years.[30]
- For all of its difficulties, the role of special rapporteur is of great value in this setting as a means of shaping the legitimacy discourse and of informing governments, NGOs, and public opinion as to issues of moral significance in relation to human rights and of legal significance with respect to the behavior of states and the rights of people. The independence of the special rapporteur is a great asset if used in a proactive spirit that is not intimidated by the contested nature of this political setting. Offsetting such pressures are a variety of compensations, including warm sentiments of appreciation from the Palestinian people and their supporters around the world. In the end, the function of this particular special rapporteur is to lend credibility and commitment to the hope for a just and sustainable peace that allows these two peoples to live together benevolently.[31]

With the benefit of a reflective interval, I now realize that John Dugard gave me misleading guidance: in retrospect, I am grateful for the opportunity to have served as special rapporteur on Palestine and to shed whatever light I could on the Palestinian struggle for their rights under international law. Until that struggle is brought to a just end, none of us deserve a peaceful sleep.

1. It is important to note the differences between the Human Rights Council (HRC), composed of forty-nine states selected by vote for three-year terms, and the Office of the High Commissioner for Human Rights (OHCHR), which is part of the overall UN bureaucracy. The former is less susceptible to geopolitical pressures than the latter, which is subject to the overall civil service discipline of the UN as a whole, with the secretary-general particularly sensitive to the political dimensions of his office, and none more so than the current secretary-general, Ban Ki-moon. Of course, the effectiveness of these pressures also depends on the outlook, ambitions, and character of a particular high commissioner.

2. Another NGO that focuses almost all its energy on defending Israel from criticism is NGO Monitor, which, unlike UN Watch, engages in polemical research on substantive issues to present Israel's side of the story, straining the interpretation of both facts and law. Rather than attack individuals, NGO Monitor saves its fury for NGOs critical of Israel.

3. For instance, Saree Makdisi's influential book, *Palestine Inside Out: An Everyday Occupation* (New York: Norton, 2008), relies heavily on Dugard's reports.

4. The United States was not a member of the HRC in 2008, and although Canada had spoken against my selection during the open debate, it abstained when it came to the vote.

5. Richard A. Falk, "Slouching toward a Palestinian Holocaust," *Daily Zaman,* July 13, 2007.

6. See David Ray Griffin, *New Pearl Harbor: Disturbing Questions about the Bush Administration and 9/11* (Northampton, MA: Olive Branch Press 2004); see also Griffin's critique of the 9/11 Commission report, *9/11 Commission Report: Omissions and Distortions* (Northampton, MA: Olive Branch Press, 2005).

7. Isabel Kershner, "U.N. Rights Investigator Expelled by Israel," *New York Times,* December 15, 2008; my version of the events is in Richard Falk, "My Expulsion from Israel," *Guardian,* December 19, 2008.

8. For a comprehensive narrative of Cast Lead, see Adam Horowitz, Lizzy Ratner, and Philip Weiss, eds., *The Goldstone Report: The Legacy of the Landmark Investigation of the Gaza Conflict* (New York: Nation Books, 2011).

9. My actual views on these events can be found in Richard Falk, "A Commentary on the Boston Marathon Murders" April 19, 2013, https://richardfalk.wordpress.com/2013/04/19/a-commentary-on-the-marathon-murders/.

10. It was extraordinary to find myself so highlighted on the 2013 Wiesenthal list, and I can only assume that it was a kind of backhanded recognition of the importance of the special rapporteur role and reports. Since my term as special rapporteur came to an end, much less attention has been given to my writings by groups shielding Israel from all criticism, whether well founded or not.

11. The secondary effects from the UN Watch onslaught continue to cause me distress wherever I speak anywhere in the world, regardless of topic. It has probably

been invisibly responsible for various organizations' failures to extend some speaking invitations, but no scheduled event has been cancelled.

12. Often country special rapporteurs are refused approval, as these mandates are usually created in reaction to situations of severe violations of human rights when the territorial government anticipates critical appraisal. This requires the rapporteur to gather information for reports without the benefit of a mission to the country. The case of Palestine was different to the extent that the governing authorities of the Palestinian territories were eager to expose Israeli violations, but access depended on Israeli cooperation, which in my experience, and that of my successor, has not been forthcoming.

13. UN General Assembly Resolution 67/19, A/Res/67/19, November 29, 2012, www.securitycouncilreport.org/atf/cf/%7B65BFCF9B-6D27-4E9C-8CD3-CF6E4FF96FF9%7D/a_res_67_19.pdf.

14. Each of these three Palestinian territories has a distinct legal status according to Israeli law—East Jerusalem is annexed; the West Bank is administered as a case of "disputed sovereignty"; and Gaza since Israel's "disengagement" in 2005 is treated as a hostile foreign entity. From the perspective of international law and the UN, these three entities should continue to be treated as both occupied and integral parts of a unified "Palestine."

15. Since April 2014 Palestine has adhered to a series of international treaties as further steps in the process of establishing the reality of its statehood and its entitlement to participate in international society as a state.

16. See Richard A. Falk and Burn H. Weston, "The Relevance of International Law to Palestinian Rights in the West Bank and Gaza: In Legal Defense of the Intifada," *Harvard International Law Journal* 32, no. 1 (Winter 1991): 129–57.

17. For this background, see Victor Kattan, *From Coexistence to Conquest: International Law and the Origins of the Arab-Israeli Conflict, 1891–1948* (New York: Pluto Press, 2009).

18. UN General Assembly Resolution 181 (II), "The Future Government of Palestine," A/Res/181 (II), November 29, 1947, https://unispal.un.org/DPA/DPR /unispal.nsf/5ba47a5c6cef541b802563e000493b8c/7f0af2bd897689b785256c33006 1d253?OpenDocument.

19. For a devastating assessment of the US diplomatic role, see Rashid Khalidi, *Brokers of Deceit: How the US Has Undermined Peace in the Middle East* (Boston: Beacon Press, 2013).

20. Several reliable reports express similar interpretations of facts and legal responsibility. See "Report of the Independent Fact Finding Committee on Gaza to the League of Arab States," April 30, 2009, www.tromso-gaza.no/090501ReportGaza .pdf; "Israel/Gaza: Operation 'Cast Lead': 22 Days of Death and Destruction," *Amnesty International,* July 2, 2009; "I Lost Everything: Israel's Unlawful Destruction of Property during Operation Cast Lead," *Human Rights Watch,* May 13, 2010; "White Flag Deaths," *Human Rights Watch,* August 13, 2010.

21. For text and commentary, see Horowitz, Ratner, and Weiss, *Goldstone Report.*

22. See the Geneva Convention on Belligerent Occupation, Art. 33 (1949).

23. For background, see John J. Mearsheimer and Stephen M. Walt, *The Israeli Lobby and U.S. Foreign Policy* (New York: Farrar, Straus and Giroux, 2008); other commentators emphasize a convergence of strategic interests between the Israeli lobby and American grand strategy in the Middle East. In my view, both interpretations of Israel's extraordinary influence on US policy are relevant to an adequate understanding.

24. See Richard A. Falk, *Palestine: The Legitimacy of Hope* (Washington, DC: Just World Books, 2015); compare with the tragic situation of Kashmir, which has never found its way onto the UN agenda and is virtually invisible internationally as a result or is at most seen as a by-product of the conflict between India and Pakistan.

25. See Peter Bauck and Mohammed Omer, eds., *The Oslo Accords: A Critical Assessment* (Cairo: American University Press in Cairo, 2012).

26. Though there were attempts at creating Palestinian unity, their partial and only temporary success was cited by the Israel government as its explanation for ending participation in the 2014 Kerry peace talks; also, the PA marginalized the relevance of the refugee communities living in neighboring countries and the rights of return of Palestinians dispossessed in 1948 and 1967.

27. See Noam Chomsky and Ilan Pappé, *On Palestine* (Chicago: Haymarket Books, 2015); see also Ali Abunimah, *The Battle for Justice in Palestine* (Chicago: Haymarket Books, 2014); Richard A. Falk, *Humanitarian Intervention and Legitimacy Wars: Seeking Peace and Justice in the Twenty-First Century* (New York: Routledge, 2015).

28. Reports of Special Rapporteur for Occupied Palestine, Human Rights Council, 2013–14, addressing in detail issues of corporate responsibility: for example, Richard Falk, "Report of the Special Rapporteur on the Situation of Human Rights in the Palestinian Territories Occupied since 1967," Human Rights Council, twenty-fifth session, agenda item 7, A/HRC/25/67, January 13, 2014.

29. Over the years the disillusioning impact of UN resolutions supportive of Palestinian claims but unimplemented have made many skeptical of the role and relevance of the UN. This background adds significance to efforts to take tangible steps that support coercive nonviolent tactics in the cause of Palestinian rights.

30. For an attempt to interpret these developments, see Richard A. Falk, *Chaos and Counterrevolution: After the Arab Spring* (Charlottesville, VA: Just World Books, 2015).

31. See Jacques Derrida's illuminating formulations in *Living Together: Jacques Derrida's Communities of Violence and Peace*, ed. Elisabeth Weber (New York: Fordham University Press, 2013).

FOUR

The UN Statehood Bid

PALESTINE'S FLIRTATION WITH MULTILATERALISM

Noura Erakat

IN MAY 2011, the Palestine Liberation Organization (PLO)/Palestinian Authority (PA) announced that it would seek membership as a state within the United Nations. The UN statehood bid, as it came to be known, would alter the PLO's status as a nonmember observer entity, conferred upon it by the UN General Assembly in 1974. For an entity to be admitted as a member state in the United Nations, the UN Security Council must also first make a recommendation to the General Assembly. According to the International Court of Justice, admission into the United Nations as a member state is impossible without a Security Council recommendation. It was clear from day one that the United States, a permanent member of the Security Council, would veto such a recommendation. Alternatively, the PLO could circumvent the Security Council and upgrade its status to nonmember observer state by garnering the vote of two-thirds of the 193 UN member states.[1]

In the lead-up to the much-anticipated September 2011 bid, it was widely expected that the majority of UN member states would recognize Palestine within the General Assembly, thereby granting Palestine statehood but not UN membership. In fact, more than 130 states had already recognized Palestine in bilateral agreements. In the unlikely scenario that the United States did not block a Security Council recommendation and that Palestine also achieved membership, it was also largely understood that this would change little on the ground; Israel would still prevent Palestinians from exercising control over their natural resources, ports of entry, movement, security, education, and economy.

While the benefits of UN membership, or in the alternative, a UN upgrade, are manifold, none of them guarantee Palestinian self-determination or freedom from Israeli control. In and of itself, the statehood bid was not promising. It did, however, signal a potentially significant, and necessary, shift within the PLO. Namely, this could have been a pivot away from complete reliance on the United States to deliver independence and a return to multilateralism that positioned the world superpower as part of the problem rather than the solution. A shift to multilateralism would have marked a return of sorts. The United Nations had been a primary site of Palestinian advocacy until the early 1990s, when the Oslo Accords and the attendant peace process began.[2]

The promise of multilateralism, signaled by Palestinians in 2011, has not been fulfilled. As several analysts rightly highlighted, the statehood bid was a tactical move aimed at rescuing the Palestinian leadership from irrelevance and the throes of the Arab uprisings rather than a decisive and strategic shift.[3] Since the early 1990s, the PLO/PA has placed its bets on the United States. Despite its flirtations with internationalization of the conflict, the PLO/PA remains committed to a US-led and dominated bilateral process. That commitment, however, is steadily waning in direct correlation to the diminishing, if not diminished, potential of the 1993 Oslo Accords and its US-led process to deliver independence.

PALESTINE AND THE UNITED NATIONS

Palestine has always had a relationship with the United Nations, though not always by choice. Like all colonial holdings following the First World War, Palestine came under the trusteeship of the League of Nations. The United Nations' predecessor aimed to guide colonial mandates to independence. However, rather than see to the establishment of an independent Arab Palestinian state, the League of Nations and, later, the United Nations oversaw the dispossession and displacement of the Palestinian people.

Were it not for the UN's failure to oversee the transition of Mandate Palestine from British trusteeship to an independent Arab state, there might not exist an ongoing struggle for Palestinian self-determination today.[4] In 1947, rather than rectify its fundamental errors, the United Nations proposed a partition of Palestine that corresponded neither to land ownership by Jews and Arabs nor to their respective populations.[5] Following the failure of partition and the lack of proper stewardship, Zionist forces executed premeditated plans to remove the Palestinian population and established a national homeland for Jews by force.[6]

In response, the UN General Assembly established the Conciliation Committee on Palestine (UNCCP). It empowered the commission, constituted of Turkey, France, and the United States, to reconcile Israel and the Palestinians and to facilitate the return, reparation, rehabilitation, compensation, or resettlement of Palestinian refugees.[7] Within two years of its establishment, the UNCCP reported to the General Assembly that conditions in Palestine "have made it impossible for the Commission to carry out its mandate."[8] In particular, the United States posed a key challenge to any terms unfavorable to the future of the newly established Israeli state. The General Assembly extended the UNCCP's mandate annually without result until it was finally declared obsolete in 1966.[9] Since the UNCCP became defunct, there has been no legal or political body dedicated to achieving the return, integration, or resettlement of Palestinian refugees.[10] Although nearly all states supported the return of Palestinian refugees, including the United States, the paralysis of the UNCCP left Palestinian refugees in a political limbo and extremely vulnerable to the whim of host states.[11]

The UN never resolved this condition. The most significant UN agency created to address the needs of Palestinian refugees, the UN Relief and Works Agency (UNRWA), provided relief and works programs. The UN General Assembly limited UNRWA's mandate to five areas of operation: Jordan, Lebanon, Syria, and the Occupied Palestinian Territory, namely the West Bank and Gaza.[12] Since it commenced its operations in 1950, UNRWA's mandate, derived from General Assembly resolutions and requests from other organs, has evolved and expanded in response to events in the Middle East.[13] Together, UNRWA and the UNCCP may have been adequate and even equivalent to the global refugee agency the UN High Commissioner for Refugees, but on its own UNRWA's protection for Palestinian refugees is geographically truncated and insufficient.[14]

UNRWA does not have a protection mandate on behalf of Palestinian refugees, and it explains that such a solution for the Palestinian refugee problem is the responsibility of the parties to the conflict.[15] The most that UNRWA has been able to do in this regard is to "highlight the urgent need for a solution and to help ensure that in its elaboration, the rights, views, and interests of the refugees are heard and safeguarded."[16]

Thus the international community of states as well as the UN subsidiary bodies they created regarded Palestinian refugees of the 1950s and 1960s as passive recipients of humanitarian relief. This began to change after the establishment of the PLO in 1964, which politicized the cause of Palestinian refugees, who subsequently demanded political solidarity rather than charitable aid.

The political shift ushered in a new era for Palestinians at the UN. In particular, they leveraged the UN General Assembly as a site of bold advocacy campaigns. This was especially true in 1974, when the General Assembly extended an invitation to the PLO to join its plenary meetings on the question of Palestine.[17] In November of that year it invited Yasser Arafat, the PLO's chairman, to address the Assembly,[18] and it passed two resolutions: one affirming the inalienable rights of the Palestinian people to national self-determination, national independence, and return and another extending observer status to the PLO at the General Assembly.[19] A year later, in 1975, the General Assembly passed a resolution (3379) finding that Zionism was a form of racism.[20] Notably, this was perhaps the apex of UN advocacy on behalf of Palestinians. In 1991, when the tide had changed, the General Assembly rescinded Resolution 46/86 as a result of US pressure to support the peace process.[21] In addition to resolutions and invitations, the General Assembly established—in 1975—a working body to fill the political and protection gap that afflicted Palestinian refugees: the Committee on the Exercise of the Inalienable Rights of the Palestinian People (hereafter "the Committee").[22]

The UN General Assembly established the Committee because of the lack of progress in fulfilling self-determination and the right to return to their homes and properties. Within a year, the Committee submitted a proposal of implementation to the UN Security Council that included a two-phase plan to return and restitute Palestinian refugees displaced in 1948 and 1967; a timetable for the withdrawal of Israeli forces from the Occupied Palestinian Territory; the presence of a temporary peacekeeping force to protect Palestinian civilians; the temporary stewardship of the Occupied Territory by the UN and the Arab League before these were handed over to the PLO; the cessation of all Israeli settlement activity; the recognition by Israel of the applicability of the Fourth Geneva Convention; and the creation of all means necessary to establish self-determination and independence of the Palestinian people. The United States vetoed the resolution. In response, the General Assembly institutionalized the role of the Committee by establishing the UN Division for Palestinian Rights within the UN Secretariat in 1977 to provide substantive support.

The question of Palestine was not unique for its specialized focus within the UN. The UN General Assembly had previously established other committees aimed at garnering international support to end foreign colonization. The two most prominent were the Special Committee on Apartheid, established in 1962 to end apartheid in South Africa (Resolution 1761), and the UN Council for Namibia, established in 1967 to be the legal administering authority of Namibia until independence (Resolution 2248). Both committees have long been dissolved, having achieved their mandate. By contrast, the Committee on the Exercise of the Inalienable Rights of the Palestinian People, now in its fortieth year, continues to function but has not effectively mobilized the General Assembly to challenge the intransigent UN (read US) opposition to resolving the conflict in line with international law. In its initial recommendations to the Security Council in 1976, the Committee wrote, "If the Security Council was unable to act because of a veto, the Committee should, in its subsequent report, recommend to the General Assembly that it carry out its own responsibilities in accordance with the Charter of the United Nations and in the light of precedents. It was also suggested that if Israel persisted in its refusal to implement General Assembly resolutions 194 (III) and 181 (II), this would constitute a violation of the conditions of its admission to the United Nations, which would then have to reconsider the matter."[23]

However, far from raising controversial issues such as the legitimacy of Israel's inclusion in the UN given its failure to meet its conditional terms of acceptance, the Committee has been conservative in fulfilling its mandate. In effect, its function has become more ceremonial than political. According to Joseph Schechla, coordinator for the Housing and Land Rights Network, Habitat International Coalition, who attended the Committee's meetings, "The Committee does not operate as a political body within the General Assembly. Their structure, in a way, is insignificant and of the member states none are particularly influential. There is no desire for this group to be effective."[24]

The lack of robust civil society participation has also limited the Committee's efficacy. In 1983, eight years after the Committee's establishment, the UN opened its doors to nongovernmental organizations by affording them special consultative status to the Economic and Social Council. That same year, the Committee convened an International Peace Conference on the Question of Palestine that featured civil society organizations. It thereafter coordinated civil society participation in the form of formal regional bodies whose elections were facilitated by the United Nations. This arrangement hit its first speed bump in the early 1990s when civil society actors used the space afforded by the Committee to condemn and reproach the diplomatic missions for their participation in the Oslo peace process.

Consequently, in 1999, the Committee ended its formal relationship to civil society in a letter where it announced the cessation of UN-coordinated elections as well as financial support.

Wolfgang Grieger, secretary for the Committee, explains that the "regional committees took votes that contradicted the Committee mandates . . . so no more elections, no more meetings, you go to Geneva for human rights issues, and come to the Committee to proceed with the national rights discussions."[25] Grieger's observation highlights a stark bifurcation of human rights and national rights in the strategic approach to the question of Palestine. While the two sets of rights are, and have been, mutually reinforcing, in the years that followed the Oslo Accords the pursuit of national rights would proceed uninfluenced by any external forces, including human rights norms.

Indeed, since the Oslo peace process began in 1993, nongovernmental organizations' participation in the Committee's sponsored activities and conferences have been dismal. Grieger explains that after Oslo civil society participation dropped by half. The reasons include a loss in financial support as well as internal Palestinian political strife. However, the fundamental issue is that Oslo split Palestinian aspirations for self-determination into two tracks: a narrow political track defined by realpolitik and a rights-based one that included legal, grassroots, and media strategies.

Legal strategies would include advocacy within the UN General Assembly, advancement of human rights norms, insistence upon adherence to international law, and cooperation with multilateral human rights organizations. They would also include support for civil society representatives among human rights treaty bodies, and innovative claims within the International Court of Justice as well as in foreign national courts. Grassroots strategies comprise support for local efforts aimed at building solidarity, including but not limited to boycott, divestment, and sanctions efforts. A media strategy involves globally taking on Israeli *hasbara* efforts through print, audio, television, and social media.

The PA turned its back on these strategies and adopted a narrow political emphasis rooted in an unequivocal faith in realpolitik. This faith effectively positioned the United States, in its capacity as world superpower and Israel's primary patron, as the only party capable of delivering a Palestinian state. In practice, this strategy is the strict adherence to the US-brokered bilateral process, which lacks any reference to international law or external review mechanisms and is dictated by expedience and pressure. In this iteration, the political is a narrow realm that dismisses the law and its attendant normative values as impediments to the possibilities of a political solution. Since 1993, at least, the Palestinian leadership has bought into this understanding of the political and left itself with no negotiating leverage.

THE PIVOT TO US TUTELAGE AND
THE PEACE PROCESS

The bifurcation between politics and rights, including the abandonment of all the rights established by PLO advocacy at the UN since the 1970s, was not inevitable. It reflects the weakness of the PLO, by 1994, in accepting the debilitating terms presented by the United States. That weakness reflects at least two significant trends evident by the late 1980s. The first is the rise of US primacy as indicated in its internationally backed war on Iraq during the First Gulf War. The end of the Cold War and the advent of a unipolar global order led by the United States diminished the UN's potential to challenge US hegemony in the Middle East.[26] The Gulf War also realigned political interests among Arab states. In this reordering, member states of the Gulf Cooperation Council shunned Yasser Arafat, then chairman of the PLO, for his support of Saddam Hussein's invasion and occupation of Kuwait, thus directly and significantly decreasing financial support for the PLO.

This trend dovetails with another: the waning influence of a transnational Palestinian leadership primarily located beyond the Occupied West Bank and the Gaza Strip. The Palestinian intifada, or uprising, that began in 1987, was unanticipated and was organically led by Palestinians within the Occupied Palestinian Territory, outside the purview of the PLO leadership, which at the time was located in Tunis. Israel's 1988 assassination of Abu Jihad, arguably the only PLO operative with serious connections to this organic movement, sealed the independence of an organic Palestinian resistance movement from the traditional PLO leadership.[27] Diminished financial support, new political configurations in the Middle East, the rise of a new Palestinian power center, and the personal vanities of Arafat made direct relations with Washington ever more attractive. Arafat achieved that in 1991 when US secretary of state James Baker initiated direct talks with relevant stakeholders, principally Israel and the PLO, around a single table.[28] The talks, at first promising, devolved into secret negotiations in Oslo among PLO officials who lacked both the adequate capacity to lead the negotiations and "direct knowledge of how the twenty months of Madrid and

Washington discussions had gone."[29] The result was the Oslo Accords, whose terms and stipulations have proven detrimental to the Palestinian cause for self-determination.

Neither the Oslo Accords nor any subsequent agreements that have flowed therefrom have been predicated on established international law, including the laws regulating occupation, human rights norms, or the series of Security Council and General Assembly resolutions regarding the conflict in particular.[30] Instead, the United States, Israel, and the PLO have established their own framework as the terms of reference and have stipulated that the negotiations be wholly self-referential. In doing so, the PLO has disavowed its political work within the United Nations. Moreover, in its role as the sole peace broker, the United States has precluded other parallel tracks aimed at resisting Israeli settler colonialism, like grassroots campaigns and legal proceedings, by wielding significant diplomatic and financial pressure against the PLO. By accepting the terms of Oslo, Palestinians placed their bets on the United States to deliver independence and agreed to play by its rules.

On its face, this is a flawed approach because it places undue faith in the United States, which self-avowedly proclaims that Israel is its most unique ally in the Middle East. It also discounts the restraint that the US Congress places on the US government to apply pressure on Israel even when, in the rare case, it wants to. This approach paralyzes the Palestinian leadership and prevents it from resisting US and Israeli hegemony even for the narrow aim of strengthening their negotiating leverage. Beyond the structural flaws of the peace process, the Oslo Accords themselves prioritized Israeli security interests—as defined by Israel—above Palestinian rights—as codified by the international community—by making any progress toward Palestinian freedom dependent upon an Israeli certificate of good conduct that the Palestinians were never going to obtain.

As such, since the signing of the Oslo Accords in 1993, the PA and Israel, together with the United States, have been managing a colonial reality rather than working toward its dissolution. The devastating consequences of this approach have not been lost on the Palestinian population.

The number of settlements in the West Bank doubled between 1993 and the 2000. In 1994, Israel sealed off the Gaza Strip, limited movement between the West Bank and Gaza, and ended the flow of labor from the territories to Israel, thus dealing a significant blow to the Palestinian economy. The collapse of the Camp David Accords in 2000 made increasingly clear that Israel had no intention to participate in a genuine process of decolonization. This sparked the second intifada between 2000 and 2005, resulting in the killing of over three thousand Palestinians, most of them civilians, as well as the destruction of no less than five thousand Palestinian homes. In 2002, Israel began construction of the Annexation Wall, whose length meandered through the West Bank, effectively confiscating 13 percent of it, and separated Palestinians from one another, their schools, their source of livelihood, and their access to health care. In 2005, Israel unilaterally disengaged from the Gaza Strip, relocated its twelve thousand settlers to the other side of the Green Line, and began a new era of all-out warfare against the densely populated enclave. Meanwhile, the negotiations had all but collapsed and had not come close to genuinely addressing the core issues separating the two sides.

In 2006, 58 percent of the Palestinian electorate voted for Hamas in PA parliamentary polls, in what can be described as a triple referendum: on Fatah's management of the PA and the national movement more broadly; on conditions of daily life in the Occupied Palestinian Territory; and on the Oslo peace process. Rather than signal the need for a strategic shift, Fatah's electoral defeat entrenched the PA's commitment to US sponsorship. In response to Fatah's collusion with the United States to overthrow Hamas in the Gaza Strip, Hamas launched a preemptive coup against Fatah and routed it from the coastal enclave in 2007.

Following the internecine schism between Fatah and Hamas, Washington has provided the Ramallah-based PA with substantial diplomatic and financial support, affording it considerable influence over the official Palestinian political agenda. The PLO/PA has used this authority to solidify its cooperation with the United States and Israel and has dedicated its resources to competing with Hamas rather than to resisting Israeli settler colonialism. This has exacerbated the tension between the national and the popular (i.e., human rights, grassroots, legal, media) tracks evidenced in the tension between Palestinian civil society, which has demanded accountability and pressure upon Israel, and the PLO, which has demanded support for the peace process and aid at the UN.

SETTING THE STAGE FOR THE UN STATEHOOD BID

In early 2011, *Al Jazeera* published confidential documents—called the *Palestine Papers*—leaked from the PLO's negotiations unit.[31] The *Palestine Papers* were a public affirmation of the degree to which the realpolitik approach had failed as a means to achieving independence. For those following the Oslo process, the document leaks from negotiations were not news. The PLO/PA had already demonstrated that they were more than willing to accept a land swap, to effectively abandon the right of return for Palestinian refugees, and to accept a demilitarized state as well as a truncated East Jerusalem in the midst of a territorial archipelago of mutually exclusive Bantustans. Although the PA denied the veracity of the documents, it implicitly claimed that these positions were necessary concessions and represented a pragmatic approach to conflict resolution.

The *Palestine Papers,* leaked just after the beginning of the Arab uprisings, provoked an array of responses from across the Palestinian national body. Diasporic Palestinians in the United States issued a petition calling for the resignation of the entire PA. The London Palestinian students representing the General Union of Palestinian Students occupied the Palestinian embassy and demanded to be given a vote in the Palestinian National Council elections. Haneen Zoabi, a Palestinian-Israeli Knesset member representing the Balad party, published an open letter to the PA, chastising it for making unauthorized decisions on behalf of the Palestinian citizens of Israel. And in both the West Bank and Gaza, Palestinians gathered in protest to demand the end of the Oslo Accords, all the while demonstrating in solidarity with their Egyptian brothers and sisters.

In an eerie echo of the former Mubarak regime in Egypt, plainclothes police forcefully infiltrated, punched, kicked, and detained participants in the protests in solidarity with Egyptians as well as the protests demanding an end to Oslo in the spring of 2012, again confirming what many already knew. Since Oslo, a self-ordained leadership has been working not simply to negotiate the rights of a global Palestinian national body without accountability but to steadily eviscerate the Palestinian anticolonial resistance movement in the context of a not-so-new Middle East.[32]

The US invasion and occupation of Iraq in 2003 and its subsequent support of Israel's 2006 onslaught against Lebanon were the devastating markers of the Bush administration's reconfigured new Middle East. The Fatah-dominated PA has neatly fit within the US camp, and this new configuration situates US allies, including (Sisi's) Egypt, Jordan, Saudi Arabia, Lebanon's March 14 coalition, and Fatah, at odds with Iran, Syria, Hamas, and Hizbullah. Accordingly, the Mubarak regime and the PA have worked in lockstep to cater to US prerogatives, earning them, along with Jordan, the moniker of Israel's strategic allies in the Middle East.

The PA's policies have included colluding with the United States and Israel to target Hamas at the expense of protecting over one and a half million Palestinians besieged in the Gaza Strip. The Egyptian government (during Mubarak's tenure and subsequently) has contributed to Israel's debilitating blockade regime by sealing the Rafah border. For its part, the PA has turned a blind eye to Israel's atrocities against Palestinians in Gaza during its now three extensive aerial and ground offensives. The most recent onslaught, known as Operation Protective Edge and launched in the summer 2014, left over two thousand Palestinians dead and over eleven thousand injured. Much like the Mubarak regime, Sisi has taken on Fatah's power struggle with Hamas as its own, given its ties to the Muslim Brotherhood, now declared illegal by Egyptian courts. Egypt has also declared the Qassam Brigades a terrorist organization.

Disdain for the PA is exacerbated by the expiration of its electoral mandate to govern. Abbas's presidential mandate expired in 2010, yet he continues to govern thanks to external financial and diplomatic support. If anything, what Abbas and the PA have successfully orchestrated is the consolidation of their political structure as an accomplice of empire. Within the current status quo, Palestinians benefit neither from a status as a dispossessed people entitled to self-determination nor from a status as citizens of a sovereign state adorned with all the duties and responsibilities of a sovereign entity. Instead, the US-brokered peace process has made the Palestinian people appear to be equal counterparts to the Israeli state, while their lived realities reflect no such parity. Worse, in its futile attempt to demonstrate its capacity to govern and maintain order, the PA/PLO has arguably relieved Israel of at least a portion of its military burden as an occupying power. In the West Bank, the PA/PLO has steadily built a security apparatus popularly known as the Dayton Forces to police Palestinians. And in the Gaza Strip, the blockade continues amid an intermittent onslaught of Israeli bombing campaigns that leave the besieged area in a chronic state of recovery from devastation.

Then there is the question of representation of Palestinians globally. Even if the PA mandate were still in force, the PA "represents" only a quarter of the global Palestinian population. Neither Hamas, nor Fatah, nor their short-lived government of national unity has ever represented the entirety of the Palestinian nation. The conflict has led friends and foes alike to ask, "Who speaks for Palestinians?"

The lack of a political program representing Palestinian national aspirations follows the steady erosion of the PLO in the aftermath of the Oslo

Accords. In his unpublished, undated paper entitled "The Rise and Fall of the PLO: A History of the Palestine Liberation Organization," Seif Da'na writes, "The Oslo agreement prepared the grounds for the demise of the PLO, both as a structure and program, initiating a conflict inside the PLO between the bureaucrats interlinked with the new ruling class, and figures professing PLO ideals and liberation and independence. This inevitable rivalry intensified as the Palestinian Authority has gradually replaced the PLO as a political structure and the nature of the Palestinian question was significantly redefined."

In 2011, these elements all came to a head. The failure of Oslo, undue faith in, and collusion with, the United States, and the momentum of change ushered by the Arab uprisings prompted Palestinians globally to revolt against the PLO/PA. It was in this context that the PLO/PA announced its bid for statehood at the United Nations.

Palestinians did not respond to the UN statehood bid enthusiastically. The bid raised concerns that if the UN granted Palestine membership, the PA, which represented only the Occupied Palestinian Territory, would supplant the PLO as the Palestinian representative body to the global community. Palestinians living in the diaspora feared that they would be excluded from Palestinian national representation altogether. The threat of such exclusion prompted many Palestinians in the diaspora to reject the statehood bid in unequivocal terms. However, despite rejections from numerous communities in diaspora, as well as skeptical youth groups and legal scholars inside and outside the Occupied Territory, Abbas's PA found a momentary reprieve due to the statehood bid as Palestinians and the international community directed their attention to the potential of a break in a stalemate.

PALESTINE RETURNS TO THE UN . . . SORT OF

The statehood bid was the PA/PLO's first direct confrontation with the Israeli occupation and US support for it since the peace process. More significantly, it indicated that Palestinians might reorient themselves toward an international stage including the United Nations and its attendant mechanisms. The primary issue was not whether the Palestinian leadership was serious about statehood but whether it was serious about a new strategic course.

Myopic focus on statehood falsely assumes that but for the lack of statehood the PA/PLO would have made significant strides in protecting Palestinian rights. Yet as demonstrated by the missed opportunities of the 2009 Goldstone Report and the 2004 International Court of Justice advisory opinion, this is not the case. Failure to further the cause for Palestinian self-determination reflects a strategic choice on the part of the Palestinian leadership and not a lack of capacity—although, it should be said, the US government actively lobbied the UN and member states to ignore the Goldstone Report.[33]

The PA/PLO did not use the Goldstone Report to hold Israel to account for its alleged war crimes during Operation Cast Lead. Instead the PA/PLO delayed its review by the Human Rights Council for the sake of obtaining the United States' offer of a better negotiating position. While the Palestinian leadership waited for the United States to deliver on its empty promises, international civil society worked furiously to sue alleged Israeli war criminals in European courts under universal jurisdiction. While no trials have ensued, their efforts have deterred Israelis from traveling to Europe.

Similarly, the 2004 International Court of Justice advisory opinion held the route of Israel's separation barrier to be illegal for being built inside the Occupied West Bank as opposed to on the 1949 Armistice Line, and it affirmed the illegality of Israel's settlements. Accordingly, the world's highest judicial tribunal recommended that all state parties to the Fourth Geneva Convention cease to, or refrain from, aiding in Israel's expansion of the wall. The PA/PLO had the perfect opportunity to run a diplomatic marathon and encourage the signatories of the Geneva Conventions to impose sanctions on Israel for its ongoing constructions, cease the sale of any materials intended for the development of the wall, or refuse to purchase Israeli goods produced in the illegal settlements.

Yet as a result of intense US pressure, the PA/PLO did nothing of the sort and seemingly shelved the monumental decision. Exactly one year later, on July 9, 2005, a broad swath of Palestinian civil society organizations launched the Boycott, Divestment, and Sanctions (BDS) campaign against Israel. To date, this scarcely funded international movement has made tremendous strides in fulfilling the International Court of Justice's recommendations. Most notably, it has encouraged several European banks to sell their holdings in Veolia, a French multinational company set to build Jerusalem's light rail to connect illegal Israeli settlements. The campaign's gains have been so great that in 2011 the Israeli Knesset passed a new law prohibiting Israeli individuals and organizations from boycotting settlement products and Israeli enterprises, thus indicating one means of resisting Israeli transgressions and cultivating international support for Palestinians.

Statehood may afford the PA/PLO with more meaningful ways to challenge Israel's occupation and apartheid. However, the lack of state status and UN membership was not the sole factor limiting the PA/PLO's resistance to injustice. The missing link has been a commitment to resist rather than appease Israeli and US prerogatives. The statehood bid did not mark this shift.

The diplomatic maneuver was little more than a slight diversion before resumption of the status quo of US-brokered bilateral negotiations in July 2013, this time led by Secretary of State John Kerry and Middle East envoy Martin Indyk. For the statehood bid to have been significant for Israel, for the United States, and for the Palestinian people, it needed to be part of a much larger reorientation in strategy and aims. In particular, it should have marked a genuine pivot away from US sponsorship and back toward the United Nations, or more generally, toward internationalization of the Palestinian struggle for self-determination.

If the lack of a long-term and strategic shift by the Palestinian leadership was not entirely obvious in 2011, the Palestinian leadership confirmed it many times over in the year leading up to the 2012 General Assembly vote for nonmember observer state status. Consider first that the bid for full membership status died a quiet death in the Security Council. To save face, the US and Palestinian leaderships agreed to spare the statehood application from a Security Council vote and the US veto it would have entailed. The standoff would have embarrassed the United States, which proclaims support for a two-state settlement, as well as the Palestinian leadership, because it has not disavowed the US-brokered peace process. What survived this process and what was gained was recognition within the General Assembly, which upgraded Palestine from an "observer mission" status at the United Nations to an "observer state" one.

The overwhelming UN General Assembly vote in support of Palestine diplomatically affirmed the Palestinian cause for self-determination as a just one among the community of nations, thereby rebuffing Israel's insistence that the conflict is a national security issue. Unfortunately, absent diplomatic lobbying by the Palestinian leadership, those states will not place the necessary pressure upon Israel to thwart its structurally violent practices. More importantly for the Fatah-dominated PA, the vote to upgrade its status saved it from the specter of complete irrelevance. This was critical for the political body at a moment when Hamas had emerged as a viable political player in the region together with the admission that the peace process had failed. However, to mark a meaningful shift, the Palestinian leadership could and should have used this opportunity to confront the United States' intransigent support of Israel. Instead, it chose not to and continued to pursue a political program under US tutelage in the hope that a global superpower would deliver independence.

After leaving UN headquarters in 2012, the Palestinian leadership did little to indicate a move away from Oslo's debilitating terms. Even its most significant achievement of earning acceptance as a member state within UNESCO became another opportunity to reify Oslo's structure. Palestinian diplomats used Palestine's state status within UNESCO to add the Church of the Nativity in Bethlehem to the list of endangered world heritage sites. While recognition of the church as a Palestinian site is indeed positive, it also marked a missed opportunity for Palestinians to use their UNESCO membership to add other sites that are under graver threat within the West Bank. For example, it would have been optimal for Palestinians if their leadership had used the opportunity to add Battir, a village in the Bethlehem district that sits in Area C, to the list of World Heritage Sites. Most of Battir is now under threat because it is about to be destroyed by the route of the Annexation Wall. The Jewish National Fund has also designated lands alienated from the village by the Israeli state as a green park for exclusive use by Israeli citizens— in effect, Jewish settlers and their fellow travelers. By contrast, the Nativity Church is located within Area A, which is under full Palestinian civilian and security jurisdiction and is not in imminent danger. Palestine did not add Battir to the list of World Heritage Sites until three years later in June 2014, after the collapse of the latest round of peace talks.[34]

EPILOGUE

In 2011 the PA made a bid for UN statehood. On the last day of 2014, by a vote in the UN Security Council, a Jordanian resolution failed to set a timetable for the end to the occupation of Palestine. Between these dates, Israel continued to encage Gaza and to conduct a policy of ethnic cleansing in East Jerusalem and settlement construction in the West Bank. By its acts on the ground, Israel is nullifying the possibility of a Palestinian state. UN agencies have expressed their despair at the acts of Israel but are otherwise powerless to do anything about it.

The Palestinian leadership has responded to the ever-diminishing potential of the US-brokered peace process with incremental steps into international forums. In response to Israel's failure to release a fourth and last batch of Palestinian political prisoners as promised, it acceded to fifteen international treaties.[35] In response to Israel's attacks on the Gaza Strip as well as the West Bank, it requested that Palestine be placed under an international protection system.[36] In response to Israel's intensified encroachment on the Occupied Territory, it declared an intention to set a deadline for the end of Israel's occupation by way of a Security Council resolution. In response to the collapse of the peace process (again), it began a diplomatic initiative to achieve recognition among European states. In response to the failure of a UN Security Council resolution aimed at ending the occupation, it acceded to the Rome Statute, thereby establishing jurisdiction within the International Criminal Court. There seems to be a direct inverse correlation between the weight of Oslo and internationalization of the conflict. This does not amount to a move away from US tutelage; rather, it indicates a more nuanced approach whereby Palestine does not keep all its eggs in the US basket.

Is there a value in the multilateralism that the UN provides? This question cannot be answered from the Palestinian example. It is a problem intrinsic to the politics of the UN, where US suffocation of any political process remains prevalent. Only if there were a truly multilateral commitment within the UN bodies, especially the UN Security Council, would the UN be able to provide support for the political aims of the Palestinian people.

Though the UN's efficacy has been diminished by the ascent of US domination and an era of global unipolarity, that alone cannot adequately explain the Palestinian leadership's near disavowal of a resistance platform. The return to multilateralism is a return to a position of resistance. It suggests internationalization of the conflict in ways that would marginalize the United States' role and seek to diminish its debilitating intervention. Multilateralism suggests radically deploying legal, popular, and media strategies to challenge the status quo.

Numerous mechanisms and tools are available to the Palestinian leadership to effectively lead a full-court press aimed at resisting Israeli settler colonialism. None of these mechanisms, severally or together, guarantee liberation. Indeed, even bold engagement with the UN in the seventies failed to overcome US and Israeli intransigence. All of them are, however, part of an arsenal aimed at resistance, which has been sorely lacking for more than two decades. Perhaps this approach is more reasonable today than it was in the nineties in the direct aftermath of the Cold War and the entrenchment of US global supremacy. Today the United States' declining influence, vividly evidenced in its inability to rein in its client state, together with the steady reestablishment of a multipolar world, signals the possibility of effective politics within the UN. It is up to the Palestinian leadership to recognize the significance of these shifts and reorient itself strategically to effectively resist Israeli settler colonialism and to reify the legitimacy of its own struggle against it.

For its part, Palestinian civil society has never lost sight of these goals and has continued to leverage legal and extralegal mechanisms aimed at accountability and resistance. This segment of Palestinian society has continued to protest within the United Nations as well as against it, knowledgeable that the UN is merely one site of contestation. The UN in Palestine has been both a source of the problem and an available forum for its resolution. The onus on any successful Palestinian leadership, formal or otherwise, is to recognize that the national struggle and the rights-based one are not mutually exclusive but mutually reinforcing. Successfully internationalizing the Palestinian struggle rehabilitates these strategies and continues to leverage the United Nations and its mechanisms as necessary but not as a matter of course.

NOTES

I would like to thank Nour Joudah for her excellent research assistance. Thanks also to Mouin Rabbani for ever-enlightening discussions and productive disagreements. Finally, thank you to the editors of this volume for the opportunity to participate in this necessary exchange on the role of the UN in the Arab world.

1. For a wide range of essays on the context of the UN statehood bid, see Noura Erakat and Mouin Rabbani, eds., *Aborted State? The UN Initiative and New Palestinian Junctures* (Washington, DC: Tadween, 2013).

2. The full story of US involvement in the "peace process" is in Rashid Khalidi's two books *Sowing Crisis: The Cold War and the American Dominance in the Middle East* (Boston: Beacon Press, 2009) and *Brokers of Deceit: How the US Has Undermined Peace in the Middle East* (Boston: Beacon Press, 2013).

3. See, for example, Ali Abunimah, "A Formal Funeral for the Two-State Solution: How the PA's Statehood Bid Sidelines Palestinians," *Foreign Affairs,* September 19, 2011, and Samah Sabawi, "September and Beyond: Who Speaks in My Name," *al-Shabaka,* September 13, 2011.

4. The classic account to go over Article 22 of the Covenant of the League of Nations—which implicitly affirmed the right of Palestinian statehood—and the question of international law in general is W. Thomas Mallison and Sally V. Mallison, *The Palestine Problem in International Law and World Order* (London: Longman, 1986).

5. UN General Assembly Resolution 181 (II), A/Res/181 (II), November 29, 1947, https://unispal.un.org/DPA/DPR/unispal.nsf/5ba47a5c6cef541b802563e000 493b8c/7f0af2bd897689b785256c330061d253?OpenDocument, allocated 55 percent of the best land for 6 percent of the population and 45 percent of the land for 94 percent of population.

6. Walid Khalidi, "Plan Dalet: Master Plan for the Conquest of Palestine," *Journal of Palestine Studies* 18, no. 1 (1988): 4–33.

7. UN General Assembly Resolution 194, "Palestine—Progress Report of the United Nations Mediator," A/Res/194, December 11, 1948, sec. 11, http://daccess-dds-ny.un.org/doc/RESOLUTION/GEN/NR0/043/65/IMG/NR004365.pdf?OpenElement; Brenda Goddard, "UNHCR and the International Protection of Palestinian Refugees," *Refugee Survey Quarterly* 28 (2009): 475, 480.

8. Goddard, "UNHCR," n. 36.

9. Noura Erakat, "Palestinian Refugees and the Syrian Uprising: Filling the Protection Gap during Secondary Forced Displacement," *International Journal of Refugee Law* 26, no. 4 (2014): 581–621.

10. Mark Brailsford, "Incorporating Protection in UNRWA Operations," in *UNRWA and Palestinian Refugees,* ed. Sari Hanafi, Leila Hilal, and Lex Takkenberg (New York: Routledge, 2014), 81.

11. See Grandi's chapter in this volume.

12. UNRWA and Office of the UN High Commissioner for Refugees, "The United Nations and Palestinian Refugees," January 2007, www.unrwa.org /userfiles/2010011791015.pdf.

13. Lance Bartholomeusz, "The Mandate of UNRWA at Sixty," *Refugee Survey Quarterly* 28, nos. 2 and 3 (2010): 452–74.

14. On protection being geographically truncated, see ibid., 459. (The Six-Day War catalyzed one of the mandate's most significant expansions. Israel's occupation of the West Bank, including East Jerusalem, the Gaza Strip, the Golan Heights, and the Sinai Peninsula in 1967, resulted in the displacement of over 300,000 persons, including 120,000 registered Palestine refugees. In response, UNRWA provided humanitarian assistance to all persons in the area who were in need of emergency assistance regardless of their registration with UNRWA. In July 1967 the UN General Assembly endorsed this activity and restated UNRWA's mandate to include assistance to the "1967 displaced." UNRWA responded similarly to other emergencies in subsequent years, and by 2008 the General Assembly had expanded the UNRWA's mandate to assist persons displaced by the "1967 and subsequent hostilities.") On protection being insufficient, see ibid., 471. (UNRWA does not have a mandate to search for durable solutions. It did have a mandate to engage in activities that promoted the integration of Palestinian refugees into their host countries, although that was suspended in 1960.)

15. Brailsford, "Incorporating Protection."

16. Ibid., 81.

17. UN General Assembly Resolution 3210, "Invitation to the Palestine Liberation Organization," A/Res/3210 (XXIX), October 10, 1974, https://unispal

.un.org/DPA/DPR/unispal.nsf/0/0D024B3225278456852560DE0056AA64. See also George Bisharat, "Justice for All: Toward an Integrated Strategy for the Liberation in Palestine," *Palestine Yearbook of International Law* 17, no. 1 (2014): 28–56.

18. For text of the speech, see "Yasser Arafat's 1974 UN General Assembly Speech," 1974, Wikisource, http://en.wikisource.org/wiki/Yasser_Arafat%27s_1974_UN_General_Assembly_speech.

19. UN General Assembly Resolution 3236, "Question of Palestine," A/Res/3236, November 22, 1974, https://unispal.un.org/DPA/DPR/un.ispal.nsf/0/025974039ACFB171852560DE00548BBE; UN General Assembly Resolution 3237, "Observer Status for the Palestine Liberation Organization," A/Res/3237 (XXIX), November 22, 1974, https://unispal.un.org/DPA/DPR/unispal.nsf/0/512BAA69B5A32794852560DE0054B9B2.

20. UN General Assembly Resolution 3379, "Elimination of All Forms of Racial Discrimination," A/Res/3379 (XXX), November 10, 1975, https://unispal.un.org/DPA/DPR/unispal.nsf/0/512BAA69B5A32794852560DE0054B9B2.

21. UN General Assembly Resolution 46/86, "Elimination of Racism and Racial Discrimination," A/Res/46/86, December 16, 1991, www.un.org/documents/ga/res/46/a46r086.htm.

22. UN General Assembly Resolution 3376, A/Res/3376 (XXX), November 10, 1975, https://unispal.un.org/DPA/DPR/unispal.nsf/0/B5B4720B8192FDE3852560DE004F3C47.

23. Noura Erakat, "Unmet Potential: The UN Committee on Palestine," *al-Shabaka,* January 19, 2011.

24. Ibid. Schechla attended committee meetings between 1986 and 1991 and again in 1999.

25. Grieger, a career UN officer, is the head of the Division for Palestine Rights at the UN's Department of Political Affairs.

26. Vijay Prashad, *The Poorer Nations: A Possible History of the Global South* (London: Verso, 2012).

27. Helena Cobban, e-mail interview by author, January 26, 2015. Cobban is the author of *The Palestinian Liberation Organization: People, Power, and Politics* (Cambridge: Cambridge University Press, 1984).

28. Rashid Khalidi, *Resurrecting Empire: Western Footprints and America's Perilous Path in the Middle East* (Boston: Beacon Press, 2004).

29. Ibid., 137.

30. There was no discussion of Articles 49 and 147 of the Fourth Geneva Convention, and no discussion of the UNSC Resolutions 181 (II), 194, 242, and 338.

31. Clayton Swisher, *The Palestine Papers: The End of the Road?* (Chicago: Hesperus Press, 2011).

32. Toufic Haddad, "Palestine," in *Dispatches from the Arab Spring,* ed. Paul Amar and Vijay Prashad (New Delhi: LeftWord Books, 2013), 325–55.

33. Phil Weiss, "US Threw Its Body Down to Block Goldstone Report's Progress to the Hague," *Mondoweiss,* April 19, 2011.

34. Ryvka Barnard, "The Palestinian Authority, UNESCO, and the Illusion of Triumph," in Erakat and Rabbani, *Aborted State?*, 215–18.

35. "Palestinians Plan to Join 60 U.N. Bodies, Treaties," *Al Arabiya News*, April 28, 2014, http://english.alarabiya.net/en/News/middle-east/2014/04/28/Palestinians-plan-to-join-60-U-N-bodies-treaties-.html.

36. Vijay Prashad, "Holding Out," *Frontline*, September 19, 2014, cites Mahmoud Abbas's letter to UN secretary-general Ban Ki-moon of July 13 requesting international protection. Wolfgang Grieger of the UN Department of Political Affairs said that the UN "takes the request very seriously" and added, "A reply will be forthcoming, but I cannot speculate on the timing."

FIVE

The Wrong Kind of Intervention in Syria

Aslı Bâli and Aziz Rana

MAKING SENSE OF UN FAILURE

Since 2011 various United Nations institutions and actors have sought to intercede in the unfolding events in Syria, with the hopes of securing both a peaceful resolution to the conflict and some measure of justice for those subject to repression and abuse. But despite these efforts, circumstances on the ground have continued to deteriorate, with growing reports of starvation conditions, escalating death tolls, and an ever-deepening militarization of the conflict. In effect, the UN experience in Syria has been one of profound failure, either in offering an internationally mediated solution to the crisis or in safeguarding Syrian civilians. The question then is, why has the UN been so unsuccessful in achieving these objectives? And as a related matter, what has led to the persistent and worsening status quo within the country?

Among commentators inside and outside the region two dominant narratives have emerged to explain the UN's inability to secure peace or justice for Syrians. The first maintains that the UN's various peace initiatives have actually precluded rather than fostered a definitive settlement of the conflict. According to this view, the UN diplomatic framework, particularly the so-called Geneva process, fundamentally obstructed a decisive and external military intervention. By pressing powerful states toward the bargaining table, so the argument goes, UN actors have undermined the political will in the United States, the European Union, or the Gulf Cooperation Council to pursue the type of direct armed strategies—from no-fly zones to boots on the ground—that would produce an actual tipping point against the Assad regime. Thus, with some degree of irony, the UN's very peace process has undermined the fostering of peace and compromised the organization's presumptive responsibility to protect civilians from imminent violence.[1] More recently, as the United States and a handful of allies have taken up air strikes against the Islamic State (IS) in Syria—a strategy distinct from strikes directed against Syrian regime targets that were previously contemplated—while Russia has used aerial intervention in favor of regime forces, the UN has been sidelined. To critics of earlier UN efforts at peace initiatives, this outcome has been a satisfying vindication of their view that the path forward in Syria required removing the organization from the equation and abandoning the quixotic pursuit of a political resolution to the conflict.

The second narrative offers a parallel critique of the UN's governing approach to Syria, focusing instead on the justice implications of any diplomatic framework that includes the Assad regime. According to this position, the UN's basic orientation—since it has taken as given the need to engage with Assad as a party to the diplomatic process—has done little more than legitimate a brutal dictator and his cronies. This view asserts that rather than creating channels to negotiate with the regime, the international community should be holding regime actors accountable for their atrocities, for instance through referral to the International Criminal Court (ICC).[2] By refusing to do so, the UN's practices not only have actually made peace less likely but also have provided cover for wartime perpetrators and left victims without any recourse to justice.

Despite the extent to which both narratives have shaped commentary about the UN's role in Syria, neither adequately captures the central forces undermining UN efforts, let alone the basic dynamics intensifying the conflict. There is no doubt that if UN actors are responsible for anything, they are responsible for raising false hopes among ordinary Syrians that a settlement is on the horizon. But the primary reason these hopes continue to be undermined has little to do with the UN's basic approach. Instead, key regional and external actors (particularly the United States, the Gulf states, Turkey, Iran, and Russia) have systematically compromised the viability of a diplomatic process or political accommodation by prioritizing their own strategic goals over basic humanitarian needs. This focus especially by regional powers on their strategic ends has fundamentally hamstrung UN efforts in two ways: first, by placing preconditions on any diplomatic process that have emptied the process of any real capacity to reach an inclusive and negotiated agreement; and second, by shaping realities on the ground that further militarize the conflict and thus work at cross-purposes with the possibility of diplomatic engagement—regardless of the nominal participation of the parties. In essence, events in Syria speak to the deep difficulties that develop when powerful states read the humanitarian needs of local civilians through the prism of a driving security discourse. For external players, although humanitarian goals are often cited, Syria above all has become a site for influencing the overall regional balance of power. The result is an entangling of security with humanitarian frameworks in ways that effectively nullify precisely those prescriptions for the conflict that could provide local communities with either peace or justice.

Over the following pages, we will examine the UN's role in Syria since early 2011, focusing on its efforts to address the crisis's international security dimensions, to respond to the urgent humanitarian needs of the civilian population, and to create a political framework for conflict resolution. In so doing, we will analyze how local and external forces have generated cyclical dynamics within Syria that not only have compromised each prong of the organization's work but also have led to increasingly catastrophic results. We begin by addressing the two dominant narratives advanced of the UN's failure and why neither properly accounts for events on the ground. We then turn to an extended analysis of the UN's approach to Syria through the Security Council, the work of the organization's humanitarian agencies, and the efforts to create a political framework for conflict resolution through the Geneva process and beyond. We conclude by reflecting on the repeated failure of peace and humanitarian efforts in Syria, especially by highlighting the multiple forms of foreign intervention currently at play in Syria and the extent to which such intervention—working to prolong the military character of the conflict—is fundamentally divorced from and at odds with UN initiatives.

THE FALSE PROMISE OF A MILITARY SOLUTION

Before we turn to a discussion of the specifics of the UN's actual involvement in Syria, it is useful to make clear precisely why both pervasive narratives of UN failure are flawed. The problem with the UN's approach is not that it has foreclosed direct military involvement or compromised international criminal prosecution for the Assad regime. Especially to the extent that the critics' underlying concerns revolve around the humanitarian welfare of the civilian population, both of these alternative strategies are counterproductive at best and at worst would escalate violence further.

To begin with, even if it were true that acting within the UN framework served for a period as a significant roadblock to direct intervention, it is essential to appreciate that there would likely be no form of direct armed involvement by external actors that would spare civilians or promote sustainable peace. This is because there are too many external actors and too many strategic interests at stake for any side to allow too great a tipping of the balance. Precisely because of Syria's centrality as a strategic asset to the dominant regional powers, new, more coercive military options risk significantly worsening the situation. Replacing the Assad regime through force with a new government allied with the United States and Gulf states would mean flipping a key Iranian ally and fundamentally reordering the regional balance of power. This, in turn, would occasion escalating Russian and Iranian military support to maintain the regime. As a result, in order to defeat the regime militarily, the United States and its allies would have to dramatically heighten the magnitude of destruction wrought on the country, resulting in even greater civilian casualties.

And given the hardening divides within Syria, direct military involvement sets the stage for escalating internecine conflict. Not only does such conflict pit Sunni constituencies backed by Western and Gulf actors against opponents that they increasingly identify in sectarian or ethnic terms, but it also has the real potential to escalate the intermilitia warfare currently consuming neighborhoods across Syrian cities. The emergence of a new configuration of Islamist forces in Syria—bringing together deeply alienated Sunni factions that emerged as a direct result of the United States' earlier intervention in Iraq with a host of Sunni Islamist forces on the ground in Syria—is emblematic of the escalation of the conflict and the damage wrought by external intervenors. Sunni militias now find themselves pitted against one another in addition to being engaged in the various interethnic and intersectarian conflicts that had already devolved into a multiparty civil war well before the consolidation of the IS.

The distribution of power on the ground in Syria and among external intervenors has been reshuffled as the apparent strategies of the erstwhile anti-Assad alliance, including such actors as Turkey, Saudi Arabia, and the United States, have diverged. While the United States pursues direct air strikes against the IS for its own purposes—purposes that have little or no direct relationship to ending or containing the Syrian civil war—Turkey continues to insist that strikes are more appropriately directed at regime targets or Kurdish forces. All the while, Saudi Arabia is caught between support for Sunni actors in Syria and increasing worries about blowback from those same actors at home. At the same time, forms of anti-Assad intervention may have triggered Russia's recent use of aerial power, ostensibly as part of the fight against IS but in fact to the advantage of Assad's forces. As these various strategies of aerial intervention unfold, air strikes are further devastating the remaining civilian infrastructure of Syria, occasioning new waves of massive refugee flows and escalating the violence that has engulfed the country. Divorced from a clear set of objectives in relation to the ultimate outcome of the Syrian civil war or even in relation to a more localized balance of power among the Sunni militias, the air strikes are a potent symbol of how external actors have allowed tactics to triumph over strategy in their policies toward Syria. The result has been the further destabilization of the country—which borders on Israel, Turkey, Jordan, Iraq, and Lebanon—creating the conditions for a long-term proxy war not only between regional Sunni and Shiite political forces but also among the various Sunni actors, one likely to continue spilling over beyond Syria's borders.

The scenarios unfolding on the ground in Syria today speak to the profound complications of direct military intervention by external players and the extent to which, perhaps unsurprisingly, further ratcheting up of the violence cannot be counted on to generate peace. Indeed, one can well see the rise of the IS itself as the product of past interventions. The very first Iraqi city captured by the IS was none other than Fallujah, the notorious site of intense US counterinsurgency operations in 2004. Indeed, many of the cities now under IS control in Iraq were those at the heart of the insurgency against the American occupation as well as those later opposed to the US-backed Iraqi government.[3] If anything, the way in which the Iraq occupation has triggered cycles of deepening regional violence underscores a comparable truth about Syria, where the eventual outcome of today's interventions will have no clear winner but a multitude of losers—most crucially ordinary civilians.

For similar reasons, the effort to pursue international criminal prosecution of Assad and other regime members in the midst of the ongoing crisis is also likely to further intensify the conflict rather than to provide victims meaningful justice. Especially given that the conflict remains unresolved, we believe that an ICC referral would likely heighten militarization, above all by reinforcing the sense within the regime that its relevant choices are to prevail militarily or face total defeat and prosecution. If criminal prosecution were seriously pursued while the conflict continues to rage, Assad might well appreciate that his final days would more closely resemble those of the deposed Iraqi dictator Saddam Hussein or Libya's Muammar Qaddafi than the comfortable exile in Saudi Arabia of Tunisia's Zine El Abidine Ben Ali. By reinforcing Assad's sense, along with that of those around him, that there are no viable options besides fighting to the death, an ICC focus in the present could lead to even greater willingness to unleash violence on Syrian civilians. Thus, shifting the regime's incentives by offering an option that is neither death nor prosecution—such as engagement in the UN's inclusive political process—may well be the most humanitarian of currently available options for international involvement.

There is no doubt that the failure to pursue immediate prosecution defers justice ends. But this missed opportunity pales in comparison to the death and destruction that may follow if the regime's sense of threat is further intensified and if nonmilitary alternatives to the crisis are foreclosed. Moreover, putting aside ICC referral does not mean closing the possibility of international criminal accountability down the line. In truth, international prosecutions take significant time and resources and do not in any case represent an immediate alternative. Further, to the extent that prosecutions have been successful in previous conflicts, their success has overwhelmingly been predicated on a preceding resolution to the underlying conflict and on meaningful political transition. Threatening Assad and his allies with war crimes prosecutions today in the context of escalating violence—rather than anything remotely resembling actual transition—may create perverse incentives with little likelihood of achieving justice for victims.

THE UN'S MANY ROLES IN SYRIA

If the central narratives of UN failure rest on faulty assumptions about the viability of either military options or criminal prosecution, what accounts for the UN's persistent inability to shift the underlying dynamics on the ground toward either peace or justice? To make sense of this, it is necessary first to appreciate the variety of roles played by the UN in Syria and the extent to which the UN should be understood not as a single undifferentiated entity but rather as a multitude of overlapping institutions and actors pursuing a range of strategies. In this section, we provide an in-depth account of the distinct aspects of UN involvement in Syria—the diplomatic process, the security framework, and humanitarian relief—and how these roles in the country have evolved over the last five years.

UN Diplomatic Initiatives

The UN's most significant and visible role in Syria has been its attempt to forge a diplomatic framework for resolving the crisis. To assess the UN's efforts to mediate between the parties to the Syrian civil war, we begin with a quick review of the course of the conflict, which began as a civil uprising in March 2011 but quickly devolved into an armed confrontation as the year proceeded. From March until July of 2011, the Syrian protests were largely nonviolent and centered on mass demonstrations demanding an end to police brutality and torture, the freeing of political prisoners, and democratic reforms. The regime responded during this period by deploying the army to quell unrest, leading to military operations in a number of cities that resulted in hundreds of civilian deaths. By the summer, some soldiers began defecting from the military to avoid firing at civilians and to protect protesters from further attack. At the same juncture protesters began to take up arms in large numbers, shifting the nonviolent uprising to an armed rebellion.

On July 29, 2011, a group of officers who had defected from the Syrian military announced the formation of the Free Syrian Army (FSA), an umbrella group that sought to represent all of the military units fighting against the regime on the ground. At the end of August, a coalition of antigovernment groups formed a governing council allied with the FSA—the Syrian National Council—which declared itself the political wing of the opposition to the Assad regime. From September to November, fighting between the FSA and the Syrian security forces steadily escalated, with the rebel units launching increasingly effective attacks and seizing control of towns near the Turkish border. Turkey allowed the FSA to establish its headquarters in the Turkish province of Hatay, bordering Syria, marking the beginning of open regional involvement in the military dimension of the conflict. By December, the ranks of the FSA had grown, as had its capacities, with increasingly effective attacks against military bases, intelligence headquarters, and airfields. In January, the Assad regime heightened its counterattacks, launching major artillery operations against the rebels in densely populated urban areas, leading to large-scale civilian deaths. By February 2012, the estimated death toll of the conflict had reached eight thousand and demands for United Nations action to stem the killing were mounting.

On February 23 of that year UN secretary-general Ban Ki-moon issued a statement jointly with the secretary-general of the League of Arab States, Nabil Elaraby, announcing that they had appointed Kofi Annan to serve as their joint special envoy on the Syrian crisis.[4] Annan's appointment was in keeping with a UN General Assembly resolution passed in the previous week endorsing the Arab League "Plan of Action" for the cessation of violence and calling for an inclusive Syrian-led political process to address the legitimate demands of the Syrian people. Annan's mandate was to provide a framework for promoting a peaceful solution to the Syrian crisis and to concretize international guidelines for the terms of the political process.

On March 16, 2012, Annan submitted a six-point plan to the UN Security Council laying out the minimum commitments necessary from all sides in the conflict to facilitate an end to violence, secure humanitarian assistance, and initiate a Syrian-led political process.[5] The plan gained the endorsement of the Security Council within one week, but no specific timetable was set for its implementation. Annan worked behind the scenes from March to June to secure a meeting that would involve Syrian participation on all sides as well as that of the regional and external supporters of the Syrian parties to the conflict. One obstacle to the inclusion of all of the Syrian parties was the public call by the external sponsors of the opposition that Assad step down. This complicating factor had actually been present from the beginning of UN efforts, since by February 2012 key states in the Arab League—the very entity cosponsoring the peace initiative—had already issued high-profile demands for Assad's ouster. Such demands translated into a sort of precondition as to the nature of the diplomatic process envisioned under the six-point plan and triggered public opposition by Russia to any suggestion of a political transition conditioned on Assad's departure. An additional complicating factor was the emergence of a contemporaneous call that the Assad regime face referral to the ICC for war crimes investigation. In response, Annan sought to delink these demands from the diplomatic process to secure the Syrian government's participation in talks—a prerequisite for any cease-fire to take hold—and to avoid the conflation of the diplomatic process with calls for regime change.

Following months of diplomatic wrangling, Annan finally succeeded in convening the parties in Geneva in June 2012, but only after meeting the American requirement that Iran be excluded from the talks. The parties in attendance were the foreign ministers of the United States, Russia, France, Britain, China, Iraq, Kuwait, Qatar, and Turkey and representatives of the EU and the Arab League—known collectively as the Action Group for Syria. Iran's exclusion was accepted by the Assad regime in exchange for Saudi Arabia also being kept out of the meeting.[6] At the same time, the chief UN spokesperson made clear that Annan recognized "the need for Iran to be part of the solution" and asserted that the special envoy would brief the Iranians about the outcome of the Geneva meeting.[7] The conference, which came to be known as Geneva I, resulted in a final document laying out the basic framework for a political settlement of the conflict. This document, known as the Geneva Communiqué, remains the basic reference point in international negotiations on the Syrian conflict some four years after the meeting.[8]

The objective of the process initiated by Annan was to develop international support for a plan that would include a political transition preserving the integrity of key state institutions and offering assurances to business communities and minorities that they would be included in the process and shielded from any retribution by opposition groups. Unfortunately, meaningful international support for the plan did not materialize after Geneva I, notwithstanding the nominal commitments of those who attended the meeting. Instead of backing the transition plan, the priority of the Arab League participants and their Western partners appeared to be the removal militarily of the Assad regime. This basic goal was manifest in the continued supply of arms, logistical support, and finance to opposition forces. What was not clear, however, was whether those supporting the opposition had agreed on any strategy as to the nature or sequence of the political transition that would follow should Assad be toppled. Moreover, the opposition's backers seemed largely uncertain as to how to produce regime change. Apparently reluctant to shift definitively the military balance through a direct intervention—one that might leave them responsible for the bloody aftermath of the regime's collapse or might trigger destabilization that would spread across Syria's borders—the regional and Western backers of the opposition limited their efforts to publicly expressing outrage, supplying weapons, escalating economic sanctions, and continuing attempts to isolate Iran.

The purpose of this strategy may have been to suspend the diplomatic process in order to give the opposition time to unite and shift the balance of power on the ground, thereby improving their negotiating position. In fact, the passage of time produced the opposite effect: greater fragmentation among the groups fighting against the regime and a deepening military stalemate. On August 2, 2012, Annan announced that he would step down as special envoy at the end of the month.[9] In a news conference that day, he stated plainly that absent international buy-in, no mediator could bring about a political process on his or her own. Annan's point was that while the major powers had called upon the UN to provide a diplomatic framework, they had not determined to support a political process. The combined effect of the six-point plan and the Geneva Communiqué were to fulfill the role assigned to the UN; that this framework would have no effect on the course of the conflict was due to the absence of political will to support it, not the failure of the UN to define a path forward. He went on to say that a political settlement of the conflict would be possible only "if the international community can show the courage and leadership necessary to compromise on their partial interests for the sake of the Syrian people."[10] By the end of August 2012, the estimated death toll of the conflict stood at twenty thousand, more than double the count from when Annan was first appointed.

Annan's successor as special envoy was another seasoned UN veteran, Lakhdar Brahimi.[11] Brahimi spent his first sixteen months in office attempting to reconvene a meeting on the basis of the Geneva Communiqué, with an emphasis on securing immediate access for humanitarian aid. Working behind the scenes, Brahimi encouraged the new US secretary of state, John Kerry, to seek a meeting with his Russian counterpart, Sergey Lavrov, in the summer of 2013 to iron out a joint approach for relaunching the diplomatic process.[12] In September 2013, Brahimi secured for the first time the Security Council's official endorsement of the Geneva Communiqué as the framework for talks. The endorsement in Security Council Resolution 2118, which came fourteen months after the communiqué was first issued, received unanimous support largely because the resolution also defused a crisis concerning Syria's chemical weapons arsenal, which we discuss below. Under the resolution, a second meeting was to be held in Geneva in the fall of 2013 with the goal of ensuring access to aid for internally displaced populations within Syria, facilitating prisoner exchanges between the sides, and securing both sides' commitment to the basic guidelines for political transition defined at Geneva I. The meeting was postponed several times before finally being convened as the Geneva II meeting on January 22, 2014. Estimates of the death toll in Syria by that date stood at 130,000.

Opposition groups attended Geneva II under pressure from their external backers, who threatened to withhold assistance should they boycott. The Assad regime similarly attended under pressure from Russia and perhaps to underscore its position as the recognized government of Syria. Yet one of the critical shortcomings of Geneva I remained in place: Iran was excluded from the talks. In a complicated prelude to the meeting that reflected continuing deep divisions in the international approach to diplomatic settlement, Iran was first publicly invited to the meeting by the UN secretary-general and then very publicly disinvited under pressure from the United States.[13]

There had been considerable hope prior to Geneva II that American insistence on excluding Iran had dissipated. The Iranian presidential elections in June 2013 replaced the widely reviled Mahmoud Ahmedinejad with the more internationally acceptable figure of Hassan Rouhani. President Rouhani's first few months in office witnessed a flurry of diplomatic outreach by Iranian officials, which was met with some enthusiasm in the West. President Rouhani's visit to New York for the September 2013 General Assembly meeting was dubbed an Iranian "charm offensive." The end of the weeklong visit witnessed an unprecedented phone call between the US and Iranian presidents.[14] The initiation of the first serious negotiations between the United States and Iran concerning that country's nuclear program formed the backdrop against which observers hoped that Iran might be included in the talks at Geneva II. Iran's participation was the subject of intense diplomatic wrangling largely because Brahimi and Secretary-General Ban Ki-moon were convinced that the Iranians must be included given their influence over the Assad regime. In the end, however, American objections could not be overcome. The apparent belief that keeping Iran at the margins of negotiations would diminish Iranian influence in Syria inverts the basic logic of negotiations. Instead, the likely result of Iran's exclusion was the weakening of the negotiations themselves by virtue of the removal of a principal from the talks intended to resolve the conflict.

The Geneva II talks ended in disarray just over two weeks after they began. By the end of the meetings, the sides had not even agreed on a common agenda for discussion. For his part, Brahimi closed the meeting by apologizing to the Syrian people for raising their expectations and delivering so little after so many months of preparation.[15] Brahimi's comments reflected the essential dilemma of the UN's position. Tasked with providing a diplomatic forum to bring the parties together, the UN labored mightily to make the meetings happen. Once they were convened, however, the absence of a common position among the international sponsors of the talks meant that neither of the Syrian sides was required to engage seriously with the process.

After the talks, the United States and Russia traded accusations, with the Americans claiming that the Assad regime had paralyzed efforts in Geneva while Russia claimed that the Syrian rebels and their backers remained committed to a military solution rather than a diplomatic one. Geneva II ended without setting a date for the next round of talks. Within a few months, rumors emerged of Brahimi's plans to follow Annan's example and step down out of frustration over the lack of international support for the mediator's role, as he eventually did in May of 2014.[16] In a telling sign of how far the original framework for the special envoy position had fallen apart, it was expected that the next person to hold the office would serve solely as the UN's envoy because of divisions within the Arab League over the Syrian conflict. Further, at least one candidate under serious consideration for the position had previously called for Assad's ouster when serving as an Australian government official and was reportedly pursuing the envoy position in the hopes that the role might strengthen his campaign to succeed Ban Ki-moon as UN secretary-general.[17] In short, the UN's efforts to furnish a diplomatic framework to resolve the Syria conflict produced a sensible plan and a platform for talks, but without the international political will for a settlement no progress was possible. By 2014, the leadership of the special envoy had become sufficiently insignificant that the discussion of potential candidates centered on their career ambitions rather than the demands of the Syrian people.

In the end, Brahimi was succeeded by Staffan de Mistura, an Italian-Swedish diplomat whose career with various United Nations agencies spans four decades. Though de Mistura lacked both the high profile and the credibility of his two predecessors, he did, at least, have some knowledge of the region, having served in United Nations positions in Iraq, Afghanistan, and Lebanon in the period preceding his appointment. As a measure of the reduced expectations for his role, at the time of his appointment supporters of his candidacy called for him to focus his efforts on "building international support for locally negotiated ceasefires."[18] Indeed, de Mistura has had little to show for his tenure as UN special envoy for Syria other than a series of local cease-fires, and more recently a wider but exceedingly fragile pause in hostilities, and reconciliation efforts given the limited international political support for what remains of the Geneva process.[19] To shore up international support, de Mistura has also made apparent concessions that neither of his predecessors countenanced, lending tacit support to the strategy of direct external intervention in Syria against IS targets. He has requested that the Turkish government allow Kurdish fighters to cross into Syria from Turkey— to strengthen "self-defense" forces against the IS on the ground in the border town of Kobane while American-led air strikes pursue IS forces from above.[20] And in his local cease-fire efforts in cities like Aleppo, Mistura has argued that "reaching an agreement 'akin to a cease fire' between opposition forces and the Syrian army would strengthen the city against an IS onslaught."[21] In effect, de Mistura has seized on the emergence of an enemy—the IS—identified as a threat by most of the principal international actors supporting or opposing the Assad regime in order to forge international consensus. But as a result his actions have in practice diverged quite dramatically from the traditional role of mediator, with its presumptions of neutrality.

Like his predecessors, de Mistura is still a proponent of bringing the Assad regime to the table with the Syrian opposition factions. He appears to be wagering that shared antipathy to the IS can provide a basis to unite external intervenors around a political framework while also isolating the IS sufficiently from other Sunni opposition groups on the ground to sustain the claim that all meaningful stakeholders will have a place at the negotiating table. In de Mistura's words, "Truce measures may be favorable to moderate rebels and government forces as they face a common threat from Islamic State militants."[22] Though de Mistura has expressed optimism that this strategy of distinguishing between moderate and extreme rebels—with military attacks proceeding against the latter—will advance the goal of resolving the conflict, in fact the odds for such a resolution have rarely been worse. Given that de Mistura has been dealt a far weaker hand than Annan or Brahimi, his notion that the escalation of violence through air strikes together with the even greater fragmentation of the actors on the ground in Syria—with intra-Sunni fighting emerging as an additional axis of division—will precipitate conflict resolution seems naive at best. More than two years into his appointment as envoy, de Mistura has mainly conducted a series of "consultations" with Syrian government and opposition forces that conclude with his own forceful condemnation of ongoing violence against besieged civilians, setting the stage for the next set of consultations. This picture shifted slightly at the end of 2015, as the UN Security Council approved a framework for peace talks, scheduled to begin in January 2016, that signaled the resumption of a diplomatic process, albeit without evidence of serious engagement by local or regional parties.[23] Indeed, within weeks of formulating this new initiative Saudi Arabia and other Gulf states cut diplomatic ties with Iran, undermining hopes for constructive peace talks.

The UN Security Council's Role

Besides the organization's efforts to provide a diplomatic framework for a political settlement, the UN has interceded in the Syrian conflict in a number of other ways, starting with Security Council involvement. The conventional wisdom on Security Council action in Syria focuses on the four instances when Russian and Chinese vetoes blocked proposed initiatives. In fact, the more interesting story about Security Council involvement is the cover it has provided for the permanent members on the Council to issue strong public statements despite their own limited appetite for any decisive intervention in the conflict that might definitively tilt the balance between the regime and opposition forces.

Three of the vetoes came during the first year of the conflict, while the last occurred in May 2014. These were not vetoes of resolutions contemplating military intervention, no-fly zones, or the securing of humanitarian corridors. No such resolutions have been proposed by any party to date. Rather, in October 2011 and again in July 2012, Russia and China blocked Western-backed resolutions threatening Syrian authorities with sanctions if they did not halt the violence.[24] Of course, multilateral sanctions against the regime by the EU, the United States, and allies like the Gulf states, Turkey, Japan, Korea, and Australia were already firmly in place outside the UN framework. The goal of the resolutions was to force countries like China and Russia to cut off trade with Syria, which they were not prepared to do. The third veto was exercised in February 2012—immediately prior to Annan's appointment as special envoy—against an Arab League–initiated draft resolution calling for Assad to hand power to a deputy as part of a compulsory, internationally enforced transition.[25] Russia publicly described the resolution as an attempt at Security Council–mandated regime change. Both China and Russia also argued that a precondition that Assad hand over power would preclude the regime's participation in peace talks, resulting in a counterproductive delay in diplomacy that would prolong the conflict. Finally, the fourth veto took place in May 2014, with China and Russia again blocking a resolution to refer the conflict in Syria to the ICC. As Russia's foreign ministry had previously stated, they believed such referral was "ill-timed and counterproductive" because it would further highlight the perceived internal need for military victory at all costs and in the process escalate the crisis.[26]

Despite the persistent divisions on the Council that led to these four vetoes, the Council adopted six substantive resolutions on the Syrian civil war prior to the emergence of the IS and has added a number of additional counterterrorism-based resolutions since. The scope of the resolutions directly tied to the Syrian civil war reflects the narrow grounds of international consensus on the conflict. The first three resolutions were nominally in support of Annan's efforts to broker a cease-fire, and the last two were attempts to defuse discrete crises on the ground. Resolution 2042, adopted by the Council over a year into the conflict, reflected unanimous agreement to send a small team of unarmed military observers to monitor a cease-fire negotiated by Annan between the parties in April 2012.[27] That unarmed UN observer mission was enlarged to a delegation of three hundred monitors a week later in a second resolution.[28] The initial drafts of these resolutions were circulated by the United States; then, in a compromise with Russia, the "demand" that Syria comply with the terms of the cease-fire was softened and replaced with a call on "all parties, including the opposition, to immediately cease all armed violence."[29] The third resolution, adopted three months later, extended the mandate of the monitoring mission in the wake of a failed bid to impose sanctions on Syria that had been blocked by Russia and China. The extension of the mission, despite the near-immediate breakdown of the brief April cease-fire it had originally been sent to monitor, was largely an attempt to keep alive the faltering Annan plan.[30] Annan's resignation as envoy despite the passage of the resolution attested to the widely held view that the monitoring mission had come to symbolize the failure of diplomatic efforts rather than their extension. The UN observer mission's mandate lapsed at the end of August as Brahimi succeeded Annan as envoy.

Another year went by before the Council acted again on Syria. This time the Council's action came against the backdrop of an American threat to launch strikes against Syria in response to a sarin gas attack in a Damascus suburb. The vagaries of American and British foreign policy on the use of weapons of mass destruction (WMDs) in Syria brought to mind the run-up to the 2003 Iraq war. As a consequence of the disastrous aftermath of that war, the prospect of WMD-based strikes against Syria laid bare the resistance to further military interventions in the region among American and British publics. President Obama had declared that chemical weapon use by the Syrian government would cross a "red line" triggering military strikes. In the face of evidence of a chemical weapons strike, however, the president proved unable to follow through on his threat.

The Obama administration insisted it was entitled to strike Syria unilaterally—without Security Council authorization—on the grounds that chemical weapons use represented a sufficiently grave violation of international law to trigger a right of response. The argument had little international law credibility outside Beltway circles (perhaps even within such circles), and a strike on Syria would have been seen as an unauthorized American intervention. Yet the sequence of events following American confirmation that the administration's "red line" had been crossed illustrates that neither international law nor the absence of Security Council authorization explains the lack of Western military intervention in Syria. Rather, the Obama administration's inability to follow through on the threatened strikes was a consequence of a British parliamentary vote against military action and opposition to such strikes in the American Congress.[31] The United States could not engage in even the limited "pinprick" air strikes that it had threatened against Syria—much less a full-blown and decisive intervention—as a result of the lack of political will *in Washington* to become militarily entangled in another Middle Eastern conflict.

The aftermath of the failed bid to strike Syria did, however, produce an interesting turn in the course of international intervention in the conflict. Russia, long accused of intransigence by the United States and the EU, acted to address the chemical weapons "red line." Seizing on a statement by Secretary Kerry that nothing short of the destruction of Syria's chemical weapons arsenal would deter an eventual American action, Russia persuaded the Assad regime to relinquish its arsenal. After weeks of intense diplomacy between the United States and Russia, a deal was hammered out under which international inspectors were dispatched to Syria to rapidly verify and destroy its chemical weapons stockpile. The Russian-brokered deal to destroy Syria's chemicals weapons arsenal was unanimously endorsed by the Council's fourth resolution on the Syrian conflict on September 27, 2013.[32] Though the Syrian government's capacity to prosecute its military campaign against the rebels did not depend on its chemical arsenal, the deal to remove the stockpile from the regime's arsenal was a modest success for international diplomacy.[33]

The last set of the Council's resolutions directly addressing the Syria civil war to date again represented discrete initiatives rather than elements of a broader strategy or evidence of deepening consensus. While the Geneva II talks ended without progress in February 2014, one limited accomplishment of the talks had been to secure a thirty-six-hour cease-fire in the Old City of Homs, where civilians had been cut off from food supply and medical care for months as a result of siege warfare. The cease-fire was dubbed a "humanitarian pause" to enable medical and food aid to get into the city and civilians a chance to leave the besieged neighborhoods and was eventually extended for a couple of days, enabling thousands of civilians to be evacuated.[34] Following the collapse of Geneva II, the Council adopted a resolution demanding that all parties lift the sieges on specific population centers in the provinces of Homs, Aleppo, and Damascus and allow unfettered humanitarian access for UN agencies and their implementing partners.[35] The identification of particular neighborhoods and towns under siege offered a level of specificity with respect to the Council's demands that empowered the UN's humanitarian agencies to better negotiate access to those areas with the Syrian government. The resolution also signaled the possibility that external backers of the parties might be willing to exert pressure on their local Syrian allies to allow humanitarian access in areas they controlled. This effort to leverage pressure to secure humanitarian access was repeated in a second resolution in July, this time specifying particular roads to be used for humanitarian supplies without the state's consent and also establishing a monitoring mechanism for implementation.[36] But while there is some evidence that the resolutions have enabled a measure of relief in besieged areas, their principal terms—calling for a cessation of violence and unfettered humanitarian access—have not been implemented.[37] Finally, in March 2015, the Council issued a resolution reiterating its condemnation of the use of toxic chemicals (in this instance, chlorine) against civilians and supporting the Organisation for the Prohibition of Chemical Weapons in its fact-finding mission concerning the use of chlorine as a weapon in Syria.[38] This was followed up by a second resolution in August, calling for the creation of a joint investigative mechanism by the UN and OPCW to determine responsibility for the use of chemical weapons in Syria.[39]

By contrast to this record of ineffective resolutions concerning the Syrian conflict, however, the Council rapidly forged a consensus on counterterrorism measures once a set of Sunni factions in Iraq and Syria united as the Islamic State in Syria and Iraq, later renamed the Islamic State. From the summer of 2014 through the end of 2015, the Council issued two presidential statements and four resolutions directly targeting the IS and expanding a counterterrorism framework for cooperation among international actors.[40] These resolutions, together with American-led air strikes on Syrian territory directed strictly against IS forces and affiliated targets, provide a stark contrast to the absence of will on the Council until after the Paris attacks to take measures meaningfully connected to resolving the underlying political conflict in Syria.[41] This disconnect underscores the extent to which the offensive against the IS has been motivated less by addressing the basic welfare of Syrian civilians and far more by worries that allowing the IS's spectacular acts of violence (above all against Western hostages and later in Western cities) to go unanswered would be taken as a sign of political and military weakness. In the immediate aftermath of the Paris attacks, however, an international initiative to address the Syrian conflict was added to the panoply of measures being taken against the IS. Only in this context did the Council finally address, for the first time, the subject of a political solution to the Syrian crisis.[42]

The foregoing overview of the UN Security Council's role in the Syria conflict offers two lessons: first, the UN's diplomatic efforts, through the good offices of the secretary-general and his envoys, are almost entirely divorced from the actions of the organization's executive organ, a political body distinct from the UN's standing civil service secretariat. Second, the Council's actions reflect the pursuit of partisan interests by the powers backing different sides in the conflict. Rather than suggesting shared interest in a diplomatic settlement of the conflict, the Council has been the forum in which Western powers and Russia forestall political resolution while continuing the flow of arms to their local proxies. When it was expedient, the United States and Russia were able to make common cause to address a discrete aspect of the conflict—as in the cases of the chemical weapons crisis, the desire to alleviate some measure of suffering for besieged civilians following the failure of Geneva II, or the consensus on counterterrorism measures against IS forces. But more often the Council has served the role of blocking either side from securing definitive international support. This is not a failure of the Council but a built-in feature of its design. In the absence of great-power unanimity, the organization is designed to block international military action in favor of providing a standing diplomatic forum—in the form of the Council itself as well as ad hoc diplomatic conferences—to hammer out differences and forge a political compromise. So long as the backers of the two sides to the conflict are represented on the Council and remain committed to a military strategy to achieve their objectives, the Council cannot be expected to play an effective role in ending the violence. Even in the wake of a unanimous resolution on the Council supporting a political solution, tensions between the regional allies of the United States and Russia—Saudi Arabia and Iran respectively—flared, dashing hopes that the new diplomatic framework could succeed or that the Council could sustain a consensus out of the fleeting moment of unity produced by the Paris attacks.

UN Humanitarian Assistance

Ultimately, the aspect of the UN's role that may receive the least public attention but has been most efficacious in affecting conditions on the ground is the work of its humanitarian agencies. The Syrian conflict has produced the largest refugee crisis since the Rwandan genocide. As of June 2015, estimates of Syrian refugees living outside the country range from four to five million, and estimates of the internally displaced population add another six million to those who have been uprooted from their homes by the fighting. The UN's Office for the Coordination of Humanitarian Affairs (OCHA) coordinates the activities of all UN humanitarian agencies and is responsible for the Syria Humanitarian Assistance Response Plan, which is the overarching framework for meeting the humanitarian needs of Syrian civilians. The principal responsibility for aiding refugees outside of Syria falls to the Office of the UN High Commissioner for Refugees (UNHCR) working together with the World Food Programme (WFP), while other agencies address the needs of civilians who remain in Syria.

UNHCR registered over 4,837,208 refugees outside Syria by April 2016, with tens of thousands of additional refugees awaiting registration.[43] As of the spring of 2016, the total appeal for humanitarian assistance funding for the Syrian refugees issued by the UN system had topped $5 billion, though less than 10 percent of that amount had been funded according to the UNHCR.[44] The interagency and regional aid coordination managed by UNHCR to assist Syrian refugees involves partnerships with over 150 organizations beyond those in the UN system.[45] Further, an important proportion of the assistance to these refugees has been provided directly by the neighboring countries that have absorbed the fleeing population. Lebanon and Turkey lead these countries with over one million refugees located in Lebanon and 2.8 million registered by the government of Turkey, followed by Jordan (630,000) and Iraq (250,000). Although these countries have no choice but to absorb some costs, they have also sought international assistance from the outset. While these countries have borne a tremendous burden in housing enormous refugee populations, the international assistance they require has been staggering and coordinated entirely by the United Nations system.

The principal international sources of food and medical assistance—as well as provisions for housing in refugee camps and schools in the case of Jordan—for hundreds of thousands of Syrian refugees have been UNHCR and the WFP. As an example, in Lebanon, UNHCR spent close to $400 million in 2013 on shelter, health, water, and education access for the Syrian refugee population, while the WFP was able to reach a quarter of the Syrian refugees living in Lebanon with food aid in the same period.[46] The work of both agencies was rendered more challenging by the fact that most Syrian refugees in Lebanon are not living in formal camps but have found shelter through extended family or the use of private resources, making access to the population more challenging. In Jordan, where a larger proportion of Syrian refugees are housed in UNHCR camps, the WFP was able to provide food aid to over half a million refugees there, including three-quarters of the 120,000 inhabitants of the sprawling Zaatari refugee camp.

In addition to serving the needs of the Syrian refugee population, UN humanitarian agencies have been among the few organizations able to assist internally displaced populations within Syria and besieged civilians who have remained in their homes but have been cut off from all access to food, water, and medical care. As of 2014, the UN estimated that there were more than 9 million people living in Syria in need of humanitarian aid, of whom 3.5 million were in areas that were hard to reach and 250,000 were cut off entirely as a result of the siege warfare tactics practiced more widely by the Syrian regime than the opposition.[47] With the occupation of large swathes of territory by the IS in 2015, the toll on besieged civilians has only risen. As we discussed above, UN humanitarian agencies were given a mandate by Security Council Resolution 2139 to help civilians in need of aid—especially those nearly four million who are hard to reach or completely isolated. Yet without action to enforce the resolution in the face of intransigence by the warring sides, UN relief workers have been operating under extremely precarious circumstances, negotiating access at checkpoints with all sides and facing severe constraints. While there has been some international criticism of the cautious interpretation of their mandate by these relief workers, the dangerous conditions of their work and their dependence on the regime and the rebels for access have left few options beyond negotiating with the warring factions or coordinating assistance with local nongovernmental organizations.[48]

On the one hand, almost all of the international aid that has reached the most vulnerable civilian populations in Syria has been coordinated by UN humanitarian agencies. On the other hand, their access to such populations remains hostage to the military and political framework dictating the terms of their presence on Syrian soil. As with the UN's other roles, the success of the organization's humanitarian assistance work is predicated on the international political will to support that work politically and financially. Such support has been intermittent at best. Moreover, as in any civil war context, the provision of humanitarian assistance will redound to the benefit of the more militarily powerful party able to dictate the terms of access. This intrinsic challenge of assistance in the presence of an ongoing conflict exposes the

UN's humanitarian efforts within Syria to withering criticism. Absent a framework for a political settlement, aid remains hostage to the military balance of power on the ground, regardless of how aggressively relief workers may choose to interpret their mandate.

Across the board, then, the UN's capacity to serve an effective role in the Syrian conflict depends on the existence of sufficient international consensus to provide the organization with a consistent mandate and to offer it the authority to see that mandate through. In the absence of such international consensus, the UN's work is doomed to serve as an international scapegoat for the persistence of a conflict being fueled by the very conditions that undermine the capacities of the organization. As Annan indicated when he resigned from his position as envoy, the UN cannot be tasked to accomplish ends not supported by its taskmasters.

CONCLUSION: CYCLES OF FAILURE AND INTERVENTIONISM IN SYRIA

Ultimately, a defining feature of the UN experience in Syria is the extent to which the primary regional and external parties to the conflict have interceded systematically in the country in ways fundamentally divorced from and at odds with political settlement efforts. The result has been a persistent cycle of failures to achieve a peaceful resolution to the violence. Each new round of diplomacy is initially given superficial support, only to be fatally compromised down the line by the unwillingness of states to subordinate their security objectives to the goal of ending the crisis. In these final paragraphs, we explore two implications of this cyclical feature of the conflict. First, we highlight how debates about whether to "intervene" in Syria through direct military action actually obscure the extent to which all of the UN initiatives unfold against a background of permanent external intervention. Given a continuous record of powerful regional and international players shaping outcomes on the ground, we then discuss whether and how the UN can still facilitate either peace or justice.

To begin with, over the last five years, the principal external actors in Syria have hardly "failed" to intervene. Instead they have fundamentally transformed the conflict into a regional proxy war by providing arms, equipping and paying the salaries for soldiers, imposing sanctions, and even threatening military strikes. The direct intervention now under way—in the form of

American-led air strikes against IS targets—is just the most recent example of the ways in which external actors have continuously deployed military tactics in Syria in pursuit of their own ends. The result is that for all the talk of "nonintervention," a basic dynamic in Syria concerns how powerful states have stepped into and out of UN processes in order to facilitate their other preexisting modes of intervention. For instance, UN-led diplomatic initiatives have been employed as a delaying tactic in the conflict to give the opposition or the government time to shift the balance of power on the ground. On other occasions, states have denounced the very same initiatives when they seem to require compromises viewed strategically as less preferable to the militarized status quo. Finally, the principals have also been willing to step out of processes entirely, as when the United States declared that the Syrian regime had crossed a "red line" with its use of chemical weapons and asserted a unilateral right to strike militarily at its own discretion. The overall effect for UN efforts has been not only cyclical failure but also a discrediting of its basic role in the country. The UN is seen as either instrumentalized to serve the interests of powerful players or marginalized through unilateral state action. In this way, the United States' red line on chemical weapons was reminiscent of how WMD arguments concerning Iraq intervention placed the UN in an untenable bind. In that context as well, the UN found itself as alternately the principal forum for discussion or entirely peripheral to the international agenda, depending on what served the central intervenors' objectives.

Perhaps this last point has been most powerfully illustrated by revelations attendant to US-Iran nuclear negotiations. It appears that those talks may have encompassed behind-the-scenes discussions about Syria. But crucially the purpose of the "grand bargain" that the United States has been purportedly discussing with Iran concerns American preferences for stabilizing the regional order in the Arab world, with at best collateral effects for peace in Syria (and other conflicts from Palestine to Yemen). For that reason it is not surprising that these grand bargain negotiations were proceeding while the United States was simultaneously seeking to exclude Iran from the diplomatic framework for Syria structured by the UN. The UN framework was designed to facilitate an inclusive political process that could generate a durable peace and that all the relevant parties would agree to. Such a process is not necessarily coincident—and under certain circumstances may not even be consistent—with the US pursuit of its favored ordering for the region. What this highlights is the extent to which external actors treat the Syrian conflict as a matter of securing their own interests rather than as an urgent humanitarian crisis or as being principally about the goals of Syrian actors. In addition, this speaks to the ways in which UN diplomatic efforts centered on civilian welfare and engaging Syrian actors on the ground are treated as marginal at best to the strategies pursued by the United States and other intervening states.

What does all this suggest about the role for the UN in Syria going forward? At the most basic level, one key function of the UN—underscored by the very composition and structure of the Security Council—has always been to serve as the secretariat of the great powers in matters of peace and security. As a result, critiquing the UN for failing to rein in the security commitments and intervening practices of the United States, Russia, and the other regional powers is fundamentally misplaced. The UN cannot serve as an independent liberating agent because the outcomes of its diplomatic initiatives are ultimately subject to the agendas and goals of key states. This is not to say that the UN is *only* the secretariat of great powers. Given the multiplicity of institutional settings within the UN—as well as the relative autonomy from state interests exercised by different organizational actors—care needs to be taken in analyzing how the organization as a whole relates to Syria (as to any context). Nonetheless, the very nature of the UN's security function means that when diplomatic initiatives face the entrenched and conflicting strategic commitments of powerful states they are almost inevitably bound to fail.

The UN can nonetheless preserve the possibility or space for local and external parties to the Syrian conflict to negotiate a political settlement. In effect, this has been the organization's principal goal in facilitating the Geneva process. It has sought to work in coordination not only with great powers represented on the Security Council but also with the Arab League and the Gulf Cooperation Council to create a procedural mechanism within which actors could reach diplomatic agreement. Again, because of the dual tracks of intervention in the country, with external actors interceding on the ground outside processes created by the UN, such a space cannot hold out the promise of independently resolving the underlying conflict. In other words, the UN's process role does not create the conditions for an actual willingness by the relevant players to compromise; its practical value exists only to the extent that the primary actors are otherwise motivated to make meaningful use of such a mechanism. Still, the importance of preserving an international negotiating space should not be underemphasized. The Syrian conflict is inherently transnational, shot through with multiple external intervenors. As a result, no settlement can emerge in the absence of some international setting for the principal stakeholders to develop and commit to a political process.

It is thus essential to appreciate the fundamental difference between a UN-led diplomatic effort and the modes of militarized intervention pursued contemporaneously by key states. In a simplistic sense, both may be viewed as forms of foreign (perhaps illegitimate) intervention. But the very transnational nature of the conflict means that if local communities are to have the political opportunity to shape their own future they will necessarily have to confront the competing external states currently directing the course of the conflict. As a result, such an international space can actually facilitate domestic decision making and control. In a sense, as all options in Syria embody one form of intervention or another, the question is not *whether* the international community should intervene but how and on whose terms. Whereas the militarized interventions of key states have transformed a local uprising into a regional proxy war, international diplomatic frameworks still hold out the best available possibility, however tenuous, for refocusing transnational politics in Syria around local needs.

NOTES

This chapter was substantially completed in November 2014, with modest revisions in June and December 2015. We would like to thank the participants at the Yale Law School Middle East Legal Studies Seminar for helpful feedback.

1. See, e.g., Erika Solomon, "Syria Killing Accelerates as Peace Talks Falter," Reuters, February 12, 2014, www.reuters.com/article/2014/02/12/us-syria-crisis-talks-idUSBREA1B0TX20140212 ("More Syrians have been killed in the three weeks since peace talks began than at any other time in the civil war. . . . It is unclear how far the bloodshed is a consequence of the talks as both sides seek to improve their bargaining positions"); "Diplomat to UN: Security Council Has Failed Syria," CNN, September 28, 2012, www.cnn.com/2012/09/28/world/meast/syria-civil-war/; and Peter S. Goodman, "International Intervention Needed to End Syrian Catastrophe," *Huffington Post*, January 23, 2014, www.huffingtonpost.com/peter-s-goodman/syria-international-intervention_b_4653395.html ("And the architects of this horror [of atrocities in Syria] sit at a hotel in Geneva, airing out the same arguments that reinforce stalemate, a status quo that condemns more to their deaths. As comforting as a parallel humanitarian solution may be, it will not happen without international action that effectively challenges the political situation").

2. "UN Syria Resolution 'Fails to Ensure Justice': HRW," Agence France Presse, September 28, 2013, www.straitstimes.com/breaking-news/world/story/un-syria-resolution-fails-ensure-justice-human-rights-watch-20130928 (citing comment by Human Rights Watch director Philippe Bolopion that the UN must "refer the situation in Syria to the International Criminal Court").

3. Alireza Doostdar, "How Not to Understand ISIS," *Jadaliyya*, October 2, 2014, www.jadaliyya.com/pages/index/19485/how-not-to-understand-isis.

4. "Kofi Annan Appointed Joint Special Envoy of United Nations, League of Arab States on Syrian Crisis," UNSG/SM/14124, press release, February 23, 2012, www.un.org/News/Press/docs/2012/sgsm14124.doc.htm.

5. The six points constituting the plan were (1) an inclusive Syrian-led political process to address legitimate aspirations and concerns of the Syrian people with an empowered mediator; (2) a cease-fire under UN supervision (with parallel commitments from the government and opposition forces to desist from attacks in population centers and to halt troop movements); (3) unfettered access to all areas affected by the fighting for the provision of humanitarian assistance to the civilian population; (4) release of arbitrarily detained persons by both sides; (5) freedom of movement for journalists; and (6) ensuring the freedom of association for civilians.

6. Nick Cumming-Bruce and Rick Gladstone, "Syria Talks Won't Include the Saudis or Iranians," *New York Times*, June 28, 2012.

7. Ibid. "Mr. Annan, who had said he wanted the Iranians to be part of such a meeting, offered no explanation for why they were not invited. Asked about it later, the chief United Nations spokesman, Martin Nesirky, told reporters in New York that Mr. Annan 'has been clear about the need for Iran to be part of the solution' and that Mr. Annan would brief the Iranians about the outcome of the Geneva meeting. Mr. Nesirky declined to comment on speculation that Hillary Rodham Clinton, the American secretary of state, had threatened to cancel her participation if Iran were invited."

8. The communiqué referenced the six-point plan as its basic framework, centering its focus on cessation of armed violence by all sides, full humanitarian access to areas affected by the fighting, and a plan for a "Syrian-led transition" with the formation of a transitional governing body that "could include members of the present government and the opposition and other groups . . . formed on the basis of mutual consent." For the full text of the communiqué, see "Final Communiqué of the Action Group for Syria," June 30, 2012, www.un.org/News/dh/infocus/Syria/FinalCommuniqueActionGroupforSyria.pdf.

9. Rick Gladstone, "Resigning as Envoy to Syria, Annan Casts Wide Blame," *New York Times*, August 3, 2012.

10. "Opening Remarks by Kofi Annan, Joint Special Envoy for Syria, at Press Conference—Geneva," UN News Centre, August 2, 2012, www.un.org/apps/news/infocus/Syria/press.asp?sID=41.

11. Brahimi had previously served the Arab League special envoy to Lebanon in the early 1990s and as a UN special envoy to South Africa (1993–94), Haiti (1994–96), Afghanistan (1997–99, 2001–4), and Iraq (2004).

12. Hillary Clinton had reportedly been less friendly to the diplomatic framework provided by the UN when she was secretary of state, making the appointment of John Kerry to the position a welcome opportunity to reset the special envoy's relationship with the US representative to the planned talks.

13. Somini Sengupta and Michael R. Gordon, "U.N Invites Iran to Syria Talks, Raising Objections from the U.S.," *New York Times*, January 20, 2014; and Michael R. Gordon and Anne Barnard, "Talks over Syria Are Set to Begin, but Iran Is Not Invited," *New York Times*, January 21, 2014 (noting that "after a day of intensive consultations in which American officials made clear their unhappiness with Mr. Ban's move, Iran was disinvited").

14. Barbara Slavin, "Call with Obama Caps Rouhani's UN Charm Offensive," *Al-Monitor*, September 27, 2013, www.al-monitor.com/pulse/originals/2013/09/rouhani-un-visit-reception-message.html#.

15. "Brahimi Apologises to Syrians after Failure of Geneva II Peace Talks," *Middle East Monitor*, February 16, 2014, https://www.middleeastmonitor.com/news/middle-east/9781-brahimi-apologises-to-syrians-after-failure-of-geneva-ii-peace-talks/.

16. "UN Mediator on Syria Quits; French Envoy Says Chemical Weapons Were Used," *New York Times*, May 13, 2014.

17. Ian Black, "UN Looking for Syrian Envoy as Brahimi Prepares to Quit after Failed Peace Talks," *Guardian*, May 1, 2014, www.theguardian.com/world/2014/may/01/un-search-syria-envoy-lakhdar-brahimi-quit (noting that former Australian prime minister Kevin Rudd "is said to have his eye on become secretary general of the UN.... The Syria envoy position could be seen as a stepping stone to that").

18. "Oxfam Reacts to Appointment of Staffan de Mistura as New UN Peace Envoy on Syria," July 10, 2014, www.oxfam.org/en/pressroom/reactions/oxfam-reacts-appointment-staffan-de-mistura-new-un-peace-envoy-syria.

19. Michele Kelemen, "In Syria, UN Promotes Local Ceasefires to Offer Relief from Civil War," NPR, November 11, 2014, www.npr.org/2014/11/11/363342249/in-syria-u-n-promotes-local-ceasefires-to-offer-relief-from-civil-war.

20. "UN Envoy Urges Turkey to Allow Kurds to Protect Kobane," *Hurriyet Daily News* (Turkey), October 10, 2014 (from Agence France Presse), www.hurriyetdailynews.com/un-envoy-urges-turkey-to-allow-kurds-to-protect-kobane.aspx?PageID=238&NID=72795&NewsCatID=359.

21. Ziad Haydar, "Staffan de Mistura's Aleppo Plan," *Al Monitor*, November 11, 2014, www.al-monitor.com/pulse/security/2014/11/syria-agreement-international-aleppo-homs-de-mistura.html#.

22. "Syria Conflict: UN's Staffan de Mistura Hopeful," BBC, November 11, 2014, www.bbc.com/news/world-middle-east-29999157.

23. "UN Syria Mediator Aims to Convene Peace Talks on January 25," Reuters, December 26, 2015, www.reuters.com/article/us-mideast-crisis-syria-talks-idUSKBN0U90CO20151226.

24. "Security Council Fails to Adopt Draft Resolution Condemning Syria's Crackdown on Anti-government Protestors, Owing to Veto by Russian Federation,

China," UN Department of Public Information, meetings coverage, SC/10403, October 4, 2011, www.un.org/News/Press/docs/2011/sc10403.doc.htm; and "Security Council Fails to Adopt Draft Resolution on Syria That Would Have Threatened Sanctions, Due to Negative Votes of China, Russian Federation," UN Department of Public Information, meetings coverage, SC/10714, July 19, 2012, www.un.org/News/Press/docs/2012/sc10714.doc.htm.

25. "Security Council Fails to Adopt Draft Resolution on Syria As Russian Federation, China Veto Text Supporting Arab League's Proposed Peace Plan," UN Department of Public Information, meetings coverage, SC/10536, February 4, 2012, www.un.org/News/Press/docs/2012/sc10536.doc.htm.

26. "Russia Opposes Syria Crisis War Crimes Court Referral," Reuters, January 15, 2013.

27. UN Security Council Resolution 2042, S/Res/2042, April 14, 2012, www.securitycouncilreport.org/atf/cf/%7B65BFCF9B-6D27-4E9C-8CD3-CF6E4FF96FF9%7D/Syria%20SRES%202042.pdf.

28. UN Security Council Resolution 2043, S/Res/2043, April 21, 2012, www.securitycouncilreport.org/atf/cf/%7B65BFCF9B-6D27-4E9C-8CD3-CF6E4FF96FF9%7D/Syria%20SRES%202043.pdf.

29. Louis Charbonneau and Michelle Nichols, "UN Council Approves Syria Monitors, Divisions Persist," Reuters, April 14, 2012, www.reuters.com/article/2012/04/14/syria-un-vote-idUSL2E8FE1VM20120414.

30. Michelle Nichols, "UN Approves 30-Day Extension for Syria Monitors," Reuters, July 20, 2012, www.reuters.com/article/2012/07/20/syria-crisis-un-idUSL2E8IK6LT20120720.

31. Steven Erlanger and Stephen Castle, "Britain's Rejection of Syrian Response Reflects Fear of Rushing to Act," New York Times, August 30, 2013 (noting that the "stunning parliamentary defeat on Thursday for Prime Minister David Cameron, which led him to rule out British military participation in any strike on Syria, reflected British fears of rushing to act against Damascus without certain evidence ... [and] reawaken[ed] British resentment over false assurances from the American and British government that Saddam Hussein had weapons of mass destruction"); Peter Baker and Jonathan Weisman, "Obama Seeks Approval by Congress for Strike in Syria," New York Times, September 1, 2013 (noting that "congressional officials said ... that if a vote were taken immediately, the Republican-controlled House would not support action"); and Paul Steinhauser and John Helton, "CNN Poll: Public against Syria Strike Resolution," CNN, September 9, 2013 ("As President Obama presses his case for a strike on Syria, a new national survey shows him swimming against a strong tide of public opinion that doesn't want the United States to get involved").

32. UN Security Council Resolution 2118, S/Res/2118, September 27, 2013, www.securitycouncilreport.org/atf/cf/%7B65BFCF9B-6D27-4E9C-8CD3-CF6E4FF96FF9%7D/s_res_2118.pdf.

33. By the end of April 2014, over 92 percent of Syria's chemical arsenal had been destroyed under international supervision. "As Deadline Passes, UN Joint Mission

Urges Syria to Complete Chemical Weapons Removal," UN News Centre, April 27, 2014, www.un.org/apps/news/story.asp?NewsID=47663#.U2ayjPldXTd. The deadline set by the Security Council to complete destruction of the arsenal was June 30, 2014.

34. "Syria: Valerie Amos on Aid Convoy to Homs," UN Office for the Coordination of Humanitarian Affairs, February 10, 2014, www.unocha.org /top-stories/all-stories/syria-valerie-amos-aid-convoy-homs; "At Least 500 Children among Civilians Evacuated from Old City Homs, Syria," UNICEF, February 11, 2014, http://childrenofsyria.info/2014/02/11/at-least-500-children-among-civilians-evacuated-from-old-city-homs-syria/.

35. UN Security Council Resolution 2139, S/Res/2139, February 22, 2014, www .securitycouncilreport.org/atf/cf/%7B65BFCF9B-6D27–4E9C-8CD3-CF6E4 FF96FF9%7D/s_res_2139.pdf. Of particular note are paragraph 5, calling upon all parties "to immediately lift the sieges of populated areas" and enumerating specific cities and areas; and paragraph 6, demanding that all parties and particularly Syrian authorities "promptly allow rapid, safe and unhindered humanitarian access for United Nations humanitarian agencies."

36. UN Security Council Resolution 2165, S/Res/2165, July 14, 2014, http:// unscr.com/en/resolutions/doc/2165.

37. An example of the measure of success achieved by the resolution is evident in the case of Yarmouk, a refugee camp outside Damascus that was among the areas specifically referenced by UN Security Council Resolution 2139. Since the resolution, the UN Relief and Works Agency reports that it has had intermittent access to the camp and has been able to deliver some food assistance to the eighteen thousand civilians trapped under starvation conditions in the camp. "The Crisis in Yarmouk Camp," UN Relief and Works Agency, April 27, 2014, http://reliefweb .int/report/syrian-arab-republic/crisis-yarmouk-camp-27-april-2014.

38. UN Security Council Resolution 2209, S/Res/2209, March 6, 2015, www .securitycouncilreport.org/atf/cf/%7B65BFCF9B-6D27–4E9C-8CD3-CF6E4FF96 FF9%7D/s_res_2209.pdf.

39. UN Security Council, Resolution 2235, S/Res/2235, August 7, 2015, www .securitycouncilreport.org/atf/cf/%7B65BFCF9B-6D27–4E9C-8CD3-CF6E4FF 96FF9%7D/s_res_2235.pdf.

40. UN Security Council, Resolution 2170, S/Res/2170, August 14, 2014, www .securitycouncilreport.org/atf/cf/%7B65BFCF9B-6D27–4E9C-8CD3- CF6E4FF96FF9%7D/s_res_2170.pdf (imposing sanctions on individuals affiliated with ISIS/IS); UN Security Council Resolution 2178, S/Res/2178, September 24, 2014, www.un.org/en/sc/ctc/docs/2015/SCR%202178_2014_EN.pdf (imposing obligations on all states to address the threat of foreign terrorist fighters traveling to Syria to join ISIS/IS); UN Security Council Resolution 2199, S/Res/2199, February 12, 2015, www.securitycouncilreport.org/atf/cf/%7B65BFCF9B-6D27–4E9C-8CD3-CF6E4FF96FF9%7D/s_res_2199.pdf (requiring all states to participate in an oil and arms embargo on ISIS/IS and their affiliates, prohibiting ransom payments to the IS, and calling for the protection of cultural heritage in Syria); and UN

Security Council Resolution 2249, S/Res/2249, November 20, 2015, www .securitycouncilreport.org/atf/cf/%7B65BFCF9B-6D27–4E9C-8CD3-CF6E4FF96FF9%7D/s_res_2249.pdf (calling on all states to act on the territory controlled by ISIS/IS to prevent the group from committing terrorist acts).

41. "Paris Attacks: What Happened on the Night," BBC, December 9, 2015, www.bbc.com/news/world-europe-34818994.

42. UN Security Council Resolution 2254, S/Res/2254, December 18, 2015, www.securitycouncilreport.org/atf/cf/%7B65BFCF9B-6D27–4E9C-8CD3-CF6E4FF96FF9%7D/s_res_2254.pdf (unanimous resolution supporting the 2012 Geneva Communiqué and the diplomatic efforts of the newly convened International Syria Support Group to pursue a political solution to the conflict through a UN-facilitated process led by di Mistura).

43. The UNHCR website (http://data.unhcr.org/syrianrefugees/regional.php) tracks the numbers of registered refugees from the Syrian crisis. When it was last accessed for this chapter (June 22, 2015), the total number registered stood at 3,984,393.

44. Coverage of the UNHCR funding requirement for Syria as of June 2015 was at 20 percent; see the UNHCR website at http://data.unhcr.org/syrianrefugees /regional.php. Underfunding has been a persistent problem. See, e.g., "UN Chides Donors for Not Enough Aid to Syrian Refugees," Agence France Press, May 4, 2014, www.globalpost.com/dispatch/news/afp/140504/un-chides-donors-not-enough-aid-syrian-refugees.

45. For a list of all the partner agencies with which the UN was coordinating relief efforts, see UNHCR's website at http://data.unhcr.org/syrianrefugees /partnerlist.php.

46. For updated information on these programs, see UNHCR's website at http:// data.unhcr.org/syrianrefugees/regional.php and the World Food Programme's web-site at www.wfp.org/crisis/syria.

47. Julian Borger, "Syria: UN Chief Calls for Action to Get Aid to 3.5 Million People Cut Off by War," *Guardian*, April 24, 2014, www.theguardian.com /world/2014/apr/24/syria-un-chief-action-aid-people-cut-off-war.

48. Julian Borger, "Syria: UN Urged to Defy Assad on Aid or Risk Lives of Hundreds of Thousands," *Guardian*, www.theguardian.com/world/2014/apr/28 /legal-experts-urge-united-nations-ignore-assad-ban-aid-syria-rebels.

PART TWO

Enforcement and Peacekeeping

Constructing Security Council Resolution 1701 in Lebanon in the Shadow of the "War on Terror"

Karim Makdisi

THE JULY 2006 WAR BETWEEN Israel and Lebanon—and the subsequent truce contained in United Nations Security Council Resolution 1701 that also authorized the deployment of a more "robust" contingent of UN peacekeepers—received extensive attention in international media, policy circles, and scholarly work. The bulk of this attention occurred in the war's immediate aftermath and focused on drawing lessons from the military dimensions of nonconventional warfare, explaining the nature of the Hizbullah "threat" and its relationship to Syria/Iran, analyzing the role of the UN in terms of "lessons learned" in peacekeeping and peacebuilding in Lebanon, or situating the 2006 war within general trends of international law.[1] With some notable exceptions, however, most of this work provides a static reading of both the conflict's fluid international-domestic nexus and the complex social and political dynamics that underpin the construction of the Lebanese state and its fragmented mode of foreign and security policy making. Much of this literature is based on preserving the existing order and is framed within problem-solving analyses that assume a given received problem (e.g., Hizbullah as "spoiler," Lebanon as "weak state") and prescribe one-size-fits-all solutions (e.g., strengthening Lebanon's "sovereignty" through an European scheme to create "integrated border management").[2] It also largely writes away Lebanese agency and assumes the Lebanese state to be a passive victim of either Hizbullah/Syrian cooptation or Israeli violence.[3]

This essay seeks to complicate this received view of the problem by contextualizing the battle over Lebanon between 2004 and 2008 within the larger "war on terror," which, in effect, ruptured the stable Pax Syriana and grounded a global struggle for and against US domination of the region in a bitter but essentially local Lebanese power dispute. The global battle over

Lebanon, in this sense, briefly condensed from a political/ideational struggle into a military one during the 2006 war; and Israel's failure to defeat Hizbullah returned it once more to the political/ideational realm now centered on the postwar interpretation of Resolution 1701 and the role of the Lebanese state and UN peacekeepers in its implementation. It further analyzes how the UN itself, through a series of resolutions on Lebanon, beginning with Resolution 1559 in 2004 and culminating in Resolution 1701, was conscripted into this localization of a global struggle. It shows how the UN mediated between the imperatives of the war on terror, with its violent, post-Westphalian implications for the Lebanese state, and its own mission to preserve the Westphalian order in which it operates.

To understand how and where meaning is produced, this essay adopts a critical discursive approach. Like all texts, UN resolutions have embedded in them a particular discourse, defined by one scholar as a "cohesive ensemble of ideas, concepts and categorizations about a specific object that frame that object in a particular way and, therefore, delimit the possibilities for action in relation to it."[4] Of course, resolutions like 1701 are not, in and of themselves, meaningful without other, related texts "upon which they draw in constructing identities and policies, in which they appropriate as well as revise the past, and in which they establish authority by reading and citing others."[5] In this case, the series of resolutions, statements, and diplomatic activities during the 2004–6 period collectively sought to frame Hizbullah and Lebanon/Syria in a way that would make an attack on them legitimate or normal.

The construction of official foreign policy texts, and by extension UN resolutions, forms a web of discourses that, in turn, are bound up with notions of power and thus are invariably contested.[6] Accordingly, competing texts vie for legitimation so that UN resolutions, for instance, are ultimately given meaning through what Charlotte Epstein has called a "powerful discourse," that is, one that "makes a difference" in interpreting the text itself.[7] This essay explores the overlapping material and ideational contests to define this "powerful discourse" and, in so doing, to define what constitutes a legitimate Lebanese state, the role of the UN within it, and the nature of resistance to American hegemony and Israeli dominance over the region. The outcome of these contests in the Lebanese case that this essay tracks between 2004 and 2008 can help us understand the notion of a "hegemonic articulation" that signals the victory of a particular configuration of meanings and social relations.[8]

The elimination of Hizbullah, and thus of the very idea of resistance, can be seen not just as a material objective but also as an ideational one on which Israeli domination and US hegemonic stability in the region depend. Moreover, while most conventional treatments of Hizbullah in Western literature begin with the apparently objective observation that it is a "terrorist" organization, this elides the lack of definition of the term *terrorism* and the fact that there is a bitterly contested struggle in Lebanon and the region focused on the idea of a legitimate resistance.

Indeed, it must be remembered that during the immediate post–civil war period in Lebanon (1990–2004) Hizbullah was officially regarded as a legitimate and protected "resistance" group and therefore, unlike other armed groups, entitled to carry arms as long as the state of war with Israel persisted. Syria's hegemonic position in Lebanon, accepted by the United States and the international community in this period as a reward for Syria's support for the US-led coalition's 1990 attack on Iraq, had prevented any global debate over this special status. Between 2004 and 2008, however, following the eviction of Syria from Lebanon and an escalation in the US-led war on terror, Hizbullah's standing in relation to the state was sharply disputed within Lebanon and, globally, at the level of the Security Council in both ideational and material terms. The war on terror discourse, as we shall see, essentially tried to "denaturalize" this resistance,[9] deny it any agency of its own, represent Hizbullah as merely a proxy of the "terror" axis run by Syria/Iran, and reinterpret it as a "militia" that undermined, rather than protected, the Lebanese state. Hizbullah's counternarrative, which of course depended on its material survival, projected itself as a "Lebanese" subject working to protect Lebanon's sovereignty.

The first section of this essay will provide an interpretative framework showing how the "powerful discourse" that emerged after September 11, 2001, connected Hizbullah and its assumed patron, Syria, with global terrorism. Next, the essay analyzes the construction of a UN-legitimated international regime, centered on Resolution 1559, that translated this war on terror discourse into domestic Lebanese terms and describes the buildup toward war in 2006. It then examines the construction of Resolution 1701, arguing that this resolution comprised two conflicting narratives about the meaning of the 2006 war and the role of the UN that made further violence in Lebanon inevitable. In the final section, the essay shows how the discursive contest over interpretations of the resolution transformed the conflict in Lebanon from an international to a domestic one and how the production of a hegemonic national discourse emerged following the signing of the 2008 Doha Agreement that precipitated the formation of a national unity government.

THE GLOBAL DISCOURSE OF THE WAR ON TERROR: FRAMING THE 2006 ISRAEL-LEBANON WAR

The historical roots of the 2006 Israel-Lebanon war lie within the larger Arab-Israeli conflict, but it was the US-led war on terror that framed the breakdown in Lebanon from 2004 to 2008 and gave the 2006 war its seminal status and, ultimately, its most significant meaning.[10] As has been well documented, Western security interests were reimagined in the post–Cold War era.[11] The new enemy was now embodied in nonstate networks that could take advantage of weak or collapsing states to undermine the existing order and, potentially, acquire weapons of mass destruction (WMDs). Liberal interventionists and neorealists in the United States and Europe advocated proactive Western and UN intervention in the Third World within a global liberal paradigm and in post-Westphalian terms that increasingly intertwined military and humanitarian/development agendas.[12]

Protected by great powers' interest in regional stability, Arab states initially remained largely immune to these changes. By the late 1990s, however, they were clearly in an internal "state of crisis": liberal reforms were exposed as failures and oppositional Islamist groups gained in popularity, utilizing the discourse and institutions of democracy to their advantage.[13] Arab states were no longer reliable security partners, and democracy was producing the wrong results. The September 11 attacks thus allowed what Michael Mann refers to as the "new imperialists" in the Bush administration to launch "global adventures" and operationalize plans for a "new Middle East."[14] As David Hirst notes, the United States now desired to "tackle the whole Arab/Muslim milieu from which the diabolical deed had sprung: to invade, subdue, shape and utterly transform it."[15]

Between 2001 and 2003, the Bush administration issued a series of seminal texts in order to consolidate and take advantage of America's "traumatized identity."[16] Targeting a "radical network of terrorists and every government that supports them," Bush made it clear that the defeat of "terrorists" entailed that the United States "pursue nations that provide aid or safe haven to terrorism. Every nation in every region now has a decision to make: either you are with us or you are with the terrorists."[17] The notion that there could be, for instance, liberation struggles or resistance groups independent of global terrorism was now removed conceptually from this discourse, as organizations as disparate as Hizbullah and Al Qaeda were lumped together.[18] In 2002, Bush invoked an "axis of evil" to rebuke states such as Iraq and Iran that were supported by a "terrorist underworld," including Hizbullah and Hamas.[19] One of Bush's goals was "to prevent regimes that sponsor terror from threatening America or our friends and allies with weapons of mass destruction." Syria was soon added to a list of "rogue states" that "sponsor terror" and sought WMDs.[20]

The 2002 *National Security Strategy* (NSS), which operationalized the US war on terror, legitimated the logic of militarism, proactive regime change, and the doctrine of preemptive attacks in the name of "self-defense" against those deemed part of the "terror" network.[21] The document stated unequivocally that the "war against terrorists of global reach is a global enterprise of uncertain duration." Accordingly, "America will help nations that need our assistance in combating terror. And America will hold to account nations that are compromised by terror—because the allies of terror are the enemies of civilization."[22] As such, these allies in the region would now include not just Israel and pro-Western Arab states (which until then had been publicly criticized in the United States for being undemocratic) but, crucially, Arab domestic political parties and alliances within "weak" states such as Lebanon that could be represented as "democratic." As we shall see below, Lebanon's pro-US "March 14" alliance, formed during this period, appealed to the United States in these very terms, projecting itself as the democratic alternative to Hizbullah (and thus Syria and Iran) in Lebanon.

The "powerful discourse" produced by these speeches and texts was prerequisite for the series of ideational battles and wars the Bush administration embarked on in the Arab region. After the 2003 Iraq War, the US gaze turned to Syria and Lebanon.[23] The testimonies of key figures in the US administration to Congress in the fall of 2003 typically sought to establish Syria as a global "security concern," since it, like Iraq, was said to be developing WMDs and since it also engaged in state-sponsored terrorism.[24] These testimonies uniformly represented Lebanon simply as under Syrian "occupation," with Hizbullah as a Syrian (and Iranian) proxy, a "terrorist organization" with "global reach."[25] By December 2003, President Bush signed the Syria Accountability and Lebanese Sovereignty Restoration Act.[26] This act called on Syria to stop "undermining international peace and security," sponsoring "international terrorism," and developing WMDs. It also called for Syria to end its "occupation" of Lebanon so that Lebanon could achieve "full restoration of its sovereignty," "deploy its army in the South," and evict all "terrorist and foreign forces, including Hizbullah and the Iranian Revolutionary Guards."[27] In effect, this act concretely linked the long-standing efforts of the neoconservatives within the US administration to isolate Syria and destroy Hizbullah to the war on terror discourse.[28]

LOCALIZING THE WAR ON TERROR DISCOURSE IN LEBANON: THE RESOLUTION 1559 REGIME

The next stage in the Bush administration's Syria-Lebanon policy was to local-ize its war on terror discourse in Lebanese domestic terms, which it did via a series of Security Council resolutions targeting Syria and its allies in Lebanon. In so doing, these interventionist UN resolutions became a pivot around which pro- and anti-Western Lebanese politics mobilized. The most impor-tant text within this discourse was Resolution 1559, adopted on September 2, 2004. This resolution—and the regime it set up, comprising biannual imple-mentation reports, Security Council presidential statements, related Security Council resolutions, and diplomatic pressure—unequivocally set forth the basic US war on terror narrative that the UN, for the first time, appeared to legitimize in Lebanon. In essence, Resolution 1559 called for the withdrawal of Syrian army units ("foreign forces") from Lebanon, on the one hand, and the disarming of Hizbullah, as well as Palestinian groups ("militias") operat-ing within Palestinian camps, on the other.[29]

The resolution had been hastily arranged to pressure Syria and the Lebanese parliament to halt the latter's imminent scheduled vote to amend the Constitution in order to extend the term of pro-Syrian president Emile Lahoud by three additional years (until 2008).[30] For the Lebanese representa-tive at the UN, this resolution's unprecedented interference with Lebanon's internal affairs called into question the UN's neutrality and was summarily rejected.[31] That there was a split between Lebanon's pro-Syrian alliance, which still had control of the Foreign Ministry, and Prime Minister Rafiq Hariri, who had close ties with Saudi Arabia and the West, was clear. The disagreement illustrated the deep division in Lebanon's policy-making proc-ess, which traditionally depends on consensus among the sectarian elites on matters of high politics and security, during the unfolding political and constitutional crisis. That the Security Council proceeded with the vote despite these political tensions underscored the Council's unprecedented activist agenda in this case and its intent to take sides with one particular domestic group over another.[32]

The most controversial and divisive element within Resolution 1559 was its stipulation that Hizbullah must disarm, thus internationalizing Hizbullah's status in Lebanon. The US ambassador to the UN considered "the continued presence of armed Hezbollah militia elements, as well as presence of Syrian and Iranian forces in Lebanon," to be the main obstacle in Lebanon, and his French counterpart decried Lebanon's "occupation and persistent presence of armed militias." The crucial implication of such statements, incorporated into Resolution 1559, was that Hizbullah was merely a proxy "militia" and not a legitimate resistance group. The Lebanese representative at the Council made this distinction a central plank of Lebanon's official dissent, stating: "There are no militias in Lebanon. The Lebanese national resistance appeared following the Israeli occupation of Lebanese territory and will remain as long as the Israelis occupy parts of Lebanon.... The resistance forces exist alongside the Lebanese national forces; our military authorities determine their presence and their size according to our needs. The authority of the Lebanese State extends over all of Lebanese territory except the Israeli occupied areas."[33]

The resolution thus interposed a Security Council interpretation into a long-standing but inconclusive national Lebanese debate about the nature of the state and its role in the Arab-Israeli conflict. Indeed, the Council's overtly interventionist agenda meant that the US-French drafted resolution mustered only a slim majority of 9 within the Council, as states such as China, Russia, Brazil, and Algeria (representing Arab states) all denounced the resolution's interference in the internal affairs of a sovereign state.[34]

Once passed, Resolution 1559 embodied and deepened the civil conflict in Lebanon. Lebanon's parliament convened in defiance of the Security Council to approve President Lahoud's extension, prompting Hariri to resign but vow to return to power. Hariri's assassination in a huge car bomb on February 14, 2005, paved the way for rival mass demonstrations and the formalization of two deeply divided Lebanese coalitions, the March 14 and Opposition blocs, who were nonetheless still partners in a coalition government.[35] March 14 representatives echoed US, European Union, and Israeli accusations that Syria and its Lebanese allies within the Lebanese-Syrian security apparatus were behind Hariri's murder and called for the implementation of Resolution 1559.[36] For its part, the Opposition blamed those powers behind Resolution

1559 as the main beneficiaries of the assassination. Indeed, for Hizbullah leader Hassan Nasrallah the "option of the resistance" and "1559" projects were mutually exclusive.[37]

The Security Council once again controversially intervened in domestic Lebanese matters, internationalizing Hariri's murder and its investigation in a manner that was then unprecedented in UN history.[38] Mobilized by the United States and France, the Security Council immediately dispatched a fact-finding mission to Beirut, which within one month had issued a controversial report, based largely on circumstantial evidence, blaming Syrian and Lebanese security agents for Hariri's murder.[39] This, in turn, led to the adoption in April 2005 of Resolution 1595 setting up a UN investigating commission with a mandate to help the Lebanese government find the "perpetrators, sponsors, organizers and accomplices" behind this "act of terrorism."[40]

The UN appointed the controversial German prosecutor Detlev Mehlis, whose name was to become synonymous in opposition circles with US neoconservative and Israeli agendas, as its first investigator.[41] In October a ministerial meeting of the Security Council passed Resolution 1636 under Chapter VII of the UN charter, defining Hariri's murder as a "terrorist" act, calling for Syria's "unconditional cooperation" with the investigation, and insisting "that Syria not interfere in Lebanese domestic affairs."[42] In effect, the Council's internationalization of the Hariri assassination investigation, which now also included periodic reports and high-profile diplomatic activity against Syria and Lebanon's pro-Syrian allies, led to its overt politicization and incorporation into Resolution 1559's regime.

Semiannual secretary-general reports, associated Security Council presidential statements, and actions by Western diplomats in 2005–6 further reinforced the Resolution 1559 regime. Indeed, the UN special envoy appointed to follow up on Resolution 1559 was the controversial Norwegian diplomat Terje Roed Larsen, who like Mehlis was viewed by the Lebanese opposition as a core part of the US neoconservative team. In effect, Larsen's reports enabled the Security Council to actively interpret Lebanon's constitutional provisions and pronounce on convoluted domestic Lebanese matters at a time of deep and potentially violent constitutional and political crisis in the country. In his very first implementation report, Larsen appeared to override Lebanon's national decisions, as well as its ongoing political process, by considering Hizbullah a "militia" rather than a legitimate "resistance" group and by suggesting that the resolution to Lebanon's problems with Israel lay with disbanding Hizbullah rather than ending Israeli aggression.[43] Further reports and related diplomatic action by Western states effectively delegitimized the extension of President Lahoud's term as president; insisted that Lebanon hold parliamentary elections on schedule and without delay in 2005 despite warnings by many civil society groups that "free and fair" elections could not be held without electoral reforms; and called for the "disbanding and disarming of Lebanese and non-Lebanese militias and the extension of government control over all Lebanese territory." The Security Council also pressured Lebanon to establish full diplomatic relations with Syria, demarcate the Lebanese-Syrian border, and deploy its armed forces throughout southern Lebanon.[44] Not surprisingly, these provisions constituted the core of the March 14 political agenda in Lebanon.

On the eve of the 2006 War, Security Council pressure on Lebanon and Syria to fully implement Resolution 1559 was unrelenting.[45] In March the UNSC passed Resolution 1664 establishing a tribunal of "international character" to try the Hariri assassins, still presumed to be Syrian and Lebanese security officials.[46] In May, Resolution 1680 called on Syria to take measures "against movement of arms" into Lebanon, to delineate its common borders, and to establish "full diplomatic relations and representation" with Lebanon.[47] All in all, from the adoption of Resolution 1559 to the start of the 2006 War, the Security Council adopted ten different resolutions and seven presidential statements—and published ten highly visible secretary-general implementation reports—dealing with Lebanon (and Syria).[48] This discourse, framed within the larger discursive context of the war on terror, substantively shifted the global context within which Hizbullah's actions would now be interpreted, something Hizbullah apparently failed to grasp in the summer of 2006.

THE 2006 ISRAEL-LEBANON WAR: "POWERFUL DISCOURSE" ELEVATES SOUTH LEBANON FROM LOCAL TO GLOBAL

During the 1990s, Israel maintained its two-decade occupation of southern Lebanon, launched two minor invasions, and engaged in a war of attrition against the Lebanese resistance. Although these events were extremely important on the domestic level in Lebanon and Israel, their impact remained contained, as the great powers did not confer meaning to them. The Clinton presidency (1992–2000) was, after all, focused on Iraq and the "peace process," and the international community thus took little interest in Lebanon's sovereignty.[49] Even Israel's May 2000 withdrawal from Lebanon after twenty-two years of occupation, so significant in local terms, did not elicit a global reaction beyond UN technical certification of the withdrawal to the "Blue Line" and rhetoric about the need for Lebanon to deploy its army along the border.[50] With the regional order unchanged, Lebanon firmly rejected the UN certification claim, pointing to Israel's frequent incursions into Lebanon's territory, airspace, and territorial waters. Lebanon's deployment of a "Joint Security Force" to southern Lebanon in August 2000 remained deliberately outside the border area: "The Government of Lebanon has taken the position that, so long as there is no comprehensive peace with Israel, the army would not act as a border guard for Israel and would not be deployed to the border."[51] Successive Lebanese governments, supported by Syria, continued to unequivocally uphold Lebanon's right to resist Israel's occupation and retrieve prisoners held in Israeli jails.

Southern Lebanon remained generally calm during the period immediately following Israel's withdrawal, with the United Nations peacekeepers (UN Interim Force in Lebanon [UNIFIL]) recording no serious breaches of the cease-fire in populated areas between May 2000 and November 2005.[52] The root causes of the Lebanon-Israeli conflict, however, had not been resolved. Israel maintained its objective of pacifying Lebanon and creating a demilitarized zone in the south, and Hizbullah openly declared its intention to secure the release of Lebanese prisoners held in Israeli jails. After several botched operations in 2004–5 to capture Israeli soldiers to exchange for Lebanese prisoners, Hizbullah declared 2006 the "year of the prisoners."[53] On July 12, 2006, a Hizbullah unit crossed the Blue Line and attacked an Israeli army patrol near the border, capturing two Israeli soldiers and killing three others.[54] Israeli prime minister Ehud Olmert accused Lebanon of an "act of war," while the Lebanese government officially requested that the UN broker a cease-fire.[55] Hizbullah, however, agreed to return the Israeli prisoners only through "indirect negotiations," leading to the "trade" with Lebanese prisoners illegally detained by Israel.[56] For its part, the secretary-general condemned Hizbullah's raid but called for all sides to "exercise maximum restraint" to "avoid any further escalation."[57] The following day, the secretary-general dispatched a team of three senior UN diplomats to travel to the region to reinforce his "call to exercise restraint and to do whatever possible to help contain the conflict."[58]

Given the new war on terror imperatives and discourse, however, Hizbullah's raid took on new meaning in global terms. The UN's calls for restraint were ignored by Israel and dismissed by the United States. The apparent failure of the Resolution 1559 regime to produce results (namely disarm Hizbullah and weaken the Syrian regime) was blamed by US neoconservatives on the more pragmatic, diplomatic side of a US administration hoping for a "slow-motion" toppling of the Syrian/Lebanese regime, or "regime change on the cheap."[59] They supported, instead, Israel's use of force to ensure the implementation of Resolution 1559.[60] In this sense, Hizbullah's July 12 raid represented an appropriate policy opportunity for the US administration, increasingly frustrated in Iraq, to reinvigorate its plans for a "new Middle East" with a quick victory in Lebanon. The 2006 war thus became a defining battle in the "war on terror." By July 14, Israel's declared aims included the elimination of Hizbullah and implementation of Resolution 1559.[61] Israel now explicitly framed its war in Lebanon within the war on terror discourse. Accordingly, senior Israeli foreign ministry spokesmen such as Gideon Meir repeated that Israel "views Hamas, Hezbollah, Syria and Iran as primary elements in the axis of terror and hate, threatening not only Israel but the entire world." For Israel, Meir explained, Hizbullah's actions proved it was part of "an international effort to wage holy war against the infidel."[62]

During the first week of the war, the United States insisted that no UN action should be taken before Israel could accomplish its objectives.[63] Following the war on terror logic, it was imperative that Hizbullah be destroyed but, equally, that the pro-US Lebanese government remain protected: Prime Minister Siniora was "on a list of 'good guys' working against the axis of evil."[64] Accordingly, the United States vetoed Israel's initial plan to destroy Lebanon's civilian power stations, government buildings, and affluent areas in the downtown district, which would have immediately damaged Siniora's standing in Lebanon.[65] The G-8 Summit communiqué of July 16 further supported Israel's actions, blamed the "extremist" Hizbullah for the war, and called for the implementation of Resolution 1559 but warned Israel not to undermine Lebanon's government by attacking civilian infrastructure.[66]

In his first briefing before the Security Council on July 20, Secretary-General Kofi Annan legitimized Israel's war against Hizbullah but drew the line at what the UN, along with European and Arab states, saw as Israel's unnecessarily "disproportionate" violence that had caused a humanitarian disaster and, more importantly, had weakened the standing of the Lebanese government: "I have already condemned Hezbollah's attacks on Israel, and acknowledged Israel's right to defend itself under Article 51 of the UN Charter. . . . I also condemn Hezbollah's reckless disregard for the wishes of the elected Government of Lebanon, and for the interests of the Lebanese people and the wider region."[67] Given that, at best, the debate within the international legal community was divided over Israel's claim of self-defense and Lebanon's right to resist, Annan's unilateral and unreserved support of the US-Israeli position can be seen as an important symbolic reinforcement of the "powerful discourse" of the war on terror. The debate was now about the extent to which Israel's violence and resulting civilian casualties undermined the ability of Lebanon's government to play its role as a "good" actor within the Westphalian order of sovereign states in the postwar phase. In other words, for Annan the UN role was now limited to ensuring that the US administration's post-Westphalian intervention in Lebanon did not repeat the catastrophic breakdown of order and security vacuum in postwar Iraq. This, in turn, would support rather than expose what David Chandler refers to as the post–Cold War practice of an "empire in denial" and its "invasive" core project of statebuilding. This project, reflecting a "new hierarchy of Western power," creates what Chandler calls a "phantom state whose governing institutions may have extensive resourcing but lack social and political legitimacy."[68]

On July 26, Annan finally called for an "immediate cessation of hostilities because we face a grave humanitarian crisis," blaming Hizbullah's "reckless" actions for the war and accusing it of "deliberate targeting of Israeli population centers" but also requesting that Israel "end its bombardments, blockades and ground operations." Annan also called for the deployment of an "international force" that could play a "vital role" and "assist" the Lebanese government in implementing Resolutions 1559 and 1680, "in particular by helping the Government to extend its authority—including a monopoly on the use of force—throughout the country, strengthen the Lebanese Army, and disarm all Lebanese and non-Lebanese militias."[69] At the end of his speech, the secretary-general revealed the key role he felt the UN could play in the region to keep US support: "We need a new push for a comprehensive Middle East peace. . . . We need a peace track here [in Lebanon], too—not least to help remove a pretext used by extremists throughout the region, including in Lebanon." In other words, the UN role would be to build "peace" in Lebanon and the region to "remove" pretexts used by "extremists" and thus preserve an order that fit Western security interests. This formula, behind which the UN, the EU, and some Arab governments rallied, was premised on a growing realization that Hizbullah could not be defeated and thus sought above all else to preserve Lebanon's government within the Westphalian order.

By the end of July, the tide of the war had shifted decisively against Israel, and the United States was losing faith in Israel's capability to destroy Hizbullah. The United States tried to salvage its position by cosponsoring a draft resolution on August 5 authorizing the deployment of a North Atlantic Treaty Organization (NATO)-style peace enforcement operation under explicitly Chapter VII terms with a main objective to disarm Hizbullah.[70] The Lebanese government, which was under huge domestic pressure given the civilian casualties, could now no longer accept such terms without the explicit approval of Hizbullah. After several more days of negotiations amid increasing Israeli military frustration, the UN Security Council on August 11 unanimously passed Resolution 1701, which came into effect three days later.

A TALE OF TWO NARRATIVES: (DE)CONSTRUCTING RESOLUTION 1701

The negotiation of Security Council Resolution 1701 reveals two deeply contested and apparently contradictory narratives that are embodied in the resolution's final text. This contradiction, in turn, resulted in a heated postwar battle over Resolution 1701's interpretation and UNIFIL's new role. The first narrative draws from the Resolution 1559 regime discourse and represents Lebanon as a weak state and Hizbullah as the principal threat to both Israel's security and Lebanon's sovereignty. The resolution holds Hizbullah fully responsible for the war and effectively recognizes Israel's right to self-defense in pursuing the war option.[71] Thus, according to the secretary-general, Hizbullah's "unprovoked attack on Israel" resulted in Israelis being "newly awakened to a threat" they thought they had "escaped" with Israel's unilateral withdrawal from Lebanon in 2000.

In this UN account, Hizbullah, unlike Israel, "launched its fire indiscriminately, to sow the widest possible terror, making no effort to distinguish between military and civilian targets and also endangering civilians on its own side by firing from the midst of heavily populated areas."[72] UN and US narratives on the causes of the war had fully converged, with Secretary Rice adding that Hizbullah "and its sponsors" have "brought devastation upon the people of Lebanon, dragging them into a war that they did not choose and exploiting them as human shields."[73] The crucial part of this narrative was to reaffirm the constructed split between Hizbullah and Lebanese "citizens," who, in the words of the secretary-general, were trying to "consolidate their country as a sovereign, independent, and democratic State." Lebanon, as a result of this split, "has been a victim for too long." To make the distinction between Hizbullah as spoiler and Lebanon as "victim" in need of "empowering" even more explicit, the resolution's text and sponsors deliberately contrast Hizbullah's role with the positive one played by the Siniora government in negotiating the terms and extending its authority "such that there will be no weapons" without its consent and "no authority" other than that of the government.[74]

Operationally, Resolution 1701's core objective according to this narrative, premised on Lebanon's assumed status as a "weak state," is to strengthen Lebanon's "sovereignty" by sealing (and delineating) its border with Syria and by disarming Hizbullah and replacing it with up to fifteen thousand members of Lebanon's armed forces: in other words, to implement Resolutions 1680 and 1559. As the secretary-general explained, "Only when there is one authority, and one gun, will there be a chance of lasting stability."[75] To accomplish its task, Resolution 1701 called for the deployment of an "enhanced" contingent of up to fifteen thousand UNIFIL troops, largely composed of and led by EU and NATO members Italy, Spain, France, and Germany.[76] UNIFIL's new "robust" mandate authorized it to "take all necessary action . . . to ensure that its area of operations is not utilized for hostile activities of any kind."[77] As Rice made clear, Resolution 1701 allows the "democratic Government of Lebanon to expand its sovereign authority, as called for in Resolution 1559. It will do so by creating a new international force" that "will not be the same force" as the "current" UNIFIL. This "new stabilization force" was to deploy with Lebanon's armed forces to "protect the Lebanese people and to ensure that no armed groups like Hizbullah can threaten stability." Indeed, despite Resolution 1701 being a Chapter VI resolution, its text includes language that clearly recalls the Chapter VII provisions of the defeated August 5 draft resolution.[78]

The second narrative that emerged during the negotiation of Resolution 1701 contested the one-sided language and interventionist impulse of the resolution's final text. Resolution 1701, according to the Qatari foreign minister at the Security Council, "lacks balance and overlooks the accumulated, complicated, historical, social and geopolitical factors" that contextualize the war; fails to condemn "Israeli aggression against innocent civilians in Lebanon and Lebanese infrastructure"; and "does not clearly spell out Israel's legal and humanitarian responsibility for that destruction or address in a balanced manner the question of Lebanese prisoners, detainees, and abducted persons in Israeli jails."[79] In this narrative, the main problem is not Lebanon's "weakness" and Hizbullah's "terrorism" but rather, in the words of Lebanon's acting foreign minister, Israel's "perennial threat to Lebanon's security" and the failure to achieve what Resolution 1701 refers to in its penultimate paragraph as a "comprehensive, just and lasting peace in the Middle East" based on long-standing UN resolutions.[80]

Operationally, this dissenting narrative rejects the post-Westphalian elements borrowed from Resolution 1559 and thus all international interference in Lebanon's domestic sphere. As a result, all direct references to Chapter VII of the UN Charter were removed from the final text, and instead of the deployment of an "international force" with a peace enforcement mandate to disarm Hizbullah and secure the Lebanese-Syrian border, as the August 5 draft had demanded, the existing UNIFIL was expanded in terms of scope and mandate but remained a traditional operation. As French foreign minister Douste-Blazy made clear, "The mandate that the Security Council is giving UNIFIL is not one that imposes peace. UNIFIL will help Lebanese Government in several of its missions."[81] Crucially, as the Qatari foreign minister stressed, the resolution "assigns sole responsibility to the Lebanese Government for dealing with the armed phenomena in the South," an area "subject to the exclusive control of the Lebanese Government." Thus UNIFIL could be authorized only to "monitor the cessation of hostilities," "accompany and support the Lebanese army as they deploy throughout the South," and otherwise assist in humanitarian issues.[82]

In this narrative, then, UNIFIL could not "secure the border" with Syria or actively seek to disarm Hizbullah without *explicit* instructions from the Lebanese government, in which Hizbullah and its allies were still represented. Finally, in this narrative, it was the Westphalian substantive elements incorporated vaguely into Resolution 1701 to which UNIFIL was expected to devote itself, namely Israeli withdrawal from remaining Lebanese territory, including Sheba'a farms; the return of Lebanese prisoners; and the halting of all air, land, and marine violations of Lebanese territory.

THE BATTLE FOR HEGEMONIC ARTICULATION OF RESOLUTION 1701 IN LEBANON

Israel's failure to defeat Hizbullah militarily and thus allow the United States to impose the Resolution 1559 regime on Lebanon, and Hizbullah's inability to challenge the war on terror discourse on the global level, produced a Security Council resolution with no apparent hegemonic narrative at its adoption. Resolution 1701 had effectively evolved over the course of its negotiation from one whose interpretive fate would have been determined by an activist Security Council operating under the shadow of the war on terror to one in which the main interpretive responsibility lay on the Lebanese government, in which Hizbullah continued to participate and over which Hizbullah continued to have some leverage. Israel, Hizbullah, and the Lebanese government all understood that, shorn of explicit Chapter VII and peace enforcement references that earlier drafts had flirted with, the text of Resolution 1701 was mere words on paper. The devil would be in the resolution's official interpretation by the Lebanese state, a site that would now witness violent contest for representation. Indeed, the often violent political and ideational battle for "hegemonic articulation" of the two conflicting narratives embedded in Resolution 1701 dominated Lebanon for nearly two years until the conclusion of the Doha Agreement in 2008.

In Lebanese discourse, Resolution 1701, and with it the role of UNIFIL peacekeepers, was contested from the start. The pro-US March 14 coalition warmly welcomed Resolution 1701 as a key political instrument with which to restore Lebanon's sovereignty, leverage international support against Hizbullah domestically, and extricate Lebanon, once and for all, from both the Arab-Israeli conflict and the Iranian/Syrian sphere of influence.[83] The Hizbullah-led Opposition coalition, for its part, considered the American-Israeli "project" to crush the resistance and create a pliant Lebanese state as the main threat to Lebanon's sovereignty and only reluctantly accepted Resolution 1701. The months after the passage of Resolution 1701 were very tense ones in Lebanon, focusing, on the one hand, on UNIFIL's new mandate and, on the other, on the nature and role of the resistance in Lebanon. Unlike the pre-2006 UNIFIL and its new, much publicized "rules of engagement," the "robust" peacekeepers were viewed with deep suspicion by residents of southern Lebanon and by Hizbullah.[84] Spanish and French contingents, in particular, faced local protests as they attempted to impose their own proactive interpretation on the UNIFIL mandate by searching homes aggressively in search of illegal weapons. However, following a roadside car bomb in June of 2007 that killed four Spanish peacekeepers, UNIFIL troops as a whole retreated to their bases and have largely adopted a much less aggressive posture in southern Lebanon since then. Indeed, the UN's rapidly expanding political office increasingly turned to statebuilding exercises as it effectively accepted the Westphalian limits to Resolution 1701's mandate.

Hizbullah's victory on the battlefield during 2006, however, did not immediately translate into domestic political terms as the March 14 coalition, neoconservatives within the US administration, and UN envoy Terje Roed Larsen continued to promote the Resolution 1559 regime and its campaign to force Hizbullah's disarming and to isolate Syria. Effectively, the conflict that had taken on an international military dimension during 2006 had now shifted to Lebanon's constitutional institutions and their authority to legitimate, or deny the claims of, an armed resistance and its relationship with the national armed forces. This bitter internal conflict resulted in sectarian clashes, the collapse of the national unity government in November 2007, and the creation of an unprecedented constitutional vacuum in which the Siniora government continued to be recognized by the West and yet was denied legitimacy by the domestic opposition.[85]

In May 2008, after the Siniora government unilaterally passed a controversial decree to dismantle Hizbullah's communication network, a move Hizbullah claimed threatened its very survival, Opposition militias took to the streets of Beirut and within hours had routed the March 14 militias, while the Lebanese army remained neutral. The United States protested, but did not interfere, and, with the Bush administration's second term coming to an end, Lebanese politicians signed an agreement in Doha, Qatar, under Qatari and Arab League patronage and endorsed by the UN Security Council.[86] This agreement set out the terms of a new national unity government, the election of a compromise president, and the dates for new parliamentary elections. The result of the Doha Agreement was thus the reincorporation of Hizbullah into the Lebanese government and the reaffirmation of the resistance as a national project that could coexist with the Lebanese armed forces. As Hizbullah parliamentarian Ali Fayyad made clear, the deployment of the Lebanese army to southern Lebanon did not represent any strategic shift in army or government doctrine, as March 14 leaders, and the United States, had wanted.[87] Moreover, a new government of national unity was formed in November 2009 with a clear mandate to implement the noncontroversial elements of Resolution 1701, that is, shorn of the remnants of Resolution 1559, and asserting Lebanon's right to resist Israel's occupation and threats.

The May 2008 Doha Agreement, and the subsequent replacement of George Bush with Barack Obama as US president, represented the end of a violent phase in which Lebanon's meaning in global war on terror terms receded as it returned, in discursive terms, to its local frame of conflict.

Hizbullah had decisively won the battle for "hegemonic articulation" of Resolution 1701 in Doha, but the threat of renewed war continues to loom, and with it the possibility of Lebanon once more becoming "meaningful" in global terms.

NOTES

1. On lessons from the military dimensions of nonconventional warfare, see, e.g., Anthony H. Cordesman, *Lessons of the 2006 Israeli-Hezbollah War* (Washington, DC: Center for Strategic and International Studies, 2007); and Stephen Biddle and Jeffrey A. Freidman, *The 2006 Lebanon Campaign and the Future of Warfare: Implications for Army and Defense Policy* (Carlisle, PA: US Army Strategic Studies Institute, 2008). On the Hizbullah threat, see, e.g., Patrick Devenny, "Hezbollah's Strategic Threat to Israel," *Middle East Quarterly* 13, no. 1 (2006): 31–38; Mehdi Khalaji, "Iran's Shadow Government in Lebanon," Policy Watch No. 1124, 2006, Washington Institute for Near East Policy, Washington, DC, www.washingtoninstitute.org/policy-analysis /view/irans-shadow-government-in-lebanon. On UN lessons learned in peacekeeping and peacebuilding, see, e.g., Karim Makdisi et al., "UNIFIL II: Emerging and Evolving European Engagement in Lebanon and the Middle East," EuroMeSCo Paper No. 76, 2009, European Institute of the Mediterranean, Barcelona, www.aub.edu.lb/ifi /Documents/images/paper76eng.pdf; William K. Mooney, "Stabilizing Lebanon: Peacekeeping or Nation-Building," *Parameters* 37 (Autumn 2007): 28–41; and Hitoshi Nasu, "The Responsibility to React? Lessons from the Security Council's Response to the Southern Lebanon Crisis of 2006," *International Peacekeeping* 14, no. 3 (2007): 339–52. On the 2006 war in the context of international law, see, e.g., Karim Makdisi, "Israel's 2006 War on Lebanon: Reflections on the International Law of Force," *MIT Electronic Journal of Middle East Studies* 6 (Summer 2006): 9–26; and Richard Falk and Asli Bali, "International Law at the Vanishing Point," in *The War on Lebanon: A Reader,* ed. Nubar Hovsepian (Northampton, MA: Olive Branch Press, 2008), 208–24.

2. On the difference between "problem-solving" and "critical" approaches, see Michael Pugh, "Peacekeeping and Critical Theory," *International Peacekeeping* 11, no. 1 (Spring 2004): 40.

3. Hizbullah, in this context, is often portrayed as a "foreign" force, essentially an Iranian proxy.

4. Charlotte Epstein, *The Power of Words in International Relations: Birth of an Anti-whaling Discourse* (Cambridge, MA: MIT Press, 2008), 2.

5. K. M. Fierke, *Critical Approaches to International Security* (Cambridge: Polity Press, 2007), 93.

6. David Howarth, *Discourse* (Buckingham: Open University Press, 2000), 9.

7. Epstein, *Power of Words,* 10.

8. Ibid.

9. Ibid., 163.

10. Israel's previous invasions in 1978 and 1982 were denounced by the UN Security Council in the form of numerous resolutions, as was its subsequent occupation of southern Lebanon. See, for instance, Paul Salem, "Reflections on Lebanon's Foreign Policy," in *Peace for Lebanon? From War to Reconstruction,* ed. Dierdre Collings (Boulder, CO: Lynne Rienner, 1994), 79.

11. Barry Buzan, "Rethinking Security after the Cold War," *Cooperation and Conflict* 32, no. 1 (1997): 5–28.

12. See Mark Duffield, *Global Governance and the New Wars: The Merging of Development and Security* (London: Zed Books, 2001).

13. Fawaz A. Gerges, *America and Political Islam: Clash of Cultures or Clash of Interests?* (New York: Cambridge University Press, 1999), 15–16.

14. Michael Mann, *Incoherent Empire* (London: Verso, 2003), 5. See also David Hirst, *Beware of Small States: Lebanon, Battleground of the Middle East* (New York: Nation Books, 2010), 280.

15. Hirst, *Beware of Small States,* 276.

16. Fierke, *Critical Approaches,* 134–35.

17. George W. Bush, "Transcript of President Bush's Address," CNN, September 21, 2001, www.archives.cnn.com/2001/US/09/20/gen.bush.transcript.

18. In the memorable words of a senior Bush administration official, "Hezbollah may be the A-team of terrorists and maybe al-Qaida is actually the B-team." See Richard L. Armitage, "America's Challenges in a Changed World," remarks at the US Institute of Peace Conference, Washington, DC, September 5, 2002, US Department of State Archive, http://2001–2009.state.gov/s/d/former/armitage /remarks/2002/13308.htm.

19. George W. Bush, "2002 State of the Union Address," George W. Bush White House Archives, http://georgewbush-whitehouse.archives.gov/news/releases/2002 /01/20020129-11.html.

20. John Bolton, "Beyond the Axis of Evil: Additional Threats from Weapons of Mass Destruction," speech to the Heritage Foundation, May 6, 2002, www .heritage.org/research/lecture/beyond-the-axis-of-evil.

21. George W. Bush, *The National Security Strategy of the United States of America,* September 2002, George W. Bush White House Archives, www .georgewbush-whitehouse.archives.gov/nsc/nss/2002/index.html.

22. Ibid.

23. See, for instance, Charles Glass, "Is Syria Next?," *London Review of Books,* July 2003, 3–6.

24. John R. Bolton, "Syria's Weapons of Mass Destruction and Missile Development Programs," testimony before the House International Relations Committee, Washington, DC, September 16, 2003, US Department of State Archive, http://2001–2009.state.gov/t/us/rm/24135.htm; Cofer Black, "Syria and Terrorism," testimony before the Senate Foreign Relations Committee, Washington, DC, October 30, 2003, US Department of State Archive, http://2001–2009.state .gov/s/ct/rls/rm/2003/25778.htm; and William J. Burns, "US-Syrian Relations,"

statement before the US Senate Foreign Relations Committee, Washington, DC, October 30, 2003, US Department of State Archive, http://2001–2009.state.gov/p/nea/rls/rm/25772.htm.

25. Burns, "US-Syrian Relations."

26. US Congress, Syria Accountability and Lebanese Sovereignty Restoration Act, Public Law 108–175, December 12, 2003.

27. Ibid. See also Hirst, *Beware of Small States*, 299–300.

28. See Robert Dreyfuss, "Syria in Their Sights: the Neocons Plan Their Next 'Cakewalk,'" *American Conservative*, January 16, 2006.

29. UN Security Council Resolution 1559, S/Res/1559, September 2, 2004, www.securitycouncilreport.org/atf/cf/%7B65BFCF9B-6D27–4E9C-8CD3-CF6E4FF96FF9%7D/Lebanon%20SRES1559.pdf.

30. Lebanon's constitution allows for a one-term presidency lasting six years.

31. UN Security Council, 5028th meeting, S/PV.5028, September 2, 2004, https://unispal.un.org/DPA/DPR/unispal.nsf/9a798adbf322aff38525617b006d88d7/c2cdf04f7bcf52a985256f0800516809?OpenDocument.

32. UN Security Council resolutions passed in the period from 1986 to 2004 dealt exclusively with routine matters related to the extension of UNIFIL's mandate.

33. UN Security Council, 5028th meeting, S/PV.5028.

34. Ibid. It should be noted that France under President Chirac went along with the United States in this case for two main reasons. First, to aid in the process of rebuilding the Franco-American relationship following the tense standoff during the 2003 US war on Iraq, which France opposed. Second, Chirac had a close personal and business relationship with Rafiq Hariri, who, by 2004, needed Syria out of Lebanon to consolidate his power within Lebanon. Indeed, in Lebanon, UN Security Council Resolution 1559 is referred to as comprising two parts: a "French" part (calling on Syria to withdraw) and an "American" part (calling on the disarming of Hizbullah).

35. Nicholas Blanford's *Killing Mr. Lebanon: The Assassination of Rafik Hariri and Its Impact on the Middle East* (London: I. B. Taurus, 2008). The March 14 movement was so named after the anti-Syrian demonstrations in Beirut on March 14, 2005.

36. Ibid.

37. Hasan Nassrallah, "You Will Today Decide the Fate of Your Nation and Country," public speech, March 8, 2005, in *Voice of Hezbollah: Statements of Sayyed Hassan Nasrallah,* ed. Nicholas Noe (London: Verso Press, 2007), 324.

38. All previous UN tribunals had dealt with genocide, war crimes, or crimes against humanity. See Samar El-Masri, "The Hariri Tribunal: Politics and International Law," *Middle East Policy* 15, no. 3 (Fall 2008): 83.

39. Omar Nashabe, "Al-Mahkama al-Khassa bi Lubnan: Ayna Takhfuq al-'Adala?" (in Arabic), *Al-Adab Magazine,* April-May 2010, www.adabmag.com/node/298.

40. UN Security Council Resolution 1595, S/Res/1595, April 7, 2005, www.securitycouncilreport.org/atf/cf/%7B65BFCF9B-6D27–4E9C-8CD3-CF6E4FF96FF9%7D/Lebanon%20SRES1595.pdf.

41. Nashabe, "Al-Mahkama al-Khassa bi Lubnan."

42. See UN Security Council, "Security Council Unanimously Endorses Findings of Investigation into Murder of Rafik Hariri, Calls for Syria's Full, Unconditional Cooperation," press release, SC/8543, October 31, 2005, www.un.org/press/en/2005/sc8543.doc.htm.

43. UN Security Council, "Report of the Secretary-General Pursuant to Security Council Resolution 1559 (2004)," S/2004/777, October 1, 2004, 7–8, www.securitycouncilreport.org/atf/cf/%7B65BFCF9B-6D27–4E9C-8CD3-CF6E4FF96FF9%7D/UNIFIL%20S2004777.pdf.

44. See, e.g., UN Security Council, "Statement by the President of the Security Council," S/PRST/2006/3, January 23, 2006, www.un.org/en/ga/search/view_doc.asp?symbol=S/PRST/2006/3.

45. Ibid.

46. UN Security Council Resolution 1664, S/Res/1664, March 29, 2006, www.securitycouncilreport.org/atf/cf/%7B65BFCF9B-6D27–4E9C-8CD3-CF6E4FF96FF9%7D/Leanon%20SRES1664.pdf.

47. UN Security Council Resolution 1680, S/Res/1680, May 17, 2006, http://unscol.unmissions.org/portals/unscol/SC%20Resolution%201680%20(2006).pdf. See also UN Security Council, "Security Council Strongly Encourages Syria to Respond to Lebanon's Request to Delineate Border, Establish Diplomatic Relations," press release, SC/8723, May 17, 2006, www.un.org/press/en/2006/sc8723.doc.htm.

48. Permanent Mission of Lebanon to the UN, "Lebanese Matters," February 21, 2015, https://www.un.int/lebanon/statements_speeches/lebanese-matters.

49. The Middle East focus of the Clinton presidency (1992–2000) was on Iraq and the Palestinian-Israeli "peace process."

50. UN Security Council, "Letter Dated 24 July 2000 from the Secretary-General Addressed to the President of the Security Council," S/2000/731, July 24, 2000, https://unispal.un.org/DPA/DPR/unispal.nsf/0/2E1E149A5C7C6B418525 69B600724CFF. The "Blue Line" is the UN designation for the temporary border between Lebanon and Israel.

51. UN Security Council, "Interim Report of the Secretary-General on the United Nations Interim Force in Lebanon," S/2000/1049, October 31, 2000, https://unispal.un.org/DPA/DPR/unispal.nsf/0/E06C472DE0025DC 985256999006C99E8.

52. UN Security Council, "Report of the Secretary-General on the United Nations Interim Force in Lebanon," secretary-general's report, S/2006/26, January 18, 2006, www.un.org/en/ga/search/view_doc.asp?symbol=S/2006/26.

53. Amal Saad-Ghorayeb, "Hizbullah's Outlook in the Current Conflict," *Policy Outlook,* Carnegie Endowment for International Peace, August 2006, 1.

54. UN Security Council, "United Nations Interim Force in Lebanon (from 21 January 2006 to 18 July 2006)," secretary-general's report, S/2006/560, July 21, 2006, www.securitycouncilreport.org/atf/cf/%7B65BFCF9B-6D27–4E9C-8CD3-CF6E4FF96FF9%7D/UNIFIL%20S2006560.pdf, 1. See also Makdisi, "Israel's 2006 War."

55. UN Security Council, "United Nations Interim Force," S/2006/560.

56. Chris McGreal, "Capture of Soldiers Was 'Act of War' Says Israel," *Guardian*, July 13, 2006.

57. UN Secretariat, "Statement Attributable to the Spokesman for the Secretary-General on the Situation along the Blue Line," July 12, 2006, www.un.org/sg/STATEMENTS/index.asp?nid=2136.

58. UN Secretariat, "Statement Attributable to the Spokesman for the Secretary-General on the Middle East," July 13, 2006, www.un.org/sg/STATEMENTS/index.asp?nid=2139.

59. Flynt Leverette quoted in Dreyfuss, "Syria in Their Sights."

60. See John Bolton, *Surrender*, 395.

61. Significantly, Israel's foreign ministry drew up an exit strategy on July 14, premised on the Security Council's ending the war by implementing Resolution 1559. See Amoz Harel and Avi Issacharoff, *34 Days: Israel, Hezbollah, and the War in Lebanon* (New York: Palgrave Macmillan, 2008), 94.

62. Quoted in Agence France Press, "Israel Blames Iran and Syria for Violence," July 14, 2006.

63. Bolton, *Surrender*, 402.

64. Harel and Issacharoff, *34 Days*, 81.

65. Ibid.

66. Ibid., 106.

67. Kofi Annan, "Secretary-General's Briefing to the Security Council on the Situation in the Middle East," July 20, 2006, www.un.org/sg/STATEMENTS/index.asp?nid=2142.

68. David Chandler, *Empire in Denial: The Politics of State-Building* (London: Pluto Press, 2006), 8–9.

69. Kofi Annan, "Secretary-General's Remarks to the International Conference on Lebanon," July 26, 2006, www.un.org/sg/statements/?nid=2150.

70. See BBC News, "Text: Draft UN Lebanon Resolution," August 5, 2006, www.news.bbc.co.uk/2/hi/middle_east/5249488.stm.

71. UN Security Council Resolution 1701, S/Res/1701, August 11, 2006, www.unsco.org/Documents/Resolutions/S_RES_%201701(2006).pdf.

72. UN Security Council, "5511th Meeting," S/PV.5511, August 11, 2006, 3, www.securitycouncilreport.org/atf/cf/%7B65BFCF9B-6D27-4E9C-8CD3-CF6E4FF96FF9%7D/Chap%20VII%20SPV%205511.pdf.

73. Ibid., 6.

74. UN Security Council Resolution 1701, S/Res/1701, August 11, 2006.

75. Ban Ki-moon, "Secretary-General's Statement to the Security Council on the Adoption of a Resolution on Lebanon," August 11, 2006, www.un.org/sg/STATEMENTS/index.asp?nid=2163.

76. Ibid., para. 11. For more on European involvement in UNIFIL, see Makdisi et al., "UNIFIL II."

77. UN Security Council, Resolution 1701, S/Res/1701, August 11, 2006, para. 12.

78. See Karim Makdisi, "The Flaws in the UN Resolution," *Counterpunch,* August 14, 2006.

79. Qatar foreign minister Sheikh al-Thani, UN Security Council, "5511th Meeting," S/PV.5511, 8–9.

80. Ibid., 19; UN Security Council Resolution 1701, S/Res/1701, August 11, 2006, para. 18.

81. UN Security Council, "5511th Meeting, S/PV.5511, 8.

82. UN Security Council Resolution 1701, S/Res/1701, August 11, 2006, para. 11.

83. See Michel Nehme, "Security Council Resolution 1701 and Its Implications," in *UN Resolution 1701: Horizons and Challenges* (Beirut: Cultural Movement and Friedrich-Ebert-Stiftung, 2007), 36–44.

84. See Makdisi et al., "UNIFIL II."

85. All Opposition cabinet members resigned following what they claimed was an unconstitutional move by the March 14 majority government authorizing an international tribunal to try the assassins of former prime minister Hariri.

86. UN Security Council, "Statement by the President of the Security Council," S/PRST/2008/17, May 22, 2008, www.securitycouncilreport.org/atf/cf/%7B65BFCF9B-6D27-4E9C-8CD3-CF6E4FF96FF9%7D/Lebanon%20SPRST200817.pdf.

87. Ali Fayyad, "Address of the Director of Consultation Center for Studies and Documentation and Member of Political Bureau of Hizbullah" [in Arabic], in *UN Resolution 1701*, 63.

SEVEN

The UN Security Council and Ghosts of Iraq

Poorvi Chitalkar and David M. Malone

IRAQ HAS OCCUPIED A PLACE on the United Nations Security Council's agenda for over three decades. In fact, the different phases of the Security Council's engagement with Iraq provide a useful lens through which to study the evolution of the Council since the end of the Cold War. It began with deplorably tentative decision making—unwillingness to recognize Iraqi aggression during the Iran-Iraq War in 1980—but shifted to a more proactive stance as the Cold War started to thaw in 1987, when the Council adopted a settlement plan that Iraq and Iran accepted in 1988, bringing active hostilities to an end. These developments foreshadowed growing cooperation among the permanent five (P5) members of the Council in the post–Cold War era.

When Iraq invaded Kuwait in 1990, the Council responded by imposing mandatory sanctions against Iraq and later that year authorized a US-led military intervention (which was carried out in early 1991). It then mandated the deployment of weapons inspectors, the creation of a complex sanctions regime to encourage compliance with the disarmament obligations the Council had imposed, and eventually an even more complex humanitarian program to mitigate the deleterious effects of those sanctions. In the next round of events in 2002–3 it proved an ultimately unsuccessful political broker. Finally, the Council became a marginal peacebuilder after 2003.

Ironically, with serious disagreements over Libya, Syria, and Crimea darkening the mood in the Council by 2013, Iraq provided a topic on which the P5 could agree when, seemingly out of nowhere, forces designating themselves as those of the Islamic State boldly captured large swaths of north-central Iraq in early 2014. The P5 hastened to condemn this nonstate actor threatening not just Iraq but, rapidly, the north of Syria as well as a terrorist menace, implicitly supporting any forces responding to the Iraqi government's call for assistance. As the fighting spread to northern Syria, the Security Council did not object when at least one foreign air force combating it acted without consulting Damascus.

With the various conflicts and tensions between Israel and its Arab neighbors largely frozen after the Camp David Accords and the peace treaties that followed between Israel and both Egypt and Jordan—although the parties were still prone to violent clashes and wars such as those in Gaza in 2008–9, 2012, and 2014, and complex entanglements in Lebanon—the UN's role in Iraq became the prism through which much of the Arab world viewed the world organization for several decades.

This essay first retraces the Council's engagement with Iraq from 1980 onwards and then explores in greater detail Security Council decision making on Iraq from 2002 to 2014. The Council's engagement with Iraq since 1980 has not only reflected wider patterns of international relations but also defined them. Further, some of the lessons from its involvement with Iraq have changed the Council's approach to promoting international security in significant ways, some of which are explored here.

TRACING HISTORY

Iran-Iraq

The Iranian revolution in 1979, during which the Western-backed shah of Iran was ousted and Ayatollah Ruhollah Khomeini established a new theocratic regime, proved to be the impetus for a decade-long Iran-Iraq war that was to claim hundreds of thousands of lives. Seeking to capitalize on the upheavals in Iran, Iraq attacked Iran, unprovoked. Among the P5, opinion overwhelmingly favored Iraq. The United States had been jolted by the loss of a key ally in the region, the shah of Iran, and pained by a long-lasting hostage crisis in Tehran affecting staff of the US embassy there. The Soviet Union had faced criticism from Iran over its 1979 invasion of Afghanistan. Iraq had been a longtime trading partner of both the Soviet Union and France. The United Kingdom and China remained more neutral, the latter supplying arms to both sides in the course of the conflict.[1]

Constrained by the Cold War standoff in the P5, the Security Council failed to take any strong action. It adopted Resolution 479 calling upon Iran and Iraq to cease hostilities and settle their dispute through negotiations but conspicuously failed to condemn Iraqi aggression. The Council thus alienated justly aggrieved Iran for many years and caused it to boycott the Security Council.[2] It also emboldened Saddam Hussein, with fateful consequences for many years.

In the absence of convincing action by the Council, UN secretary-general Waldheim offered his good offices to facilitate discussions, but to no avail. In 1984, Secretary-General Javier Perez de Cuellar appointed a former Swedish prime minister, Olof Palme, to help nudge Iran and Iraq toward a compromise. Finally, in 1987, Perez de Cuellar's efforts, coupled with a shifting dynamic within the P5 due to Mikhail Gorbachev's rise to power in the Soviet Union, led to the adoption of Resolution 598, which imposed a cease-fire (accepted by the two parties only after a further year of hostilities) to be monitored by the United Nations Iran-Iraq Observer Group. This was a classic Cold War peacekeeping operation, leveraging the political capital of neutrality to provide a buffer between warring parties.[3] The withdrawal of forces to internationally recognized borders was complete by 1990.

Iraq-Kuwait

The Iran-Iraq War is estimated to have cost Iraq over $450 billion.[4] Taking advantage of this war and Iraq's financial ruin, Kuwait began to press for concessions in its border disputes with Iraq. It exceeded the oil production quota set for it by the its Organization of the Petroleum Exporting Countries (OPEC), flooding the market and depressing prices for Iraq's oil, which plummeted from $20 to $14 between January and June 1990. At a time when Saddam Hussein needed to deliver rewards to his country, the demands of Kuwait risked further humiliating him in the eyes of the Iraqi people as well as the Arab world.

Perhaps driven by these considerations, Iraq invaded Kuwait on August 2, 1990. Now, demonstrating dynamics starkly different from those of the Cold War period, the Security Council, within a matter of hours of the invasion, condemned it, mobilized to declare a breach of the peace (under the terms of the UN Charter's Chapter VII), and demanded a complete withdrawal.[5] Four days later, Resolution 661 imposed comprehensive sanctions on both Iraq and occupied Kuwait and established the 661 Committee to implement the same. This swift action signaled a fundamental shift in the UN's capacity to act, promising a new decisiveness and effectiveness in the post–Cold War era.[6] US secretary of state James Baker stated, "That August night, a half-century after it began in mutual suspicion and ideological fervour, the cold war breathed its last."[7]

Resolution 661's sweeping sanctions regime, requiring careful monitoring and humanitarian management, represented a bold shift in the Council's approach to international peace and security. With it, the Council initiated a move beyond its hitherto preferred politico-military mode as mediator and peacekeeper between warring parties to a more legal-regulatory approach seeking to coerce compliance with its demands, an evolution in Council disposition greatly amplified in Security Council Resolution 687 some months later.[8] This new approach would play out in the Council's engagement in Iraq over the next two decades.

When sanctions did not achieve the desired results, the Security Council moved to authorizing the use of force, driven by determined and highly effective US diplomacy managed by President George H. W. Bush, Secretary of State James Baker, and their UN ambassador Thomas Pickering. In November 1990, Resolution 678 called on "Member States . . . to use all necessary means to uphold and implement Resolution 660 . . . and restore international peace and security in that region" unless Iraq were to comply with earlier resolutions by January 15, 1991.[9] When Iraq failed to comply, a military offensive, Operation Desert Storm, was unleashed by a US-led coalition importantly including leading Arab states such as Egypt and Syria, which routed Iraqi forces within one hundred hours with overwhelming firepower and organization, liberating Kuwait and driving Iraqi forces well into their own country before stopping. Bush later wrote that the decision not to move on to Baghdad was taken because the Security Council had not authorized an advance on Iraq's capital and also because it might provoke a disintegration of Iraq were its government to fall apart.[10]

As Simon Chesterman and Sebastian von Einsiedel have written: "Resolution 678 provided the template for most of the enforcement actions taken through the 1990s: it was dependent on the willingness of certain states to undertake (and fund) a military operation; it conferred a broad discretion on those states to determine when and how the enumerated goals might be achieved; it limited Council involvement to a vague request to 'keep the Security Council regularly informed'; and, most importantly, it failed to provide an endpoint for the mandate."[11]

Soon after Operation Desert Storm ended, insurgencies and humanitarian crises erupted in Iraq. Shia militias rose up in rebellion in southern Iraq, and Kurdish rebels mounted an offensive in the north.[12] Although US president Bush had called upon the Iraqi people to "take matters into their own hands and force Saddam Hussein to step aside, the United States would not intervene in the south and did so only belatedly in the north.[13] The Security Council passed Resolution 688 condemning Iraqi repression and casting the refugee flows as a threat to international peace and security. Meanwhile, close to two million Kurdish civilians fled for their lives. Under strong media pressure, the United States led a coalition effort, Operation Provide Comfort, acting unilaterally without Council authorization to address a humanitarian crisis. This effort relied on previous resolutions and on international humanitarian law for justification and was quietly accepted by Russia and China. Coalition forces, including the United Kingdom and France, imposed "no-fly zones" in both the north and the south. The UN Secretariat meanwhile devised an innovative stopgap arrangement stationing UN Guards in northern Iraq, which permitted the return of thousands of Kurdish refugees and the safe delivery of a large international assistance program carried out by several UN agencies.

Resolution 688 signaled a significant shift in the Security Council: human rights and broader humanitarian issues became prominent in the Council's decision making, with the resolution representing the first instance in which the Council explicitly stated that internal repression could lead to a threat against international peace and security.[14] However, addressing human rights issues that had hitherto been seen as internal matters of states remained controversial, and several countries including India and China voiced their reservations clearly.[15] Nevertheless, since then, the Council has increasingly invoked human rights in its decisions and has addressed them in its mandates, although its practice has remained inconsistent across the range of crises it has addressed since 1991.

Finally, the UN Iraq-Kuwait Observer Mission (UNIKOM) was established by Resolution 689 in April 1991. Once again, signaling a new post–Cold War vigor, the Council empowered the Mission with duties under a Chapter VII mandate, implying coercive powers if necessary.

All of these developments to a degree provided grist for President Bush's vision of a "New World Order," outlined in a speech to a joint session of

Congress on September 11, 1990, and prompted by the Iraqi invasion of Kuwait.[16]

SANCTIONS AND WEAPONS INSPECTION

While international attempts to address some of Iraq's humanitarian needs were being made, Iraq's military capacity remained worrying, particularly after coalition forces uncovered the previously unknown extent of Iraq weapons programs. Resolution 687, widely known as the "mother of all resolutions," among other wide-ranging provisions required Iraq to provide reparations for the damages it had inflicted and to eliminate Iraqi weapons of mass destruction (WMDs) and missiles with a range of over 150 kilometers. Unprecedented and complex regulatory machinery flowed from Resolution 687 to implement the disarmament of Iraq through weapons inspection and destruction. The Council aimed to compel Iraq's compliance and cooperation through the continued imposition of wide-ranging sanctions.[17] Together with an ambitious humanitarian program that followed, the overall result, seriously underestimated at the time, was one of regulatory and administrative overload for the UN.

The UN Special Commission (UNSCOM) was established in Security Council Resolution 687 to monitor the destruction or removal of Iraq's chemical and biological weapons. The International Atomic Energy Agency (IAEA) was charged with similar responsibility with respect to Iraq's nuclear capability. Iraq's compliance with UNSCOM was reluctant at best. The climate of controversy and brinkmanship fostered by Saddam Hussein around the weapons inspectors over time undermined faith in the inspections approach, with Washington pressing for a confrontation between UNSCOM and Saddam Hussein in 1998. Following P5 divisions over the usefulness of the inspections-plus-sanctions approach, the United States and United Kingdom once again acted unilaterally to bomb Baghdad (Operation Desert Fox) for not allowing UNSCOM access to disputed sites. By January 1999, UNSCOM was disbanded, amid much acrimony over evidence of a degree of UNSCOM collusion with the Central Intelligence Agency.[18] As Seymour Hersh succinctly put it, "The result of the American hijacking of the UN's intelligence activities was that while Saddam Hussein survived, UNSCOM did not."[19]

Although the stated aim of UNSCOM was Iraq's disarmament, it soon became apparent that for the United States the goal was different. Secretary of State Madeleine Albright confirmed this in 1997, saying: "We do not agree with the nations that argue that sanctions should be lifted. Our view . . . is that Iraq must prove its peaceful intentions. . . . Is it possible to conceive of such a government under Saddam Hussein? The evidence is overwhelmingly that Saddam Hussein's intentions will never be peaceful. Clearly, a change in Iraq's government could lead to a change in US policy."[20] Washington's stance did little to induce Saddam Hussein to cooperate with UNSCOM.

Even prior to this, the sanctions proved critically ill-suited over time to induce compliance with the UN's wider demands articulated in Resolution 687, as the Saddam Hussein regime itself suffered little from the effect of sanctions, which, worse, created the potential for a lucrative black market largely controlled by and benefiting those in power in Baghdad. The Iraqi population, on the other hand, suffered "near-apocalyptic" humanitarian consequences.[21] After the program began, many thousands of Iraqi children under the age of five are believed to have died as a result of the sanctions, and child mortality rates more than doubled. Some even compared the sanctions regime itself to a weapon of mass destruction.[22]

By 1995, the sanctions were becoming unpopular well beyond Iraq and led to a division within the P5, with France and Russia in particular, pressing to end them for humanitarian and perhaps also commercial reasons. The devastating impact and overall ineffectiveness of the sanctions regime in Iraq, which mostly remained in place, because of lack of unanimity among the P5 over ending it, until 2003 (although some measures lingered thereafter) created widespread negative perceptions globally of sanctions, one of the few coercive instruments at the Council's disposal. While, as a result, the design and application of sanctions have been refined, the overall impact on the UN's reputation of their use in Iraq was and remains singularly negative.

The vast humanitarian Oil-for-Food (OFF) program was created in 1995 under Resolution 986 to respond to the perverse outcomes of these sanctions, but the effort to graft it successfully onto other Security Council–mandated UN objectives and activities in Iraq largely failed to produce positive results (although it did relieve a degree of distress locally within Iraq). Under OFF, Baghdad was allowed to sell oil, with the export revenues devoted to purchasing humanitarian supplies under the controlling eye of the UN. A few years later, Baghdad was allowed to take over the distribution of goods within the country and choose who would buy Iraqi oil, greatly expanding the opportunities for corruption.[23] OFF over its lifetime handled $64 billion worth of Iraqi revenue and served as the main source of sustenance for over 60 percent of Iraq's population. But Iraq continued to channel oil illegally to Jordan, Turkey, and Syria (while the P5 looked the other way), while billions of dollars were stolen by Iraqi and other intermediaries in the form of kickbacks. Frustratingly for UN staff, everything about OFF, not unlike the Security Council itself, was inherently political.[24] The selection of oil sale overseers, the bank to hold the revenues in escrow, and the firms to provide the supplies were all negotiated among member states in the Council, particularly the P5.[25]

Thus the strategy of containment based on "inspections plus sanctions," buttressed by the occasional unilateral use of force, ultimately sundered P5 unity. Crumbling international support for this approach on the one hand, and its relentless pursuit by the United States and United Kingdom on the other, ultimately undermined the credibility and legitimacy of the related (and for some, wider) Council decisions for many other member states.[26] Its standing, elevated very high in 1990 and 1991, never fully recovered.

Learning from the Iraq experience, the Security Council now commonly imposes time limits on its sanction regimes. This has not only altered the power dynamics within the Council but has also forced the Council, at regular intervals and even if sometimes only formally, to assess the effectiveness of its measures in relation to other UN objectives such as the protection of human rights. Further, there has been an impetus to craft "smart sanctions" that target perpetrators and avoid adverse impact on civilian populations.

THE UN AND IRAQ, 2001–3

By 2001, the Security Council was stuck in an impasse over Iraq recalling the Cold War. Any adjustments to strategies earlier agreed without an end point were prevented by the "reverse veto"—through which any of the permanent members can veto the termination of any arrangement earlier agreed by the Council that did not provide for an explicit end date. The terrorist attacks of September 11, 2001, against the United States only strengthened Washington's resolve. The risk of proliferation of WMDs to terrorists became a driving preoccupation for the United States, as did determination to be rid of Saddam Hussein once and for all.

President Bush's National Security Strategy in 2002 advocated preemptive use of force and made clear that the United States would not hesitate to act alone.[27] This largely new doctrine suggested that the nation was free to use force against any foe it perceived as a potential threat to its security, at any time of its choosing and with any means at its disposal. In the words of legal scholar Thomas M. Franck, this "stood the UN Charter on its head."[28]

It is now clear that a decision to go to war against Iraq was taken within the Bush administration by the late spring of 2002.[29] Nonetheless, under pressure from some of its traditional allies (mainly the United Kingdom), the United States adopted the "UN route." But President Bush delivered an ultimatum to the UN: either the Security Council backed the US demand for forceful disarmament of Iraq and regime change or it would be sidelined and, in effect, deemed irrelevant.

Seeking a "middle ground" between unarmed inspections and military intervention, the Security Council adopted Resolution 1441 in November 2002. It decided that Iraq had been in "material breach" of its disarmament obligations and gave it one final opportunity to comply, failing which it would face serious consequences. It required Iraq to allow inspections of the UN Monitoring and Verification Commission (UNMOVIC) to operate freely, as well as provide a complete disclosure of its WMD activities. However, Resolution 1441 suffered from creative ambiguity—it was unclear what would constitute a failure by Iraq to comply, what would happen in the event of the failure, and, most importantly, who was to decide. Mainly, it begged the question of whether "failure" by Iraq would automatically permit states to enforce the resolution or whether a second resolution would be necessary for that purpose.

Following the resolution, UNMOVIC was deployed to Iraq under Hans Blix, an energetic leader. In January 2003, Blix told the Council that, while cooperating fitfully, Iraq had not accepted the disarmament demanded of it. Nevertheless, UNMOVIC was doubtful of Iraq's possession of biological and chemical weapons. Mohammad El Baradei of the IAEA told the Council that Iraq was not in the process of reconstituting its nuclear program. Further, both UNMOVIC and IAEA pointed to Western intelligence failures in Iraq. Sharp divisions within the P5 flared up, with France threatening to veto any attempt to go to war, supported by Germany, Russia, and China. In a final attempt along the "UN route," the United States, Britain, and Spain introduced a resolution stating that Iraq had failed to take the "final opportunity" afforded by Resolution 1441 (which had not in its text provided more than a threat of further measures). If passed, this resolution would have provided a rationale for the use of force. However, the deadlock within the P5 persisted, and on March 19, 2003, the invasion of Iraq by a US-led coalition began absent Security Council authorization. (The United Kingdom and the United States had withdrawn their draft resolution not because of a veto but because they had been unable to secure the nine positive votes among Council members required for an affirmative vote.)

A number of episodes of sharp diplomatic confrontation over a six-month period in 2002–3, particularly in February 2003, involving foreign ministers and ambassadors, unfolded under the eyes of the world, broadcast by television all over the globe. The UN Security Council chamber and its surroundings offered nonstop drama, becoming a crucible for world politics as it had been before only during the Cuban missile crisis of 1962 and in the run-up to Operation Desert Storm in 1990–91. Counterintuitively, the decision by Washington and London to attack Iraq without a UN mandate proved highly negative for the UN in world public opinion. Publics in many countries seem to have thought that the UN should somehow have actively prevented the invasion of Iraq.

In this sidelining of the UN, the United States signaled a new approach. It would look to the UN as one potential source of legitimacy and support— one coalition among many—but if the UN could not contribute to the achievement of US foreign policy goals, the United States would act without its support. Debate over policy on Syria in 2013 suggests that this has not changed under President Obama, although his administration has engaged with the UN positively overall.

THE OCCUPATION OF IRAQ AND BEYOND (2003–13)

With the coalition-led invasion under way, both the coalition powers and other member states, shocked by the sudden complete irrelevancy of the UN in Iraq, were left to decide what its future role there could be. While a continuing UN presence in Iraq now risked retrospectively lending legitimacy to the coalition's purposes and methods, its absence would represent an abdication of its essential humanitarian and peacebuilding roles. Striking a balance, once the major coalition military campaign to occupy and subdue the country was over, the Security Council adopted on May 22, 2003, Resolution 1483, which recognized the United States and the United Kingdom as occupying powers and appointed a special representative of the secretary-general to Iraq, Sergio Vieira de Mello. Secretary-General Kofi Annan envisaged a broad multidisciplinary assistance operation, to be carried out by the new United Nations Assistance Mission for Iraq (UNAMI), including constitutional, legal and judicial reform, police training, demobilization and reintegration of former military forces, public administration, and economic reconstruction. However, on the ground, the United States resisted any significant role for Vieira de Mello.

On August 19, 2003, the UN suffered the largest loss of its civilian employees to date. A truck bomb detonated outside UNAMI headquarters in Baghdad, killing Vieira de Mello and twenty-one others. The terrorist attack shocked the UN community and cooled its ardor to play a leading role in Iraq but also carried implications for its approach to peace operations elsewhere thereafter. Any notion of the UN and its staff somehow rising above conflict and enjoying a degree of immunity from attack due to its humanitarian mission vanished.

Soon after securing Baghdad, the slow and rocky task of nation (re-)building began for the coalition. A Coalition Provisional Authority (CPA), headed by US administrator Paul Bremer, was established, and with the special representative of the secretary-general it was tasked with appointing an Interim Iraqi administration. The appointed Iraqi Governing Council served as a provisional government for Iraq, albeit without meaningful powers, and on November 15, 2003, the CPA and the Iraqi Governing Council entered into an agreement on the political process, involving several steps: a transitional national assembly would prepare a constitution; an interim government would be formed by June 2004; and national elections for a post-transition government would be held by December 2005. However, finding support for this arrangement, particularly amongst the Shias and the Kurds, proved challenging.

Recognizing the difficulty of the task, the United States called upon the UN to play a role in gaining acceptance for the plan. The UN's most respected mediator, and the architect of the Taif Agreement that ended the Lebanese civil war, Lakhdar Brahimi, working with the CPA and the Iraqis as a UN special envoy, was able to engineer an acceptable interim government until elections could be held and, importantly, injected much-needed legitimacy into the political process. Nevertheless, at his mission's end in May 2004 he expressed some frustration over the difficulty of working with the CPA, characterizing Bremer as "dictator of Iraq" in a parting shot.[30] British officials working within the CPA and in London expressed similar reservations, more privately.

On March 8, 2004, a Transitional Administrative Law was signed to serve as a constitutional framework until elections allowed for drafting a new constitution.[31] At the same time, the Iraqi Governing Council was replaced by a transitional government, which would prepare for elections. On June 28, 2004, sovereignty was at least formally restored to the Iraqis, and a transitional government headed by Iyad Allawi took over.

Throughout this period, the security situation remained tenuous. The CPA disbanded the Iraqi military and oversaw de-Baathification of the security forces. In the resulting security vacuum, the coalition was unable to meet the most basic security needs of Iraq's citizens. Further, the effect of a disenfranchised Sunni community was underestimated. An energetic insurgency that destabilized an already fragile Iraq with an intense cycle of conflict ensued (also involving elements of the Al Qaeda terrorist movement).[32] Ten years later, domestic security is still seriously impaired by patterns of sectarian and insurgent violence, with murderous crescendos of bombings punctuating political life in ways often difficult to decode from outside the country.

The humanitarian costs of the decade of war continue to burden Iraq. About five million Iraqis have been displaced from their homes since 2003. While hundreds of thousands fled to Jordan and Syria, nearly three million are displaced within Iraq.[33] While estimates vary, in all likelihood one hundred thousand civilians lost their lives during these years.[34] Minority ethnic and religious groups, including the Baha'is, Christians, Shabaks, and others, have been and continue to be particularly vulnerable in the face of insecurity.[35]

UNAMI

Since 2003, the UN's role in Iraq has been that of a peace builder. UNAMI was established by Resolution 1500 in 2003, and its role greatly expanded in 2007. Its mandate included supporting political dialogue and national reconciliation, assisting in electoral processes, facilitating regional dialogue between Iraq and its neighbors, and promoting the protection of human rights and judicial and legal reform.[36] Between 2003 and 2005 UNAMI remained seriously handicapped by the bombing of its headquarters and the lack of policy space to play a meaningful role. Ben Rowswell, senior program manager of the National Democratic Institute in Erbil and then Canada's diplomatic resident representative in Baghdad from 2003 to 2005, recalls: "After de Mello's death the UN played important technical roles such as with the surprisingly successful organization of three national polls in 2005, but exercised little significant political influence."[37] Sir Jeremy Greenstock, the United Kingdom's senior representative in the CPA in 2003, notes: "The main stumbling blocks for greater UN involvement were a), of course, big power disagreement but also b) the Iraqi people's distaste for the UN after sanctions."[38]

However, UNAMI played an important role in the process of drafting and adopting a constitution in 2005 as well as with elections in 2009 and 2010. In 2006, the Iraqi government and the United Nations, with the support of the World Bank, entered into the International Compact for Iraq—an agreement aimed at normalizing the security environment, reconciling the political environment, and revitalizing the economy.[39]

Taking nothing away from individual, sometimes significant achievements of the UN in Iraq, it has not, overall, been able to much improve the quality of life, justice, or politics in the country, despite considerable public expense. Regular reports from the secretary-general to the Security Council document UN activities in Iraq as the country stumbles from crisis to crisis, UN efforts notwithstanding.[40]

Current signals from the ground are hardly encouraging, except perhaps for developments in the Kurdish provinces. There is widespread recognition that at times, on politically sensitive issues such as the status of Kirkuk, UNAMI has made real contributions. That said, like much else in Iraq, Kirkuk's status remains unresolved. UNAMI represents one of the UN's largest political deployments, along with its cousin, UNAMA, in Afghanistan (which equally wrestles with unpromising local circumstances). As of March 2015, UNAMI included 214 troops responsible for protecting UN buildings and staff, 326 international civilian staff, 460 national civilian staff, and a projected budget of $137.2 million.[41] Depressingly, in spite of hard and at times bold and effective work by UN staff, no meaningful reconciliation has been achieved; the Kurdish territories continue their transition toward complete autonomy; the economy is still hamstrung; and violence remains endemic.

Writing in 2013, Joost Hilterman, who has contributed so much to the International Crisis Group's excellent analytical work on Iraq, concludes: "On balance, within Iraq, the UN has made the best of a bad hand, lying low when it was most vulnerable to US manipulation, then playing to its strength on issues that the US was willing to hand over, such as disputed territories. Now, with US troops gone and the situation deteriorating partly as a result of developments in neighbouring Syria, the UN could play a more prominent role but would probably achieve less due to local dynamics."[42]

RENEWED COMBAT IN IRAQ: THE ISLAMIC STATE AS SALVE TO P5 DIVISIONS?

Further chaos was to engulf Iraq, precipitated by civil war in Syria. In August 2014 the Council unanimously adopted Resolution 2170, under Chapter VII of the Charter, condemning in the strongest terms "gross, systematic and widespread abuse" of human rights by the insurgent jihadist Islamic State in Iraq and the Levant (ISIL, also known as ISIS [Islamic State in Iraq and Syria]) and the Al-Nusra Front. In an annex to the text, building on earlier practice after the events of September 11, 2001, it named individuals subject to the travel restrictions, asset freezes, and other measures.

Along somewhat similar lines, the Council united over the humanitarian plight of many Syrian citizens still in their country. On July 14, 2014, the Council adopted Resolution 2165, calling on all parties (rather than primarily the Syrian government, as some previous attempts had done) to facilitate humanitarian access to distressed civilian populations, and—an important breakthrough given strong concerns over sovereignty entertained by some Council members—authorized cross-border access for the UN and its partners to deliver humanitarian aid in Syria without referring to the receiving state for consent.

While the Ottoman Empire has long since evaporated, the past twenty-five years have revived the geo-strategic centrality of Turkey and its potential clout in a neighborhood of failing and failed states. The only meaningful resistance in Iraq to the Islamic State at first arose from Kurdish forces, with the American-trained Iraqi army having been undermined by corruption and internal dysfunction. Turkey, long at odds with ambitions for Kurdish autonomy and, worse, independence—but today having adopted a more qualified Kurdish policy—has emerged under its president, Recep Ayyip Erdoğan, as the key modern state (other than Israel) standing in the region (albeit one still constrained by its own limited economic capabilities and its sometimes challenged internal governance). Should Erdoğan's rule endure some years more, in spite of a significant electoral setback in June 2015, Turkey could wind up playing a significant role in influencing the redrawing of any borders further to the recent collapse of the Sykes-Picot dispensation of 1916 in Asia Minor.

UNILATERALISM

The sidelining of the UN by the United States prompted widespread criticism not only of the United States but also of the UN. Many argued that there had been a twin failure on the part of the UN: failure to contain Iraq and failure to contain the United States. Further, the UN's failure was seen as a sign of an international system that was insufficiently responsive to the needs of the day and that did not mirror the evolving realities of world power. James Traub describes the catch-22 situation that the Security Council found itself in: "Containing the Bush administration has meant finding a middle ground between rubber stamping American policy—and thus making the Council superfluous—and blocking American policy, and thus, provoking America to unilateral action, which of course would make the council irrelevant."[43]

However, the sidelining of the UN did not come without its costs for the United States, both financial and reputational. When it acted unilaterally without explicit authorization from the UN, the United States showed disregard for the principles (and benefits) of collective decision making. Soon after its intervention, the United States began to realize that it needed far more resources and troops than previously anticipated.[44] Embarrassingly, the claims of WMDs that justified its decision to go to war have since been proven unfounded. International skepticism of US intelligence-based assertions was bound to be greater in the future and affected the United States and international calculus on alleged use of chemical weapons in Syria in mid-2013.[45]

IMPLICATIONS FOR INTERNATIONAL PEACE AND SECURITY

The 2003 invasion also held important lessons for postconflict reconstruction and statebuilding. In the case of Operation Iraqi Freedom, the insufficient number of boots on the ground to secure key locations, coupled with a lack of postwar planning, resulted in widespread looting and collapse of basic services like electricity, medical care, and local security services. In face of multiple failures by the invading coalition, Larry Diamond articulated important lessons for postconflict reconstruction. These include preparing for a major commitment, committing enough troops with the proper rules of engagement to secure the postwar order, and mobilizing international legitimacy and cooperation as well as generating legitimacy and trust within the postconflict country. Perhaps most importantly, he advises humility and respect, since the act of seizing the sovereignty of a nation is a particularly bold and assertive one.[46] These recommendations apply to the Security Council in planning UN operations just as much as to Washington in planning US interventions. Similarly, Iraq scholar Phebe Marr warns: "If you cannot garner adequate resources and public opinion at home and abroad to rebuild a nation, don't start."[47]

A number of lessons emerge from the narrative above, of which we suggest a few here.

Egypt, Syria, and Iraq, in varying forms, with widely varying borders, have mattered in the Middle East throughout most its recorded history. The UN has been much engaged with all three since the slow-moving Arab revolt of the 1950s. The latter held out the hope of democratizing and modernizing polities that had remained essentially postcolonial. But such hopes were betrayed as regimes coarsened and proved self-perpetuating, corrupt, and, in the case of both Iraq and Syria, murderous. They were essentially repressive, with Saddam Hussein's Iraq and Hafez al Assad's Syria vying with each other as to which would prove the most ruthless.

In the region composed of Israel and its immediate Arab neighbors, UN political, observer, and peacekeeping missions overlap, with an astonishing number of senior UN players sharing political space. Alas, few concrete results have ensued in advancing peace, as the politics of Israeli-Arab differences remain largely frozen (while on the ground, the balance of force, demographics, varying levels of economic development, and much else have changed a great deal for residents of the region). None of this seems to have alarmed the great powers unduly. Each, with the possible exception of the Russian Federation, has seen its own interests in some ways advanced or comforted by the status quo, while each except China, which cultivates good relations with all local parties, has offered some ideas for altering it.

The UN's ideals, and notions such as the sovereign equality of states promoted in much of the UN Charter, may have inspired hopes that the UN would validate Arab claims and extend effective assistance—beyond the humanitarian and refugee spheres—to Arab peoples. Not surprisingly, weak and vulnerable Arab states have alternately been lulled by the great powers—occasionally supported by them and sometimes shocked by their advancement of interests at odds with those of Arab regimes.

The Iraq experience demonstrates that the Security Council unsurprisingly is subject to the ebb and flow of international politics, especially the relationship among P5 countries at any given time. P5 members alienate each other at considerable risk, as happened during the 1990s and until 2003 with respect to Iraq. When the Iran-Iraq War broke out, Cold War divisions prevented an effective Council response. By contrast, freed from the Cold War stasis, the Council acted swiftly and effectively in addressing Iraq's aggression against Kuwait. Today that former comity has been curdled by disagreements over Libya, Syria, and Crimea. Although their capitals have continued to be capable of cooperation on most Security Council files, the evolution of great-power relations is, at the time of writing, unpredictable.

The Iraq case from the mid-1990s to 2003 points to serious limitations in the Security Council's ability to oversee with impartiality and effectiveness the implementation of its often ambitious decisions. For example, with active collusion of leading Council members, the awarding of contracts under OFF was highly politicized, with benefits "carved up" between member states. These have been addressed to some extent through the professional staffs of several of the Council's committees, notably those of Security Council Resolutions 1373 and 1540, but the instinct in P5 capitals to advance national objectives, including commercial ones, through Council decisions remains strong. Administrative probity lost out to diplomatic realpolitik in the Council on Iraq. But most of the blame of the Volcker report fell on the secretary-general and others in the Secretariat. Not much has changed since then.

The evolution of the Security Council's role on Iraq during the 1990s points to a significant shift, one pregnant with lessons—from a mainly politico-military approach to international peace and security to a greater reliance on a legal-regulatory approach. In its legal-regulatory approach, the Council establishes detailed rules governing the behavior of states or other entities and devolves power to implement and monitor those rules to administrative delegates.

UNSCOM, UNMOVIC, the sanctions regime, and the OFF program are examples of this legal-regulatory approach, and each provides examples of the Council's failures of oversight. But the Council is not likely to abandon this approach. Contemporary threats, which are diffuse, global, and often propagated through nonstate actors, require collaborative, proactive, and complex solutions for which the politico-military approach is insufficient.

Just as agencies in the domestic national spheres are bound by administrative law principles in regulatory decision making, so should be institutions of global governance, like the Security Council, when they act in legal-regulatory capacities. In adopting this perspective, the Council would be not only upholding the rule of law but also enhancing its own legitimacy and credibility. The Council's effectiveness ultimately rests on UN member states recognizing its authority—and a Council seen to be accountable and responsible has a better chance at that.

There are important lessons from Iraq for the Council's effectiveness in this legal-regulatory approach. First, regulatory agencies need clear mandates. Resolutions must be precise, specifying what rules the delegated agent is to implement, the powers available to it in implementing them, and the process by which they should be enforced. The Iraq sanctions regime was the biggest, most complex, and longest lasting ever implemented by the UN. Yet whether its goal was disarmament, regime change, or achieving broader regional stability in the Middle East was not clear, and the P5 disagreed among themselves on this key point. The duration of the sanctions regime was also not specified, and the "reverse-veto" dynamic, requiring P5 unanimity for change, turned it into an indefinite one long after support for it had evaporated internationally.

Second, member states as well as regulatory agents must be accountable. UNSCOM is an excellent example of an ambitious regulatory attempt by the Security Council encumbered by muddled lines of accountability. The chairmen of UNSCOM were appointed by the secretary-general but were to report to the Council. The triangular relationship became highly problematic when UNSCOM head Richard Butler and Secretary-General Kofi Annan differed on issues of substance. When claims arose that the United States was using UNSCOM for its own intelligence purposes, there was no clarity on whom UNSCOM was answerable to. Similarly, the Volcker inquiry report found "egregious lapses" in the management of OFF both by the UN secretariat and by member states, also noting that neither the Security Council nor the Secretariat was in clear command, producing evasion of personal responsibility at all levels.[48]

Third, agents must be independent and adequately resourced so as to maintain their capacity to perform effectively. For example, the 661 Sanctions Committee, which consisted of Council members, was required to oversee extremely lengthy and complex contracts under Resolution 611. However, with some exceptions, members did not have the expertise or the resources to perform this task. The Secretariat also was apparently somewhat at sea. No wonder problems set in.

This sorry case equally suggests lessons for the United States. Even for the most powerful nation, the quality and quantity of member states it keeps in its company in its international ventures, such as military coalitions, matter.

In 1990, the US administration, working closely with P5 capitals, Arab governments, and many others, patiently built the consensus necessary for the formidable military and political coalition with significant regional participation, to which Operation Desert Storm gave expression under an expansive but nevertheless well-defined Council mandate. It stopped well short of toppling the government and taking over the country. The result was, overall, a very good one for Coalition members and for the UN. In 1999, facing a Russian veto threat, the North Atlantic Treaty Organization (NATO) acted without Council authorization in launching air strikes against Serb forces in Kosovo (and, eventually, in Serbia) but enjoyed significant support in the Muslim world and beyond, while Moscow's attempt to have the Council condemn NATO could garner only three of the Council's fifteen votes.

But in 2003, the United States and the United Kingdom led a narrowly gauged coalition involving no active Arab participation (although several Gulf countries did provide quiet support). Washington and London overestimated their own capacity to govern a country of which they knew all too little, and they failed in all but the narrow objective of overthrowing Saddam Hussein, at huge cost to Iraq, the region, and themselves. The very lack of broadly based (particularly regional) company in this venture should have served as a warning flare that the venture was highly risky. A Security Council authorization of force, because of the legitimacy through legality it confers, tends to produce company.

Deliberately vague resolutions seeking to bridge very deep differences can be dangerous. The lack of clarity about what amounted to "material breach" of Resolution 687 and the "serious consequences" threatened by Resolution 1441, as well as about who would enforce those provisions and what powers were available to actors, made it tempting for the United States (if not the United Kingdom) to undertake unilateral military action relying on implied authorization as justification. Short-term diplomatic cleverness in the form of sleight of hand in capitals and within the Council carries great risk.

Meaning of mandates needs to be clear and widely shared, at the very least among the P5.

The Security Council engaged in a flight forward on Iraq as of 1991, imposing ever sterner restrictions and conditions on the country, hoping against the evidence that these would compel cooperation with its objectives. The humanitarian costs of the strategy caused France to defect from the critical P3 consensus, which the United Kingdom and the United States, in their agitation, hardly seemed to notice. And they hardly seemed to notice that international public opinion had abandoned them. This speaks to the isolation of chanceries that can convince themselves of almost anything. Reflecting on a failure to secure the Security Council's approval for invasion of Iraq in 2003 might productively have prompted second thoughts. But it only increased US and UK truculence (as it had increased French excitement in the run-up to the climax, during which France alienated many of its East European Union partners by seeking to speak for them). The United States and the United Kingdom largely lost the 2003 Iraq war, after briefly winning it. In international public opinion the Security Council also lost a great deal of legitimacy for failing to prevent the war. There were thus no winners from this fiasco.

Challenged by European courts, the Council has recently become more attentive to considerations of due process in relation to its sanctions regime against individuals and groups suspected of terrorism. The belief that the Council can act in any way it chooses is neither supportable in law nor acceptable to international public opinion. The Council's failure to tend carefully to oversight of its legal-regulatory strategies in Iraq likewise eroded its credibility, a fragile asset that now more than ever needs careful nurturing.

The Council's renewed comity over Iraq in 2014 after so much discord over Libya, Syria, and Crimea suggests there is no cause that can more rapidly unite the P5 than the fight against terrorism, which, together with separatism, can threaten even the most powerful states. To a lesser extent, the P5 can also agree that humanitarian distress should be relieved where feasible as long as this contravenes no central interests of their own and breaches as few of their principles with respect to sovereignty as possible.

On Iraq's legacy within the Council, Lord Mark Malloch Brown, formerly the UN deputy secretary-general, later a minister in the UK government of Gordon Brown, sums up:

> The Security Council is inhabited by the Ghost of Iraq. Crisis after crisis seems to re-open the distrust sowed by that conflict. The West is branded as

having manipulated intervention into a means of projecting its power and influence under a UN banner. The opposition, notably Russia and China, is portrayed as having turned its back on the Responsibility to Protect and human rights more generally. The result is a broken-backed unreformed Council no longer representative of the distribution of global power, let alone the Charter Principles, but only of the world's basest fears and suspicions.[49]

NOTES

This essay draws on David Malone, *The International Struggle over Iraq: Politics in the United Nations Security Council, 1980–2005* (New York: Oxford University Press, 2005), and on the scholarship and ideas of James Cockayne, who has written extensively on the UN Security Council's involvement in Iraq.

1. David M. Malone and James Cockayne, "The UNSC: 10 Lessons from Iraq on Regulation and Accountability," *Journal of International Law and International Relations* 2, no. 2 (Fall 2006): 4.

2. Javier Perez de Cuellar, *Pilgrimage for Peace: A Secretary-General's Memoir* (New York: St. Martin's Press, 1997), 132.

3. David M. Malone and James Cockayne, "Lines in the Sand: The United Nations in Iraq, 1980–2001," in *The Iraq Crisis and World Order: Structural, Institutional and Normative Challenges*, ed. Ramesh Thakur and Waheguru Pal Singh Sidhu (Tokyo: United Nations University Press; Delhi: Pearson Longman, 2006), 20.

4. Kamran Mofid, *Economic Consequences of the Gulf War* (London: Routledge, 1990), 133.

5. UN Security Council Resolution 660, S/Res/660, August 2, 1990, http://fas .org/news/un/iraq/sres/sres0660.htm.

6. Cockayne and Malone, "Lines in the Sand," 21.

7. James A. Baker, *The Politics of Diplomacy: Revolution, War and Peace, 1989–1992* (New York: G. P. Putnam's Sons, 1995), 16.

8. Malone, *International Struggle over Iraq;* Malone and Cockyane, "UNSC."

9. UN Security Council Resolution 678, S/Res/678, November 29, 1990, http:// fas.org/news/un/iraq/sres/sres0678.htm.

10. George H. W. Bush and Brent Scowcroft, *A World Transformed* (New York: Alfred A. Knopf, 1998), 303.

11. Simon Chesterman and Sebastian von Einsiedel, "Dual Containment: The United States, Iraq and the U.N. Security Council," in *September 11, 2001: A Turning Point in International and Domestic Law,* ed. Paul Eden and Thérèse O'Donnell (Ardsley: Transnational Publishers, 2005).

12. Cockayne and Malone, "Lines in the Sand," 23.

13. George H. W. Bush, "Remarks to the American Association for Advancement of Science," February 15, 1991, www.presidency.ucsb.edu/ws/?pid=19306.

14. Resolution 688 was not explicitly adopted under Chapter VII of the UN Charter, which would have made it more binding.

15. Joanna Weschler, "Human Rights," in *The UN Security Council: From the Cold War to the 21st Century,* ed. David Malone (Boulder, CO: Lynne Reiner, 2004), 58.

16. George H. W. Bush, "Address before a Joint Session of the Congress on the Persian Gulf Crisis and the Federal Budget Deficit," September 11, 1990, http://en.wikisource.org/wiki/Toward_a_New_World_Order.

17. This is addressed more comprehensively in the chapter by Coralie Hindawi in this volume.

18. David Malone, "Iraq: No Easy Response to 'the Greatest Threat,'" *American Journal of International Law* 95, no. 1 (January 2001): 239.

19. Seymour M. Hersh, "Saddam's Best Friend," *New Yorker*, April 5, 1999, 32.

20. Madeleine Albright, "Preserving Principle and Safeguarding Stability: United States Policy Toward Iraq," March 26, 1997, http://secretary.state.gov/www/statements/970326.html.

21. Javier Perez de Cuellar, "Report to the Secretary-General on Humanitarian Needs in Kuwait and Iraq in the Immediate Post-crisis Environment by a Mission to the Area Led by Martti Ahtisaari, Under-Secretary-General for Administration and Management," S/22366, March 20, 1991, para. 8, www.un.org/Depts/oip/background/reports/s22366.pdf.

22. See, for example, Jay Gordon, "When Economic Sanctions Become Weapons of Mass Destruction," March 26, 2004, SSRC Series on Contemporary Conflicts, Social Science Research Council, New York, http://conconflicts.ssrc.org/archives/iraq/gordon.

23. James Traub, "The Security Council's Role: Off Target," *New Republic,* February 21, 2005, 14.

24. For more on the Oil-for-Food program as a humanitarian exception, see the chapter by Hans von Sponeck in this volume.

25. Traub, "Off Target," 16.

26. Malone, "Iraq," 240.

27. George W. Bush, "The National Security Strategy of the United States of America," September 2002, http://georgewbush-whitehouse.archives.gov/nsc/nss/2002/.

28. Thomas Franck, "What Happens Now? The UN after Iraq," *American Journal of International Law* 97, no. 3 (July 2003): 619; Jonathan Steele, "Bush Doctrine Makes Nonsense of the UN Charter," *Guardian*, June 7, 2002.

29. Walter Pincus and Dana Priest, "Some Iraq Analysts Felt Pressure from Cheney Visits," *Washington Post*, June 5, 2003. See also Nicholas Lehman, "How It Came to War: When Did the President Decide to Fight," *New Yorker*, March 31, 2003, 36.

30. Tom Lasseter, "UN's Brahimi: Bremer the 'Dictator of Iraq' in Shaping Iraqi Government," Knight Ridder News, June 3, 2004.

31. Iraq's Transitional Law, May 25, 2004, US General Accounting Office website, www.gao.gov/assets/100/92639.html.

32. Freedom House, "Country Report—Iraq," *Freedom in the World 2013*, www
.freedomhouse.org/report/freedom-world/2013/iraq.

33. Ibid.

34. For one serious estimate slightly above this, see figures available at Iraq Body
Count, www.iraqbodycount.org/database/.

35. Samer Muscati, *Iraq at a Crossroads: Human Rights in Iraq Eight Years after
the US-Led Invasion* (New York: Human Rights Watch, 2010), 65; Bill Bowring,
"Minority Rights in Post-war Iraq: An Impending Catastrophe," *International
Journal of Contemporary Iraqi Studies* 5, no. 3 (2011): 332.

36. "UN Assistance Mission for Iraq," n.d., UN Iraq website, accessed February
25, 2016.

37. Ben Rowswell to authors, September 7, 2013.

38. Sir Jeremy Greenstock to authors, August 29, 2013.

39. UN, "United Nations, Iraq Jointly Announce Launch Of Five-Year
International Compact Aimed at Achieving National Vision of United, Federal,
Democratic Country," press release, IK/552, July 27, 2006, www.un.org/News
/Press/docs/2006/ik552.doc.htm.

40. The most recent, at the time of writing, is "Third Report of the Secretary-
General Pursuant to Paragraph 6 of Resolution 2061 (2012)," S/2013/408, July 11,
2013, www.securitycouncilreport.org/atf/cf/%7B65BFCF9B-6D27–4E9C-8CD3-
CF6E4FF96FF9%7D/s_2013_408.pdf. Much more user-friendly than the UN's
website is the excellent Iraq archive of the research nongovernmental organization
called Security Council Report, accessible at www.securitycouncilreport.org
/un-documents/iraq. Equally useful complementary assessments are now produced
annually by New York University's Center on International Cooperation, documenting both UN peace missions, at http://cic.es.its.nyu.edu/content/annual-
review-global-peace-operations.

41. United Nations, "Factsheet: United Nations Political and Peacebuilding
Missions," March 31, 2015, www.un.org/en/peacekeeping/documents/ppbm.pdf.
For budget figures, see UN Advisory Committee on Administrative and Budgetary
Questions, Report to the General Assembly, A/69/363, October 17, 2014.

42. Joost Hilterman to authors, August 29, 2013.

43. James Traub, "Who Needs the UN Security Council?" *New York Times*,
November 17, 2002.

44. US Department of Defense, testimony of Deputy Secretary of Defense Paul
Wolfowitz, July 29, 2003, www.globalsecurity.org/military/library/congress/2003_
hr/wolfowitztestimony030729.pdf.

45. Kenneth Pollack, "Spies, Lies, and Weapons: What Went Wrong?" *Atlantic
Monthly*, January/February 2004, 92.

46. Larry Diamond, "Building Democracy after Conflict: Lessons from Iraq,"
Journal of Democracy 16, no. 1 (January 2005): 20.

47. Phebe Marr, "Occupational Hazards: Washington's Record in Iraq," *Foreign
Affairs* 84, no. 4 (2005): 186.

48. The Volcker Report, formally the report of the Independent Inquiry Committee into the United Nations Oil-for-Food program, *Report on the Management of the Oil-for-Food Program,* September 7, 2005, www.iic-offp.org /documents.htm.

49. Lord Mark Malloch Brown to authors, August 30, 2013.

EIGHT

Iraq

TWENTY YEARS IN THE SHADOW OF CHAPTER VII

Coralie Pison Hindawi

WITH THE INVASION AND ANNEXATION of Kuwait in August 1990, Iraqi decision makers had to expect an international reaction. However, they surely could not anticipate that this move would place Iraq in the shadow of Chapter VII's enforcement measures for the two decades to come.

Occurring at the very beginning of the post–Cold War era, Iraq's blatant violation of international law—an act of aggression in the view of many—generated almost universal condemnation. And given the particular historical and geopolitical context, Iraq's invasion of Kuwait quickly became, to put it in slightly cynical terms, a perfect opportunity to demonstrate the potential of the resurrected United Nations collective security system. After decades of Cold War–related paralysis, the UN Security Council was back to the front of the scene. More importantly for this chapter's focus, the Council had recovered the ability to use its Chapter VII powers to react to threats to the peace, breaches of the peace, or acts of aggression.

Shortly after the invasion, the Security Council adopted a very ambitious approach backed by unprecedented enforcement measures. How these turned progressively into a trap from which Iraq had no chance to escape is the paradox that will be studied here. And while many argue that the UN collective security system was reborn in Iraq, this country might as well be seen as the place in which the system was buried again. Eventually, I will claim that, rather than illustrating the potential effective uses of Chapter VII in a post–Cold War environment, the Iraq case in fact illustrates Chapter VII's illusory nature.

REAWAKENING OF THE UN COLLECTIVE
SECURITY SYSTEM

Iraq's invasion of Kuwait on August 2, 1990, is the textbook example of an international behavior that endangers international peace and security. It was a blatant violation of one of the UN Charter's most fundamental rules: the prohibition of the use of force in international relations.[1] Accordingly, it comes as no surprise that the attack and proclaimed annexation of Kuwait triggered the intervention of the UN Security Council. Such violent actions are precisely what the UN Charter empowers the Security Council to react to. Thus to a great extent the Security Council's use of its enforcement powers to secure the Iraqi retreat from Kuwait suggested a return to the traditional collective security framework: the Council seemed to follow almost religiously Chapter VII's letter and spirit.

The Security Council first adopted a resolution calling the Iraqi invasion of Kuwait "a breach of international peace and security" and demanding "that Iraq withdraw immediately and unconditionally all its forces to the positions in which they were located on 1 August 1990."[2] Four days later, with the passing of Resolution 661 (1990), the Council started to act "under Chapter VII of the UN Charter." It established a complete economic boycott: states were expected to prevent "the import into their territories of all commodities and products originating in Iraq or Kuwait." This measure was accompanied by a virtually all-inclusive embargo: states were to prevent "the sale or supply . . . of any commodities or products, including weapons or any other military equipment," as well as any transfer of funds or resources, to Iraq and Kuwait. The only exceptions to this embargo were "supplies intended strictly for medical purposes, and, in humanitarian circumstances, foodstuffs." In addition, the Security Council established a committee to monitor the implementation of the resolution.[3] And throughout the following weeks and months, the isolation of Iraqi and Kuwaiti territories was reinforced through a succession of additional resolutions: Resolution 665 (1990) established a naval blockade, asking member states to "use such measures commensurate to the specific circumstances as may be necessary under the authority of the Security Council to halt all inward and outward maritime shipping in order to inspect and verify their cargoes."[4] Resolution 670 (1990) insisted that the embargo encompass "all means of transport, including aircraft."[5]

Finally, as months passed, the Security Council resorted to the ultimate coercive measure: the use of military force. In typical UN euphemisms, it authorized the countries cooperating with the government of Kuwait "to use all necessary means to uphold and implement resolution 660 (1990) and all subsequent relevant resolutions and to restore international peace and security in the area." Remaining apparently true to the UN principle that military force be used only as a last resort, the Security Council granted Iraq a "final opportunity" to comply with its resolutions by January 15, 1991. By the end of this "pause of goodwill," Iraq had still refused to withdraw, automatically triggering the UN mandate to use force.[6] Two days later, Operation Desert Storm was launched, with more than 540,000 military personnel from thirty-one countries participating in a coalition led by the United States.[7]

Only ten days after the start of the military air campaign, the coalition had achieved absolute supremacy by defeating the Iraqi army and systematically destroying Iraqi infrastructure. And on February 27, 1991, six weeks after the start of the military intervention, and after only one hundred hours of ground offensive, the permanent representative of Iraq at the United Nations addressed two letters to the president of the Security Council to announce the withdrawal of the Iraqi troops from Kuwait and Iraq's acceptance of all relevant resolutions.

Overall, the Security Council exercised the full extent of its Chapter VII powers, after having proved unable to do so for decades of Cold War–related paralysis. The Council deviated from the UN Charter's letter in one regard, though: upon establishment of the United Nations, the UN Charter originally foresaw the establishment of UN armed forces that would be ready to intervene, should the Security Council decide that the use of military force was necessary.[8] While these forces were never established, the Council progressively developed a practice of delegating its power to use military force to member states. Following the Korean War in 1950, Resolution 678 (1990) was the second time the Council authorized member states to use military force on its behalf to react to breaches of the peace. Though much more restricted in scope and time, numerous such authorizations have subsequently followed the Korean and Iraqi precedents. Lawyers now generally agree that "given the lack of any significant opposition and the widespread resort to such practice," this "authorization regime" resorted to by the Council in Iraq has since turned into customary law and become part of a reinterpreted Chapter VII.[9]

Therefore, one could assess the Security Council's involvement in the crisis as appropriate and ultimately successful: following a short military campaign under de facto US leadership, which was launched only after all nonviolent options had been exhausted, Iraq had been defeated militarily. Interestingly, though, the fact that Iraq had been efficiently coerced into compliance with the Council's demands and that its attack had come to an end did not lead to the termination of the enforcement measures. On the contrary, Iraq's military downfall actually marked the beginning of a new round of coercive measures, which were based upon an expanded definition of what constituted a threat to international peace and security. As we shall see, those measures signaled an increasingly ambitious interpretation of the UN Security Council's powers under Chapter VII.

AN AMBITIOUS SECURITY COUNCIL FOR A NEW WORLD ORDER?

While one would have expected the Security Council to progressively disengage from the Iraq/Kuwait question following Iraq's defeat, the Council retook the lead once the fighting stopped. With its Resolutions 686 (March 2, 1991) and 687 (April 3, 1991), the Council did not only establish an at first temporary, then permanent cease-fire. Continuing to act under Chapter VII, the Council went extremely far in its role of primary guarantor of international peace and security. With Resolution 687 (1991) in particular, at the time the longest and most complex resolution ever adopted, the Council entered new territory. It created a set of extraordinary obligations designed to force Iraq to resolve all pending issues left from the conflict (related in particular to the Iraq/Kuwait border's delimitation, restitution of property, and responsibility for the damage). Further, the adopted measures aimed at preventing renewed aggression from Iraq and building sustainable peace in the region.

Terminating the Conflict

Eager to definitively terminate the conflict, the Security Council dedicated the first two parts of Resolution 687 to the inviolability of the Iraq/Kuwait boundary. A demilitarized zone was created near the border, and a peacekeeping mission—the UN Iraq-Kuwait Observation Mission—was established to monitor the area. Furthermore, the Council called for the secretary-general's assistance to make arrangements with Iraq and Kuwait to demarcate the boundary between the two countries.[10] Soon, a demarcation commission with representatives of both countries was created to serve this purpose. It is important to note, though, that the final agreement on the exact points delimitating the boundary—which led to a loss of Iraqi territory—was made in spite of Iraq's abstention during the votes. As such, the Council inaugurated in its Resolution 687 a new way of dealing with territorial conflicts, basically imposing a decision upon one of the parties.[11]

This coercive touch to resolve boundary issues seems benign, however, in comparison with the system established by the Security Council to force Iraq to pay for the damage related to its invasion of Kuwait. Not only did the Council insist that Iraq return all Kuwaiti property it seized; it also reaffirmed in Resolution 687 that Iraq was "liable under international law for any direct loss, damage—including environmental damage and the depletion of natural resources—or injury to foreign Governments, nationals and corporations as a result of its unlawful invasion and occupation of Kuwait." The Council also created a fund to pay compensation for claims and a commission to administer the fund.[12] Interestingly, while the text of the resolution allowed for several interpretations, the Compensation Commission later on opted for a very extensive understanding of Iraqi responsibility. While Iraq was not asked to pay for the losses resulting from the embargo or to support the cost of the allied military intervention, the commission deemed it responsible for all losses suffered not only as a result of Iraqi actions and direct consequences thereof but also as a result of military operations conducted by either side between August 2, 1990, and March 2, 1991.[13]

According to Pierre D'Argent, author of a detailed study on war reparations in international law, among the truly unusual features here is that, in addition to forcing Iraq to pay an appropriate compensation to Kuwait, the Security Council allowed itself to "reaffirm" that Iraq was "liable" for all damages caused by its illicit behavior. Second, the Council not only asked Iraq to honor its debt but also took it upon itself to create a mandatory mechanism to guarantee compensation.[14]

The broad framework designed in Resolution 687 progressively turned into a sophisticated reparation system administered by a Compensation Commission composed of representatives of the Security Council members. The commission established detailed compensation procedures based upon the type of requests and found—here again—unprecedented ways to ensure that Iraq would start contributing to the fund in spite of its limited financial means throughout the 1990s. All in all, the Compensation Commission received about 2.7 million claims seeking approximately US$352.5 billion. And by June 2015 Iraq had paid roughly US$47.7 billion, out of about US$52.4 billion ultimately awarded by the commission.[15] This is an impressive amount for a country that spent nearly thirteen years under strict UN economic sanctions and that has been struggling since to escape military conflict and rebuild its infrastructure, administration, and society.

Preventing Future Conflicts

Beyond those far-reaching measures designed to terminate the conflict and ensure that Iraq would pay for the consequences of its invasion and occupation of Kuwait, the Security Council adopted in Resolution 687 a second set of exceptional measures whose primary purpose was to address the Iraqi threat and prevent future conflicts. Given its aggressive record and use of or work on the development of nonconventional weapons the Council decided that one of the ways to secure sustainable peace in the region was to reduce significantly Iraq's military potential.[16] At the conventional level, the embargo on arms and related materiel of all types was to continue (§ 24). At the nonconventional level, Iraq was required by Resolution 687 to disarm and abstain from developing new armaments or military programs in the biological, chemical, and nuclear fields. Furthermore, it had to renounce the use of ballistic missiles with a range greater than 150 km.[17]

To implement these extraordinary obligations, the Security Council had—here again—to adopt additional, practical measures to design a workable system. This started with Resolution 687 and was developed subsequently, particularly in Resolutions 705 and 711 adopted in August and October 1991, respectively. Those resolutions defined more precisely the legal and organizational framework within which the process was to take place. First, Iraq had the obligation to quickly submit a declaration of the location, amount, and type of all forbidden items. In a second phase, onsite inspections were to be carried out by two bodies created for the purpose of disarming Iraq: a special commission (UNSCOM) in charge of the biological, chemical, and missile fields and a special team from the International Atomic Energy Agency (IAEA). These two bodies were charged with the additional task of supervising the destruction of the prohibited items or their rendering harmless. Finally, an ongoing monitoring and verification process had to be set up to ensure that Iraq would not resume its prohibited programs after the completion of the first two steps. UNSCOM and the International Atomic Energy Agency were granted extensive rights and privileges in order to accomplish their mandates. Iraq had to allow them 'immediate, unconditional and unrestricted access to any and all areas, facilities, equipment."[18] UNSCOM had the right to conduct interviews, install equipment, take aerial photographs, and so on.

Acknowledging probably the unlikelihood of Iraq complying gracefully with such an intrusive disarmament process, the Security Council included a short paragraph in Resolution 687 whose wording suggested that economic sanctions adopted originally by the Council to force Iraq to withdraw from Kuwait were to be maintained pending "Council agreement that Iraq has completed all actions contemplated in paragraphs 8 to 13."[19] In essence, this meant that the economic isolation of Iraq would persist until the Security Council assessed that Iraq had complied fully with its disarmament obligations in the nonconventional and ballistic missiles fields.

A Super–Security Council?

Many may have come to naturally accept the notion of the Iraqi regime of the 1980s and 1990s as a "rogue" actor that had to be subjected to special obligations and "contained" for the sake of regional security. It is crucial, however, to understand that the way in which the Security Council dealt with Iraq after the end of the 1990–91 Gulf War was completely unprecedented. At the time of its adoption, Resolution 687 was—and still is—a milestone in terms of UN Security Council action. This is obvious if one considers not only the diversity of issues that the Council tackled but also, more importantly, the very authoritative way in which the Council treated these issues: resorting to original and creative solutions, but also solutions that ultimately rested on extreme forms of coercion. The dilemma triggered by the Security Council's awakening has been well captured by a joke, allegedly originating from UN circles, observing that the Council, once a vegetarian, had now become a carnivore and was at risk of turning anthropophagic.[20]

Surely, the very ambitious approach taken by the Security Council in dealing with Iraq cannot be properly understood outside its singular historical context. Many will remember the statement of US president Bush in September 1990:

The crisis in the Persian Gulf, as grave as it is, also offers an opportunity to move toward an historic period of cooperation. Out of these troubled times ...a new world order can emerge: ... A world where the rule of law supplants the rule of the jungle. A world in which nations recognize the shared responsibility for freedom and justice. A world where the strong respect the rights of the weak. This is the vision that I shared with President Gorbachev in Helsinki. He and other leaders from Europe, the Gulf, and around the world understand that how we manage this crisis today could shape the future for generations to come.[21]

Without taking such statements at face value, one ought to recall that the abrupt end of the Cold War really triggered—perhaps naively—hopes for a new international order based upon international law and a functioning collective security system. The words of the Austrian representative probably give a fair picture of many of the perspective of many Security Council members on their adoption of a text as far-reaching as Resolution 687, a mixture of cautious hope and humility: "History will be the judge of whether we have chosen the right approach. Today, we can only say, in all honesty, we did what seemed best."[22]

The extraordinary status created for Iraq by Resolution 687 is therefore to be read within this particular context of hopes for a new, different world order in which a strong Council would play a much more decisive role in the maintenance of international peace and security.

THE CHAPTER VII TRAP: DESTROYING THE COLLECTIVE SECURITY SYSTEM AGAIN?

These hopes notwithstanding, the ambitious approach adopted to tame the Iraqi threat progressively turned into a trap from which there was no way out and that triggered renewed insecurity instead. Explaining how this happened is crucial, as it has a lot to teach about the potential and pitfalls of the collective security system that was deemed reborn in Iraq.

Iraq had to abide by numerous obligations before being allowed to regain its prewar and pre–Chapter VII status. As already mentioned, the most important obligations seemed to be those related to the disarmament process, as the termination of the economic sanctions was made conditional upon Iraq's compliance with the resolution's measures in this domain. Interestingly, though, while the vast majority of the stockpiles of prohibited weapons were destroyed unilaterally or under UN supervision in the early 1990s and the prohibited programs were all brought to an end by the mid-1990s the process continued and actually turned more confrontational *after* that date.[23] As a result, the economic sanctions remained in place up until the 2003 invasion of the country, while other coercive measures—originally adopted following Iraq's invasion of Kuwait—were maintained until as late as December 2010!

Endless Disarmament

The maintenance of this extraordinary status in spite of Iraq's de facto compliance with most of its disarmament obligations is intriguing.[24] By the mid-1990s, the economic and humanitarian impact of the sanctions had become increasingly well documented—including several hundred thousand Iraqi deaths as a result of Iraq's economic isolation.[25] Still, some Security Council members continued to insist on the need to maintain these measures given the threat represented by Saddam Hussein's regime.[26] Even opponents to the US project of military invasion would lament, in late 2002 and early 2003, Iraq's lack of "full cooperation" with its disarmament obligations.[27] The last resolution adopted by the Council before the invasion—itself presented by the attacking countries as the only way to address the Iraqi threat after more than a decade of multilateral failure—also declared that Iraq was in "material breach" of its obligations and would be afforded "a final opportunity to comply with its disarmament obligations."[28]

But while the goal of the process seemed to be straightforward, a close look at the disarmament obligations shows that it was never clear exactly what complete disarmament meant. The Security Council did not define the duration of any of the disarmament's phases (declaration and inspections / destruction or rendering harmless of prohibited goods / ongoing monitoring and verification) or set a deadline for their completion. It even seemed that the final monitoring and verification phase was to continue ad infinitum. In addition, the constant evolution of the legal basis through the Council's repeated adoption of new, additional obligations generally meant that the Iraqi state had little prospect of a return to normality.[29] And with time, the absence of any palpable way to end the process fostered the Iraqi belief that whatever the form of cooperation, it would not lead to the release from external coercion that the regime was looking for. Of course, this reduced considerably the incentive for cooperation and led to repeated Iraqi posturing and provocations.[30] At the same time, any form of Iraqi resistance to the process was interpreted as further evidence that the Iraqis were trying to hide some prohibited activities, which, as stressed previously, had almost ceased by the mid-1990s. Consequently the confrontational nature of the process had increased by the time Iraq had basically complied with most of its obligations.

But how to explain, still, that this effective compliance was not acknowledged by the Security Council? One needs to consider the coercive nature of the process, its politicization, and the dual-use possibilities of biological, chemical, and nuclear technologies (the fact that many materials and techniques can be used for both civil and military purposes). Given the coercive nature of the process, while Iraq had fulfilled most of its obligations, it had done so in a nontransparent, reluctant, and sometimes defiant manner, trying to keep some useful knowledge or material to preserve its potential to restart its programs at a later point, once international scrutiny would have faded. And as we were dealing with nonconventional, dual-use technology, this was indeed a possibility that inspectors had to consider and that explains how difficult it was for the disarmament bodies to ever assess with certainty that Iraq had "fully complied" with its obligations. But while this justified the need for an indefinite monitoring phase, it also meant that the process would in essence be insatiable and of ever-increasing intrusiveness, regardless of any achievements. Consequently, the economic sanctions had little chance of ever being lifted, since it was unlikely, in the context described above, that the Security Council would ever decide that Iraq had "fully complied" with its disarmament obligations. And this, in turn, paved the way for a subjective interpretation and instrumentalization of Chapter VII–based measures for political purposes.

Fulfilling or Destroying the Collective Security System?

The repeated declarations by US and British representatives according to which the sanctions would be lifted only after Saddam Hussein's removal from power hinted at the fact that these countries' opposition to the termination of the sanctions was only partially related to the disarmament process.[31] Over the years, it became increasingly obvious that certain permanent members of the Security Council were using the Chapter VII measures of Resolution 687 to implement a policy of containment that was only loosely connected to the actual threat posed by Iraq, even going as far as infiltrating the UN bodies for espionage and regime destabilization activities.[32] In the end, caught as it was in Chapter VII, Iraq became perhaps the first and most spectacular case of "reverse veto," a situation in which the lack of consensus among the permanent members "does not block the Security Council from authorizing or ordering an action but, rather, blocks it from terminating or otherwise altering an action it has already authorized or ordered."[33] Indeed, in spite of growing unease over the humanitarian impact of the sanctions, even within the Security Council and the permanent members' circle, the reluctance of the United States and the United Kingdom to lift the sanctions prevented the coercive measure from being terminated.[34] The best that the Council could achieve was a progressive relaxation of the boycott with the Oil-for-Food program, which started operating in 1997,[35] and in 2001/2002—a decade after Resolution 687 was adopted—the Council introduced additional measures designed to make the sanctions more "targeted" and "smart."[36]

The inability of the Security Council to lift the sanctions was decried by some as a violation of human rights. Because of their well-documented adverse humanitarian impact, the argument went, the measures adopted by the supreme international body had become unlawful and no longer required states' obedience. Some even went as far as suggesting that the maintenance of the sanctions in knowledge of their deadly impact amounted to a form of genocide.[37]

But while the sanctions alone raised serious questions related to the Security Council's role in Iraq, the picture would not be completely accurate without mentioning the repeated use of military force against Iraq after the end of the 1991 allied intervention and up until the invasion of the country in 2003. Throughout the 1990s, a number of states patrolled and bombed Iraqi territory in two no-fly zones (NFZs), which were established first in the northern and later in the southern parts of Iraq.[38] While it is often said that the northern NFZ was established by Security Council Resolution 688 (1991) to react to the Iraqi regime's harsh repression of its Kurdish population, this text was not adopted under Chapter VII of the Charter, and it neither mentions an NFZ nor authorizes the use of military force. The southern NFZ, from its side, was first established in August 1992 south of the thirty-second parallel and was expanded in September 1996 to the thirty-sixth parallel, allegedly in reaction to a military attack in the north of Iraq. By that time, the NFZs covered more than 60 percent of Iraqi territory. Within that framework, foreign patrols conducted over 250,000 flights in the northern and southern zones,[39] regularly striking Iraqi defense sites as well as, sometimes, civilians.[40] Beyond the reference to Resolution 688 (1991), UK and US representatives justified these operations as a way to monitor the Iraqi forces and reduce their capacity to threaten neighboring countries or regional security. The United Kingdom also mentioned the objective of protecting the Iraqi civilian population. It was even argued regularly that the military patrols operating in the NFZs were resorting to armed force in self-defense.[41]

In addition to the NFZs, the United States and the United Kingdom used military force against Iraq on several occasions throughout the 1990s, a couple of times with French participation. In January 1993, for example, in parallel with joint US, British, and French strikes in the southern NFZ, the United States struck an alleged nuclear site in Baghdad's vicinity.[42] Later on that year, the United States targeted Iraqi intelligence buildings in retaliation for an alleged Iraqi involvement in an assassination attempt of former US president Bush. The most spectacular and massive resort to military force was the December 1998 joint US-UK Desert Fox operation that led to four days of intensive bombing of about a hundred Iraqi sites. The attack was launched following the release of a report from the disarmament body UNSCOM, which, once again, deplored Iraq's lack of cooperation. Interestingly, though, the attack started as the Security Council was discussing the report and before the multilateral body could make any decision, which triggered anger within the Council, in particular from Russia and China.

From a legal point of view, it is worth noting that while the authorization to use military force against Iraq granted by Security Council Resolution 678 (1990) had clearly ended with Resolution 687, the lethal operations that took place after that day were presented most of the time as designed to enforce the Security Council's will. The argument was often made that the Council "implicitly" authorized the use of force against Iraq. More precisely, the United Kingdom and the United States claimed in an increasingly sophisticated manner that the cease-fire established by Resolution 687 was conditional upon Iraq's acceptance of and compliance with its obligations. Borrowing the concept from the law of treaties, they developed the argument that because Iraq was in "material breach" of its obligations under Resolution 687 this suspended the cease-fire and "revived" the authorization to use military force granted by the Council in Resolution 678 (1990).[43] Interestingly, the United States and the United Kingdom employed the exact same reasoning in their official legal justification of the March 2003 invasion of Iraq.

Such an argument, of course, demonstrates to the extreme the absurdity of the claim that to achieve durable peace—what Resolution 687 was supposed to be all about—one had first to wage limited and then full-scale war. But it also raises the question of the role that the Chapter VII framework played in allowing for the progressive destruction of Iraq.

THE CHAPTER VII CHIMERA

If the multilateral reaction to Iraq's invasion of Kuwait symbolized the revival of the collective security system in a post–Cold War world, and if Security Council action under Chapter VII did indeed have its successes, the Iraqi case tells an important story.

It tells the story of an overly ambitious project designed to build sustainable peace that turned into a trap. It tells the story of economic sanctions maintained to promote a less threatening regional order that led to the destruction of an entire economy and to the deaths of hundreds of thousands. It tells the story of UN Security Council measures being instrumentalized for political, national, and, to a great extent, bellicose purposes, ultimately reaching their Orwellian apex with the invasion of Iraq: a war of aggression, the very same crime that had opened the door to the Security Council involvement in Iraq to start with. But of course, given that the invasion was launched by two of its permanent members, the Council was unable to react forcefully this time. In a nutshell, the Iraqi case symbolizes all at once the great potential, but also great danger, of Chapter VII, and it should serve as a reminder of the probably irremediable limitations to UN Security Council action.

True, the Security Council made history in Iraq. It proved able to use all of Chapter VII's tools, and from a distance it may seem that these tools achieved many of their stated objectives: Iraq did withdraw from Kuwait, it did pay for the damage incurred both by its own invasion and by the allied military response, it did disarm against its will, and it never again engaged in an aggression against any of its neighbors.

But at what cost? The unilateral disarmament of Iraq did not lead to greater regional security; on the contrary, it paved the way for more insecurity. Hundreds of thousands died as a result of the sanctions, and hundreds of thousands more died as a result of the 2003 invasion of the country and the armed conflicts it unleashed. Iraq became a cradle for the most violent nonstate armed groups, and the political transition orchestrated under foreign occupation failed to produce the inclusive and balanced system that might have allowed Iraqis to live at peace with each other following the fall of Saddam Hussein's regime. At the international level, Iraq showed the danger of pushing forward too strongly an overambitious collective security system whose implementation is decentralized and left to the states able and willing to act. Retrospectively, one might actually wonder why, if the will to build a new world order was that strong, back in 1990, the decision was not made to establish UN armed forces that would have been able to use military force when decided by the Security Council. In the absence of a truly multilateral regime, and given both the particular geopolitical context of post–Cold War US hegemony and US obsession with Iraq, the framework created by the Security Council, with all its weaknesses, lent itself perfectly to instrumentalization.

One should note, of course, that this particular combination of both far-reaching and vague Chapter VII measures with a superpower's determination to push a political agenda against an adversarial regime is quite unlikely to repeat itself. Within the Security Council, numerous lessons were learned out of Iraq: the Council members became much more cautious in their resort to and drafting of authorization to use military force, economic sanctions, and other coercive measures. At the same time, this very approach of caution points at a persistent dilemma: whenever the UN Security Council resorts to its Chapter VII powers, it opens the door to coercive measures whose termination, unless the measures are limited in time, will be subject to the Council's agreement. Thus the Council's action continues to be constrained not only by the veto power of permanent members preventing any action from being taken but also by the (reverse) veto power of permanent members preventing coercive measures from being terminated. Given both the impossibility for the Council to involve itself productively in some situations crucial to international peace and security—because of the inherent selectivity of its interventions—and the risk for any Chapter VII action taken to be hijacked by permanent members, the Iraq case and post–Cold War practice teach us, once again, the importance of humility. The UN Security Council's political constraints are so great that the international body is extremely limited in its ability to take appropriate action in the collective interest to preserve international peace and security. It might be about time to start looking elsewhere for more tangible solutions.

NOTES

Funding for the research behind this chapter was provided by the Gerda Henkel Stiftung. The author would like to thank Timothy Eddy for the editing, as well as Hans-Christoph von Sponeck, whose outrage at the UN's role in Iraq back in the early 2000s encouraged me to pursue this line of research. Thanks to Karim Makdisi and Vijay Prashad for putting together this important book.

1. UN Charter, 1945, Article 2(4), www.un.org/en/charter-united-nations/.

2. UN Security Council Resolution 660, S/Res/660, August 2, 1990, www .un.org/en/ga/search/view_doc.asp?symbol=S/RES/660(1990).

3. UN Security Council Resolution 661, August 6, 1990, S/Res/661, paras. 3–4, www.un.org/en/ga/search/view_doc.asp?symbol=S/RES/661(1990).

4. UN Security Council Resolution 665, August 25, 1990, S/Res/665, para. 1, www.un.org/en/ga/search/view_doc.asp?symbol=S/RES/665(1990).

5. UN Security Council Resolution 670, September 25, 1990, S/Res/670, para. 2, www.un.org/en/ga/search/view_doc.asp?symbol=S/RES/670(1990).

6. UN Security Council Resolution 678, November 29, 1990, S/Res/678, para. 2, www.un.org/en/ga/search/view_doc.asp?symbol=S/RES/678(1990).

7. Despite being officially presented as being under "strategic" Saudi headship.

8. UN Charter, 1945, Articles 43–47, www.un.org/en/charter-united-nations/.

9. See, e.g., Antonio Cassese, *International Law*, 2nd ed. (Oxford: Oxford University Press, 2005), 346–50, in particular 350.

10. UN Security Council Resolution 687, S/Res/687, April 3, 1991, paras. 2–6, www.un.org/Depts/unmovic/documents/687.pdf.

11. These measures are precisely what led Ecuador to abstain during the vote on Resolution 687, fearing the precedent might weaken the principle according to which borders are to be sovereignly agreed upon by states.

12. UN Security Council Resolution 687, S/Res/687, paras. 15–19.

13. UN Compensation Commission, "Criteria for Expedited Processing of Urgent Claims," February 8, 1991, S/AC.26/1991/1, § 18, www.uncc.ch/decision/dec_01.pdf.

14. Pierre D'Argent, *Les réparations de guerre en droit international public* (Brussels: Bruylant; Paris: LGDJ, 2002), 333.

15. UN Compensation Commission, "Summary of Awards and Current Status of Payments," n.d., accessed June 6, 2015, www.uncc.ch/summary-awards-and-current-status-payments.

16. Biological, chemical, and nuclear weapons, also sometimes referred to as weapons of mass destruction.

17. UN Security Council Resolution 687, S/Res/687, paras. 7–14.

18. UN Security Council Resolution 707, S/Res/707, August 15, 1991, § 3, www .un.org/Depts/unmovic/documents/707.pdf.

19. UN Security Council Resolution 687, S/Res/687, para. 22.

20. S. Sur, "La résolution 687 (3 avril 1991) du Conseil de sécurité dans l'affaire du Golfe: Problèmes de rétablissement et de garantie de la paix," *Annuaire Français de Droit International* 37 (1991): 89.

21. George H. W. Bush, Address before a Joint Session of the Congress, September 11, 1990, http://millercenter.org/president/bush/speeches/speech-3425.

22. UN Security Council, "Provisional Record of the 2981st Meeting," S/PV.2981, April 3, 1991, http://repository.un.org/handle/11176/55543.

23. UN Monitoring and Verification Commission, "Summary of the Compendium of Iraq's Proscribed Weapons Programmes in the Chemical, Biological and Missile Areas," S/2006/420, June 21, 2006, www.un.org/Depts/unmovic/new/documents/compendium_summary/s-2006–420-English.pdf; Iraq Survey Group, *Iraq Survey Group Final Report*, vol. 2, section "Nuclear," subsection "Key Findings," September 30, 2004, www.globalsecurity.org/wmd/library/report/2004/isg-final-report/.

24. For a more detailed analysis, see C. Pison Hindawi, "The Controversial Impact of WMD Coercive Arms Control on International Peace and Security: Lessons from the Iraq and Iranian Cases," *Journal for Conflict and Security Law* 16, no. 3 (2011): 417, from which this section is drawn.

25. According to the most conservative estimate, 227,000 children under five died as a direct consequence of the sanctions between August 1991 and March 1998; R. S. Garfield, *Morbidity and Mortality among Iraqi Children from 1990 through 1998: Assessing the Impact of the Gulf War and Economic Sanctions* (Notre Dame, IN: University of Notre Dame, Joan B. Kroc Institute for International Peace Studies, 1999). Most assessments reach much higher figures.

26. One will recall Madeleine Albright's infamous reply when asked by journalist Lesley Stahl whether she believed that the death of half a million Iraqi children under the sanctions regime was worth it: "I think this is a very hard choice, but the price—we think the price is worth it." Lesley Stahl, "Punishing Saddam," *60 Minutes,* CBS, May 12, 1996.

27. See, e.g., the statements made during a Security Council meeting, UN Security Council, "4644th Meeting," S/PV.4644, November 8, 2002, http://daccess-dds-ny.un.org/doc/UNDOC/PRO/N02/680/99/PDF/N0268099.pdf?OpenElement.

28. UN Security Council Resolution 1441, S/Res/1441, November 8, 2002, §§ 1 and 2, www.un.org/Depts/unmovic/documents/1441.pdf.

29. In addition to Resolutions 707 (1991) and 715 (1991), which specified the legal frame of the inspections, one should point out subsequent texts in which the Security Council not only reminded Iraq of its initial obligations but also established new requirements, such as its Resolutions 949 (1994), 1051 (1996), 1137 (1997), 1284 (1999), and 1441 (2002).

30. G. Cottereau, "Rebondissement d'octobre en Iraq: La résolution 949 du Conseil de sécurité (15 octobre 1994)," *Annuaire Français de Droit International* 40 (1994): 192.

31. See, e.g., the declaration made by Sir D. Hannay, UK representative at the UN Security Council, in UN Security Council, "2981st Meeting," S/PV.2981, April 3, 1991, http://repository.un.org/handle/11176/55543?show=full, or by US president Clinton declaring, a few years later, that the sanctions "will be there until the end of

time or as long as [Saddam Hussein] lasts," quoted in B. Crossette, "For Iraq, a Dog House with Many Rooms," *New York Times,* November 23, 1997, 4.

32. See, e.g., Susan Wright, "The Hijacking of UNSCOM," *Bulletin of the Atomic Scientists* 55, no. 3 (1999): 23–25, or "Spying on Saddam," *Frontline,* PBS, April 27, 1991, www.pbs.org/wgbh/pages/frontline/shows/unscom/.

33. D. Caron, "The Legitimacy of the Collective Security of the Security Council," *American Journal of International Law* 87 (1993): 552–94. For the quote, see 577.

34. For expressions of unease with the humanitarian impact of the sanctions, see, e.g., the debate within the Council on October 17, 1994, recorded in UN Security Council, "3439th Meeting," S/PV.3439, October 17, 1994, www.un.org/en/ga/search /view_doc.asp?symbol=S/PV.3439; the statement of the Russian representative on May 21, 1999, recorded in UN Security Council, "4008th Meeting," S/PV.4008, May 21, 1999, p. 2, www.un.org/en/ga/search/view_doc.asp?symbol=S/PV.4008; or the debate on economic sanctions that took place on June 26 and 28, 2001, recorded in UN Security Council, "4336th Meeting," S/PV.4336, June 26, 2001, www.un.org /en/ga/search/view_doc.asp?symbol=S/PV.4336, and June 28, 2001, www.un.org /en/ga/search/view_doc.asp?symbol=S/PV.4336%20(Resumption%201).

35. For a critical insider account of the humanitarian program, see von Sponeck's chapter in this volume.

36. UN Security Council Resolution 1382, S/Res/1382, November 29, 2001, http://daccess-dds-ny.un.org/doc/UNDOC/GEN/No1/668/53/PDF/No166853 .pdf?OpenElement, and UN Security Council Resolution 1409, S/Res/1409, May 14, 2002, www.un.org/Depts/unmovic/documents/1409.pdf.

37. Marc Bossuyt, "The Adverse Consequences of Economic Sanctions on the Enjoyment of Human Rights," working paper, Commission on Human Rights, UN Economic and Social Council, E/CN.4/Sub.2/2000/33, June 21, 2000, §§ 71–73 and 109, http://daccess-dds-ny.un.org/doc/UNDOC/GEN/Goo/140/92/PDF /Goo14092.pdf?OpenElement.

38. The countries involved in these operations were the United States and, to a lesser extent, the United Kingdom, but also France, Turkey, Saudi Arabia, and Kuwait.

39. According to the information provided on Operations Provide Comfort, Northern Watch, and Southern Watch on the Global Security website, www .globalsecurity.org.

40. While the Global Security website does not provide any assessment of civilian casualties, it seems that the frequency of strikes grew exponentially from 1999 onward, a year for which a UN report initiated by then humanitarian coordinator von Sponeck counted 144 civilians killed and 446 injured in 132 days of strikes. UN Office of the Humanitarian Coordinator for Iraq, "Air Strikes in Iraq and Reported Civilian Casualties and Damages, 28 December 1998—31 December 1999," Baghdad, 1999, internal document.

41. For a detailed analysis of these uses of military force and the legal arguments presented to justify them, see C. Pison Hindawi, *Vingt ans dans l'ombre du chapitre*

VII: Eclairage sur deux decennies de coercition a l'encontre de l'Iraq (Paris: L'Harmattan, 2013), 151–203.

42. M. Weller, ed., *Iraq and Kuwait: The Hostilities and Their Aftermath* (Cambridge: Grotius, 1993), 745.

43. See, e.g., the statement of the US and UK representatives to justify Operation Desert Fox in UN Security Council, "3955th Meeting," S/PV.3955, December 16, 1998, 7 and 10, www.un.org/en/ga/search/view_doc.asp?symbol=S/PV.3955.

NINE

Libya: A UN Resolution and NATO's Failure to Protect

Jeff Bachman

ON FEBRUARY 25, 2011, the United Nations Security Council held its first formal meeting on the situation in Libya. Secretary-General Ban Ki-moon opened the meeting, stating, "Today, clashes broke out again, with high casualties reported. In their public statements, Colonel Al-Qadhafi and members of his family have continued to threaten citizens with a civil war and the possibility of mass killing if the protests continue."[1] At the same meeting, Libyan ambassador Abdel Rahman Shalgam, in an about-face, claimed that on February 15 peaceful protesters had "faced gunfire aimed at their heads and chests, as if the soldiers who opened fire did not know that human beings have heads, hearts and legs, or that there are other parts that can be shot at, that there are such things as tear gas bombs or roadblocks that can contain demonstrations."[2] Shalgam compared Qaddafi to Pol Pot and Hitler, and he reminded those in attendance that during the 2005 World Summit the international community had pledged to "protect populations by preventing genocide, war crimes, ethnic cleansing and crimes against humanity, as well as their incitement," a clear reference to the responsibility to protect.[3]

Testimony such as that given by the secretary-general and Shalgam began the campaign that would be expanded upon and utilized by many of the North Atlantic Treaty Organization (NATO) powers to ensure the adoption of Security Council Resolutions 1970 and 1973. Resolution 1970 was adopted by the Security Council on February 26, eleven days after the first protests. Adopted unanimously, it referred to "widespread and systematic attacks . . . against the civilian population" that may constitute crimes against humanity.[4] It also expressed concern "at the plight of refugees forced to flee the violence" and reminded Libyan authorities of their "responsibility to protect its population."[5] Finally, the resolution referred the situation in Libya to the

International Criminal Court and authorized an arms embargo, as well as other sanctions.

Following the adoption of Resolution 1970, prointervention members of NATO did their best to anchor the narrative presented by the secretary-general one day earlier. The ambassador from the United Kingdom proclaimed, "[We] presented the text of this resolution because of our grave concern about the appalling situation in Libya. The violence we have seen and the incitement to further violence by Colonel Al-Gadhafi are totally unacceptable."[6] The United States added, "When atrocities are committed against innocents, the international community must speak with one voice and today, it has. . . . The international community will not tolerate violence of any sort against the Libyan people by their Government or security forces."[7] France made explicit reference to the responsibility to protect, establishing the pretext for military intervention: "The text unanimously adopted today, recalls the responsibility of each State to protect its own population and of the international community to intervene when States fail in their duty."[8]

Russia and China, traditional allies at the Security Council in their mutual opposition to interference in internal matters of state, were among those who voted to adopt Resolution 1970. Support for the resolution from regional stakeholders, such as the Arab League, the African Union, and the Organization of the Islamic Conference, played a key role in gaining their backing. Also key was the absence of any language in the resolution that could have been interpreted as authorizing the use of force against Libya. Russia emphasized this point, arguing that "it does not enjoin sanctions, even indirect, for forceful interference in Libya's affairs."[9]

The Security Council did not meet again to discuss Libya until about three weeks later on March 17. France opened the discussion by recalling Resolution 1970 and declaring that the sanctions implemented were insufficient: "Throughout the country, violence against the civilian population has only increased. . . . We must not give free rein to warmongers; we must not abandon civilian populations, the victims of brutal repression, to their fate."[10] Following France's statement, a vote was held on Resolution 1973. The new resolution was adopted with ten votes for, none against, and five abstentions. Resolution 1973 reiterated or strengthened a number of the sanctions first implemented under Resolution 1970. More significantly, it authorized member states "through regional organizations or arrangements . . . to take all necessary measures . . . to protect civilians and civilian populated areas under threat of attack in the Libyan Arab Jamahiriya."[11]

Those who abstained from voting on Resolution 1973 included four of the five BRICS countries—Brazil, Russia, India, and China—and Germany. Brazil argued that Resolution 1973 went far beyond what was called for by the League of Arab States. Germany expressed its concern that military intervention would end up causing more harm than good. China and Russia noted with frustration that they had sought answers to legitimate questions—such as how the no-fly zone would be enforced, what the rules of engagement would be, and whether there would be specific limits on the use of force—all of which went unanswered.[12] Further, Russia warned that the "inevitable humanitarian consequences of the excessive use of outside force in Libya will fall fair and square on the shoulders of those who might undertake such action."[13] Finally, India implied that it had been asked to vote on the resolution without first having adequate information for making an informed judgment, noting that Resolution 1973 authorized "far-reaching measures under Chapter VII of the United Nations Charter, with relatively little credible information on the situation on the ground in Libya."[14]

Each of the abstaining states raised concerns over issues that would prove to be relevant to the NATO-led intervention in Libya. Yet the intervention has been labeled by advocates of the responsibility to protect as an unequivocal success. Gareth Evans cites the passing of Resolutions 1970 and 1973 as proof of an appropriate incremental increase in the coerciveness of the international response. According to Evans, "That was a major breakthrough itself because you had the Responsibility to Protect principle expressly invoked and you had a set of really strong measures agreed on to apply that. And that [Resolution 1970] was a unanimous decision. However, of course, it didn't work, it didn't stop the violence."[15] James Pattison states that the moral permissibility of the intervention in Libya turned on the assessment that the situation was serious enough at the time of the intervention. He cites the number of individuals killed prior to the intervention as between one thousand and ten thousand. Pattison uses the death toll as evidence of the Qaddafi administration's "willingness to use force against its own people."[16] Simon Chesterman describes the case of Libya as unusually clear, citing the clarity of Qaddafi's intent.[17]

The narrative presented as the principal justification for the use of military force against a sovereign state did not go unchallenged. Alan Kuperman has conducted extensive research into the veracity of the generally accepted narrative that preceded the authorization of the use of military force. Kuperman's initial challenge to the narrative was published in the *Boston Globe,* less than one month into NATO's intervention.[18] Citing a Human Rights Watch (HRW) report, Kuperman argues that Qaddafi's battles with rebels provide evidence that he was not intentionally targeting civilians and that the claims of an imminent massacre were unfounded.[19] While investigating the impact of the conflict on the populations of three cities, including Misrata, where heavy fighting had taken place, HRW reported a total of 257 deaths and 949 wounded. Of the 1,206 physically affected by the fighting, 22 were women.[20] That amounts to only 3 percent of the total affected, hardly what would be expected from the use of indiscriminate force.

Kuperman does note that Libyan forces "did kill hundreds as they regained control of cities. . . . And strict laws of war may have been exceeded." However, "Khadafy's acts were a far cry from Rwanda, Darfur, Congo, Bosnia, and other killing fields. Libya's air force, prior to imposition of a UN-authorized no-fly zone, targeted rebel positions, not civilian concentrations. Despite ubiquitous cellphones equipped with cameras and video, there is no graphic evidence of deliberate massacre. Images abound of victims killed or wounded in crossfire—each one a tragedy—but that is urban warfare, not genocide."[21]

Academics were not the only ones who challenged the Libya narrative. Four days after the Security Council adopted Resolution 1973, on March 21, David Kirkpatrick of the *New York Times* reported, "And like the chiefs of the Libyan state news media, the rebels feel no loyalty to the truth in shaping their propaganda, claiming nonexistent battlefield victories, asserting they were still fighting in a key city days after it fell to Qaddafi forces, and making vastly inflated claims of his barbaric behavior."[22] Yet neither Kuperman's analysis nor Kirkpatrick's reporting succeeded in permeating the popular narrative.

Kuperman and Kirkpatrick were not alone. Vijay Prashad was not convinced that there would have been a massacre at Benghazi. He notes that there were well-trained troops among the rebel opposition. Some of the rebels had been trained and armed by the Libyan regime. Additionally, the rebels had already repelled a previous attempt by Qaddafi to take Benghazi. In a debate with Juan Cole, Prashad argued, "The real humanitarian intervention there would have been to have conducted the creation of a corridor, a momentary ceasefire, let people leave as war refugees, and then see what happens, because this is not strictly the case in Benghazi of unarmed civilians fighting against a state. It is precisely why General Ham of the African Command said that from a cockpit it is very hard to know whether you're defending civilians or whether you're assisting rebels."[23]

Legal scholar Mary Ellen O'Connell also disagrees with the categorization of the crisis in Libya as a one-sided imminent humanitarian emergency. She points to the rapidity with which events in Libya escalated. Though President Obama told Americans on March 29, 2011, that the use of force was to stop "violence on a horrific scale," O'Connell argues that the use of force stopped "the defeat of the rebels, allowing them to continue fighting. The United States has intervened in a civil war."[24] In doing so, NATO exceeded the mandate it was provided under Resolution 1973, likely crossing the line that stands between the lawful use of force and the unlawful use of aggressive force in violation of Article 2(4) of the UN Charter.

The arguments advanced by Kuperman, Prashad, and O'Connell raise serious questions over whether NATO abandoned its primary duty to protect all members of the civilian population in Libya because it was committed first and foremost to ensuring the overthrow of Qaddafi. The following critical analysis of the NATO-led intervention in Libya seeks to determine whether there is further evidence that ulterior motives for the intervention adversely affected NATO policy during and subsequent to the intervention, thus putting civilians at greater risk of serious injury or death.

NATO'S VIOLATIONS OF INTERNATIONAL HUMANITARIAN LAW

While carrying out its intervention in Libya, NATO not only potentially committed the crime of aggression by employing force for purposes beyond those that were authorized but also committed multiple violations of international humanitarian law (IHL) by (1) intentionally directing attacks against civilians and civilian objects; (2) attacking Libyan state television despite the special protection awarded to journalists; and (3) failing to come to the aid of refugees despite its knowledge of their distress and contact with them.

Intentionally Directing Attacks against Civilians and Civilian Objects

The principle of distinction is one of the most important rules of IHL because it requires that civilians not be intentionally targeted. When determining whether to launch an attack against a perceived threat, one must distinguish civilians from combatants. When there is doubt, individuals must be assumed to be civilians unless there is clear evidence that they are participants in the hostilities. This is well established in both customary and treaty law. Rule 1 of the International Committee of the Red Cross's study of customary IHL states, "The parties to the conflict must at all times distinguish between civilians and combatants. Attacks must not be directed against civilians."[25] Articles 50(1) of the "Protocol Additional to the Geneva Conventions of August 12, 1949, and Relating to the Protection of Victims of International Armed Conflicts (Protocol I), June 8, 1977," further establishes the principle of distinction. Article 50(1) states, "In case of doubt whether a person is a civilian, that person shall be considered to be a civilian."

Intentionally directing attacks against civilian objects is also prohibited by Additional Protocol I. Article 52 defines civilian objects as "all objects which are not military objectives."[26] Military objectives are "limited to those objects which by their nature, location, purpose or use make an effective contribution to military action and whose total or partial destruction, capture or neutralization, in the circumstances ruling at the time, offers a definite military advantage."[27] Further, when there is doubt as to "whether an object which is normally dedicated to civilian purposes, such as a place of worship, a house or other dwelling or a school, is being used to make an effective contribution to military action, it shall be presumed not to be so used."[28]

In 2012, HRW published a report titled, "Unacknowledged Deaths: Civilian Casualties in NATO's Air Campaign in Libya." HRW investigated eight sites that were bombed during the campaign. According to the report, "Extensive field investigations by Human Rights Watch uncovered no or only possible indications of Libyan government forces, such as military weaponry, hardware or personnel, or communications equipment, at seven of eight sites."[29] The eight NATO air strikes investigated resulted in the deaths of twenty-eight men, twenty women, and twenty-four children. Dozens of others were wounded in the strikes. At two of the strike sites, HRW did not find any evidence to suggest that they were valid military targets. In five of the remaining six sites, HRW "found only possible signs of a military presence, such as a military-style shirt or coat amidst the rubble."[30] At the remaining site, an individual believed to be a high-ranking member of the Libyan military may have been killed along with seven civilians.

To summarize, seventy-two people were killed and dozens injured in strikes on sites at which (1) there was no valid military target; (2) the only evidence that there was potential military presence was military-styled shirts or coats; and (3) there may have been one high-ranking member of Libya's military. Further, according to HRW's report, "Satellite imagery taken before the strikes at five of the sites revealed no signs of military presence that would have rendered the areas struck as lawful military targets."[31]

Not only did NATO commit IHL violations through attacking civilian objects and killing civilians, it also imported the use of "double-taps," a tactic commonly used in the Obama administration's targeted killing program. A double-tap involves the launching of an initial attack, which is then followed by a second attack. The first attack aims to kill the intended target(s), and the second attack aims to kill any survivors of the initial attack, along with those who converge on its scene. In its report, HRW documents the use of a double-tap in a small rural village about one hundred miles east of Tripoli. The two attacks launched by NATO resulted in thirty-four deaths and an additional thirty wounded. According to the report, "NATO bombs hit two family compounds, one of them hosting dozens of displaced persons. This attack was followed by another bomb that struck outside one of the compounds as neighbors and relatives were retrieving the wounded and dead."[32] In response to HRW's investigation, NATO claimed the compounds attacked were a staging base for Qaddafi forces. Evidence in support of this claim has not been provided. The only evidence HRW found of any possible military presence at the scene of the attacks was a single military-style shirt.

The *New York Times* also documented the employment of double-taps. According to the *New York Times,* in an April 7 attack NATO mistakenly attacked a rebel convoy. Following the initial attacks on the convoy, the "attack continued as civilians, including ambulance crews, tried to converge on the craters and flames to aid the wounded. Three shepherds were among them."[33] Double-tap strikes were reported several times by survivors of other distinct attacks and were also cited as a reason why some civilians refrained from aiding wounded individuals at strike sites.

Double-taps are clear violations of IHL because they (1) intentionally target wounded individuals and (2) intentionally target first responders and rescuers. The Convention (I) for the Amelioration of the Condition of the Wounded and Sick in Armed Forces in the Field requires that individuals "placed hors de combat by sickness, wounds, detention, or any other cause, shall in all circumstances be treated humanely."[34] Launching a second attack against wounded individuals cannot satisfy this obligation. Attacks on rescuers and first responders also fail to distinguish between civilians and combatants. Further, such attacks undermine the special status rescuers are awarded under IHL.

Despite all of the evidence that suggests NATO violated IHL on multiple occasions, it has refused to investigate the allegations and, where appropriate, hold those responsible accountable. Fred Abrahams, an investigator with HRW and principal author of the report on Libya, stated, "We have questions that NATO has not yet answered, and we're calling for prompt, credible and thorough investigations to understand why these 72 civilians died. And until now, NATO has taken a position of denial. They refuse to acknowledge that civilians died. They refuse to give information about how they died. And they refuse to investigate. And it's this lack of transparency that's deeply troubling.... It's crystal clear that civilians died in NATO strikes. But this whole campaign is shrouded by an atmosphere of impunity."[35]

South Africa, holder of the Security Council presidency for the month of January 2012, called for an investigation into human rights abuses during NATO's intervention in Libya. Ambassador Baso Sangqu stated, "There must be investigations of human rights abuses in Libya across the board: by Gadhafi regime supporters, by the rebels, by NATO, anybody who was involved in that conflict as mandated by the resolution 1973 and 1970 should be held accountable especially those that were mandated."[36] Failure to investigate credible allegations of IHL violations that resulted in civilian casualties is itself a violation of international law.

Intentional Targeting of Journalists

On July 30, NATO intentionally attacked Libyan state television facilities, killing three media workers and injuring twenty-one others. In a statement aimed at justifying an act that could constitute a war crime, NATO said, "The strike, performed by NATO fighter aircraft using state-of-the art precision guided munitions, was conducted in accordance with the UN Security Council Resolution 1973, with the intent of degrading Qadhafi's use of satellite television as a means to intimidate the Libyan people and incite acts of violence against them. Our intervention was necessary as TV was being used as an integral component of the regime apparatus designed to systematically oppress and threaten civilians and to incite attacks against them. In light of our mandate to protect civilian lives, we had to act."[37]

NATO's defense of its attack against the civilian infrastructure was based on the belief that state propaganda justified launching air strikes against a civilian-populated facility in a civilian-populated area. Thus NATO launched an attack with full knowledge that the only possible victims from the attack would be civilian. The director-general of UNESCO, Irina Bokova, referred to the attack on Libyan state broadcasting facilities as unacceptable, stating, "I deplore the NATO strike on Al-Jamahiriya and its installations. Media outlets should not be targeted in military actions. U.N. Security Council Resolution 1738 (2006) condemns acts of violence against journalists and media personnel in conflict situations."[38] Bokova continued, "The NATO strike is also contrary to the principles of the Geneva Conventions that establish the civilian status of journalists in times of war even when they engage in propaganda."[39]

Robin Geiss, an International Committee of the Red Cross legal expert, agrees with Bokova's assessment of the civilian status of journalists under the Geneva Conventions, which would make attacks on journalists violations of the laws of war. In a 2010 interview, Geiss was asked what protection media professionals have under IHL. Geiss responded, "Article 79 of Additional Protocol I provides that journalists are entitled to all rights and protections granted to civilians in international armed conflicts. . . . Thus, in order to perceive the full scope of protection granted to journalists under humanitarian law one simply has to substitute the word 'civilian' as it is used throughout the Geneva Conventions and their Additional Protocols with the word 'journalist.'"[40] Geiss was then asked whether attacks against journalists amount to war crimes. According to Geiss, "In as much as they are civilians, journalists are protected under international humanitarian law against direct attacks unless and for such time as they take a direct part in hostilities. Violations of this rule constitute a grave breach of the Geneva Conventions and Additional Protocol I. What is more, intentionally directing an attack against a civilian—whether in an international or in a non-international armed conflict—also amounts to a war crime under the Rome Statute of the International Criminal Court."[41]

UNSC Resolution 1738 condemns "intentional attacks against journalists, media professionals and associated personnel, as such, in situations of armed conflict, and calls upon all parties to put an end to such practices"; recalls that "journalists, media professionals and associated personnel engaged in dangerous professional missions in areas of armed conflict shall be considered as civilians and shall be respected and protected as such, provided that they take no action adversely affecting their status as civilians"; and notes that "media equipment and installations constitute civilian objects, and in this respect shall not be the object of attack or of reprisals, unless they are military objectives."[42]

While Security Council Resolution 1738 repeatedly calls upon states to recognize the civilian status of journalists and, therefore, to make every effort to protect them in situations of armed conflict under their IHL obligations, the resolution also condemns "all incitements to violence against civilians in situations of armed conflict" and indicates the willingness of the Council, "when authorizing missions, to consider, where appropriate, steps in response to media broadcast inciting genocide, crimes against humanity and serious violations of international humanitarian law."[43]

NATO failed to bring its concerns about Libyan state television to the Security Council prior to launching the air strikes that killed or injured two dozen journalists and media workers. Therefore, NATO decided unilaterally what steps would be taken in response to what NATO alleged to be Libyan state television's active role as an inciter of violence. NATO was authorized by Security Council Resolution 1973 to take all necessary measures to "protect civilians and civilian-populated areas under threat of attack in the Libyan Arab Jamahiriya." To stretch its mandate to include bombing Libyan state television facilities, a wholly civilian structure, NATO had to demonstrate when and why the civilian structure became a legitimate military target. Failure to do so could make the attack a war crime.

A week after the attack, Joel Simon, the executive director of the Committee to Protect Journalists, wrote NATO a letter of inquiry, seeking an explanation for the attack. Noting NATO's initial justification for the attack, Simon wrote, "Such attacks can only be justified under International Humanitarian Law if the media facility is being used for military purposes or to incite violence against the civilian population. For this reason, we believe it is essential for NATO to provide a more detailed explanation as to the basis for the attack on Libyan broadcast facilities."[44]

Seeking the specific evidence needed to justify NATO's attack, Simon asked NATO to respond to the following: (1) Has NATO carried out systematic monitoring of Libyan state television; (2) Are there specific broadcasts or programs that were intended to incite violence against civilians; (3) Can NATO describe the content of these programs and note precisely when they were aired; (4) Have any broadcasts or programs been linked to actual, specific violence carried out against the civilian population; and (5) Since the initial strike failed to achieve its intention of knocking Libyan state television off the air, are further strikes being considered, including attacks on broadcast facilities?

Regarding the first question, NATO responded, "Extensive monitoring of Libyan TV broadcasting was a key element that led to this decision. In the assessment of the operational commander, several Gaddafi speeches broadcast through the targeted installation clearly called for the conduct of acts of violence against the population in Libya."[45] Clearly, NATO failed to provide any information in response to the substantial questions it was asked.

Purposeful Neglect of Refugees

Article 3(2) of the Convention (II) for the Amelioration of the Condition of Wounded, Sick and Shipwrecked Members of Armed Forces at Sea states, "The wounded, sick and shipwrecked shall be collected and cared for."[46] Therefore, under the Geneva Conventions, states have an affirmative obligation to rescue and care for individuals, including refugees. The UN High Commissioner for Refugees stated that 2011 was the "deadliest year" in the Mediterranean since it had begun keeping such statistics in 2006. It estimated that more than 1,500 migrants had died at sea while attempting to flee the conflict in Libya. According to the authors of the report "Forensic Oceanography: Left-to-Die Boat Case," "The loss of lives at sea in 2011 occurred despite the significant naval and aerial presence in the area due to the military intervention in Libya launched by an international coalition of States and NATO under the United Nations Security Council Resolution 1973."[47] The "left-to-die" case is significant because it provides evidence that NATO may have purposefully neglected refugees in violation of its treaty obligations under the Geneva Conventions, as well as its obligations under Resolution 1973.

The "Forensic Oceanography" report summarizes the "left-to-die" case as follows:

> 72 migrants fleeing Tripoli by boat on the early morning of March 27 2011 ran out of fuel and were left to drift for 14 days until they landed back on the Libyan coast. With no water or food on-board, only nine of the migrants survived. In several interviews, these survivors recounted the various points of contacts they had with the external world during this ordeal. This included describing the aircraft that flew over them, the distress call they sent out via satellite telephone and their visual sightings of a military helicopter which provided a few packets of biscuits and bottles of water and a military ship

which failed to provide any assistance whatsoever. The events, as recounted by these survivors, appeared to constitute a severe violation of the legal obligation to provide assistance to any person in distress at sea, an obligation sanctioned by several international conventions.[48]

The "Forensic Oceanography" report estimates that throughout the two weeks that the "left-to-die" boat was adrift at least thirty-eight NATO naval assets had been deployed at one point or another. Additional aerial assets were also deployed during this time. The authors of the report found that (1) NATO was informed of the migrants' distress call; (2) NATO was provided with the migrants' location on at least two occasions; and (3) NATO, despite its denials, probably had multiple encounters with the migrants, including two points of contact from military helicopters and one from a military ship. The report concludes, "Despite all this, none of these actors intervened in a way that could have averted the tragic fate of the people on the boat."[49]

Though Libya shares responsibility for the deaths that occurred at sea because the deaths occurred within Libya's search-and-rescue zone, NATO's bombing campaign created a surge in persons seeking refuge. Further, under Resolution 1973, NATO was mandated with the task of taking all necessary measures for the protection of Libya's civilian population. In a separate report presented to the Council of Europe's Committee on Migration, Refugees and Displaced Persons, Rapporteur Tineke Strik described a "catalog of failures."[50] Strik wrote that

> NATO failed to react to the distress calls, even though there were military vessels under its control in the boat's vicinity when the distress call was sent (including the *Mendez Núñez* which was estimated to have been 11 miles away although this distance is disputed by Spain). The flag States of vessels close to the boat also failed to rescue the people in distress.... Perhaps of most concern in this case is the alleged failure of the helicopter and the naval vessel to go to the aid of the boat in distress, regardless of whether these were under national command or the command of NATO.[51]

NATO COMPLICITY IN CRIMES COMMITTED BY THE REBELS

One week into the intervention, David Zucchino reported that the rebels had begun utilizing the same tactics they decried. Zucchino wrote, "Rebel forces are detaining anyone suspected of serving or assisting the Kadafi regime, locking them up in the same prisons once used to detain and torture Kadafi's opponents."[52] Zucchino also quoted Abdelhafed Ghoga, an opposition spokesperson, as saying that suspected Qaddafi loyalists who did not surrender would face revolutionary "justice."[53]

The rebels' previous commission of violations of IHL did not stop NATO members from arming, training, and militarily supporting the rebels. In the middle of March 2011, President Obama signed an intelligence finding that authorized covert aid to the rebels. At the time of Resolution 1970's adoption, the United States was aware that Egypt was already arming the rebels. By the beginning of April, the British were aiding the rebels in the establishment of a command structure and defense ministry. In mid-April, France transferred weapons to the rebels, using Qatar as a middleman. By May, France began "air-dropping weapons to opposition forces in western Libya, who were being trained by operatives from France, Italy, and the United Kingdom."[54]

In May 2011, the *Guardian* published a report that provides data on NATO's direct involvement in Libya's civil war on behalf of the rebels during the first two months of the intervention. The report states that NATO hit three thousand targets while flying over fourteen thousand sorties in twelve different civilian-populated cities.[55] Further, NATO members openly spoke of their support for the rebels and their commitment to seeing Qaddafi overthrown. In March, Secretary of State Clinton proclaimed, "Khadafy has lost the legitimacy to lead, so we believe he must go. We're working with the international community to try to achieve that outcome."[56] In August, President Sarkozy stated, "We are prepared to continue military operations as long as our Libyan friends need them. So long as there are pockets of resistance we will be at your side."[57] Also in August, Prime Minister Cameron said, "His regime is falling apart and is in full retreat. Gaddafi must stop fighting, without conditions, and clearly show that he has given up any claim to control Libya. Our task now is to do all we can to support the will of the Libyan people which is for an effective transition to a free, democratic and inclusive Libya."[58]

In the end, the rebels overthrew Qaddafi with NATO's support. NATO's apparent indifference to the crimes committed by the rebels during the conflict, including Qaddafi's summary execution, continued in its immediate aftermath. HRW paints a clear picture of rampant lawlessness. Four days after Qaddafi was killed, HRW issued a press release titled "Libya: Apparent Execution of 53 Gaddafi Supporters." According to Peter Bouckaert, emergencies director at HRW, "We found 53 decomposing bodies, apparently Gaddafi supporters, at an abandoned hotel in Sirte, and some had their hands bound behind their backs when they were shot."[59] Daniel Williams, a senior HRW researcher, described attacks on Qaddafi loyalists as "part of a vast revenge killing spree." According to Williams, "Members of these militias have engaged in torture, pursued suspected enemies far and wide, detained them and shot them in detention."[60]

The town of Tawergha, a town that had been populated mainly by citizens loyal to Qaddafi, was abandoned by its residents after the fall of Tripoli. On October 30, 2011, HRW reported that none of the thirty thousand residents remained and that militias from Misrata were terrorizing the displaced persons. HRW interviews with displaced persons revealed "credible accounts of some Misrata militias shooting unarmed Tawerghans, and of arbitrary arrests and beatings of Tawerghan detainees, in a few cases leading to death."[61]

In January 2012, Doctors without Borders (MSF) halted its work at Misrata detention centers because its medical staff were being brought patients who had been tortured. The medical staff was being asked to treat detainees who had been tortured so that they would be able to hold up under further abuse. "Patients were brought to us in the middle of interrogation for medical care, in order to make them fit for more interrogation," MSF general director Christopher Stokes said in a statement. "This is unacceptable. Our role is to provide medical care to war casualties and sick detainees, not to repeatedly treat the same patients between torture sessions."[62]

Amnesty International reported on February 16, 2012, that African migrants had been targeted by attacks, forcibly displacing entire communities. According to Donatella Rovera, senior crisis response adviser at Amnesty International, "Militias in Libya are largely out of control and the blanket impunity they enjoy only encourages further abuses and perpetuates instability and insecurity."[63] On February 21, 2012, HRW reported that villages were being razed and that displaced persons were being barred from returning to their homes. According to Bouckaert, "Tomina and Kararim are ghost towns because Misrata officials are blocking thousands of people who fled from returning home. Armed groups from Misrata are openly looting and destroying their homes, as they have been doing for months in Tawergha."[64]

The International Commission of Inquiry on Libya summarized the crimes committed by the rebels in its March 2012 report to the Human Rights Council. The commission concluded that the rebels "committed serious violations, including war crimes and breaches of human rights law, the latter continuing at the time of the present report."[65] Specifically, during the civil war, the commission found that the rebels committed "acts of extrajudicial executions of those perceived to be loyalists, suspected merce-naries and captured Qadhafi soldiers, particularly when towns first came under control of *thuwar* [anti-Qaddafi forces]."[66] Further, the commission stated that allegations of violations of IHL and human rights law were not being treated equally. The commission concluded, "Failure to apply criminal law to crimes committed by *thuwar* during and after the end of the conflict creates an environment of impunity and leaves the victims of *thuwar* viola-tions without protection of the law, justice and redress."[67]

The UN Security Council authorized the NATO-led intervention in Libya under Resolution 1973 because of the reports that Qaddafi's forces were indis-criminately attacking civilian-populated areas and intentionally targeting civilians. Though the narrative used to gain support for Resolution 1970 and to deter China and Russia from vetoing Resolution 1973 has been challenged, even if the narrative were accurate it would not justify the ways in which NATO simultaneously exceeded its mandate and failed to fulfill it. Because NATO members had the self-interested objective of overthrowing the Qaddafi regime, NATO likely committed the crime of aggression against Libya and violated IHL while doing so. Further, NATO materially sup-ported the rebels with the knowledge that the rebels were committing their own IHL violations. Rather than protect civilians and civilian-populated areas, NATO's intervention put civilians at greater risk. If the United Nations is truly committed to civilian protection, it must not allow states to use the organization to legitimize actions carried out on behalf of their own interests, causing more harm than good.

NOTES

1. UN Security Council, "Provisional Record of the 6490th Meeting," S/PV.6490, February 25, 2011, 2, www.securitycouncilreport.org/atf/cf/%7B65BFCF9B-6D27–4E9C-8CD3-CF6E4FF96FF9%7D/Libya%20S%20PV%206490.pdf.

2. Ibid., 4.

3. Ibid.

4. UN Security Council Resolution 1970, S/RES/1970, February 26, 2011, 1, www.securitycouncilreport.org/atf/cf/%7B65BFCF9B-6D27–4E9C-8CD3-CF6E4FF96FF9%7D/Libya%20S%20RES%201970.pdf.

5. Ibid., 1–2.

6. UN Security Council, "Provisional Record of the 6491st Meeting," S/PV.6491, February 26, 2011, 2, www.securitycouncilreport.org/atf/cf/%7B65BFCF9B-6D27–4E9C-8CD3-CF6E4FF96FF9%7D/Libya%20S%20PV%206491.pdf.

7. Ibid., 3.

8. Ibid., 5.

9. Ibid., 4.

10. UN Security Council, "Provisional Record of the 6498th Meeting," S/PV.6498, March 17, 2011, 2, www.securitycouncilreport.org/atf/cf/%7B65BFCF9B-6D27–4E9C-8CD3-CF6E4FF96FF9%7D/Libya%20S%20PV%206498.pdf.

11. UN Security Council Resolution 1973 (2011), S/RES/1973, March 17, 2011, 3, www.securitycouncilreport.org/atf/cf/%7B65BFCF9B-6D27–4E9C-8CD3-CF6E4FF96FF9%7D/Libya%20S%20RES%201973.pdf.

12. UN Security Council, "Provisional Record of the 6498th Meeting," S/PV.6498.

13. Ibid., 8.

14. Ibid., 6.

15. Nayan Chanda, "Former Foreign Minister Gareth Evans: Responsibility to Protect," *YaleGlobal Online*, April 15, 2011, http://yaleglobal.yale.edu/content/gareth-evans-responsibility-protect-transcript.

16. James Pattison, "The Ethics of Humanitarian Intervention in Libya," *Ethics and International Affairs* 25, no. 3 (2011): 272.

17. Simon Chesterman, "'Leading from Behind': The Responsibility to Protect, the Obama Doctrine, and Humanitarian Intervention after Libya," *Ethics and International Affairs* 25, no. 3 (2011): 279–85.

18. Alan Kuperman, "False Pretense for War in Libya?," *Boston Globe*, April 14, 2011.

19. Ibid.

20. Alan Kuperman, "A Model Humanitarian Intervention? Reassessing NATO's Libya Campaign," *International Security* 38, no. 1 (2013): 105–36.

21. Kuperman, "False Pretense."

22. David Kirkpatrick, "Hopes for a Qaddafi Exit, and Worries of What Comes Next," *New York Times*, March 22, 2011.

23. Democracy Now, "A Debate on U.S. Military Intervention in Libya: Juan Cole v. Vijay Prashad," *Democracy Now*, March 29, 2011, www.democracynow.org/2011/3/29/a_debate_on_us_military_intervention.

24. Mary Ellen O'Connell, "What Is the Goal?," *America: The National Catholic Review*, April 18, 2011, http://americamagazine.org/issue/773/100/what-goal.

25. International Committee of the Red Cross, "Protocol Additional to the Geneva Conventions of 12 August 1949, and relating to the Protection of Victims of International Armed Conflicts (Protocol I), 8 June 1977," https://www.icrc.org/ihl/INTRO/470.

26. Ibid., Art. 52, no. 1.

27. Ibid., Art. 52, no. 2.

28. Ibid., Art. 52, no. 3.

29. Human Rights Watch (hereafter HRW), "Unacknowledged Deaths: Civilian Casualties in NATO's Air Campaign in Libya," 2012, 4–6, https://www.hrw.org/report/2012/05/13/unacknowledged-deaths/civilian-casualties-natos-air-campaign-libya.

30. Ibid., 10.

31. Ibid.

32. Ibid., 12.

33. C. J. Chivers and Eric Schmitt, "In Strikes on Libya by NATO, an Unspoken Civilian Toll," *New York Times*, December 17, 2011.

34. International Committee of the Red Cross, "Convention (I) for the Amelioration of the Condition of the Wounded and Sick in Armed Forces in the Field. Geneva, August 12, 1949," https://www.icrc.org/ihl.nsf/7c4d08d9b287a421 41256739003e636b/fe20c3d903ce27e3c1256410004a92f3.

35. HRW, "NATO: Investigate Civilian Deaths in Libya," press release, May 14, 2012, https://www.hrw.org/news/2012/05/14/nato-investigate-civilian-deaths-libya.

36. "Incoming U.N. Diplomat Calls for Libya NATO Investigation," *USA Today*, January 4, 2012.

37. Roland Lavoie, "NATO Strikes Libyan State TV Satellite Facility: Statement by the Spokesperson for NATO Operation Unified Protector, Colonel Roland Lavoie, Regarding Air Strike in Tripoli," North Atlantic Treaty Organization, July 30, 2011, www.nato.int/cps/en/natolive/news_76776.htm.

38. UNESCO, "Director-General Deplores NATO Strike on Libyan State Television Facilities," UNESCO press release, August 8, 2011, www.unesco.org/new/en /no_cache/unesco/themes/pcpd/dynamic-content-single-view/news/director_ general_deplores_nato_strike_on_libyan_state_television_facilities/#.VtEjGza4mqQ.

39. Ibid.

40. Robin Geiss, "How Does International Humanitarian Law Protect Journalists in Armed-Conflict Situations?," interview, International Committee of the Red Cross, July 27, 2010, https://www.icrc.org/eng/resources/documents/interview /protection-journalists-interview-270710.htm.

41. Ibid.

42. UN Security Council Resolution 1738 (2006), S/RES/1738, December 23, 2006, www.securitycouncilreport.org/atf/cf/%7B65BFCF9B-6D27-4E9C-8CD3-CF6E4FF96FF9%7D/Civilians%20SRES1738.pdf.

43. Ibid.

44. Joel Simon, executive director, Committee to Protect Journalists, to Secretary General Anders Fogh Rasmussen, NATO Headquarters, August 4, 2011, https://cpj.org/blog/Libya%20letter%208%204%2011%20final%20PDF.pdf.

45. Martin Howard, assistant secretary-general for operations, NATO, to Joel Simon, executive director, Committee to Protect Journalists, August 12, 2011, https://cpj.org/8–12–11%20Nato%20Letter.pdf.

46. International Committee of the Red Cross, "Convention (II) for the Amelioration of the Condition of Wounded, Sick and Shipwrecked Members of Armed Forces at Sea. Geneva, August 12, 1949," https://www.icrc.org/applic/ihl/ihl.nsf/385ec082b509e76c41256739003e636d/44072487ec4c2131c125641e004a9977?openDocument.

47. Charles Heller, Lorenzo Pezzani, and Situ Studio, "Report on the Left-to-Die Boat," Forensic Oceanography project, 2012, https://www.fidh.org/IMG/pdf/fo-report.pdf.

48. Ibid.

49. Ibid.

50. Tineke Strik, "Lives Lost in the Mediterranean Sea: Who Is Responsible?," Committee on Refugees and Displaced Persons, April 5, 2012, http://assembly.coe.int/CommitteeDocs/2012/20120329_mig_RPT.EN.pdf.

51. Ibid.

52. David Zucchino, "Libyan Rebels Appear to Take Leaf from Kadafi's Playbook," Los Angeles Times, March 24, 2011.

53. Ibid.

54. Kuperman, "Model Humanitarian Intervention?"

55. "NATO Operations in Libya: Data Journalism Breaks Down Which Country Does What," Libya Datablog, Guardian, May 22, 2011, www.theguardian.com/news/datablog/2011/may/22/nato-libya-data-journalism-operations-country.

56. "Diplomats in London Agree Gadhafi Must Go," NPR, March 29, 2011, www.npr.org/2011/03/29/134945359/libyan-rebels-shelled-outside-gadhafis-hometown.

57. Kareem Fahim, "Libya Rebels Fight Loyalists, and Put Bounty on Qaddafi," New York Times, August 24, 2011.

58. Andrew Sparrow, "Libya: Cameron Urges Gaddafi to Give Up Fight Immediately," Guardian, August 22, 2011.

59. HRW, "Libya: Apparent Execution of 53 Gaddafi Supporters," press release, October 24, 2011, https://www.hrw.org/news/2011/10/24/libya-apparent-execution-53-gaddafi-supporters.

60. Daniel Williams, "The Murder Brigades of Misrata," HRW, October 28, 2011, https://www.hrw.org/news/2011/10/28/murder-brigades-misrata.

61. HRW, "Libya: Militias Terrorizing Residents of 'Loyalist' Town," October 30, 2011, https://www.hrw.org/news/2011/10/30/libya-militias-terrorizing-residents-loyalist-town.

62. Ian Black, "Libyan Militias Accused of Torture," Guardian, January 26, 2012.

63. Amnesty International, "Libya: 'Out of Control' Militias Commit Widespread Abuses, a Year On from Uprising," February 15, 2012, https://www.amnesty.org/en/latest/news/2012/02/libya-out-control-militias-commit-widespread-abuses-year-uprising/.

64. HRW, "Libya: Displaced People Barred from Homes," February 21, 2012, https://www.hrw.org/news/2012/02/21/libya-displaced-people-barred-homes.

65. International Commission of Inquiry on Libya, "Report of the International Commission of Inquiry on Libya," March 2, 2012, 2, www.ohchr.org/Documents /HRBodies/HRCouncil/RegularSession/Session19/A.HRC.19.68.pdf.

66. Ibid., 197.

67. Ibid., 195.

TEN

Peacekeeping and the Arab World

INDIA'S RISE AND ITS IMPACT ON
UN MISSIONS IN SUDAN

Zachariah Mampilly

THE END OF THE SECOND WORLD WAR ushered in momentous changes across the globe. Amid the ashes, in 1945, the United Nations was created to help turn a page and foster a new era of global peace. Just two years later, it confronted its first major challenge when British-ruled India was partitioned in an orgy of bloodshed. A year later, the UN was again at the forefront as Israel was carved out of British-ruled Palestine, triggering a regional war with four Arab states. In response to both crises, the UN began developing a peacekeeping capacity, seeking to play a productive role in these ongoing conflicts. By 1956, when Israel invaded Egypt with the support of the British and French, in what became known as the Suez Crisis or the Tripartite Aggression, Indian troops participated in the first armed peacekeeping mission organized by the international body. From its inception then, UN peacekeeping has been intertwined with the fates of the South Asian and Arab worlds.

This essay considers Indian involvement in UN peacekeeping in the Arab world, with a focus on the country's involvement in missions in Sudan and South Sudan. Participation in peacekeeping has always been shaped by broader geopolitical trends, most prominently the division between those countries that provide troops to staff missions and those that define the mandate and pay the bills. South Asian countries continue to occupy the top three spots on lists of troop-contributing countries (TCCs) as they have for decades. Meanwhile, the ability to define the mandate of UN missions has long been controlled by England, France, and the United States, the so-called P3. As India seeks a greater role on the global stage, it has destabilized this traditional binary that has defined UN peacekeeping since its inception.

India's involvement with peacekeeping in the Arab world and its peripheries has a long history. By the second half of the nineteenth century, Indians were deployed as part of the British Royal Army to quell nativist uprisings throughout the Indian Ocean rim. Indian soldiers frequently served as part of various "pacification" campaigns, service that garnered high praise from Winston Churchill during his term as undersecretary of state for the colonies. By many accounts, the involvement of Indian troops was not supplemental but "at the very centre of the defence system of the British Empire."[1]

Indian troops first arrived in Sudan in September 1940 as part of Britain's East Africa campaign against Italian-controlled Eritrea and Ethiopia. The numerically superior Italians threatened Egyptian supply routes that ran through Sudan from the Red Sea. The Indian Fifth Infantry Division, under the command of Major-General Lewis Heath, was sent to reinforce a British force under pressure from attacks by Italian troops in Eritrea. In December, the Indian Fourth Infantry Division joined the fray. During the Battle of Keren in early 1941, the combined force of British, Indian, and French troops defeated the Italians, taking control of the capital Asmara and the key Red Sea port of Massawa. The two Indian divisions suffered great losses with approximately four thousand casualties, of which around four hundred lost their lives. But Allied forces emerged victorious in a battle considered a key turning point in the larger war.

Richhpal Ram, a forty-one-year-old soldier from Haryana affiliated with the Rajputana Rifles, was a subahdar with the Fourth Division during the campaign. During the Battle of Keren, Ram was a subcommander of an Indian company, which, like most such companies, was under the ultimate control of a British officer. On February 7, 1941, with his commanding officer wounded, Ram assumed command of the company, leading thirty troops to achieve their objective and then fighting off a series of counterattacks through the night. A few days later, while Ram was again leading the company, his right foot was blown off. According to the official citation for the Victoria Cross, the British Empire's highest military award offered for bravery in battle, after losing his foot Ram suffered further wounds but continued to encourage his men to fight. "We'll capture the objective," were his final words, according to the declaration by King George VI in his posthumous awarding of the medal to Ram.[2]

More than seventy years later, in December 2013, some two thousand rebel soldiers ransacked a base in Jonglei State, South Sudan. Two soldiers from the

Indian Battalion serving with the UN Mission in South Sudan (UNMISS) were killed. Subahdar Kanwar Pal Singh, deployed with the Army Medical Corps, was a forty-six-year-old father of two who hailed from Gurgaon. Subahdar Dharmesh Sangwan of 2 Rajputana Rifles, a thirty-four-year-old father of two from Haryana, was a successful rower who had earned India a silver medal at the 2006 Asian Games. At the time, the temporary base in Akobo hosted a small contingent of forty-three Indian soldiers working alongside six UN political officers and twelve civilian staff. Thirty civilians fleeing the fighting fled to the base. Reports suggest that rebels fighting with a Lou Nuer ethnic militia demanded that the civilians be handed over, a request denied by the Indian soldiers. The militia men then opened fire.[3]

Singh and Sangwan were cremated with state honors amid much fanfare and praise for their "martyrdom."[4] But in Singh's case the cremation took place only after family members held a demonstration (*rasta roko*) to force the government to return the body. As one demonstrator told a reporter: "Many soldiers of the Indian army belong to our village and we have never stopped our sons from joining the service. But this attitude is shocking. The authorities have neither acknowledged the death, nor have they made any efforts to bring back the martyr."[5] The deaths of Singh and Sangwan were not the only incidents of violence against Indian peacekeepers in South Sudan. In April 2013, five soldiers, including a lieutenant colonel, were killed alongside seven civilians during an attack on a convoy in Jonglei State.

Two different governments operating in two different eras sent Indian soldiers to Sudan in pursuit of a broader geopolitical agenda. In both, Indian soldiers paid the ultimate price, receiving little more than ceremonial recompense. Why do Indian troops keep dying in the broader Arab world for often murky and unproductive reasons?

India has long had multiple motivations for its involvement in peacekeeping. During the Cold War, its primary concern was to bolster the UN as a neutral institution through which the countries of the Third World could articulate claims to equity within the international system. In addition, involvement in peacekeeping missions was seen as a means both to improve the capacity of the Indian military and to secure lucrative mission reimbursements. More recently, the country has used peacekeeping to bolster its claim for a seat on the UN Security Council. By exploring this history, this chapter seeks to make sense of the current Indian involvement in the missions in South Sudan, where Indian troops make up the largest contributor.

By the nineteenth century, England had emerged as the global hegemon, underwriting and sustaining the burgeoning international order. Though other European states vied for supremacy, it was the British Empire, and its economic and political institutions, that dominated the global system. Threats to British hegemony, which began to pick up steam during the latter half of the century, were treated as threats to global order itself. To quell these uprisings, England cobbled together various multiethnic military forces composed of disparate recruits from the colonies. While England underwrote the costs and provided officers, the rank-and-file troops were drawn from and deployed throughout the Afro-Asian world in a bid to preserve British hegemony and the global order it sought to entrench.

By the early part of the twentieth century, Indian troops represented a significant share of the British Royal Army, deployed to suppress nativist challenges to British rule from Kenya in the west to Malaya in the east. With the advent of the world wars, recruitment of Indian soldiers into the British-controlled Indian Army accelerated, and various Indian divisions were deployed throughout multiple theaters in service of the Allied powers. More than one million Indian soldiers served under British command in the two world wars, representing the largest volunteer army in history.

The successor states to undivided India remain at the forefront of global peacekeeping operations and have ranked among the top three contributors to UN missions for decades. Yet this lineage that ties Indian, Bangladeshi, or Pakistani peacekeeping to European colonial projects is not one that the postindependence governments were enthusiastic to embrace. Much like the African soldiers who served bravely within the French army during World War II only to face ambivalence upon their return home, Indian troops were stained by the colonial connection, and independent South Asian governments ignored their legacy, even as European colonial powers sought to deny them the rightful benefits from their service.

But Britain's reliance on South Asian troops also left each country with large volunteer armies and a strong military tradition posing a dilemma for the new regimes. While some called for the demilitarization of India, including Martin Luther King Jr. during his 1959 visit to the country, the emergence of UN peacekeeping provided an opportunity for independent governments to continue their overseas military engagements, dressed in a new noble garb.

India's first prime minister, Jawaharlal Nehru, was a staunch believer in the potential of the UN to serve as a space through which the Afro-Asian nations could achieve equity on the global stage. Influenced by liberal internationalism, Nehru believed in strengthening the UN system as a means to achieve world peace. By contributing troops to UN peace operations, Nehru sought to demonstrate India's active support for the emerging global body.

Nehru's involvement with the Nonaligned Movement (NAM) provided ideological coherency to this strategy. Historically, 80 percent of all personnel participating in UN missions come from NAM countries, providing the organization a significant voice on peacekeeping matters.[6] India through NAM articulated a doctrine that called for support for UN peacekeeping while also insisting on respect for state sovereignty, the independence and territorial integrity of states, peaceful settlement of disputes, and a last resort to the use of force. Such support for peacekeeping operations, manifested through troop contributions, bolstered India's claim to nonalignment and its positioning of the UN as a politically neutral space for the countries of the Third World.

By 2009, over 100,000 Indians had served in forty-three operations around the world, with 130 having lost their lives during their deployments abroad, securing for the country the tragic position atop the list of countries that have lost personnel on UN missions.[7] Currently, India is the third-largest contributor of troops, with over eight thousand personnel deployed operating in eight of the sixteen UN peacekeeping operations globally, trailing only Pakistan and Bangladesh in total numbers.[8] This figure represents almost 10 percent of all personnel in UN missions and is more than double the contributions of China and Brazil combined, two other rising powers that have sought to leverage their involvement in UN missions. India's total number of troops represents more than double the amount of peacekeepers deployed by the five permanent members of the Security Council.[9]

The country touts its long-standing record of contributing to various missions across Africa and the Arab world, including in Egypt, Somalia, Mozambique, Angola, Sierra Leone, and more recently, Democratic Republic of Congo (hereafter, Congo), Sudan, and South Sudan. Indeed, India's first major involvement in a complex peacekeeping operation was as part of the UN Operation in Congo from 1960 to 1964. The Congo intervention was unique in that it was the first UN operation in a domestic conflict as opposed to the interstate wars that defined peacekeeping efforts throughout most of the Cold War. India deployed a large contingent of soldiers, including an air force bomber detachment.[10] The mission took heavy casualties and India lost thirty-nine men.

As part of its push to build stronger ties with both African and Arab countries over the past decade India has redoubled its commitment to peacekeeping efforts in both regions. Thus the bulk of Indian troops are currently concentrated in South Sudan (2,047) and Congo (4,001). In both cases, India is the largest troop contributor. By many accounts, the capacity of Indian military contingents makes them central to both of these ongoing peacekeeping efforts.

Positions abroad are highly sought after by Indian officers and troops. According to Indian officers I interviewed in Congo in 2012, positions in peacekeeping missions provide an opportunity to gain field experience that is highly valued upon their return to India. Every year, approximately fifteen thousand troops are selected for a first interview, with five thousand eventually deployed to various missions following a "preinduction training" at the Centre for United Nations Peacekeeping in New Delhi. Most troops have little awareness of the specific country to which they will be deployed. They receive a series of briefings prior to departure where they learn the background of the specific mission, the activities of Indian troops, and a general history of the country. But the focus is primarily operational and offers little insight into the culture of local communities.

Once the Indian troops are in country, life is often difficult for them. They work six days a week and are prohibited from socializing with the local population because of Department of Peacekeeping Operations restrictions. One informant compared working with a UN mission to "remaining in an Indian bubble" and suggested that "the personal connection is not there" when asked about relations with local communities.[11] Troops interviewed also suggested that it was "not an easy life over here" and complained that the "UN is never concerned about the working life of peacekeepers—he's like a slave."[12]

Indian troops abroad are sometimes thought to exist within a more permissive UN culture that allows for higher degrees of corruption and other nefarious activities than what is permitted while they are stationed at home.[13] In Congo, which hosts the largest Indian contingent in the world, troops have been accused of a long litany of infractions and have met with a variety of criticisms related to their performance from both Congolese and international observers. Foremost among these is a consistent inability to carry out the mission's mandate of civilian protection. In addition, the mission has been accused of corruption, sexual misconduct, and favoritism toward the various antigovernment militias operating in the region. Indian peacekeepers have also been accused of extensive involvement in the region's illicit trade in natural resources, especially gold.[14] When asked about accusations of peace-keepers engaging with local sex workers, one Indian officer blithely explained that "soldiers have no outlets."[15] The criticism of Indian performance became so loud that after a particularly brutal attack on civilians in 2008 near an Indian-staffed based in Kiwanja, the Congo government asked India to with-draw its troops from the mission.

Yet despite the lackluster performance of many missions with large num-bers of Indian troops, it is incorrect to assume that all Indian troops are corrupt or that the country has only instrumental reasons for participating in UN operations. The country possesses several unique competencies that it touts in relation to its peacekeeping efforts. In addition to its history of peacekeeping and the fact that officers know English (making them accessi-ble for all UN employees), the country possesses the capacity to provide well-trained troops accustomed to operating in diverse terrains. This is generally credited to the extensive number of operations the military engages in domestically, often in terrains comparable to other conflict zones.[16]

Most importantly, unlike other leading TCCs such as Pakistan and Bangladesh, India possesses "stand-alone capability" to support a peacekeep-ing operation on its own. Such a capability is the product of a national army possessing the appropriate military hardware necessary to provision a mission without having to rely on supplies from other countries or the UN. Its history as one of the leading arms buyers—as of 2012, the largest in the world—means that the Indian military remains among the best stocked. By early 2011, India provided more attack and utility helicopters to UN missions than any other country, for example. Further, Indian troops are familiar with state-of-the-art equipment, including a wide variety of weapons and systems supplied by all the major arms-producing countries such as the United States, the United Kingdom, and importantly, because of the lack of interoperability between their systems and those of the Western powers, Russia. As one recent study put it, "India is the backbone of UN peacekeeping operations."[17]

INDIAN PEACEKEEPING IN SUDAN / SOUTH SUDAN

The UN currently is involved with three distinct missions in Sudan: UNMISS, the UN Interim Security Force for Abyei (UNISFA), and the joint African Union / UN Hybrid Operation in Darfur (UNAMID). Of the three, India contributes troops primarily to UNMISS. UNAMID is primarily staffed by troops from the African Union drawn from African countries, and UNISFA is largely staffed by Ethiopian troops. Of the almost nine thousand personnel within UNMISS, India's contribution constitutes almost a quarter, making the country the largest contributor by far. Beyond personnel, India has provided much of the advanced weaponry for the mission, including desperately needed attack and transport helicopters. The approximately 2,100 Indian army and police personnel make up two battalions in South Sudan, one based in Jonglei State near Ethiopia and the other in Malakkal, Upper Nile, on the southeastern border with Sudan.

In January of 2005, the Khartoum government signed a comprehensive peace agreement with the rebels of the Sudan People's Liberation Movement/ Army (SPLM/A), which fought the government to a stalemate after three decades of brutal warfare. The agreement called for a six-year transition period during which both sides would work to resolve their issues, followed by a referendum during which South Sudanese could decide whether to remain within a united Sudan or to break apart. In support of the agreement, the Security Council authorized the UN to establish the UN Mission in Sudan (UNMIS) with up to ten thousand troops. UNMIS had a broad mandate, including supporting the implementation of the comprehensive peace agreement; facilitating and coordinating the voluntary return of refugees and internally displaced persons and humanitarian assistance; assisting the parties in the mine action sector; and contributing toward international efforts to protect and promote human rights in the Sudan.[18]

Following the January 2011 referendum, during which over 98 percent of the population voted for secession, the Security Council authorized Resolution 1996, establishing UNMISS as a successor to UNMIS. The new mission had a similarly broad and challenging mandate. In addition to "peace consolidation" and "protect[ing] civilians," it was tasked with supporting the newly created government of South Sudan with "economic development," "conflict prevention, mitigation, and resolution," "establishing the rule of law," and "strengthening the security and justice sectors in the country." In short, the mandate called for UNMISS to support the government in "longer-term statebuilding." Yet the mission was vastly weaker than was necessary for achieving even its most basic function of stabilization. The initial authorization called for only some seven thousand military personnel augmented by nine hundred police personnel in a country the size of Texas.

South Sudan has faced an unending stream of crises since its independence in July 2011. In 2012, a conflict with Sudan over the border and oil revenues set off a deep economic crisis in South Sudan, which derives more than 95 percent of revenues from the petroleum sector. Furthermore, the state remains far from consolidated, and the central government, led by a corrupt and nepotistic militarized elite, has never been able to assert full control over armed groups that challenge its rule. Prior to independence, internal divisions, often along ethnic lines, bedeviled the coalition that made up the SPLA, frequently leading to brutal internecine conflicts. In the run-up to the referendum, the ruling SPLM sought to bring these violent militias into the government by offering concessions. But even after independence, various armed militias have continued to challenge the SPLM/A, rendering the newly birthed nation a space of almost constant violence.

In April 2013, a UN convoy traveling within Jonglei State was attacked by militants suspected to be loyal to an SPLA dissident named David Yau Yau. Indian troops escorting the convoy came under fire by a group of close to two hundred militants armed with small arms and rocket-propelled grenades. Indian troops were outnumbered by six to one during the hour-long attack, according to eyewitnesses. Five soldiers were killed alongside two UN staff members and seven civilian contractors. Four other Indian troops were injured.

But the largest attack on the mission occurred in December 2013 following a violent schism within the ruling coalition. During a meeting of the SPLM's National Liberation Council, fighting broke out between units loyal to President Salva Kiir and Vice President Riek Machar. Machar, a Nuer, accused the president, a Dinka, of seeking to purge the SPLM leadership of critical voices and orchestrating violence against Nuer living in Juba, the capital. Machar, rumored to receive support from the government of Sudan, retreated with a segment of the SPLA and took control of several Nuer areas of the country, including significant parts of Jonglei, Unity, and Upper Nile States.

The outbreak of war initiated a sequence of events that led to the December attack on the UN base in Jonglei State. Four days after Machar's split, some two thousand Nuer youth overran the UN base in Akobo County, hunting down the thirty to forty members of the Dinka community who had fled to the base seeking refuge. Despite the efforts of the forty-three Indian soldiers present within the base, at least ten Dinka civilians were killed along with two Indian soldiers. After the killings, the Security Council altered the mission's mandate, increasing the total troop level to 12,500 troops and 1,323 police personnel. With the crisis still not resolved, the mandate was extended again in March 2014. The revised mandate reduced the ambition of the mission, moving away from statebuilding toward a less ambitious agenda of civilian protection and support for the ongoing peace process.

The bigger question that remains is whether Indian peacekeepers could ever have made a positive impact on the two Sudans in the first place. Four years after independence, it is clear that South Sudan owes its independence to the machinations of the United States, not to any particular readiness for statehood. During the administration of George W. Bush, Sudan was a potential target of military action for its involvement, real and imagined, in supporting Islamic terrorism. Under pressure from his evangelical constituency, Bush signaled to Sudan's leaders that negotiations with the SPLA were a precondition to avoiding military action, a threat made credible by the invasions of Afghanistan and Iraq. Though there were many internal reasons that Omar al-Bashir, the Sudanese president, agreed to participate in the peace process, it is clear that American pressure was paramount. Nothing signifies the appreciation of South Sudanese leaders for the American intervention quite as clearly as the black cowboy hat that always adorns the head of President Kiir, a gift from Bush during a 2006 White House meeting.

This is not to suggest that South Sudan's claim for independence was invalid. Decades of war and the historic marginalization of the region provided southern secessionists no shortage of credibility. But beyond the normative claim for autonomy, how ready was the country for independence? And should the "international community" be absolved for its inability to predict the multiple political crises that have bedeviled the country since independence?

A useful comparison is the last state to successfully secede globally: East Timor from Indonesia in 1999. Like East Timor, southern Sudan was a culturally distinct part of a majority-Muslim country. Like East Timor, the region was a political and economic backwater that had been marginalized by the central authority for decades. Both witnessed the development of armed resistance movements that sought to project themselves as the natural political authorities within their territories. Both movements fought for decades in wars that cost tens of thousand of lives. Like South Sudan, East Timor confronted a number of political crises immediately after the vote for independence in a referendum. Beyond economic deprivation, the nascent Timorese government faced violent challenges from militias supported by the Indonesian government, much as Khartoum has supported violent militias such as those controlled by David Yau Yau.

But the key difference between the two countries has been the response of the international community, and specifically the UN. Soon after East Timorese overwhelming voted for independence, leading to violent clashes, an Australian-led international peacekeeping force was sent in to restore order. Most importantly, the UN Transitional Administration in East Timor was created and given sovereign control over the young nation in order to shepherd the country through the secession process. Its mandate was expansive—to administer East Timor's territory, exercise legislative and executive authority during the transition period and support capacity building for self-government—and it was provided the resources necessary to engage in a broad process of statebuilding. Specifically, the mission possessed a maximum strength of 9,150 troops and 1,640 police to control a territory of less than fifteen thousand square kilometers and a population about a million strong.[19]

In contrast, UNMISS was initially provided fewer soldiers to control a territory more than forty times as large and home to more than eight times as many people, but with a mandate only slightly less challenging. In this context, it is hard to deny that the mandate defined for UNMISS far outpaced the resources that were provided to it. It is no surprise that the mission has largely failed to fulfill its mandate.

THE P3 VERSUS NAM: WHITHER INDIA?

The crisis in South Sudan again throws into stark relief the fundamental tension gnawing at Indian foreign policy makers. The country's position as a leading contributor of troops to UN missions often conflicts with its ambition to become a permanent member of the Security Council, the body primarily responsible for funding and designing the mandate of UN peacekeeping missions. The basic tension for India is how to reconcile its role in contributing troops to peacekeeping missions—undertaken without the country playing a direct role in devising mission mandates—and its historic support for the centrality of sovereignty in the current international order, particularly when it is perceived as being abrogated by the P3. The key challenge is whether India can achieve its objectives while retaining its position alongside other TCCs and NAM or whether it must move away from these positions as a precondition for having a greater say over the design of mandates.

To understand this tension, it is necessary to examine how UN missions are funded and staffed. After the decision has been made to authorize a peacekeeping mission, the UN faces two related challenges: Who will pay for the mission, and who will contribute troops? On one side of the equation is the question of who pays for UN peacekeeping missions. According to Article 17 of the UN Charter, all members of the General Assembly are required to pay a share. While the Assembly apportions peacekeeping expenses to each member on the basis of a complex formula that takes into consideration the relative economic wealth of each country, the five members of the Security Council are apportioned an additional share on the basis that they have a special responsibility for the maintenance of global peace and security.[20] In practice, this creates a tiered system in which permanent members of the Council, the so-called P5, not only have disproportionate political influence over peacekeeping operations (i.e., every mission must get the approval of all Security Council members) but also bear a substantially higher proportion of the costs. Yet while the top ten financial contributors provide approximately 80 percent of the costs of UN missions, they contribute less than 10 percent of the personnel to staff those missions.[21]

So who does staff UN peacekeeping missions? The UN Charter calls for all member states to contribute troops and other military resources. Since its founding, close to 130 members states have complied, with 117 currently contributing personnel. In practice, however, the vast majority of personnel are drawn from a much smaller set of countries. Currently, out of the 106,506 personnel contributed, fully 57,819 come from just ten countries, accounting for 54 percent of the total. More than 37 percent are drawn from just the top five countries.[22]

Why do countries choose to contribute troops? Scholarship suggests states contribute to UN missions because of a complex mix of motivations and constraints, including the size of their military force, the amount of concurrent commitments, the risk of casualties, their belief in the UN mission, their relative wealth, and, relatedly, the economic incentives on offer.[23] These studies generally agree that while other motivations are important the most common profile of troop contributors is relatively poor countries with large militaries and few concurrent commitments.[24] Yet while the economic incentive is essential for understanding the broader universe of cases, it ignores the political forces that may shape the participation of certain countries. While accurate at the aggregate level, a narrow focus on economic incentives does not offer much insight into the behavior of a rising power like India, which has a complex set of political motivations for its participation in UN missions.

Why does India contribute troops? In a recent study, Richard Gowan and Sushant Singh examine four prominent explanations—Nehruvian ideals, pursuit of national economic interests, showcasing of force projection, and financial gain—and find them all wanting.[25] Instead, they point to India's evolving diplomatic entanglements as the key driver of the country's contradictory approach to UN peacekeeping.

Within the debate around peacekeeping mandates, India has consistently positioned itself on the side of the troop contributors, despite its aspirations to ascend to the Security Council. The relationship between the two sides is complex. While basic directions for individual missions come from the Security Council, the TCCs are not powerless. Despite the disproportionate share of the costs borne by Council members, budgetary discussions take place in the Fifth Committee of the General Assembly, giving NAM countries a significant voice. In addition, systems and norms of peacekeeping are debated by a Special Committee on Peacekeeping Operations (Committee of the 34 or C34) that is open to any country. The net effect is that, despite not having formal influence over the mandate of peacekeeping mission, TCCs do have considerable influence over events on the ground through conditions placed on how they use their forces or by their threat to withdraw their troops altogether.[26]

During the Cold War, reflecting India's limited strength as a middling global power, the country could participate in peacekeeping on the basis of being a good citizen within the global community, as long as peacekeeping did not abrogate NAM's central tenets. But the end of the Cold War and the increasing politicization of the humanitarian discourse means that India can no longer participate in "neutral" humanitarian interventions without contradicting many of its central and long-standing foreign policy positions. Equally important, India's ambition to be viewed as a major power is in direct tension with many of the values that it has sought to advance through NAM and other institutions representing the global South. Western countries including the United States, the United Kingdom, and France have worked to garner India's support for more robust interventionist policies, thereby getting the country to challenge NAM on peacekeeping, but with little to show for their efforts.

At different points, India has sought to resolve this tension by advocating on behalf of the TCCs. In 2008–9 India played a major role in demanding that TCCs be given a greater say over the mandates for operations.[27] In response the Security Council agreed to improve consultations with TCCs over the renewal of mandates affecting their forces. The UN Secretariat also offered India a greater share of command posts in operations. In 2011, India advocated a change in the reimbursement formula for troops, which had remained at the same level since 2002 ($1,028 per month). Although India called for a raise of 57 percent, it was able to secure only an increase of 7 percent and a commitment to appoint a Special Advisory Group in 2012.

That same year, India assumed a seat as a rotating member of the Security Council and sought to use its position to advocate for greater reforms to the mandate design process. Soon after India began its term, however, the debate over the UN-authorized North Atlantic Treaty Organization (NATO) intervention in yet another Arab country, Libya, set the stage for a standoff between the two sides. After days of strained negotiations, ten members, including the P3, voted in favor of an intervention in Libya, while five others, including India, Brazil, Germany, and two permanent members, China and Russia, abstained. On March 17, 2011, the Security Council passed Resolution 1973, establishing a no-fly zone in Libya and authorizing the use of force for the protection of civilians.

The actual conduct of the Libya campaign further incensed the abstaining Council members. Once the campaign began, it became clear that the P3 countries, which possess the power to draft Security Council resolutions (short of a veto by China or Russia), were pushing for regime change, a position that the abstainers felt superseded the boundaries of the mandate itself. Though the abstainers were helpless to stop the intervention once it had begun, the Libyan war triggered a broader debate about one of the central questions driving peacekeeping missions in the contemporary period, the meaning and practice of the evolving international norm of the Responsibility to Protect (R2P).

Within the C34, there have been intense debates regarding the amount of force peacekeepers can and should use, and R2P further enflamed these concerns. NAM countries have long resisted the idea of making missions more robust out of fear of real or imagined neocolonial ambitions on the part of Western nations. But they also have expressed doubts about what greater force can accomplish. Beyond NAM, the BRICS (Brazil, Russia, India, China, South Africa) grouping continues to "advocate a 'light footprint' approach rather than a heavier approach that risks generating dependence, insist on local ownership and the responsibilities of the host state; and warn against transplanting models from one region to another."[28]

India's concern is whether its participation in peacekeeping missions was merely designed to advance the agendas of Western powers or is truly in line with its historic foreign policy values and objectives. As one leading Indian foreign policy figure suggested, R2P is perceived by many developing countries "as yet another attempt by the more powerful members of the developed world to impose their value systems on the weaker states."[29] For India, blindly supporting R2P through its contributions to peacekeeping missions while allowing the P3 to retain control over defining peacekeeping mandates triggers a deep sense of unease. Many in the foreign policy establishment feel that Indian troops are being deployed to bolster the foreign policy preferences of Western powers. As the Indian Permanent Representative to the UN, Hardeep Singh Puri, bluntly put it, "The principle of R2P is being selectively used to promote national interest rather than protect civilians."[30]

India sought to retain some commitment to its professed values by retaining ties to the Qaddafi regime even after it was clear that the P3 was intent on its removal, going as far as inviting a Libyan delegation to attend the second Africa-India Forum Summit held in Addis Ababa in May 2011. During the summit, India's external affairs minister, S. M. Krishna, met on the sidelines with Libya's foreign minister, Abdal al Latti al Obedi, expressing regret for the NATO-led air strikes and urging an immediate cease-fire. The declaration that ended the conference chastised NATO, calling for its efforts to remain "within the spirit and letter of those resolutions." It also urged both parties to the conflict to strive for a political resolution and expressed support for the marginalized African Union High-Level Ad Hoc Committee initiative and the African Union road map for the peaceful and consensual resolution of the conflict.[31]

During India's term as president of the Security Council, the Council was set to host an "Open Debate on Peacekeeping." In addition, both Brazil and South Africa, India's rising power allies through groupings such as IBSA (India, Brazil, South Africa) and BRICS, were also rotating members of the Council with similar misgivings about the Libyan intervention. With the IBSA countries in agreement, both China and Russia might feel compelled to agree. Prior to the debate in August, India circulated a memo entitled "Peacekeeping: Taking Stock and Preparing for the Future." In the memo, India highlighted the importance of host government consent and R2P's implications for state sovereignty, calling for peacekeeping missions to be treated as a "partnership" between the Security Council, the General Assembly, and the TCCs, rather than the preserve of the P3. In addition, in a clear nod to criticism leveled against Indian troops in Congo and Sudan, the memo repeated India's long-standing concern that peacekeeping mandates continued to underestimate the resources necessary, with TCCs bearing the bulk of the blame when these missions failed.[32]

The leverage the Indians possessed to push for a greater voice around peacekeeping missions was their capacity and willingness to deploy aerial power, a crucial contribution to the African missions. Toward this end, parallel to the debate unfolding around Libya and R2P, in July of 2011 India began threatening to withdraw its Mi-35 helicopters from Congo and Sudan when its contract expired on July 4 unless TCCs were given a greater say in designing future missions, much to the chagrin of the P3. One close observer of the Council noted that the debate was the "most acrimonious" she had ever witnessed.[33]

With few exceptions, notably South Africa and Ukraine, no other country has the capacity or the will to provide helicopters for extended periods, hence making the Indian threat a substantive one.[34] Although the government claimed that it faced a domestic need for the helicopters to fight its internal Maoist insurgency—a position bolstered by a damning comptroller and auditor general report that suggested that operational shortages faced by the Indian Army in its battle with domestic insurgents were directly linked to its participation in UN missions—it was widely perceived as a power play by the Indian government to assert more influence over the direction of future peacekeeping mandates.[35] Leading Indian voices have long called for leveraging India's contributions to peacekeeping in order to "insist on adequate representation at the UN Headquarters and on decision-making mechanisms there."[36] India's deputy ambassador to the UN, Manjeev Singh Puri, also spoke openly about the need for "more consultation" with key TCCs, directly linking the provision of helicopters to the debate around the mandates of peacekeeping missions. The debate is far from resolved, but India's decision to withdraw its helicopters demonstrates its willingness to challenge the existing binary between the TCCs and the P3, even to the detriment of UN peacekeeping and the country's reputation.

Despite the moral claims articulated by India at the UN, the country does not have a coherent position regarding its involvement in peacekeeping missions. There is an ongoing debate in India about whether support for peacekeeping is in line with its national security priorities and its ambitions to be taken seriously as an emerging power or if its commitment to contributing troops is a relic of an earlier era of Indian foreign policy making. In places like Sudan and Congo, these debates between New Delhi and New York have often undercut the effectiveness of mission commanders and troops, transforming them into pawns within India's larger geopolitical ambitions. As violent crises continue to transform the broader Arab world, UN peacekeeping is likely to be expected to help bring durable resolutions. Yet without resolving the tensions between the TCCs and the P3, a tension that can be solved only with India's consent, UN peacekeeping itself is likely to suffer.

NOTES

1. C. Raja Mohan, "India and International Peace Operations," *SIPRI Insights on Peace and Security,* no. 2013/3 (April 2013): 1.

2. *London Gazette,* July 4, 1941.

3. "Two Indian Soldiers Killed in Attack on UN Base in South Sudan," *Times of India,* December 20, 2013.

4. "Indian Soldiers Killed in Sudan Cremated with State Honours," *Indo Asian News Service,* December 24, 2013.

5. Sanjay Yadav, "Relatives Demand Body of Soldier Killed in South Sudan," *Times of India,* December 23, 2013.

6. Richard Gowan and Sushant Singh, "India and UN Peacekeeping," in *Shaping the Emerging World: India and Multilateral Order,* ed. Waheguru Pal Singh Sidhu, Pratap Bhanu Mehta, and Bruce D. Jones (Washington, DC: Brookings Institution Press, 2013), 179.

7. T. S. Chinna, "For the Honour of India: A History of Indian Peacekeeping," *Journal of the United Service Institution of India,* no. 576 (2009).

8. United Nations, "UN Missions' Contribution by Country," May 31, 2015, www.un.org/en/peacekeeping/contributors/2015/may15_5.pdf; United Nations, "UN Missions' Summary Detailed by Country," June 30, 2015, www.un.org/en/peacekeeping/contributors/2015/jun15_3.pdf.

9. Colum Lynch, "India's Withdrawal of Helicopters from Congo Points to Wider Trend," *Washington Post,* June 14, 2011.

10. N. K. Pant, "India's Peacekeeping Missions," Institute of Peace and Conflict Studies, Article No. 340, March 23, 2000, www.ipcs.org/article/india/indias-peacekeeping-missions-340.html.

11. Anonymous Indian officer, interview, Goma, Congo, 2012.

12. Anonymous MONUSCO troops, interviews, Goma, Congo, 2012.

13. Gowan and Singh, "India and UN Peacekeeping," 184.

14. O. Ahmad, "Rotting Olives: Corrupt Indian Peacekeepers in the Congo Are Marring a Legacy," *Outlook,* June 2, 2008, 20–22; Bally Mutumayi, Ashish Sen, and Saikat Datta, "The Peacekeeper's Child: Sexual Misconduct by Indian Soldiers and Officers on UN Duty in Congo Raises Disturbing Questions," *Outlook,* August 8, 2011; Human Rights Watch, "UN: Tackle Wrongdoing by Peacekeepers: Letter to Secretary-General Ban Ki-Moon," April 30, 2008, https://www.hrw.org/news/2008/05/01/un-tackle-wrongdoing-peacekeepers.

15. Anonymous Indian officer, interview, Goma, Congo, 2012.

16. India Strategic, "India to Continue Supporting UN Peacekeeping Operations," 2011, www.indiastrategic.in/topstories172.htm.

17. Gowan and Singh, "India and UN Peacekeeping," 184.

18. Description drawn from the official UNMIS Web page, n.d., accessed May 8, 2016, www.un.org/en/peacekeeping/missions/past/unmis/background.shtml.

19. The UN Transitional Administration in East Timor remained the sovereign authority of East Timor from October 1999 to May 2002, when sovereignty was passed to the East Timor government. It was replaced by the UN Mission of Support to East Timor.

20. UN General Assembly Resolution 55/235, A/Res/55/235, December 23, 2000, www.un.org/documents/ga/docs/55/a55235.pdf.

21. Vincenzo Bove and Leandro Elia, "Supplying Peace: Participation in and Troop Contribution to Peacekeeping Missions," *Journal of Peace Research* 48 (2011): 700.

22. These figures as well those in table 1 are drawn from United Nations, "UN Missions' Contribution" and "UN Missions' Summary."

23. Laura Neack, "UN Peace-Keeping: In the Interest of Community or Self?," *Journal of Peace Research* 32, no. 2 (1995): 181–96; James Lebovic, "Uniting for Peace? Democracies and United Nations Peace Operations after the Cold War," *Journal of Conflict Resolution* 48, no. 6 (2004): 910–36; Jonah Victor, "African Peacekeeping in Africa: Warlord Politics, Defense Economics, and State Legitimacy," *Journal of Peace Research* 47, no. 2 (2010): 217–29; Bove and Elia, "Supplying Peace."

24. Bove and Elia, "Supplying Peace."

25. Gowan and Singh, "India and UN Peacekeeping," 185–88.

26. Ibid., 184.

27. Ibid., 188.

28. Ibid., 189.

29. Satish Nambiar, "Robust Peacekeeping Operations, Rapid Deployment Capability of the UN: An Indian Perspective," *Journal of the United Service Institution of India,* no. 566 (2012).

30. Vijay Prashad, "Syria, Libya and Security Council: Interview with Hardeep Singh Puri, Permanent Representative of India to the United Nations," *Frontline,* PBS, March 10–23, 2012.

31. Siddharth Varadarajan, "India, Africa Call for End to Libya Bombing," *Hindu,* May 26, 2011.

32. Security Council Report, "Peacekeeping Debate Preparations," What's in Blue, August 12, 2011, www.whatsinblue.org/2011/08/peacekeeping-debate.php.

33. Kirsten Hagan, OXFAM, interview, Goma, Congo, March 6, 2012.

34. Ibid.; see also Lynch, "India's Withdrawal."

35. "No Conspiracy to Snub the UN," *Pragmatic Euphony* (blog), September 11, 2010, and "Indian Helicopter Back in UN Peacekeeping," *Pragmatic Euphony* (blog), September 8, 2011.

36. Nambiar, "Robust Peacekeeping Operations."

PART THREE

Humanitarianism and Refugees

———

The UN Human Rights Game and the Arab Region

PLAYING NOT TO LOSE

Fateh Azzam

THE UNITED NATIONS HUMAN RIGHTS system has grown significantly over the past sixty years, and with it the demands for human rights protection and their respect around the world, including in the Arab region. The revolts that first hit the region in 2011 focused on demands for dignity, economic justice, and political freedoms, which are fundamentally human rights demands. As the protests unfolded and spread from one country to another, their chants gained remarkable consistency in rejecting unaccountable leadership, severe limitations on the exercise of civil and political freedoms, and exclusionary economic and development policies that had failed for decades. Thus the Arab revolts brought into sharp focus the interdependence of development, democracy, and human rights, first articulated in the outcome document of the World Conference on Human Rights in Vienna in 1993.[1] The UN Programme for Reform in 1997 reaffirmed the centrality of human rights to "peace and security, economic prosperity and social equity" and started the UN on the road to mainstreaming human rights.[2]

The Arab revolts can be understood as a collective demand for speedier implementation of this human rights–based approach, especially since the warning signs have been there all along in the UN Development Programme's (UNDP's) Arab Human Development Reports, in the statistics of the World Bank's reports, and certainly in reports of national and international human rights organizations.[3] The warning signs were also present in the comments and observations of the UN human rights mechanisms, charged with supporting the implementation of states' international obligations under human rights law.

This essay will look at the role played by the international human rights protection system and its mutual interactions with countries and societies of the region. It will begin with a restatement of the normative framework of human rights, followed by a review of how Arab states engaged with this framework and how the UN bodies and processes have dealt with rights issues in the region. This in turn will be followed by a discussion of Arab civil society's interactions with and usage of the UN human rights system.

The discussion below is neither exhaustive nor comprehensive but will provide an initial sketch of those interactions. Much more empirical research and analytical study is needed to arrive at evidence for the impact and proper assessment of how seriously the Arab region takes its human rights obligations and how well the UN-based protection system has worked to protect rights in the region.

THE UN NORMATIVE FRAMEWORK
FOR HUMAN RIGHTS

The most significant value added by the human rights approach is that it frames governance, policies, and development goals as a fulfillment of entitlements rather than simply a meeting of needs. In the human rights paradigm, individuals and communities are therefore seen as *rights holders* and governments as *duty bearers,* who are bound by international law to respect, protect, and fulfill those rights. The scope of these legal obligations may vary depending on the international treaties that each state has signed and ratified and on the specific right in question.[4]

There are currently nine core conventions and treaties within the human rights system. They cover a range of issues such as civil and political rights, economic, social, and cultural rights, racial discrimination, torture, women, children, migrant workers, persons with disabilities, and enforced disappearances. States enter into those human rights conventions voluntarily; once they do so, they become bound to implement the conventions as a matter of international contractual obligation. Human rights treaties also establish committees known as treaty bodies to oversee the implementation of the provisions of each treaty.[5] These committees are composed of human rights experts who, although nominated by the states parties to each convention, do not represent their states but serve in their personal professional capacity. The committees' role is to review state reports as well as parallel reports offered by nongovernmental organizations (NGOs) and others and to make recommendations that aim to assist states to meet their legally established obligations under those treaties in the spirit of international cooperation. These committees are also tasked with explaining the scope and common understanding of the specific rights guaranteed by the human rights treaties.[6]

The UN human rights system also includes mechanisms established under the 1945 Charter of the United Nations, the most important of which is the Human Rights Council, reinvented in 2006 from its previous incarnation, the Human Rights Commission under the Economic and Social Council.[7] The Human Rights Council has in place several mechanisms, primary among which is the Universal Periodic Review (UPR), which reviews the human rights record of each UN member state once every four years and provides recommendations for improvement. It also includes the system of Special Procedures: thematic and geographic experts known as mandate holders, appointed by the Human Rights Council and by the secretary-general of the United Nations to provide expert assessment and recommendations to states.[8] Altogether, these mechanisms constitute the international human rights protection system as it currently stands.

It is important to remember that the international human rights system is built on the premise of international cooperation rather than coercion. It is consequently weak on effective enforcement measures to ensure compliance with legally binding obligations. This cooperation takes the form of discussion of states' periodic reports under each treaty and other public debates on states' human rights record in the Human Rights Council or through cooperation with the Special Procedures and the treaty bodies. Under the rubric of "international cooperation," these public discussions provide little more than a soft (and politically acceptable) form of "naming and shaming." Indeed, the entire international legal system is based on respect for sovereignty and noninterference, and the human rights system does not stray far from that paradigm. The only exceptions, sometimes, are extreme cases of genocide, crimes against humanity, war crimes, and "gross and systematic violations of human rights," which may allow states to prosecute them under a universal jurisdiction—a very rare occurrence—or may trigger an investigation and indictment by the International Criminal Court.[9]

Human rights implementation, then, becomes a process that combines legal requirements with societal and political pressure from within and without the state. In pointing to shortcomings and violations, civil society within the region and internationally continues to galvanize and increase international pressure on states to conform to human rights standards. This pressure is growing despite—and probably because of—weaknesses in implementation; Arab states are hesitantly but increasingly responding to this pressure. They have had patchy but active engagement with the UN's various mechanisms and processes in a game of push-and-pull that they are becoming increasingly adept at.

THE ENGAGEMENT OF ARAB STATES WITH THE UN HUMAN RIGHTS SYSTEM

Ratification of Treaties

The level of ratification of human rights treaties by Arab states is the first indicator of their willingness to engage with the system. The vast majority of the twenty-two states who are members of the Arab League are in fact party to nearly all of the nine core human rights treaties, as table 11.1 demonstrates.[10]

Judging by their ratification of treaties, most Arab states are committed to international human rights standards, and their level of ratifications is consistent with global trends. Sudan, Somalia, and the Comoros appear to be the least willing to sign on, bringing the total ratifications down from universal acceptance of the Convention against Torture (CAT), the Convention on the Elimination of Discrimination against Women (CEDAW), and the Convention on the Rights of the Child (CRC). In addition to the Comoros, four of the countries of the Gulf Cooperation Council are not parties to the International Covenant on Civil and Political Rights (ICCPR) and the International Covenant on Economic, Social and Cultural Rights (ICESCR): Oman, Qatar, Saudi Arabia, and the United Arab Emirates. The problematic convention is the International Convention on the Protection of the Rights of All Migrant Workers and Members of Their Families (ICRMW), and indeed the issue of migrant workers and their rights is a serious problem in the region, where they constitute from 40 percent to as much as 88 percent of the populations of those countries. Finally, the few ratifications of the International Convention for the Protection of All Persons from Enforced Disappearance (ICCPED) may be due to the fact that it is the newest convention, having entered into force only on December 23, 2010, and we may see further Arab ratifications in the coming years.

The fact that Arab states are parties to human rights treaties, however, is not necessarily an indicator of a serious commitment. The picture differs

TABLE 11.1 Arab States Who Have Ratified the Nine Core Human Rights
Treaties

Convention	Arab State Ratifications
International Covenant on Civil and Political Rights (ICCPR)	17
International Covenant on Economic, Social and Cultural Rights (ICESCR)	17
International Convention on Elimination of Racial Discrimination (ICERD)	22
Convention against Torture (CAT)	19
Convention on the Elimination of Discrimination against Women (CEDAW)	20
Convention on the Rights of the Child (CRC)	21
International Convention on the Protection of the Rights of All Migrant Workers and Members of Their Families (ICRMW)	6
Convention on the Rights of Persons with Disabilities (CRPD)	16
International Convention for the Protection of All Persons from Enforced Disappearance (ICPPED)	3

when we consider their record on the required periodic reporting to the treaty bodies. Data from the Office of the UN High Commissioner for Human Rights show that over half of the states in the region are seriously late in presenting their reports, some by as many as thirteen years or more. For the ICCPR, for example, ten states are late, two of them by one or two years and the rest for at least five years or more. Interestingly, the only conventions where Arab states appear to be more diligent about reporting and discussing their implementation records are CEDAW and the CRC. On the former, only two states, Bahrain and Mauritania, are late by one and two years respectively. Similarly, six countries are only about one to two years late in reporting on the CRC.[11] This is generally consistent with global trends, however, as being a few years late is a common practice across the globe in human rights reporting, and it becomes a problem when delays increase by more than three or four years.

States can voluntarily sign onto optional protocols to the various treaties, most of which allow the treaty bodies to examine individual complaints of human rights abuses by the signatory state and to communicate with the state in question about redress. In this, Arab states demonstrate a clear lack of willingness to be subject to such international scrutiny. Only five states have ratified the Optional Protocol to the ICCPR,[12] and none to the

Optional Protocol to the ICESCR. Four have declared that they accepted the Committee against Torture's competence to review individual complaints as provided by Article 22 of that convention,[13] and only three have ratified the Optional Protocol to CAT, committing themselves to create a national torture prevention mechanism and accepting the authority of the international Sub-Committee for the Prevention of Torture to investigate allegations of torture.[14]

Engagement with Special Procedures

As of May 2015, there were forty-one working groups and independent experts appointed by the Human Rights Council or directly by the secretary-general of the UN to work with states on specific human rights themes and issues.[15] These are called Special Procedures and are mandated to communicate with states and offer observations and recommendations aimed at improving the enjoyment of the specific human right under their individual mandates.

The working groups and mandate holders receive information and complaints from any sources and may communicate with the concerned state regarding this information. The state is expected to reply to these communications with explanations, clarifications, and, ideally, measures of implementation. Arab states' rates of response can only be described as patchy and inconsistent. Here too the frequency of replies from Arab states does not differ markedly from the global trend, which is also patchy and inconsistent.[16]

What can be noted from table 11.2 is that Bahrain and Morocco are the only states that appear to take this communication seriously, while the rest, particularly Saudi Arabia and the United Arab Emirates, do not. Interestingly, it appears that the average Arab state response rate for all of the Special Procedures Communications has been in steady decline, from 41 percent (2011) to 31 percent (2012) to a mere 20 percent in 2013, when 110 communications were sent and only 22 responses provided.[17]

Mandate holders may also visit countries that specifically invite them to engage proactively and constructively with them. The records show that Arab states are generally not very willing to host visits by the various experts and working groups for purposes of discussing their human rights record under the various thematic headings. To date, only five countries in the region have standing invitations to those independent experts,[18] but this does not necessarily mean that they will agree to the specific requests for visits.

TABLE 11.2 Arab States' Response to Queries on Their Human Rights Records

Special Procedures Communications	2011		2012	
	Sent	*Replies*	*Sent*	*Replies*
Bahrain	18	18	12	12
Egypt	13	5	17	5
Iraq	7	2	7	3
Libya	7	0	0	0
Morocco	8	7	0	0
Saudi Arabia	8	0	13	0
Sudan	0	0	8	3
Syria	15	3	11	1
UAE	8	0	8	0
Total	84	35	76	24

Engagement with the UN Human Rights Council's Universal Periodic Review

The UPR mechanism was included in the very same resolution that established the Human Rights Council. Its unique addition to the international human rights protection system lies in its universal and periodic character and its potential for follow-up. First, all states undergo the review regardless of which human rights treaties they have signed or ratified.[19] Second, the Human Rights Council reaffirmed the universal and interrelated nature of all human rights, and thus all rights enumerated in the Universal Declaration and human rights treaties are considered in the UPR.[20] Third, all concerned parties and stakeholders may contribute, including national institutions and NGOs, whether or not the latter have consultative status with the Economic and Social Council.[21] Finally, the process is repeated for each state once every four years, thus its periodic nature. In sum, the UPR involves all countries, it is about all rights, all those concerned are involved, and it happens at regular intervals. It is an interactive mechanism where the summary of each state review contains a set of recommendations to be implemented over the course of the following four years.

Since the Human Rights Council is a political body composed of state representatives, it is not immune to political dynamics as any other such body is, and groupings of states with shared interests tend to work together and support one another. Nevertheless, one of the surprising aspects of the Council's UPR process is that it has managed to keep those dynamics within reasonable bounds, despite the usual mutual praise and soft-pedaling on issues and accusations of overpoliticization, particularly for keeping human rights in the Occupied Palestinian Territory permanently on its agenda.[22] The political dynamics do have a direct effect on the discussions and recommendations made in the interactive dialogue of the UPR, and Arab states' reviews are certainly no exception.[23] The tone and sometimes hidden (or not so hidden) assumptions in the language of a particular recommendation can affect the attitude of the state under review and whether this recommendation is accepted or rejected.

The recommendations in the first cycle of the UPR were numerous, highly nuanced, and of varying degrees of specificity. A review of ten Arab states' UPRs shows that they accepted around 71 percent of all recommendations made, a third of which came from fellow Arab states, while rejecting 17 percent.[24] The bulk of the recommendations accepted by the ten Arab states reviewed related to improving economic, social, and cultural rights, improving women's rights, strengthening the institutional protection of human rights, and instituting human rights education programs. These issues also represented the bulk of Arab states' recommendations to one another as well. Nearly a quarter of all Arab states' recommendations revolved around noncontroversial issues like child rights and the right to education. In contrast, hardly any comments were made on citizen security, torture, elections, democratic participation, or freedoms of expression, association, and assembly.[25]

However, a closer look at those recommendations reveals that nearly 80 percent of all of the recommendations those states accepted did not demand any more than general suggestions to share experiences, continue current actions and policies, "review" actions or policies, request assistance or cooperation with others, undertake or "consider" action of a general nature, or "enhance efforts" without specifying how. Only 1.7 percent of the recommendations accepted called for a specific action or measure to protect a particular right or set of rights. Interestingly, it worked the other way round as well; Arab states' recommendations to fellow Arab states for specific measures to take accounted for only 5.4 percent of their total recommendations.[26]

Recommendations were rejected for a variety of reasons, some of which had more to do with the language or tone of the recommendation than with the subject matter. Several observations and recommendations were rejected because the reviewed state considered them technically or factually incorrect or simply because of the country making them (such as Israel), even while the reviewed state accepted the same or very similar recommendations from others. The Arab states reviewed rejected nearly 90 percent of the recommendations that they undertake or consider undertaking a specific act or measure like revoking a law or a practice. This leaves little room for interpretation: states clearly did not wish to commit themselves so specifically to taking steps or measures that they would later have to be accountable for.

Interestingly, no recommendations made by fellow Arab states were rejected. This was most likely because the vast majority of the recommendations made by other Arab states were general and required no real commitment to change on the part of the receiving state, so were quite easy to accept. We can also assume that the quid pro quo nature of these discussions was a major factor: states put some effort towards being supportive and nonconfrontational in the expectation that the same will be done for them when it is time for their own UPR review.

All recommendations made by states on abolishing the death penalty were rejected, including calls for establishing a moratorium on its use, as were all recommendations on sexual orientation. Needless to say, no Arab state made such recommendations either. Also rejected were many recommendations for improvements in the areas of women's rights—the bulk of which related to questions of family or personal status rights, including the right of women to pass nationality to their families, migrant and refugee rights, and labor rights. Of all the recommendations rejected, 14.5 percent called on the states to ratify optional protocols to treaties, most of which required state acceptance of individual complaints and other forms of international scrutiny.[27]

UN ENGAGEMENT WITH ARAB STATES ON HUMAN RIGHTS

The treaty bodies, special rapporteurs, and the UPR process provided substantive comments and observations to the Arab states designed to assist them in improving their human rights practices. Most observations took note of serious shortcomings in the areas of the equal enjoyment of rights by men and women; the rights of noncitizens, especially migrant workers; poverty and discrepancies between rural and urban areas; and serious problems in the exercise of freedoms of expression and association.

UN human rights bodies noted wide variance in the standards of living and levels of poverty between countries and an urban-rural divide in many. Populations living in the urban areas where services are more accessible and political attention focused generally fare better than their counterparts in the outlying and rural areas. The observations made by the Committee on the Rights of the Child for Syria may be instructive when correlated to the uprising there in 2011, where the committee noted its concern "that a more sustained strategy to address the structural determinants of poverty is not being adopted ... [as well as] ... poor management of and deterioration of natural resources that have led to constant migration from rural to urban areas and has contributed to the increasing prevalence of poverty."[28]

States were criticized for not guaranteeing equality of access and equal enjoyment of rights. For example, Gulf states offer significant social and economic benefits to their citizens, but not for their large populations of migrant workers and other noncitizens. Child labor came in for much criticism as well, with poverty being a major cause of child labor. As the Committee on the Rights of the Child pointed out in the case of Jordan, disparities exist in the enjoyment of the rights to health and education by children belonging to vulnerable groups, including those living in rural regions of the country and those living in unrecognized Palestinian refugee gatherings.[29]

According to the treaty bodies and independent experts, states were seriously remiss in managing the right to work. In particular, women's rights to work and to equal treatment in wages and benefits received a significant share of treaty bodies' attention, pointing to the inadequacy of legislation to guarantee equality and nondiscrimination in the labor sector. For example, the Committee on the Elimination of Discrimination against Women (hereafter CEDAW committee) criticized the labor code in Jordan for not prohibiting discrimination against women or guaranteeing the same entitlements for female employees as for males, and noted the exclusion of migrant domestic workers, nearly all women, from the law,[30] a point it also made for Lebanon, Bahrain, and several other countries.[31] Along with other treaty bodies like the Committee on the Rights of the Child, the Committee on Racial Discrimination, and the Committee on Economic, Social and Cultural Rights, the CEDAW committee singled out the sponsorship (*kafala*) system as an egregious violation of the rights of migrant domestic workers.[32] It should be noted and emphasized that human rights law is clear on the legal obligations of states under human rights law to protect the rights of noncitizens as well as citizens, without prejudice to citizenship-related political rights such as the right to vote and be elected.

UN human rights comments also focused on the right to political life and the formation of political parties, as was the case for Kuwait and Bahrain, for example.[33] Concerns were particularly expressed on the issue of women's participation in public and political life in several countries. For example, the special representative on human rights defenders called on Saudi Arabia not to target those working for political reform and democratic rights, especially those advocating for greater rights for women.[34] The treaty committees, special rapporteurs, and other bodies also have been noting the greatly restricted freedoms of expression, association, and assembly in the region for many years, recommending improvements to state practice and amendments of the current laws, which are vaguely framed and repressive.[35] To give a few examples: in early 2011, the UN Educational, Scientific and Cultural Organization (UNESCO) noted in its submission to the UPR that Syria prohibits publication of material that "harms national unity, tarnishes the image of the State or threatens the goals of the revolution."[36] The secretary-general's representative on human rights defenders criticized Bahrain, charging that the use of criminal charges such as "encouraging hatred of the state" and "distributing falsehoods and rumors" effectively suppresses legitimate free speech.[37] Similarly in Oman, a 2009 amendment to the press law further tightened censorship that already included any material deemed "politically, culturally or sexually offensive," including making it illegal to criticize public officials, according to court judgments.[38] In the United Arab Emirates as well, lawyers and human rights activists have been arrested on charges of insulting public officials, including a well-known case in 2005 that was criticized by a number of thematic mandate holders.[39] The special representative of the secretary-general on the situation of human rights defenders has also reported on these violations in Bahrain, Saudi Arabia, and Yemen.[40] The Committee against Torture criticized persistent acts of harassment and persecution of activists in Syria,[41] and the Human Rights Committee expressed concern over the Syrian government's regular blocking of Internet websites used by activists and rights defenders.[42]

Arab states' attack on democracy activists and human rights defenders has intensified since the revolts of 2011. There are daily arrests and prosecutions of activists in Egypt, and Egyptian activists have appealed to the UN for support.[43] In the Gulf region, dozens have been subjected to long-term imprisonment and lashings for blogging, writing in social media, and calling for reforms, "crimes" that are fundamentally protected by human rights laws binding on the Gulf states.[44] Violent conflict in Syria, Libya, Iraq, and Yemen has put community activists and human rights defenders at even greater risk of life and limb.

Freedom of association is also tightly regulated across the region, making it difficult for like-minded civil society activists to join forces to promote or defend their common interests. Instead of simple registration, associations and NGOs need to be approved and licensed under restrictive conditions. UN bodies have been repeatedly calling upon countries in the region to review this legislation and open the space for civil society participation in public life. Criticism of limits on NGO registration in Bahrain has been expressed by the Committee against Torture, for example,[45] and the special representative of the secretary-general encouraged the country to review the law and relevant legislation in order to protect the right to organize.[46] According to Oman's regulations, approval of the Ministry of Social Development is needed for associations to join international coalitions or to invite outside experts to their functions,[47] and the Committee on the Rights of the Child recommended in 2006 that Oman open the space for NGOs and involve them systematically in all stages of implementing the CRC.[48] The Committee on the Rights of the Child also called on Qatar to do the same in 2009.[49] In 2007 the CEDAW committee encouraged Syria to amend its law of association and to lift the restrictions on NGOs, particularly women's organizations, to enable them to operate independently of government.[50]

These concerns were echoed in the UPR reports and recommendations, as civil and political rights concerns were raised twice as frequently by international NGOS and four times more by non-Arab states than they were by the Arab states.[51] For Arab national and regional NGOs, problems in the areas of freedom of conscience, expression, association and assembly, and torture topped the list of their concerns in their contributions to Arab states' UPR reviews. In contrast, Arab states were almost silent in their recommendations on those rights.[52] In the area of economic and social rights, this trend was reversed, with region-based national NGOs and Arab states focusing on those rights twice as frequently as non-Arab states and NGOs did. Arab states focused in their recommendations on improving education, protecting children and reducing poverty but focused less on labor rights.

THE ROLE OF CIVIL SOCIETY

Civil society organizations at the national, regional, and international levels have worked toward holding states accountable for their actions in the human rights field; it is their raison d'être. For the past four decades, national, regional, and international NGOs have been submitting shadow reports to the treaty bodies and meeting with the mandate holders appointed by the

Human Rights Council. They have taken advantage of the space opened up by the UPR process and have engaged actively with the review of each of the states. In the absence of democratic participation, effective judicial recourse, and access to influence domestic policy within their own countries, the UN becomes a crucially important forum where civil society hopes for pressure to bear on governments.

Between 2004 and 2009, national NGOs within the region made 66 submissions to nine treaty bodies, more than a third of which were to the CEDAW committee and the Committee on the Rights of the Child alone.[53] For the four years of the first cycle of the UPR, national NGOs offered 192 organizational and joint submissions to the UPR process for ten Arab countries only. Further evidence of the increasing engagement and growing importance of NGOs in the UPR process is that for four of the countries that have undergone a second cycle of the UPR, NGO submissions nearly doubled, from 35 in the first cycle to 60 in the second.[54]

In the first cycle of the UPR review processes, the end of which coincided with the beginning of the revolts in 2011, national and regional NGOs demonstrated the highest concern with the status of civil and political rights in the region, followed immediately by economic, social, and cultural rights and administration of justice and recourse issues. They also advocated for improvements in women's rights and the protection of vulnerable groups, including migrants, refugees, and stateless persons.[55]

Put together, the freedoms of opinion and conscience, expression, and association topped the list of issues of concern for national and regional organizations. These are all rights essential for civic participation in public life, without which any kind of democratic practice is simply not possible. Their comments and recommendations ranged from freedom of the press and imprisonment of journalists to publication and censorship laws and Internet freedoms, including blogs, website blocking, and free access to information. National and international NGOs both identified this as the highest priority in this set of rights. Arab NGOs also noted concerns with most of the specific economic and social rights far more often than international NGOs did, on average more than 4.5 times the frequency. Topping the list were generalized references to economic and social rights, social security and issues of poverty and an adequate standard of living, and housing rights. Most of those comments were aimed at countries that are large in populations and poorer in resources.[56] Concerns with the rights of children were evident in the comments of all civil society organizations. The comments spanned a range of issues from child labor to education to child victims of trafficking and children of migrants and disadvantaged communities. NGOs raised problems with human rights protection in the context of states' counterterrorism efforts 2.5 times more frequently than states did, but the reverse was true for human rights education and institutional capacity building.

Interestingly, several NGOs contributed to the preparations of some governments' national reports to the UPR, which on the face of it seems a contradiction. In the UPR, this is an expectation built into the modalities of the process.[57] One positive aspect is that, arguably, it was the first time that some governments opened their doors to direct discussions with civil society and the first opportunity for civil society actors to engage directly with them on human rights issues.

While there may still be some general resistance to the human rights paradigm in some circles, states and societies in the Arab region have recently moved on from the view that human rights are a form of Western neocolonialism. This is evident in the discussion of ratifications and engagement above. The more common discourse now is that Arab and Islamic culture are equally valid sources of human rights concepts and that Islam already guarantees rights in a manner largely consistent with human rights law. This debate, while important to help encourage states to sign and ratify human rights treaties, becomes immaterial to the fact that once they do ratify those treaties (as most have done), they become legally obligated to implement them. Despite some protestations to the contrary, Arab countries are cognizant of these legal obligations. This has been demonstrated in their engagement, albeit hesitant, with the treaty bodies and in their active engagement with the Human Rights Council's UPR. Yet the impression is created that it is primarily a political effort to appear engaged that is not complemented by serious measures on the ground to implement those obligations.

It is safe to say that despite all this activity within UN human rights circles and forums, where states' human rights practices are discussed, the UN has not been able to effectively influence policy decisions on human rights in the Arab region. Arab states have been willing to engage with the system, but in a limited fashion. They will discuss, debate, and make recommendations to one another, but the system meets with resistance whenever action is required or whenever direct scrutiny and specific criticisms or sanctions are involved. The most honest and clearest of the UN comments on human rights realities in the Arab states come from the treaty bodies and Special Procedures, which is not surprising since these bodies and individuals act in their individual expert capacities and not as representatives of states. The same issues come up in the Human Rights Council's UPR, where the discussion is among states and where the potential for action and decision making is greater. However, they do so only in generally diplomatic, noncommittal terms, and the willingness and capacity to take serious action are minimal, so that the outcomes are inconclusive. Clearly, the more political the body, the more of a game the human rights system becomes. The Arab states demonstrate willingness to discuss the issues but far less willingness to commit themselves to implementation as a result of recommendations by any power outside their own sovereignty.

Yet the UN remains a crucially important forum for calling states to account for their human rights practices. One should not discount entirely the ongoing effects of "naming and shaming" or the possibility that at certain moments in global interaction a human rights issue gathers sufficient critical mass and energy to pressure states to act. Arab states have indeed taken several steps in the past decade to appear positive and engaged vis-à-vis human rights discourse, and this is evident in some practices. For example, with global attention focused on the serious problem of trafficking in persons, five Arab countries passed anti–human trafficking laws between 2006 and 2009.[58] As noted earlier, Arab states in the UPR process have highlighted the importance of institutionalizing human rights education and strengthening the institutional protection of human rights, both of which have long-term effects.

Arab states have taken other proactive steps to "own" human rights. They were instrumental in the adoption by the Organisation of Islamic Cooperation of the 1990 Cairo Declaration on Human Rights in Islam.[59] The long moribund Arab Charter on Human Rights, originally adopted in 1994 but never ratified, was dusted off, rewritten, and adopted in 2004,[60] but only about half of the Arab states have ratified it. More recently, the Gulf Cooperation Council adopted its own Human Rights Declaration.[61] Both of those documents have been criticized by Arab and international organizations and experts as falling below the standards of the Universal Declaration of Human Rights, notwithstanding Qatar's assertion that "the declaration stems from the member states' deep belief in human dignity and respect for his [sic] rights as well as their commitment to protecting human rights guaranteed by Islamic Shariah, which embodies the values and noble principles entrenched in the conscience of the GCC communities, as well as the foundations of their policies at all levels."[62]

Another important example is the growing role of national human rights institutions. To date, fourteen of the twenty-two Arab states have national human rights institutions as official state institutions charged with improving human rights practices.[63] Those state institutions vary a great deal in their ability to act independently of their executive authorities, but the potential for their having some effect on state practice cannot be discounted.

Yet even with this engagement, state practice seems not to improve, and it has even taken a turn for the worse in several countries, particularly after the revolts of 2011. Of special note is Bahrain, the first country to undergo the UPR in 2008, which it embraced enthusiastically.[64] Bahrain has actively engaged with the UN human rights system, rarely failing to respond to queries and recommendations, as mentioned earlier in this paper. Yet in substance, it has come under severe criticism for its human rights practices and has harassed and imprisoned human rights defenders for several years, failing to respond to UN calls for their release.[65]

The UN is also an indispensable forum for civil society organizations, which are continually trying to push the limits of state—and UN— responses. As seen above, regional and national NGOs have increasingly relied on the UN forums to raise human rights issues to bring pressure to bear on states to improve their human rights practices, despite their frustrations when the human rights system fails to respond. Before the UPR of Egypt was presented to the Human Rights Council on November 5, 2014, nineteen Egyptian human rights organizations published a joint report decrying the deteriorating situation of human rights in the country and inviting the Egyptian government to discuss this report as well as its own report to the Council before the UPR took place,[66] and several of them decided not to participate in the proceedings at all for fear of reprisal.[67]

Arab governments will most likely continue on this current path of discussing but not implementing human rights obligations or accepting any international scrutiny in doing so. The question is whether the UN system in its entirety can do more to affect changes on the ground. The forum for doing so is not limited to the Human Rights Council and its Special Procedures, the UPR, or the committee mechanisms of the human rights treaties. The connection needs to be made between international development cooperation more generally and domestic and international legal obligations, with human rights standards as central to those efforts. All stakeholders, including NGOs, UN agencies, and aid agencies, have the potential to frame their work in the context of assisting states in the duty to implement human rights, relying on the advice of the treaty bodies, Special Procedures, and the UPR recommendations that states have accepted during their review.

Incorporating a human rights lens and practical strategies and approaches in any new human development model is imperative, not only because of the legal requirements to do so, but because of the opportunity it offers to try something new.[68] The challenge before the UN is to consider how to work cooperatively with governments in the context of diplomatic relations, while at the same time insisting that governments change their methods of work and do what they legally must do.

Indeed, mainstreaming human rights is now a requirement for the UN, which has been moving toward a human rights–based approach, formalized in 2003 as "A Common Understanding among UN Agencies," which laid out the elements of this approach.[69] Moreover, in the Outcome Document of the 2010 Millennium Summit states recognized the interconnectedness of human rights, development, peace, and security (paras. 3 and 13), gender equality (12 and 53), participatory, community-led strategies (23e), and reform of international financial institutions and their role in development (40). "Inclusive and equitable economic growth" appeared throughout the text, (43, 47, and elsewhere), and the document reaffirmed that "respect for and promotion and protection of human rights is an integral part of effective work towards achieving the Millennium Development Goals" (53 and 55).[70] This document essentially reiterates the interconnectedness and indivisibility of rights, which were clarified in particular by the Declaration on the Right to Development adopted by the General Assembly twenty-six years ago, and which Arab states played a significant part in adopting.[71]

UN organizations, funds, and programs like UNESCO, the UN Office on Drugs and Crime, UNDP, and others must therefore consider the legal protection of human rights in this cooperation, be guided by its laws and standards, and ensure their enjoyment by everyone. Whether they are doing so as part and parcel of their programming is arguable and deserving of more elaborate and detailed research, to include a review of UN efforts to promote human rights in the region, including the promotional work of the Office of the High Commissioner for Human Rights; technical assistance programs of agencies like Economic and Social Commission for West Asia; the International Labour Organization; and the UNDP and its development policies on mainstreaming human rights. These are crucial studies if we are to learn whether the UN has been able to influence policy decisions on human rights in the Arab region.

The uprisings in North Africa and the Middle East in 2011 were clear expressions of people's frustrations with unaccountable government, ineffectual economic policies, rampant corruption, and the exclusion of the intended beneficiaries of development from any participation in the debates on public policy. None of this should have been surprising, of course, and the human rights reports and discussions within the United Nations had been noting these problems for years, as the first part of this essay notes. Yet despite some successes in some countries at regime change, the situation has significantly worsened and deteriorated into armed conflict and destruction that have set countries like Iraq, Libya, Syria, and Yemen back many years. Only Tunisia appears to be on the path to a people-powered democratic statebuilding process that is predicated on respect for human rights.[72]

To date, what the UN human rights mechanisms have added is to remind states in the region that they have a legal obligation, as duty bearers, to take measures to ensure the enjoyment of human rights within their jurisdiction and to propose specific recommendations and actions to help them do so. UN agencies must also do their part, whether or not they work directly in human rights, governance, or related fields. They can play a crucial bridging role between governments, their civil societies, and international forums for debate and discussion, provided they can maintain trust as neutral arbiters that nevertheless insist on the human rights–based approach as mandated by the international community.

Failing that, and given the continued absence of enforcement mechanisms, human rights processes at the UN become little more than a diplomatic game, and Arab states are becoming good players, with their efforts focused on simply staying in the game and not losing. In fact, in such a diplomatic game, a state loses only if it becomes a complete pariah without support in the international community, a rare occurrence. In the domestic sphere, meanwhile, states continue business as usual, and human rights defenders continue their uphill struggle to make the human rights system work.

NOTES

This essay is based in large part on a previous research report by the author: Fateh Azzam, "Arab States and U.N. Human Rights Mechanisms," Research Report,

Issam Fares Institute for Public Policy and International Affairs, American University in Beirut, July 2013, https://www.aub.edu.lb/ifi/public_policy/rapp /Documents/20130710ifi_RAPP_rr_Arab_States_and_UN_Human_Rights_ Mechanisms.pdf.

1. United Nations, "Vienna Declaration and Programme of Action, Adopted by the World Conference on Human Rights," A/CONF.157/23, June 25, 1993, www .ohchr.org/EN/ProfessionalInterest/Pages/Vienna.aspx.

2. UN General Assembly, "Renewing the United Nations: A Programme for Reform, Report of the Secretary General," A/51/950, July 14, 1997, paras. 78–79.

3. See UN Development Programme, "Regional Arab Human Development Reports," www.arab-hdr.org/reports/regionalarab.aspx; World Bank, "Data: Arab World," accessed April 6, 2016, http://data.worldbank.org/region/ARB; and, e.g., Cairo Institute for Human Rights Studies, "Delivering Democracy; Fifth CIHRS Annual Report on the Human Rights Situation in the Arab World," May 16, 2013, www.cihrs.org/?p=6590&lang=en. See also the annual reports of Amnesty International relevant to the Arab region, www.amnesty.org/en/region/middle-east-and-north-africa.

4. For an overview of UN human rights mechanisms, see UN Office of the High Commissioner for Human Rights (hereafter OHCHR), "Working with the United Nations Human Rights Programme: A Handbook for Civil Society," accessed April 6, 2016, www.ohchr.org/EN/AboutUs/CivilSociety/Pages /Handbook.aspx. The International Criminal Court, established in 2003, is also part of the system, but its purview is not considered here.

5. See, e.g., Article 28(3) of the International Covenant on Civil and Political Rights, and Article 17(1) of the Convention on the Elimination of Discrimination against Women.

6. See OHCHR, "Monitoring the Core International Human Rights Treaties," n.d., accessed April 6, 2016, www.ohchr.org/EN/HRBodies/Pages/TreatyBodies .aspx.

7. The Human Rights Council was established by UN General Assembly Resolution 60/251, A/Res/60/251, March 15, 2006, http://www2.ohchr.org/english /bodies/hrcouncil/docs/A.RES.60.251_En.pdf; see UN Human Rights Council, "Welcome to the Human Rights Council," n.d., accessed April 8, 2016, www.ohchr .org/EN/HRBodies/HRC/Pages/AboutCouncil.aspx.

8. See OHCHR, "Special Procedures of the Human Rights Council," n.d., accessed April 8, 2016, www.ohchr.org/EN/HRBodies/SP/Pages/Welcomepage .aspx.

9. The UN Diplomatic Conference of Plenipotentiaries on the Establishment of an International Criminal Court adopted the Statutes of the International Criminal Court in Rome, Italy, on July 17, 1998. International Criminal Court, "Rome Statute of the International Criminal Court," A/CONF.183/9, July 17, 1998, accessed April 8, 2016, http://legal.un.org/icc/statute/romefra.htm.

10. For more detailed information, see OHCHR, "Ratification of 18 Human Rights Treaties," n.d., accessed April 8, 2016, http://indicators.ohchr.org. Palestine,

after its recognition as a state nonmember of the UN in 2012, has now signed seven of the nine treaties; see OHCHR, "Press Briefing Notes on Palestine, Spokesperson for the UN High Commissioner for Human Rights: Rupert Colville," May 2, 2014, https://unispal.un.org/DPA/DPR/unispal.nsf/0/262AC5B8C25B364585257CCF0 06C010D.

11. See OHCHR, "Late and Non-reporting States," on global reporting status, n.d., accessed April 8, 2016, http://tbinternet.ohchr.org/_layouts/TreatyBodyExternal /LateReporting.aspx.

12. Algeria, Djibouti, Libya, Somalia, and Tunisia.

13. Algeria, Bahrain, Morocco, and Tunisia.

14. Lebanon, Mauritania, and Tunisia.

15. List of thematic mandates available at OHCHR, accessed April 8, 2016, http://spinternet.ohchr.org/_Layouts/SpecialProceduresInternet/ViewAllCountry Mandates.aspx?Type=TM.

16. See OHCHR, Annual Reports of Special Procedures, Publications on Special Procedures, www.ohchr.org/EN/HRBodies/SP/Pages/Publications.aspx.

17. OHCHR, "United Nations Special Procedures, Facts and Figures 2013," February 2014, www.ohchr.org/Documents/HRBodies/SP/Facts_Figures2013.pdf.

18. Jordan, Kuwait, Lebanon, Qatar, and Tunisia.

19. Human Rights Council Resolution 5/1, A/HRC/Res/5/1, June 2007, para. 3(c) and (d), paras. 5–14, www.refworld.org/docid/4ae9acbbd.html.

20. Ibid., paras. 1, 3, and 3(a).

21. Ibid., para. 3(m).

22. See, e.g., Rosa Freedman, "The United Nations Human Rights Council: More of the Same?," *Wisconsin International Law Journal* 31, no. 2 (December 2013): 208–51, http://hosted.law.wisc.edu/wordpress/wilj/files/2014/01/Freedman_final_v2.pdf.

23. See Edward R. McMahon, *The Universal Periodic Review: A Work in Progress; An Evaluation of the First Cycle of the New UPR Mechanism of the United Nations Human Rights Council*, Dialogue on Globalization Series (Berlin: Friedrich Ebert Stiftung, September 2012), 14–15, http://library.fes.de/pdf-files/bueros /genf/09297.pdf.

24. Azzam, "Arab States," 25. The states reviewed were Algeria, Morocco, Tunisia, Egypt, Jordan, Lebanon, Bahrain, Kuwait, Oman, and Yemen (19).

25. Ibid., 24. See also Annex II, chart 4, 44.

26. Ibid., 27.

27. Ibid., 28.

28. Committee on the Rights of the Child, "Consideration of Reports submitted by States Parties under Article 44 of the Convention: Concluding Observations: Syrian Arab Republic," CRC/C/SYR/CO/3–4, February 9, 2012, 15, http:// tbinternet.ohchr.org/_layouts/treatybodyexternal/Download.aspx?symbolno=CRC /C/SYR/CO/3–4&Lang=En.

29. Committee on the Rights of the Child, "Concluding Observations on Jordan," CRC/C/15/Add.125, 2000, paras. 31, 43, 45, 47.

30. UN Committee on the Elimination of Discrimination against Women (hereafter CEDAW committee), "Concluding Comments: Jordan," CEDAW/JOR/CO/4, August 10, 2007, paras. 31 and 33.

31. CEDAW committee, "Concluding Comments: Lebanon," CEDAW/C/LBN/CO/3, para. 30, http://www2.ohchr.org/english/bodies/cedaw/docs/co/CEDAW.C.LBN.CO.3.pdf; CEDAW committee, "Concluding Observations: Bahrain," CEDAW/BHR/CO/2, November 14, 2008, para. 34, www.refworld.org/pdfid/494ba8cd0.pdf.

32. CEDAW committee, "Concluding Observations: Oman," CEDAW/C/OMN/CO/1, October 21, 2011, paras. 27 and 42, http://www2.ohchr.org/english/bodies/cedaw/docs/co/CEDAW-C-OMN-CO-1.pdf; CEDAW committee, "Concluding Comments: Saudi Arabia," CEDAW/C/SAU/CO/2, April 8, 2008, p. 7; CEDAW committee, "Concluding Observations: United Arab Emirates," CEDAW/C/ARE/CO/1, February 5, 2010, para. 36, http://www2.ohchr.org/english/bodies/cedaw/docs/co/CEDAW-C-ARE-CO-1.pdf.

33. United Nations, "Report of the Human Rights Committee," vol. II, chap. IV, sec. M, "Kuwait," A/55/40, paras. 493–94, www.un.org/documents/ga/docs/55/a5540vol2.pdf; Committee on the Elimination of Racial Discrimination, "Bahrain: Concluding Observations," CERD/C/BHR/CO/7, April 14, 2005, www.refworld.org/publisher,CERD,,BHR,42de64fd4,0.html.

34. "Compilation of Developments in the Area of Human Rights Defenders: Saudi Arabia," E/CN.4/2006/95/Add.5, March 6, 2006, para. 1424, https://documents-dds-ny.un.org/doc/UNDOC/GEN/G06/122/53/PDF/G0612253.pdf?OpenElement.

35. See the following compilations prepared by the OHCHR in accordance with paragraph 15 (b) of the annex to Human Rights Council resolution 5/1: for Bahrain, A/HRC/WG.6/1/BHR/2, March 14, 2008, https://documents-dds-ny.un.org/doc/UNDOC/GEN/G08/116/54/PDF/G0811654.pdf?OpenElement; for Jordan, A/HRC/WG.6/4/JOR/2, November 21, 2008, https://documents-dds-ny.un.org/doc/UNDOC/GEN/G08/168/85/PDF/G0816885.pdf?OpenElement; for Kuwait, A/HRC/WG.6/8/KWT/2, February 12, 2010, https://documents-dds-ny.un.org/doc/UNDOC/GEN/G10/116/11/PDF/G1011611.pdf?OpenElement; for Lebanon, A/HRC/WG.6/9/LBN/2, September 2, 2010, www.univie.ac.at/bimtor/dateien/lebanon_upr_2010_info.pdf; for Oman, A/HRC/WG.6/10/OMN/2, November 12, 2010, http://www.refworld.org/pdfid/4d551cod2.pdf; for Qatar, A/HRC/WG.6/7/QAT/2, November 23, 2009, www.refworld.org/pdfid/4b264e3e0.pdf; for Saudi Arabia, A/HRC/WG.6/4/SAU/2; for Syria, A/HRC/WG.6/12/SYR/2, September 5, 2011, https://documents-dds-ny.un.org/doc/UNDOC/GEN/G11/156/35/PDF/G1115635.pdf?OpenElement; for A/HRC/WG.6/3/ARE/2, September 29, 2008, https://documents-dds-ny.un.org/doc/UNDOC/GEN/G08/161/44/PDF/G0816144.pdf?OpenElement; and for Yemen, A/HRC/WG.6/5/YEM/2, March 9, 2009, https://documents-dds-ny.un.org/doc/UNDOC/GEN/G09/119/38/PDF/G0911938.pdf?OpenElement. Note that states'

adherence to International Labour Organization conventions they have ratified relevant to freedom of association is not considered here.

36. UNESCO, "Universal Periodic Review, Contribution of UNESCO, Syrian Arab Republic," October 3–14, 2011, paras. 2–24, 26, www.upr-info.org/sites /default/files/document/syrian_arab_republic/session_12_-_october_2011/unesco-eng.pdf. See OHCHR, "Compilation Prepared by the Office of the High Commissioner for Human Rights in Accordance with Paragraph 15 (b) of the Annex to Human Rights Council Resolution 5/1: Syrian Arab Republic," A/HRC/ WG.6/12/SYR/2, September 5, 2011, para. 70, https://documents-dds-ny.un.org /doc/UNDOC/GEN/G11/156/35/PDF/G1115635.pdf?OpenElement.

37. Hina Jilani, (former) special representative of the secretary-general on human rights defenders, "Summary of Cases Transmitted to Governments and Replies Received," E/CN.4/2005/101/Add.1, March 16, 2005, para. 48, https://unispal .un.org/DPA/DPR/unispal.nsf/1ce874ab1832a53e852570bb006dfaf6/2f2c9ff72352f 63d85256fd2005199b3?OpenDocument.

38. OHCHR, "Compilation Prepared by the OHCHR in Accordance with Paragraph 15 (b) of the Annex to Human Rights Council Resolution 5/1: Oman," November 12, 2010, A/HRC/WG.6/10/OMN/2, para. 40, www.refworld.org /pdfid/4d551c0d2.pdf.

39. Human Rights Council, "Report of the Special Rapporteur on the Independence of Judges and Lawyers, Leandro Despouy," A/HRC/4/25/Add.1, April 5, 2007, para. 376, https://documents-dds-ny.un.org/doc/UNDOC/GEN /G07/128/12/PDF/G0712812.pdf?OpenElement.

40. The citations here are all from the Reports of the Special Representative of the Secretary-General on the Situation of Human Rights Defenders, "Summary of Cases Transmitted to Governments and Replies Received." For Bahrain, A/ HRC/4/37/Add.1, March 27, 2007, para. 35, http://www2.ohchr.org/english /bodies/hrcouncil/docs/4session/A-HRC-4–37-Add-1.pdf. For Saudi Arabia, E/ CN.4/2006/95/Add.5, March 6, 2006, para. 1424, https://documents-dds-ny .un.org/doc/UNDOC/GEN/G06/122/53/PDF/G0612253.pdf?OpenElement; E/ CN.4/2005/101/Add.1, March 16, 2005, para. 473, https://documents-dds-ny.un .org/doc/UNDOC/GEN/G05/129/65/PDF/G0512965.pdf?OpenElement; A /HRC/4/37/Add.1, March 27, 2007, paras. 584, 585, and 586, http://www2.ohchr .org/english/bodies/hrcouncil/docs/4session/A-HRC-4–37-Add-1.pdf; and A /HRC/7/28/Add.1, March 5, 2008, paras. 1738, 1741, 1744, and 1746, https:// documents-dds-ny.un.org/doc/UNDOC/GEN/G08/114/44/PDF/G0811444 .pdf?OpenElement. For Yemen, E/CN.4/2006/55/Add.1, March 27, 2006, paras. 1117–18 and 1121, https://documents-dds-ny.un.org/doc/UNDOC/GEN /G06/121/12/PDF/G0612112.pdf?OpenElement; and A/HRC/7/14/Add.1, February 25, 2008, paras. 745–47, https://documents-dds-ny.un.org/doc/UNDOC /GEN/G08/109/89/PDF/G0810989.pdf?OpenElement.

41. UN Committee against Torture, "Concluding Observations: Syrian Arab Republic," CAT/C/SYR/CO/1, May 25, 2010, para. 34, https://documents-dds-ny .un.org/doc/UNDOC/GEN/G10/426/23/PDF/G1042623.pdf?OpenElement.

42. UN Human Rights Committee, "Concluding Observations: Syrian Arab Republic," CCPR/CO/84/SYR, August 9, 2005, para. 13, https://documents-dds-ny.un.org/doc/UNDOC/GEN/G05/435/11/PDF/G0543511.pdf?Open Element.

43. "Joint Appeal by Egyptian Human Rights Organizations to the UN OHCHR," April 3, 2013, www.cihrs.org/?p=6479&lang=en.

44. See, e.g., only some of the Gulf Center for Human Rights press releases: "Saudi Arabia: Raif Badawi Facing 1000 Lashes in Public for His Human Rights Works," October 24, 2014, http://gc4hr.org/news/view/792; "Update: Bahrain: Another Case Brought against Jailed Human Rights Defender Zainab Al-Khawaja," October 21, 2014, http://gc4hr.org/news/view/789; "Oman: Writer and Online Activist Saed Al-Darodi Held Incommunicado," October 20, 2014, http://gc4hr .org/news/view/786; "Update: Kuwait: Human Rights Defender Sulaiman Bin Jasim Sentenced to One Month in Prison," October 19, 2014, http://gc4hr.org/news /view/784; and "UAE: Postponement of Trial of Human Rights Defender Osama Al-Najjar," September 26, 2014, http://gc4hr.org/news/view/762.

45. UN Committee against Torture, "Conclusions and Recommendations: Bahrain," CAT/C/CR/34/BHR, June 2005, paras. 6–7, http://docstore.ohchr.org /SelfServices/FilesHandler.ashx?enc=6QkG1d%2fPPRiCAqhKb7yhshvVcmWTu l6%2fu%2bWl9YGTVqCesQ6ZOBJNgo%2bxntePMzgdo2%2feTrGzToTMLKJ6 GVRh%2fcw9F2ySSAGZkGPuCRxyBnJgosT%2fqFUqoBhTR%2fN3tsi3.

46. Jilani, "Summary of Cases," E/CN.4/2005/101/Add.1, para. 49.

47. UN General Assembly, Human Rights Council, "Compilation," para. 41.

48. Committee on the Rights of the Child, "Concluding Observations: Oman," CRC/C/OMN/CO/2, September 29, 2006, para. 21, https://documents-dds-ny .un.org/doc/UNDOC/GEN/G06/451/19/PDF/G0645119.pdf?OpenElement.

49. Committee on the Rights of the Child, "Concluding Observations: Qatar," CRC/C/QAT/CO/2, October 14, 2009, paras. 21–22, http://repository.un.org /bitstream/handle/11176/280116/CRC_C_QAT_CO_2-EN.pdf?sequence=3&is Allowed=y.

50. CEDAW committee, "Concluding Observations: Syrian Arab Republic," CEDAW/C/SYR/CO/1, June 11, 2007, para. 36, www.un.org/womenwatch/daw /cedaw/cdrom_cedaw/EN/files/cedaw25years/content/english/CONCLUDING_ COMMENTS_ENGLISH/Syrian%20Arab%20Republic/Syrian%20Arab%20 Republic%20CO-1.pdf.

51. Azzam, "Arab States," Annex II, charts 1–6, 43–45.

52. Ibid., 22.

53. Joseph Schechla, "The Use of Human Rights Mechanisms by Human Rights Defenders in the Middle East, 2004–09," unpublished research commissioned by the Middle East Regional Office of the High Commissioner for Human Rights, Beirut, June 2010, 12.

54. Azzam, "Arab States," 37.

55. Ibid., Annex II, charts 1 and 2, 47.

56. Egypt, Morocco, and Yemen.

57. Human Rights Council Resolution 5/1, June 2007, A/HRC/Res/5/1, para 3(m), www.refworld.org/docid/4ae9acbbd.html.

58. Bahrain (2008), Djibouti (2007), Jordan (2009), Oman (2008), and the United Arab Emirates (2006). See UN Inter-Agency Project on Human Trafficking, Resources page, accessed 2015, www.no-trafficking.org/resources_int_tip_laws .html.

59. Adopted at the Nineteenth Islamic Conference of Foreign Ministers in Cairo, Egypt held July 31-August 5, 1990. See text of the Declaration at Organisation of Islamic Cooperation, "The Cairo Declaration on Human Rights in Islam," www .oic-oci.org/english/article/human.htm.

60. See text of the Charter at www.refworld.org/cgibin/texis/vtx/rwmain? docid=3ae6b38540.

61. GulfNews, "Gulf States Urged to Act on Human Rights," December 10, 2014, http://gulfnews.com/news/gulf/qatar/gulf-states-urged-to-act-on-human-rights-declaration-1.1425060. For an Arabic text of the GCC Human Rights Declaration, see http://24.ae/print-article.aspx?ArticleId=123304.

62. Qatar Ministry of Foreign Affairs, "GCC Supreme Council Approves Declaration on Human Rights," December 9, 2014, www.mofa.gov.qa/en /SiteServices/MediaCenter/News/Pages/News20141210194504.aspx.

63. For a list by region, see International Coordinating Committee of National Institutions for the Promotion and Protection of Human Rights, "Directory of National Human Rights Institutions," accessed April 8, 2016, http://nhri.ohchr .org/en/contact/nhris/Pages/default.aspx.

64. See Bahrain's UPR website at www.upr.bh.

65. See OHCHR, "UN Experts urge Bahrain to Release Human Rights Defender Maryam al-Khawaja," press release, September 5, 2014, www.ohchr.org /EN/NewsEvents/Pages/DisplayNews.aspx?NewsID=14992&LangID=E. See also OHCHR, "Press Briefing Notes on Bahrain and Destruction of Places of Religious Significance by ISIL," October 3, 2014, www.ohchr.org/EN/NewsEvents /Pages/DisplayNews.aspx?NewsID=15135&LangID=E. For more information, see Bahrain Center for Human Rights website at www.bahrainrights.org.

66. "19 Rights Organizations Declare: A Dramatic Deterioration in the Status of Human Rights in Egypt over the Past Four Years," October 29, 2014, www.cihrs .org/?p=9589&lang=en. The full report, "Joint Submission by Forum of Egyptian Independent Human Rights Organizations," 2014, can be found at www.cihrs.org /wp-content/uploads/2014/10/Joint.Stakeholderssubmission.UPR_.Egypt_ .TheForum.EN_.pdf.

67. "As a Result of a Direct Threat to Their Work: Egyptian Human Rights Organizations Have Decided Not to Participate in Egypt's UPR before the UN," November 5, 2014, www.cihrs.org/?p=9836&lang=en.

68. See, e.g., OHCHR, "Summary of the Draft Guidelines on a Human Rights Approach to Poverty Reduction," March 2004, www2.ohchr.org/english/issues /poverty/docs/SwissSummary1.doc. See also "The Right to Development and Practical Strategies for the Implementation of the Millennium Development Goals,

Particularly Goal 8," E/CN.4/2005/WG.18/TF/CRP.1, November 2, 2005, and more recently UN Economic and Social Commission for Western Asia, "A Human Rights Approach to Sustainable Development in the Arab Region," ESCWA Expert Report, May 2015, http://css.escwa.org.lb/SDPD/3572/8-AzzamSD.pdf.

69. See "The Human Rights Based Approach to Development Cooperation: Towards a Common Understanding among UN Agencies," n.d., HRBA Portal, accessed April 8, 2016, http://hrbaportal.org/the-human-rights-based-approach-to-development-cooperation-towards-a-common-understanding-among-un-agencies.

70. UN General Assembly, "Keeping the Promise: United to Achieve the Millennium Development Goals," A/65/L.1, September 17, 2010, https://documents-dds-ny.un.org/doc/UNDOC/LTD/N10/537/31/PDF/N1053731.pdf?OpenElement.

71. UN General Assembly, Declaration on the Right to Development, A/RES/41/128, December 4, 1986, www.un.org/documents/ga/res/41/a41r128.htm.

72. See "The Tunisian Pact on Rights and Liberties," FIDH website, June 5, 2013, www.fidh.org/en/north-africa-middle-east/tunisia/the-tunisian-pact-on-rights-and-liberties-13237.

TWELVE

The Politics of the Sanctions on Iraq and the UN Humanitarian Exception

Hans-Christof von Sponeck

UN SANCTIONS AND THE HUMAN RIGHT FOR DIGNIFIED SURVIVAL

Sanctions were imposed on Iraq by the United Nations four days after Saddam Hussein invaded Kuwait, on August 2, 1990.[1] They were lifted two months after the United States/United Kingdom invaded Iraq on March 19, 2003.[2]

There had to be a strong international response to Iraq's invasion of its neighbor Kuwait. The UN Security Council's decision to impose sanctions for such aggression was justified. However, these should have been accompanied by a carefully crafted humanitarian exemption to ensure that the civilian population would receive what they needed for a dignified survival, especially food, medicines, clean water, and electricity. The fact that the UN so clearly failed to do so eventually led to the successive resignations of Denis Halliday and myself as Baghdad-based UN assistant secretaries-general and humanitarian coordinators.

During almost thirteen years of the most comprehensive economic sanctions ever imposed by the United Nations, the Iraqi civilian population's life changed from a high level of well-being to an abject level of ill-being.[3]

The initial years of sanctions (1990–95) passed without the adoption of a UN humanitarian exemption designed to prevent malnutrition, disease, and poverty. Signs of a deepening human catastrophe—identified as early as 1991 by two UN missions—were largely ignored by the UN Security Council. Forgotten were the conclusions of UN under-secretary-general Martti Athisaari that the Iraq conflict had "wrought near-apocalyptic results" and had "relegated Iraq to a pre-industrial age."[4] Even though all fifteen governments represented in the Security Council knew that outside help was urgently needed, the Council had introduced comprehensive sanctions without any concern for a social safety net.

The Security Council had abrogated the fundamental principles of justice and human rights as enshrined in the UN Charter and had ignored the demands of international humanitarian law. Mitigation against the adverse impact of UN sanctions was left entirely to voluntary external initiatives. It must be recalled here that during the 1991 war civilian infrastructure—electricity, water and sanitation facilities, bridges and roads—especially in southern Iraq had been deliberately targeted and destroyed. This in turn made outside humanitarian help even more important but also more difficult to deliver.

It was clear that the United States with support from its allies made sure that UN politics of disarmament took precedence over humanitarian concerns. "Although the flow of humanitarian and civilian goods to Iraq was a matter of strong interest to the US government, it should be emphasized that an even greater pre-occupation throughout the period of sanctions was to ensure that no items be permitted for import which could . . . contribute to Iraq's WMD program."[5]

The UN Secretariat, not the UN Security Council, issued five appeals during the years 1992–96 calling for voluntary contributions totaling $1.2 billion. The response was sobering: only $420 million was actually collected.[6] The international public and many governments had difficulty looking beyond what they perceived as the ruthlessness of the dictatorial regime of Saddam Hussein. They also failed completely to understand the negative impact of Security Council sanction policies. It eluded them that there was an innocent population that urgently required outside help.

TENSIONS BETWEEN THE UN SECURITY COUNCIL AND THE UN SECRETARIAT

Neither the UN Office of the Coordinator for Humanitarian Affairs (OCHA) nor the rest of the UN system were able to convincingly convey this reality. The UN Department of Public Information, the voice of the UN Secretariat, was kept from making the case for the Iraqi people. Years of "political animosity between Iraq and the West . . . prevented the development of a bargaining dynamic and unnecessarily prolonged both the political crisis and the agony of the Iraqi people."[7]

What evolved was a multilateral sanctions regime irrevocably tied to Iraq's disarmament. It is important to remember that following Operation Desert Storm in early 1991 the decision to impose an import embargo of "weapons or any other military equipment" had been replaced by major new demands.[8] Sanctions, the UN Security Council then decided, would continue until Iraq had eliminated all its weapons of mass destruction and had agreed to pay compensation for all those—individuals, firms, and governments—who had claims against Iraq as a result of its invasion into Kuwait.[9] This new conditionality deepened the confrontation between the government in Baghdad and the governments in Washington and London.

The welfare of the people remained a negotiable commodity. Human suffering, the world was told, had to be accepted as unfortunate but unavoidable collateral damage.

DISAGREEMENTS WITHIN THE UN SECURITY COUNCIL

UN Security Council resolutions, more often than not conceived and formulated by the US and the UK missions to the UN in New York, became helpful facilitators for the two governments in pursuing their Iraq agenda—"helpful" because as so-called consensus resolutions they allowed a flexible and convenient interpretation of wording to suit the majority of Council members. Sanctions would remain until Iraq "had completed all actions contemplated" and had "cooperated in all respects."[10]

The one issue of seemingly common concern within the Security Council had to do with Iraq's weapons of mass destruction. This may explain why Council members went along with the United States/United Kingdom by either supporting or abstaining rather than voting against "their" resolutions.

What these resolutions did not, and could not, reveal, for obvious reasons, was the US/UK determination to achieve, at all costs, regime change in Iraq. It took many years for the United States to publicly admit such intentions as revealed in the 1998 Iraq Liberation Act.[11] When this happened, the polarization of the Iraq debate in the UN Security Council, especially within the P5 group, intensified.[12]

For China, France, and Russia as well as elected (non-Western) Council members, "regime change" was clearly a subject that had no place on any UN agenda. There was also no agreement on the admittedly controversial issue of including, at least confidentially, a time frame for ending sanctions. This allowed two permanent members (the United States and the United Kingdom) to prolong sanctions indefinitely.

TENSIONS WITHIN THE UN SECRETARIAT

Tensions within the UN Security Council were not without fallout for the UN Secretariat. From the perspective of the UN in Baghdad, it often looked as if divisions within the Council had mirror effects on senior UN officials in New York.

A case in point: during my visits to New York, UN deputy secretary-general Louise Fréchette, a former Canadian deputy minister of defense, always insisted that she wanted "nothing but facts" when discussing with me conditions in Iraq. To collect credible data, I tried to explain, in the Iraq of Saddam Hussein was a tough undertaking at any time. Efforts were made to sort out, as best as we could, spurious information from more convincing data.

To cite one important example: food distribution. While the US government insisted that monthly food rations were deliberately withheld by the Iraqi government from certain segments of the population, the World Food Programme was fully satisfied with the equitable distribution as confirmed by regular spot checks of the fifty-four thousand distribution centers across the country. Fréchette seemed to consider US accusations more credible than the information provided by UN staff on the ground.

There, however, was another dimension. It had to do with Iraqi suspicion that information collected by the United Nations would be politicized, if not by the UN itself, by individual governments. The Iraqi government would cite, not without some justification, child mortality statistics from the UN Children's Emergency Fund (UNICEF) and education statistics from the UN Educational, Scientific and Cultural Organization (UNESCO) as evidence not of biased data but of data misuse.

Throughout the years, US authorities, including some academics, kept arguing that UNICEF's child mortality data were in fact Iraqi government data. They argued that for this reason such data did not take into account that the prime cause for the excessive child mortality was the Iraqi government's deliberate neglect of child nutrition programs rather than with sanctions. In the context of the enormously bureaucratized and politicized Oil-for-Food (OFF) program, there was no evidence to support such an accusation.

THE OIL-FOR-FOOD PROGRAM AS THE UN'S HUMANITARIAN EXEMPTION

After five years of frustrating negotiations at two levels, the UN Security Council and the government on the one hand and, on the other hand, UN and Iraqi officials in Baghdad, an agreement about a humanitarian exemption was finally reached. In January 1996, UN secretary-general Boutros Boutros-Ghali and deputy prime minister Tariq Aziz had agreed on what became known as the Oil-for-Food program to ensure for twenty-three million Iraqis a "dignified survival" under sanctions. Four months later, in May 1996, an agreement was signed by the UN legal counsel and Iraq's ambassador to the UN.[13] The OFF program would be "temporary" and would be managed "under the overall authority of the [UN] Department of Humanitarian Affairs." Largely unnoticed by many in the Security Council as well as the UN system of humanitarian agencies, OCHA was quietly replaced by the newly created UN Office of the Iraq Program (OIP) to manage the humanitarian exemption "as an operation separate and distinct from all other activities."[14]

Given the size of OFF—it was the largest humanitarian program ever undertaken by the United Nations—it did make sense to create a special unit within the UN Secretariat in New York. What made no sense whatsoever was that this unit did not form part of OCHA, where until then all sanction programs had been located. The question that remains unanswered is who was behind this decision. What is clear is only that such a special unit could be more easily controlled.

As it turned out, OFF operated throughout its existence in total and deliberate isolation from OCHA. Though it was initially located on the same floor in the UN Secretariat building, there was no contact at all between the two humanitarian units. On one occasion a young OCHA officer was told: "You refrain from contact with the Iraq program, they are too political."

It is remarkable and worrisome that senior UN management had agreed to such a separation. To run two units was costly and dysfunctional, and, most significantly, it deprived the Iraq program of making use of the extensive and global OCHA sanctions experience.

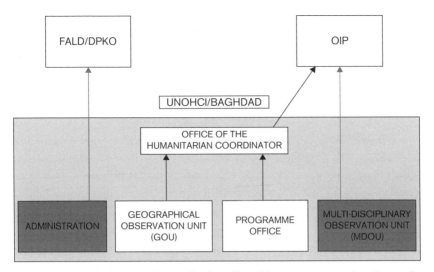

FIGURE 12.1. Organizational diagram for the Office of the Humanitarian Coordinator for Iraq (UNOHCI). Baghdad, 10 October 1999. FALD = Field Administrative and Logistics Division; DPKO = Department of Peacekeeping Operations; OIP = Office of the Iraq Program; UNOHCI = UN Office of the Humanitarian Coordinator for Iraq.

Another structural anomaly with negative consequences for the "effective" running of the humanitarian exemption was in place in Iraq. It had to do with the management setup of the OFF program in Baghdad. The Office of the Humanitarian Coordinator for Iraq (UNOHCI), headed by an assistant secretary-general, was made up of four units (see figure 12.1).

Such a disjointed structure had to result in disarray and conflict. It did indeed and once again prevailed at the expense of running an "effective" humanitarian exemption.[15]

It quickly became evident that the limited sale of Iraqi oil during the initial years of OFF (1996–97), amounting to a mere $2.6 billion for six months, made a "dignified" survival for a majority of Iraqis all but impossible. Even the doubling of this amount to $5.2 billion in 1998, as agreed in Baghdad between UN secretary-general Kofi Annan and President Saddam Hussein, did not significantly change the prevailing conditions of misery.[16]

The OFF program had as its stated objective the "equitable" and "effective" distribution of humanitarian supplies based on "adequate" resources. As it turned out, OFF during six and a half years of operation (1996–2003) was neither effective nor adequate. What can be confirmed is that "inadequacy" was not equitably distributed! More favorable sanctions conditions for Iraqi Kurdistan came much closer to "adequate," as will be detailed later.

DELIBERATE DIS- AND MISINFORMATION

In December 1999, the UN Security Council, under increasing pressure because of the deepening humanitarian crisis in Iraq, passed Resolution 1284, which suggested an end to the period of sanction cruelty.[17] The UK government announced that this resolution "removed the ceiling ... of oil Iraq is allowed to export."[18] Should Iraqis continue to suffer, so the UK and the US governments argued, it would confirm yet again that Saddam Hussein and his government were the sole cause of Iraqi suffering. This was a malicious political ploy. These two governments knew very well from their intelligence and from annual UN oil sector review missions, first, that Iraq's oil industry—the only licit source of income—was in a very precarious or, as oil experts pointed out, even "dangerous" state, and second, that rehabilitation beyond minor repairs had not been permitted under sanctions. It was obvious that Iraq would not be able to increase its oil output beyond 2.2 million barrels per day, the amount they had been able to sell on the international oil market prior to the Security Council decision to remove the prevailing oil ceiling.

Deliberate misinformation conveyed by the US and UK governments and often repeated by major media outlets in the West covered up the fact that increased oil revenue in 1999/2000 was entirely due to higher oil prices on the world market and not at all because of a higher volume of production![19] Equally misleading was the US State Department contention that "Iraqi oil exports [in 1999] were now at near pre-war levels."[20] The State Department also ignored the fact that oil revenue in the years of sanctions was the sole source of legal income in the absence of a normal private sector and state economy.

Throughout the thirteen years of sanctions, all those in the UN system and the community of nongovernmental organizations implementing humanitarian assistance were continuously faced with the power of false information in a wide range of areas. Examples of such planted information included the accusation that the food basket the government and the UN had agreed to distribute had been systematically withheld from those Iraqis considered in opposition to government. The UN World Food Programme countered by stating that the food distribution program, involving 440,000 tons of food every month, was one of its best anywhere, with no signs of systematic politicization. Another US/UK false and serious accusation was that the government of Iraq purposely hoarded medicines and other much-needed supplies. The storing of medicines was in fact in accordance with global World Health Organization guidelines for times of epidemics. Other OFF supplies often had to be stored because either they had failed quality control tests or complementary items had not yet arrived or were blocked by the UN Iraq Sanctions Committee.[21] What alternatives were there but to store syringes without vaccines, equipment for irrigation and water purification without engines and chemicals, agricultural implements without seeds and pesticides?

The US and UK governments regularly pointed out that in Iraqi Kurdistan the OFF program was implemented efficiently "because the government of Saddam Hussein was not in control there."[22] The humanitarian exception in the three Kurdish governorates indeed functioned more smoothly but for very different reasons, including the fact that the 13 percent of Iraq's population who lived there received almost 20 percent of the oil income and had access to cash payments. Oil-for-Food projects with a cash component were not available in the area under Baghdad's control. Cash was needed to pay contractors installing water pipes and electricity and sanitation equipment or to purchase locally made spare parts.

Moreover, in contrast to the large volume of items that were delayed or permanently blocked by the United States in the UN Sanctions Committee for areas under government administration, not a single item was withheld from the Kurdish areas![23] In addition, Iraq's borders with Iran and with Turkey on the Kurdish side were much more porous, allowing large amounts of smuggling. Finally, thanks to the higher altitude of much of Iraqi Kurdistan, a better epidemiological situation existed. Waterborne diseases, for example, were much less prevalent there than in the warmer and humid central and southern parts of the country. All of these factors explain why OFF worked better in the Kurdish areas, rather than the widely accepted perception promoted by the US and the UK authorities that the Iraqi regime was punishing its own people.

Efforts by senior UN officials in Baghdad, New York, and elsewhere to clarify, correct, or challenge flawed information by governments, often ably assisted by self-proclaimed investigative journalists, were feeble and ineffective. Unfortunately, all of us feared the repercussions that would come our way from powerful single-minded political authority in Washington and London.

THE OIL-FOR-FOOD PROGRAM WAS NOT
MEANT TO WORK

Apart from the systematic disinformation campaigns by individual governments, other measures involving the UN Security Council as a whole had a damaging impact on the delivery of the humanitarian program. Among these was the increasingly fine-tuned bureaucratization of OFF. The UN Sanctions Committee for Iraq was meant to be an oversight body to monitor the implementation of the humanitarian exception. Instead it became a micromanaging authority and a major cause for delays of arrivals of urgently needed supplies.[24] Worse than that, the US government continuously increased the volume of supplies it decided to withhold. In August 2002 the volume of blocked contracts peaked at the extraordinary amount of $5.2 billion. These involved such products as vaccines, chemicals, pesticides, electrical equipment, and spare parts for the oil industry. Repeated reassurances by the UN in Baghdad to the US/UK authorities that the UN capacity to monitor the deployment of such supplies existed made no difference. Blocking items was part of a deliberate effort to derail any "effective" functioning of OFF. Exceptions were made when this was considered politically opportune. In 2002 such a situation arose. Eighteen months earlier, the US authorities had withheld urgently needed electricity spare parts that Iraq had ordered from Russia. In May 2002 the US government wanted to introduce revised procurement rules and for that purpose had drafted Security Council Resolution 1409.[25] In return for Russian support, the US authorities released this blocked electricity equipment in its entirety. This was pure political opportunism. It had nothing to do with humanitarian concerns for the people of Iraq or with the 1996 UN memorandum of understanding calling for "adequate," "efficient," and "equitable" implementation of the humanitarian exemption!

THE OPERATIONAL DIVIDE AND THE
MORAL DILEMMA

The untenable situation provoked by the UN Security Council added to the confrontational relationship between UN operational staff, especially at the Baghdad level, and the Security Council policy makers in New York. There was little trust and much frustration on both sides. UN staff felt that dialogue and mediation had given way to hard-core power politics and a definite reluctance on the part of the US and UK governments to interact with "the other side" to find a solution to the Iraq crisis.

As the German ambassador Tono Eitel revealed in a confidential report to the UN Security Council on the situation in Iraq in 2002, "it is necessary for the targeted state . . . to be able to interact with the Security Council!" Yet such a basic demand was again and again prevented by individual council members for "procedural reasons."[26]

Consistent with the dominating mind-set of distance and exclusion, the UN Security Council, in violation of its oversight mandate, refrained from visiting Iraq to obtain a firsthand picture of conditions in the country as a result of its sanctions policies. Baghdad-based UN officials were regularly blocked by the US and UK representatives in the Council from coming to New York for Iraq briefings. The two governments feared that presentations of the facts on the ground by Baghdad-based UN officials could derail their Iraq intentions.

US/UK OPERATION DESERT FOX IN DECEMBER 1998—AN INTENSIFICATION OF PLANNED DESTABILIZATION

At the time when the Clinton/Blair administrations carried out Operation Desert Fox, which involved four nights of heavy bombing, especially over Baghdad, an illegal intrusion causing loss of life and property, aggressive destabilization of Iraq intensified at two levels. First, there were more and more intelligence operations across Iraq's borders into Iraqi Kurdistan, mostly by foreign agents stationed in Ankara (with cooperation by the Iraqi Kurdish authorities). This, of course, was in violation of UN Security Council resolutions confirming the country's sovereignty and territorial integrity. Such operations encouraged local acts of resistance and sabotage against Saddam Hussein's government in Baghdad. Second, the two no-fly-zones (NFZs), established by the United States, the United Kingdom, and France in 1991–92, witnessed a steep increase in US and UK air strikes. The NFZs were justified as a way of protecting Shiites in southern Iraq and Kurds in the northern part of the country from air strikes by the Saddam Hussein government. Allied air strikes within and outside (!) these zones were justified without exception as necessary to protect allied pilots from Iraqi ground-to-air missile threats.[27]

Here is another example of serious disinformation. The two governments were well aware that their aircraft were flying at altitudes at which they could not possibly be reached by the dilapidated Iraqi air defense force. The real aim of these attacks was to provoke and destabilize the Iraqi regime. This also affected the safety of Iraqi civilians as well as UN staff traveling daily throughout the area in connection with the distribution of oil-for-food supplies.

In response to these tensions, I decided as the UN official responsible for the security of UN personnel to restrict UN travel on Iraqi roads. While Secretary-General Kofi Annan supported my decision, others in the UN Secretariat in New York, including the head of the OIP, Benon Sevan, strongly objected. This showed again the fateful disunity within the UN Secretariat, with all the consequences for the Iraqi people and a professionally managed humanitarian exemption!

To raise awareness of the externally induced worsening security situation (on average one air strike every three days), which had been largely ignored by the UNSC and mainstream Western media, my office furthermore began to compile in Baghdad periodic air-strike reports.

It came as no surprise that the governments in Washington and London expressed outrage that the UN in Baghdad dared to document the civilian damage caused by their air strikes.[28] The US/UK governments reprimanded me in the strongest terms, pointing out that it was not my business to issue such reports and that I had neither the mandate nor the competence to do so. They took the unusual step to jointly ask the UN secretary-general to withdraw me from Iraq. Their contention: all the coordinator in Baghdad was doing was "to repeat Iraqi propaganda."[29]

The OFF program, inadequate as it turned out to be, nevertheless constituted an improvement over the chaotic and haphazard manner in which the government of Iraq and the UN Security Council had dealt with the Iraqi people until then. As the humanitarian exemption evolved, it appeared as if at the end of 1999 a more humane Security Council approach was emerging. The US/UK governments would argue that more funds were becoming available, the sanctions bureaucracy was being reduced, imports could reach Iraq in larger volumes and faster—"all for the benefit of the Iraqi people." Yet "Baghdad's refusal to cooperate with the oil-for-food program and its deliberate misuse of resources are cynical efforts to sacrifice the Iraqi people's welfare."[30] This certainly was not how the UN system in Iraq perceived the reality in the country. The uncompromising posture of the US and the UK governments continued unabated, though this was not obvious to the public eye. More funding and speedier clearance of some supplies meant neither a larger volume of arrivals nor the release of critical supplies in such "survival" sectors as water supply, sanitation, electricity, and agriculture. The US/UK claims that they had removed all obstacles for the effective running of OFF were false and dishonest. The concurrent steep increase of items mainly blocked by the United States offset completely the debureaucratization of procurement.

Against the backdrop of a US policy of regime change, the political and security context described earlier became significantly more confrontational. Under these circumstances, UN staff had considerable difficulty in making a difference for the benefit of the people of Iraq. It was the people who continued to pay the price. A dramatic example had to do with compensation Iraq was obliged to pay for its invasion into Kuwait. As a result, 30 percent of Iraq's oil income was automatically transferred to the UN Compensation Commission (UNCC) in Geneva from Iraq's bank account, which the UN Treasury administered under sanctions regulations. Such transfers were made regardless of the financial needs of the OFF program and therefore regardless of the state of suffering of the Iraqi people. What this meant was that the UNCC had an assured income while there was no guarantee that minimum funding for the humanitarian exemption would be available. Funds for OFF were determined, not by an agreed UN allocation, but by the vicissitudes of the international oil market! In 1999 UNICEF reported that Iraq had become one of the countries with the highest mortality rates for children under five in the world.[31] Had the UN Security Council at the time been humanitarian-minded, it could have intervened without any difficulty to temporarily halt, or at least reduce, the 30 percent transfers to the UNCC and could have added these amounts to the OFF program. Well-to-do governments, especially Kuwait, and firms could have been told that their compensation claims would be considered at a time when Iraq's human condition had sufficiently been improved. At no time did the UN Security Council even consider such an option, nor was it raised by the UN Secretariat. Criticism of the OFF program was the same as "propping up a dictator." This was the view of Peter Hain, British minister of state for foreign affairs.[32] Even though the US and the UK governments must primarily be held accountable for the irresponsible implementation of the OFF program, the other thirteen members of the UN Security Council cannot evade responsibility. They had equal access to UN reporting on the continually deteriorating physical conditions in Iraq. They were as aware as the UN staff of the existing disinformation about the impact of a flawed OFF program. They knew of the destabilizing overt and covert measures taken by members of the UN Security Council. The question that has no good answer yet is, Why did they not intervene more forcefully in fulfillment of their mandate? To a lesser extent, the same question can be raised about the role played at the time by the three UN secretaries-general de Cuellar, Boutros-Ghali, and Annan, whose voices were often too faint to be heard. Of course, policies were made in the Security Council, and UN officials were expected to follow these. At the same time, senior UN officials had a considerable margin of freedom in shaping the OFF program and influencing the humanitarian impact of sanctions. They also had the responsibility to remind the Security Council of Article 25 of the UN Charter, which states that "the members of the United Nations agree to accept and carry out the decisions of the Security Council in accordance with the present charter."

THE DYSFUNCTIONAL UN POLITICS OF
IRAQ UNDER SANCTIONS

An independent UN civil service existed that was committed to the fulfillment of its humanitarian mandate in Iraq. Yet intervening forces within the UN Secretariat, allied with powerful members in the UN Security Council, made the smooth running of OFF next to impossible.

A serious and deliberate impediment had to do with the relationship between the four UN operational entities the UN Security Council had created to implement the overall UN disarmament and humanitarian programs in Iraq.[33] Even though an Iraq policy team chaired by UN deputy secretary-general Louise Fréchette existed at UN headquarters, these four units operated in complete isolation. In Baghdad, all UN agencies with a humanitarian mandate cooperated effectively and argued for similar integrated approaches with the other three units as steps to reduce the conflict and improve the welfare of people. They were ignored. The UN Special Commission wanted no contact, even though they were located in the same UN building in Baghdad as staff concerned with the humanitarian programs. The UNCC in Geneva also wanted no contact with UN offices in Iraq.

Not even the UN human rights rapporteur in Geneva, a former foreign minister of the Netherlands, Max van der Stoel, was receptive to our suggestion to cooperate with the UN humanitarian agencies in Baghdad. In hindsight, his refusal had to do with the rapporteur's unfortunate mandate, which subjected to review only the government of Iraq's human rights record and not the harms inflicted by other factors, especially the sanctions policies of the UN Security Council.

After nine years and only one visit to Iraq, van der Stoel was replaced in 2000 by a former foreign secretary from Cyprus, Andreas Mavromatis.[34] The new rapporteur immediately understood the problem and had the courage that his predecessor lacked to broaden the mandate without clearance from anyone and to include in his review UN sanctions policies and their impact on human conditions in Iraq. In doing so he showed the necessary impartiality, established close working relations with the UN system in Baghdad, and was able to visit Iraq to discuss human rights issues with the government in Baghdad. In other words, this expansion of mandate gave the UN rapporteur the needed credibility to cover the whole range of human rights violations rather than merely the constrictive and politicized mandate followed by his predecessor.

Dysfunctional structures at UN headquarters (OCHA and OIP) and in the field (within UNOHCI), the ineffective Iraq policy committee at the UN headquarters, and isolated operations of UN entities working in Iraq with different mandates (disarmament, compensation, human rights and humanitarian support) reflect a major leadership vacuum within the UN Secretariat and stymied efforts to deescalate the conflict. They also contributed to a deepening of suffering.

Other disturbing features cast serious doubts on the impartiality with which Iraq issues were handled at UN headquarters in New York. These included OFF reporting to the UN Security Council. The UN team in Baghdad (the UN Development Programme, UNICEF, the World Health Organization, the World Food Programme, UNESCO, and the Food and Agriculture Organization), led by the UN humanitarian coordinator, had repeatedly made it known that it found unacceptable a UN reporting format that focused on supplies and distribution of goods, that is, UN humanitarian accomplishments rather than on the impact on people's welfare. The description of the human face of the Iraqi recipients was largely absent. In early 1999 we were finally asked to comment on the existing reporting format. We welcomed this opportunity. It coincided with a general review of the humanitarian situation in the country by a panel appointed by Ambassador Celso Amorim of Brazil, then president of the UN Security Council in January 1999.[35]

A revised reporting format proposed by the UN team in Baghdad was forwarded to the OIP in New York. It suggested sector assessments of the implications of inadequate medical services, water supply, sanitation, electricity services, nutrition, and education materials made available by the OFF program. Our proposals were not taken into account in New York at the time because they mysteriously "got lost" in transition![36] During a subsequent meeting in New York, the UN humanitarian coordinator was told by the deputy secretary-general, Louise Fréchette, that the disappearance of our proposals was "most unfortunate." With this the issue seemed closed as far as UN headquarters was concerned.

The UN team in Baghdad was horrified but not discouraged. With little time available, we decided to prepare for the UN Security Council, without further consultation with UN headquarters, a comprehensive UN Baghdad statement outlining the desperate human conditions in Iraq for which the UN Security Council was largely responsible. Brazilian ambassador Amorim's report to the Security Council and his statement to the media made it clear that our message had been understood: there was urgency for additional funding, the rehabilitation of the oil industry, the freezing of compensation payments, and the direct procurement of medical equipment and agricultural and educational supplies.[37]

The UN humanitarian agencies in Baghdad greatly appreciated the warning Amorim conveyed to the Security Council: "Even if not all the suffering in Iraq can be imputed to external factors, especially sanctions, the Iraqi people would not be undergoing such deprivations in the absence of the prolonged measures imposed by the UN Security Council and the effects of war. But even if all the humanitarian supplies were provided in a timely manner the humanitarian program ... can admittedly only meet a small fraction of the priority needs of the Iraqi people. The gravity of the human situation of the Iraqi people is undisputable and cannot be overstated."[38]

Immediate implementation of the Amorim Panel report in early 1999 certainly would have helped belatedly to ease Iraqi suffering. The UN team in Baghdad regrettably saw no evidence that the OIP management in New York vigorously pursued with the Security Council the adoption of the panel's report. The Council itself lacked the political and moral fortitude to redress its faulty Iraq policy. It took almost a year before the Security Council responded to the Amorim proposals in December 1999 and reacted to the recommendations made by Secretary-General Kofi Annan by adopting Resolution 1284.[39]

Among other things, Resolution 1284 provided for the allocation of cash and the temporary lifting of sanctions on condition that Iraq "continued to cooperate in all respects." For the Iraqi authorities this resolution constituted a step backwards from their demand for the permanent lifting of sanctions altogether and therefore was rejected altogether. The government felt that it had fully complied with preceding resolutions on disarmament.

Other troubling anomalies faced the UN's largest-ever humanitarian exception. Besides the skewed reporting on OFF operations, there was no political reporting at all, not even informal reviews of political developments in the country as seen by senior UN officials resident in Iraq.[40] That such reporting was a sensitive matter and had to be handled with great care and confidentiality is unquestioned. Such reporting, however, would have been valuable in shaping the secretary-general's ability to influence the Iraq debate. Sir Kieran Prendergast, the British under-secretary-general heading the Department for Political Affairs, did not show any interest in interacting with the UN humanitarian staff in Baghdad.[41]

Attempts to give tangible meaning to the importance of protecting Iraq's territorial integrity, a point stressed in every major UN resolution on Iraq, were vigorously opposed by the OIP in New York. For example, as the UN coordinator for Iraq as a whole, and not just for the area under control of the government of Saddam Hussein, I discouraged demands in the three Kurdish governorates of Dohuk, Erbil, and Sulemaniah for UN support in establishing an electricity grid separate from the rest of the country, and in issuing Kurdish car license plates and the printing of currency notes other than Iraqi dinars. Instead, I tried to bring Kurdish officials together with their government of Iraq counterparts to jointly find alternatives that would prevent further separation between the Kurdish north and the Arab center and south. I was convinced this was doable. We organized meetings between the two sides in Baghdad. The Kurdish delegation came with unease. To cross the "green line" dividing the Kurdish north from the Iraq of Saddam Hussein was difficult for them. One outcome: an agreement that the sole electricity link between Mosul, on the Arab side and Dohuk, on the Kurdish side, would be maintained. It was a victory for everyone, including the UN as the mediator. The OIP in New York saw it differently. Instead of support we earned a reprimand: "Your predecessor burnt his fingers do not burn yours," was the written message from the responsible under-secretary-general in New York.[42] The preference of the OIP in New York seemed to be to show no concern for the protection of Iraq's territorial integrity as demanded in

Security Council resolutions. Not getting involved as we did would have contributed to a deepening of the existing divide between Baghdad and the Kurdish north.

Mention also needs to be made of dubious personnel decisions confronting us in Baghdad. Unlike the more rigorous appointment process for regular staff positions at UN headquarters, selection for so-called Iraq "mission assignments" often involved applicants who came from outside the UN system, who had little relevant experience but useful connections, and who were looking for lucrative jobs.[43] More difficult to discover were appointments of individuals with "intelligence" interests. We had little doubt that they were among us and in some cases not even difficult to discern. For instance, someone on loan from the UK Ministry of Defense to the UN's humanitarian program charged with editing the reports we prepared in Baghdad could not escape being considered by us to be among those.

Were all these unfortunate "realities" that we faced in managing the humanitarian exception due to incompetence, lack of commitment, a laissez-faire attitude, an absence of vision and leadership, or remote controls involving non-UN parties? The answer: They were attributable to a concoction of all of these factors!

Under normal circumstances, the United Nations has difficulties in securing adequate financial resources for the tasks it is asked to undertake. In the case of Iraq's OFF program, however, inadequate resources were determined by the politics of sanctions rather than by a shortfall of finance. "Adequate resources" promised for OFF in the 1996 memorandum of understanding were available but only to meet the UN's administrative expenses. While there was not enough to cover the needs of innocent civilians, there was more than enough to finance generous salaries, rental of premises, travel, office equipment, and so on. The largest-ever UN "project" turned out to be the cheapest: all UN costs were paid with Iraqi oil revenue![44]

The overall pictures that emerges includes five years of confrontation between the dictator in Baghdad and the rulers in the UN Security Council in New York (1990–95), six and a half years of a severely limited humanitarian exception, a dysfunctional Iraq policy group at UN headquarters, and the absence of collaboration between key operational UN units charged with disarmament, human rights observation, compensation, and humanitarian assistance. In addition the structural disarray and mismanagement within

OIP in New York as well as in Baghdad had an impact. All of this confirms the deliberate international contribution to the human catastrophe that prevailed at the time when the UN Security Council pronounced the end of economic sanctions in May 2003 following the US/UK 2003 invasion.[45]

Ending almost thirteen years of the most comprehensive sanctions ever imposed on a country was good news for the Iraqi people. However, the UN Security Council failed to admit that lifting these sanctions constituted an act of illegality because the Council had not yet confirmed that Iraq had "completed all actions contemplated" and "co-operated in all respects," especially with regard to Iraq's weapons of mass destruction. Earlier Security Council resolutions had made such confirmation a precondition for the lifting of sanctions.[46]

Acknowledgment of Iraq's full cooperation would have constituted admission that the US and UK governments had invaded Iraq in 2003 on false premises, as had been argued all along by many in Europe, the Middle East, and elsewhere. This would have been highly embarrassing for the Security Council and, for two of its permanent members, the United States and the United Kingdom, not without a serious internal and external political fallout.

In terminating UN sanctions, the UN Security Council also should have undertaken an in-depth review of the impact of its fateful Iraq sanctions policies. Such a review was only partially carried out. It showed that Iraq during the period of the OFF program (1996–2003) had earned $61 billion from the sale of oil. Of this amount, $43 billion was available to finance the humanitarian programs, but only $28 billion of humanitarian supplies was actually distributed to the Iraq people. Had the UN further disaggregated the financial picture, it would have revealed that on a per capita basis Iraqi citizens had been getting $185 per year or 51 cents per day as "humanitarian" assistance. The extreme inadequacy becomes even clearer when it is pointed out that 60 to 70 percent of Iraqis were totally dependent on the OFF program.

Little was said in the UN review about the adequacy of the total amount made available by the Security Council, the deduction of 30 percent for compensation payments to Kuwait and other parties, the disproportionate allocation of oil revenue to the Kurdish provinces, the debilitating UN bureaucracy that added to Iraqi misery, and the fact that the funds used were not external contributions but money earned from the sale of Iraqi oil.

There was another serious gap not often mentioned in the capitals of those responsible for the failure of protection of the Iraqi people. In April 1995, the

P5, the five permanent members of the Security Council, had issued a general statement on the humanitarian impact of sanctions in whatever country they were imposed.[47] In this statement they made the crucial points that "adverse side-effects of sanctions should be minimized," that "short- and long-term humanitarian consequences should be assessed," and that the "simplest possible authorization procedures should be developed for essential supplies." In other words, the P5 knew very well what had to be done to protect citizens in any sanction circumstances. Yet in the context of Iraq sanctions all of this was discarded. What emerged was an iron fist and an inhuman implementation of UN sanctions in Iraq.

The conclusion by Ambassador Dato Agam Hasmy, representing Malaysia in the UN Security Council in 2000, on the impact of UN sanctions in Iraq makes for somber reading: "How ironic is it that the same policy that is supposed to disarm Iraq of its weapons of mass destruction has itself become a weapon of mass destruction." This conclusion, I have to say with much discomfort, is consistent with the experience I had as a UN civil servant in Iraq at the time.

The OFF program was an innovative and important addition to UN sanction policy. The comprehensive nature of Iraq sanctions demanded such a humanitarian exemption. International political pressure on the government of Saddam Hussein had to be accompanied by a responsibility to protect innocent people.

The stark reality, however, has been that powerful bilateral interests for regime change in Iraq took precedence. The UN Security Council became divided and unable or unwilling to change the prescribed course. The UN secretary-general Kofi Annan, despite his best efforts, could not prevent serious divisions within the UN Secretariat and ensuing dysfunctionality between the UN in Iraq and the UN in New York. During the thirteen years of UN sanctions the Iraqi people emerged as the major victim. Iraq remains a reminder and a major challenge of the urgency of a fundamental overhaul of the United Nations and the international security architecture.

NOTES

1. UN Security Council Resolution 661, S/Res/661, August 6, 1990, https://www.treasury.gov/resource-center/sanctions/Documents/661.pdf.

2. UN Security Council Resolution 1483, S/Res/1483, May 22, 2003, https://www.treasury.gov/resource-center/sanctions/Documents/1483.pdf.

3. The World Health Organization estimated that in 1990 alone the average caloric intake per person quickly changed from over 3,000 kcal prior to August to an estimated 1,300 kcal at the end of the year!

4. UN secretary-general Pérez de Cuellar had dispatched Under-Secretary-General Martti Athisaari and Prince Sadruddin Aga Khan, executive delegate, to Iraq in February and June 1991 respectively. *UN Blue Book Series* 9 (1996): 38 and 56–60.

5. US ambassador to the UN John Negroponte, statement before the Committee on Foreign Relations, US Senate, April 7, 2004.

6. *UN Blue Book Series* 9 (1996): 59.

7. David Cortright and George A. Lopez, introduction to *The Sanctions Decade: Assessing UN Strategies in the 1990s,* ed. David Cortright and George A. Lopez (Boulder, CO: Lynne Rienner, 2000), 37.

8. UN Security Council Resolution 661, S/Res/661, August 6, 1990.

9. See UN Security Council Resolution 687, S/Res/687, April 8, 1991, www.un.org/Depts/unmovic/documents/687.pdf; H. C. von Sponeck, *A Different Kind of War: The Sanctions Regime of the UN in Iraq* (New York: Berghahn, 2006), chap. 2.

10. UN Security Council Resolution 687, S/Res/687, April 8, 1991 (twelve Security Council members voted for this resolution, including all P5 members; Cuba voted against; Yemen and Ecuador abstained); UN Security Council Resolution 1284, S/Res/1284, December 17, 1999, www.un.org/Depts/unscom/Keyresolutions/sres99–1284.htm (eleven Security Council members voted for this resolution; three permanent members—China, France, and Russia—and Malaysia abstained).

11. The US House of Representatives passed this act by 360 to 38 votes; the US Senate voted unanimously in support, and US president Clinton signed the act into law on October 31, 1998.

12. *P5* refers to the five permanent members of the UN Security Council (China, France, Russia, United Kingdom, and United States).

13. Memorandum of Understanding, signed May 20, 1996, in New York in New York by Iraq's ambassador Abdul Anbari and UN legal counsel Hans Correll.

14. OCHA and OIP were both headed by UN under-secretaries-general. The head of OCHA, Viero Sergio de Mello (killed in 2003 in a bomb attack on UN premises in Baghdad), remarked to the author in 1999 in New York that he had never understood why the OIP had not been made part of OCHA!

15. Repeated requests to end this counterproductive management invariably led to the same response from the head of the OIP: "Do not argue, the Security Council wants to have a more direct link with field operations!" When the author brought this to the attention of Secretary-General Kofi Annan, he reacted with "I cannot believe that such a structure exists at the UN in Baghdad!" The structure was ultimately revised but by that time had done irreversible damage.

16. On April 14, 1995, the Security Council had passed Resolution 986 "to meet the 'humanitarian needs' of the Iraqi people."

17. UN Security Council Resolution 1284, S/Res/1284, December 17, 1999.

18. Statement at Chatham House in London by the minister for Middle East affairs in the British Foreign Office, Peter Hain, November 7, 2000.

19. Sponeck, *Different Kind of War*, 111–13.

20. US State Department, "Saddam Hussein's Iraq," September 1999, http://nsarchive.gwu.edu/NSAEBB/NSAEBB167/13.pdf, a compilation of incorrect information, false interpretations, and half-truths. UN/Baghdad efforts to correct such information had no effect!

21. The Security Council establishes special sanctions committees for all countries under UN sanctions, for Liberia, Haiti, Iran, etc.

22. US State Department, "Saddam Hussein's Iraq."

23. The US government was responsible for over 95 percent of blocked items. Vaccines, chemicals for water purification, and electricity equipment were withheld for "technical reasons" or on account of their dual-use character (their capacity to be put to military or civilian use).

24. It took on average a year and twenty-three procurement steps for nonfood items to reach their destination in Iraq.

25. UN Security Council Resolution 1409, S/Res/1409, May 14, 2002, www.un.org/Depts/unmovic/documents/1409.pdf.

26. In violation of Article 32 of the UN Charter, Iraqi diplomats were barred from joining Iraq debates when the UN Security Council had decided to hold "informal" meetings. Such meetings of "exclusion," as the author experienced repeatedly when in New York on consultations, had become the norm rather than meetings in "public," which would have allowed Iraqi participation.

27. A northern (thirty-sixth parallel) NFZ and a southern (thirty-third parallel) NFZ were maintained by the US and UK air forces without UN Security Council agreement. These zones were justified on the basis of UN Security Council Resolution 688, S/Res/688, April 5, 1991, www.securitycouncilreport.org/atf/cf/%7B65BFCF9B-6D27-4E9C-8CD3-CF6E4FF96FF9%7D/IJ%20SRES688.pdf, passed under UN Charter Chapter VI (Pacific Settlement of Disputes), which does not allow the use of military force!

28. For 1999, we recorded 132 air strikes with 144 civilian deaths and 446 civilian injuries.

29. This US/UK contention was incorrect. The fact was that we investigated in situ major air-strike incidents and discovered that there was at times even an Iraqi undercount of casualties. In an air-strike incident in Basra, for example, the Iraqi count referred to eleven killed while I personally had counted fifteen coffins. On another occasion, the author carried out an onsite visit involving an air strike near Mosul in which six shepherds and 101 sheep were killed. Instead of admitting this crime, the US European Command issued a press release indicating that the US Air Force had "successfully destroyed" Iraqi antiaircraft facilities!

30. US State Department, "Saddam Hussein's Iraq," 6.

31. In the late 1990s, Iraq's child mortality rate for children under five was 132 out of 1,000.

32. Peter Hain, "I Fought Apartheid. I'll Fight Saddam. My Critics Are Wrong: They Are Merely Propping Up a Dictator," *Guardian,* January 6, 2001.

33. The units were (1) the UN Special Commission / the UN Monitoring, Verification and Inspections Commission; (2) the UN special human rights rapporteur; (3) the UN Compensation Commission (UNCC); and (4) the UN Office of the Humanitarian Coordinator for Iraq (UNOHCI).

34. As early as 1991, Max van der Stoel had been barred by the Iraqi authorities from visiting the country because of his narrow terms of reference and his focus on secondary (expatriate) Iraqi sources.

35. Such an initiative was not welcomed by the United States and the United Kingdom, as it interfered with their hard-line Iraq agenda. For this courageous decision, Brazil's ambassador Amorim, facing strong US pressure, was subsequently "punished" and transferred out of New York to Geneva. The panel members included Staffan di Mistura, a former UN high commissioner for Iraq, Sergio Vieira de Mello, under-secretary-general and head of OCHA, and Benon Sevan, under-secretary-general and head of OIP.

36. For details, see von Sponeck, *Different Kind of War,* 117–18.

37. UN Security Council, "Letters Dated 27 and 30 March 1999, Respectively, from the Chairman of the Panels Established Pursuant to the Note by the President of the Security Council of 30 January 1999," UN S/1999/356, March 30, 1999, 45–46, www.securitycouncilreport.org/atf/cf/%7B65BFCF9B-6D27-4E9C-8CD3-CF6E4FF96FF9%7D/Disarm%20S1999356.pdf.

38. Ibid., 45.

39. UN Security Council Resolution 1284, S/Res/1284, December 17, 1999, www.un.org/Depts/unscom/Keyresolutions/sres99-1284.htm; UN Security Council, "Review and Assessment of the Implementation of the Humanitarian Programme Established Pursuant to Security Council Resolution 986 (1995) (December 1996-November 1998)," S/1999/481, April 28, 1999, http://fas.org:8080/news/un/iraq/oip/twoyearreview.htm.

40. The focus on reporting UN accomplishments rather than the impact of OFF on people's welfare remained a serious controversy between the UN in Baghdad and the UN in New York. The UN in Baghdad also objected strongly to the fact that "their" reporting responsibilities were usurped by the OIP, since OIP sent their staff to compile the reports rather than letting the UN Baghdad offices be in charge of the drafting.

41. It is a curious anomaly that the author's consultations in New York never included Kieran Prendergast, under-secretary-general for political affairs (formerly British diplomat with assignments inter alia in the British Foreign Office's NATO Department in London, as consul-general in Tel Aviv and the UK Mission to the UN in New York).

42. This is a reference to UN humanitarian coordinator Denis Halliday, whom I had replaced in Baghdad after his resignation in September 1998.

43. In the case of the UN Iraq mission, every staff member received a mission bonus of $100 per day in addition to generous salary payments. During 1998/2000 several ambassadors and one former foreign minister joined UN staff in Baghdad as UN observers.

44. The Security Council set aside 2.2 percent of Iraq's oil revenue to cover the entire UN overheads. Funds available to the UN amounted to more than what was needed! While UN offices in Baghdad had at their disposal top computer technology paid for by Iraqi oil revenue, the Iraq Ministry of Health, for example, had to resort to manual management of its medicine stores, as computers were not allowed under sanctions. On one occasion, UN offices in Baghdad were instructed by the UN in New York to destroy functioning computer equipment to make room for more recent models available in Western markets. We found this scandalous and also illegal, since the equipment was legally Iraqi property on loan to the UN. We ignored this order, accepted the latest version of computers, and without telling New York handed over to selected ministries a good number of the items to be replaced and stored the rest in our offices.

45. UN Security Council Resolution 1483, S/Res/1483, May 22, 2003, para. 10, https://www.treasury.gov/resource-center/sanctions/Documents/1483.pdf: "all prohibitions . . . shall no longer apply."

46. UN Security Council Resolution 687, S/Res/687, April 8, 1991, and Resolution 1284, S/Res/1284, December 17, 1999.

47. Ambassador Sergev Lavrov, today's Russian foreign minister, and Ambassador Madeleine Albright, subsequently US secretary of state, signed on behalf of their two countries.

THIRTEEN

An Agency for the Palestinians?

Jalal Al Husseini

"HOW UNRWA CREATES DEPENDENCY," "Congress Should Withhold Funds from [UNRWA]," "UNRWA's Anti-Israel Bias," "UNRWA Employees Protest against Reduced Services," "How UNRWA Supports Hamas," "UNRWA Strongly Condemns Placement of Rockets in School," "Hamas to UN: Your Textbooks Are 'Too Peaceful'" . . . These headlines randomly selected from recent articles found on the Internet in 2014–15 illustrate the dilemmas that the United Nations Relief and Works Agency for Palestine Refugees in the Near East (UNRWA) has faced since the start of its activities in May 1950. These dilemmas result to a large extent from the competing roles it has come to assume in the absence of a comprehensive Israeli-Arab peace agreement.

Tasked to provide educational, medical, social and relief, microfinance, and camp upgrading services to the "Palestine refugees" in Jordan, Lebanon, Syria, the Gaza Strip, and the West Bank, UNRWA has recently reshaped itself as a "human development" organization that also covers the protection of the refugees' human rights and promotes their active participation in the planning and implementation of its activities to the fullest extent possible.[1] "The Agency" (as UNRWA is commonly known) has also been a prime witness of the refugees' plight and a staunch advocate of their rights as prescribed by UN resolutions, which has brought Israel and Western governments to question its influence on the Israeli-Palestinian peace process.

The essay seeks to determine how UNRWA has assumed these roles and reflects on their impact on the Palestine refugees and the overall Near East context. In so doing, it offers insight into the interplay of humanitarian/developmental concerns, as articulated by UNRWA, and of political objectives as pursued by its main stakeholders (from the donor and host countries to the refugees and their representatives) that have determined the course of UNRWA's evolving mandate. In this regard, the Agency may be considered a site of conflicting claims its staff has had to reconcile for the sake of preserving the delivery of humanitarian assistance.

The two first sections trace the dynamics behind the creation and the evolution of its mandate in terms of institutional and operational development and overview of the impact of its assistance programs. The third section focuses on the political dimensions attached to the concepts of community participation and of protection that UNRWA has recently mainstreamed across its various activities.

THE MAKING OF A SEMIPERMANENT TEMPORARY AGENCY

The Arab States' Lasting Imprint on UNRWA's Mandate

UNRWA was created in December 1949 by virtue of Resolution 302 of the UN General Assembly as a subsidiary, temporary UN body tasked to cater to the basic needs of the Palestine refugees. In 1949, the West Bank of River Jordan, which would be formally annexed to the Hashemite Kingdom of Jordan in 1950, was the main host territory with an estimated 280,000 refugees, followed by the Gaza Strip then administered by Egypt (200,000), Lebanon (97,000), Syria (75,000), and Jordan (East Bank—70,000).[2] The Agency was endowed with a twofold objective: first, to prevent conditions of starvation and distress among refugees through a short-term relief program including the provision of food rations, housing, basic health, and educational services; second, to reduce their dependency on such humanitarian assistance by promoting their economic integration through their involvement in small-medium irrigation, agricultural, and construction works projects.

Geopolitical considerations also mattered. For the United States, UNRWA's main initiator and donor country since 1950, the durably stabilizing impact of its assistance programs was explicitly seen as a tool against the spread of communism in West Asia, for "the presence of . . . destitute, idle refugees provides the likeliest channel for [communist] exploitation."[3] In order to assuage the refugees' concerns that UNRWA's works program might contradict General Assembly Resolution 194 (para. 11) of December 1948, which recommended the refugees' return to their homes or their compensated resettlement elsewhere, Resolution 302 (IV)—and following resolutions—claimed that UNRWA's mandate did not prejudice the provisions of Resolution 194.[4]

Despite these reassurances, the works program failed to meets its objectives. Very few refugees agreed to give up their UNRWA registration card that represented the only international document attesting to their status as refugees;[5] they also viewed UNRWA, the only UN body actively involved in their issue, as a prime symbol of the international community's commitment to implement the right of return.[6] The prevalence of such perceptions among refugees, together with the situation of political turmoil that prevailed in the host countries, also explains the failure of the larger-scale reintegration schemes envisioned by UNRWA until the late 1950s, be it through major irrigation schemes in the Jordan Valley, the Sinai, and North Syria (1952–55) or through mass transfer toward the Gulf countries (1959–60). Even UNRWA's upgrading interventions in the camps, home to the most destitute refugees, were opposed on the same grounds.

Ultimately, the provisions of Resolution 302 that would define UNRWA's refugee assistance in the next decades bore the signature of Arab countries. While most of them (except Lebanon) consented in principle to the works program, their main concern was to prolong the relief program that alleviated the refugees' burden on their economies. The Arab countries also wanted to reassure the refugees and their own citizens, who were then hugely supportive of the Palestinian cause, about their commitment to the "right of return." Using their status as indispensable players in the implementation of UNRWA's mandate, the Arab states managed to impose, during the discussions that preceded the adoption of Resolution 302, several key amendments that organically linked it to the implementation of Resolution 194 (paras. 5, 20). The Arab amendments also allowed for the possible extension of the relief program, its termination initially set "not later than 31 December 1950" being qualified by the eventuality that "*the General Assembly determines otherwise*" (para. 6).[7]

Makeshift Institutional and Operational Development

The practical implications of the Arab amendments to allow the extension of the Agency's services pending the resolution of the refugee issue were largely ignored by the stakeholders. These included the registration (or not) of the refugees' descendants and the adaptation of UNRWA's budget and activities to the evolving needs of the refugees, which required a possible prioritization among its activities. The UN General Assembly has systematically refused to engage in such issues, reflecting its uneasiness at tackling the long-term, political dimensions of UNRWA's mandate. Its resolutions have generally endorsed steps taken beforehand by the latter's headquarters.

The lack of guidance has resulted in UNRWA's incremental and distorted administrative and institutional development. For instance, the registration of the descendants of the original 1948 refugees owes more to UNRWA's concern about having to bear alone the refugees' and the host countries' hostility to a termination of registration than to a belief in a transgenerational need for assistance. For that matter, the criterion of "being in need" that was initially conceived as a key registration criterion determined only eligibility for services (not registration per se) as early as 1953, precisely as a means of encouraging refugees to find jobs without affecting their "self-perceived" status as Palestine refugees; in 1991–92, the "need" criterion was even dropped as a requirement for access to services except relief.[8] These steps have resulted in the continuous increase in the number of registered refugees, beneficiaries of services or not, that today stands at over five million, one-third of them being camp refugees.[9] Simultaneously, its services have taken a semipermanent character, turning UNRWA into a regional, "quasi-governmental" institution currently manned by some thirty thousand employees, the vast majority of whom come from the refugee communities.[10]

Yet UNRWA still officially operates under the original, outdated "works" wording and institutional mechanisms of Resolution 302, which results in a lack of clarity about its current goals and objectives. Its mandate, regularly extended for periods of time not exceeding three to five years, has prevented any long-term planning. Moreover, the Agency's budget, covering the costs of both regular and emergency interventions, has depended quasi-exclusively on the voluntary contributions of donors, particularly the United States and the European countries. Since the mid-1970s, these contributions have not kept pace with the needs of the growing numbers of refugees, leading to a deterioration of the quantity and quality of services and the latter's subsequent dissatisfaction.[11]

Policy-wise, the Agency's main decisions have been based on the lowest common denominator of agreement among refugees, host countries, and donor countries. The reorientation of its mandate in the early 1960s from the refugees' collective to individual reintegration through primary education and vocational/technical training is a case in point. A subsidiary relief activity in 1950, education has been the Agency's main program since the late 1960s. It now consumes nearly one-half of UNRWA's budget and employs two-thirds of its staff. This reorientation has suited the interests of all stakeholders: the refugees welcomed it as a means of leading productive lives that did not jeopardize their "right of return"; the host countries considered it a fruitful investment in the human resources of a sizable proportion of their resident population; and although donor countries resented the transformation of UNRWA into a "semipermanent" institution, they have since the late 1950s endorsed it as a bulwark against instability caused by such "subverting" ideologies as communism, radical nationalism, and Islamism. Last, while Israel has relentlessly criticized UNRWA for contributing to perpetuate the refugee problem, it has nevertheless sought to entertain harmonious operational relations with the organization during Israel's (full) occupation of the West Bank and the Gaza Strip between 1967 and 1994, when it acted as a "host" country: In any case, UNRWA's programs de facto reduced the material costs of the occupation while contributing to preserve stability in these territories.

CONTRIBUTING TO THE INTEGRATION OF REFUGEES IN THE OVERALL MIDDLE EAST

UNRWA's Functional Educational System

The United States' acceptance of UNRWA's reorientation toward education was not unconditional. As its acting secretary of state put it in 1960, "[While] its government [was] fully aware of the grave alternatives which might result were outside aid to the Palestine refugees suddenly stopped, UNRWA was to be operated so as to stimulate the resettlement in every way possible [including through] vocational training."[12] This means that, unlike national education systems that endeavor to promote a civic culture predicated on the identification to collective nation/state values among children, UNRWA's education system has been based on the host country curriculum and steered toward refugees' professional integration in the local and regional job markets.

The first outcome of UNRWA education was a dramatic increase in literacy levels among refugee children, from 27 percent in 1951 to nearly 100 percent in the early 1980s. Females benefited from the gender balance policy pursued by the Agency, with the proportion of female pupils jumping from 26 percent at the primary level and 0 percent at the preparatory level in 1950 to about 50 percent at both levels across the Agency's five fields in the 1980s.[13] Within a few decades, UNRWA and host state education institutions (for the secondary and university levels) were instrumental in turning the refugee population into skilled professionals that contributed to the development of the entire Middle East. Indeed, given the dearth of available jobs in the first host countries, emigration toward labor-importing countries such as the booming oil-exporting Gulf countries became a traditional professional outlet for thousands of young qualified refugees. Conversely, relations between migrants and their relatives were maintained through marriages and remittances, forming the linchpin of an integrated and dynamic diaspora that contributed to and was reinforced by the Palestinian national movement that emerged across the Arab world in the late 1960s.

However, the "reintegration through emigration" trend has proven vulnerable to any decision made by the receiving countries. The downturn in the economic activity of the Gulf countries in the mid-1980s and again in Dubai in 2008 led to a (temporary) contraction of demand for foreign labor, including among Palestinians. More spectacularly, in 1991 Kuwait expelled three hundred thousand Palestinians, many of whom were UNRWA-registered refugees, toward Jordan and the West Bank as a retaliation against the ambiguous stances of the Palestine Liberation Organization (PLO) and Jordan during Iraq's invasion of its territory in 1990/1991. Nevertheless, work migration has remained an essential socioeconomic pillar of the refugees' domestic economy. However, its political significance has changed since the start of the peace process and the establishment of a Palestinian Authority in the West Bank and the Gaza Strip. The Palestinian Authority's failure to create a viable state/homeland for all Palestinians, together with the demise of the PLO's social institutions across the Middle East, has weakened the ideological links that bound the dispersed communities together. As a result, the Palestinian diaspora today tends to turn into the fragmented series of communities it was in the early years of the Nakba.

Refugees' Various Levels of Dependency on UNRWA

Since work-related emigration involved only a portion of Palestine refugees, questions remained as to the fate of those, more numerous, who stayed in UNRWA's fields of operations. By the late 1950s, roughly 20 percent of employable men, mostly of urban origin, had managed to find durable employment. Refugees of rural origin failed to find jobs because they moved into areas already saturated with farmers and unskilled laborers.[14] In the following decades a gradual, employment-led reintegration process developed, based on two sources of jobs. First, UNRWA itself turned into one of the largest employers of the region, hiring refugees as local staff performing tasks under the aegis of senior international employees. From 1951 to 2014, their number increased sixfold from about 5,800 to over 30,000 (in contrast to only 150 international staff, some of them former Palestinian local staff).[15] In addition, as a reminder of the "works" program of the 1950s, UNRWA has since 1990–91 developed a microfinance program designed to provide sustainable income generation opportunities to refugees. This program, which has been especially successful in the Gaza Strip, is also accessible to nonrefugees living in "refugee clusters."

A second source of employment has been the host country job markets, where access has depended on the legal status local authorities have ascribed to Palestine refugees, from the granting of citizenship and employment opportunities in the private and public sectors in Jordan to the imposition of a discriminatory regime in Lebanon where refugees are excluded from public and most of private sector employment. Available data show that refugees are on average less economically active in the formal employment sector and are poorer than the host population. They also tend to be subject to informal social discrimination. This is especially the case of the dwellers of the fifty-eight official refugee camps across the region—about one-third of the refugee population overall—who have traditionally constituted its poorest segment.[16]

The gradual socioeconomic reintegration process that has nevertheless taken place is reflected by the refugees' decreasing dependency on UNRWA's services. For instance, the proportion of refugees benefiting from the ration program (today labeled the "social safety net program") dwindled from about 100 percent in 1950 to some 5 percent in 2014, with highs of 12 percent in Lebanon and 8 percent in Gaza and lows of 2 and 3 percent in the West Bank and Jordan, respectively.[17] To some extent, such material autonomy has been imposed by the austerity measures imposed by UNRWA, in particular its 1982 decision to limit the "general distribution of rations" to the most vulnerable refugee families. Moreover, because of budget constraints, the Agency has not been able to adapt its services infrastructure to the refugee population growth. In Jordan and the West Bank, the insufficient number of UNRWA schools outside camps has led an increasing number of noncamp refugee children—a majority of them since the early 2000s—to attend governmental schools.[18]

But voluntary or constrained material autonomy has not detached the refugees from UNRWA. For most refugees, registration with the Agency serves primarily—though not exclusively, especially in conflict areas—as a proof of status as refugees endowed with rights according to Resolution 194.[19] This explains why refugees not using UNRWA services tend to maintain their registration.[20] Sixty years on, the refugees' relation with the Agency is thus defined primarily in terms of political dependency.

NEGOTIATING THE LONG-TERM RELATIONSHIP BETWEEN UNRWA AND REFUGEES: PARTICIPATION AND PROTECTION

The Oslo Peace Agreement of 1993 foresaw the resolution of the refugee issue and the handover of UNRWA's activities to the host countries by 1999–2000. Its failure brought the Agency's donor countries to face an *ad aeternam* perpetuation of the refugee issue and that of UNRWA. This translated into the former's open frustration at the latter's incremental, "vision-less" management of its programs and pressures on its headquarters to inscribe them within a coherent developmental framework. The organizational development scheme that UNRWA launched in 2006 set its operations within a human development framework that promoted the refugees' full potential as individuals and members of the community. The redefinition of UNRWA's relationship with the refugees that such a framework entailed revolved around "participation," a methodological concept referring to the involvement of refugees in the planning and implementation of programs, and "protection," a programmatic concept covering "all activities aimed at obtaining full respect for the rights of the individual in accordance with the letter and spirit of relevant bodies of international law."[21] Presented as modern governance tools, "participation" and "protection" have, however, marked the relations between UNRWA and the refugees for decades, less by design (through related activities) than by default, namely through debates and controversies about their legal, political, and operational significance.

Community Participation and Its Political Implications

Participation was never considered a central component of UNRWA's operational mandate. Reflecting in 1970 on the growing demands by refugees—

and their yet informal representative institution, the PLO—to be consulted on the Agency's orientations and programs, UNRWA stated that "under successive resolutions of the General Assembly there [was] no reference to consultation with the refugee community. Consultation [took] place . . . either through the host Governments or informally between headquarters staff or field directors and individuals or groups, who have some—but not necessarily a continuing—representative quality."[22] In the field, community participation has taken place on the margins of UNRWA's relief activities, either through the establishment in the early 1950s of community-based social welfare organizations tasked to raise the morale of socially marginalized camp residents, in particular among the young, the women, and the disabled persons, or through grassroots small-scale "self-help" initiatives aimed at improving housing conditions as well as the camps' amenities.

More generally, the low status of participation betrays the fact that, despite its close relations with the refugees, UNRWA has actually remained relatively estranged from them. At stake here lies the Agency's traditional "top-down" managerial approach whereby its assistance is provided exclusively for, not with, refugees; to some extent, such an approach has also defined its relationship with the local staff generally relegated to implementation tasks. The involvement of refugees in PLO-affiliated politico-military organizations from the mid-1960s, and later in Islamist groups, further complicated matters. It not only questioned the Agency's authority over its serviced population and local staff but also affected the Agency's impartiality in the eyes of its stability-driven donors. Since 1966, the US Congress has passed several laws conditioning its approval of funding for UNRWA to guarantees that its aid would not benefit members of any Palestinian military group.[23] Allegations that local staff employees had used the Agency's facilities as ideological and military props against Israel, more especially in Lebanon until 1982 and in the Gaza Strip since 2000, have led to additional pressure on UNRWA's management to thin out those employees affiliated to "terrorist" organizations and more generally to limit the local staff's political activities inside and even outside the Agency's premises.[24]

It took a radical transformation of the Palestinian-Israeli conflict, triggered by the outbreak of the first Palestinian uprising (intifada) against the Israeli occupation of the West Bank and the Gaza Strip (the Occupied Palestine Territory, OPT) in 1987 to see UNRWA and the refugees engage in a durable, yet sectorial rapprochement. Requested by Security Council Resolution 605 (December 1987) to examine the situation in the OPT, the

UN secretary-general explained that consultations with camp refugees had revealed a change in their perceptions of UNRWA. Not only were they now favorable to a durable improvement of the camps' infrastructure, provided this did not prejudice any future political settlement and compromise their right of return; they also demanded that such work be implemented by UNRWA.[25] This paved the way for a new participatory approach to camp interventions in the OPT, which was later replicated in the other host countries in the early 2000s, combining infrastructural development /reconstruction works with grassroots social activities.[26]

UNRWA has since 2006 extended the participatory approach to the management of its entire range of programs as a double-edged tool of operational efficiency and of refugee empowerment. In this vein, school parliaments have been established and health teams tasked to encourage community members to participate in creating healthy environments at home and in public life. The Agency has also sought to alert the international community about the need to enhance the status of refugee youths in their host societies. In this spirit, it organized a conference, "Engaging Youth: Palestine Refugee Youth in a Changing Middle East," in Brussels in 2012 that resulted in a list of "Ten Youth Commitments" around which pro-youth inclusion efforts of all should crystallize. Remarkably, these commitments comprise, together with the improvement of UNRWA's services (education at large, health, microfinance), other themes requiring partnerships with other stakeholders, including UN sister organizations, local governments, and civil societies: the use of youth's views in Agency programming, scholarships, skills development, and more generally the promotion of youth's rights as individuals and as refugees.[27]

For all these efforts, UNRWA's participatory approach is still considered in its incipient phase. Echoing the voices of many refugees and local staff employees, a recent assessment of UNRWA's operations found its level of communication with the refugees wanting: "The planning, including the reform of services [still] has limited participation by the front-line UNRWA staff and refugee beneficiaries. . . . UNRWA is more accountable to donors and hosts than it is to the Palestine refugees."[28] At an implementation level, the participation of refugees in the upgrading/reconstruction of their camps or in cultural and social programs, for instance, has proven to be a time-consuming and costly process that also requires an adequate representation of the various political, social, and economic segments of the community: a difficult challenge in the heavily politicized atmosphere prevailing in refugee communities. In addition, the repeated setbacks of the peace process, together with the marginalization of the "right of return" on the Palestinian leadership's agenda and persistent rumors about UNRWA's possible termination of services, have refueled fears among refugees about the possible adverse repercussions of development projects on the right of return and compensation.

Other challenges stem from the host authorities' (and part of the local staff's) scant experience and interest in social development, which they tend to see as a potentially uncontrollable process likely to question the refugees' legal status and thus the political and social discriminations related to it. These risks to stability, especially when it comes to empowering young refugees, may explain why participation has so far remained carried out in a rather cautious, "top-down" way, leaving little formal space for refugee autonomy. For that matter, UNRWA's ambitious "ten youth commitments" initiative of 2012 has not been followed up by any significant step. In sum, UNRWA's participation process has not (yet) turned into the genuine partnership it aspires to be in principle.

Protection and Its Challenges

The unique status that the Palestine refugees were granted within the international refugee regime owes more to political considerations, namely the acknowledgment of their specificity as a group for whom the United Nations bore a responsibility based on Resolution 194, than to humanitarian values. They have been excluded from the international refugee protection regime embodied in the Convention Relating to the Status of Refugees (1951) and the Statute of the Office of the UN High Commissioner for Refugees (1950).[29] And while UNRWA was considered a substitute, its mandate does not provide for the protection tasks carried out by the Office of the UN High Commissioner for Refugees and related legal instruments. Initially supported by the Arab countries, such "positive discrimination" has proved to be a heavy but durable legacy whenever refugees have faced discrimination or have been exposed to armed violence. Resisting the demands of the PLO and refugee communities for an expansion of its mandate of human rights protection in the 1980s, at a time when refugees were becoming increasingly exposed to armed violence in Lebanon and the OPT, UNRWA repeatedly insisted that the only ways it was able to provide protection in such contexts were "to report, to warn and to make representations to the authorities responsible," it being understood that "the responsibility for the protection of the civilian population lies with the territorial sovereign or, in the case of occupied territory, the occupying Power."[30]

The outcome of such informal diplomatic representations has depended on the goodwill of the protagonists involved in conflicts. They have sometimes yielded positive results, especially when the lives of local employees were at stake. But diplomatic representations are of little value when refugees are engaged as actors in armed violence, as has been amply evidenced over the past decades in the OPT, in Lebanon, and more recently since the outbreak of the Syrian conflict in 2011. Citing the example of the Palestinian refugees stranded in the Yarmouk refugee camp of Damascus since 2012, UNRWA's commissioner-general noted how "Yarmouk has come to represent all places where—for Palestinians and especially refugees—control over one's life is an illusion, where the safety of decades can disappear overnight, where land is confiscated, homes are demolished, rights are denied, travel is restricted, jobs are lost, resentments and prejudices prevail."[31]

Two other protection methods have proven more sustainable. The first is protection through the information UNRWA provides to the international community about the violations of the Palestinian refugees' human rights. The second is direct protection through regular and emergency programs targeting discriminated or endangered refugees. It is precisely upon the notion that protection was what the Agency already did but without necessarily being fully aware of it that UNRWA has since 2008 turned "protection" into an essential cross-cutting theme across its programs with a view to safeguarding the refugees' physical integrity, freedom of movement, and protection from arbitrary displacement, as well as their social and economic rights in accordance with relevant bodies of law.[32] This has required constant attention to and reporting about any breach of such rights, and advocacy consultations with the relevant authorities.

That long-overdue protection framework may contribute to reuniting UNRWA and the refugees around shared objectives and goals, thereby alleviating the mutual mistrust that has often plagued their relationship. But such a framework seems constrained by two serious challenges. A first challenge stems from UNRWA's restricted margins of manoeuver vis-à-vis the host countries with which it is bound to harmonize its services but that do not necessarily share similar protection values. A second challenge is the lack of financial resources necessary to endorse the promotion of the refugees' socioeconomic rights. Quite the opposite: the austerity measures the Agency has been compelled to take in the form of curtailments or suspension of services in all programs are seen as having undermined such rights. Looking at the future, wouldn't UNRWA's failure to deliver on the various dimensions of its protection framework fuel among refugees additional frustration and resentment likely to develop into violence within a depressed political and socioeconomic regional context?

UNRWA represents a unique international investment in the promotion of the social and economic rights of one particular category of refugees: the Palestine refugees. However, beyond the indisputable operational achievements of its "quasi-governmental' services in the fields of education, health care, social welfare, microfinance, and camp improvement, UNRWA has played several, often contradictory, political roles that far exceeded the scope of its humanitarian mandate according to Resolution 302 of the UN General Assembly. Because it has long been the only UN agency active within the framework of the Palestine refugee issue, UNRWA has, as seen throughout this chapter, become a site of contest among different stakeholders and agendas. The refugees understand UNRWA as a major symbol of the international community's responsibility for finding a just solution based on Resolution 194 and fulfilling their claims to a right of return. Western powers have financially supported the Agency for the sake of regional stability and certainly not to support the refugees' right of return. For their part, the Arab host countries have oscillated between supporting the refugees' right of return and mitigating their adverse impact on their societies' political and socioeconomic balance. Since 1950, UNRWA has successfully striven to strike a balance between these contradicting claims for the sake of its preservation and the continuation of humanitarian services to its registered population.

The evolution of the Palestinian agenda since the first intifada have led to a significant change in UNRWA's mandate. With the support of its main stakeholders, including the host countries and the refugee communities, UNRWA has explicitly incorporated a developmental dimension into its humanitarian tasks. Moreover, since 2008, it has engaged in a human development paradigm, elevating community "participation" and the "protection" of the refugees' human and socioeconomic rights to the core of its agenda.

However, the persistence of challenges to the Agency's operations, such as dwindling per capita donor support and continuous outbreaks of violence in the host and neighboring countries, may undermine such a valuable effort and erode again its relations with the refugees. Ultimately, as often suggested by the Agency itself, only a breakthrough in the current Israeli-Palestinian negotiations toward a permanent status solution may allow for a rapprochement between UNRWA and all its stakeholders around shared objectives and values. While UNRWA is not mandated to trigger such a breakthrough, it is nevertheless well placed to contribute to it, notably through the active promotion of its human development framework.[33]

NOTES

1. UNRWA defines a Palestine refugee as a person "whose normal place of residence was Palestine between June 1946 and May 1948, who lost both their homes and means of livelihood as a result of the 1948 Arab-Israeli conflict" UNRWA, "Palestinian Refugees," n.d., UNRWA website, accessed March 1, 2016, www.unrwa.org/palestine-refugees.

2. Until 1952, UNRWA's operations also covered the needs of thirty-one thousand displaced "Arabs of Palestine" and seventeen thousand "Jewish" refugees, mainly from East Jerusalem, that resided in Israel after 1948; see "First Interim Report of the United Nations Economic Survey Mission for the Middle East," November 16, 1949, https://unispal.un.org/DPA/DPR/unispal.nsf/0/648C3D9C F58AF0888525753C00746F31.

3. See, among many other documents explaining the political importance of UNRWA's operations, "Policy Paper Prepared in the Department of State," March 15, 1949, in *Foreign Relations of the United States, 1949*, vol. 6 (Washington, DC: Government Printing Office, 1977). The Soviet Union and its allies at the UN General Assembly were excluded from all discussions leading to UNRWA's creation.

4. Paragraph 11 of Resolution 194 resolves "that refugees wishing to return to their homes and live at peace with their neighbours should be permitted to do so at the earliest practicable date, and that compensation should be paid for the property of those choosing not to return and for loss of or damage to property." UN General Assembly Resolution 194, A/Res/194, December 11, 1948, www.securitycouncilreport.org/atf /cf/%7B65BFCF9B-6D27–4E9C-8CD3-CF6E4FF96FF9%7D/IP%20ARES%20194 .pdf.

5. As will be seen below, the Palestine refugees were excluded from the international refugee protection regime. On refugee attitudes, see Jalal Al Husseini, "UNRWA and the Palestinian Nation-Building Process," *Journal of Palestine Studies* 29, no. 2 (Winter 2000): 51–64.

6. The other UN body involved in the search for a solution to the refugee issue, the UN Conciliation Commission for Palestine, has been dormant since the early 1960s.

7. UN General Assembly Resolution 302, A/Res/302, December 8, 1949, www .unrwa.org/content/general-assembly-resolution-302.

8. See UNRWA, "Report of the Commissioner-General of UNRWA (1 July 1991–30 June 1992)," Supplement no. 13, A/47/13, June 30, 1992, para. 35.

9. Jordan is the largest host country (over two million registered persons) but has the lowest percentage of camp dwellers (18 percent); Lebanon records the smallest registered population (less than half a million) but has the largest proportion of camp refugees (about over half of them). In absolute terms, Gaza has the largest camp refugee population (over half a million persons). UNRWA, "UNRWA in Figures," January 2014, UNRWA HQ Jerusalem, www.unrwa.org/sites/default /files/2014_01_uif_-_english.pdf.

10. Ibid.

11. Since the start of the Oslo peace process in particular, UNRWA's budget per capita decreased from $98 in 1994 to about $70 since the early 2000s. For more on the funds and donors, see Grandi's chapter in this volume.

12. "Memorandum of a Conversation, Department of State, Washington, October 5, 1960," in *Foreign Relations of the United States*, 1958–1960, vol. 13 (Washington, DC: Government Printing Office, 1992), 378.

13. Jalal Al Husseini et al., "The Educational Profile of the Palestine Refugees in the Near East," Thematic Report, UNRWA, May 2007, www.academia .edu/5888993/The_Education_profile_of_the_Palestine_refugees_in_the_Near_ East.

14. "Annual Report of the Director of UNRWA (1 July 1959–30 June 1960)," A/4478, June 30, 1960, para. 5, https://unispal.un.org/DPA/DPR/unispal.nsf/0 /886668A541861089052565AA0051333C.

15. The number of international staff has remained stable: from 133 in 1951 to 150 in 2014. Sources: "Annual Report of the Director of UNRWA (1 July 1950–30 June 1951)," A/1905, June 30, 1951, para. 110, https://unispal.un.org/DPA/DPR/unispal .nsf/181c4bf00c44e5fd85256cef0073c426/8d26108af518ce7e052565a6006e8948?O penDocument; and UNRWA, "UNRWA in Figures."

16. F. Lapeyre and M. Bensaid, "Socio-Economic Profile of UNRWA Registered Refugees," UNRWA Thematic Report, May 2007, Social Science Research Network, http://papers.ssrn.com/sol3/papers.cfm?abstract_id=1646853.

17. UNRWA, "UNRWA in Figures."

18. Conversely, over 80 percent of refugee camp children in Jordan and the West Bank continue to attend neighboring UNRWA schools; see Al Husseini et al., "Educational Profile."

19. As indicated in a survey implemented across the Near East in 2005, see Jalal Al Husseini and Riccardo Bocco, "Dynamics of Humanitarian Aid, Local and Regional Politics: The Palestine Refugees as a Case Study," in *Palestinian Refugees, Identity, Space and Place in the Levant,* ed. Sari Hanafi and Are Knudsen (London: Routledge, 2011), 128–46.

20. This is the case of those refugees from Lebanon who have migrated to Europe, mostly since the late 1970s. According to surveys, they constitute the

majority Palestinians registered in Lebanon. See Ole Fr. Ugland, ed., *Difficult Past, Uncertain Future: Living Conditions among Palestinian Refugees in Camps and Gatherings in Lebanon* (Oslo: Fafo, 2003).

21. See UNRWA, *UNRWA Programme / Project Management Handbook* (Amman, Jordan, 2008).

22. UNRWA, "Annual Report of the Commissioner-General of UNRWA (1 July 1969–30 June 1970)," A/8013, June 30, 1970, para. 19, https://unispal.un.org/DPA/DPR/unispal.nsf/0/519871909FA2913885256A5700565639.

23. See, e.g., Foreign Policy Assistance Act of 1969, Public Law 91–175, s. 108 (a), 83 Stat. 819, December 30, 1969, and Foreign Policy Assistance Act of 1966, Public Law 89–583, September 19, 1966, AFPCD (1966).

24. See Department of State [and UNRWA], "Actions to Implement Section 301(c) of the Foreign Assistance Act of 1961," November 17, 2003, www.gao.gov/htext/d04276r.html. The education program has been affected by UNRWA's political mainstreaming process. Started in the wake of the 1967 war (after Israel complained about the anti-Jewish material found in the host country textbooks used by UNRWA in the West Bank and Gaza), the process has been reinvigorated since the late 1990s by the inclusion of "peacebuilding" material in the curriculum: a bone of contention between UNRWA and Hamas in past years, revolving notably since 2009 around the inclusion of a course on human rights that speaks about the Holocaust; see "Statement by UNRWA on Holocaust Education," September 4, 2009, www.unrwa.org/newsroom/press-releases/statement-unrwa-holocaust-education?id=434.

25. The investigation mission was headed by M. Goulding, under-secretary-general for political affairs. "Report Submitted to the Security Council by the Secretary-General in Accordance with Resolution 605 (1987)," S/19443, January, 21, 1988, https://unispal.un.org/DPA/DPR/unispal.nsf/0/1109F4C12D7E478F852560E6004D9DFB.

26. In 2006, UNRWA inaugurated a new core (general) program: the Infrastructure and Camp Improvement Program (ICIP), aimed at ameliorating the urban management of the camps through the establishment of recreational areas and the strengthening of the refugees' capacity to launch local social activity initiatives.

27. See UNRWA, "UNRWA's Ten Youth Commitments," April 27, 2012, www.unrwa.org/newsroom/features/unrwas-ten-youth-commitments.

28. Independent Commission for Aid Impact, "DFID's Support for Palestine Refugees through UNRWA," September 2013, www.oecd.org/derec/unitedkingdom/UK_DFID_ICAI%20UNRWA_Palestine_Refugees.pdf.

29. Office of the UN High Commissioner for Refugees, Convention Relating to the Status of Refugees, July 28, 1951, www.ohchr.org/EN/ProfessionalInterest/Pages/StatusOfRefugees.aspx; Statute of the Office of the UN High Commissioner for Refugees, A/RES/428(V), December 14, 1950, https://documents-dds-ny.un.org/doc/RESOLUTION/GEN/NR0/060/26/IMG/NR006026.pdf?OpenElement.

30. UNRWA, "Annual Report of the Commissioner-General of UNRWA (1 July 1982–30 June 1983)," A/38/13, June 30, 1983, para. 7, https://unispal.un.org /DPA/DPR/unispal.nsf/0/9B371B1E35E5B30985256866006A88EC. The only exception occurred within the context of the first intifada in the OPT (1987–93) when, on the basis of above-mentioned Security Council Resolution 605, UNRWA implemented the Refugee Affairs Officers program, whereby international staff in the field were tasked to report brutalities committed by the Israel Defense Forces during clashes with the population. The program ended in 1994 at the start of the peace process.

31. ee Grandi's chapter in this volume.

32. For instance, the Convention on the Rights of the Child and the Convention on the Elimination of Discrimination against Women.

33. See UNRWA, "Medium Term Strategy, 2010–2015," n.d., www.unrwa.org /userfiles/201003317746.pdf.

FOURTEEN

Challenged but Steadfast

NINE YEARS WITH PALESTINIAN REFUGEES AND THE UN RELIEF AND WORKS AGENCY

Filippo Grandi

PROLOGUE: YARMOUK, SYRIA, 2014

On February 24, 2014, as part of my last visit to Syria as commissioner-general of the United Nations Relief and Works Agency (UNRWA), I was able to enter the embattled Damascus suburb of Yarmouk. Syria, at the start of the civil war, had been refuge to approximately half a million Palestinians. The largest Palestinian community in the country lived in Yarmouk, until 2011 a vibrant social and economic hub in the outskirts of the capital, where refugees had lived side by side Syrians for decades.

Most Palestinians had been extremely cautious in not taking sides in the course of the war. Unfortunately, however, war had caught up with them. Some—a small minority—had eventually taken up arms, with either progovernment or opposition groups, and during 2013 fighting had engulfed most of the areas in which Palestinian communities had lived in relative peace.

In the course of a career spanning three decades as a UN and humanitarian official, I have witnessed much suffering; but I was hardly prepared for the desperate sight that awaited me when we reached the food distribution point. Palestinian refugees who emerged like ghosts from the ruins, as in a medieval siege, described how they subsisted on grass, spices mixed in water, and animal feed and how they burned furniture on their balconies to keep warm. They were suffering severe malnutrition and dehydration. Sixty-five years after the expulsion from their homes in Palestine, they were again dying from readily treatable conditions.

Lyse Doucet of the BBC, who accompanied me into Yarmouk, aptly said in her reportage: "Yarmouk has become the byword for all the suffering in Syria." But Yarmouk also clearly symbolizes the much larger, unresolved plight of all refugees from Palestine; and its humanitarian and political complexity reflects the challenges, dilemmas, and contradictions facing UNRWA as it strives to support Palestinian refugees throughout the region.

That morning in Yarmouk I was well aware that wherever I went, and whatever I said to journalists, carried the risk of being used as propaganda by one side against another. For UNRWA, staying neutral in that war was a desperate necessity and its greatest challenge, just as in the various situations of conflict or occupation that it must confront daily in many places throughout its fields of operation, which also include Lebanon, Jordan, and the Occupied Palestinian Territory.

I was also aware that I had to speak out, and speak out forcefully, to draw the world's attention to the humanitarian plight of the suffering refugees. All sides in the Syrian war have legal and moral responsibilities in that tragedy, of course. However, the reflex I developed after many years of work with UNRWA told me that I had to mix force and clarity with prudence and tread carefully on the issue of attributing fault because the next day my colleagues would still be there, struggling to bring desperately needed relief to the population under conditions in which access was dependent on those fighting in Yarmouk. To advocate courageously but to be politically guarded was a crucial balance that I was acutely aware of not only in Yarmouk but throughout my work with UNRWA.

However, by far the most difficult thing about my Yarmouk experience was seeing the people. Their physical suffering was bad enough, but it was the fear in their eyes that was unbearable, the realization of profound loss when they looked around and saw only blackened shells where they had built their lives, and also their disbelief that the world was unable to prevent this from happening. Syria had been a country in which Palestinians had found a secure and stable refuge and where UNRWA had established forward-looking programs that focused on empowerment of youth, on community participation, and on self-reliance. All this, I knew, was being swept away by violence, mirroring the fate of other UNRWA innovative projects in Gaza, the West Bank, and Lebanon.

Another immediate thought was that the immensity of Yarmouk's needs would require us to appeal for massive resources for years to come, amid all the other priorities in this destroyed country. Raising those funds, pressing as it would be, would make it more difficult to obtain resources also desperately needed in Gaza, the West Bank, and Lebanon. On the other hand, I knew what an uphill battle it would be—if peace ever returned—to convince donors to invest in the rebuilding of houses and structures in the Palestinian refugee camps in Syria. I knew that such funding would inevitably decline after the first surge but that unless we raised adequate reconstruction funds for a number of years we would witness in Syria the same hardship and tensions caused by the delays in reconstruction experienced in other Palestinian refugee communities affected by conflict and military operations, such as the Nahr el-Bared camp in Lebanon.

As I left Yarmouk on that cold February day, it occurred to me that Yarmouk symbolizes the persistence of the Palestinian refugee question. In a region beset by overlapping crises, and with resources and political attention stretched to the limits, the presence of a large refugee population, highly exposed to the consequences of war, poverty, and political tensions, is not just creating hardship for the refugees; it is also an element of instability, and of political fragility, that will not go away until it finds a just and durable solution.

THE LARGER PICTURE

The issue of refugees from Palestine has been a compelling political and humanitarian crisis since 1948. It is a crisis inscribed in the broader history of all Palestinians over the last century. One could say that of the constant crises that have affected Palestinians in the past decades, none has carried more tragic significance than their original dispossession and dispersion.

It is a crisis the international community has too often forgotten, although it is part of a conflict that has become, unfortunately, a global household name amid the many conflicts of our time. In the 1948 Arab-Israeli war, about 750,000 Palestinians either fled or were forced to flee from their homes in what would become the state of Israel. UNRWA was created by the General Assembly in 1949 to address the needs of the refugees from Palestine until a political solution was found to their plight.

It was, and remains, one of the largest refugee situations in contemporary history; and it has become one of its most protracted. Today, five million refugees are registered with UNRWA and eligible for its basic services, mainly education and health care, in the Occupied Palestinian Territory, Jordan, Lebanon, and Syria.

UNRWA's original task was to try and move from "relief" to "works" and to do so by progressively weaning refugees from dependency on relief assistance and creating opportunities for self-reliance. This mission has become much more complicated over the decades, not least because the refugees have constantly found themselves involved in (or at least affected by) other conflicts— Gaza and Syria being the most recent—thus continually rekindling the need to resume "relief" and making attempts at "works" increasingly difficult.

I was involved with UNRWA for nearly a decade. I served first as the deputy commissioner-general from October 2005 (just after the unilateral Israeli "disengagement" from Gaza) to 2010 and then as its commissioner-general until March 2014 (during the continuously escalating war in Syria, and a few weeks before a new, devastating explosion of conflict in Gaza). During these years, the Middle East was propelled into considerable upheaval, affecting all Palestinians but especially Palestinian refugees in all of UNRWA's fields of operation.

Even leaving aside the complicated political context, leading UNRWA is a unique experience: certainly one of the UN's most challenging management tasks. The commissioner-general, although a nonelected official, runs quasi-governmental services larger than in many small countries. Unlike governments, however, UNRWA is funded not by taxes but by precarious voluntary financing. And although UNRWA does not represent refugees (something it is not equipped and authorized to do), it is frequently urged to carry out this role given the institutional and credibility gap left by weakened Palestinian political bodies and especially the Palestine Liberation Organization, which has the actual mandate to represent all Palestinians.

As the commissioner-general of UNRWA, I was often told by sympathetic interlocutors that leading UNRWA "must be a tough job." This actually sums it up simply and accurately. In the observations that follow, I will focus on four areas that in my view are crucial to understanding UNRWA, its mission, and its future: the challenge of scarce resources; neutrality in an environment of conflict or occupation; the question of whether UNRWA is part of the problem instead of contributing to solutions; and the opportunities of (and threats to) UNRWA's development potential.

These observations are not meant to be exhaustive, and they reflect my own experience at the helm of the organization.

THE ISSUE OF RESOURCES

Managing UNRWA is like chairing a company board with little money, a polarized membership, and combative employees. Although the funding gap in the core budget is relatively small in global financial terms—an extra US$50 to 100 million a year would suffice to at least keep things going, although not to make quality investments—it is a huge problem for UNRWA, which kept me busy (and worried) most of the time.

Unlike organizations that can pace or even suspend their programs depending on the availability of funds, UNRWA is confronted, relentlessly, with a payroll supporting over thirty thousand staff and requiring about US$46 million per month in 2014. This has to be honored if, among much else, half a million children are to continue to go to school and five million people are to have access to basic health care. Because UNRWA essentially provides services through its teachers, health staff, and social workers, salaries represent almost 90 percent of the agency's core budget.

The centrality of salaries in UNRWA's budget structure points to another challenge: the formidable pressure exercised by staff unions. UNRWA is an important employer of Palestinians, the second largest in Palestine after the Palestinian National Authority and the largest in other host countries. The unions' leverage over management in frequent discussions on salary increases and other benefits is quite extraordinary and absolutely without comparison in the UN system. From the perspective of the unions, UNRWA's "W," or "works," stands for "employment," which they consider a priority for the organization. Resistance by management to union demands has often resulted in strikes and other industrial action, especially in the West Bank. Confrontations can be harsh, and exacerbated by the context. There were times when I even felt that the unions perhaps unconsciously framed UNRWA in these debates as a proxy for the Palestinians' frustrated struggle against the occupation.

UNRWA has tried to regulate the issue of salaries by pegging them to those of public services in the respective host countries. Unions' acceptance of this approach has been erratic at best, with frequent disagreements on how to calculate the comparator value of public salaries, and additional demands regarding benefits. Western donors have been concerned by the constant increase of salaries to match corresponding increases in the public sector. Host countries have been worried about resources being channeled increasingly to staff salaries but have been reluctant to intervene in support of management in addressing union demands, for fear of alienating a large constituency, especially in Palestine and Jordan. Amid these contrasting pressures, UNRWA's leadership has usually been alone in making difficult compromises that allow the organization to continue its work but often leave the unions, or government stakeholders—or both—dissatisfied.

Many states finance UNRWA in a fairly regular manner, but a broad element of uncertainty always exists because of the voluntariness of funding. This is UNRWA's greatest operational contradiction. The argument has often been made by refugees and their advocates that donors wish to progressively strangle UNRWA by cutting the money flow. This is sometimes true: under the Harper administration, for example, Canada decided to stop funding UNRWA, going from a total yearly contribution of about US$35 million to zero.

Fortunately, this is the exception to the rule. Generally, reasons for funding shortages are more financial than political. But the fact remains that UNRWA's contractual and therefore regular obligation to pay its staff is supported by contributions that are voluntary and thus unpredictable. This fragility is quite common in the UN system, but it has more serious and compelling consequences in UNRWA than in other agencies: an interruption in the cash flow at any given time would cause a suspension of essential services to millions of people. We came excruciatingly close to such a disruption many times during my tenure at UNRWA, but we always managed, sometimes at the eleventh hour, to avoid interruptions by deferring some expenditure and convincing one or two donors to contribute additional funds or to advance funds against the following year's budget.

Like other UN agencies, UNRWA's funding base is narrow: in 2014, over 70 percent of its regular funding was pledged by only seven governmental donors—the United States, the European Commission, the United Kingdom, Sweden, Norway, Japan, and Switzerland. Enlisting the support of states perceived as more politically neutral—BRICS (Brazil, Russia, India, China, South Africa) governments, for example, or other emerging economic powers—would help ease tensions between traditional donors and refugee hosting governments, but widening the donor base has proven a difficult task. Although endowed with resources, Latin American and East Asian states, for example, have relatively nascent aid structures; they may not perceive that they have a direct stake in issues related to the Israeli-Palestinian conflict; and their relationship with the UN and multilateral bodies is less close than that of traditional donors.

With the support of the Arab League, UNRWA has also spent the last few years vigorously pursuing larger and more predictable contributions from

Arab states and charities. That would seem an appropriate fit, given UNRWA's exclusive focus on Palestinians. While yielding considerable results, especially from Saudi institutions, the preference of Arab donors to fund infrastructure projects and give high-profile, emergency grants, however, does not ease UNRWA's structural and financial problems.

The funding patterns of Arab donors are also quite unpredictable. In January 2009, for example, I traveled to Kuwait for an emergency Arab summit, to present an urgent US$34 million funding appeal for Gaza after the start of Israel's invasion under Operation Cast Lead. As is often the case, and in spite of waiting for hours for promised meetings to materialize, I was not received by even one Arab delegation. However, as I was leaving the country, feeling frustrated and confused, I discovered that the emir of Kuwait had in fact just contributed to UNRWA exactly US$34 million.

Arab aid is not designed to support the functioning of international agencies, even when, as in the case of UNRWA, "functioning" means running very concrete programs. For example, Arab donors' allocation of an additional US$50 million a year to UNRWA's core budget (not a major financial burden, surely, for these states) would go a long way in addressing some of the organization's basic funding problems and (as importantly) would add balance to UNRWA's stakeholder group.

There are also political implications to Arab funding limitations. The traditional argument was that since the West helped create the Palestinian refugee problem it is responsible for supporting refugees financially. While this argument has been somewhat diluted by the geopolitical shifts over the past decades, it remains strong. Many times, as I presented my frequent, often fruitless and frustrated pleas for additional funding to Arab princes and officials, I was reminded that supporting Palestinian refugees was something they considered a humanitarian gesture, not a responsibility as members of the UN and of the international community.

Thus UNRWA remains dependent on a small group of Western donors. Such reliance has become even riskier from the financial point of view after the 2008 global economic crisis, given the increased budget constraints of traditional donors and their understandable reluctance to fund what (for all intents and purposes) is public services at a time of cuts in state bureaucracies at home. This has not substantially improved even after the worst of the economic downturn ended. Increasingly donors rely on special funds allocated on an ad hoc basis to respond to humanitarian emergencies, especially when political efforts to shore up the gaps in regular aid budgets fail (in Gaza, for example, or in Syria). The shift of resources toward emergency funding has meant that while UNRWA's humanitarian activities have been by and large sustained, its longer-term investments in education, health, and poverty alleviation have been weakened, preventing UNRWA from fostering the very self-reliance of refugees that donors expect the organization to encourage.

ON THE FRONT LINES

Doing nonpolitical work in a highly politicized environment also produces difficult challenges for UNRWA. Many are linked to operating in situations of conflict and occupation; others are more specific to UNRWA.

Working in Syria, as already mentioned, has illustrated some of these challenges since the start of the civil war in 2011. UNRWA has delivered services to Palestinian refugees in and around almost all major cities for over six decades. Maintaining access to Palestinians, often displaced by conflict, has therefore been the agency's main task. Keeping distance from those in control of the territories in order to maintain neutrality, but being in sufficiently close contact to facilitate operations, has exposed UNRWA to criticism: opponents to the government have accused it of supporting the regime; and vice versa, the government has complained that UNRWA is not forceful enough in denouncing obstacles created by opposition groups to the delivery of aid.

In the Occupied Palestinian Territory, pressure by the United States, Israel, and other governments for UNRWA to maintain its neutrality has been intense, especially in Gaza. Working in an area controlled by Hamas often led detractors to say that UNRWA was "supporting terrorism." This is of course a facile and futile criticism. The reality is different.

Since 2007, the United Nations has applied a "no contact" policy with respect to Hamas: in my personal view, this policy is counterproductive, as the UN should speak to all players in a conflict if it is to fulfill its role in promoting peace and security. Nevertheless, the policy has been observed by all parts of the UN, including UNRWA, though taking into account operational needs. Shortly after being appointed commissioner-general, I received a call from the Israeli government asking me whether I intended to deal with Hamas and cautioning me against "legitimizing" it. I responded, as I did many times afterwards, that UNRWA deals with Hamas as it deals with any authority, be it de jure or de facto: there are operational matters, such as security, water and sanitation, or land use, in which UNRWA has no choice but to talk with those in control. This position was generally accepted by Western donors and by Israel.

I was also challenged many times by interlocutors who criticized what they perceived as UNRWA's inadequate upholding of "neutrality": the US Congress, for example, or pro-Israeli groups in Europe and North America. Many of the negative observations relate to the view that UNRWA's facilities are misused by combatants and specifically by Hamas. In fact, in the overwhelming majority of cases these accusations have been proven untrue, or worse, fabricated; and on the rare occasions when UNRWA's facilities were compromised, the agency took decisive and public measures to assert their inviolability.

Another frequent target of criticism is UNRWA's school curriculum. Supporters of Israel, and at times some Israeli government representatives, have claimed that it incites violence. UNRWA's, curricula, however must follow those of host countries. These—and the manner in which they are taught—are continually and thoroughly reviewed to guard against any element of incitement and are complemented by an UNRWA-specific syllabus teaching human rights and tolerance that is unique in the region. Of course, the curriculum follows the historic narrative of the Arab countries in which it is taught. This alone attracts unjustified but often very sharp criticism. But which schools, in which country, do not teach history from the national perspective?

In the debate on neutrality, there are lines to be drawn. Both Karen Abuzayd, my predecessor as commissioner-general, and I were frequently accused of acting "politically" when we spoke publicly about the need to uphold the rights of Palestinian refugees. We systematically rejected this accusation, insisting that advocacy on behalf of Palestinian refugee rights was a key aspect of our protection work and that protection, in turn, was an integral and explicit part of UNRWA's mandate. I think that we would have actually been remiss in fulfilling our responsibilities had we not, for instance, spoken out against the Israeli settlers encroaching on Palestinian land or against the blockade in Gaza as yet another unnecessary, illegal, and counterproductive manifestation of occupation. We would have been equally remiss had we failed to speak out frequently about the need for Palestinians in Lebanon to have access to a better regime of rights or about disparities of treatment among Palestinians in Jordan.

But the most complicated issue concerns accusations that some of UNRWA's Palestinian staff members were violating the neutrality rules. I never hesitated in explaining to critics that UNRWA's efforts to uphold neutrality had to be seen in the proper context: Palestinians are party to the conflict, so to ask a Palestinian member of UNRWA's staff to be neutral is a tough, even unfair demand. This is true of course for any organization working through local staff in situations of war. The specific challenge of the Occupied Palestinian Territory is that UNRWA staff there, just like all other Palestinians, live and suffer under the unique and stifling burden of occupation, so to demand neutrality raises difficult questions: How far can a staff member go in criticizing occupation measures on his or her Facebook page, for example, without becoming "political"? Should a staff member be forbidden from participating in a rally against house demolitions or to celebrate the liberation of Palestinian prisoners?

These dilemmas have not deterred UNRWA from pursuing efforts to promote neutrality in accordance with UNRWA's staff rules and regulations. The key approach is to insist that all activities related to work must be seen as nonpolitical and that no staff member can carry out political activities, either at work or outside work. We also asked staff to not partake in violence and insisted that their jobs required a considered restraint. This is a viable position, and one that we managed to enforce during the last few (and difficult) years.

But it is not a position that can be taken for granted. To do so would be, somehow, disrespectful. Neutrality has to be explained, debated, and even argued. If UNRWA is to be "neutral," it must do so in a manner that is as acceptable as possible to those who are told to be neutral in a situation in which they are also the victims of the occupation, and whose adherence to neutrality, no matter how great their understanding of the context, will always and inevitably require that they overcome strong personal emotions and maintain thoughtful balance and vigilance.

This is a difficult issue for the UN in many countries beset by war; but it will uniquely continue to challenge UNRWA in Palestine for years to come.

AIDING OR ABETTING

One of the most difficult UNRWA-related questions I frequently confronted was whether the Agency was part of the problem rather than of a solution to the question of the Palestine refugees and thus was fueling conflict instead of promoting peace. Not surprisingly, this criticism of UNRWA comes from two, completely opposite directions.

There are those—some Israelis or supporters of Israel, mostly—who say that through its very existence UNRWA perpetuates the refugee question, the logic of this argument being that if UNRWA ceases to exist, so does the question of refugees. This is a very obstinate criticism. Those biased against UNRWA ensure that it is dealt with in a manner that causes maximum damage. The argument, however, finds support even among many apparently without political bias. Protracted refugee situations generate discomfort, confusion, and fatigue; the temptation is to deny the fact that they persist because their root causes have not been solved.

The institutional objection, of course, is that for UNRWA to (gradually) end its work, political decisions must be made to solve the Palestinian refugee question, in full respect of refugee rights, and (we always argued, though many would say that it was wishful thinking) in consultation with refugees themselves. The practical counterargument is that without UNRWA not only would Palestinian refugees be worse off, and even, in some places, abandoned, but their ensuing inevitable marginalization and exclusion would also expose the region, including Israel, to more instability and perhaps also insecurity.

The completely opposite point of view is that UNRWA, by de facto fulfilling some of Israel's responsibilities as occupying power, exempts Israel from carrying out functions for which it should be responsible under international law. In so doing, the argument goes, it abets, albeit unwittingly, the Israeli occupation and its consequences.

This is not an abstract dilemma: it is generated by very practical situations. Since 2010, for example, when under international pressure the blockade of Gaza was partly relaxed and UNRWA (like other agencies) was allowed to bring some building materials into Gaza, Israel has demanded that, for this to happen, organizations must comply with cumbersome control measures. Lengthy negotiations were conducted on these measures in the hope of obtaining more flexible conditions. However, the question was often asked: Should UNRWA help develop Israeli-imposed control mechanisms to allow building materials into Gaza (and thus, somehow, reinforce the blockade) or refuse to do so (and thus prevent even a limited quantity of materials from entering)?

Such criticism is not unique to Palestine. Humanitarian organizations have long been accused of favoring violations of rights by helping the victims, for example in situations of ethnic cleansing in the former Yugoslavia during the war.

So, in this case, are humanitarian agencies aiding or abetting? I doubt that there is an answer, because I believe that the criticism is directed at the wrong target. As long as political actors (the parties to the conflict, the mediators, regional organizations, the Security Council, and so on) do not address the causes of a war, humanitarian agencies will continue to be faced with the dilemma of either helping those in need but potentially strengthening violations of human rights as collateral damage, or denouncing such violations, withdrawing, and leaving victims to their fate.

In general, agencies will opt for the former if and until reasonable compromises can be reached. In so doing, organizations like UNRWA will continue to be accused of acting politically. But the target is wrong. The brunt of criticism should be directed instead at the failure of politics in finding solutions to conflicts that, inevitably, will continue to transfer these intractable dilemmas to those working on addressing their consequences.

DEVELOPMENT AND WAR

UNRWA has always been conscious of the narrow space that it is allowed to navigate amid contrasting pressures and agendas. The lack of a political solution to the plight of refugees over the past six decades has been its biggest limitation. There have been positive phases, for example in the mid-1990s after the Oslo Accords, during which expectations of a solution to the Palestinian-Israeli conflict grew to the point that some initial steps to wind down UNRWA were taken.

But the failure of peace negotiations at Camp David in 2000, Israel's increasingly right-wing shift, and the onset of the second intifada ushered in a long period of great instability and uncertainty. Solutions appeared, once again, remote, both to the overall conflict and specifically to the question of the Palestinian refugees. UNRWA thus carried on its regular work but supplemented it by adopting the "human development" discourse forged by the United Nations to define a form of development directed essentially at individuals or communities rather than—for example—at state institutions or macroeconomic policies. This new discourse provided a longer-term, constructive perspective to UNRWA's vision and practical action and allowed the agency to put its work on education, health, and social protection in a more strategic framework that was aligned with the rest of the UN.

Initially, there was resistance to this concept, due to the fear that promoting any form of development would lead to *tawteen*—the politically unacceptable integration of refugees in host countries. Such resistance, however, was eventually overcome, especially in more stable situations. Interestingly, it was in Syria—whose government has always been conservative in terms of interpreting UNRWA's mandate, but which, until 2011, was a relatively stable and confident regime—where the organization was able to go furthest in promoting ideas and practices of human development, from the camp improvement project in the Aleppo province to Engaging Youth, a European Union–funded initiative aimed at fostering a business culture among young refugees.

UNRWA is the only UN agency that does not have a global mandate. Given its regional scope and proximity to sensitive political issues (uncomfortable to many), its relative isolation in the UN system will not come as a surprise, even in the humanitarian sphere. Thus embracing human development was a way for UNRWA to link up with the broader UN development agenda and to focus more explicitly on some of the global developmental challenges such as the youth bulge, the decline in the quality of education, and the rise of noncommunicable diseases. But the human development framework also defined a useful space and a balanced role for UNRWA, whose role is to provide developmental opportunities to refugees in the absence of a traditional, state-based development context.

As part of human development, UNRWA also developed the notion of "camp improvement," an attempt to shift the focus of infrastructural work, one of UNRWA's main activities, from a technical, engineering approach to one that involves the community as a whole in planning and decision making. Such a shift represents the closest an organization like UNRWA can get to promote participation and democracy in refugee camps and communities. This, in turn and unsurprisingly, generated some nervousness among host authorities.

Adopting a human development approach also indicated that in spite of its limited focus and mandate UNRWA could be a very useful, experimental instrument in the hands of responsible stakeholders. This was especially important at a time when uprisings in many Arab states (starting in 2010) opened a new debate on the relationship between governments and citizens in the region, and in particular on the importance of human development.

UNRWA's greatest potential is thus arguably its recent human development work. But such work has one fundamental enemy: war. During my time at UNRWA, between 2005 and 2014, at least five major conflicts erupted in one or another of UNRWA's fields of operation: the war between Israel and Hizbullah in 2006, the destruction of the Nahr el Bared refugee camp in northern Lebanon in 2007, two Gaza wars in 2008 and 2012 (with one more soon to follow after I left), and the civil war in Syria starting in 2011.

In Syria, for example, UNRWA's human development experiments came to an almost complete halt once the war spread. Most of UNRWA's Syria program became a large emergency relief operation focusing on cash and food handouts. The Syria war also had clear negative consequences on human development for Palestinians living in Lebanon. Progress made through excruciating negotiations with the government on expanding labor rights for Palestinians, a fundamental precondition for increasing their self-reliance, all but ended once the war started in Syria and Lebanon became flooded with refugees, making a discussion on this sensitive matter practically impossible.

IS UNRWA SUSTAINABLE?

UNRWA has existed for sixty-five years, showing, just like the refugees whom it serves, remarkable resilience. But although one should always be wary of comparing the present with the past, it is not an exaggeration to say that in the last few years a significant number of negative regional developments have overlapped with the institutional and financial problems described above, creating one of the most difficult contexts for the organization since its inception and threatening its sustainability.

UNRWA will continue to be needed and relevant in the foreseeable future. The Oslo Accords defined the question of Palestine refugees as one of the "final status" issues. This designation has inextricably linked a solution to the refugee problem—and thus the future of UNRWA itself—to a peace process that is clearly destined to fail, barring some (unlikely) fundamental political changes. The UNRWA machinery is hence here to stay, but in a relatively expensive context of refugee population increase, rising inflationary costs, and parallel crises that have a direct impact on refugees and UNRWA's work.

Apart from some exceptional cases, donors have never asked for UNRWA's operations to wind down. The international community has accepted UNRWA's importance and continued usefulness. However, since there is worry that UNRWA's operational model may become difficult to finance, donors have focused on what they call "prioritization." In practical terms, they have pushed for services to be limited to needy refugees, as opposed to the current system in which all registered refugees have access to UNRWA's schools and health clinics. They have also encouraged positive reforms, some of which, however, would entail significant changes in the type and number of beneficiaries.

These donor demands have met with strong resistance by other stakeholders: host authorities, refugees, and in some instances UNRWA's staff. Any retrenchment in the scope of assistance—even any change in the modalities of delivery—is usually interpreted as UNRWA relinquishing its mandate and politically abandoning refugees.

UNRWA's leadership has been consistently confronted with these often contradictory dynamics and has tried to find a way forward to sustain the organization with a realistic view of resource limitations and other constraints. This includes defending universal access to schools and clinics while also supporting the call for reforms. It has proven a difficult mediation, given the insistence by some donors, at least, to go all the way and that of hosts—and others—to maintain the politically neutral, but precarious, status quo.

Having to contend with contrasting interests has always been a difficult task for UNRWA. Recent developments in the region, however, have made this issue more complicated. In the past, UNRWA could chart a relatively autonomous way forward because there was a balance of forces between donor and host pressures. But in the past few years, the ability of host governments to weigh forcefully in policy and strategy discussions at UNRWA has diminished. Only Jordan continues to substantively represent the interests of host countries, with Syria at war, Lebanon increasingly dysfunctional, the Palestinian leadership fragmented and weakened, Egypt preoccupied with its own transition, and the Arab League struggling with major upheavals and divisions in the region. Thus the counterweight provided by hosts to the donor agenda—so important not just to the refugees themselves but also to UNRWA's ability to carve out a space to work in—is less effective than before the Arab uprisings and the Syria war. This reality, paradoxically, added to UNRWA's sustainability problems, at least during my tenure as commissioner-general.

More than once, I thought I should send back to donor and host governments the question they anxiously asked us all the time: Do you think UNRWA will remain viable? I also asked myself, countless times, as we were pondering what balancing act we could perform to keep UNRWA going, how long this precarious situation could last and where the boundary was between doing the UN's job of reconciling diverse agendas and perpetuating a system based on precarious support, the collapse of which would expose millions to renewed hardship.

LEARNING FROM *SUMUD*

The picture, therefore, is grim, and the task is difficult. This (partial) digest of the challenges that UNRWA must face to carry out its work raises a question that I certainly asked myself over and over again in my UNRWA years: Why continue to support and promote a project that is sixty-five years old, difficult to reform and improve, with scarce resources and amid a range of contrasting pressures and crippling limitations?

Yet the effort simply must continue, and—I dare say—it is worthwhile. The UNRWA project will always be imperfect, beset by contradictions and confronted by seemingly insurmountable difficulties. My observations have dwelled on those difficulties but have also pointed to the directions that I think must (and can) be followed: a relatively modest increase in core contributions, especially by Arab states; an approach to neutrality that takes into account the realities of working in multiple conflicts and under occupation; the acceptance by UNRWA's stakeholders that the Agency addresses the consequences of a protracted refugee crisis but that only governments can end it; and the importance of allowing UNRWA to fully deploy its developmental potential.

All this is feasible, and UNRWA will persist in this direction. In doing so, the Agency will remain inspired by the Palestinian refugees themselves, as I was, and the resilient attitude that they have shown over all these decades as they were faced with exile, violence, rejection, poverty, and shattered hopes. That "chin up" response to an adverse fate is what Palestinians call *sumud,* a term that roughly translates as "steadfastness," though the English word does not carry the depth and complexity, even urgency, of the Arabic one.

While I was head of UNRWA, my patience was often undermined and my optimism severely tested by the array of hostile circumstances. And not only in Palestine: I remember, for example, how difficult it was to start the reconstruction of Nahr el Bared, a Palestinian camp in northern Lebanon razed to the ground by the Lebanese army in 2007 to dislodge a group of (non-Palestinian) militant extremists who had taken refuge in it. Everything was problematic, including getting funds from donors, obtaining construction permits from the various parts of the Lebanese bureaucracy, reconciling the demands of the community with those of the army, ensuring that the Palestinian factions were on board, and finding the right contractors. At one point, the Lebanese authorities halted the reconstruction of the camp ostensibly because antiquities had been discovered under the construction site, though in reality it was clear that reconstruction had become a pawn in the broader political wrangling of the Lebanese parties. In early 2015, reconstruction had not yet been completed.

Despite all these challenges, I always felt that our frustrations were inconsequential when compared to the suffering of the refugees, who increasingly faced renewed displacement and a devastating depletion of their reservoirs of hope for a better future. Yet when I went to meet them in their temporary homes and shelters, though sometimes their customary courtesy, patience, and hospitality were swept away by anger and frustration, I was always inspired by how determined they were to rebuild once again, awaiting the end of their exile.

Those supporting Palestinian refugees should draw strength from their *sumud*. Steadfastness will continue to be severely tested in the years to come, in a context that is probably one of the most difficult since 1948. I have had a growing sense that, year after year, Palestinian refugees are increasingly stuck in dangerous places without exit, as in Gaza and Syria. We have even seen Palestinians board boats by the hundreds to cross the Mediterranean in pursuit of better lives in Europe, often tragically perishing at sea.

The men, women, and children who met me in Yarmouk on that winter morning in February 2014 proved once again, as if proof were needed, that Palestinian refugees, in their long, unresolved exile, remain an acutely vulnerable population. This alone, and their determination not to give in, should be reason enough for the international community to fulfill its obligations and ensure that UNRWA remains sustainable in spite of its inevitable fragility, and for UNRWA's leadership to face its challenges with realism but also with the courage and determination inspired by the people it serves.

FIFTEEN

The UN High Commissioner for Refugees and the Iraq Refugee Operation

RESETTLING REFUGEES, SHIFTING THE MIDDLE EAST HUMANITARIAN LANDSCAPE

Arafat Jamal

AS THE ARAB UPRISINGS OF 2010 descended into the forced displacements of subsequent years, the United Nations—for so long a marginal humanitarian protagonist in the Middle East—assumed an unfamiliar aspect: prominent, operational, and on the side of war victims. In December 2014, combined UN agencies launched an appeal for over US$8 billion to help nearly eighteen million Syrians—a huge shift from the modest pre-2007 programs and budgets. For an entity frequently associated in the region with partition, sanctions, the Oil-for-Food program, or military interventions, the new image of the UN and other international agencies firmly implanted in the region, and sheltering and aiding displaced people, demonstrated just how much the humanitarian space in the Middle East had opened. While the trigger for the Syria refugee response was mass displacement and the staggering burden this imposed on neighboring countries, the foundations for trust and effective action had been laid earlier, during the reaction to the protracted outflow of Iraqis (from 2003) into neighboring countries, at the time the largest refugee movement in the Middle East since the Palestinian exodus of 1948.

The operational and legal responses chosen to deal with the post-2003 Iraqi displacement of Iraqis engendered a fundamental shift in the perception of Office of the UN High Commissioner for Refugees (UNHCR) and its engagement with refugee hosting states, bringing with it major, positive consequences for the post-2011 outflows of Syrians in the region. UNHCR, mandated by the United Nations to lead and coordinate international protection of refugees and the resolution of refugee problems, played a key if at times unexpected and unplanned role in redefining the image of the UN and paving the way for a new partnership. Its normal responses to refugee situations—such as large-scale emergency operations or structured legal protection—proved largely unsuited for the Iraqis, given the nature of the outflow and the prevailing legal and political climate, and instead UNHCR enacted new procedures to protect an urban, scattered, and middle-class population that had found asylum in legally and culturally complex host states. Recognizing a changed environment, where the long-standing Palestinian refugee situation was overshadowed by Iraqi outflows that threatened to overwhelm existing national reception and assistance resources, UNHCR exercised its humanitarian and nonpolitical character to fill a void and to stake out a space for a multilateral humanitarian approach to forced displacement.

Resettlement, a staple but at times underused tool at UNHCR's disposal, was deployed to great effect in 2007 and 2008, giving UNHCR a tangible means of sharing burdens and solving individual problems. Resettlement was but one element in a multipronged response, and while its direct impact was limited to a minority of refugees its activation was instrumental in building confidence and trust between the UN and host governments and in pioneering the use of innovative ways to respond to urban refugees.

This essay examines the changing role of the UN in the Middle East by focusing on the Iraqi refugee situation and by homing in on the actions of one organization (UNHCR) with respect to one activity—resettlement. After examining the pre-2007 context, it explains how the recognition of the existence of a massive refugee population, combined with the choice of UNHCR to recognize all Iraqis as prima facie refugees, enabled UNHCR—with support from donor countries, in particular the United States—to seize the initiative and stake out a new mode of operation involving both resettlement and new urban approaches. While resettlement is most obviously a highly individualized means of resolving a refugee problem, it is also recognized as having a strategic value beyond those directly affected by it. In the Middle East, resettlement helped improve the general asylum climate for Iraqi refugees and was used by the UNHCR to begin carving out a larger humanitarian space in the region. The chapter will conclude by noting the initial response to the Syrian refugees (beginning in 2011), reflecting on the limitations of humanitarian action in the face of mass displacement and in the absence of political solutions.

Whereas the notion of asylum and the status of refugee have a long lineage in Arab and Islamic tradition, recent history and practice have diverged from prevailing international norms; one consequence of this has been the curtailment of space for independent humanitarian action and refugee protection. Before the second Iraqi outflow (beginning in 2003), the UNHCR, along with other international humanitarian actors, was in a weak position in the region.[1] Its explicitly nonpolitical, humanitarian mandate has not been well understood, and the grant of refugee status—also a nonpolitical act—has not always been interpreted in this manner.[2]

The UNHCR has a global mandate and operations around the globe but until around 2005 was not especially active in the Middle East. There are several reasons for this, including the exclusion of Palestine refugees from its mandate; the weak legal regimes concerning non-Palestine refugees in the Middle East; and the relative absence of major humanitarian emergencies in the region and consequent lack of opportunities for the display of independent humanitarian action.

Regarding the first, for decades the term *Palestinian* has been synonymous with *refugee*, yet the UNHCR—"the UN Refugee Agency"—does not deal with the majority of Palestinian refugees. Its 1950 Statute and the 1951 Refugee Convention exclude "persons who are at present receiving . . . protection or assistance" from other UN organs or agencies.[3] The UN Relief and Works Agency (UNRWA) predates the UNHCR and was already dealing with Palestinians in Lebanon, Syria, Jordan, the West Bank, and the Gaza Strip; thus the UNHCR does not normally deal with Palestinians unless they are outside this area of operation.[4] A major difference between UNRWA and the UNHCR is that while the UNHCR has a strong protection and solutions mandate, whereas UNRWA is focused on assistance.

Unlike other UN entities, UNRWA—with its large-scale and enduring assistance and institutional activities and its periodic emergency interventions—is viewed in a largely positive light in the region. It is "the single most trustworthy institution in the eyes of the people in the West Bank and Gaza Strip," for example.[5] But UNRWA occupies a special niche as a UN organization with a specific geographical focus that stands apart from the 1951 Refugee Convention and some of the more global UN and multilateral bodies, such as the Inter-Agency Standing Committee, which is viewed as the "primary mechanism for inter-agency coordination of humanitarian assistance."[6]

So strong is the association of the term *Palestinian* with *refugee* that it used to be very difficult for the UNHCR to advocate or work on behalf of non-Palestinian refugees. In 2005/2006, for example, it was almost impossible to discuss non-Palestine refugees with Lebanese or Jordanian officials without first listening to government positions on Palestine refugees and then allaying concerns about any overlap between UNRWA and UNHCR mandates.

The second reason the UNCHR has been weak in the region is that legally, apart from Egypt and Yemen, none of the Middle Eastern nations are party to the main international refugee instrument, the 1951 Convention Relating to the Status of Refugees. A strong tradition of reciprocity among Arab states with regard to movement of citizens, coupled with a deep reluctance to confer refugee status on non-Palestinians, had meant that issues of forced migration were handled as immigration and national security issues rather than as refugee ones, effectively restricting the UNHCR's actions in the region.

The final reason why the UNHCR did not have a high profile in the region is that, prior to 2003 it had little opportunity to demonstrate its nonpolitical, humanitarian profile in the region. In other places—Europe, Africa, and Asia—the UNHCR responded to Cold War, independence struggles, and boat people situations, and through these operations people and governments there came to observe and understand and value the humanitarian and operational aspects of the UNHCR's work. In these situations, the UNHCR evolved from a largely European entity formed in the aftermath of the Second World War, and shaped by the Cold War, to become a truly global entity, practicing international protection in an independent and impartial manner. This was not the case for the Middle East, where, UNRWA excepted, the UN was more likely to be associated with Security Council resolutions, inefficiency, and scandals such as Oil-for-Food.

In the Middle East, 1991 was the first instance when the UNHCR undertook a major operation in the region, also concerning Iraq. In what was the "first explicit use of UN enforcement action to contain refugee crises," UN Security Council Resolution 688 of April 5, 1991, provided the basis for Operation Provide Comfort, which ensured assistance to Iraqi Kurds while preventing them crossing the border into Turkey.[7] This operation was highly politicized and militarized, was played out in the international media, and profoundly shaped the UNHCR's approaches to emergency response and working in such environments. It was not, however, the type of operation that would carve out a humanitarian space for the agency in the region.[8]

STATUS: VISITORS AND GUESTS

In such a context, where historic traditions of sanctuary are strong but where the Palestine issue looms large, forced migrants—including those considered refugees by the 1951 Convention definition—have been treated under a variety of laws and categories. Citizens of Arab nations have been able to enter neighboring countries without visas for varying periods. Renewing this status in most cases was a matter of exiting and immediately reentering the host country, without a need to actually enter a third country (be it the country of origin or another neighbor). In Jordan, those with greater means could regularize this status by making a hefty payment and deposit, but the majority subsisted in a legal limbo, where they were able to escape persecution and war, but without a firmly grounded status. They enjoyed "temporary refuge," a condition "between non-*refoulement* and admission which self-consciously distinguishes them from one another."[9]

Jordan addressed the status issue by referring to all Iraqis in the Kingdom as "guests." It was a novel approach, ensuring that Iraqis were treated in a "traditional" mode, sidestepping the issue of refugee status. In many ways this status worked well, enabling the Iraqis to stay in safety for long periods, not formalizing their settlement and—when required for resettlement purposes—also permitting the UNHCR to undertake and pronounce on formal refugee status. However, just as a houseguest can overstay his welcome, so too can a "refugee-guest."

The UNHCR's relations, and the status of non-Palestinian refugees, were governed in both Lebanon and Jordan through memoranda of understanding, which, while affording some legal protections to refugees, were quite restrictive and emphasized that refugees could not enjoy long-term status in either country by stipulating time limits within which they were expected to be resettled by the UNHCR.

RESPONDING TO THE IRAQI OUTFLOW, 2003–6: ANTICIPATED INVASION, UNEXPECTED POPULATION MOVEMENTS

The 1991 intervention in Iraq undid the annexation of Kuwait, created the foundations for Kurdish autonomy, and ushered in a period of sanctions, low-intensity displacement, and stagnation. Following an emergency operation in northern Iraq in 1991, the UNHCR largely reverted to dealing with Iraqis fleeing the Saddam Hussein regime on an individual basis.

In 2003, the United States geared up for a second military intervention in Iraq, one that was both announced and anticipated. The UNHCR, together with the International Federation of the Red Cross, prepared for an expected refugee outflow in model, textbook fashion. They had stockpiled enough relief items and emergency staff to respond to an anticipated outflow of some six hundred thousand persons. Yet the expected outflow never occurred; instead, several thousand Iraqi exiles moved in the opposite direction, repatriating to Iraq. The UNHCR, on alert for an emergency, was wrong-footed. Then the August 19, 2003, Canal Hotel bombing in Baghdad—which killed twenty-one UN staff—discouraged high-profile approaches in the region. Rather than being involved in a large humanitarian operation, the UNHCR offices in the region reverted to small operations that focused on individual Iraqi and African asylum seekers.

Yet by 2005, as any casual visitor to Amman or Damascus would have remarked, the Iraqi outflow that initially eluded the UNHCR had occurred. What had happened? Iraqis were leaving their country, but not in a mass exodus. With unrestricted access to neighboring Arab countries, as visitors, Iraqis departed in an orderly fashion. Some were indeed visitors, or businesspersons, undertaking routine travel and intending to return to Iraq. But among these travelers were some who had been forced to leave—who had sold their belongings and were escaping from war, persecution, or worse. They were initially "invisible" in that they crossed without visa and, as Arab state visitors, did not apply for special refugee status (with some exceptions, who came directly to the UNHCR), lived in rented urban housing (not camps), and were physically similar to their hosts. Some were wealthy, others appeared wealthier than they were because they brought with them the proceeds of property they had sold before departure. In Jordan, those who could afford it placed a hefty deposit into a special fund that entitled them to annual residency; others kept their visas current by making regular exits and reentries.

Thus Iraqis, many of whom were leaving their country for refugee-like reasons, had entered Syria and Jordan in large numbers, but without appearing as victims of persecution in search of sanctuary.

Largely urban, educated, and middle class, the Iraqis rented apartments throughout their host cities and did not generally congregate in separate neighborhoods. From a behavioral standpoint, the Iraqis could confound international officials used to other relief contexts. They did not initially seek out assistance, and when they did they sought levels and standards much higher than those usually provided by aid agencies. They were not initially attracted by the idea of resettlement and—problematically from a conventionally interpreted legal standpoint—they went back to Iraq periodically to complete exams, attend funerals, or dispose of property.

Thus, at the beginning of 2006, the UNHCR was present and active in the three main hosting countries but was stymied by the lack of an international legal regime, restrictive memoranda of understanding, and the atypical urban refugee population. It ran medium-sized programs but did not have a level of activity commensurate with the increasingly evident scale of the refugee problem. Relationships with host governments varied from good but limited (Syria and Lebanon) to rocky (Jordan in 2006 suspended UNHCR operations for two weeks).

2006–7: INTENSIFIED VIOLENCE INSIDE IRAQ, ALL IRAQIS CONSIDERED AS PRIMA FACIE REFUGEES

In February 2006, the golden-domed Shiite shrine of Samarra was bombed, and the violence in Iraq ignited into a ruthlessly sectarian civil war. Minorities, secularists, people in mixed marriages, and those who would not take sides in the new, divided Iraq were increasingly targeted and often compelled to seek safety across borders.[10]

The UNHCR had been scaling up its presence in the region, and while the magnitude of the Iraqi exodus was becoming clearer, it did not yet have a sharp response focus or international profile. Although from a humanitarian viewpoint it was evident that violence was so intense inside Iraq that almost anyone leaving would have a compelling reason to do so, the legal status of the Iraqis remained ambiguous: visitors with permission to stay, overstayers with fines to pay, asylum seekers with applications pending with the

UNHCR or, for a small number, UNHCR-registered refugees who—in Jordan and Lebanon—were to be resettled within a short period of time.

By December 2006, with Iraq engulfed in bloodshed, the high commissioner for refugees declared that all "Iraqis fleeing their country (with the exception of the three provinces of northern Iraq under the control of the Kurdish Regional Government) and who are unable or unwilling to return" were deemed to have international protection needs, making them "persons of concern to UNHCR as *prima facie* refugees."

This was a major initiative, with far-reaching consequences. The UNHCR sent a signal that the situation inside Iraq was so serious that everyone in that country had grounds for being considered a refugee. The use of prima facie status by the high commissioner is rare; a notable example of its application in the past concerned Vietnamese and Lao refugees, who were considered to enjoy this status in the 1970s and 1980s, including under the multilateral Comprehensive Plan of Action agreement. The declaration did not of itself change the Iraqis' legal status in the countries of asylum—indeed, some host governments categorically rejected this classification. However, it sent a strong signal that the situation of Iraqi displacement was a major, international humanitarian issue. This declaration alone would not have been enough, though. The UNHCR had previously tried to consider Iraqis as benefiting from "temporary protection," with no results. This time, the high commissioner had a tool to concretize this declaration: resettlement.

To reach a new level, the UNHCR had to overcome tangled legal issues and the image of the UNHCR and the UN in the region and had to devise means of effectively responding to the largest urban refugee population it had ever dealt with. Over the next few years, the UNHCR was to hone its approaches, eventually putting in place innovative and efficient programs—including the use of cash transfers, Big Data, and biometrics—that would serve as models for other urban situations. But at that moment it needed to build credibility and confidence with host governments, and in 2007 it did so in two critical ways: through the organization of an international conference on Iraqi refugees (April 2007) and through a massively expanded resettlement program.

The two-day conference, which gathered some 450 delegates representing sixty countries, drew attention to the humanitarian dimensions of the crisis then affecting some two million Iraqi refugees. High Commissioner Guterres appealed for a sustained, comprehensive, and coordinated international response to the humanitarian crisis. While the immediate outcomes of the conference appeared modest (most concretely, a US$25 million pledge by Iraq toward its own people), in retrospect the conference was a key event in getting Iraq's refugees onto the international agenda.

The greatly expanded resettlement program, which was to accelerate from 2007 to 2009, was an instrument for the UNHCR to provide durable solutions[11] for individual refugees, to demonstrate concrete international burden sharing, and to fit into national frameworks where the UNHCR was expected to resettle recognized refugees. Resettlement surged in 2007–9 and decreased thereafter, but during this peak it helped focus UNHCR energies, emphasized the human face of the refugee crisis, and enlarged the humanitarian space for the UNHCR and other actors in the Middle East.

RESETTLEMENT: A MATERIAL EXPRESSION OF HUMANITARIANISM IN THE IRAQI REFUGEE CONTEXT

Resettlement is the "selection and transfer of refugees from a State in which they have sought protection to a third State which has agreed to admit them—as refugees—with permanent residence status." It is characterized as serving three important functions: providing international protection and meeting the specific needs of individual refugees whose life, liberty, safety, health, or other fundamental rights are at risk in the country where they have sought refuge; providing a durable solution for larger numbers or groups of refugees, alongside the other durable solutions of voluntary repatriation and local integration; and tangibly expressing international solidarity and responsibility sharing, and allowing states to help share responsibility for refugee protection and reduce problems affecting the country of asylum.[12]

Resettlement is also seen to bring strategic benefits. A group of resettlement countries suggested the following definition for the strategic use of resettlement: "The planned use of resettlement in a manner that maximizes benefits, directly or indirectly, other than those being received by the refugee being resettled. These benefits may accrue to other refugees, the hosting state, other states or the international protection regime in general."[13]

Historically, resettlement has been used for large numbers in the cases of White Russians out of China; in 1956, for Hungarian refugees (two hundred thousand resettled); in 1972, for expelled Uganda Asians; in 1973, for Chileans; and in the long-lasting and massive resettlement program for

Indo-Chinese "boat people" (two million resettled). As resettlement is not an obligation on par with the grant of asylum by neighboring countries, the resettlement country must be actively involved in bringing refugees to its territories. Motivations have varied over time, including solidarity, a commitment to international burden sharing, and a need for labor.

Resettlement in a given year rarely covers more than 1 percent of the global refugee population, yet used in the right situations it is a powerful tool in assisting needy cases and in opening up protection space. During the 1990s, resettlement numbers fell, and this solution was sometimes viewed as less equal to the other two durable solutions of voluntary repatriation or local integration. In 2002, resettlement submissions by the UNHCR dipped to twenty thousand, and they remained below thirty thousand through 2006. Iraqi resettlement during this period was similarly low; from April 2003 through early 2007, the United States—eventually the main resettlement country for this population—took in only 692 Iraqi refugees. During this period, the total number of Iraqis resettled to all resettlement countries totaled 3,183. By 2008, in part reflecting the increased Iraqi submissions, the UNHCR submitted 121,000 persons for resettlement globally.

RESETTLEMENT OF IRAQIS: UPPING THE ANTE

In February 2007, in recognition of the scale of the problem, and following consultations with relevant resettlement countries—in particular the United States—the UNHCR announced that it would submit twenty thousand Iraqi refugees for resettlement that year. This was a watershed. Externally, it brought pressure to bear upon states that professed a desire to share responsibility but that had not yet done so.

While other resettlement countries played an important role, the United States, by dint of numbers and influence, was the motor behind it. It has always been the largest resettlement country, and it pledged to be the same for Iraqis. US ambassador James Foley, subsequently designated as the State Department's senior coordinator for Iraqi refugee issues, set a "target" of twenty thousand submissions by the UNHCR to the United States of Iraqi refugees in 2007.[14] Other resettlement countries followed suit, with enlarged quotas for Iraqi refugee resettlement.

Foley was later to reflect on the actions that the United States needed to take:

At the time UNHCR decided to start referring Iraqis for resettlement, the U.S. Government had virtually no refugee processing infrastructure in the two major asylum countries, Syria and Jordan. Neither country had been a location where UNHCR and the United States had collaborated on resettlement operations. No in-country staff or facilities were in place to process resettlement requests, whether they belonged to UNHCR, the host countries, the United States, or any other resettlement country. Immediately after UNHCR's decision to refer cases to the United States, however, we took the steps needed to establish processing operations in both countries, hired and trained local and international staff, and prepared thousands of cases for presentation to adjudicators from the Department of Homeland Security. Since the expansion of our program began less than a year ago, the USRAP [US Refugee Admissions Program] has received some 23,000 referrals of Iraqis. The DOS OPEs [Department of State/Overseas Processing Entities] have prepared for interview and DHS/USCIS [Department of Homeland Security/US Citizenship and Immigration Services] officers have interviewed more than 13,000 individuals.[15]

The US decision represented a significant shift in policy. Iraqis who had fled Iraq under Saddam Hussein had been admitted to the United States as refugees, but following his overthrow in 2003 very few Iraqis had been taken in for resettlement. Now, in 2007, as the Americans surged some twenty thousand extra troops into Iraq, it paralleled this with what some referred to as the "resettlement surge." With the situation on the ground in Iraq messy and military action inconclusive, and with an increasing number of interpreters and minority groups at risk, US officials in Washington and Iraq focused on alleviating the humanitarian consequences of the war. In Washington, the State Department's Ellen Sauerbrey testified that the United States had "a moral obligation to protect Iraqi refugees, particularly those who belong to persecuted religious minorities, as well as those who have worked closely with the United States government since the fall of Saddam Hussein."[16] Also in September 2007, the US ambassador in Iraq, Ryan Crocker, urged the United States to speed up resettlement processing times.[17]

Observed from Amman, Beirut, or Damascus, it was a strange moment, bringing out the contradictions between the political and military consequences of US intervention in Iraq and the humanitarian impulses and actions of that same state. Inside Iraq, a massive US military force was waging war as the country roiled in waves of violence. Some Iraqi refugees fled as a direct result of the US intervention, whether because of association with the

US forces (interpreters in particular), or whether as a result of action against them. Among the refugees, anti-American sentiment was palpable. Yet for thousands the most attainable, durable solution lay in making a new life in the United States. For many, it was deeply uncomfortable to be faced with a choice between a state of insecure asylum or resettlement to a country that many Iraqis blamed for their nation's current plight and even for their specific exile. The number of refugees who had undergone the lengthy interview and vetting process and were accepted for resettlement to the United States, and who failed to turn up at the final departure stage, was higher than in any other resettlement operation (where no-shows were practically unheard of).

By the end of the year the UNHCR had submitted over 21,300 Iraqi refugees from the region to the United States, and the following year it submitted a total of 33,500 Iraqis. In total, during the height of the resettlement submission process (2007 to March 2009), the UNHCR submitted over 75,000 Iraqis for resettlement. Compared to the estimated two million Iraqis in the region in 2007, the percentage of those submitted for resettlement was 3, higher than the global average of 1 percent; however, as a percentage of registered Iraqis in need of resettlement the proportion was considerably higher.

HOW IT WAS DONE

The process of resettling a refugee is intensely individual, intimate, and frequently heartbreaking. It is often through the resettlement procedure that UNHCR staff grasp the contours of horrific conflict and persecution; and it is also through this process that refugees come into contact with the international resettlement machinery, during which they may find themselves revealing, and then repeating, the details of their trauma. To interview an Iraqi refugee for resettlement is to be confronted with a searing narrative of personal suffering; to read through the records of thousands of resettlement interviews is to begin to understand the depth of the national catastrophe that has befallen Iraq.

The following example is just one of thousands that brings out the nightmare from which refugees were fleeing:

> On 24 June 2006, four militants came in a car at 6:00 p.m. and took the [applicant's son] with them from his house. The next day the PRA [principal applicant] and her husband were informed by their neighbor that [their

son] had been killed and his corpse was in the morgue. The neighbor who informed her was close to ——militia and often worked as an informer to —— militia. The PRA's husband and her two brothers ... went to the morgue to receive [the son's] corpse—on the way they were ambushed, attacked and killed.... PRA does not know exactly how her husband and two brothers were killed. She never received the corpse of her son ... or of her husband or brothers. Immediately after the murder of PRA's husband and brothers, militants came to the PRA's house and threatened her, ordering her to vacate the house. PRA fled to the house of her deceased brother.... While in ——, PRA received threatening SMS [short messaging system, i.e., text] messages stating that if she organizes a funeral, the place would be blown up and all the attendants would be killed.

Incredibly, stories such as this became routine fare, and staff who had to interview dozens of applicants each month often burned out from the emotional toll and secondary trauma of listening to and transcribing such narratives.

Resettlement involves sorting among different levels of need and qualification. In the Iraq case, all Iraqis were considered prima facie refugees, but not all Iraqi refugees were ipso facto in need of resettlement. Internal guidance prescribed eleven categories of Iraqi refugees who could qualify for resettlement. These included victims of torture, women at risk, people with urgent protection needs, members of particularly vulnerable communities, and persons associated with the multinational forces in Iraq, such as interpreters.[18]

Interviewing a person for resettlement is difficult and time consuming. The applicant, having already been registered and then screened for possible resettlement, comes to the UNHCR office with his or her entire family and is asked detailed questions about the persecution endured. There then follows a complex process involving verifications, further interviews, and an interface between UNHCR-determined resettlement needs, resettlement country quotas and criteria, and host state interests and visa requirements for assessors from resettlement countries.

This required, on the one hand, a tightly functioning, labor-intensive capability to interview thousands of applicants in Beirut, Damascus, Amman, and elsewhere; and on the other hand a finely tuned ability to negotiate for places with resettlement countries, manage resettlement country missions (or "circuit rides"), and liaise with host governments. The UNHCR chose to dedicate the resources and leadership to successfully manage the mass Iraq resettlement program, both ensuring that it ran an individualized, credible operation for those directly involved and enabling it to serve as a tool through which to leverage greater protection space and embark on more activities.

EX-IRAQI PALESTINIANS, MINORITIES, AND OTHERS

One aspect of the resettlement program was that it included submissions of significant numbers of minority groups, each with their specific needs and risks, who were in need of resettlement. From Iraq alone, people with Iranian, Kurdish, Darfuri, Ahwazi, and other backgrounds came under this rubric; and in a wider context, a typical UNHCR office in the Middle East might end up interviewing a defecting athlete, a disaffected diplomat, a member of a tiny religious minority, or a victim of a brutal sexual assault. Two groups from Iraq—Palestinians and Christians—were of particular sensitivity.

Ex-Iraqi Palestinians

The case of Palestinian refugees from Iraq was in the first instance an illustration of the callous politics surrounding the Palestinian issue and an example of a creative and humanitarian solution to a specific and seemingly insoluble humanitarian problem.

Prior to the fall of Saddam Hussein, some thirty-four thousand Palestinian refugees were registered with the UNHCR inside Iraq. That they were signed up with the UNHCR rather than UNRWA was a result of the fact that UNRWA was mandated to assist Palestine refugees in Lebanon, Syria, Jordan, West Bank, and Gaza, while the UNHCR dealt with those outside this area. With the change of regime in Iraq in 2003, the Palestine refugees—perceived to have benefited under the Baath government—were persecuted and caught up in the sectarian conflict. Chased out of Baghdad, many sought refuge in Jordan or Syria. Owing to political and demographic concerns, they were not welcome in either place, and many were restricted to harsh border camps in Al Tanf, Syria, and Ruwaished, Jordan.[19] The UNHCR initially advocated for their admission to these countries, and, while a limited number were permitted entry (notably to Jordan, where a royal decree was issued to this effect), the others were stranded and without prospects.

For most Palestinian refugees, who come under the UNRWA mandate, resettlement is not an option, as it is seen to negate the right of return.[20] Those under the UNHCR's mandate, however, could benefit from this.

While historically this had not previously been attempted, in the case of the ex-Iraq Palestinians the situation was becoming desperate, and the UNHCR decided to try resettlement.

Given the sensitivities, UNHCR made sure to liaise very closely with both regional governments and the Palestinian Authority. Its approach included calling for acceptance of refugees to neighboring countries, advocating for the repatriation of refugees to their original homes in Palestine (unsurprisingly, this was unsuccessful), attempting to resettle them in League of Arab State countries such as Sudan and Yemen, trying resettlement to "nontraditional" countries, and finally also streaming some—particularly very vulnerable cases—to standard resettlement countries known to have treatment facilities for victims of violence.[21]

For the UNHCR it was a departure, both in dealing with Palestinian refugees and in attempting unconventional solutions. Ultimately, Brazil and Chile unblocked these situations with their offers of resettlement spots for Palestinians in the Ruwaished and Tanf camps. Both countries took their decisions in order to demonstrate solidarity and at the cost of straining their social reception systems. The government of Chile, in particular, recalled that many of its members had themselves been refugees in the 1970s, and now that the situation had changed they wished to offer sanctuary to the Palestinian group.

As a result of these efforts, the UNHCR was able to work with the new resettlement countries to empty the border camps and provide the 1,300 ex-Iraq Palestinians from Tanf with a new start. On the one hand, it was an encouraging example of true international solidarity, flexibility, and burden sharing. On the other, it was a sobering example of just how perniciously the politics of Palestinian refugees can stand in the way of simple, humane treatment of individuals.

Iraqi Christians and Other Minorities

Resettling Iraqi Christians also raised issues of need, politics, and perception. It was clear that in post-2003 Iraq minorities of all stripes faced grave persecution owing to their affiliation. In Iraq, this covered a particularly rich, ancient, and diverse group of communities—Assyrians, Chaldeans, and other Christians; Mandeans, Jews, Bahai, Kakai, and Yezidis; and Muslim sects who were in the minority in their regions and under threat. Given the targeted nature of the threats these groups faced, it was inevitable that they would figure prominently among those submitted for resettlement. But while submitting them responded to real needs, it also risked playing into domestic agendas of resettlement countries, the fears and perceptions of Middle Eastern host states, and the status of these communities inside Iraq.

The UNHCR adopts a principled approach with respect to submissions. It does not tailor submissions to meet subjective requests from resettlement countries, including for specific groups, or for those with good "integration potential."[22] In the case of Iraqis, it explicitly cited nondiscrimination as a key principle governing its resettlement strategy.[23] While resettlement countries have generally respected this principle, in the Iraq case some of them did lobby with the UNHCR to receive more submissions of Christians and other minorities. The UNHCR did not, of course, comply with this. Doing so not only would have gone against its own principles but would have fueled perceptions in the region of the UN as having a "Western" agenda.

But even those minorities that were resettled contributed, inadvertently, to the impoverishment of the cultural landscape in the region. Forced departure was part of the plan for some insurgent and other groups in Iraq, and resettlement played into this. Leaders of tiny groups, such as the Mandeans, would sometimes come to the UNHCR, making the case for resettling their refugees, yet anguished with the knowledge that this was also eradicating them from their ancestral homes.

THE STRATEGIC USE OF RESETTLEMENT: OPENING SPACE FOR REFUGEE OPERATIONS?

The resettlement of Iraqi refugees in 2007–9 was successful in helping to open humanitarian space and can be considered an example of the strategic use of resettlement. In planning the resettlement "surge" of 2007, the UNHCR was clear that one objective was to "create protection dividends for Iraqi refugees who will not be resettled." Indicators for this included "continuous access to the territory, non-*refoulement* access to refugees in detention, access to basic services/rights such as primary education, basic health care, adequate housing, access to informal and gradually the formal labour market."[24] The United States, the largest resettlement country, also linked its program to strategic goals, as the assistant secretary of state for population, refugees and migration put it in March 2007: "Our support for UNHCR's refugee protection mandate and our bilateral diplomatic efforts with host governments have been and will remain essential tools in preserving the principle of first asylum, maintaining humanitarian space in refugee hosting countries and ensuring that assistance reaches vulnerable refugees."[25]

Success or otherwise according to these specific indicators cannot be attributed to resettlement alone. Access to territory, non-*refoulement,* and access to health care and education, for example, were already largely granted to Iraqis. However, viewed with a wider lens, resettlement did contribute to enlarging the humanitarian space available to Iraqis.[26] For the first time, the UNHCR was able to demonstrate a sustained commitment to refugee protection in the Middle East. Making use of a tool both accepted and desired by host states, and now offered in quantity by resettlement countries, the UNHCR invested the resources required to reach out to, register, interview, and submit thousands of Iraqis from several host countries over multiple years. Here at last was a humanitarian UN entity committed to the region and to a resolution of the problem. This was recognized by host countries; as an evaluator of the operation observed:

> In interviews with government officials and other stakeholders in the three countries of asylum, it became apparent that the resettlement programme is regarded as both a substantive and symbolic gesture of support for their effort to deal with the refugee influx.... By alleviating the pressure that the refugee influx was placing on the three countries of asylum, and by showing that UNHCR and its partners were serious in their efforts to support those states which had admitted large numbers of Iraqi refugees, the resettlement programme has undoubtedly contributed to the expansion of protection space in the region.[27]

STRATEGIC REPERCUSSIONS OF AN EXPANDED HUMANITARIAN PRESENCE IN THE MIDDLE EAST

What are we to make of the resettlement surge of 2007–9, in which some seventy-five thousand Iraqi refugees were submitted for resettlement? First and foremost, it provided a durable solution for these individuals; it protected and rescued some of the most vulnerable Iraqi refugees. Undoubtedly, even after resettlement many Iraqis who found themselves in unexpectedly difficult circumstances in their new homes. But from a legal standpoint, a period of limbo was replaced by one in which the refugee enjoyed a firm legal status and a clear path to naturalization in the country of resettlement.

Beyond that, resettlement activities appear to have laid the groundwork for an expanded and temperamentally different UN involvement and presence in the region. In those years, the UNHCR went from being a small entity bound by restrictive memoranda of understanding and largely unknown to the general public to being a prominent operator on the ground, providing protection and services to hundreds of thousands of refugees and enjoying the increased confidence of host and donor governments alike.

The UNHCR used resettlement as a means to expand operations, share burdens, and build trust. Resettlement was a known procedure and—once quotas were known—largely within the UNHCR's remit and control. The resettlement gave an impetus to registration and with that an increased awareness of the profile of the refugees. These were urban refugees, scattered throughout large cities rather than sequestered in camps. Registering with the UNHCR was the main means of contact between refugees and the organization, but prior to the resettlement operation there was little incentive for them to register. Resettlement began to draw people in, and with that the UNHCR became more and more aware of the characteristics, vulnerabilities, and size of this population. As the registration databases grew, the UNHCR was better able to map the locations of refugees within the cities and to begin more targeted assistance.

By 2009, resettlement was waning as a solution for large numbers; the sense of urgency had passed, and many of the desperately vulnerable had already resettled. Political will and absorption capacity had diminished in some resettlement countries, and other obstacles—such as the inability of US resettlement officers to obtain visas for Syria—also contributed. But by then the UNHCR and a host of other UN and nongovernmental organization partners were receiving relatively generous funding that enabled them to run an array of targeted, creative programs, such as cash assistance, psychosocial support, tertiary health treatments, and extensive trainings of law enforcement officials.[28]

In the spring of 2011, as the first protests erupted in Syria and the first wave of refugees fled from Deraa into Jordan, the UNHCR was in a very different position than in 2003. Present, prepared, and trusted, it worked discreetly and collaboratively with governments in the region to ensure access and care for the new arrivals. The habit of working together and the urban interventions used for adapted from the Iraqi context made the first phase of this exodus go smoothly.

Resettlement was not, of course, the only action that determined the narrative of the Syria crisis response. The outflow and the effect of that very soon surpassed those of the Iraq exodus and imposed astounding burdens and challenges, to which a vast array of UN and other humanitarian entities reacted. The countries in the region were overwhelmed and needed international support. That they could turn, in the first instance, to the UNHCR was in large part determined by the working methods, infrastructure, and goodwill built up during its response to the 2003 Iraq outflow, for which resettlement played a central role.

CONCLUSION: THE LIMITS OF THE HUMANITARIAN MODE

In 2006–7, the UNHCR responded to a new, non-Palestinian and urban refugee crisis by asserting its magnitude (prima facie declaration), providing durable solutions (resettlement), and running innovative programs financed by international donors. It had entered an area dominated by sovereign concerns and often ineffectual subregional approaches and had brought it into an internationalist, humanitarian fold.

The terms of engagement between the UNHCR and refugee-hosting states had changed. In 2006, the very term *refugee* was taboo in reference to non-Palestinians, and governments were deeply suspicious of UN interference in security-related matters. By mid-2011, UNHCR officials would be sought out and taken to sensitive border areas to interview and begin to assist the Syrians who had begun to cross over, and *refugee* became a term in common use.

Yet just as a culture of international humanitarianism was taking root in the region, the resources and tools of that system were being overwhelmed. The scale of the new Syrian outflow surpassed the bounds of traditional humanitarianism and shook the economic and societal underpinnings of Lebanon, Jordan, and Turkey, and—urging in 2015—going beyond the immediate region and entering Europe in large numbers. Resettlement emerged both as a desperately needed and supported solution for the Syrians (at March 2016, thirty countries had made humanitarian pathways for admission available to more than 162,000 Syrians) and as a path foreclosed by refugee decisions (to travel to Europe) and political deals on admission, readmission, and barriers to movement.

Not only did refugees need help but what were being termed "refugee-affected countries" were in dire need of support. "The consequences have been stark, with over 4 million refugees, effecting unprecedented social and economic impacts on host countries in the region, affecting their stability and reversing years of hard-won development gains; exacerbating pre-existing vulnerabilities; overstretching basic social services such as health, water, sanitation and education; aggravating unemployment; diminishing trade and investment; and creating competition for limited and declining resources."[29]

Rising to this challenge, the UNHCR, together with the UN Development Programme and some two hundred humanitarian and development partners, has tried to go beyond traditional humanitarianism. In December, the high commissioner and the UNDP administrator launched the Regional Refugee and Resilience Plan in Response to the Syria Crisis (3RP), a "consolidated framework to address refugee protection needs, the humanitarian needs of the most vulnerable, and the longer-term socio-economic impacts of the Syria crisis on neighboring countries." UN high commissioner for refugees Antonio Guterres, inaugurating the plan, stated that host countries were at "breaking point" and that a new aid architecture linking support to refugees with stabilization for host countries was needed. The cost for assisting the six million people covered under this plan was put at US$5.5 billion—almost double the UNHCR's annual budget for assisting refugees worldwide.[30]

While the 3RP offers hope, it does not address the root causes of the problem. In the 1990s, then high commissioner Sadako Ogata used to refer to the "humanitarian alibi," the focus on humanitarian action to take attention away from the inability or unwillingness of states to take political action. In the same month that the 3RP was launched, the two dozen heads of the main humanitarian organizations—the UN, the Red Cross Movement, the International Organization for Migration, and nongovernmental organizations—reflected upon the collective humanitarian response in 2014 at a gloomy gathering in Geneva. Downcast at the lack of global leadership, one felt that "there had never been so much pressure to politicize the humanitarian agenda" as in Syria and Iraq; others noted the "lack of accountability of politicians and the gap between rhetoric and action of Security Council . . . members."[31] To them, the limits of humanitarianism, and the unassumed political action needed to make a real difference, were clear. Yet confined to a nonpolitical space, the assembled heads of agency soon moved on, focusing on what action they could take, collectively, in their constrained yet available humanitarian sphere.

In retrospect, the Iraq refugee operation may appear as a brief moment when international humanitarianism, with its principles of humanity and impartiality, was practiced for the first time on such a scale in the Middle East. But the subsequent Syria refugee situation, with its crushing numbers and complex political agendas, surpassed the "classic" humanitarian phase early on. As this chapter has argued, a strong foundation for humanitarian action was laid during the Iraq refugee operation. The ability of the UNHCR and the humanitarian community to continue to innovate, deliver, and draw in the development and political actors will determine to what extent this foundation will hold and accommodate an even stronger response.

NOTES

I would like to thank the resettlement teams in the Middle East and at headquarters, whose dedication and humanity is the inspiration for this chapter. I wish also to thank the many colleagues who assisted with this article through providing information and answering questions. While drawing on my professional experience and observation, this chapter is written in a personal capacity and does not purport to represent an official UNHCR standpoint.

1. For general reference on the history of the UN Office of the High Commissioner for Refugees (hereafter UNHCR), two books are of particular relevance: Gil Loescher, *The UNHCR and World Politics: A Perilous Path* (Oxford: Oxford University Press, 2001), and UNHCR, *The State of The World's Refugees 2000: Fifty Years of Humanitarian Action* (Oxford: Oxford University Press, 2000).

2. The UNHCR Statute, enshrined in General Assembly Resolution 428(V) of December 14, 1950, defines the work of the high commissioner as being "of an entirely non-political character; it shall be humanitarian and social and shall relate, as a rule, to groups and categories of refugees." UNHCR, Statute of the Office of the UN High Commissioner for Refugees, A/Res/428(V), December 14, 1950, https://documents-dds-ny.un.org/doc/RESOLUTION/GEN/NR0/060/26/IMG/NR006026.pdf?OpenElement.

3. Office of the UN High Commissioner for Refugees, Convention Relating to the Status of Refugees, July 28, 1951, www.ohchr.org/EN/ProfessionalInterest/Pages/StatusOfRefugees.aspx; Statute of the Office of the UN High Commissioner for Refugees, A/RES/428(V), December 14, 1950.

4. Palestinians who are refugees as a result of the 1948 or 1967 Arab-Israeli conflicts, and who receive protection or assistance from the United Nations Relief and Works Agency for Palestine Refugees in the Near East (UNRWA), do not benefit from the protection of UNHCR under paragraph 1 of Article 1D of the 1951 Refugee Convention. However, should a person be outside UNRWA's area of operations, he or she may no longer enjoy the protection or assistance of UNRWA and would

therefore fall within the scope of paragraph 2 of Article 1D. Consequently such a person would automatically be entitled to the benefits of the 1951 Convention and would fall within the competence of UNHCR. Therefore, Palestinian refugees in Iraq, being outside the UNRWA's area of operations, fall within UNHCR's competence by virtue of paragraph 2 of Article 1D of the 1951 Convention Relating to the Status of Refugees.

5. Åge A. Tiltnes, Jon Pedersen, Silje Sønsterudbråten, and Jing Liu, *Palestinian Opinions about Governance, Institutions and Political Leaders: Synthesis of Results of Fafo's Opinion Polls in the West Bank and Gaza Strip, 2005–2011* (Oslo: Fafo Institute for Applied International Studies, 2011), 19.

6. See the Inter-Agency Standing Committee website, https://interagency standingcommittee.org/.

7. Loescher, *UNHCR and World Politics*.

8. In the wider Arab world, UNHCR has had a history of operations in the Algerian war of independence, the western Sahara, and Sudan. Looking further, at Muslim countries, it has had and continues to have extensive operations in such places as Afghanistan, Somalia, and more, and some two-thirds of refugees are Muslims. However, in the Middle East operations have tended to be small and often restricted in scope.

9. David Kennedy, *The Dark Sides of Virtue: Reassessing International Humanitarianism* (Princeton, NJ: Princeton University Press, 2004), 230. Non-*refoulement* is cited in Article 33 of the 1951 Refugee Convention as follows: "No Contracting State shall expel or return ('refouler') a refugee in any manner whatsoever to the frontiers of territories where his life or freedom would be threatened on account of his race, religion, nationality, membership of a particular social group or political opinion."

10. For a view of the sectarian violence of the period and the displacement caused by it, see Deborah Amos, *The Eclipse of the Sunnis: Power, Exile, and Upheaval in the Middle East* (New York: PublicAffairs, 2011).

11. UNHCR defines durable solutions for refugees as comprising voluntary repatriation, local integration into host communities, and resettlement to third countries.

12. UNHCR, *UNHCR Resettlement Handbook*, rev. ed. (Geneva: UNHCR, 2011), www.unhcr.org/46f7c0ee2.pdf.

13. UNHCR, "The Strategic Use of Resettlement," EC/53/SC/CRP.10/Add.1, June 3, 2003, www.unhcr.org/3edf57cd4.html.

14. The figure of twenty thousand submissions was not official or binding but served as a challenge and a goal for both UNHCR and the United States.

15. Helsinki Committee Hearing, US Commission on Security and Cooperation in Europe, testimony of Ambassador James Foley, April 4, 2000, www.csce.gov /index.cfm?FuseAction=ContentRecords.ViewWitness&ContentRecord_id=970 &ContentType=D&ContentRecordType=D&ParentType=H.

16. Ellen Sauerbrey, Assistant Secretary for Population, Refugees, and Migration, "Sectarian Violence and the Refugee Crisis in Iraq," remarks to the US Commission

on International Religious Freedom Hearing, Washington, DC, September 19, 2007, http://2001–2009.state.gov/g/prm/rls/92551.htm.

17. Spencer S. Hsu and Robin Wright, "Crocker Blasts Refugee Process," *Washington Post,* September 17, 2007.

18. In certain situations a group methodology is used, enabling certain categories of refugees to be considered en bloc, without the need for probing individual interviews. This was difficult to effect in the Iraq case, owing to what are termed exclusion concerns—the need to vet individuals who might have been involved in nefarious acts that would exclude them from refugee status.

19. Others did not even make it across the border and were stuck in the rough Al Waleed camp inside Iraq.

20. Legally, this is incorrect. Resettlement does not void a refugee's right to eventually return to his or her country of origin.

21. In parallel to, and complementary with, UNHCR efforts were those of independent actors, most notably Adam Shapiro and Perla Issa, who worked tirelessly to get nontraditional countries to offer places to the ex-Iraq Palestinians.

22. UNHCR, *UNHCR Resettlement Handbook.*

23. This internal Iraq refugee resettlement strategy elaborates that "UNHCR's approach to submissions for resettlement if Iraqi refugees will be determined strictly on the basis of identified needs. . . . This approach will ensure broad recognition of Iraqis in need and will not be restricted to any particular groups that may be defined on the basis of their ethnic, socioeconomic, religious, political or ethnic profiles." UNHCR, "Resettlement of Iraqi Refugees," March 12, 2007, www.unhcr .org/45f80f9d2.pdf. See also Inter-Agency Standing Committee, "Preserving Humanitarian Space, Protection and Security," Background Document: IASC 70th Working Group Meeting, March 11–13, 2008, www.refworld.org /pdfid/48da506c2.pdf, and Anne Evans Barnes, "Realizing Protection Space for Iraqi Refugees: UNHCR in Syria, Jordan and Lebanon," New Issues in Refugee Research, UNHCR Research Paper No. 167, January 2009, www.unhcr.org/4981d3ab2 .html.

24. UNHCR, "Resettlement of Iraqi Refugees."

25. Ellen Sauerbrey, assistant secretary for the Bureau of Population, Refugees, and Migration, statement before House Foreign Affairs Sub-committee on Middle East and South Asia, March 26, 2007, "Iraqi Volunteers; Iraqi Refugees: What Is America's Obligation?," https://www.gpo.gov/fdsys/pkg/CHRG-110hhrg34477 /pdf/CHRG-110hhrg34477.pdf.

26. The UNHCR's working definition of humanitarian space is "a social, political and security environment which allows access to protection, including assistance, for populations of concern to UNHCR, facilitates the exercise of UNHCR's non-political and humanitarian mandate, and within which the prospect of achieving durable solutions to displacement is optimized." Vicky Tennant, Bernie Doyle, and Raouf Mazou, "Safeguarding Humanitarian Space: A Review of Key Challenges for UNHCR," PDES/2010/01, February 2010, www.unhcr.org/4b68042d9 .html.

27. Jeff Crisp, "Surviving in the City: A Review of UNHCR's Operation for Iraqi Refugees in Urban Areas of Jordan, Lebanon and Syria," PDES/2009/03, July 2009, www.unhcr.org/4a69ad639.pdf.

28. UNHCR expenditure in the Middle East in 1999 came to US$20 million; by 2010 this had reached US$318 million, and in 2013—with the Syria crisis at hand—US$430 million. The United States has consistently been the top donor for UNHCR activities in this region; in 2010, it provided US$229 million, while the second largest contributor—the European Commission—gave some US$18.5 million.

29. UNHCR, "Regional Refugee and Resilience Plan 2015–2016 in Response to the Syria Crisis: Regional Strategic Overview," December 2014, www.3rpsyriacrisis .org/wp-content/uploads/2015/01/3RP-Report-Overview.pdf.

30. The 3RP was launched together with the Strategic Response Plan for operations inside Syria. Combined, the 3RP and the Strategic Response Plan appealed for US$8 billion to reach eight million affected Syrians.

31. "Inter-Agency Standing Committee Principals Meeting, 9 December 2014: Final Summary and Action Points," https://www.interaction.org/sites/default /files/16012015Final%20Summary%20Record%20IASC%20Principals%209%20 December%202014.pdf.%20meeting%202122May.pdf.

SIXTEEN

The Syrian Refugee Crisis in the Middle East

Shaden Khallaf

The Syria crisis has become the biggest humanitarian emergency
of our era, yet the world is failing to meet the needs of refugees
and the countries hosting them.

—ANTONIO GUTERRES, *former United Nations
high commissioner for refugees*

ACROSS THE WORLD, the number of people displaced every day has risen
from 14,000 in 2011 to 23,000 in 2012, to 32,000 in 2013, and to 42,500 in 2014,
with a current global tally of 59.5 million persons[1]—close to the total population of the United Kingdom. In the Middle East and North Africa, displacement has become a more prominent feature of dynamics in the region than ever
before. The latter half of the twentieth century witnessed significant inter- and
intranational strife that, in turn, created some of the largest displacement crises
in the world, including the most protracted refugee situation of them all: the
Palestinian refugees under the mandate of the United Nations Relief and
Works Agency for Palestine Refugees (UNRWA).[2] Ironically, as we move forward into the twenty-first century, rather than see solutions emerge for serious
displacement crises, we see another humanitarian catastrophe unfolding during one of the most tumultuous and complex times in contemporary Middle
Eastern history, namely the Syrian displacement crisis that began in 2011. The
Syria crisis has been a transformational development, a "game-changer," on a
number of levels, including the impact on local and regional dynamics, the
scope and nature of the international response, and the challenges to the global
refugee protection regime it has triggered. Hence, a qualitative and quantitative
shift in approach to dealing with displacement in the region seems to herald the
way forward, with a pressing need for innovative outlooks and meaningful
partnerships that give primacy to refugees' own perspectives.

As the conflict in Syria raged on over the past few years, the humanitarian needs and the human cost of the crisis rose with every day that passed. With alarming speed, Syria became the world's largest refugee-producing country: there were 9.3 million people (constituting almost 40 percent of the population) in need of assistance inside Syria by early 2015, and since the end of that year over 4.5 million Syrians have crossed borders into neighboring countries seeking safety.[3] In the space of four years, the Syrian situation became the most dramatic humanitarian crisis the world faced in decades. The consequences for Syria's developmental trajectory as well as for the neighboring countries— Lebanon, Jordan, Turkey, Iraq, and Egypt—have been enormous.

Economies, public services, the social fabric of communities, and the welfare of families have been all greatly affected, in addition to the security impact of the Syria conflict on the region as a whole. For a country renowned for its historic cultural legacy, its proud and generous people, and its firm place as a pillar of stability in the Arab world, the destruction and despair continue to send shock waves throughout the region and to have direct and acute impact on its future. A total of 16.4 million people have been displaced in the Syria and neighboring Iraq crises, including 6.6 million displaced within Syria and 4.8 million Syrian refugees abroad.[4] In Iraq, 1.9 million were displaced in 2014 alone by internal fighting and the advance of militant extremists in both countries, adding to the 1 million previously displaced and the 220,000 who left the country to seek safety abroad. As of mid-2015 the total of internally displaced Iraqis had reached 3.9 million, with 377,747 persons having sought refuge abroad.[5] The figures are staggering by any standard, even within the world of humanitarian crises familiar to organizations such as the Office of the UN High Commissioner for Refugees (UNHCR).

One of the most challenging features of this crisis has been its sheer magnitude, as the figures above demonstrate. But its complexity has likewise been daunting. Against a background of highly volatile and politicized regional conflict, the humanitarian crisis has required a sophisticated emergency response to the immediate needs of those fleeing their homes and abandoning their ordinary lives to seek safety; parallel tracks of stabilization to those who have already reached their destinations but continue to require protection and assistance; and programs to support the communities hosting them, so that both immediate needs and medium- to long-term requirements are addressed simultaneously. While thinking ahead to possible solutions, the organization has also had to develop contingency plans for scenarios entailing further deterioration given the current regional climate.

COMPLEX DISPLACEMENT PATTERNS

Multiple displacements have been a striking feature of the Syria crises as conflict zones have shifted and as areas previously considered safe inside Syria have become less so. The emergency phase of the Syrian refugee crisis continued throughout 2014 and 2015, with an average of ninety thousand refugees arriving in host countries in the region every month, almost half of them being refugee children.[6] Families fled for a number of reasons, including the absence of food and medical supplies, a lack of services, such as health care, and the loss of livelihoods. Members of religious and ethnic minority groups likewise fled abuses committed by parties to the conflict. The expansion of control by extremist militant organizations and the brutality with which they dealt with population groups have resulted in significant displacement as well.

Fleeing the violence and persecution in Syria and seeking international protection in neighboring countries have become more difficult as the conflict has become more entrenched and protracted. With more than 1 million registered Syrian refugees in Lebanon, this small country had in 2015 the highest per capita concentration of refugees in recent history. The number of Syrian refugees registered by the end of September 2014 was 375 times what it had been in December 2011. Other neighboring countries also have hosted significant numbers, with more than 2.7 million in Turkey, according to the government, and with UNHCR registering over 638,000 in Jordan, 245,000 in Iraq, and 119,000 in Egypt.[7] Host countries are experiencing real demographic, economic, political, and social pressures. The sudden increase in population, particularly in Lebanon, has affected health care, education, the economy, the labor market, infrastructure, traffic, and waste management systems. In September of 2013, the World Bank estimated that by the end of 2014 Syria's conflict would have cost Lebanon $7.5 billion in cumulative economic losses.[8] Additionally, a February 2016 report by the World Bank estimated that the average cost of hosting Syrian refugees in Jordan is $2.5 billion a year.[9] "Jordanians are suffering from trying to find jobs," said King Abdullah in early 2016. "The pressure on infrastructure and for the government, it has hurt us when it comes to the educational system, our healthcare. Sooner or later I think the dam is going to burst."[10]

INTERNATIONAL RESPONSE

The contribution of host countries in allowing Syrians access to safety has been fundamental to the international community's global refugee protection framework, making them the largest humanitarian donors in the Syrian context. While international support to alleviate the burden has been generous, it has been neither proportionate to nor commensurate with the immense needs created by this crisis. In 2014, a total of almost US$800 million was received by UNHCR, which, while a high figure, amounted to 62 percent of the funds appealed for in Regional Response Plan 6.[11] The 2015 Regional Refugee and Resilience Plan (3RP) yielded similar results, with UNHCR receiving $785 million, which amounts to 59 percent of the required sum.[12]

Beyond the immediate region, some non-neighboring countries have shared the responsibility by granting Syrian refugees access to safety on their territory. Calls have been made for this to be widened through a variety of channels, including through resettlement, humanitarian admission schemes, simplified family reunification, or more flexible visa regulations. Between April 2011 and January 2016, 935,000 asylum applications were submitted by Syrians in European countries (other than Turkey).[13] Advocacy and lobbying, as well as awareness campaigns directed toward sensitizing the European public and policy makers about the need for Syrian refugees to be admitted to Europe and their strategic impact on widening protection space in the Middle East/North Africa, are building up, yet need to continue to expand. The numbers of persons losing their lives in attempts to reach safety in Europe have increased dramatically, with over 2,600 deaths in 2015.[14] The human cost of their seeking safety is testing the collective global conscience. "Refugees fleeing conflict and violence and arriving in Europe carry an important message," says Filippo Grandi, UN high commissioner for refugees in 2016. "Addressing their plight cannot only be the task of countries and communities that are close to wars. It is a global responsibility that must be widely shared until peace prevails again."[15]

As the neighboring countries offering protection space for Syrian refugees in the region begin to face considerable strain, they need massive and concrete aid to support the resilience of hosting communities and to prevent further and deeper humanitarian tragedy. One of the greatest structural challenges the international community has faced during this period has been to reconcile addressing the most pressing humanitarian needs of those fleeing conflict with the considerable impact of the displaced on host countries and communities.[16] It has thus become imperative to establish a solid link between the humanitarian, resilience, and development dimensions of this crisis. Bridging the relief-to-development gap, discussed by scholars, practitioners, and analysts for many years, is integral to conducting humanitarian operations in the years ahead. This comprehensive vision has developed in close cooperation with the United Nations Development Programme to strengthen the respective national response plans through the Regional Refugee and Resilience Plan, which represents the first international response of its kind on this scale.

In the context of the Syria crisis, where the conflict and displacement are likely to remain protracted, major organizational change is also required to bridge the gaps in governments', agencies', and international financial institutions' planning and delivery of assistance. Greater realignment of priorities in development cooperation policies is required for such processes to become more adapted to the complexity of the Syrian refugee crisis and its impact on host countries. This approach requires closer collaborative and comprehensive planning for communities, incorporating both refugees and local citizens and adopting a multiyear and multistakeholder approach.

POLICY CHALLENGES

Numerous challenges continue to face the international community as it grapples with the magnitude and scope of the Syria refugee crisis and its complexity. Among them are ensuring that access to safety remains a viable reality for Syrians fleeing their homeland; strengthening the ability of national institutions to absorb the shock of such large-scale arrivals and needs; dealing with the largely urban nature of displacement; searching for durable solutions that allow refugees a long-term lifeline; closer collaboration between humanitarian and development actors; and more meaningful engagement in local and regional partnerships. In terms of carrying capacity, absorbing the sheer magnitude of the crisis in countries receiving refugees, organizations providing services, and donors providing funds has been and will probably continue to be a massive undertaking. This is likely to require redefining the international humanitarian aid architecture as we know it.[17]

Some 90 percent of Syrian refugees reside outside camps,[18] in urban and rural areas, and addressing their protection and assistance needs requires different approaches from the ones adopted in camps. These widely dispersed refugees have found it increasingly difficult to cope as their resources dwindle. Refugees have faced increased debt as they struggle to pay for soaring rent and rising costs for food, water, and other basic essentials. Many refugees in urban areas have been living in unheated or unfurnished apartments or garages, often overcrowded, with as many as twenty people, normally from extended family groups, sharing rooms. Negative coping mechanisms, such as taking children out of school, relying on child labor, begging, reducing food intake, and marrying early have been on the rise across the region. A study undertaken in Jordan by UNHCR and International Relief and Development, entitled "Living in the Shadows," indicated that "two-thirds of refugees across Jordan are now living below the national poverty line, and one in six Syrian refugee households is in abject poverty, with less than $40 per person per month to make ends meet. Almost half of the households researchers visited had no heating, a quarter had unreliable electricity, and 20 per cent had no functioning toilet. Rental costs accounted for more than half of household expenditures, and refugee families were increasingly being forced to share accommodations with others to reduce costs."[19] "I don't have enough money to buy painkillers for my wife who can barely walk," said Talaal, a Syrian refugee in Jordan. "The only food we have right now is a bag of bread that is three days old."[20]

The vast majority of Syrians who have sought asylum in the neighboring countries are women and children. "Can you imagine? Losing your child in a foreign country, when you're running from war?" asks Reem Al-Hayek, a Syrian refugee who lost her daughter upon crossing the Greek border.[21] With loss of, or separation from, family members, women often become the primary caretakers of their family members, despite the accompanying heightened risk of abuse and exploitation. Along with other key protection areas such as admission to safety and protection from *refoulement,* registration and documentation, and child protection and education, preventing and responding to gender-based violence remain a significant challenge.

Greater efforts are needed to ensure that, in addition to the refugees themselves, the communities hosting Syrian refugees and sharing their already limited financial and natural resources are included in the design of relief programs. Host countries have spent billions of dollars responding to the crisis. The cumulative economic and social consequences of hosting the refugees, including the impact on the communities, public services (health and education) and job markets, should not be underestimated. As a result of the refugee influx, Lebanon's population, for instance, grew to the level it was expected to reach only in 2050.[22] The scattered nature of the Syrian refugee population in Lebanon across some 1,700 locations posed even greater challenges in providing assistance in often remote areas, which required innovation and increased outreach through community-based forms of protection, associations, and volunteers. To make interventions as cost-effective as possible, cash-based programs, which also have the advantage of preserving dignity and freedom of choice for refugees, where possible, are increasingly being turned to as the basis of assistance in Lebanon, Jordan, and Egypt.

Given the vastness of the needs to be met, concerns about sustainably funding and maintaining programs on such a massive scale cannot be overlooked. Resource requirements will continue to be enormous given the magnitude of the outflow and the complexity of the impact on host communities. The risk of donor fatigue, especially in the absence of hope for peaceful solutions to the conflict, is high. Unfunded components of the response plan for refugees are likely to result in reduced and limited household assistance and a reduced number of projects to support affected host communities.

Forging closer relationships with development actors as the crisis moves into its sixth year has become an intrinsic part of strategic planning for the region. Early recovery, the preservation of social cohesion, and the provision of support to government counterparts, local municipalities, and communities in such sectors as water and sanitation, health, education, small-scale infrastructure, and solid waste management have become critical areas of intervention. Collaboration between host community needs assessments and the alignment of assistance with main development priorities and with national systems for planning, programming, and implementation have had to become components of humanitarian planning. Out of the US$4.3 billion required by agencies and organizations participating in the 2015 Regional Refugee and Resilience Plan, some US$2 billion is allocated to helping host countries and communities.[23] The World Bank has also been attempting to bring a more long-term and evidenced-based outlook to the support provided to host countries receiving such large refugee populations in a manner that helps address their socioeconomic impact. World Bank assistance to Lebanon and Jordan has focused on supporting services and institutions and on helping local communities to endure the challenges they have faced as a result of the crisis.

In addition to all the above points, ensuring the protection of displaced Syrian children and youth is a priority in the international response. In host countries, some 1.2 million Syrian children have become refugees, and in 2014 the UN Children's Emergency Fund (UNICEF) estimated that one in ten children were working and that one in every five Syrian girls in Jordan were forced to marry early.[24] Also in 2014, UNHCR announced further reinforcements of its support to Syrian refugee children through significant increases in funding for the education of refugees, mass information campaigns on education, and birth registration.[25] Over ten thousand government officials, civil society workers, and humanitarian workers were provided training on refugee protection, child protection, and gender-based violence throughout the region. In January 2014, UNICEF, Save the Children, and other humanitarian organizations, including UNHCR, issued an open letter to the Geneva II peace talk participants, calling for urgent action to protect Syrian children.[26] The "No Lost Generation" interagency initiative seeks to further galvanize global attention and resources to highlight the plight of displaced Syrian children.

As the crisis becomes protracted, reflections on the search for durable solutions take on increasing prominence. With this in mind, the international community continues to monitor the situation inside Syria and to gather information on areas of origin of refugees, with a view to better understanding the dynamics on the ground in terms of changing demographic composition of specific areas, the viability of residential buildings and homes, property ownership, functioning services, and other elements that refugees would want information about in order to make a decision about voluntary return when the day comes. Voluntary repatriation to refugees' countries of origin is promoted only when conditions there are deemed conducive and when specific benchmarks for physical, legal, and material safety are met. In the meantime, other solutions, such as resettlement and humanitarian admission programs for Syrians beyond the region, have been actively pursued. Since 2014 UNHCR has been hosting resettlement pledging conferences to call upon states to provide the most vulnerable Syrian refugees with resettlement or other forms of humanitarian admission.[27] In March 2016, 179,179 places were pledged by thirty countries toward this goal, against a plan to resettle 130,955 by the end of 2016.[28] While this is a small proportion of the massive numbers of refugees in the region, UNHCR will continue to advocate for a widening of this resettlement base and to consider other innovative solutions.

In light of the continued volatility of the conflict in Syria and unpredictable developments on the ground that may spur additional waves of refugee outflows or further deterioration in the conditions of those already displaced, and given the overall security climate in the region, which remains tense, fragile, and unpredictable, the international community continues to keep a watchful eye on the range of scenarios that may continue to unfold.

THE WAY FORWARD

As long as we were safe I knew I could improve our situation. I just see opportunities.

—JIHAD, *a Syrian refugee in*
Azraq Refugee Camp, Jordan

No matter what obstacles I face in life, they can be overcome.

—MUZON, *a seventeen-year-old Syrian refugee in*
Azraq Refugee Camp, Jordan

The people of Syria have experienced and witnessed tremendous suffering over the past five years and have demonstrated remarkable resilience in the face of tragedy and trauma.[29] It is clear that the challenges posed by the Syrian refugee crisis are beyond what can be managed by one agency or entity alone, and concerted and collaborative efforts on the part of UNHCR, other UN agencies, governments in the region bearing the brunt of the responsibility, donors, nongovernmental organizations, and other actors engaged with this massive undertaking remain critical.

To widen its support base and to ensure sustained, influential, and meaningful support for Syrian refugees, collaboration with existing partners and continual outreach to new partners at different levels have become necessary. Emphasis has been placed on public awareness and advocacy through the media, both traditional and social, including reality TV programming, targeted campaigns, and humanitarian documentaries; on the development of a private sector partnerships platform; and on the planning of greater synergies with civil society, academia, think tanks, and research institutions, with a focus on youth, particularly across the Middle East/North Africa region. Building a network among emerging and well-established civil society actors in the countries concerned and beyond in the Middle East/North Africa to address displacement might be a way to widen protection space by empowering the voices of local individuals and organizations who are best placed to define the responses and future directions from an organic and homegrown, grassroots approach.

The paradigm shift brought about through the Syria crisis has been a model in terms of innovation in the design, implementation, and coordination of such a massive response among over two hundred partners. Yet challenges remain: Will long-term resilience and development components of the response be sufficiently funded, even as humanitarian needs for daily life-saving assistance persist? Will newly recognized actors and donors from across the region continue to be engaged with addressing the impact of the Syria crisis in the years ahead? How will their role evolve, and how will they relate to international structures and planning/funding/coordination mechanisms? Will the new activists and advocates for rights-based governance that erupted onto the regional scene in 2011 continue to play a role in policy making, and will they be advocates for refugee rights? Can Syrian refugees one day be considered less as an "existential threat" and more as an opportunity or a pool of resources that can contribute to national development? Has the next generation of Syrians already become "lost," and if not, how can much more be channeled into investing in the future of Syria through its youth? Will the voices of Syrian refugees be heard more clearly, and can more concerted effort be made to incorporate their perspective in planning for the future? The questions abound.

The Syrian displacement crisis highlights every day that the global refugee protection regime is predicated on a system of solidarity and responsibility sharing. Humanitarian assistance, which serves to address immediate and potentially medium-term needs of persons affected by conflict, does not end the refugee plight—given that it does not address the reasons for flight, it is merely a bandage on a bleeding wound. Likewise, development assistance, while addressing the longer-term and institutional needs of states hosting refugees, does not end refugees' plight of exile and dispossession. Only through political solutions to the root causes of displacement can hope spring for reconciliation in and rehabilitation of nations with wounds as deep as Syria's. Until such political solutions are reached, and until there is a climate conducive to voluntary return to Syria in safety and dignity, the dramatic humanitarian tragedy of Syrian displacement will continue to need concerted regional and international attention. In the meantime, Syrian refugee women, children, and men, who continue to pay the heaviest price imaginable, have been impressing us with their strength, resilience, and determination to go on and to keep hoping for a brighter future. They are the real and largely unsung heroes of this crisis. We cannot let them down.

NOTES

Views in this chapter do not necessarily reflect positions of any organization I may be affiliated with.

This chapter's epigraph is from "Syrian Refugees Biggest Humanitarian Crisis," *Middle East Star*, August 30 2014, www.middleeaststar.com/index.php/sid /225225113.

1. Office of the UN High Commissioner for Refugees (hereafter UNHCR), "Worldwide Displacement Hits All-Time High as War and Persecution Increase," June 18, 2015, www.unhcr.org/558193896.html; UNHCR, *World at War: UNHCR Global Trends: Forced Displacement in 2014* (Geneva: UNHCR, 2015), www.unhcr .org/556725e69.html.

2. For UNRWA, see the chapters by Jalal Husseini and Filippo Grandi in this volume.

3. UNHCR, "Syria Regional Refugee Response," updated 4 April 4, 2016, http://data.unhcr.org/syrianrefugees/regional.php.

4. UN Office for the Coordination of Humanitarian Affairs, "Syrian Arab Republic," n.d., April 4, 2016, www.unocha.org/; Syria Regional Refugee Response Inter Agency Information Sharing Portal, http://data.unhcr.org/syrianrefugees /regional.php.

5. UNHCR, "Country Operations Profile—Iraq," June 2015, April 4, 2016, www.unhcr.org/pages/49e486426.html#.

6. UNHCR, "Syrian Refugees," Inter-Agency Regional Update. November 20, 2014, https://data.unhcr.org/syrianrefugees/download.php?id=7644.

7. UNHCR, "UNHCR Syria Regional Refugee Response," Syria Regional Refugee Response Inter-agency Information Sharing Portal, n.d., accessed April 4, 2016, http://data.unhcr.org/syrianrefugees/regional.php.

8. Dominic Evans, "Syria War, Refugees to Cost Lebanon $7.5 Billion," Thomson Reuters, September 19, 2013, www.reuters.com/article/syria-crisis-lebanon-idUSL5N0HF3I220130919.

9. World Bank, "Economic Effects of War and Peace in the Middle East and North Africa," press release, February 3, 2016, www.worldbank.org/en/news/press-release/2016/02/03/economic-effects-of-war-and-peace-in-the-middle-east-and-north-africa.

10. Michael Holden, "Jordan Needs International Help over Refugee Crisis: King Abdullah," Thomson Reuters, February 2, 2016, www.reuters.com/article /us-mideast-crisis-jordan-idUSKCN0VB0WI.

11. UNHCR, "2014 Syria Regional Response Plan: Strategic Overview," December 2014, www.unhcr.org/52b170e49.html.

12. UNHCR, "2015 Regional Refugee and Resilience Plan—3RP Funding Snapshot (All Agencies)," December 29, 2015, https://data.unhcr.org/syrian refugees/download.php?id=10032.

13. UNHCR, "UNHCR Syria Regional Refugee Response."

14. "Migration to Europe: Death at Sea," *Economist*, September 3, 2015, www .economist.com/blogs/graphicdetail/2015/09/migration-europe-0.

15. "UNHCR: 1 in 10 Syrian Refugees Will Need Resettling," *UNHCR News*, March 29, 2016, www.unhcr.org/56fa71f39.html.

16. See, e.g., Rabih Shibli, *Reconfiguring Relief Mechanisms: The Syrian Refugee Crisis in Lebanon*, Research Report (Beirut: Issam Fares Institute for Public Policy and International Affairs, 2014), https://www.aub.edu.lb/ifi/public_policy/pal_ camps/Documents/research_reports/20140224ifi_pc_unrwa.pdf.

17. More localized forms of response, greater accountability to persons of concern, and earlier and more specific linkages between resilience-oriented interventions and immediate humanitarian assistance have been priority issues emerging from a multistakeholder analysis conducted ahead of the World Humanitarian Summit, planned to take place in Istanbul in the spring of 2016.

18. UNHCR, "UNHCR Syria Regional Refugee Response."

19. UNHCR, "Living in the Shadows: Jordan Home Visits Program, 2014," January 14, 2014, ReliefWeb, http://reliefweb.int/report/jordan/living-shadows-jordan-home-visits-report-2014.

20. Frances Voon and Skandar Keynes, *Living in the Shadows: Jordan Home Visits Report 2014* (Amman: UNHCR, 2014), 28.

21. Tanya Karas, "Lost and Found," *UNHCR Tracks*, March 11, 2016, http:// tracks.unhcr.org/2016/03/lost-and-found/.

22. Josh Wood, "Lebanon's Population Already What It Was Projected to Be in 2050," *Next City*, January 29, 2014, https://nextcity.org/daily/entry/lebanons-population-already-what-it-was-projected-to-be-in-2050.

23. UNHCR, "2015 Regional Refugee and Resilience Plan."

24. UNICEF/Jordan, A Study on Early Marriage in Jordan (Amman: UNICEF/ Jordan, 2014), www.unicef.org/mena/UNICEFJordan_EarlyMarriageStudy2014(1) .pdf.

25. UNHCR, "What We Do: Education," n.d., accessed 2014, www.unhcr.org /pages/49c3646cda.html.

26. Xinhua News Agency, "UN Relief Agencies Call for Protection of Syrian Children," *REF Daily* (UNHCR), January 22, 2014, www.unhcr.org/cgi-bin/texis /vtx/refdaily?pass=52fc6fbd5&id=52e0b8635.

27. UNHCR, "Geneva Conference on Syrian Refugees Ends with New Pledges of Places, Recognition of Challenges Ahead," press release, March 30, 2016, www .unhcr.org/56fc0cf06.html.

28. UNHCR, "Resettlement and Other Forms of Legal Admission for Syrian Refugees," n.d., accessed March 18, 2016, www.unhcr.org/52b2febafc5.pdf.

29. This section's two epigraphs are from UNHCR, *Jordan: The Syrian Mousetrap Inventor*, video, uploaded March 16, 2015, YouTube, https://www .youtube.com/watch?v=tyyePqog9Gc, and Charlie Dunmore, "A Teenage Refugee Champions Girls' Education," *UNHCR Tracks*, November 25, 2015, http://tracks .unhcr.org/2015/11/a-teenage-refugee-champions-girls-education/, respectively.

SEVENTEEN

The Middle East

A MANDATORY RETURN TO
HUMANITARIAN ACTION

Caroline Abu Sa'Da

THE SYRIAN REVOLT AND THE CONSEQUENT CONFLICT starting in 2011 have had a tremendous impact on the lives of millions of people in need of both political action and humanitarian assistance, either in the country itself or in neighboring countries. The scale of needs inside Syria is enormous, while the ability of international organizations to provide aid there has been severely restricted. Because of this inability, most international agencies focus attention and resources on the massive and continuing flows of Syrian and Palestinian refugees who have crossed the borders into Turkey, Lebanon, Jordan, and Iraq. The political framework in which the Syrian crisis evolved during the first five years (2011–15) severely hindered medical and humanitarian activities. The blurring of lines between political and humanitarian action has been, once again, rightly questioned.[1]

This essay argues that the Syrian crisis has clearly shown the limitations of mixing political and humanitarian activities and its damaging impact on the delivery of much-needed assistance to Syrian civilians. Some actors, such as United Nations and some of its agencies, have faced challenges in their ability to provide aid to people on the ground because their political mandate has largely overruled the humanitarian imperative. Other actors, such as Médecins Sans Frontières (or Doctors without Borders; MSF), a nongovernmental medical humanitarian organization, are compelled to challenge this political frame, even if they face huge difficulties in delivering aid in an impartial and independent manner. The first part of this chapter will show how the Middle East challenges conventional actors—in particular MSF and the UN—over the limits of their mandates and/or actions. In the second part, it uses case studies to demonstrate how these limits have influenced the delivery of humanitarian assistance in Syria.

New Humanitarian Actors Emerging

The Middle East is considered today as a region where new trends in the humanitarian sector are appearing. It is now widely acknowledged that the population affected by a crisis is first and foremost responsible for delivering assistance to its members. In Syria, while some areas have been besieged, Syrian citizens themselves have provided much of the aid and support to their population.

UN agencies, donors, and nongovernmental organizations (NGOs) form the current humanitarian aid system. The Syrian crisis shows the deficiencies of this system to contribute adequately to humanitarian assistance for several reasons: either it is seen as part of the problem, or it does not have the willingness, the funds, or the capacity to respond, or its mandate restricts it. Other actors are therefore willing or able to fill in some of the gaps: Gulf states massively donate to UN agencies. For example, charitable, local, and/or religious organizations show their ability to work in specific Syrian areas, and diaspora networks are very much involved in various sectors, including the medical one. Regional charitable organizations, diaspora networks, and donor countries from the Gulf are reshaping the way humanitarian action has been envisaged over the last few decades. The region is also seen as a very challenging place for humanitarian actors in terms of understanding the working environments and the specificities of the populations targeted by humanitarian assistance; gaining access to populations in need; and negotiating with armed groups and nonstate actors. The inability of so-called traditional humanitarian actors to provide aid efficiently also reveals the shortcomings of the current humanitarian aid system and how this affects the response to the Syrian conflict.

The Syrian context represents a kind of crisis situation that humanitarian agencies will increasingly encounter in terms of difficulties of accessing populations in need, insecurity for teams on the ground, and unwillingness of states and nonstate actors to respect the basic rules of international humanitarian law.

Traditional Actors Being Tested

MSF and UN agencies have different organizational identities and natures, and these have significantly affected their ability to respond to the Syrian conflict since 2011.

Created in 1971 by a group of French doctors and journalists, MSF is a humanitarian medical organization that aims at combining relief action and the capacity to speak out whenever a situation requires it. Today it is a movement of five operational centers that manages a budget of over a billion dollars and is present in over sixty countries.[2] Its principles are to be fundamentally independent from any political power, though it acknowledges the political nature of humanitarian action: "If we consider that humanitarian aid is not an exact science but an art, then the essence of this art is to create and maintain the conditions of its existence—to generate interest, make itself useful, identify conjunctures that could be propitious for change—and to be capable at all times of modifying the balance of power, creating a hiatus, permanently maintaining the right conditions for pacific conflict with forms of power that may sometimes be partners, and sometimes adversaries, to our action."[3] It stays independent by relying on private funding for close to 90 percent of its total budget and refusing to accept funding from certain governments considered too politically involved, such as the United States or France. MSF is a "principled Dunantist" organization, often compared to the International Committee of the Red Cross (ICRC) in terms of values.[4] It tries to be transparent about the difficulties, dilemmas, and tensions it faces while conducting operations on the ground. As a medical NGO specialized in emergency operations, it has been involved in the Middle East for decades. This region is an atypical context for the organization in that negotiating an independent operational space there is very difficult.[5]

Although MSF has a great deal of experience in responding to acute crises, the Middle East suffers mostly from an acute conflict taking place against a background of chronic health and political issues, and the burden of noncommunicable diseases in the region is definitely a challenge for an organization used to emergencies in low-income countries. The medical organization therefore has had to adapt its operational ways in the last few years. Noncommunicable diseases are now one of the medical priorities addressed by MSF in the region. Currently the organization is looking at innovative ways of treating these medical conditions in emergency situations.

In addition to medical challenges, MSF faces institutional challenges. The organization has identified the requirement to engage in networking activities with all stakeholders as a starting point for the acceptance, acknowledgment, and recognition of its humanitarian action.[6] Because of the difficulties in negotiating an independent operational space with both governments and nonstate actors, MSF has had to adapt its institutional and medical strategies to be more relevant to these contexts.

MSF has indeed recognized the connections between humanitarian work and "politics," and this has influenced its strategies and actual on-the-ground operations. For two decades, MSF has had a regional office in the United Arab Emirates with the task of forming longer-term relations with donor countries and regional state and nonstate players. An office has been opened in Beirut in 2010 under the umbrella of MSF International with the aim of creating and maintaining communication channels with the major actors in the region. Therefore, in recent years, MSF has also engaged in creating partnerships with less "traditional" actors, such as charitable societies, diaspora networks, and Red Crescent societies. However, some partnerships are difficult to establish because of the lack of operational capacity of potential partners.

MSF was already present in Lebanon, Jordan, Iraq, and Palestine before the Syrian conflict. But it scaled up its activities in the region in 2011 to be able to answer medical needs in Syria's neighboring countries and started supporting Syrian medical networks. Its relations with the Syrian government were tense, since the organization set up activities responding to the influx of Iraqi refugees in 2003. The Syrian government has not granted MSF authorization to work officially inside the country since the beginning of the conflict, though it has done so for thirteen other international NGOs and though MSF has consistently asked for it.

In contrast, the UN, an intergovernmental organization made up of 193 member states, has an agenda that is mainly political. Syria is one of the member states. While MSF's charter stresses the humanitarian principles of independence, impartiality, and neutrality, the UN Charter states, among other things, in Article 2 that "the Organization is based on the principle of the sovereign equality of all its Members."[7] The article also states, "Nothing contained in the present Charter shall authorize the United Nations to intervene in matters which are essentially within the domestic jurisdiction of any state." Moreover, MSF has the ability to discuss with all parties in place, which is sometimes impossible for UN agencies. "MSF's freedom of action is not rooted in a legal and moral 'space of sovereignty' that simply needs to be proclaimed in order to be automatically acknowledged and respected. It is the product of repeated transactions with local and international political and military forces. Its scope depends largely on the organization's ambitions, the diplomatic and political support it can rely on and the interest taken in its action by those in power."[8] Since the natures of MSF and the UN are fundamentally different, their mutual relation is a dynamically evolving one. Indeed, the humanitarian purpose of the UN is just one among others (security, peace, development, etc.). The multifaceted mandate of the UN is an issue in highly politicized situations. The Syrian conflict may have exacerbated tensions between MSF and the UN. However, what is important here is to understand to what extent these different values have proven to be efficient or not in Syria.

The reform of the UN some years ago (in 2005) came from a perceived need to improve the coordination of the humanitarian actors under the UN umbrella. Both the ICRC and MSF decided to stay out of this new arrangement because of fear that they would lose their independence and impartiality. They also worried about being perceived as part of the UN world—which raises important security issues. Being both a political and a humanitarian body has definitely blurred the lines when it comes to the perception of the UN in the Middle East. MSF has therefore clearly made a point of not participating in the UN-led reform and the cluster system of coordinating humanitarian action.[9] The ability to be operational, and particularly hands on, is also a major point of discussion between the two organizations. In a recent review of the so-called traditional aid system, MSF stated that the humanitarian system is not good at responding to new or hard-to-reach humanitarian needs because it has a low threshold of reactivity and has poor commitment to coverage. There is a strong tendency to move away from difficult populations, areas, or needs, with organizations increasingly averse to risk and avoiding difficult interventions for security, logistics, costs, and reputational or just practical considerations.[10] Therefore, MSF has taken an insider/outsider position toward the institutionalized aid system and has sometimes taken a harsh stand vis-à-vis the UN. However, as rightly mentioned by Bernard Taithe, "It seems contradictory to wish simultaneously for greater UN presence and more nimble field responsiveness. The UN was never and never will be nimble. Whether or not it is humanitarian is another debate."[11]

The strategic choices and the modalities of the operations of humanitarian organizations on the ground have also significantly influenced the delivery of assistance. The relation to the state is a major component of the capacity of humanitarian organizations to operate choices of assistance. As mentioned by Rami Khouri, three trends are at work today in the Middle East: the slow deterioration of conditions in Middle Eastern countries over the past quarter century; the gradual fraying of state authority in the region, which has created zones of nongovernability or even chaos that provide an ideal environment for (nonstate) armed groups; and the steady deterioration of the significance of official borders between countries. These phenomena, a "frightening symptom of erratic modern Arab statehood," explain why some violent armed groups are at work today in this region.[12] They have a significant impact on how much MSF and UN agencies are actually able to operate in such a context. As an NGO, MSF has much more room to maneuver here, since it has the ability to discuss the situation with all parties involved in a conflict. On the other hand, the UN has had to work within the frame of sovereignty of its member states, for instance, the Syrian regime in this crisis, even with regard to delivering much-needed assistance to populations.

Funding is a second major issue that confronts all agencies at work in these conflicts. The Consolidated Appeal Processes, the UN funding mechanisms for the Syrian crisis, have been only partially funded (around 25 percent, comparable to the funding levels for other emergencies in the Central African Republic or South Sudan). UN agencies channel funds through international and local NGOs, while MSF does not because it favors a "hands-on" approach and because its funding for the Middle East is exclusively private. The delegation of tasks implied by the UN cluster approach still has to be monitored, since there is no real accountability for such delegation at the moment. For example, if the organization in charge of the water sector in a refugee camp does not deliver properly, it can take a while before action is taken.

Strategic working choices are also important to consider. MSF is very much committed to an emergency approach, so it favors life-saving activities over a longer-term approach, and this is also a serious discussion point with some other organizations, such as UN agencies. While "a titanic 'shift in focus' in the United Nations' response to the Syrian crisis is occurring, leading aid agencies to incorporate more development-focused projects into their humanitarian work as they settle in for the long haul," MSF's response keeps its "emergency DNA."[13] The main issue here is more that emergency response should be scaled up and not forgotten, even as it is necessary to employ mid- to long-term strategies, since the crisis seems unending.

THE IMPACT ON HUMANITARIAN ASSISTANCE DELIVERY IN SYRIA

Mobilization of assistance inside Syria has been extremely difficult, and most NGOs have chosen instead to invest in neighboring countries. As Shaden

Khallaf has noted, the refugee flows into Syria's neighboring countries have posed the challenge of balancing refugee needs and national sovereignty, especially in countries already very much affected by previous refugee flows, The threat to regional security, considered to be posed by massive refugee numbers, is often emphasized, and "Many are starting to consider the presence of such large numbers of displaced persons as a destabilizing element in the region."[14] It has been and still is extremely difficult to negotiate with the Syrian government and with armed groups to gain access for humanitarian aid operations.

In fact, since the beginning of the Syrian conflict in 2011, heated discussions have taken place between UN agencies (mainly the World Health Organization [WHO], UNHCR, and the Office for the Coordination of Humanitarian Assistance [OCHA]) and MSF, primarily regarding their differing political understandings of the crisis and their differing modes of operation (including engagement strategies, such as cross-border operations vs. Damascus-centered operations, the ability to conduct operations on the ground, reactivity, and planning). MSF, for example, has criticized the UN's delayed and sometimes inappropriate response to major crises and failure to give the needs of an entire population priority over political discussions and pressure.

Globally, the failure of humanitarian assistance toward the people affected by the Syrian crisis has multiple causes: the crisis has been largely underestimated since the beginning; huge planning errors have been made; and there has been an incapacity to foresee scenarios and plan assistance accordingly. Many of the debates occurring at the moment on aid delivery in Syria are also symptomatic of the frustration of humanitarian actors over not being able to do more.

Two examples of institutional tensions will now be analyzed to show the difficulties that this crisis has created. The first deals with the discussions that occurred around the best way to address the needs inside Syria for the entire population and not for a specific part of it. Since the early stages of the crisis, MSF advocated for cross-border operations, while the UN and the ICRC stayed Damascus centered in their approach because of their mandate. Only in June 2012, after six weeks of negotiation, was the UN able to produce a Syrian government response plan. This plan "allowed nine UN agencies and seven international NGOs to provide aid for one million people affected by more than 15 months of unrest in Syria. . . . The plan also allows the UN to set up field offices in four locations of unrest and the government has promised to lift bureaucratic blockages to aid . . . but it has not allowed new international NGOs to enter Syria to scale up aid, and has limited the response to 44 specific projects. It also maintains a strong level of control in all relief operations."[15] International aid within Syria is only officially delivered through Damascus by the ICRC, ten UN agencies, and eight international NGOs that were present before the crisis, dealing with Iraqi refugee programs. All assistance has to be delivered in partnership with the Syrian Arab Red Crescent. UN agencies and their partner NGOs operate under the umbrella of the foreign ministry, which leads a steering committee responsible for the evaluation of the needs and the implementation of projects.

MSF has been asking the Syrian government for authorization to be operational inside the country since the beginning of the crisis. Until November 2015, this authorization has not been granted. However, considering that the needs of the populations inside Syria were too great to be left unattended, the medical organization decided to start providing assistance anyway, first by supporting Syrian diaspora medical networks, then by supporting hospitals and health centers within Syria, and finally by opening its own medical structures in several governorates.[16]

The legality of such actions has been discussed. According to Cédric Ryngaert, it is broadly accepted that "states cannot deny access for arbitrary or capricious reasons. In the face of such inhumanity, humanitarian actors may decide to enter the conflict or disaster zone regardless. The legality of such operations is contested under international law. Yet is it arguable, at least in a progressive reading of the law, that a customary international law norm has formed, or is forming, that allows for such clandestine humanitarian action."[17] According to Michael Bothe, "another key player remains the United Nations where the most relevant actor is the Security Council: it could and should adopt a resolution obliging all States (i.e. Syria and third States) concerned to allow, facilitate and protect relief actions."[18] International humanitarian law also states that humanitarian action carried out by impartial humanitarian organizations and the ICRC cannot be considered as interference in state internal affairs or as hostile acts.[19] No formal requirement or consent should be therefore required to carry out medical relief activities.

The MSF has been opposed to the UN's position since the beginning of the conflict. As an intergovernmental organization, the UN, in the first moments of the crisis, maintained that cross-border operations were illegal without the formal consent of the Syrian government. It was not until January 2013 that OCHA advocated publicly for such operations:

"Humanitarians must obtain access to all areas and by whatever routes are most effective. Our experience of the past 22 months has convinced us that cross-line access from within Syria, while vital, is just not enough to reach everyone, everywhere. We therefore need agreement to cross borders, irrespective of whose control they are under."[20]

In an editorial published by the French newspaper *Le Monde*, MSF argued that international aid in Syria was suffering from a severe imbalance: "Zones under governmental control are receiving the quasi-totality of international assistance, while zones under the opposition are only receiving a tiny part. Without cross-border operations towards opposition-held areas, millions of Syrians will be deprived of a much needed aid."[21] It also called on the participants to the pledging conference in Kuwait City to recognize the legitimacy of humanitarian cross-border operations to Syria and to give them the necessary funding and logistical and administrative support. One day later, Valerie Amos, head of OCHA, said that aid to Syrian civilians was equitably distributed, although it recognized that the UN could not reach certain areas controlled by the opposition.[22]

This cross-border issue triggered a heated debate between OCHA, the ICRC, and MSF, with the former two advocating for the necessity to obtain governmental consent to launch cross-border operations and the latter arguing that this was not mandatory, since the government was no longer in control of these areas. On December 16, 2013, MSF addressed this matter publicly in a letter to the member states of the High Level Group on Syria, stating the urgent need to significantly increase cross-border assistance and to include this issue in negotiations on humanitarian aid. The letter emphasized that if the government of Syria remained the sole distribution channel for international humanitarian relief efforts, then millions of Syrians would continue to be deprived of adequate assistance, particularly essential medical services: "The United Nations agencies and the international aid organizations providing this aid are subjected to strict control measures by the government. . . . Fewer than a dozen international NGOs, including MSF, are able to provide assistance through neighboring countries to the populations living in these opposition-controlled areas. The UN agencies do not provide such cross-border aid, fearful that their operations in Damascus will suffer reprisals. . . . UN agencies appear to have given up negotiating cross-border access to people living in opposition-held areas."[23]

The Security Council presidential statement of October 2, 2013, reaffirms the Council's "strong commitment to the sovereignty, independence, unity and territorial integrity of Syria"; it "calls on all parties to respect the UN guiding principles of humanitarian emergency assistance and stresses the importance of such assistance being delivered on the basis of need, devoid of any political prejudices and aims." It also "urges all parties, in particular the Syrian authorities, to take all appropriate steps to facilitate the efforts of the United Nations, its specialized agencies and all humanitarian actors engaged in humanitarian relief activities."[24] It was followed by Resolution 2139, unanimously adopted on February 22, 2014, in which the Council demanded "that all parties, in particular the Syrian authorities, promptly allow rapid, safe and unhindered humanitarian access for UN humanitarian agencies and their implementing partners, including across conflict lines and across borders."[25] These were two steps toward the improvement of aid delivery.[26] However, they will have an impact on the ground only if they are operationalized. They showed that UN agencies were using only a fraction of their leverage on the ground and should have been much more vocal when dealing with access to populations in need. Up until the end of March 2014, only one OCHA convoy was allowed to cross from Turkey into northern Syria.[27] When MSF asked if it could be allowed to ship medical supplies with this convoy, the UN declined this request, explaining that the equilibrium with the government was too fragile.

The second example is the imbroglio around the polio outbreak in Syria. The engagement of UN agencies with the Syrian government has especially been contested because of the dire effects on the health system. While health care providers and facilities have been directly targeted by all the fighting parties in the entire country, an assessment in northern Syria identified the lack of health care services as the greatest risk Syrians face aside from direct conflict-related injuries.[28] In fact, "64% of Syria's public hospitals, 38% of public healthcare centers and 92% of ambulances are damaged or out of service due to the crisis. Over 80,000 medical staff have left the country resulting in shortages of qualified health personnel."[29]

Some argued that the UN should have seen the collapse of the health system coming:

> The collapse of the health system and a lack of basic sanitation in opposition-held areas have created prime conditions for outbreaks of vaccine-preventable diseases. . . . It was no surprise to medical practitioners that a polio outbreak occurred. The question is why the international community did not prepare better for this eventuality. A disturbing part of the answer is that the United Nations itself has aggravated the situation. Like other United Nations agencies, the World Health Organization works directly with the Syrian

government. . . . A recent Reuters report on how the Assad government uses red tape and threats to prevent the provision of aid in opposition areas has raised doubts about the ability of the WHO to act with impartiality.[30]

Furthermore, organizations, including MSF, pointed out that WHO had excluded the governorate of Deir-Ez-Zor from a polio vaccination drive that began in December 2012 because the government had told them that the governorate was now almost empty. Yet this governorate was where the polio outbreak started months later. The WHO country office has also obstructed the testing of polio samples from the Deir-Ez-Zor region because they were presented by the Aid Coordination Unit (ACU), the aid coordination body of the Syrian National Coalition.[31] As Adam Coutts and Fouad Fouad conclude, "The situation is extremely challenging, but humanitarian agencies in the region should be independent and transparent. There are real challenges for United Nations staff members working in Syria, but the World Health Organization must respond to the claims that it refused to test the Deir-Ez-Zor polio samples, explain why it took three months to confirm a suspected case in July 2013 and give a better account of why the area was excluded from its vaccination drive."[32] Many aid actors failed to understand why there was no strong UN position regarding either the collapse of the Syrian health system or the deliberate neglect of opposition-controlled areas.

Even when WHO accepted and announced the polio outbreak following permission from the Syrian government, and even as it had made the issue a major priority by the end of 2013, it failed to secure the most effective form of vaccination campaigns, especially in opposition-held areas such as Raqqa and Deir Ez Zour. In a meeting that included a high-ranking WHO official and MSF Middle East senior medical personnel, WHO urged MSF to not attempt to bring polio vaccine to those areas without permission from the Syrian government, despite MSF's protest that the vaccines would arrive late and the proposed vaccination campaign was designed for catch-up rather than outbreak control. At the same time, high-ranking WHO officials kept appearing in Damascus and accepting without a clear challenge their being used by the Syrian government media as proof of its effective and timely response to the polio outbreak.

MSF's own capacity to deal with the extent of the crises in the Middle East has also been discussed both internally and externally. For some, MSF, which once gained legitimacy in dealing with massive refugee operations, has lost part of its ability to respond in refugee camps in displacement emergencies. Too focused on secondary and hospital-level care in emergencies, MSF has been questioned on its ability to put into place primary health care structures, and deal with the refugee camps. For example, with regard to water and sanitation, MSF has recently adopted a much more gap-filling approach that has only created confusion among other actors and further delayed the response.

As seen in this essay, several issues are sources of tensions within the aid system, but the main difficulty is the ongoing blurring of lines between different mandates and its harsh impact on assistance provision. MSF's limited capacity to provide assistance stems from the operational choices made while adapting to an unknown context (middle-income countries with health care systems already in place), such as the Middle East. The UN's shortcomings in providing assistance, on the other hand, stem from a political positioning concerning the legitimacy of the exercise of sovereignty of the regime in power. This positioning is inconsistent with the principle of neutrality inherent to humanitarian action and provokes an imbalance in the distribution of aid, a blatant feature of UN agencies' pattern of operation.

Because of their mixed mandate, UN agencies are sometimes wearing different hats at the same time. The management of acute emergencies is an example of this. UNHCR has a triple function as a donor, coordinator, and implementer of assistance. This creates confusion and therefore delays the provision of assistance. Each agency has a different role according to the specificity of the crisis. For example, OCHA is currently leading the response inside Syria, while UNHCR has the mandate to lead the refugee crisis in the neighboring countries. This sometimes creates tensions between UN agencies themselves. Their links to political powers, consubstantial of their identity, cannot permit them to act as neutral and impartial humanitarian actors.

The Syrian conflict demonstrates more than any other the limits of a humanitarian approach, which has relied only on governmental sovereignty. It is also a stark reminder of states' responsibilities toward populations in need. Therefore, this chapter has shown that the political mandate of the UN must be completely independent from humanitarian action. It is illusory to think that both can be done by the same actors, for the sake of the efficiency of humanitarian assistance and its ability to reach people in need. When confronted with a multifaceted crisis, the UN approach is challenged because of its political nature. The complexity of the response then only adds to the challenges of dealing with the crisis.

NOTES

I am grateful to Tammam Aloudat, Sergio Bianchi, Philippe Calain, and Maude Montani for their feedback on earlier drafts of this essay and their support throughout the editing process.

1. Several contexts, such as Somalia or Afghanistan, have been examples of this blurring of lines. This essay's title is a reference to the report *Afghanistan: A Return to Humanitarian Action,* by Michiel Hofman and Sophie Delaunay (Geneva: Médecins Sans Frontières [hereafter MSF], 2010), whose main argument is that the blurring of lines between political and humanitarian actions by the Coalition operating in Afghanistan has severely damaged the ability of independent and impartial humanitarian actors to properly deliver assistance to people in need.

2. For the budget figure, see MSF, "Médecins Sans Frontières Financial Report 2013: Key Figures," 2013, www.msf.org/sites/msf.org/files/international_financial_report_2013_summary.pdf. On operation in sixty countries, see Caroline Abu Sa'Da, *In the Eyes of Others: How People in Crisis Perceive Humanitarian Aid* (New York: MSF-USA, 2012), 1–3.

3. Marie-Pierre Allié, "Introduction: Acting at Any Price," in *Humanitarian Negotiations Revealed: The MSF Experience,* ed. Claire Magone, Michaël Neuman, and Fabrice Weissman (London: Hurst, 2011), 10.

4. Rony Brauman, "Médecins Sans Frontières and the ICRC: Matters of Principle," *International Review of the Red Cross* 94, no. 888 (December 2012), www.msf-crash.org/en/sur-le-vif/2013/07/15/7229/medecins-sans-frontieres-and-the-icrc-matters-of-principle/: "In short, their 'Dunantist' mission—inherent for one, acquired for the other—seems to bring them together to the point where there is no need to talk about the difference or differences between them, the main point being what they have in common."

5. Caroline Abu Sa'Da, "MSF in the Middle-East: A Challenging Context," *Humanitarian Exchange Magazine,* March 2012, www.odihpn.org/humanitarian-exchange-magazine/issue-53/msf-in-the-middle-east-a-challenging-context.

6. Ibid.

7. MSF Charter, accessed April 9, 2014, www.msf.org/msf-charter-and-principles; UN Charter, 1945, Chapter I, "Purposes and Principles," www.un.org/en/sections/un-charter/chapter-i/index.html.

8. Allié, "Introduction."

9. According to the UN Office for the Coordination of Humanitarian Affairs (hereafter OCHA), "The Humanitarian Reform of 2005 introduced new elements to improve capacity, predictability, accountability, leadership and partnership. The

most visible aspect of the reform is the creation of the Cluster Approach. Clusters are groups of humanitarian organizations (UN and non-UN) working in the main sectors of humanitarian action, e.g. shelter and health. They are created when clear humanitarian needs exist within a sector, when there are numerous actors within sectors and when national authorities need coordination support." OCHA, "Cluster Coordination," n.d., accessed April 28, 2014, www.unocha.org/what-we-do /coordination-tools/cluster-coordination.

10. Tiller Sandrine and Healy Sean, "Where Is Everyone? Reflections on Emergency Response," MSF, December 2013, www.bond.org.uk/where-is-everyone-reflections-on-emergency-response.

11. Bertrand Taithe, "The Poverty of Humanitarian Critique?," July 7, 2014, http:// bertrandtaithe.wordpress.com/2014/07/07/the-poverty-of-humanitarian-critique/.

12. Rami G. Khouri, "Why Salafist-Takfiris Should Worry Us," *Daily Star,* February 15, 2014.

13. Venetia Rainey, "UN Shifts Focus to Development, but Can It Work?," *Daily Star,* April 4, 2014.

14. Shaden Khallaf, "Displacement in the Middle East and North Africa: Between an Arab Winter and the Arab Spring," Working Paper Series No. 17, American University of Beirut, Issam Fares Institute, August 2013, 11.

15. "Analysis: Principles or Pragmatism? Negotiating Access in Syria," *IRIN Middle East,* June 12, 2012, http://news.trust.org//item/20120612084000-yucin /?source=search.

16. "Since June 2012, MSF has been providing healthcare in parts of Northern Syria where needs were identified and where it was possible to set up makeshift hospitals and clinics. To date (12 March 2014), the teams have provided more than 140,000 consultations, many of them for trauma wounds and life-threatening chronic diseases. Nearly 7,000 surgical procedures have been performed and more than 1,900 women have been assisted with safe deliveries. . . . We are providing medical supplies and technical support to 50 hospitals and 80 health centers across seven governorates, covering opposition-controlled, government controlled and contested areas." MSF, "MSF Response to Syrian Crisis," March 12, 2014, www.msf.org/article/msf-response-syrian-crisis.

17. Cédric Ryngaert, "Humanitarian Assistance and the Conundrum of Consent: A Legal Perspective," *Amsterdam Law Forum* 5, no. 2 (2013): 5–19.

18. Michael Bothe, "Access for Relief Operations in Syria," Legal Expert Opinion, Frankfurt, November 2013, 5.

19. International Committee of the Red Cross, Additional Protocol I, 1971, Art. 70.1, https://www.icrc.org/ihl/INTRO/470, and Additional Protocol II, 1977, Art. 18, https://www.icrc.org/applic/ihl/ihl.nsf/Treaty.xsp?documentId=AA0C5BCBAB5C 4A85C12563CD002D6D09&action=openDocument; Françoise Bouchet-Saulnier, "Cross Border Humanitarian Operations in Syria: Legality and Legal Consequences of Acting without the State Consent," Internal MSF document, October 2013.

20. OCHA, "OCHA Operations Director: Humanitarians Must Have Access to Make Sure Aid Reaches Syrians in Desperate Need," January 29, 2013, ReliefWeb,

http://reliefweb.int/report/syrian-arab-republic/ocha-operations-director-humanitarians-must-have-access-make-sure-aid.

21. Marie-Pierre Allié and Fabrice Weissman, "Syrie: Soutenons les opérations humanitaires transfrontalières," January 29, 2013, MSF, www.msf.fr/actualite /publications/tribune-marie-pierre-allie-et-fabrice-weissman-syrie-soutenons-operations-hum.

22. "Aide en Syrie: L'ONU dément privilégier les zones tenues par le régime," Agence France-Presse, January 30, 2013, http://quebec.huffingtonpost.ca/2013/01 /30/aide-en-syrie-lonu-dme_n_2580854.html.

23. Dr. Joanne Liu, president of MSF International, "Letter to the Member States of the High Level Group on Syria," December 18, 2013, www.doctorswithoutborders .org/news-stories/speechopen-letter/letter-member-states-high-level-group-syria.

24. UN Security Council, "Statement by the President of the Security Council," S/ PRST/2013/15, October 2, 2013, www.un.org/en/ga/search/view_doc.asp?symbol=S /PRST/2013/15.

25. UN Security Council, "Security Council Unanimously Adopts Resolution 2139 (2013) to Ease Aid Delivery to Syrians, Provide Relief from 'Chilling Darkness,'" SC/11292, February 22, 2014, www.un.org/News/Press/docs/2014/sc11292.doc.htm.

26. The Security Council's "Report of the Secretary-General on the Implementation of Security Council Resolution 2139," S/2014/208, March 24, 2014, http://reliefweb.int/sites/reliefweb.int/files/resources/N1427034.pdf, shows that very little progress has been made on the ground on humanitarian access.

27. OCHA, "Syria: Cross-Border Aid Convoy Arrives in Northern Syria," March 20, 2014, www.unocha.org/top-stories/all-stories/syria-cross-border-aid-convoy-arrives-northern-syria.

28. Andrew Bossone, "Planning for a Syrian Refugees Health Crisis," *Nature Middle East,* August 19, 2013, www.nature.com/nmiddleeast/2013/130819/full /nmiddleeast.2013.129.html.

29. UNHCR Syria, "Syria: A Year in Review, 2013," 26, www.unhcr .org/52eb7a7a9.html.

30. Adam Coutts and Fouad Fouad, "Syria's Raging Health Crisis," *New York Times,* January 1, 2014.

31. Annie Sparrow, "Syria's Polio Epidemic: The Suppressed Truth," *New York Review of Books,* February 20, 2014, www.nybooks.com/articles/archives/2014 /feb/20/syrias-polio-epidemic-suppressed-truth/. See also "The Truth about Polio in Syria," an exchange between Bruce Aylward of the World Health Organization and Sparrow on Sparrow's article "Syria's Polio Epidemic," *New York Review of Books,* March 6, 2014, www.nybooks.com/articles/archives/2014/mar/06/truth-about-polio-syria/, and Hernan de Valle, "Paralysis: How Political Deadlock Is Failing to Stop Polio in Syria," *Off-the-Cuff* (MSF blog), December 11, 2013, MSF www.msf-crash.org/en/sur-le-vif/2013/12/11/7254/paralysis-how-political-deadlock-is-failing-to-stop-polio-in-syria/.

32. Coutts and Fouad, "Syria's Raging Health Crisis."

PART FOUR

Development

The UN, the Economic and Social Commission for West Asia, and Development in the Arab World

Omar Dahi

ON AUGUST 9, 2013 THE UNITED NATIONS' Economic and Social Commission for West Asia (ESCWA) celebrated its fortieth anniversary. A year later it released a major study titled *Arab Integration: A 21st Century Development Imperative.*[1] As a UN organization whose mandate is regional integration, it is expected to produce such reports. Yet the report emerged precisely at a time when the region, unlike many others in the global South, was heading toward further fragmentation.

Throughout the Arab world, the political opening that had seemed possible just a few years earlier seemed to be shutting down and in some cases, such as Egypt, in even more suffocating fashion than before. About 100 km to the south of ESCWA's headquarters in Beirut, the troops of the UN Interim Force in Lebanon remained stationed along the border between Lebanon and Israel; they had been there since March 1978's Security Council Resolutions 425 and 426, but their size and scope had increased since August 2006, the last round of major Israeli aggression against Lebanon.[2] A little closer, less than 80 km to the east of its headquarters, a civil war was raging within Syria that had resulted—by ESCWA estimates—in up to a 40 percent reduction in Syria's gross domestic product by the end of 2012. Closer still to the Riad Solh Square in downtown Beirut where ESCWA was located, and throughout the city and country, hundreds of thousands of Syrian refugees were seeking shelter and sustenance.

Unsurprisingly, the celebrations of the fortieth anniversary were muted, the conditions under which they took place ominous and unprecedented. Nevertheless the anniversary provides an opportunity for a critical reappraisal of the UN's role in economic development throughout the Arab world. If one adds UNHCR and other UN implementing organizations, the UN's presence has become a multi-billion-dollar operation in the region whose role is impossible to escape. Yet a full appraisal is no easy task for several reasons. Much of the academic literature has focused on the UN's political and social role, unsurprisingly given the legacy of the Israeli-Arab conflict.[3] As a result the overwhelming majority of literature dealing with the economic side of UN intervention in the Arab world emanates from the UN's massive documentary output itself, and most of this output explains the UN's goals and what it does rather than its actual impact.

Second, interventions into development have not been marked by historic events or grand turning points. Of course various UN agencies provide crucial economic and technical support for many Arab countries with very low infrastructure and technological development, and millions of Arabs depend on the UN in some form or another (whether for material, educational, or health aid). There is, however, no economic equivalent to the 1947 plan for the partition of Palestine. Nothing dramatic such as that. Economic development is more staid. To compound matters, it is widely understood that the developmental path of the Arab states has not been influenced decisively by the UN.

In and of itself this is not a bad thing. While the UN may not have had a crucial role in improving human development, it has not had the negative role associated with International Monetary Fund and World Bank policy advice and structural adjustment either.[4] Compared to these multilateral agencies, the UN has always been the most receptive to global South grievances and the most in favor of socially inclusive development. Whether resulting from its more democratic nature, the legacy of pressure from the global South, and the fact that many of its staff are more likely to be drawn locally (for implementing organizations) and from outside the rigid confines of top-tier neoclassical economics departments of the US academy (though this has increasingly changed), the UN has been more receptive to heterodox economic policies or the particular grievances that exist in the region. The UN Development Programme (UNDP) and the UN Conference on Trade and Development (UNCTAD), for example, have continued to publish studies on industrial decline and the need for some industrial policy long after these fell out of fashion in the economic mainstream.[5] They also provide technical advice and infrastructure to the poorest countries, often along the grain of the mandates of the people in those countries and not of the Washington Consensus.

This point should not be pushed too far. All multinational institutions are by their very nature conservative even at their most radical, being as they are creations of states and subject to the pressure of big powers. Moreover, the UN does not operate outside the confines of the respectable ideological spectrum in global North (and Washington, D.C., in particular) policy circles, and as that spectrum lurched dramatically to the right in the 1980s, so did the UN itself. As *efficiency, business climate, market-led, growth-oriented*, and *inflation targeting* became some of the keywords of the neoliberal era, they in turn seeped into UN knowledge production and policy advice. The militancy of both the UNDP and UNCTAD was reined in or simply ignored by the West over the years, particularly in the late 1980s and early 1990s, the heyday of the ideological shift into neoliberalism. Even after the Great Recession of 2007/2008, the West fought to limit UNCTAD's purview at its Thirteenth Ministerial Quadrennial Conference in Doha in 2012, to keep it away from critiques of finance, mute its advocacy on larger state intervention, and prevent it from discussing "root causes" of the global financial crisis, which would implicate the West.[6]

The combination of the heterodox and critical impulse with the neoliberal turn has often made for schizophrenic knowledge production. The UN has been forced to come to terms with the particular grievances of the region. For example, the *Arab Human Development Report 2002*, which subjected the Arab countries to withering criticism, also mentioned Israeli policies and the occupation of Palestine as the key obstacles to human development in the entire region, not just in Palestine.[7] Yet the same report's rather refreshing critical analysis mixed radical critique with bland and mainstream policy advice.

This essay will discuss three time periods in the postwar era in the Arab world. The first was from the 1950s to the 1970s, which witnessed the rise of the developmental state in several parts of the Arab world and coincided with the rise of the Third World Movement in the Global South, when developing countries came together to demand political and economic reforms as well as nuclear disarmament. Next came an even longer thirty-year period, from the late 1970s to 2010, which witnessed state retrenchment and rising poverty and inequality alongside persistent authoritarianism and increased imperial intervention. The dawn of the Arab uprisings marks the third period. Despite the setbacks and turmoil since the early hopeful days of the Tunisian revolution, the uprisings that swept the Middle East and North Africa region have had a profound impact on the political economy of authoritarian regimes within the region as well as frameworks used to explain them. This ongoing phase signals the possibility of a new era of Arab participatory politics and political projects.

In each of the three eras a different UN report is referenced: the 1949 "United Nations Economic Survey Mission for the Middle East" (henceforth the Survey Mission Report), the 2002 *Arab Human Development Report*, and ESCWA's *Arab Integration* report. Each of these reports represents an aspect of those three time periods, either for what it contains or for what it omits. The aim is not to give an exhaustive account of UN development in those periods nor of the full impact of the reports themselves, but to draw attention to certain aspects that are necessary for a richer understanding of the UN's role over the years.

POSTWAR RADICALIZATION, ARAB NATIONALISM, AND NONALIGNMENT

The first major UN document on Middle Eastern economic development in the postwar period was also the most pessimistic. "Much has been written about the possibility of reorganizing land and water resources of the Middle East," runs the introductory text of the "United Nations Economic Survey Mission for the Middle East" of December 1949. "At the beginning of its task [the Mission] cherished a hope . . . that several large development projects . . . could be recommended." Unfortunately the Mission's hope was not realized. "The region is not ready, the projects are not ready, the people and Governments are not ready" for large-scale development of rivers and underdeveloped land areas.[8]

Headed by Gordon R. Clapp, chairman of the Board of the Tennessee Valley Authority, the mission was sent (with the support of President Harry Truman) mainly to monitor the economic conditions of the Palestinian refugees in the aftermath of the Nakba and to examine the regional Arab context within which the refugees now found themselves. The "Interim Report" issued by the same mission had recommended an assistance program of $54.9 million to what would become the UN Relief and Works Agency (UNRWA), a recommendation supported by all UN members, including Israel, who hoped that assistance would be coupled with permanent resettlement of the refugees. The report's authors did not include any local economists, but its spirit was developmentalist while recognizing the necessity of massive external aid. Nevertheless, its conclusions were that industrial development on a mass scale was impossible: "Basically the area is, and for a long time to come will remain, agricultural ... but to talk or plan now of the industrialization of any of the five countries in terms appropriate to the great industrial centers of the world would be to fly in the face of nature and common sense."[9]

The report is notable for many reasons. Among them it refers to the "Arab world," an early recognition of the regional interconnections. It captures the extreme inequality and almost feudal setting, and it discusses at length the agricultural nature of most societies. Yet it misses the potential for mass mobilization: the region was in fact ready for popular participation.

Shortly after the initial shock of the Nakba and in large part propelled by it, the Arab world was shaken up. The Free Officers Revolution of 1952 and the rise of Gamal Abdel Nasser and the Arab Nationalist Movement, Abdel Karim Qasim's July 14th Revolution in 1958, the United Arab Republic, and later the rise of a more radical Ba'ath Party in Syria under the leaderships of Yasin al-Hafiz, Jamal Atassi, and Salah Jadid radically transformed the region.[10]

In all those countries the "few individuals" with a great amount of wealth saw their power cut down with mass land redistribution schemes that put an end to the traditional landed oligarchy in the Levant as well as Egypt. The postwar international economic architecture ("Bretton Woods") that these movements found themselves integrated into once they came to power was designed in a way that reflected the power and interests of its chief architects, primarily the United States and secondarily the United Kingdom. The International Monetary Fund, the World Bank, and the General Agreement on Tariffs and Trade were viewed in the Arab world and the global South as the rich men's clubs.

The bipolar world of the Cold War coupled with the energies unleashed by the anticolonial movements created a space for maneuver for elites in the global South out of which emerged the Third World and Nonaligned Movements (NAM). UNCTAD was also a result of the Third World Movement and was a site for some of its most bitter struggles. Along with UNCTAD these institutions sought to carve out a more independent political and cultural space and ambitiously an alternative economic program.[11] The 1956 Suez-Hungary crisis, the largest confrontation between radical nationalism and the major powers in the first twenty years of the postwar era, solidified nonalignment and brought Egypt, Yugoslavia, and India closer together.[12]

Together these movements that came to power in the Arab world along with their counterparts elsewhere in the global South had a radicalizing influence on the international arena, and particularly in the United Nations, to which many of them turned after having been shut out of the Bretton Woods institutions. This created a dynamic that is astutely documented by Balakrishnan Rajagopal. Rajagopal argues that mainstream accounts of the success or failure of organizations such as UNCTAD dwell endlessly on whether they achieved their declared goals, a question that misses the crucial way in which southern elites have used these institutions to radicalize the international discourse and make claims and demands against the great powers. "The most important 'lesson' that should be learned from the UNCTAD example is that international institutions should no longer be thought of merely in terms of whether they successfully carry out the functions that they have been assigned but rather they should be thought of in their own terms of occupying and politicizing the space of international law."[13] The Arab world played a prominent role in this radicalization, which culminated in the unveiling in Algiers of the New International Economic Order (NIEO), a plan to democratize multinational institutions, establish international cartels to prop up commodity prices, impose restrictions on the power of multinational corporations, and achieve massive technology transfer and industrialization of the South.[14]

Mohammaed Bedjaoui, Algeria's ambassador to the UN, authored one of the key texts to explain the role of the NIEO: *Towards a New International Economic Order*. Bedjaoui played a central role in keeping together the Third World Coalition and pushing the NIEO in his capacity as chair of the G77. He delivered scathing indictments in the UN and elsewhere of the exploitative and imperialist "poverty of the international order" that places Western "civilization" and capitalist development as end goals of a linear process of development. This process, he argued, united "the Darwinians and the school of Marx and Hegel." For this latter point, Bedjaoui invoked Lebanese political economist George Corm's critique of Marxism itself as a "protest within the Western system, not a protest against it."[15]

The radicalizing attempts of the Third Worldist movements inside the UN carried their own limitations. The other side of taking the fight to multinational institutions was the "institutionalization of radicalism" and solidification of multinational institutions as inherently legitimate terrains of deliberation and policy making.

There is no doubt that economic performance in the early postwar period was impressive and that radical nationalist forces in Egypt, Syria, Algeria, and Iraq launched relatively large-scale industrialization programs. The first country in the region to launch such programs was in fact Turkey (which launched the first Five-Year Plan with the help of Soviet advisers). Starting from the early 1930s, despite some flirtation with a more liberal regime in 1950s, Turkey based its development model on the import-substituting industrialization regime, with state economic enterprises playing a pivotal role in the industrial sector.[16]

Leading the pack in the Arab world after 1952 was Egypt. Egypt was a model for the populous Arab countries in combining authoritarian rule with a redistributive welfare state served by a large bureaucracy. The state owned industrial and other enterprises employing an urban workforce, provided agricultural support to the peasantry, and supplied extensive subsidies for basic consumer goods.[17]

James Rauch and Scott Kostyshak argue that economic performance during this period was impressive.[18] They divide the Arab countries into three groups, the Arab Mediterranean (countries similar to other countries of the middle-income global South with relatively large populations and a substantial resource base for development); Arab oil-rich (very high resource-to-population ratio so that rentier conditions prevail); and Arab sub-Saharan Africa (countries with geographic and developmental experiences similar to those of other African states). When comparing these three groups of countries with other similar countries in the global South, they find that each has made substantial progress on health, education, and income levels, the three components of the Human Development Index (HDI).

Though demonstrating impressive overall growth from the 1950s to the 1970s, the import-substituting industrialization model was exhausted by the early 1980s. Many countries quickly became primary or secondary oil economies, relying either on direct sales of oil or on indirect aid and remittances from oil-rich countries. Large inflows of oil wealth had the predictable Dutch Disease effects of turning the terms of trade against industry, and the industrial base never became a major self-sustaining source of capital accumulation in any Arab country.[19]

New alliances formed between a liberalizing capitalist class and the ruling regimes; the elites found an avenue for personal enrichment in state-sponsored and -managed economic liberalization. There was a reordering of state-society relationships in which the traditional constituencies of workers and peasants were sidelined in favor of merchants and domestic and foreign capital. Nevertheless, substantial youth unemployment, increasing levels of inequality, and corrupt and authoritarian rule persisted throughout. This created a pattern of economic decline, resentment, and further authoritarian consolidation that would mark the region for a thirty-year period.

FALL OF DEVELOPMENTALISM: RETRENCHMENT AND DECAY

The Arab world was not unique in terms of its developmental failures. Of all the regions of the developing world, only East Asia maintained high levels of growth after the 1980s. Repeated and devastating wars of aggression in the region, whether by Israel or the United States, not to mention other devastating conflicts (such as the Iran-Iraq War), have hardly helped the task of human development. Throughout the 1990s and early 2000s at least five or more Arab states were under US sanctions, more so than any other region in the world. However, what tells the story of failed development is the interplay between domestic and foreign dynamics rather than simply foreign intervention or internal failure.

Many Arab states, having long placed themselves in the US orbit, found new ways of being useful in the post–Cold War era of US hegemony, particularly after the war on terror, where they continually tried to recast their local enemies as foes of the United States. The key common denominator was authoritarian rule. One can make the same observation that Thandika Mkandawire did with respect to sub-Saharan Africa, that Arab rulers hung the same banner on their societies' doors: "Silence, development in progress!"[20]

The imperative of silence, however, remained long after "development" was dropped, and as many Arab states took the neoliberal turn, managing the contradictions of liberalizations and privatization required more, not less, repression. As Samuel Bowles and Arjun Jayadev have shown in the US case, the numbers of those they call "guard labor"—workers whose primary task is policing, securing, and maintaining the capitalist system—have dramatically increased primarily as a result of increasing inequality and exclusion.[21] Similar processes were taking place in the Arab world, particularly in places with traditions of independent militant labor unions and other social movements, such as Egypt.[22]

Confronted with this claustrophobic and repressive climate, UN agencies in the Arab world were faced with the dilemma of how to navigate economic development crises against a backdrop of an Arab world marked by repressive and corrupt rule, stunted social movements, and foreign bellicosity in a manner that does not exist elsewhere.

The tensions and paradoxes of UN attempts at influencing development and the development discourse in the modern Middle East are illustrated in the UNDP's *Arab Human Development Report 2002*, which was an unrelenting indictment of social, economic, and political backwardness in the Arab world. The critical tone was set by the opening statement in the report, "The Arab region might . . . be said to be richer than it is developed."[23] Anticipating the likely backlash, the report's authors went to great lengths to emphasize that Arab scholars wrote the report: "The report was prepared by a team of Arab scholars, with the advice of a distinguished panel of policymakers in the region. As with all HD Reports the conclusions are not in any way a statement of UNDP policy. This disclaimer is particularly important on this occasion, as it is independent experts from the region rather than UNDP who have placed their societies under a sympathetic but critical examination and have exposed strengths, weaknesses, opportunities and threats about themselves in a way that perhaps only Arabs should."[24]

As Asef Bayat argued, the *Arab Human Development Report 2002*, along with the follow-up reports in 2003, 2004, and 2005 (on women's empowerment), "represents the most significant 'manifesto of change' produced by the Arabs for the Arab world."[25] Context here is crucial. The events of 9/11 had put the entire Arab and Muslim world under attack, and the report can only be seen as the best attempt at a sympathetic yet critical self-study.

The report begins with acknowledgment that the Arab world faces external challenges and that the Israeli occupation is a problem but then immediately switches to a full-scale diagnosis of the developmental and political ills of the Arab world. The discussion of external challenges and Israeli occupation passes as almost a token nod rather than being integrated into the full analysis. In fact these issues are brought up in the Overview, with an implicit message being, "Enough using Israel and the West as excuses, the problem lies in ourselves."

The core of the problem, according to the report, lies in three deficits: the freedom deficit; the women's empowerment deficit; and a deficit in human capabilities/knowledge relative to income.[26] The report goes on to marshal an impressive array of qualitative and quantitative indicators that demonstrate these deficits.

One curious approach of the report was to propose an Alternative HDI that includes, in addition to life expectancy and years of schooling, freedom score, gender empowerment measures, Internet hosts per capita, and carbon dioxide emissions but that removes income per capita.[27] Predictably, when the Arab country data are tabulated according to the Alternative HDI, their global rankings drop precipitously compared to the regular HDI ranking. The Alternative HDI was not, however, used for any other region in any other Human Development Report, so it was created for the explicit purpose of showing the poor performance of the Arab countries.

The report was widely acclaimed in the West, particularly in US media and policy circles. It was downloaded more than a million times within a year of its publication, and its website received two million hits during the same period.[28] It was named by *Time* magazine as the best publication of 2002. The report also coincided with the neoconservative onslaught in US politics. Senator Lugar cited the 2002 report nine times in his concept paper on the Greater Middle East Initiative.[29]

There were major problems with the report. The Alternative HDI was created to presumably underscore the need to highlight women's rights, the failures of democratization, pollution, and the lack of a knowledge economy. However creating a unique index out of a mishmash of indicators does not work methodologically and is not particularly illuminating. As Rauch and Kostyshak demonstrated, if one adds homicide rates and Gini coefficient to the traditional HDI, the Arab countries all rank in the top third of the global HDI ranking table.[30] The idea of creating statistical indicators used only for the Arab region to show its poor performance solidified the idea that the report was merely intent on embarrassing the region.

Second, the report's withering critiques of the Arab states' performance contrasted with mainstream and bland prescriptions. Regarding the idea of freedom deficit, the report offered the following prescriptions: civil society and nongovernmental organizations must be tolerated or encouraged; regarding technological acquisition, there must be more investment in information and communications technology. As for women's empowerment, the report proposed the promotion of education, women's associations, and labor participation. Though indubitably important, the policy prescriptions did not square with the immense magnitude of the diagnosed problem.

Third, the report does not depart from the liberal economic model that was being packaged and sold throughout the region. This was in a context when even mainstream development circles—including the World Bank—incorporated critiques of unfettered liberalization.[31] And though the report criticizes lack of freedoms, there is little mention of elite capture, corruption, and siphoning off of public wealth. However, the deepest problem with the report can be surmised from Thomas Friedman's enthusiasm for it: "We should stop talking about 'terrorism' and W.M.D. and make clear that we're in Iraq for one reason: to help Iraqis implement the Arab Human Development Reports, so the war of ideas can be fought from within. Then we should get out of the way. Just one good model—one good Arab model that works—and you will see more than just municipal elections in Saudi Arabia."[32]

After demonstrating how the Arab countries were authoritarian basket cases, the report calls on these countries to implement policies meant to overcome the three deficits without tackling the central contradiction of how such failed states could possibly reform themselves. Friedman's conclusion, that these countries must be reformed from the outside, was not a giant leap.[33]

Nevertheless, despite these limitations, the *Arab Human Development Report* was a shout of protest against the claustrophobic and suffocating environment that had enveloped the Arab world. It stirred debate, ruffled feathers, and opened a space for some debate where none had previously existed. In its limitations, it was a product of its time. Like the UN Survey Mission Report, it failed to see the potential in mass mobilization, in the people of the region themselves.[34] Eight years after the *Arab Human Development Report,* the Arab Spring opened a new possibility. The Arab masses asserted themselves as a significant, even if not yet powerful enough, force on the stage of world history.

ESCWA, THE ARAB UPRISINGS, AND THE ARAB INTEGRATION REPORT

If the *Arab Human Development Report 2002* was a desperate cry in desperate times, ESCWA's 2014 *Arab Integration* report emanated from the revolutionary possibilities unleashed by the Arab uprisings. It is perhaps one of the most ambitious and radical documents issued by a UN institution in the post–debt crisis era.

Such a report could emanate only from ESCWA. The UN Economic and Social Commission for West Asia was established on August 9, 1973, and was fully launched in 1974 in Beirut, its first and current headquarters after stints in Baghdad (1982–91) and Amman (1991–97) because of the displacements of war. The regional designation in its official title is misleading; this was really a commission intended for the Arab world, with seventeen Arab countries, several of which (Tunisia, Libya, Egypt, Morocco, Sudan) are in Africa and the rest in Asia (Bahrain, Iraq, Jordan, Kuwait, Lebanon, Syria, Palestine, Qatar, Saudi Arabia, United Arab Emirates, Yemen, Oman). ESCWA's formal mandate, like that of the other regional commissions, was to improve social and economic development and promote regional integration. The mandate was also for ESCWA to be a conduit or representative of the region and its concerns in the wider UN system, thus transmitting knowledge from the peripheries to the center. In reality, ESCWA has tried to come to terms with the specific issues animating the region while transmitting to the region international consensus knowledge.

The creation of ESCWA itself is indicative of the complexities of the UN's role in the region, especially as it relates to the Arab-Israeli conflict. Though ESCWA was founded in 1974, its establishment had been set in motion about ten years earlier with the creation of the United Nations Economic and Social Office in Beirut (UNESOB), which was established directly under the Department of Economic and Social Affairs of the Secretariat rather than as a regional commission. Though Arab countries had been pushing for a regional commission, their requests had stalled because inclusion of Israel was a nonstarter. Yet launching a regional commission while excluding Israel would violate the UN's charter of universality of participation on an equal basis of all member countries in intergovernmental bodies of the UN.[35]

As narrated by Paul Berthoud, the first director of UNESOB, establishing UNESOB under the Secretariat's own department rather than as a regional commission was credited to Philippe de Seynes, then under-secretary for economic and social affairs, as a middle ground to circumvent the problem. Israel vehemently protested this exclusion. There was a discussion to move the headquarters to Cyprus. This back and forth came to a head in the Nineteenth Session of the General Assembly in September 1964. The Assembly refused to challenge the establishment of UNESOB and thus reaffirmed the exclusion of Israel.

Berthoud accurately captures the divergence between diplomatic isolation of Israel and its actual power:

> Ever since 1964, even before the Six Day War, you had a complete dichotomy between the loss of grip by the Israelis on the diplomatic scene in New York, and their constantly increasing power on the ground. Israel was becoming weaker and weaker in the General Assembly, where it was very isolated, often

left with the support of only the United States. But that constant weakening on the diplomatic scene was accompanied by a very strong spreading of its power in the reality of the terrain. The divergence between those two trends did for a long time interest me as a notable aspect of the conflict, alas indicative of the loss of weight of the United Nations in world affairs.[36]

It is telling that ESCWA was the last of the five regional commissions to be established. The other commissions are the Economic Commission for Europe (established in 1947); the Economic and Social Commission for Asia and the Pacific (in 1947); the Economic Commission for Latin America and the Caribbean (in 1948); and, the Economic Commission for Africa (in 1958). These previous commissions were established not just in earlier time periods but in earlier ideological eras.

ESCWA was launched in 1973, and thus at the peak of the Third World Movement, coinciding with the unveiling of the NIEO. Unlike the Economic Commission for Latin America, ESCWA did not have the towering figure of Raul Prebisch and Latin America's developmentalism to work with, nor did it deal—as the Economic Commission for Asia and the Pacific did—with the relatively high-performing economies of East Asia. ESCWA itself makes little attempt to study its own impact or to track its work over time in a systematic way. It has had meaningful impacts not through grand events but through the minutiae of daily agenda setting, the microprocesses of needs assessment, the building of databases, the provision of support and technical cooperation for government ministries, and the gradual addition of progressive elements to the inter-Arab agenda.[37] Therefore the boldness and ambition of the *Arab Integration* report make it a significant milestone and a departure from ESCWA's cautious approach. Subtitled *A 21st Century Development Imperative*, the report is a throwback to the Third Worldist era in vision if not in rhetorical overkill.

The first four chapters develop the conceptual framework of the report. They diagnose past successes and failures of joint Arab cooperation at the political, economic, cultural, and social levels. Chapters 5 through 9—the heart of the report—lay out the details of the integration plan. Arab integration is defined in nonexclusionary and nonchauvinistic terms as a progressive and voluntary unification of the people in the region into an independent entity capable of achieving human development and competing effectively with other regional groups. The four dimensions focused on are economic, political, cultural, and educational development. The report sets its tone at the outset: "This group believes that a history of fragmentation, actively encouraged by outside forces, combined with some flawed policy choices by Arab countries, have left the region vulnerable to oppression, foreign intervention and stifled development. A disruptive legacy that has affected every Arab country's prospects will not be overcome through further discord. Rather, it requires a consolidated response from all: nothing less than the comprehensive integration and renewal of the region in all dimensions of its political, economic, cultural and educational life."

The report is remarkable for a number of reasons. First, its analysis contains a real sense of path dependency in a way that rarely factors into ahistorical documents usually produced by multinational institutions. This sense of history is integrated into almost every chapter but is most prominent in chapter 4, "Arab Integration: The Causes of Failure." Containing perhaps the best short summary of the legacy of Western imperialism in the region, the chapter starts with the view that both major drives for Pan-Arabism started with Egyptian rulers: Muhammad Ali Pasha's modernization drive in the first Nahda and Gamal Abdel Nasser's Arab Nationalist and Nonaligned movements. In both cases "The great powers of the era crushed these endeavors, exerting economic and political pressures against their regimes and even taking up arms against them."[38] The chapter documents how the Western countries have been undermining attempts at Arab integration since Ali Pasha's time, passing through the Treaty of Versailles and ending with the free trade agreements peddled by the United States and the European Union starting in the 1990s. These agreements were signed between the United States or the EU and individual Arab states, and then the individual signatories would be encouraged to establish relations with one another, an underhanded way to pick off the Arab countries one by one, advance Western commercial interests, and promote normalization of relations with Israel—also a signatory to a US and EU bilateral free trade agreement.

Israel's role in the region is given particular focus and a severe critique, a feature that marks the second major distinctiveness of the report. The *Arab Human Development Report* contained eleven mentions of Israel, whereas the *Arab Integration* report mentions it over 150 times. Also unlike the *Arab Human Development Report,* the *Arab Integration* report does not limit Israel's role to negatively affecting Palestinians through the occupation: its presence in the region as a bellicose power is shown as having a destructive impact on the entire Arab region and on Arab integration in particular. In that sense the report lays out an argument that was first advanced in the 1950s and 1960s by the Arab Nationalist Movement—that Israel is a threat to development in the region as a whole and not just a problem for the Palestinians. The report also digs back into history to show how the Palestinian cause was a major unifying factor for the Arab populations. In chapter 6, "Arab Popular Integration in the Political and Civic Space," the Arab fedayeen (men/women of sacrifice) are recalled as an example of how the Arab population as a whole saw in the fight against Israel a universal fight against injustice: "The *fedayeen* had an aura in the late 1960s and 1970s that attracted Arab youth.... The freedom fighters represented the universal concept of struggle for justice" (121).

The most trenchant criticism in the report is reserved for the idea that the Palestinians and Arabs in general need to recognize Israel as a Jewish state in return for a peace settlement: "Israel insists on being recognized by the world and the Arabs as an exclusively Jewish state. It imposes this recognition as a condition for reaching settlement with the Palestinians. This policy is based on the concept of the religious or ethnic purity of States, which brought to humanity the worst crimes and atrocities of the twentieth century" (132). In offering these critiques and historical examples, the report stands as a sharp rebuke to Israel and the West but also to the Arab countries who over the years have "toned down their position towards Israel and its occupation of Arab territories" (84). Indeed, the trenchant critique of Israel found in the report can no longer be found in the official discourse of any Arab state.

The third and perhaps most salient feature in the report is that unlike both the Survey Mission Report and the *Arab Human Development Report,* it recognizes the potential for mass movements to act as an agent for social change. The *Arab Integration* report would have been impossible in its current form without the Arab uprisings of 2011. "The Arab civil revolts drew their dynamism from these young people's passion, shared experiences and abilities. In many countries, young activists organized themselves into an autonomous opposition movement independent of muzzled political parties. They created new tools of organization and team-work through the Internet, resorting to horizontal outreach (in contrast to the vertical chains of command within political parties) and multiple initiatives coordinated in real-time. Although often leaderless, each national movement nevertheless had a clear plan of action and specific, unambiguous and inclusive demands" (124).

Fittingly, rather than the three "deficits" of the *Arab Human Development Report,* the *Arab Integration* report lays out three freedom goals—rights, dignity, and security—which according to the report start with liberation and end with good governance, freedom from unproductive, weak, or uncompetitive economies, the unshackling of Arab culture from self-inflicted limits and conflicts, the restoration of the vigor of Arab language and culture, and a revival of thought based on the restoration of independent reason. The report's strategic vision for accomplishing integration is both ambitious and pragmatic, starting with concrete steps that focus on solidifying the common space: unrestricted mobility for all Arabs in Arab states, common holidays, and the building of a transportation infrastructure. Developing joint institutions and youth organizations, boycotting Israeli products in the Occupied Territory, and taking diplomatic action against Israeli actions constitute the next steps. Finally, the report calls for building a League of Arab Peoples (akin to the European Community Parliament) directly electable by Arab citizens and building countries based on full citizenship while building knowledge economies and reviving the Arabic language.

The report is not perfect. It is undoubtedly colored by the excessive optimism of the onset of the Arab uprisings. Though opinion polls are marshaled to show the strength of Arab identity, the sectarianization of the uprisings coupled with revival of Arab interstate rivalries has dampened the enthusiasm of early days. The economic section (chapter 8) dwells too much on the potential payoffs of tariff liberalization (though the discussion showing only limited payoff from the unfettering of trade and advocating regional production chains is important).

Just over two and a half decades, between 1990 and 2015, two major Arab countries with an official ideology of Arab nationalism, Syria and Iraq, have been effectively destroyed by sanctions, foreign invasion, and civil war. Their people are divided, many millions of them refugees. The Arab Gulf countries for the most part have resorted to consolidating power by creating military and economic linkages among themselves. They have mobilized Arab identity not as a progressive political project but in a chauvinistic attempt to demonize what they consider their primary enemy of Iran. The most important and largest Arab country, Egypt, seems to be heading toward a full military dictatorship; the political space that opened in Egypt closed with the Sisi coup.

The radical Islamist movements in the Levant offer an exclusionary political project. Neither these radicals nor the moderate Islamist parties offer a viable economic alternative to neoliberal policy. The Arabian Gulf oil-rich countries offer an economic vision based on megaprojects and large-scale retail, construction, and tourism completely divorced from human development. In this landscape the report offers what no other state or mass movement in the region seems to be offering: a political project and a progressive cultural, social, and economic vision that have the capacity to inspire and mobilize the Arab populations. As regional blocs have become the norm in the global economy rather than the exception, Arab integration is perhaps not a utopian pipe dream for the region but a necessity for its survival.

This essay has provided an overview of postwar development in the region divided into two phases: the rise and fall of the developmental state and the dawn of the Arab uprisings. It has examined instances of UN involvement and attempts to influence the development process. This overview is necessarily limited and incomplete, especially without delving into particular case studies or projects. The focus has been on the evolution of the UN and its role, culminating with the *Arab Integration* report.

Though the UN economic bureaucracy is notoriously slow and inefficient, the *Arab Integration* report shows a two-way relationship between the UN organizations and their subjects. The UN is not immune from pressures from "above," but neither is it immune to pressures from below, as the Third World Movement and the Arab uprisings reveal.

NOTES

I would like to thank Ramla Khalidi, Rana Mitri, Bassel Kaghadou, and Maria Salem for assistance and insight at different stages of researching and writing this chapter. I am solely responsible for the content.

1. Economic and Social Commission of West Asia (hereafter ESCWA), *Arab Integration: A 21st Century Development Imperative* (Beirut: ESCWA, 2014), https://www.unescwa.org/sites/www.unescwa.org/files/publications/files/e_escwa_oes_13_3_e.pdf.

2. See the chapter by Makdisi in this volume and the chapter by Kassem in this volume.

3. Edward H. Buehrig, The UN and the Palestinian Refugees: A Study in Nonterritorial Administration (Bloomington: Indiana University Press, 1972); Walter Laqueur, The Struggle for the Middle East: The Soviet Union in the Mediterranean, 1958–1968 (Washington, DC: Center for Strategic and International Studies, Georgetown University, 1969); Nathan A. Pelcovits, The Long Armistice: UN Peacekeeping and the Arab-Israeli Conflict, 1948–1960 (Boulder, CO: Westview Press, 1993); Brian Urquhart, "The United Nations in the Middle East: A 50-Year Retrospective," *Middle East Journal* 49, no. 4 (1995): 572–81. But also see,

for a different perspective, *UNRWA and Palestinian Refugees: from Relief and Works to Human Development,* ed. Sari Hanafi, Lex Takkenberg and Leila Hilal (London: Routledge, 2014), and references in Martin Wählisch, *Research Handbook: UN in the Arab World* (Beirut: Issam Fares Institute for Public Policy and International Affairs, 2015).

4. Karen Pfeifer, "How Tunisia, Morocco, Jordan and Even Egypt Became IMF 'Success Stories' in the 1990s," *Middle East Report,* no. 210 (1999): 23–27; Jane Harrigan and Hamed El-Said, Aid and Power in the Arab World: IMF and World Bank Lending in the Middle East and North Africa (New York: Palgrave Macmillan, 2009).

5. UN Conference on Trade and Development, "Social Unrest Paves the Way: A Fresh Start for Economic Growth with Social Equity," UNCTAD Policy Brief, No. 21, February 2011, http://unctad.org/en/Docs/presspb20113_en.pdf.

6. See Robert Wade, "The West Almost Succeeds in Marginalizing the UN Conference on Trade and Development," *Triple Crisis* (blog), November 2, 2012, http://triplecrisis.com/the-west-almost-succeeds-in-marginalizing-the-un-conference-on-trade-and-development/, and Vijay Prashad, "Red Ink Holds UN Trade Challenge at Bay," *Asia Times,* April 24, 2012, for two excellent accounts on the battles and what was at stake in Doha 2012.

7. UN Development Programme (hereafter UNDP) Regional Bureau for Arab States, *Arab Human Development Report 2002: Creating Opportunities for Future Generations* (New York: UN Publications, 2002), www.arab-hdr.org/publications /other/ahdr/ahdr2002e.pdf.

8. United Nations, "Final Report of the United Nations Economic Survey Mission for the Middle East," A/AC.25/6, December 28, 1949, 3.

9. "Interim Report of the United Nations Economic Survey Mission for the Middle East," A/1106, November 16, 1949, 1, https://unispal.un.org/DPA/DPR /unispal.nsf/5ba47a5c6cef541b802563e000493b8c/3b693eff5f4e4d4b852577d6005 1ef13?OpenDocument. One main reason, the report went on to say, was that "[except Israel] the wealth of these countries from which Governments derive little revenue, is concentrated in the hands of relatively few individuals who show, at the moment, little disposition to lend their money for long-range economic projects yielding a relatively small return."

10. Hanna Batatu, *The Old Social Classes and the Revolutionary Movements of Iraq: A Study of Iraq's Old Landed and Commercial Classes and of its Communists, Ba'thists and Free Officers* (Princeton, NJ: Princeton University Press, 1978); Hanna Batatu, *Syria's Peasantry, the Descendants of Its Lesser Rural Notables, and Their Politics* (Princeton, NJ: Princeton University Press, 1999); Peter Mansfield, "Nasser and Nasserism," *International Journal* 28, no. 4 (1973): 165–78; Maxime Rodinson, Israel and the Arabs (London: Pelican Books, 2002).

11. Vijay Prashad, *The Darker Nations: A People's History of the Third World* (New York: New Press, 2007).

12. Peter Willets, *The Non-Aligned Movement: The Origins of a Third World Alliance* (New York: Nichols, 1978).

13. Balakrishnan Rajagopal, *International Law from Below: Development, Social Movements, and Third World Resistance* (Cambridge: Cambridge University Press, 2003), 88.

14. William R. Cline, ed., *Policy Alternatives for New International Economic Order: An Economic Analysis* (Santa Barbara, CA: Greenwood, 1979).

15. Quoted in Rajagopal, *International Law from Below*, 90.

16. Caglar Keyder, *State and Class in Turkey* (London: Verso, 1987); Ayse Bugra, *State and Business in Modern Turkey* (Albany, NY: SUNY Press, 1994).

17. Roger Owen and Sevket Pamuk, *A History of Middle East Economies in the 20th Century* (Cambridge, MA: Harvard University Press, 1998).

18. James E. Rauch and Scott Kostyshak, "The Three Arab Worlds," *Journal of Economic Perspectives* 23, no. 3 (2009): 165–88.

19. Tarik M. Yousef, "Development, Growth and Policy Reform in the Middle East and North Africa since 1950," *Journal of Economic Perspectives* 18, no. 3 (2004): 91–115.

20. Thandika Mkandawire, ed., *African Intellectuals: Rethinking Politics, Language Gender and Development* (London: Zed Books, 2005).

21. Samuel Bowles and Arjun Jayadev, "Guard Labor," *Journal of Development Economics* 79, no. 2 (2006): 328–48.

22. Joel Beinin, "Workers' Protest in Egypt: Neo-liberalism and Class Struggle in the 21st Century," *Social Movement Studies* 8, no. 4 (2009): 449–54; Paul Amar, *The Security Archipelago: Human-Security States, Sexuality Politics, and the End of Neoliberalism* (Durham, NC: Duke University Press, 2013).

23. UNDP, *Arab Human Development Report 2002*, 26.

24. Ibid., iii.

25. Asef Bayat, "Transforming the Arab World: The Arab Human Development Report and the Politics of Change," *Development and Change* 36, no. 6 (2005): 1225–37.

26. UNDP, *Arab Human Development Report 2002*, 27.

27. Ibid., 21.

28. Cited in Bayat, "Transforming the Arab World."

29. Richard G. Lugar, "A New Partnership for the Greater Middle East: Combating Terrorism, Building Peace," March 29, 2004, Brookings Institution, www.brookings.edu/~/media/events/2004/3/29middle-east/20040329lugar.pdf.

30. Rauch and Kostyshak, "Three Arab Worlds."

31. World Bank, *Economic Growth in the 1990s: Learning from a Decade of Reform* (Washington, DC: World Bank, 2005).

32. Thomas Friedman, "Courageous Arab Thinkers," *New York Times,* October 19, 2003.

33. For a general critique of the *Arab Human Development Report 2009*, which provides a broad context for the project, see Saseen Kawzally, "Arab Human Development Report 2009," *Menassat,* July 24, 2009, and essays in *Arab Human Development in the Twenty-First Century: The Primacy of Empowerment,* ed. Bahgat Korany (Cairo: AUC Press, 2014).

34. For accounts that suggested the importance of the "democracy deficit," see the essays in *Democracy in the Arab World: Explaining the Deficit,* ed. Ibrahim Elbadwai and Samir Makdisi (London: Routledge, 2010).

35. Paul Berthoud, "Paul Berthoud: A Professional Life Narrative," 2008, www .edinter.net/paulberthoud/narrative/.

36. Ibid., xx.

37. One useful assessment document is *The ESCWA Region: Twenty-Five Years, 1974–1999. Political, Economic and Social Developments,* ed. Riad Tabbarah, with contributions from Ahmed Youssef Ahmed, the Arab Center for Development and Futuristic Research, and Samir Makdisi (New York: United Nations, 1999).

38. ESCWA, *Arab Integration,* 77. Subsequent citations to this work are given parenthetically in the text.

NINETEEN

The United Nations, Palestine, Liberation, and Development

Raja Khalidi

THE LONG AND WINDING ROAD OF UN SUBMISSION

If the history of international aid to the Palestinian people since the 1948 Nakba is ever written, special attention should be paid to the manner with which the United Nations relinquished its unique role in development cooperation and as an enabler of liberation, at least, and was relegated to being a relief services provider, at best. The complicity of the UN system in endorsement and maintenance of the 1994 Oslo framework for Palestinian self-government amounted effectively to granting a rights-deficient, international mandate to Israel to indefinitely rule the Palestinian people in the Occupied Territory and, by extension, to continue its settler colonial project unabated. With the blessing by the Palestinian people's "sole legitimate representative" (the Palestine Liberation Organization [PLO]) of this arrangement, the UN and its agencies have by necessity collaborated since then with the panoply of its "partners for peace" in trying to manage this peculiar trusteeship awarded to Israel and the subordinate Palestinian (National) Authority (PA) on the naive assumption that it would not be permanent. In the same period, the UN was starting to witness cracks in its development mission, architecture, and resources amid the rising swell of globalization and liberalization.

The forceful entry into the Palestinian economy arena, especially after 1993, of the Bretton Woods Institutions (BWIs) and the powerful appeal of the World Bank's first (of many) publications on the subject, *Developing the Occupied Territories: An Investment in Peace,* added a new influential player to a scene that had been previously dominated by Israeli unilateralism.[1] Indeed, it appeared for a moment that the stars were aligned in favor of an international push for Palestinian development, based upon the first PLO *Programme for Development of the Palestinian National Economy*, which had just been completed in 1993, and with UN and BWI institutions working harmoniously side by side.[2] The UN agencies' mandate of "assistance to the Palestinian people" was supposed to coexist harmoniously with the BWIs' "support to the Middle East peace process" agenda that has defined the parameters of their Palestinian engagement since then. Somehow the circle was supposed to be squared by fitting this into a framework of "international legitimacy," which for the Palestinians and the UN has always meant one thing (Resolutions 181, 194, and 242) but for other partners, especially the donors, the international financial institutions (IFIs) and Israel, has been defined by Madrid, Oslo, and Paris.[3] The awkward marriage between these intrinsically opposed parties was best epitomized by the appointment of the seasoned Norwegian diplomat and Oslo negotiator Terje Rod Larsen to the newly created under-secretary-general post of UN special coordinator for the Occupied Palestinian Territory (and for the Middle East peace process. This new UN office, the UN Special Coordinator Office for the Middle East Peace Process, at once reflected the common interests of donors and IFIs, Palestinians and Israelis and was staffed accordingly. Even the heads of the two resident UN agencies, the UN Development Programme (UNDP) and the UN Relief and Works Agency for Palestine Refugees (UNRWA), longtime rivals for political leadership of the UN in the field, probably both preferred to see the top UN in-country job go to anybody but the other.

That was twenty years ago.

The landscape of international donor aid in Palestine today of course no longer resembles that of minimal UN presence and stake in local affairs that characterized the pre-Oslo period. This is not only because of the sheer scale that international engagement has acquired, especially since the second intifada and the indefinite prolongation of the five-year interim period that was supposed to be Oslo. More insidious is the manner in which donors and international institutions, including UN agencies, have become the inseparable partners, if not managers, of Palestinian development, trade, fiscal, financial, and social service policies and institutions. The corollary of this is the extent to which Palestinian dedication to the national liberation struggle has been diverted by attention to the nuts and bolts of governance at the behest and guidance of the donor community and Israel, and according to their policy preferences ("Do as we say, not as we did"). In the chorus of cheerleading by international agencies in 2011 that the PA had reached, indeed surpassed with flying colors, all the benchmarks that the agencies had established for their standards of "statehood preparedness," there were few, if any, dissenting voices. But as the UN agencies have gradually been obliged since 1994 to surrender to the BWIs and bilateral donors their pioneering role in Palestinian development cooperation, not all have bought into the neoliberal reform agendas that donors have advocated globally and in Palestine, and a handful have maybe even resisted.[4]

This is a story that cannot be easily told through available public documents, and the bureaucratic details of UN bending in the wind are probably best left in the closed files of the Secretariat. However, through a straightforward recounting of the historical record as experienced since 1985 by this author, it is possible to discern the general trajectory followed by UN agencies assisting the Palestinian people, which has straddled the thin line between compromise and resistance, faithfulness to mandates and diplomatic flexibility, and the values of international civil service versus the perks of business class travel and the power of consultancy.

THE KEY STAGES OF UN INVOLVEMENT IN PALESTINIAN DEVELOPMENT

The interplay of the geopolitical/legal dimensions of the "question of Palestine" debated in the UN for seven decades with the dimensions of its developmental and humanitarian engagement on the ground has generally led to the latter being subordinate to the former. Resolutions issued over the years by the UN General Assembly, the Security Council, the Economic and Social Council, the Human Rights Council Ministerial Conferences and Summits, and other "legislative bodies" built up the "international legitimacy" that the PLO continues to fervently embrace. Though often repetitive, these mandates have nevertheless been accumulative, since there is no "sunset clause" on UN resolutions, and collectively they have framed UN operational interventions in Palestine since 1949. However, given the generally nonbinding nature of such mandates, it falls upon the agencies and the Secretariat to do what they can, or what political circumstances permit /dictate, to implement fully and faithfully the many demands that the international community makes of Israel and, increasingly, of the Palestinians themselves (especially in areas of human rights, security, and counterterrorism). Hence, there is always wiggle room for agencies to do more or less with the mandates they are handed, depending on internal and external political pressures, operational resources, and the quality of UN leadership and technical staff on the ground, all of which can combine to make the UN an actor/convener or a simple observer/participant.

UNRWA Occupies the Scene through the 1970s: Relief before Development

With a name that encapsulates the essence of UN involvement in the question of Palestine, the UN Relief and Works Agency for Palestine Refugees was established in 1949 and continues today to be the most consistent, widespread, and concrete manifestation of the world's recognition of its share of responsibility for the creation of the Palestinian refugee problem.[5] Until 1967 at least, and for several years after the Israeli occupation of the West Bank and Gaza Strip, UNRWA was the sole UN interlocutor with the Palestinian people, through its educational and vocational training, health care, camp housing, community services, and (originally but no longer) food rations and employment generation programs. Its mandate has been unswerving and its dedication equally consistent: to provide refugees with the basic services and empower them to be able to live dignified lives until a fair and just solution may be reached to the refugee issue.

As the longest-operating UN agency in the field, UNRWA has had an impressive record, especially with regard to educating and providing essential health services to generations of Palestinians. Symbolically at least, UNRWA's presence maintains their "rights" as refugees, enshrined in the refugee ration card, which is no less sacred than the keys and title deeds that refugees still cherish in locked-away boxes of their few valuables. If any UN agency should have been nominated for the Nobel Peace Prize, it would be UNRWA, as it has been faithful to its mandate for sixty-five years and, despite dwindling resources and international support, has made a concrete difference to the lives of millions of refugees and to peace. Indeed, UNRWA continues to be a necessary humanitarian partner of those refugees who find themselves in the worst of circumstances (as most recently witnessed in the Yarmouk camp drama in Syria or in the efforts to reconstruct Gaza after the 2014 war).

UN Development Agencies: Engagement from Afar through the 1980s

The key turning point in the relation between the UN and the Palestinian people came in 1974 with admission of the PLO to the UN General Assembly as an observer national liberation movement, in its capacity as "sole legitimate representative of the Palestinian people."[6] This status not only gave the PLO access to be heard within UN legislative bodies, including the Economic and Social Council and the Security Council, but also gave them a similar status with all UN funds and programs (e.g., the UNDP, the UN Children's Emergency Fund [UNICEF], the UN Population Fund), bodies and commissions (e.g., the UN Conference on Trade and Development [UNCTAD], the UN Economic and Social Commission for Western Asia [ESCWA], the Human Rights Commission) and specialized agencies (e.g., the UN Industrial Development Organization [UNIDO], the Food and Agriculture Organization of the UN, the World Food Programme, the UN Educational, Social and Cultural Organization [UNESCO]). In the years afterwards the PLO dedicated its efforts to building up its multilateral diplomatic capacities and status. It was mainly focused on confronting Israel on political issues such as Israeli attacks on Lebanon, settlement expansion in the Occupied Territory, annexation of territory, threats to holy places in Jerusalem, and human rights violations.

In the late 1970s, the PLO made its first forays into the UN social and economic development arena, and a rash of resolutions were passed by UN conferences mandating various agencies to commence activities in Palestine under the broad rubric of "assistance to national liberation movements." UN interventions focused on the occupied West Bank and Gaza Strip, since UNRWA and the PLO catered to the social and economic needs of the Palestinians in exile.[7] By 1979, the assemblies of several agencies had tasked their secretariats with undertaking analytical or technical studies on Palestinian socioeconomic issues within their sector of purview, and soon afterwards UNCTAD, UNIDO, and the Food and Agriculture Organization had each prepared the first UN reports on Palestinian development issues.

Meanwhile, at the behest of the PLO, the Arab states members of ESCWA, based in Beirut, had decided by 1980 to prepare a comprehensive survey of socioeconomic conditions of the Palestinian people throughout the West Asia region. This undertaking, which at the time was monumental, was commissioned to the Palestinian consultancy firm TEAM International, which produced several dozen studies and reports over the following two years despite the war conditions prevailing in Lebanon through much of the period.

By the mid-1980s, the UNDP had established a distinct "Programme of Assistance to the Palestinian People" and eventually a small office in Jerusalem, followed in 1984 by an institutionalized research program established by UNCTAD with dedicated (UN regular budget) resources: the Special Economic Unit—Palestinian People.[8] Meanwhile, a full-scale Division of Palestinian Rights had commenced working in the Department of Political Affairs in the UN Secretariat to service a "Committee on the Inalienable Rights of the Palestinian People." It also was tasked with organizing a series of international and regional nongovernmental organization seminars and conferences on the question of Palestine and assistance to the Palestinian people, convened from 1983 and through the ensuing decade in UN headquarters around the world, discussing rights, peace, resistance and development.[9] In a relatively short time after entering the international scene as a recognized partner, the PLO had succeeded in mobilizing almost every and any UN agency. These included some of the most obscure or irrelevant to immediate Palestinian needs or concerns, such as the Universal Postal Union, the International Atomic Energy Agency, the International Road Transport Union, and the Conference on Law of the Sea.

Until then UNRWA had exclusively dealt with Palestinians on behalf of the international community, but now UN bureaucrats around the world were implicated through their work programs for Palestinians and were grappling with the hot potato of "assistance to the Palestinian people." They soon learned to navigate the thin line between diplomatic niceties and the harsh Palestinian realities they were charged with revealing to the world community. While this Palestinian "takeover" of UN agencies was resisted by Israel, the United States, and most Organisation for Economic Co-operation and Development countries in the voting and budget allocation processes, ultimately the "universal" and majority-rule nature of UN legislative processes meant that the question of Palestine was by the mid-1980s on everybody's agenda (and budget) and would stay there, as it has until today.

From Madrid to Oslo: The New (BWI) Sheriff in Town

By the early 1990s, almost every agency had begun to issue regular reports on its operations, and UNCTAD has issued an annual report on the state of the

Palestinian economy annually since 1985. Some dispatched technical or fact-finding missions (though Israel refused to collaborate with most or even grant them access), and most had written Palestine into their rule books and protocol procedures. Ministerial conferences were regularly deadlocked by late-night negotiations on the language and budget implications of resolutions on their Palestinian programs, and UNCTAD, the International Labour Organization, UNESCO, and the World Health Organization became favorite sites for drawn-out confrontation with Israel, while the General Assembly debated annually up to a dozen resolutions on Palestine (political and operational). Meanwhile, UNDP presence and engagement on the ground had grown as Israel tried to deflect growing pressure by allowing "technical" assistance to the Palestinian people though blocking "political" interventions (especially human rights related).

Though the Madrid Peace Conference was convened in 1991 on the basis of the concept of "land for peace" embodied in Security Council Resolution 242, it produced a series of negotiation "tracks" that excluded the UN from the bilateral Israeli-Palestinian track begun in Washington, D.C., and concluded in Oslo in 1993. Over the same period, a number of "multilateral working groups" were constituted as a way to engage all interested regional and international parties, including the UN, covering diverse areas such as regional economic development, water, refugees, and infrastructure. These not only provided the first common practical platform for "partnering for peace" by the main protagonists from the region but also opened the door to a host of other interests to insinuate themselves discreetly into the fray, especially new actors like the United States, the European Union, and of course, the IFIs.

By 1993 the World Bank had begun work on its first study of the Palestinian economy, while PLO delegates were active members of all the multilateral groups and were building up expertise and a database to serve an ever-expanding "peace process."[10] As the stature and involvement of other parties grew, so did the prominence of the UN decline. Most of its agencies (except the UNDP) had remained until 1993 on the Israeli and US blacklist because of the alleged anti-Israeli bias of its legislative mandate. Compared to the significant funding and technical support that the IFIs and bilateral donors could bring to bear, the UN's technical role became dispensable from the Palestinian point of view. Both political negotiations and regional cooperation were proceeding with the UN as no more than just another participant at an enlarging round-table.

The conclusion of the Oslo (and subsequent) Accords in a bilateral Israeli-Palestinian framework created a whole new legislative frame of reference that suited the engagement of new bilateral actors and the IFIs and that even UN agencies had to adhere to, while not abandoning their core UN mandates. Since then these "partners" have provided massive budget support, development funding, and technical assistance (over $3 billion until 2000 and over $20 billion since) under the broad rubric of "support to the peace process." This has been justified to taxpayers and above all to Israel less by the argument that the Palestinian people and their institutions required or deserved this aid in order to empower them to defend and achieve their rights—the essential rationale of UN assistance to the Palestinian people—than by the argument that donor aid is necessary in order to keep the peace process alive, credible, and worthwhile to the Palestinian people. The IFIs' exceptional involvement in this conflict situation including a nonstate actor has always been rationalized by the theme "support for the Middle East peace process."

Nevertheless, a cooperative, rather than confrontational, relation eventually emerged between the many UN agencies active in Palestine and the bilateral donors and the IFIs. The donors effectively adopted the Bank and the Fund as their technical and policy secretariat in helping them to decide their aid and sectoral interventions. Each of the institutions began to produce annual reports and in-depth studies to guide the consultations of an aid community that developed an array of sectoral and cross-sectoral coordination committees, working groups, and task forces. Meanwhile, UN agencies leveraged their technical capacities and local credibility to attract donor resources and contented themselves increasingly with a technical assistance role, leaving the politics of the question of Palestine to the UN special coordinator and the diplomats. Agencies learned to balance the dictates of international legitimacy (which considers Israeli occupation as illegal and resistance to it justified) against the new framework of Oslo. The latter entailed maintaining Israeli approval, consultation, or other endorsement of international aid to the Palestinian people, be it for relief, development, or budget support.

Geopolitical Drivers and the Lure of Globalization

An important additional dimension of the dynamics of the UN retreat from development leadership in Palestine was the rapidly transforming global and regional political and economic scene. The collapse of the Soviet bloc meant that while the PLO bought into the Madrid process with US-USSR cospon-sorship, by the time of the Oslo Accords the bilateral Israeli-Palestinian track had become dominant. Only when the second intifada threatened the peace process was some nominal multilateralism restored and a UN "Quartet" eventually created including the United States, the Russians, the EU, and the UN. Meanwhile, the PLO itself had welcomed the engagement of influential Washington and Brussels players, who came armed with money, political influence, and a textbook of technical advice.

The UN development institutions were of course undergoing their own "reform" and restructuring under the relentless Western pressure to situate the debate and action on international financial, trade, and development within the BWIs, with the establishment of the World Trade Organization in 1995 being a major victory in that direction.[11] So just when UN develop-ment agencies had to address the challenge of maintaining their relevance, functionality, and role in Palestine in the 1990s their organizations witnessed major battles (in UNCTAD and the UN General Assembly) or trade-offs (in the UNDP and UNIDO) regarding their position on globalization and liberalization. However appropriate the UN might have been from a Palestinian rights angle to lead the international development effort in Palestine, it was increasingly reminded of the need to keep in tune with developments at headquarters and to not oppose the inexorable rise of the BWIs in the Palestinian arena. Few UN reports during this period were overtly critical of continued Israeli occupation measures and impact in their sectors of operation (though a notable exception was UNCTAD's critical stance toward the Paris Protocol as early at the mid-1990s). Most instead were focused on the positive aspects of the peace process. However, at least in spirit if not in letter, UN monitoring and interventions remained faithful to the UN legitimacy script that bound them together and that differentiated them from bilateral or BWI interventions.

Collapse of Camp David and the Second Intifada: Relief and Reform the Order of the Day

UN and BWI agencies, like the PA itself, predicated their involvement in Palestine after 1994 on the expectation that the Oslo five-year interim period would conclude with an agreement on permanent status issues (borders, set-tlements, Jerusalem, refugees, and water). While international assistance during this period was mainly aimed at short-term achievements and responses to immediate humanitarian, social, and infrastructural needs, by the end of the decade a range of institution- and capacity-building projects also had commenced, on the assumption of future, indeed perhaps imminent, statehood and independence.

The fast-fix interventions of this period were generally not intended to provide strategic solutions or define permanent status issues. Both economic policy and sectoral assistance were generally less concerned with concrete results than with keeping "peacebuilding" on track until the permanent status issues could be resolved and the real business of nationhood launched. By the eve of the collapse of the 2000 Camp David Summit (including its "economic permanent status" negotiations) and the beginning of the second intifada, only a few agencies had marked the end of the "interim period" with a stock-taking and next (statebuilding) phase in mind. UNCTAD produced a study on interim-period economic "Achievements and Pending Tasks," while the UNDP funded a PA planning document for statehood infrastructure that never saw the light of day.[12]

As the implications of indefinite donor engagement became evident after 2001 with the massive humanitarian relief and PA budget support efforts managed by the BWIs on behalf of the donor community, establishing the conditions on which this rapidly increasing aid was being provided became imperative. The first "reform" push came with the highly publicized Council on Foreign Relations report of 1999 on PA governance failures, parallel to internal PA ombudsmen and parliamentary audit and scrutiny of public finances.[13] By 2001, the International Monetary Fund (IMF) had prompted PLO Chairman Arafat to establish the first PA public finance oversight body, the Higher Commission on Investment and Finance, which identified improved fiscal management as one of its key functions. The commission was short-lived, however, as political developments after 2002 entailed intensified pressure to delegate presidential financial and security authorities to the specially created post of an empowered prime minister. This included elevation of PA reform to a precondition for peace and statehood in President Bush's June 2002 statement and the further notching up of BWI influence against a UN role that was largely now confined to relief rather than development.[14]

Most UN agencies reverted after 2001 to the more critical tone toward Israeli policies and repressive measures, and even the World Bank reports had to gradually join the chorus that emphasized Israeli occupation restrictions as the root cause of violence and impoverishment. Indeed, this period witnessed the arrival of the UN Office for Coordination of Humanitarian

Affairs (OCHA) to play a new monitoring role of humanitarian conditions. OCHA has developed this vital function into an art, in a series of effective field-presence-based protection, monitoring, and advocacy activities that probably have made OCHA an even more maligned UN agency within Israeli official circles than UNRWA or UNCTAD. ESCWA led one interagency initiative that departed from the donor reform agenda of that time, actively serviced by most UN agencies. The 2004 International Forum on Assistance to the Palestinian People stressed the need to link relief to development and to exploit the Arab strategic depth of Palestine to bolster steadfastness under adverse conditions.[15] Meanwhile, a landmark study by UNCTAD issued in 2006 on Palestinian state formation, aid, and development redefined the governance and reform debate in the context of the imperative of establishing sovereign functions in the economic financial and trade policy domains.[16] In doing so, it was effectively challenging the thinking that had by then taken hold among PA policy makers and economists under the PA premiership of Salam Fayyad, as epitomized in the contemporaneous Palestinian Reform and Development Plan of 2007, followed soon after by the 2009 statebuilding program entitled "Ending the Occupation, Establishing the State."[17]

The Post-Arafat PA: Good Governance until the Fat Lady Sings

For all the historical or even transient worth of these disparate UN efforts undertaken from a different vantage point and with a markedly different content than those of the BWIs and donors, ultimately the UN has been sidelined in the Palestinian development and economic policy arena. When the UN does pronounce itself on the substance, it can be difficult to discern a major difference from the positions of the BWIs, which focus on the need to alleviate Israeli restrictions affecting development, rather than the need to end the occupation. When the World Bank and the IMF issued their 2011 reports attesting to the success of the PA "statehood preparation" phase launched in 2009 by Salam Fayyad, their more glowing reports were soon followed by a less rosy, slightly begrudging UN report that nevertheless added its blessing of statehood institutional readiness to the PA scorecard.[18] This was perhaps to be expected, since the PA itself considered such endorsement a condition for proceeding with the first attempts to obtain UN membership for Palestine later that year and since the UN's first constituency on the question of Palestine is always Palestine.

While the UN has adhered to its role as the good soldier in the international effort, it has retained the ability to depart from the peace process script (or to stick to its script of assisting the Palestinian people) when political circumstances dictate or when simple common sense prevails. One example may be found in the debate at a 2011 Bir Zeit University conference where (this former) UNCTAD expert questioned the World Bank chief economist as to what would come next after the PA had achieved all the benchmarks for statehood but political circumstances were not delivering a state. Was it really necessary to pursue reform ad infinitum as if a slightly more perfect service function here and more transparent public finances there would accelerate the day when statehood would arrive? The answer was simple: "Of course, more reform can always help and surely can't hurt? There is always more to fix."

No less indicative in the other direction is the candid statement in 2012 by the UN special coordinator Robert Serry to a Palestinian conference that while we all continue to seek the two-state solution, we are already living the "one-state reality."[19] This constitutes a recognition of realities at least that would never be forthcoming from the politically correct officials of the BWIs. The "End of Mission Report" by one of Serry's eminent predecessors, Alvaro de Soto, was a bombshell in terms of its accurate depiction of donor and UN agency complicity in intra-Palestinian conflict and their effective acquiescence in prolonged occupation.[20] Somehow, against all odds, the UN has maintained the last lines of defense of the real and enduring "international legitimacy" on Palestine in the face of the overwhelming superiority of forces represented by Israel, donors, and BWIs, not to mention Palestinian complicity at various levels.

PALESTINIAN ACQUIESCENCE IN NEOLIBERAL AGENDAS: STATEBUILDING AND REFORM AS SURVIVAL TACTICS

The full story of how and why the PLO bought into neoliberalism cannot be pursued here in enough depth and in any case needs fresh research if we are to understand the calculations that were made at the time. Certainly the discrete shift in those few years from "steadfastness for development" in the preceding era to "development for peace" (the theme of the first World Bank studies on the subject in 1993) sums up the sorts of decisions that were being made at the time.[21]

Even as PLO negotiators were quietly being drawn into a secret deal with Israel in Oslo in 1993, one of the very same officials (Ahmad Qurie—Abu Alaa', who not coincidentally was also the director general of both the Fatah productive arm, Samed, and the PLO Economic Department) was putting the finishing touches in Tunis to the monumental PLO achievement led by Yusef Sayigh and a team of Palestinian experts, begun in 1991. The *Programme for Development of the Palestinian National Economy 1994–2000* (the first so-called PDP) was fully in line with the heterodox, public goods, social justice brand of economics that was Sayigh's trademark.[22] It was intellectually consistent with the PLO's tradition of "economic nationalism" and was reflective of the actual conditions and requirements for establishing a Palestinian economy geared to ending occupation and dependency rather than accommodating to it. The PDP at once harked back and projected forward to a different era, but at a moment when the forces of global economic liberalization were being unleashed and when market fundamentalism had begun to enjoy its heyday.

There has been some recent debate among Palestinian economists, myself included, as to whether so-called "Fayyadism" in its economic dimension is only a higher stage of "Arafatism," insofar as the latter approved all the economic arrangements with Israel that the former simply took to their logical conclusions. Certainly the PA under Fayyad witnessed a greater degree of centralization and clarity of financial functions under the minister of finance/prime minister (instead of the PLO chairman), largely at the behest of donors and the IMF. But the core economic philosophy and policies of the PA dictated by their acquiescence to the Paris Protocol have been constant for the past twenty years, even if shifting gradually more to the right.

More pertinent perhaps is to consider the limited options that the nationalist leadership (and an exhausted resistance movement) had in the early 1990s. These constraints were obvious with regard to both the ability to resist the terms of an imposed "peace settlement" and the capacity to manage the lives of some three million Palestinians with only a somewhat patchy record of rough-and-ready institution building in exile. And, the opportunity that Oslo offered to expatriate Palestinian capital to link up again with the PLO, except this time inside Palestine in a shared economic and investment program, meant that the PLO could only bend with the prevailing wind, not to mention heed the cresting wave of globalization and the growing influence of the IFIs.

The PLO entered the scene after 1993 bankrupt and effectively dependent on the potentials of limited rent management and some public revenue from trade and taxation intermediated with Israel, as well as the kindness of donors after the second intifada had again brought the PLO to its knees. The 1990s did witness much rent seeking and some attempts to manage rents through public monopolies and commercial ventures in what Mushtaq Khan has analyzed as Arafat's rational strategies to counter Israel "asymmetric containment."[23] So the first IMF reform order of the day after 2001 was to establish new mechanisms for cutting off remaining sources of off-the-books income that Arafat had managed to maintain even in the confines of the Oslo framework and to privatize the remaining economic assets and rents managed by the PLO.

Looking for a Palestinian public sector in the post-Oslo period is probably a futile exercise. But to what extent was the pre-1982 goal of a "national economy" and a "public sector liberated of bureaucracy," as once stated by Yasser Arafat, simply reflective of some blurry patriotic vision of the future?[24] Or perhaps such rhetoric was more about the nature of the economic project at hand when the national liberation trajectory that the PLO had embarked upon was still predominant and the lure of power, money, and the good life had yet to entrap the PLO?

With all its limited but increasingly forgotten achievements and all its oft-cited failings in economic institution building in Lebanon and elsewhere, through the first intifada and until Oslo the PLO had remained faithful to the national liberation model of a leading public sector and social/economic policies that catered to the broad masses of the Palestinian people. Skeptics today might argue that adhering to that economic vision was superficial and more about political survival in those circumstances than ideological or intellectual sophistication, especially since it was so abruptly abandoned in the 1990s.

It would be unreasonable to expect, after so much attrition of the very concept of a Palestinian public sector, that any reversal in PA economic policy can be countenanced by the PLO and Fateh leadership today. This is not only because of how neoliberal economic thought and values have been embedded among ruling elites and even the broader middle-class constituency of the PA. Nor is it only because of the extent to which capital investment has been committed to the PA project in its current form. More importantly, a nationalist economic and social agenda presupposes a national liberation movement and struggle, something that to all intents and purposes remains suspended in an infinite "peace process." It would seem that there is no real constituency in the Palestinian political and capitalist leadership today for Arafat's fantastical independent Palestinian economy or a Palestinian public sector "liberated of bureaucracy and infused with the determination and spirit of revolution."[25]

RETAINING RELEVANCE IN A CROWDED PLAYING FIELD: WHY THE UN STILL MATTERS TO PALESTINE

It has been no mean feat for the UN and its humanitarian and development agencies to have maintained over the past two decades a distinct identity and narrative, indeed their own "audio ammunition" amid the blaring trumpets of the end of history and of the Israeli-Palestinian conflict.[26] They have designed and managed field programs that address basic needs and relief and development for the poorest communities, and their staff have largely kept the faith in UN mandates rooted in justice and rights, some dating back over sixty-five years, even as the emphasis has shifted from national liberation to human rights. The extreme degree to which donors have become implicated in managing so many aspects of Palestinians' daily lives under occupation is visible throughout the Occupied Territory. This may be seen most blatantly in the advertisements in local papers for international intergovernmental organization and nongovernmental organization jobs often already allocated, the inevitable donor cosponsorship of dozens of workshops and conferences convened monthly, or the ubiquitous signs throughout the West Bank announcing the generosity of this or that donor in providing a school, a water pump, a road, a police car, or an ambulance. Macro-level economic and fiscal policy is effectively decided in the closed rooms of consulates, international agencies, and of a handful of PA senior officials, with only lip service paid to the trendy development principles of "participation" and "ownership." So the UN's ability to retain a certain degree of street credibility because of its "pro-Palestinian" core mandate and advocacy and the absence of a political agenda, not to mention its relative cost-effectiveness as a source of technical assistance compared to BWI or donor rates, still constitutes an asset in an otherwise donor-dominated "cooperation for development" landscape.

As mentioned, the UN comparative advantage has been underpinned by a certain innate resilience of most UN institutions globally (and in this specific area) to buck certain political trends, or at least not fully buy into them, however much sometimes they have been swept along by them. But the attractiveness of the UN to Palestinian beneficiaries has also been made necessary by, or is a natural outcome of, the core UN legislative and budgeting processes and the Palestinian capacity to influence them directly. The PLO performance has waxed and waned over the years as some PA diplomats and ministers have been carried away at critical moments by the post-Oslo "peace process" euphoria (especially during the interim period and more recently during the PA statebuilding romp). In some cases, this has entailed abandoning the historical UN version of "international legitimacy" that an earlier generation of PLO and its diplomacy carved out and staunchly defended from the 1970s onward. This was owing either to a Palestinian version of the Stockholm (or perhaps, Oslo) syndrome or more likely, to simple political, historical, and legal ignorance.

In three examples outlined below from different stages at one agency familiar to me, UNCTAD, the disparities between PLO diplomacy and UN agency implementation of mandates illustrate the essential link between continued UN commitment to international legitimacy and continued PLO adherence to the same framework and some lessons (still to be?) learnt.

Never, Never Forget the Occupation

While most UNCTAD delegates and Secretariat officials at the Trade and Development Board in Geneva in September 1993 were mutually congratulating each other for the recently announced Declaration of Principles and the new era of peace it supposedly was to usher in, one dissenting voice of doom was heard in the conference room. PLO ambassador Nabil Ramlawi was the only one that day with the courage and foresight to affirm that this was an interim self-government agreement that in no way ended occupation, settlement, or Israeli restrictions on the Palestinian economy and that the only solution was a complete implementation of the relevant UN resolutions, as anything else would be palliative and deceptive.

This position was important in keeping the Secretariat on its toes in the following years so that it did not succumb to the "partners for peace" paradigm. Many at the time assumed that the program would be soon abandoned and that Palestine could integrate into the regular UNCTAD work as a full member by the end of the interim period. The same ambassador still had to remind the board in 1997 of "the continuing historic responsibility of the

United Nations, including UNCTAD, in respect of the Palestinian issue until the peace process succeeded and Palestine could take its place as a full member of the Board and other international agencies."[27] Admittedly, this was not to be. However, not all PLO declarations in diplomatic arenas have remembered that maxim: the 2009 Palestinian memorandum submitted to the World Trade Organization for consideration of observer status membership omitted references to the "occupied Palestinian territory" or to Israeli colonial practices affecting foreign trade and instead opted for a bright portrayal of the promising Palestinian liberal and modernizing economy.

Don't Empower Rookies

By 1996, when the Ninth UNCTAD Conference was convened in Midrand, South Africa, the PLO delegation that attended was headed by newly appointed PA trade officials who had never before attended a UN conference. Without checking on the status of UNCTAD's program on Palestine, they left after delivering their formal plenary statement, not realizing that negotiations on the text of the outcome document would continue until the last hours of the conference. Since there were no PLO diplomats around to insist on the now-standard paragraph on the Palestinian economy and assistance to the Palestinian people, the ministerial consensus document excluded any reference to Palestine or Israeli occupation.[28]

Soon, some in the Secretariat with Israeli and US support had interpreted this as a justification to end the mandate on Palestine, and efforts began to "lower the profile" of work on the issue and to dissemble the resources and work program that had been in place for twelve years. Only with sustained PLO and Egyptian diplomatic maneuvers over the following two years between UNCTAD meetings in Geneva and General Assembly meetings in New York were the program and resources restored and legislative catastrophe averted. This required at one point a joint PLO-Egypt "filibuster" that held up the biennial regular budget approval by the (almost sovereign) UN Fifth Committee at the eleventh hour until Arab demands were met. By the next UNCTAD conference in Bangkok in 2000, the Palestinian Unit had been restored and Israel and the United States for the first time joined a simple consensus "welcoming UNCTAD's programme of assistance to the Palestinian people" that remained solid and indeed expanded over the following conferences.

Perhaps the most awkward situation that dedicated UN secretariat officials could experience in this respect is to find that they are out of sync with the Palestinian mood of the moment. One such close encounter came in 2010, when Israeli diplomats expressed to the Secretariat their dissatisfaction with the generally downbeat tone of UNCTAD reports on the "war-torn" Palestinian economy, reports that hadn't bought into the statebuilding narrative. Israel proposed that the Secretariat might wish, when preparing their reports, to consult different sources that told the "true picture" on the ground.

This sort of monitoring by Israeli diplomats of UN reports is standard procedure and provides regular material for Israel to denounce UN "one-sidedness" and "politicization" of technical assistance. However, in this case the file of documents formally presented by Israel to the Secretariat for its consideration was composed solely of Palestinian private sector and PA documents, reports, and brochures featuring upbeat growth projections, hopeful children, yuppie entrepreneurs, and ambitious middle-class housing programs brochures with dramatic graphics of roses growing through barbed wire. As in the mid-1990s, some Palestinian peace partners had gotten caught up in the statebuilding euphoria and perhaps didn't realize how their own glossy publicity and advocacy material were being used by Israeli diplomacy to showcase how extreme and out of tune the UN was in its refusal to endorse economic peace. This is perhaps a classic, if ironic, example of when the Secretariat needed to blindly adhere to the UN version of international legitimacy in order to keep their Palestinian constituents to the same script. This awkward situation is experienced regularly in the field by other agencies, which can find themselves ahead of the curve that the PA is struggling to keep up with (the UNDP, OCHA, and UNRWA come to mind).

With the gradual collapse of the bilateral peace process in early 2014, and the sustained Palestinian struggle for national liberation, with all its failings and disappointments, the endurance of UN agencies in advocating for Palestinian rights, justice development, and peace means that all is not lost. The past twenty years might be seen by some historians as a diversion for Palestine and for the UN from the path that sought liberation as a precursor, not an outcome, of development. However, the balance of forces within Palestinian society and politics, between the Palestinian people and an increasingly belligerent but bankrupt Israeli military machine, as well as in Israel's international standing, is not fixed and appears to have been shifting since 2014.

To the extent that the bilateral peace process between Israel and Palestine dominated by one (dishonest) broker appears to be at a dead end, so must multilateralism within a multipolar setting be reasserted. The options for a better future for the Palestinian people as compared to the past twenty years very much depend on regaining the path, deserted in Oslo, of public authorities taking the lead in providing public goods, including liberation, and in returning to the fold of UN legitimacy and multilateral leadership in all aspects of the question of Palestine. Above all, if Palestinian efforts at achieving statehood are to one day succeed, the Palestinian people must become full partners, indeed leaders, in their own liberation, not acquiescent spectators to their colonial subjugation and the dismemberment of their country.

NOTES

1. World Bank, *Developing the Occupied Territories: An Investment in Peace* (Washington, DC: World Bank, 1993).

2. The document's production was led and coordinated by the late Professor Yusif Sayigh, *Programme for Development of the Palestinian National Economy for the Years 1994–2000* (Tunis: Palestine Liberation Organization, 1993).

3. UN General Assembly Resolution 181, "Future Government of Palestine," A/Res/181(II), November 29, 1947, https://unispal.un.org/DPA/DPR/unispal.nsf/5b a47a5c6cef541b802563e000493b8c/7f0af2bd897689b785256c330061d253?OpenDo cument; UN General Assembly Resolution 194, "Palestine—Progress Report of the United Nations Mediator," A/Res/194(III), December 11, 1948, https://unispal .un.org/DPA/DPR/unispal.nsf/o/C758572B78D1CD0085256BCF0077E51A; UN Security Council Resolution 242, "The Situation in the Middle East," S/Res/242, November 22, 1967, https://unispal.un.org/DPA/DPR/unispal.nsf/o/7D35E1F729 DF491C85256EE700686136.

4. For more on these developments and trends, see Raja Khalidi and Sobhi Samour, "Neoliberalism as Liberation: The Statehood Program and the Remaking of the Palestine National Movement," *Journal of Palestine Studies* 9, no. 2 (Winter 2011): 6–25; Raja Khalidi, "Reshaping Palestinian Economic Policy Discourse: Putting the Development Horse before the Governance Cart," *Journal of Palestine Studies* 34, no. 3 (Spring 2005): 77–87; Sara Roy, "De-development Revisited: Palestinian Economy and Society since Oslo," *Journal of Palestine Studies* 28, no. 3 (April 1999): 64–82.

5. James G. Lindsay, "Reforming UNRWA," *Middle East Quarterly* 19, no. 4 (Fall 2012): 85–91.

6. Seventh Arab League Summit Conference, "Resolution on Palestine," October 28, 1974, https://unispal.un.org/DPA/DPR/unispal.nsf/0/63D9A930E2B 428DF852572C0006D06B8.

7. UN Conference on Trade and Development (hereafter UNCTAD), Conf. Res. 146(VI), 199th plenary meeting, October 18, 2014, http://unctad.org/en/pages /gds/Assistance%20to%20the%20Palestinian%20People/CONF--RES--146-(VI). aspx.

8. UNDP, "UNDP's Programme of Assistance to the Palestinian People," accessed October 20, 2014, www.ps.undp.org; UNCTAD, Conf. Res. 146(VI), October 18, 2014. The program was renamed after Oslo as "Assistance to the Palestinian People Unit."

9. UN Committee on the Exercise of the Inalienable Rights of the Palestinian People, "United Nations: Committee on the Exercise of the Inalienable Rights of the Palestinian People," January 1, 2004, https://documents-dds-ny.un.org/doc /UNDOC/GEN/N04/542/31/PDF/N0454231.pdf?OpenElement.

10. Raja Khalidi, "The Economics of Palestinian Liberation," *Jacobin,* October 15, 2014, https://www.jacobinmag.com/2014/10/the-economics-of-palestinian-liberation/.

11. Vijay Prashad, *The Poorer Nations: A Possible History of the Global South* (London: Verso, 2013).

12. UNCTAD, *The Palestinian Economy: Achievements of the Interim Period and Tasks for the Future* (Geneva: UNCTAD, 2001).

13. Yezid Sayigh and Khalil Shikaki, "Strengthening Palestinian Public Institutions," Independent Task Force Report for the Council on Foreign Relations, 1999, www.pcpsr.org/sites/default/files/strengtheningpalinstfull.pdf.

14. Larry Garber, "Palestinian Reform and International Assistance," *Sada,* February 26, 2005, http://carnegieendowment.org/sada/?fa=21604.

15. See Economic and Social Commission for Western Asia, Resolution 252(XXII), "Rehabilitation and Economic and Social Reconstruction in Palestine," April 12, 2003, https://www.unescwa.org/sites/www.unescwa.org/files/ministerial_sessions /resolutions/252_xxii.pdf; Arab-International Forum on Rehabilitation and Development in the Occupied Palestine Territory, "Rehabilitation and Development in the Occupied Palestinian Territory: Towards an Independent State," October 14, 2004, https://unispal.un.org/DPA/DPR/unispal.nsf/0/6A610D7BB7D4491885256 F71006D2F6A.

16. UNCTAD, *The Palestinian War-Torn Economy: Aid, Development and State Formation* (New York: UNCTAD, 2006).

17. Palestinian National Authority, "Palestinian Reform and Development Plan, 2008–2010," December 2007, http://siteresources.worldbank.org /INTWESTBANKGAZA/Resources/PRDP08–10.pdf; Palestinian National Authority, "Palestine: Ending the Occupation, Establishing the State," August 2009, https://unispal.un.org/pdfs/PA_EndingOccupation-Statehood.pdf.

18. Office of the United Nations Special Coordinator for the Middle East Peace Process, "Palestinian State-Building: A Decisive Period," April 13, 2011, http://www

.unsco.org/Documents/Special/UNs%20Report%20to%20the%20AHLC%2013_April_2011.pdf.

19. Office of the UN Special Coordinator for the Middle East Peace Process, "Statement From Robert Serry, the United Nations Special Coordinator for the Middle East Peace Process, Following the Announcement of Further Settlement Construction in the West Bank," June 7, 2012, www.unsco.org/Documents/Statements/SC/2008/following%20the%20announcement%20of%20further%20settlement%20construction%20in%20the%20West%20Bank.pdf.

20. Edith Ballantyne, "An Equitable Solution to the Israel/Palestine Conflict: The Responsibility of the United Nations," *International Peace Update,* December 1, 2007.

21. Alaa Tarir and Jeremy Wildeman, "Persistent Failure: World Bank Policies for the Occupied Palestinian Territories," *Al-Shabaka*, October 9, 2012.

22. Yusif Sayigh, *Programme for Development of the Palestinian National Economy for the Years 1994–2000: Executive Summary* (Tunis: Palestine Liberation Organization, 1993).

23. Mushtaq Khan, with C. Giacaman and I. Amundsen, eds., *State Formation in Palestine* (London: Routledge Curzon, 2004).

24. Quoted in Ahmad Qurie, *"Abu Alaa": Samed, the Productive Experience of the Palestinian Revolution"* [in Arabic] (Amman: Arab Institute for Research and Publishing, 2007).

25. Ibid.

26. A phrase from the song "This Is Radio Clash" by the band The Clash (Mick Jones, Topper Headon, Paul Simonon, and Joe Strummer).

27. UNCTAD, "Report of the Trade and Development Board, Forty-Fourth Session (13–23 October 1997)," A/52/15, November 4, 1997, https://unispal.un.org/DPA/DPR/unispal.nsf/0/2D76A3ADDBFD9EA585257132007 65E26.

28. UNCTAD, "9th Session of the United Nations Conference on Trade and Development (UNCTAD IX), 27 April–11 May 1996, http://unctad.org/en/pages/MeetingsArchive.aspx?meetingid=4290.

TWENTY

Peacebuilding in Palestine

WESTERN STRATEGIES IN THE CONTEXT OF COLONIZATION

Mandy Turner

THE TERM *PEACEBUILDING* WAS FIRST used in 1975 by the peace scholar Johan Galtung in his development of three approaches to instituting peace, which he defined as peacekeeping, peacemaking, and peacebuilding.[1] Peacebuilding, for Galtung, constituted the actions taken to address the root causes of conflict and to support local capacities for conflict resolution toward building a sustainable peace *after* war. While this definition continues to underpin the rhetoric of peacebuilding, the way in which it has been adapted and developed by the United Nations and (largely) Western governments has given it a particular meaning and application that peace scholars such as Galtung and others could not have envisaged or indeed supported. This is one of the reasons why the term *peacebuilding* and its application can be interpreted in both negative and positive ways—because its origins are largely progressive and the language benign, but the way in which it has been developed by Western donors vis-à-vis the content and implementation is more problematic and malignant. It has been variously criticized for proffering a template neoliberal framework for development and governance that is not appropriate for war-torn societies,[2] ignoring local conditions and desires and externally imposing these frameworks,[3] and sidestepping and ignoring global economic inequalities and inequities in the structures of global governance in the application of these templates.[4]

This chapter critically analyzes the way in which peacebuilding as a policy discourse and practice has been developed and applied in the Occupied Palestinian Territory (OPT). It is split into four sections. The first section briefly charts the emergence of peacebuilding as a Western policy discourse, its development into a hegemonic project in the post–Cold War world, and the key assumptions and policies that underpin it. The second section goes on to analyze the situation in which Western peacebuilding practices and policies were applied in the OPT—inserted as they were into the framework created by the Oslo Accords and subsequent peace agreements between Israel and the Palestine Liberation Organization (PLO). The third section critically explores how these policies and practices were shaped by global structures of power as they manifest themselves in the region. The particular application of these peacebuilding policies and their impacts are then the focus of the fourth section. The chapter concludes by arguing that peacebuilding strategies in the OPT have contributed toward creating a "zombie peace." And like its namesake in the movies, this means it is neither dead nor living but is a shambling corpse that staggers on, refusing to die.

PEACEBUILDING AND STATEBUILDING: DEFINITIONS AND DEVELOPMENT

Peace building entered international policy discourse in 1992 through UN secretary-general Boutros Boutros-Ghali's report *Agenda for Peace,* which outlined the way in which the UN should respond to conflict in the post–Cold War world. This call for a more robust engagement signaled the dawn of a new world order in which the UN was able to promote, and indeed was at the forefront of promoting, a particularly Western understanding of how to build peace. Boutros-Ghali defined postconflict peacebuilding as "action to identify and support structures which will tend to strengthen and solidify peace in order to avoid a relapse into conflict."[5] So far, so benign. But as one would expect of the UN, an organization of states, the state was to be a "foundation stone" of all work, and subsequent UN reports in this area emphasized this practically through promoting certain features of peacebuilding, particularly civilian security and rule of law (the Brahimi Report, 2000) and statebuilding ("A More Secure World," 2004).[6] Between 1989 and 2007, twenty major multilateral peacebuilding missions were deployed to war-torn societies, all of which involved statebuilding and governance components.[7] The statebuilding/peacebuilding nexus thus lies at the core of UN and Western donor policy and practice,[8] and it became more pronounced after the attacks on New York City on September 11, 2001, which led to Western foreign policy strategies that focused on the issue of failing, weak, and fragile states and regarded their resulting problems, including criminality, conflict, terrorism, and migration, as being the product of such a "governance gap," and as constituting the main threat to world stability.[9] The popular donor tautology that emerged during this time which argued that "development requires security and security requires development," thus led to more and more programs directed at "rule of law," "security sector reform," "good governance," and "capacity building"—which merely justified greater donor involvement and intervention.[10] While there is indeed a long (and checkered) history of interference by powerful states in the affairs of less powerful ones, "Intervention in the present age as a means of reordering third states is in fact historically unprecedented."[11]

Decades of ideological and practical restrictions on the UN promoting a particular model of development and governance because of the lack of a consensus during the Cold War came to an end after the collapse of the Soviet Union and the perceived triumph of capitalism and liberalism.[12] The UN was thereafter able to take its place as a key player in the development of the "peacebuilding industry," which encompassed Western donors, international organizations, international financial institutions, and large international nongovernmental organizations. A vast number of matrixes and "toolboxes" were created and promoted during the 1990s and 2000s, as well as a plethora of networks and institutions, including the UN Peacebuilding Commission in 2006. The peacebuilding matrices developed by these actors and outlined in their policy documents tend to read like a wish list for the "good society," encompassing all societal aspects and processes that would plant the seeds of a particular model of Western capitalist economics and governance, and underpinned by the belief that this would create a pacific society. In essence, therefore, Western peacebuilding is a modern version of the *mission civilisatrice* in its attempt to implant Western sociopolitical and economic forms[13] (or, rather, an idealized and particularly neoliberal version). Some writers, including this one, have referred to Western programs in war-torn societies as "liberal peacebuilding" because clear neoliberal economic and governance principles underpin the discourse (both in policy documents and in practice).[14] Until the 1980s, development was defined as a state-centered process requiring a high degree of government intervention dominated by protectionist and corporatist policies.[15] After the "neoliberal turn," the type of policies that states could follow became increasingly circumscribed as the transformation of the global political economy proceeded apace—and this has been enshrined in the architecture of global governance.[16] The policies developed for war-torn societies are no different in this regard. Indeed, the "overall framing of peace by external agencies reinforces neoliberal prescriptions, particularly in the realm of political economy, that neither take account of local needs and agency, nor reflect on the role of global capitalism and structural adjustment policies as drivers of conflict."[17]

While there are, of course, differences between Western agencies involved in the peacebuilding industry, there are hierarchies of power. Compared to the United Nations Development Programme, for example, the international financial institutions have considerable power to set the agenda for policy intervention in war-torn societies.[18] The World Bank, which is widely regarded as an "ally in peacebuilding," has a seat on the UN Peacebuilding Commission, uses trust funds to exercise leverage where it has no direct role, drives donor conferences, and, backed by International Monetary Fund (IMF) conditionalities, places state institution building at the top of the agenda so that neoliberal political economies can be institutionalized.[19] While UN agencies and Western donors have slight differences in priorities and emphases, the discourse of the Washington Consensus is all-pervasive—and dominant—in peacebuilding through the liberal paradigm.[20] For instance, it is important to remember that although the UN Development Programme promotes policies of social inclusion and well-being it tends to find itself implementing World Bank programs that are driven by the promotion of neoliberal economic and governance policies.[21] So recent pieces that criticize the concept of liberal peacebuilding and suggest it is a narrative fiction are misguided,[22] because there are indeed common assumptions and policy agendas applied across the board in war-torn societies as outlined above, and you do not need to dig far to see these, replete as they are in donor reports and policy documents. The most resilient parts of this peacebuilding matrix have been those related to the pursuit of an aggressive economic liberalization agenda and governance strategies focused on enhancing instruments of state coercion and "capacity building," even while democracy and human rights components have been substantially downgraded.[23] And this is very obviously the case in the OPT, as this chapter will argue.

Peacebuilding, however, does not operate in a vacuum. It takes place in concrete socioeconomic and political settings, interacts and affects these political economies in crucial ways, and is in turn is shaped by these circumstances. Some commentators have referred to this process as creating "hybrid forms of peace";[24] others say it merely proves that peacebuilding helps to create no "pure" or replicated form but rather a multitude of different types of "liberal peaces."[25] Whatever conceptual framework is used, it should be a commonsense conclusion that the context and the different actors involved interact to create unique "types" of peace. The OPT is no different in that regard. The context for peacebuilding was provided by the Oslo Accords and the peace process, which created the framework through which the peacebuilding industry operated, and this is explored in the next section.

THE CONTEXT FOR PEACEBUILDING: THE OSLO FRAMEWORK AND ISRAEL'S OCCUPATION

The Oslo framework was the practical outcome of the peace agreements signed between Israel and the PLO, beginning with the Oslo Accord signed in 1993. These agreements committed the parties to track-one bilateral negotiations toward a resolution of the conflict (overseen by the United States), the creation of a form of partial self-government for the Palestinian people (the Palestinian Authority) with management functions over small pockets of territory that were not contiguous, an economic customs union, and a phased withdrawal of Israel's occupation forces. Though the interim period of five years has long since ended, this framework remains in place and has been crucial in creating a violent and yet manageable form of stability and victor's "peace." The stated objective of Western peacebuilding in the OPT has been to support and underpin this framework, which is one of the reasons why the UN and donors have been unwilling and unable to change their policies, despite clear evidence that Israel has continued its aims of expanding its state and securing dominance over the land and resources of historic Palestine. Indeed, the British-Israeli historian Avi Shlaim has referred to the peace process in this context as negotiating the division of a pizza while one side is continuing to eat it.[26]

Israel's colonization practices, which create a structural imperative of control and displacement, are the root cause of the continuous spiral of resistance and counterinsurgency. Israel's counterinsurgency strategies encompass direct military intervention, extensive repression through mass incarcerations, detention without trial, torture, and house demolitions as well as targeted assassinations and collective punishment. More sophisticated pacification techniques include methods of population control such as stratified citizenship and restrictions on movement, marriage, and residency; a closure regime of checkpoints, barriers, and the Separation Wall; and the use of local proxies and collaborators.[27] These techniques have neither changed nor been reduced during the two decades of "peacemaking" and "peacebuilding."

Israel retains control over 70 percent of the West Bank as well as over all the borders, including entry and exit points, and thus control over land and other natural resources. This control has meant that Israel has continued to confiscate Palestinian land to settle its own population, which by 2015 had grown to over 350,000.[28] The 2005 unilateral Israeli disengagement from Gaza, which signaled the withdrawal of settlements and checkpoints internal to the Gaza Strip, has been the only significant redeployment since the interim period (1994–99) ended, although Gaza itself remains under siege and blockade with extensive maritime restrictions and a "buffer zone" policed by boats, tanks, and watchtowers. And the West Bank remains under military control, with a multitude of internal borders created and policed by the Israeli military at checkpoints and roadblocks. However, some of the policing and internal repression was devolved to the PA, as its primary task, as codified in the Oslo agreements, was to stop attacks on Israel and ensure its security.[29] Indeed the language of security is dominant in the Oslo Accord. This has been understood by third-party actors as encapsulating the reasonable demand that violence should cease during negotiations, but what it has meant in reality is that the PA has been continually forced to prove that it can police its own people, repress internal dissent, and deliver security to Israel. If and when it does not, then Israeli military forces again take over—as indicated by Operation Defensive Shield during the second intifada and Operation Brother's Keeper during the kidnapping crisis of June 2014. Raids to arrest Palestinians in Area A (supposedly under PA control) occur on a daily basis.

An economic part was added to these geographic, governance, and security aspects of the Oslo framework. The 1994 Paris Economic Protocol, which was the economic annex to the Oslo Accord, is a framework that was instituted to govern economic relations between the PA and Israel. It did not deal with the asymmetry of power between the two parties as indicated by Israel's repeated (and unpunished) violations of the Protocol's principles, including restrictions on the free movement of Palestinian labor to work in Israel, discrimination against Palestinian products both in the Israeli market and through customs authority clearance, and tariff and dual-use lists that increase production costs and make Palestinian business uncompetitive.[30] The Protocol instituted a tax transfer scheme where Israel collects and passes to the PA the taxes and custom duties on Palestinian imports from or via Israel, and income tax from Palestinian workers in Israel. This is a hugely important control mechanism, particularly given that, in 2014, these transfers accounted for 36 to 44 percent of the PA's budget and is the single biggest source of revenue.[31] These transfers can be withheld at any time, and frequently have been, when the PA has done something of which Israel disapproves. Furthermore, the tariff structure on this "joint" trade regime is appropriate for an advanced globalized economy, such as Israel, not for an economy emerging out of military occupation.[32] By the time of the signing of the Oslo Accords, twenty-six years of occupation had taken its toll on the political economy of the West Bank and Gaza Strip. Palestinians suffered from land expropriations, restrictions on the use of natural resources, low levels of public investment, an undeveloped economic infrastructure and industrial base, poor and fragmented social services, feeble local government, a weak financial sector, and a loose legal and regulatory system.[33] Some of these problems have continued as the promised end of occupation was not fulfilled, while some have eased slightly because of the peacebuilding policies after Oslo.

And it is in this context that Western donors and peacebuilding agencies have operated. Western peacebuilding in the OPT has been framed by three dominant factors: the liberal peace assumptions and policies of the peace-building industry (as identified in the first section); the context, that is, the Oslo framework and Israel's continued occupation and colonization (as identified in this section); and the relations of power between the main actors, which will be explained in the following section.

THE "PEACEBUILDING INDUSTRY" IN THE OCCUPIED PALESTINIAN TERRITORY

Since the signing of the first Oslo Accord in 1993, around forty donor countries and dozens of UN and other multilateral agencies have provided aid for peacebuilding activities, including for governance, development, and humanitarian purposes. This section briefly maps the main Western actors and their policies. It does not analyze the agendas and impacts of non-Western aid and donors, important though they are (particularly those from the Arab world), because although they operate within a similar structural reality their ideational framework is different and they largely do not set the agenda for peace building.[34]

The UN, the World Bank, the European Union, and the United States are the dominant Western agencies involved in peacebuilding activities in the

OPT. Ultimately, the relationships and role of these main actors reflect global structures of power as they manifest themselves in the region, which is why Anne Le More characterizes their roles and influence as "The US decides, the World Bank leads, the EU pays, the UN feeds."[35] The UN has around twenty-one agencies operating in the OPT, overseen by the Office of the UN Special Coordinator for the Middle East Peace Process, which was established in the aftermath of the first Oslo Accord to enhance the involvement of the UN during the interim period.[36] Of course, the UN has been continually involved, with some agencies of longer pedigree operating in the area. For instance, the UN Relief and Works Agency for Palestine Refugees in the Near East was created in 1949 to provide assistance to the refugees created by the Nakba. And the UN Development Programme's Programme of Assistance to the Palestinian People was established in 1978 to improve the economic and social conditions of Palestinians resident in the OPT. Despite its leading role and extensive experience as an aid provider and coordinator of extensive peacebuilding and humanitarian activities, the UN has been shut out of the peace negotiations, even though it has a long history of leading these in other contexts.

The World Bank's involvement is much more recent: its 1993 study *Investment in Peace* formed the basis for the first donor pledging conference and the first strategic aid framework for the OPT in 1994. And yet, despite being a newcomer, it has become a hugely influential player: first, because it is touted as politically "neutral"; second, because it is the administrator of the multidonor trust funds; third, because it is the leading multilateral actor in donor coordination, holding positions on nearly all the key committees; and fourth, because its reports and policy recommendations shape the aid agenda and the allocation of funds.[37] As well as shaping the framework for donor involvement, the World Bank has played an important role in setting the economic and policy agenda for the PA: it helped design the first Palestinian Development Plan (1998–2000) and subsequent plans, and in 2002 former World Bank economist (and IMF representative to the PA) Salam Fayyad become a finance minister, and then in 2007 became prime minister in a technocratic government that more eagerly embraced the neoliberal economic and governance agenda that underpins Western development and peacebuilding strategies.[38]

The EU, through the European Commission and individual member states, has been the largest donor—in the initial Oslo period constituting nearly half of all donor funding.[39] However, this largesse in the form of financial support has not translated into influence at the diplomatic level. Competition and tension between the United States and the EU has been constant since Oslo, with the EU regarding the United States as being too pro-Israeli, and the United States regarding the EU as more likely to take positions that would antagonize Israel. The United States has also regarded the EU's complicated decision-making process as an obstacle to united and decisive action—which it has been, on occasion. But the lack of a united perspective from EU member states has also been rooted in different opinions and interests between them—those between Germany, France, and the United Kingdom are particularly notable. A large amount of EU aid was initially channeled into construction, infrastructure, and natural resource management. But after the second intifada this shifted toward high levels of budgetary support to the PA (as did all aid).[40] The EU has generally tried to use its role as primary donor to exert influence on the diplomatic process, but with relatively little success. Indeed, EU guidelines announced in July 2013 that restricted business and trade with settlements in the OPT indicate a level of frustration with the current structures and state of negotiations—and a desire to flex some muscle.[41]

Despite the key roles played by the UN, the World Bank, and the EU, the United States remains the most important third-party actor. The United States' dominant role is accepted by both Israel and the PLO—and all other donors have tended not to publicly challenge US positions for self-interested foreign policy reasons, although of course tensions and friction are occasionally obvious. Given the United States' unconditional support for Israel, which is cemented by generous amounts of aid (around US$3 billion annually), close military relations, and political/diplomatic support (through the UN and the US Congress), Washington's role is incredibly problematic—causing Palestinian academic Rashid Khalidi to call it the "dishonest broker."[42] The creation of the Quartet (the UN, the EU, the United States, and Russia) to oversee the implementation of the 2003 Roadmap added another layer of donor oversight and coordination, which many regard to be merely duplicating the role of other agencies. The dominant role of the United States' agenda in the Quartet is indicated by the fact that in 2013 and 2014 its primary function was to implement US secretary of state John Kerry's peace plan.[43]

Western donors have committed significant resources to peacebuilding activities in the OPT, as shown by the level of overseas development assistance. In 2013, the IMF estimated that, since its creation, the PA has received more than US$15 billion in aid from bilateral and multilateral donors, with annual per capita aid averaging $340, which constitutes 15 percent of GDP per year. Before 2001, roughly one-third of this was for budget support; by 2007, budget support used up more than 80 percent. This has come at the expense of development support.[44] To coordinate and guide this aid, an extensive layer of oversight committees was created by the donors and the multilaterals.

While these structures are typical of donor behavior in other war-torn societies, the PA is unique in that it was not given sovereignty, nor had the UN (or another multilateral agency) assumed sovereignty on behalf of the Palestinian people, as it had, for instance, in East Timor and Kosovo.[45] While it is true that the Oslo framework has blurred the boundaries, sovereignty over the land, resources, and people in the OPT remains firmly with Israel. This means that any peacebuilding and statebuilding activities have been heavily circumscribed and structured by the geographic, economic, and governance limitations imposed by the Oslo framework. Development activities have not been implemented in Area C, for instance. This has meant that only pockets of prosperity have been created—which some writers refer to as "bubbles."[46] And the Palestinian security sector, whose main role is to prevent attacks on Israeli citizens (including settlers), is forbidden to respond to attacks on its own population by Israeli settlers and the Israeli military. The particular way in which peacebuilding strategies have been implemented in the OPT, and their impacts, are further explored in the following section.

LIBERAL PEACEBUILDING POLICIES IN A COLONIAL CONTEXT

Since their first implementation over twenty years ago, donor peacebuilding policies have altered on occasion to ensure that the Oslo peace framework continues, often in the face of threatened breakdown, while the PA has been persuaded to progressively embrace liberal peacebuilding policies in a context of colonization. Donor policies have followed general peacebuilding principles as applied in other war-torn societies, but they have manifested themselves in particular ways and with certain impacts. In the realms of governance, Western strategies have focused on supporting "sympathetic" Palestinian elites and embedding their power in opposition to those who reject the vision of peace on offer. Using aid to prop up preferred "peace partners" is common in peace processes where international donors confer legitimacy on some actors and withhold it from others. But in this context, "sympathetic elites" are defined as those with whom Israel will negotiate and who are acceptable to the donors, particularly those with the most power to decide and exclude, that is, in this case, the United States.[47] The "partners for peace" discursive framework underpinned and provided the ideological rationale for two separate instances of changes in PA personnel insisted on by Israel and the donors. The first instance was during the second intifada. The first PA president, Yasser Arafat, was forced, by the Roadmap, to agree to reforms that diluted his power through, for example, the creation of the post of prime minister. The second instance was after the election of Hamas in 2006, whereby a boycott by the main peacebuilding actors and Israel created the conditions for it to be forced out of office and restricted to the Gaza Strip.

In the realms of economic development, Western strategies have focused on supporting the development of infrastructure, a more open economy tied into the world market, and a Palestinian business elite with vested interests in ensuring stability (albeit one that they wish would lead to statehood). Opening up countries to the world market is a common donor prescription, and in this context it had a broader strategy of tying the OPT into a regional economic system designed to normalize relations with Israel and the Arab states, which had the effect of also intensifying Palestinian economic dependence on Israel.[48] The West Bank is a captive market for Israel—and local companies find it impossible to compete with cheap imported goods (particularly from China). Monopolies, however, are still in existence and are often controlled by those connected to the PA, so the form of crony capitalism created under Arafat has continued, albeit in a different format. While the Western peacebuilding industry has a preference for neoliberal economic and good governance policies, their adoption in the OPT has been gradual and patchy—and has been the outcome of struggles and changes *within* the Palestinian elite, assisted and facilitated by changes in the policies of Israel and pressure from Western donors. So despite billions of dollars of peacebuilding assistance over the past two decades, the strictures of the Paris Economic Protocol, the restrictions of Israel's occupation, and neoliberal policies have all combined to create an economic climate in the OPT that is marked by weak growth in the gross domestic product, high unemployment (particularly among the youth) and pressure on wages, a massive growth in private consumer debt, and a struggling private sector.[49] The Palestinian economy is therefore "trapped on a path of low growth, economic dependence on Israel and reliance on foreign aid."[50] This clearly affects the PA, which has large and growing arrears to private suppliers and Palestinian banks, as well as recurring shortfalls in donor aid; by March 2014, the PA's debt stood at US$4.8 billion.[51]

In the security realm, peacebuilding strategies have continually focused on the creation and enhancement of a Palestinian security force capable of ensuring and enforcing stability. But in this context, this has meant promoting Israel's security first through a counterterrorism strategy that requires a tight regulation of security coordination between the PA and Israel. Under conditions of Israel's continued occupation and in a context where the Palestinians lack democratic governance, the conditions have been created for authoritarianism and the construction of a police state.[52] In 2014, the Palestinian security services employed more than seventy thousand people across the West Bank and Gaza—around one for every fifty-seven Palestinians in the OPT, which by any comparison is a high figure.[53] Democracy, human rights, and even economic development have been downgraded, or ignored, if and when they have been an obstacle, or have not been essential, to the survival of the Oslo framework.

And so a picture emerges of a political economy that is the outcome of the policies and practices of Israel, the donors, and different sections of the Palestinian elite under the auspices of liberal peacebuilding as structured by the Oslo Accords. In the first, interim, period (1994–99), the interaction of these three actors facilitated the emergence of a neopatrimonial state that used nepotism and violence to suppress opposition, created trading monopolies and unaudited accounts, and instituted a proliferation of security institutions under the direct control of the PA president, not the parliament. This period ended with the outbreak of the second intifada, during which security coordination disintegrated, the institutions of the PA were destroyed, and there was mass destruction of physical infrastructure. In the second, Roadmap period (2003–6), peacebuilding strategies focused on rebuilding the PA but removing Arafat through democratic reform, implementing "good governance" strategies, and rebuilding the security sector but this time making it more streamlined and more securely under the control of the United States. This period ended with the election of Hamas, a party that rejects the Oslo framework, in January 2006—an event that ushered in another period of instability and an internal Palestinian struggle for control that culminated in the administrative division between the West Bank and Gaza Strip. The third, West Bank First, phase (2007–present) signifies the coming to fruition of the policies introduced under the Roadmap and thus the adoption and internalization of Western peacebuilding priorities. The PA has subsequently focused on building institutions within the framework of Oslo, promoting a private sector focused on services and export-oriented activities, "good governance" (rather than democracy), and security coordination.[54]

Western peacebuilding in the OPT has been subjected to extensive and frequent criticism, particularly that there is a contradiction in promoting Palestinian institutions, governance structures, and economic development in preparation for sovereignty in the context of Israeli occupation and colonial practices.[55] It stands further accused of failing to deliver peace.[56] But if the goal of peacebuilding is to ensure stability and implement neoliberal economic and governance strategies, then it has not failed—in fact, quite the contrary, it has largely succeeded.

CONCLUSION: BUILDING AND SUSTAINING A "ZOMBIE PEACE"

The zombie has become a popular metaphor for many things in the West, from its moribund capitalist financial system (for Chris Harman), to the defunct ideas of its business leaders (for Paul Krugman), to the apparent submissiveness of its population (for Noam Chomsky).[57] Fictional creatures taken from Haitian folklore and popularized in horror films, zombies are typically portrayed as mindless reanimated corpses that stagger on neither dead nor alive, but somewhere in between.[58] With these characteristics in mind, this chapter concludes by proposing that the label "zombie peace" aptly describes the situation in the OPT: neither peace nor conflict, but something in between. This is a peace characterized by an isolated and blockaded Gaza, an East Jerusalem increasingly integrated (but in a skewed and unequal manner) into Israel, and a West Bank with widely varying political economies (from middle-class and prosperous towns such as Ramallah to desperately poor refugee camps and rural villages) living side by side with Jewish settlements integrated into Israel via an extensive road network system and with access to generous services.

Yet despite the growing fiscal problems, deepening inequality and poverty, and lack of democratic accountability, as charted in the previous section, it is clear that the PA can continue to stagger on like a zombie in a B-list movie as long as donors support it through money and practical assistance. The Oslo framework, Western peacebuilding activities, Israel's occupation and colonization strategies, and Palestinian elite strategies have all contributed to creating this "zombie peace." The PA is caught in a difficult balancing act: between retaining its international legitimacy through coordination with Israel and the donors and retaining its domestic legitimacy in the face of increasing accusations that its continued existence gives credence to a moribund negotiation process and a colonial peace. Western peacebuilding policies and practices, based as they are on enhancing institutions of state coercion, capacity building, and economic liberalization, have been a central contributing factor to the creation of this situation. The peacebuilding industry will continue its involvement in the OPT because Western foreign policy objectives in the region demand it. Under conditions such as these, the zombie peace is sadly all too sustainable—albeit unjust and fragile—because no alternative vision is being suggested or indeed contemplated.

NOTES

I would like to thank the British Academy, the Council for British Research in the Levant, and the Leverhulme Trust for grants that made this research possible. I would also like to thank Michael Pugh and Alaa Tartir for comments made on an earlier draft, but any errors are, of course, of my own making.

1. Johan Galtung, "Three Approaches to Peace: Peacekeeping, Peacemaking and Peacebuilding," in *Peace, War and Defence—Essays in Peace Research*, vol. 2 (Copenhagen: Christian Ejlers, 1975), 1075.

2. Michael Pugh, "Local Agency and Political Economies of Peacebuilding," *Studies in Ethnicity and Nationalism* 11, no. 2 (2011): 308–20.

3. Richard Caplan, *International Governance of War-Torn Territories* (Oxford: Oxford University Press, 2005).

4. Michael Pugh, Neil Cooper, and Mandy Turner, eds., *Whose Peace: Critical Perspectives on the Political Economy of Peacebuilding* (Hampshire: Palgrave Macmillan, 2008).

5. Boutros Boutros-Ghali, "An Agenda for Peace: Preventive Diplomacy, Peacemaking and Peacekeeping," A/47/277—S/24111, June 17, 1992, 6, www.unrol .org/files/A_47_277.pdf.

6. Panel on UN Peace Operations, "Report of the Panel on United Nations Peace Operations" [Brahimi Report], A/55/305–S/2000/809, August 21, 2000, www.un.org/en/ga/search/view_doc.asp?symbol=A/55/305; UN Secretary-General's High-Level Panel on Threats, Challenges and Change, "A More Secure World: Our Shared Responsibility," DPI/2367, December 2004, www.un.org/en /peacebuilding/pdf/historical/hlp_more_secure_world.pdf.

7. Roland Paris and Timothy D. Sisk, "Introduction: Understanding the Contradictions of Postwar Statebuilding," in *The Dilemma of Statebuilding: Confronting the Contradictions of Postwar Peace Operations,* ed. Roland Paris and Timothy D. Sisk (London: Routledge, 2009), 1.

8. Michael Pugh, "The Political Economy of Exit," in *Exit Strategies and State Building* ed. Richard Caplan (New York: Oxford University Press, 2012), 278.

9. Olivier May, "International Organisations and the Production of Hegemonic Knowledge: How the World Bank and the OECD Helped Invent the Fragile State Concept," *Third World Quarterly* 32, no. 2 (2014): 210–31.

10. Mark Duffield, *Development, Security and Unending War: Governing the World of Peoples* (London: Polity Press, 2007).

11. John MacMillan, "Intervention and the Ordering of the Modern World," *Review of International Studies* 39, no. 5 (December 2013): 1042.

12. Francis Fukuyama, *The End of History and The Last Man* (New York: Penguin, 1992).

13. Roland Paris, "International Peacebuilding and the 'Mission civilisatrice,'" *Review of International Studies* 28, no. 4 (2002): 637–56.

14. Neil Cooper, Mandy Turner, and Michael Pugh, "The End of History and the Last Liberal Peacebuilder: A Reply to Roland Paris," *Review of International Studies* 37, no. 4 (October 2011): 1995–2007.

15. Ha Joon-Chang, *Bad Samaritans: The Guilty Secrets of Rich Nations and the Threat to Global Prosperity* (New York: Random House, 2008), 26–28.

16. Mark T. Berger, "From Nation-Building to State-Building: The Geopolitics of Development, the Nation-State System and the Changing Global Order," *Third World Quarterly* 27, no. 1 (2006): 5–25.

17. Cooper, Turner, and Pugh, "End of History," 2001.

18. Susan L. Woodward, "The IFIs and Postconflict Political Economy," in *Political Economy of Statebuilding: Power after Peace,* ed. Dominik Zaum and Mats Berdal (Abingdon: Routledge, 2013), 140–57.

19. Cooper, Turner, and Pugh, "End of History," 2001–3.

20. Michael Pugh, "Local Agency and Political Economies of Peacebuilding," *Studies in Ethnicity and Nationalism* 11, no. 2 (2011): 309.

21. Michael Pugh, "Lineages of Aggressive Peace," in *The Politics of International Intervention: The Tyranny of Peace,* ed. Mandy Turner and Florian Kuhn (Abingdon: Routledge, 2016), 77–93.

22. Jan Selby, "The Myth of Liberal Peacebuilding," *Conflict, Security and Development* 13, no. 1 (2013): 57–86; David Chandler, "The Uncritical Critique of 'Liberal Peace,'" *Review of International Studies* 36, no. 1 (October 2010): 137–55.

23. Cooper, Turner, and Pugh, "End of History."

24. Roger MacGinty and Gurchathen Sanghera, eds., "Hybridity in Peacebuilding and Development," special issue, *Journal of Peacebuilding and Development* 7, no. 2 (2012); Oliver P. Richmond and Audra Mitchell, eds., *Hybrid Forms of Peace: From Everyday Agency to Postliberalism* (Basingstoke: Palgrave Macmillan, 2012).

25. Neil Cooper, "Picking Out the Pieces of the Liberal Peaces: Representations of Conflict Economies and the Implications for Policy," *Security Dialogue* 36, no. 4 (2005): 463–78.

26. Avi Shlaim, "Obama and Israel: The Pessimistic Perspective," *Antonian: The Newsletter of St Antony's College,* Fall 2010, 6–7.

27. Mandy Turner, "Peacebuilding as Counterinsurgency in the Occupied Palestinian Territory," *Review of International Studies* 41, no. 1 (2014): 73–98.

28. Jodi Rudoren and Jeremy Ashkenas, "Netanyahu and the Settlements," *New York Times,* March 12, 2015, www.nytimes.com/interactive/2015/03/12/world /middleeast/netanyahu-west-bank-settlements-israel-election.html.

29. Yezid Sayigh, "The Palestinian Paradox: Statehood, Security and Institutional Reform," *Conflict, Security and Development* 1, no. 1 (2006): 101–8.

30. Saed Bamya, "The Economics of the Oslo Accord," *Perspectives,* no. 5 (December 2013): 61–67.

31. Neri Zilber, "Israeli Financial Measures against the Palestinian Authority," April 11, 2014, working paper, Washington Institute for Near East Policy, Washington, DC, www.washingtoninstitute.org/policy-analysis/view/israeli-financial-measures-against-the-palestinian-authority.

32. Hiba I. Husseini and Raja Khalidi, "Fixing the Paris Protocols Twenty Years Later: Some Lessons for Diehard Reformers," *Perspectives,* no. 5 (December 2013): 56–60.

33. Rex Brynen, *A Very Political Economy: Peacebuilding and Foreign Aid in the West Bank and Gaza* (Washington, DC: US Institute of Peace Press, 2000), 40.

34. Published work on non-Western donors in the OPT in English is limited, but see Jonathan Benthall and Jérôme Bellion-Jourdan, *The Charitable Crescent: The Politics of Aid in the Muslim World* (London: I. B. Tauris, 2009), and E. Villanger, *Arab Foreign Aid: Disbursement Patterns, Aid Politics and Motives* (Bergen: Chr. Michelsen Institute, 2007).

35. Anne Le More, "Killing with Kindness: Funding the Demise of a Palestinian State," *International Affairs* 81, no. 5 (2005): 995.

36. Until 1999, it was called the Office of the Special Coordinator in the Occupied Territories.

37. Anne Le More, *International Assistance to the Palestinians after Oslo: Political Guilt, Wasted Money* (London: Routledge, 2008), 105–7.

38. Mandy Turner, "Creating 'Partners for Peace': The Palestinian Authority and the International Statebuilding Agenda," *Journal of Intervention and Statebuilding* 4, no. 1 (2011): 15; Sobhi Samour and Raja Khalidi, "Neoliberalism and the Contradictions of the Palestinian Authority's Statebuilding Programme," in *Decolonizing Palestinian Political Economy: De-development and Beyond,* ed. Mandy Turner and Omar Shweiki (Hampshire: Palgrave Macmillan, 2014).

39. Dimitris Bouris, *The European Union and the Occupied Palestinian Territories: Statebuilding without a State* (London: Routledge, 2013).

40. Le More, *International Assistance,* 88–89.

41. Dimitris Bouris and Nathan J. Brown, "Can the EU Revive the Cause of Middle East Peace," Carnegie Paper, May 29, 2014, Washington, DC, http://carnegieendowment.org/2014/05/29/can-eu-revive-cause-of-middle-east-peace.

42. Rashid Khalidi, *Brokers of Deceit: How the US Has Undermined Peace in the Middle East* (Boston: Beacon Press, 2013). On US support for Israel, see J. M. Sharp, *US Foreign Aid to Israel*, CRS Report RL33222 (Washington, DC: Congressional Research Service, 2012). See also John J. Mearscheimer and Stephen M. Walt, "The Israel Lobby," *London Review of Books,* March 23, 2006; Ilan Pappe, "Clusters of History: US Involvement in the Palestine Question," *Race and Class* 48, no. 3 (2007): 1–28.

43. Quartet official, interview by author, April 2014, Jerusalem.

44. International Monetary Fund, "West Bank and Gaza: Staff Report Prepared for the September 2013 Meeting of the Ad Hoc Liaison Committee," September 11, 2013, 17, https://www.imf.org/external/country/WBG/RR/2013/091113.pdf.

45. Caplan, *International Governance*, 2005.

46. Kareem Rabie, "Ramallah's Bubbles," *Jadaliyya*, January 18, 2013, www.jadaliyya.com/pages/index/9617/ramallah%E2%80%99s-bubbles.

47. Turner, "Creating 'Partners for Peace,'" 2011.

48. UN Conference on Trade and Development (hereafter UNCTAD), "Report on Assistance to the Palestinian People: Developments in the Economy of the Occupied Territories," TD/B/60/3, July 8, 2013, 7, http://unctad.org/meetings/en/SessionalDocuments/tdb60d3_en.pdf.

49. U. Kock (head of the IMF West Bank and Gaza office), "Between a Rock and a Hard Place: Recent Economic Developments in the Palestinian Economy," lecture at the Palestine Economic Policy Research Institute, Jerusalem, February 19, 2014; UNCTAD, "Report on UNCTAD Assistance to the Palestinian People: Developments in the Economy of the Occupied Palestinian Territory," TD/B/59/2, July 13, 2012, 3, www.un.org/depts/dpa/qpal/docs/2013Rome/P2%20Mahmoud%20Elkhafif%20addl%20EN%20TD%20B%2059%202.pdf.pdf; World Bank, "Stagnation or Revival? Palestinian Economic Prospects," report to the Ad Hoc Liaison Committee, March 21, 2012, http://siteresources.worldbank.org/INTWESTBANKGAZA/Resources/WorldBankAHLCreportMarch2012.pdf.

50. UNCTAD, "Policy Alternatives for Sustained Palestinian Development and State Formation," UNCTAD/GDS/APP/2008/1, 2009, http://unctad.org/en/Docs/gdsapp20081_en.pdf.

51. "IMF: Fund Palestinian Unity Government," YNet, July 4, 2014, www.ynetnews.com/articles/0,7340,L-4537882,00.html.

52. Yezid Sayigh, "Policing the People, Building the State: Authoritarian Transformation in the West Bank and Gaza Strip," Carnegie Papers, 2011, Carnegie Endowment for International Peace, http://carnegieendowment.org/files/gaza_west_bank_security.pdf; Tzvi Ben Gedalyahu, "US Trained Armed Forces Turning PA into Police State," *Arutz Sheva* (Israel National News), November 23, 2011, www.israelnationalnews.com/News/News.aspx/140787#.U6wqtbHvKSo.

53. The "more than seventy thousand" estimate is from "Security Agencies Consume Palestinian Authority Budget," Middle East Monitor, May 4, 2014,

https://www.middleeastmonitor.com/news/middle-east/11264-security-agencies-consume-palestinian-authority-budget. It is obviously problematic with what statistics to compare the Palestinian security services, as they expand beyond "police" but are certainly not an "army," and as all are stationed domestically. If we look at the UN figures published in 2010 for police officers, these show the world median for police officers was 300 to 100,000 inhabitants. The Palestinian figures translate into 1,754 for every 100,000 Palestinian inhabitants in the OPT. S. Harrendorf, M. Heiskanen and S. Malby, "International Statistics on Crime and Justice," European Institute for Crime Convention and Control, with the United Nations and United National Office on Drugs and Crime, Heuni Publications No. 64, Helsinki, 2010, https://www.unodc.org/documents/data-and-analysis/Crime-statistics/International_Statistics_on_Crime_and_Justice.pdf.

54. Palestinian National Authority, "The Palestinian Reform and Development Plan, 2008–2010," 2008, http://siteresources.worldbank.org/INTWESTBANKGAZA/Resources/PRDP08–10.pdf; Palestinian National Authority, "Ending the Occupation, Establishing the State: Programme of the 13th Government," August 31, 2009, https://unispal.un.org/DPA/DPR/unispal.nsf/0/FC11A804CC0C13B88525790A004CA9E1; Palestinian National Authority, "National Development Plan, 2012–14: Establishing the State, Building Our Future," April 2011, www.apis.ps/up/1332062906.pdf; Palestinian National Authority, "Palestinian National Development Plan, 2014–16: Statebuilding to Sovereignty," 2014, www.mopad.pna.ps/en/images/PDFs/Palestine%20State_final.pdf.

55. Le More, *International Assistance*; Sahar Taghdisi-Rad, *The Political Economy of Aid in Palestine: Relief from Development or Development Delayed* (London: Routledge, 2011); Mushtaq H. Khan, George Giacaman, and Inge Amundsen, eds., *State Formation in Palestine: Viability and Governance during a Social Transformation* (Abingdon: Routledge Curzon, 2004).

56. Sara Roy, *Failing Peace: Gaza and the Palestinian-Israeli Conflict* (London: Pluto Press, 2007).

57. Chris Harman, *Zombie Capitalism: The Global Crisis and the Relevance of Marx* (Chicago: Haymarket, 2010); Paul Krugman, "The Zombie Confidence Fairy," *New York Times,* January 10, 2014, http://krugman.blogs.nytimes.com/2014/01/10/the-zombie-confidence-fairy/?_r=0; "Chomsky Breaks Down the Zombie Apocalypse," *Daily Kos,* February 16, 2014, www.dailykos.com/story/2014/02/16/1278055/-Noam-Chomsky-Breaks-Down-the-Zombie-Apocalypse#.

58. Deborah Christie and Sarah Juliet Laro, *Better Off Dead: The Evolution of the Zombie as Post-human* (New York: Fordham University Press, 2011).

TWENTY-ONE

The International Labour Organization and Workers' Rights in the Arab Region

THE NEED TO RETURN TO BASICS

Walid Hamdan

THE RESEARCH ON THE WORK and the role of the International Labour Organization (ILO) in the Arab States is quasi-absent.[1] The little attention the ILO receives in the Arab states is due to its failure in influencing and shaping policies in the region. It is the United Nations specialized agency that seeks the promotion of social justice and internationally recognized human and labor rights.[2] It was founded in 1919 and is the only surviving major creation of the Treaty of Versailles, which brought the League of Nations into being. The ILO in particular stands out within the UN system by having a tripartite structure representing the voice and interests not only of governments but also of workers' organizations, and employers' organizations. It considers labor peace as essential to prosperity and has a founding mission to promote social justice and internationally recognized human and labor rights. The preamble of the ILO constitution adopted in 1919 affirms that "universal and lasting peace can be established only if it is based upon social justice."[3]

To what extent was the organization able to reflect its principles and conventions through its interventions in the Arab region? How can its role be improved? In this essay we will analytically review the organization's work and interventions in the Arab states since 2010.[4]

THE ILO IN THE ARAB STATES: MISSING PREREQUISITES

The ILO was founded on the principles of tripartism and social dialogue, which can be genuine and productive only when workers' and employers' organizations are independent, representative, democratic, and able to voice their members' interests and aspirations. To this end, the ILO issued two International Labour Conventions, C87 (1948), on freedom of association and protection of the right to organize, and C98 (1949), on the right to organize and collective bargaining, and considered them as fundamental to every context regardless of their ratification status.

Labor legislation and governments' practices in countries covered under the ILO's Regional Office for the Arab States have rendered the principle of tripartism void of its meaning and purpose because of severe restrictions put on workers' right to join and establish their organizations. In this regard, Arab states can be put in two categories: countries where workers can establish their unions, however strict the requirements of governmental permission are (Lebanon, Jordan, Oman, Bahrain, Syria, etc.), and countries where it is completely illegal for workers to form their own organizations (United Arab Emirates, Qatar, and Saudi Arabia).[5] In many countries of the first category, public sector workers cannot form unions, and migrant workers are either banned from joining unions or do not have full membership rights. Adding to that, the right to strike is either banned or severely restricted, and workers involved in trade union action are not protected from reprisals and intimidation.[6]

This has produced a situation where formal workers' organizations have fallen under government control. Instead of challenging this situation, the ILO has treated these government-controlled organizations as representatives of workers and has turned its back on workers' actions and movements outside the formal trade unions. Formal workers' organizations participated in tripartite meetings without having an independent role. Here they approved policies of privatization and dismantling of the welfare state. Workers, meanwhile, were taking to the streets opposing these policies and rejecting the legitimacy of formal trade unions. Nevertheless, the ILO rarely considered informal movements and did not take into account the formal trade unions' lack of independence and representation (they mostly represent a small fraction of national formal sector workers, leaving out migrant workers, workers in the informal economy, and migrant workers). Consequently, the ILO failed to gain the important ally and leverage of a genuine and independent trade union movement for their mission of making economies in the Arab region more just and productive.

THE EXCLUSIONARY ECONOMIES OF ARAB STATES: THE NEED FOR ILO INTERVENTIONS

The economies of the Arab states can be put in two broad categories: rentier economies in the Arab Gulf, centered on the extraction of natural resources, and quasi-rentier economies, especially in the Levant, that feed upon the former ones and are centered on financial activities, construction, remittances, and tourism. Nevertheless, features common to all of them can be identified. Arab countries have weak economic structures with a high predominance of low-productive service activities at the expense of high-productive ones, especially in the industrial sector.[7] Moreover, the public sector is important in terms of numbers employed but has a minimal function and role in leading economic development and productive infrastructure. The public sector has historically absorbed much of the workforce, offering relatively good working conditions and social protection, unlike the private sector, and has been used to defuse people's resentment over rising unemployment and job insecurity.

Economic policies and structures in Arab countries can be deemed exclusionary in that they push toward informalization, making workers vulnerable. Arab economies are trapped in a vicious circle fueled by economic growth based on rentier and quasi-rentier activities and monetary and fiscal policies nonconducive to productive employment. The region is left with weak economic structures fostering low-value activities, lack of public investment and infrastructure, low productivity, and a prevalence of small and micro enterprises. This has led to an increasing informality of employment, characterized by the lack of social protection, low wages, poor working conditions, and an increasing number of low-skilled migrant workers with poor working conditions. These dynamics have had drastic effects on workers, who often face high unemployment, vulnerability, low wages, and little prospect of career advancement and development.[8] Theoretically the ILO, by its mandate and mission, should be addressing such conditions. Nevertheless, it has failed to have a significant impact in the region.

THE DECENT WORK AGENDA: FROM RIGHTS TO A DEPOLITICIZED TECHNICALITY

The ILO operates within a region where major and powerful international organizations like the International Monetary Fund and the World Bank are promoting a neoliberal agenda that contradicts ILO conventions and principles. That agenda pushes for labor flexibility and cutting of labor costs as opposed to job security and decent wages; social safety nets instead of social protection; and privatization and deregulation as opposed to the central role of the state in securing full employment. In 1999 the ILO chose to reposition itself through the slogan of Decent Work.[9]

The concept of Decent Work has become the guiding principle of ILO interventions worldwide. According to the organization, it is based on "the understanding that work is a source of personal dignity, family stability, peace in the community, democracies that deliver for people, and economic growth that expands opportunities for productive jobs and enterprise development."[10] Decent Work is based on four main pillars: creating jobs through expanding economic opportunities and productivity; guaranteeing rights at work for all workers, especially poor and disadvantaged ones; extending social protection for all, especially informal workers; and promoting social dialogue based on freedom of association and collective bargaining. To promote the Decent Work agenda, the ILO has Decent Work Country Programmes under way in several Arab states. This concept was not promoted as an alternative to the programs of the International Monetary Fund and the World Bank; on the contrary, the ILO hoped that it would be mainstreamed in them.[11]

Thus the ILO started its technical cooperation projects as a way of integrating itself and easing the devastating impacts of the ongoing transformations. But in the midst of its attempt not to be sidelined by more powerful players, the organization lost its vision, focusing on technical services rather than the advancement and promotion of its standards. Advocacy for workers' basic rights of freedom of association and collective bargaining was set aside because the ILO feared upsetting governments in the region through trying to promote and enforce its basic standards. As workers' voices were either utterly excluded or appropriated by government-backed trade unions to legitimize unpopular policies and as official constituents (governments and their subsidiary workers' and employers' organizations) converged in favor of privatization, deregulation, and informalization, the ILO avoided tackling real issues of workers' genuine representation and participation in policy making, instead offering technical assistance meant to serve "constituent needs."

Therefore, instead of having its policies and approaches mainstreamed, the ILO found itself sidelined by governments in the region. This can be clearly observed with regard to social protection, which is one of the pillars of the

Decent Work agenda. According to the ILO, social security involves access to health care and income security, particularly in cases of old age, unemployment, sickness, invalidity, work injury, maternity, or loss of a main income earner. But although the ILO has tried to expand social security through long-lasting technical assistance and policy advice for different Arab states, governments have instead been opting for the concept of social safety nets promoted by the World Bank. According to this concept, in contrast to that of social protection, social security is not a right; it does not include all members of society and is seen as compensatory services granted to the poor and the losers of economic liberalization.

Moreover, despite calling for productive and job-rich economies and growth, the ILO has failed to influence governments to significantly reform their socioeconomic policies. The governments' resistance to economic reform has led the ILO to settle for piecemeal interventions that ease social tensions but do not introduce significant changes. In this regard, important resources have been allocated to the promotion of self-employment as one of the major solutions to unemployment. This can lead to the proliferation of micro and small enterprises fueling informality and vulnerability, given that economic institutions and policies remain unchanged and do not support productive enterprise development and expansion.[12] Moreover, significant efforts have been devoted to building the skills of workers, at a time when enterprises increasingly demand unskilled and low-skilled workers. In fact, interventions have been implemented regardless of their apparent failures. This has been especially obvious when the ILO has conducted trainings on collective bargaining and social dialogue in countries where unions are banned or in contexts where the institutions and legal framework for collective bargaining were absent.[13]

The ILO has used many pretexts to justify overlooking the prerequisites of genuine and effective tripartism. It has used the excuses of country specificities and a need for gradual change to avoid tackling fundamental workers' rights in some countries, particularly freedom of association in the Arab Gulf. Moreover, it has waived its role to ensure the implementation of labor standards on the basis that it intervenes only by the request of constituents (governments and most representative workers' and employers' organizations), ignoring the fact that workers' organizations do not exist in some countries and that where they exist they are likely to be controlled and have their coverage restricted to a small segment of workers, rendering tripartism an empty shell. Therefore, if no formal requests exist the ILO will not intervene, even when organized and unorganized workers strike and take the streets unsupported by formal workers' organizations.

Doing business through fragmented interventions under the guise of technical cooperation usually results in the ILO considering minimal improvements or the endorsement of laws that are not in conformity with International Labour Standards as achievements, on the assumption that such minimal improvements will eventually lead into the ratification and implementation of ILO conventions. Nevertheless, these approaches have failed, especially given the absence of a political will to reform and given the government enforcement of measures to prevent the labor movement from organizing itself to press for a reform process.[14] The ILO's work and respect for its mandate and standards have been reduced to a mere technicality and depoliticized, on the assumption that the problem lies in capacity and not in the absence of political will to respect workers' basic rights and enable conditions that allow social partners to voluntarily practice collective bargaining and social dialogue.

THE ARAB UPRISINGS: DESTABILIZING THE ILO'S BUSINESS-AS-USUAL APPROACH

The ILO's approach has proved to be self-defeating. This was demonstrated when millions of people took to the streets in many Arab countries, refusing governments' economic policies and oppressive practices and demanding freedom and social justice.

The demands of the Arab uprisings that swept the region—for employment, social justice, and decent jobs—were tenets at the heart of the ILO mandate and mission. The workers' movement outside formal trade unions, which the ILO had previously ignored, kept growing and by 2012 was producing popular mass protests on a scale that the ILO could no longer disregard.[15] This created a great deal of confusion for ILO officials, as their comfort zone of several years vanished and they had to face a challenging new reality. Emerging workers' groups wanted the ILO to take a bigger role and wanted more respect for its standards. At the same time, governments were seeking the organization's advice on how to soothe the explosion of workers' protests demanding the right to organize, employment, equal treatment, decent wages, and social protection. Unfortunately, the ILO, instead of using this opportunity to revise its way in doing business, was hesitant in responding to the demands of millions to have a say in socioeconomic choices and policies.

The ILO cautiously voiced the opinion that fundamental labor rights, social dialogue, and inclusive socioeconomic policies were the main deficits to be changed.[16] However, its interventions were slow, and after timidly supporting the new workers' movement it quickly changed its approach to favor government-backed organizations and justified the government's choices to continue the same socioeconomic policies that fueled increasing informality, pushing the millions of workers in the region beyond the line of poverty.

The Bureau for Workers' Activities (ACTRAV), the department within the ILO that coordinates activities related to workers and their organizations, was the first to decide to respond to the emerging realities—internally by pushing the organization to revise its approach in the region and externally by supporting the emerging workers' movement to organize itself nationally and regionally. It considered that the main task was to restore freedom of association and the right to organize, which would enable the labor movement to break away from years of containment and guardianship by governments. This would support workers to play an effective role in the democratization of their societies and would secure more justice and balanced socioeconomic policies. However, and despite ACTRAV's position to support the new workers' organizations in the region, the ILO continued to align itself with the governments, employers, and formal trade unions that refused to recognize them. In doing so, it encouraged governments' opposition and led their affiliated trade unions (regrouped in the International Confederation of Arab Trade Unions) to wage a campaign against ACTRAV and its officials in the Arab region.[17] Amid these developments, the ILO seemed uncertain, not wanting to upset governments and at the same time unwilling to support and protect its officials. Nevertheless, workers' protests grew and governmental reprisals could not be ignored anymore. For example, in Bahrain more than four thousand workers and trade unionists were fired and persecuted in response to their participation in popular protests in Bahrain in 2011. Moreover, independent trade union actions in Jordan proliferated and workers' protests exponentially grew. Adding to that, after years of inactivity, the newly emerged workers' organizations in Arab states began to use ILO supervisory mechanisms and filed five complaints against Arab governments in the year 2012, indicating high expectations for a new and bigger role for the ILO.

In fact, the position of the International Trade Union Confederation (the most representative workers' organization in the world) in supporting the Arab workers' move toward building democratic and independent unions pressured the ILO to pay attention to the ongoing popular movements and to regain its rights-based discourse enshrined in its mandate and constitution. This was clear from its active support for the fired workers in Bahrain and intervention for their reinstatement. The ILO incorporated independent trade unions into some of its activities, particularly the federation of independent trade unions in Jordan, which started to participate in different projects' activities and meetings. Moreover, it attempted to generate an alternative discourse on socioeconomic policies in the region. In this regard, in 2013 it issued jointly with the UN Development Programme a report entitled "Rethinking Economic Growth in the Arab Region: Towards Productive and Inclusive Societies." The report highlighted the structural deficiencies of the current economic models in the region and called for policies encouraging productive activities, a greater role of the state, and respect for workers' basic rights.

Nevertheless, the above-mentioned changes had little effect, as they were limited to rhetoric and remained superficial. The ILO overlooked the Jordanian government's reprisal measures, which included firings and intimidation, against independent trade union action in the private and public sectors. Furthermore, the 2013 joint report remained mere ink on paper. It was never endorsed by governments in the region as they maintained their resistance to alternative economic policies. Meanwhile, ILO projects remained unchanged in their interventions in that they avoided addressing core issues in Arab states ranging from economic policies to freedom of association and basic trade union rights. The only apparent change was that ILO specialists and project managers, as a result of ACTRAV pressure, had to recognize that new partners, independent trade unions, were to be engaged in activities.

A RACE FOR FUNDING IN THE ARAB GULF

These contradicting patterns were further intensified as donors became more interested in funding projects in Arab states as a result of the rising popular movements. The ILO began competing with other international organizations for donor funds to increase its portfolio. Thus funding became an end in itself, and the ILO started setting up ad hoc projects based on donor priorities without any clear strategy or vision and without attending to the needs and aspirations expressed by popular movements. This suggested that the ILO was changing only cosmetically and was not about to reinvent itself in light of the Arab uprisings. On the contrary, it was about to return back to its comfort zone.

The ILO's continued reluctance and hesitance to respond to the new realities was accompanied by rapid political developments in the Arab region going against the tide of popular movements. In many countries, militarism and radical Islam gained ground and Arab governments and regimes started to adapt and contain the popular movements, including workers' and trade union movements. As governments regained the initiative, the old trade union structures counterattacked independent workers' organizations in order to reaffirm their monopoly over trade unionism in Arab states. Thus, in this climate of a waning mass popular movement, the scant international support for independent trade unions and freedom of association that independent trade unions had succeeded in gaining after the uprisings was lost.

In this situation, the ILO in the Arab region quickly returned to its comfort zone and became once again aligned with governments' positions, exerting pressures on ACTRAV to reinitiate its cooperation with government-backed trade unions after years of suspension as a result of the uprisings. Once again, the rights to organize and engage in collective bargaining were put on the shelf in favor of piecemeal interventions lacking an overarching strategy. This was obvious when the ILO decided to intervene in the Gulf Cooperation Council (GCC) countries.

As a result of the Arab uprisings, the issue of freedom of association gained prominence, especially with ACTRAV's insistence on it as a prerequisite for all ILO interventions in the Arab states. Thus all interventions in the GCC, namely the Kingdom of Saudi Arabia, Qatar, and the United Arab Emirates, were put on hold until there would be a clear government commitment to secure an enabling environment for workers to establish their own organizations. Nevertheless, this situation changed as the balance of power shifted between the governments of these countries and popular movements and as the GCC countries' influence significantly grew among the Arab Labour Organization and the International Confederation of Arab Trade Unions (the regional federation regrouping mostly government-backed trade unions). In addition, GCC countries were ready to pour in important funds to finance ILO projects. Thus the ILO, which sought financing in a context of dwindling international funding, started initiating projects in Qatar, Saudi Arabia, and the United Arab Emirates, even though these countries completely banned workers from establishing unions were increasingly violating migrant workers' rights.[18]

The ILO's Regional Office for Arab States disregarded the disapproval of ACTRAV and ventured into activities according to the agendas of the main GCC countries. Thus it toned down the issue of migrant workers in the United Arab Emirates upon the request of the government; however, it maintained its normal cooperation with the country. It engaged in activities on social dialogue and provided technical advice for the Kingdom of Saudi Arabia, even though no workers' organizations exist in the country and even though social dialogue requires the presence of trade unions. Moreover, the ILO held regional and international conferences in Qatar, despite the country's record of severe human and labor rights violations. The ILO also provided technical support for Qatar to develop a charter on migrant workers' rights that failed to respect most of its International Labour Standards. These and many other examples show that the ILO not only is maintaining its business-as-usual approach but also is being used by governments to whitewash their image on the international level without making any significant changes. In fact, the unconditional ILO technical assistance provided to Arab governments, in particular the GCC, is used to legitimize the status quo without tackling the fundamental issues of workers' rights in general and migrant workers' rights in particular.

The ILO has clearly failed to improve people's lives in Arab states and to fulfill its mandate and the principles of its constitution. Its role in the region has proved to be mostly serving governments' agendas and priorities, disregarding workers' aspirations and rights. In fact, it has made little effort to push for the ratification and implementation of the ILO Conventions. Its main purpose is to promote and achieve social justice, but can this goal be achieved if the ILO maintains its current approach? The obvious answer would be that the ILO has to reinvent itself in order to respond to the challenges of the Arab region. This will be possible only when it makes genuine and effective tripartism central to its agenda and approach and promotes the reform of economic structures in the interests of productivity, decent work generation, inclusiveness, and social justice. This requires making an effort to achieve rights to freedom of association and collective bargaining so that all workers, including migrant workers, can have a genuine, free, independent, democratic, and representative voice. The ILO must not compromise on these basic rights, without which interventions will remain ineffective and self-defeating.

NOTES

1. The International Labour Organization (hereafter ILO) represents three sets of constituents—governments, employers' organizations, and workers' organizations—who debate and elaborate international labor standards and policies on the organization's level. The International Labour Office is the permanent secretariat of the ILO. It is the focal point for the ILO's overall activities.

2. The ILO formulates international labor standards in the form of conventions and recommendations setting minimum standards of basic labor rights: freedom of association, the right to organize, collective bargaining, abolition of forced labor, equality of opportunity and treatment, and other standards regulating conditions across the entire spectrum of work-related issues. It provides technical assistance primarily in the fields of vocational training and vocational rehabilitation, employment policy, labor administration, labor law and industrial relations, working conditions, management development, cooperatives, social security, labor statistics, and occupational safety and health.

3. ILO, "Constitution of the International Labour Organization," preamble [1919; constitution has been modified by amendments since, but preamble is unchanged], www.ilo.org/public/english/bureau/leg/download/constitution.pdf.

4. By *Arab states* we mean the countries covered by the ILO Regional Office for Arab States: Lebanon, Jordan, Palestine, Syria, Iraq, Bahrain, Kuwait, the United Arab Emirates, Qatar, the Kingdom of Saudi Arabia, Oman, and Yemen.

5. Mansour Omeira, Simel Esim, and Sufyan Alissa, "Labour Governance and Economic Reform in the Middle East and North Africa: Lessons from Nordic Countries," ERF (Economic Research Forum) Working Paper No. 436, September 2008.

6. See the International Trade Union Confederation annual report "Countries at Risk: 2013 Report on Violations of Trade Union Rights," June 10, 2013, www.ituc-csi.org/countries-at-risk-2013-report-on.

7. ILO and UN Development Programme, *Rethinking Economic Growth: Towards Productive and Inclusive Arab Societies* (Beirut: ILO, 2012).

8. M. Omeira, "Rethinking Informality in Light of the Arab Uprisings," paper for the ILO, March 2013, www.ilo.org/wcmsp5/groups/public/---arabstates/---ro-beirut/documents/publication/wcms_218072.pdf.

9. Guy Standing, "The ILO: An Agency for Globalization," *Development and Change* 39, no. 3 (2008): 355–84.

10. ILO, "Decent Work Agenda," n.d., accessed May 5, 2014, www.ilo.org/global/about-the-ilo/decent-work-agenda/lang--en/index.htm.

11. Paul Middlekoop, "Neutrality and Hegemony: International Institutions in a Multipolar World," MA thesis, University of Amsterdam, 2012.

12. Nabil Abdo and Carole Kerbage, "Women's Entrepreneurship Development Initiatives in Lebanon: Micro-achievements and Macro-gaps," *Gender and Development* 20, no. 1 (2012): 67–80.

13. For example, the ILO implemented capacity-building activities for labor inspectors on collective bargaining, knowing that collective bargaining is between employers and workers and does not involve labor inspectors.

14. In the first trimester of the year 2014, the Jordanian parliament discussed and approved amendments of thirty-nine articles of the labor law without touching on the issue of trade union rights, which are still severely restricted in Jordan.

15. According the Jordanian Labour Watch, workers' actions outside formal trade unions reached 901 protests in 2012 as compared to 139 protests in 2010.

16. ILO, "ILO Director-General Says Policy Makers Need to Reconnect with the Needs of Working Families and Put Job Creation at the Centre of Economic Recovery Efforts," press release, December 4, 2011, www.ilo.org/global/meetings-and-events/regional-meetings/asia/aprm-15/media-centre/WCMS_169454/lang--en/index.htm.

17. Since 2012, over forty articles and statements have been issued by leaders of the International Confederation of Arab Trade Unions attacking and defaming ACTRAV officials in the Arab region.

18. ILO, "ILO Workshop on Good Labour Inspection Practices in GCC Countries," press release, January 29, 2013, www.ilo.org/labadmin/news/WCMS_205177/lang--en/index.htm.

TWENTY-TWO

Peacekeeping, Development, and Counterinsurgency

THE UNITED NATIONS INTERIM FORCE IN LEBANON AND "QUICK IMPACT PROJECTS"

Susann Kassem

MORE INTERNATIONAL INTERVENTIONS WERE CARRIED out in the name of "peace" in the decade following the end of the Cold War than in the previous four decades put together.[1] In the era of US unipolarity, following the demise of its Soviet rival, the budget of United Nations peacekeeping missions has increased from a total of US$3.6 billion in the year 1994 to US$8.27 billion in the year 2016.[2] In fact, the peacekeeping budget is one and a half times more than the general UN budget, which in 2016 consisted of $5.4 billion.[3]

This shift in the relative importance of peacekeeping missions was most clearly outlined in UN secretary-general Boutros Boutros-Ghali's 1992 manifesto, "An Agenda for Peace," which attempted to redefine peace operations by classifying the missions in a "taxonomy of peace operations" that linked peacemaking to the establishment of the rule of law, economic development, and democracy.[4] Scholars have termed this approach a liberal peace, as it assumes that democracy, rule of law, and market economics can achieve a sustainable peace in postconflict and transitional states and societies.[5] This liberal approach to peace has since been criticized and challenged by scholars who argue it has been shaped by US geostrategic interests since the end of the Cold War.[6] Sociologist Mark Duffield argues that liberal peacemaking, as opposed to the identification and alleviation of conflicts' root causes, is a superficial process that institutionalizes the status quo.[7] Studies that have looked at the role of international peacekeeping and intervention in today's world order have further attributed the use of force in formerly colonized countries to serve geostrategic interests of the Western countries as a continuation of colonialism by other means.[8] The interventions made in the name of peace in the contemporary world order and their implications for affected countries can be understood only when situated in a theoretical and historical context of imperialism and its effects.[9]

This essay looks at the practice of one of the biggest and oldest international peacekeeping forces in the world: the UN Interim Force in Lebanon (UNIFIL), located along the Lebanese-Israeli border for almost four decades. By analyzing the function of UNIFIL's "Quick Impact Projects" (QIPs), small-scale and short-term development projects carried out with local municipalities, I will provide a practical example of the revised agenda for peace operations, in which military peacekeeping is merged with development initiatives in order to facilitate its implementation. Much in line with the studies critical of the liberal peace approach, this research contends that in the aftermath of the 2006 Israeli war on Lebanon UNIFIL became an exemplary case of a peacekeeping mission that is designed to implement a pacification approach in accordance with US geostrategic policy.[10] It suggests that UNIFIL's ideological readings of peace, the Arab-Israeli confrontation, and the internal structure of power in Lebanon all contribute to the consistent frustration of the mission's basic aims.

In particular, this essay posits that UNIFIL's QIPs clearly illustrate the mission's contradictions and its frequently thorny relations with the local population. On the one hand, UNIFIL's economic development efforts are welcomed and needed by a rural population on the fringes of a notoriously weak, embattled, and laissez-faire state. On the other hand, as I will demonstrate, locals reject UNIFIL's objective to disarm Hizbullah and delegitimize it as a resistance party within the context of the Arab-Israeli conflict. Thus most southern Lebanese, who are overwhelmingly supportive of this resistance, view UNIFIL's mission and its development projects with great suspicion.

This research is an outcome of over two years of ethnographic fieldwork in UNIFIL's area of operations.[11] It is based on qualitative analysis of the activities of the mission's Civil Affairs Department, which administers the QIPs. From February to August 2009, then during January, February, September, and October 2010, and finally between September 2014 and August 2015, I lived in southern Lebanon and conducted official semistructured and unstructured recorded interviews with the local population and municipal representatives, as well as Civil Affairs staff and Civil Military Coordination (CIMIC) officers.[12] Furthermore, I participated in several official meetings between UNIFIL and local authorities and observed their interaction with the population during the implementation of the QIPs and in several inauguration ceremonies that Civil Affairs conducted in UNIFIL's area.

UNIFIL: BACKGROUND

The UN Security Council established UNIFIL in 1978, in the midst of the fifteen-year Lebanese civil war (1975–90). In April 1978, the Israeli army invaded southern Lebanon in order to suppress the increasingly active Palestinian-Lebanese resistance movement operating there and to thwart US attempts to impose a wider Arab-Israeli peace treaty.[13] Since then, UNIFIL has attempted to serve as a buffer between Israel and southern Lebanon, even after the much larger 1982 Israeli invasion and occupation of Lebanese territory south of the Litani River. Initially, UNIFIL was deployed under the terms of Security Council Resolutions 425 and 426 as an interim force to "restore international peace and security" in the area.[14] Yet so far, despite various periods of calm and relative stability, it has not been able to achieve a long-term sustainable and enduring peace, leaving the Security Council to regularly renew its mandate.[15] While the Lebanese civil war ended in 1990, the Israeli occupation of southern Lebanon carried on until an increasingly effective local resistance led by Hizbullah forced Israel and its proxy militia to withdraw in May 2000. The United Nations certified this line of withdrawal, referring to it as the "Blue Line," basically the unofficial and disputed border between Israel and Lebanon.[16]

Nonetheless, relations between Israel and Hizbullah remained tense until a limited cross-border operation in July 2006 by Hizbullah was met with another massive Israeli military invasion of Lebanon that had the avowed objective once again of destroying the social, political, and military capabilities of the Lebanese resistance.[17] After a thirty-three-day war that resulted in a humanitarian disaster and untold damage in southern Lebanon, the Security Council passed Resolution 1701 declaring a cessation of hostilities and making a more robust mandate for UNIFIL.[18] UNIFIL's main task was now to "prevent the presumption of hostilities" and to ensure the establishment "of an area free of any armed personnel, assets and weapons other than those of the Government of Lebanon and of UNIFIL."[19] Additionally, the size of the mission was greatly expanded, from two thousand soldiers on the eve of the 2006 war to a maximum of fifteen thousand troops, notably containing large European contingents from Spain, Italy, and France.

Upon arrival, some of the European troop-contributing countries interpreted Security Council Resolution 1701 broadly to include the direct disarmament and the limitation of Hizbullah's authority and movement.[20] Indeed, some of the first European contingents that were sent to Lebanon included battle-trained military troops who duly faced rejection and resistance for what the local population interpreted as their overly aggressive behavior.[21] The population often confronted these peacekeepers as they went about actively searching homes and depots for weapons. When a car bomb killed six UNIFIL peacekeepers serving with the Spanish army in June 2007, European contingents within UNIFIL ceased this informal peace enforcement approach, brought in specifically trained peacekeepers, and enhanced their budget for mission's civilian-military coordination activities.[22] They also henceforth adhered to Resolution 1701's clear mandate that UNIFIL's disarmament activities south of the Litani River had to occur with the express authorization of the Lebanese government enacted through the Lebanese Armed Forces (LAF). By mid-May 2008, the contradictory interpretations of Resolution 1701, and thus of UNIFIL's new mandate, were largely settled as it became clear that the international community could not bring about the disarmament of Hizbullah by force.[23]

UNIFIL's original 1978 mandate, which envisioned the peacekeeping contingents as an "interim" force in southern Lebanon, has yet to reach its primary objective of establishing peace and security there and is likely further away from it than ever. The following analysis will contribute to understanding why UNIFIL has been unable to establish a lasting peace in Lebanon. It shows that when the larger military and political confrontations die down and UNIFIL's Civil Affairs staff goes about its daily activities, the divergent conceptions of peace held by UNIFIL and the local population, and embodied in the meaning of the QIPs, are clearly exposed. My analysis shows that the QIPs and their implementation are a highly political activity that reveals much about the Western-designed vision of peace in South Lebanon. I argue that this peace is one in which Hizbullah and its supporters are solely held responsible for the international conflict over South Lebanon.

UNIFIL IN PRACTICE

Kheir, a Shia village located in the easternmost part of southern Lebanon, is situated along the Blue Line, which is still unmarked in many places throughout southern Lebanon.[24] As in a number of other villages and towns, the demarcation of the Blue Line in Kheir has become a constant issue with the villagers, as it cuts through olive fields and a well. When an area is marked as being part of the Blue Line, it becomes off limits to the villagers. Hence, the Blue Line deems this particular land, ordinarily used for agriculture in Kheir, as inaccessible, a development not welcomed by the owners of the fields and patrons of the well. The borderline in Kheir constitutes one of the thirteen reservations noted by the Lebanese government against the Blue Line demarcations.[25] In 2009 UNIFIL worked toward solving this border issue by building a gate around the olive fields, which were to be accessed only by their owners. UNIFIL's interest in gating the olive groves occurred after the Israelis abducted a pair of brothers from the village in December 2008.

In the early morning hours, two brothers, Ali and Mohammad Ismail, were working in their olive groves as usual when they were suddenly attacked by Israeli army dogs. In the midst of the attack the pair were captured and taken for interrogation in Israel, where they were held for twenty-four hours. After negotiations between UNIFIL and Israel they were released.[26] Israel claimed they were in Israeli territory, while the farmers and Lebanese officials argued they were working on their land, which lies within Lebanese territory. Other significant incidents occurred when the municipality of Kheir decided to clean an old local well in May 2014. Facing a major drought, the municipality attempted to alleviate the burden for its village by restoring this well. However, the army halted the work as the Blue Line cuts right through the well.[27] In May 2014, in an expression of their opposition to this demarcation, together with the municipality, a group of villagers held a few demonstrations at the Blue Line in which they symbolically reclaimed the disputed territory while playing music and dancing. The deputy mayor of Kheir explained to me that the work was halted after the LAF intervened and talked to the municipality. The deputy said there were more pressing issues the army had to deal with at the moment (the Syrian war and the rise of ISIS) and that it was not the time to solve the issue over the well. The advice was taken seriously, and the municipality did not pursue its work on the well.[28] The protests have since been halted.

When I went to visit the well with Ali Ismail and a representative of the Kheir municipality, I was surprised to see how the villagers completely ignored the UNIFIL soldiers and the LAF who were guarding the Blue Line. The villagers maneuvered around the well freely and crossed the Blue Line several times, deliberately ignoring open warnings by the LAF. On this occasion, I was not able to spot the location of the Blue Line because it was not marked clearly. When I asked the nearby Malaysian peacekeeper monitoring the site to point out the location of the Blue Line, he replied that the UN flag he was holding in his hand was supposed to mark the Blue Line.

The villagers and I stood by the well, crossing the Blue Line, as Ismail and the representative of the municipality were informing me about the incident with UNIFIL and the LAF and telling me about the history of the well. Neither UNIFIL nor the LAF were able to prevent the villagers from visiting the well and crossing the Blue Line. During this trip I asked Ali Ismail if he had avoided going to his olive fields since his abduction in 2008.[29] He responded that his olive groves had never been better kept in his life.

On another occasion his brother, Mohammad Ismail, told me that he walked by the Blue Line every day and was not afraid of being captured again. Both Ali Ismail and the municipality representative recounted the history of the well, which has served as one of the very few water resources to the village for their fathers' and grandfathers' generation. It was unthinkable for them that it was now identified as lying outside Lebanese territory. For UNIFIL, the well and the olive groves merely constitute one of thirteen other issues along the Blue Line that they have inconsistencies with and are trying to solve. For the villagers it is considered another Israeli attempt to colonize parts of their land, as has repeatedly happened to them since the creation of Israel in 1948, when parts of Kheir were occupied, and especially during the twenty-two-year-long occupation of southern Lebanon in 1978.[30]

Demarcating the Blue Line is important from UNIFIL's perspective because it is an attempt to mark an official border between Israel and Lebanon that does not exist. The Blue Line can theoretically serve as a neutral line from which UNIFIL can monitor border violations and assign responsibility for them. However, for the villagers, having to give up this well in a country where water resources are scarce does not make them see UNIFIL in a favorable light. Many people in the south still rely on the water they can collect through rainfall in the winter, which often is insufficient, especially in years such as 2014, where there was a lack of rainfall. The villagers' deliberate crossing of the Blue Line and their intentional disregard of the LAF checkpoint during this visit—in addition to the previously described demonstrations—indicate that the Blue Line and UNIFIL itself are not taken very seriously. This prompts an important question: Considering the low regard in which UNIFIL and its mission are held, why and how do the people tolerate UNIFIL's long-term presence on their lands? To understand how UNIFIL handles such a fundamental divergence with the local population, the following section analyzes the implementation of UNIFIL's QIPs.

UNIFIL'S QUICK IMPACT PROJECTS

Although UN peacekeeping is a military and not a humanitarian intervention, the merging of peacekeeping with humanitarian and development practices is apparent in UNIFIL's work in southern Lebanon.[31] The QIPs are one of the three main functions of UNIFIL's Civil Affairs Department, alongside conflict resolution and management and engagement with the population. The QIPs are designed to produce immediate results beneficial to UNIFIL's mission and can be best described as small-scale and short-term development projects that are carried out with local municipalities and nongovernmental organizations throughout southern Lebanon.[32] Each QIP can cost up to US$25,000 and must be completed within ninety days. Additionally, individual UNIFIL troop-contributing countries carry out similar projects that can exceed this funding limit if the projects are of direct relevance to their mission. UNIFIL devotes great resources, effort, and time to the realization of these projects. UNIFIL's total budget for 2015–16, approved by the UN General Assembly, is US$506,346,400, from which only about US$500,000 is directly allocated to QIPs.[33] However, this seemingly low figure is misleading, as additional projects are funded by the troop-contributing countries that exceed this sum by far.[34] How much countries invest in QIPs varies widely and is scaled to their respective individual capacity and political will: the wealthier European countries, such as Italy, Spain, and France, send proportionally more money for development and reconstruction, while less developed countries, such as Nepal and Indonesia, contribute in-kind donations, such as medical care for the villagers and livestock. In total, UNIFIL's budget for development projects in its area of operations amounts to about US$5 million yearly.[35] Italy's budget for 2014, for example, amounted to 1.6 million euros in 2014 and 1.3 million euros in 2015.[36]

The QIPs combine the political goals of UNIFIL's peacekeeping mission with development activities. The 2013 UN Department of Peacekeeping Operations policy statement on the QIPs emphasizes that the projects should "remain in direct support of the mission's mandate."[37] The document stresses the "contribution to promoting acceptance of the mandated tasks of the mission amongst the population and/or supporting the credibility of the mission by demonstrating progress in the implementation of these tasks where confidence is lacking."[38] It further states that QIPs should contribute "to building confidence/support in/for the peace process" by demonstrating early dividends of stability to the population and that QIPs, by addressing immediate needs of the population, aim to "contribut[e] to improving the environment for mandate implementation by generating support for the mission."[39]

According to the head of the Civil Affairs Department, UNIFIL's involvement in civil society aims to address the local population's needs and to prevent misunderstandings with them through continuous communication.[40] The publicly stated goal of the QIPs is to facilitate relations between the armed peacekeepers and the local population by creating a space where UNIFIL can directly communicate with the populace in order to explain its mission and understand and eliminate the population's fears.[41] A CIMIC officer in the field also told me that the QIPs are designed to ensure the safety of the soldiers. This happens in two ways. First, the direct provision of aid to communities is intended to create a climate of support for the soldiers on the ground. The idea is that grateful communities are less likely to attack peacekeepers.[42] Second, improving village infrastructure facilitates the mobility of UNIFIL patrols. This can be seen in cases where UNIFIL funds projects such as solar-powered street lights, which, according to an officer, assist the soldiers to maneuver in the otherwise dark streets during the frequent electricity cuts.[43]

Building a Rival Power

The minimal rationale for the QIPs has been a need to establish and maintain good relations with the parties to the conflict, but UNIFIL's engagement has political implications beyond good relations. Relations are selective, strategic, and politically motivated.

One of the main goals in funding the QIPs is to build alliances with people and organizations outside local political parties. UNIFIL has to engage with municipalities whose political affiliation with Hizbullah is very obvious, because Hizbullah members are the elected and officially acknowledged representatives of the village. Yet as a Civil Affairs officer underlined during an interview, UNIFIL tries to reach out to nongovernmental, "grassroots" organizations, as well as individuals who are not politically affiliated with Amal or Hizbullah, the two main Shiite resistance parties in Lebanon.[44] According to the Civil Affairs officer, parties that are not affiliated with

Hizbullah or Amal are what UNIFIL perceives as more "neutral" to the conflict.[45]

An anticipated outcome of funding the QIPs is to build connections with politically unaffiliated groups and organizations throughout the southern Lebanese villages. UNIFIL further works with the local municipalities to win their trust for future cooperation. Its projects aim to win the support of the villages for cooperation on the implementation of its mandate.[46]

In interviews and in their media, such as the biannual UNIFIL magazine *al-Janoub*, UNIFIL often presents the QIPs as benevolent and rather spontaneous activities, as in the following description by the senior Political Affairs officer: "[QIPs] are really meant to just support the fact that, you know, you have a large peacekeeping mission in an area and [there is] your relationship with the people and that you can sometimes do something positive for the people."[47] In contrast to this description, UNIFIL's civilian activities, such as the QIPs, can be seen as the nonmilitary corollary of UNIFIL's disarmament plans. UNIFIL's QIPs are also needed in order to create alliances with local people to facilitate the implementation of their resolution. In this case, development aid is thus directly linked to military aims, and to the security concerns of the most powerful troop-contributing countries of the global North, namely France, Spain, and Italy. The linking of aid to the military and geostrategic security concerns of foreign powers needs to be understood as a form of external domination highly reminiscent of the period of classical European colonialism.[48]

Local Response to Quick Impact Projects

The local authorities are aware of UNIFIL's political ambitions. As a member of the municipality relayed to me, "They get in touch with the municipalities under the pretext that they want to help and fund projects, but in reality they are keen to get to know more villagers to spy on the village."[49] While the QIPs have been welcomed, the villagers and municipalities have refused to cooperate on key issues such as accepting the Blue Line demarcation, allowing UN peacekeepers to move freely in their village center, or allowing searches of buildings for weapons. According to Kheir's deputy mayor, the municipality sends only specific people to UNIFIL events to purposely prevent UNIFIL from building its desired relations with their villagers outside the authorities' supervision.[50] It should also be noted that there is a very apparent general apathy among villagers about being involved in such events.

From my own observations, attendance at events such as the inaugurations of completed QIPs is often very low. However, as long as the peacekeepers keep spending significant sums of money on beneficial projects for the village the municipality doesn't mind their presence.[51] Nevertheless, as we have seen with the disagreements over the Blue Line demarcations, sometimes incidents occur that reveal the tensions between diverging political projects for the village. Such incidents can also become violent, when, for example, UNIFIL troops enter the village center, even after repeated warnings by the municipality not to do so. As the deputy mayor told me, this has been a reoccurring issue in Kheir and is considered an act of surveillance. Entry into the village center has happened several times in the past few years, and as a consequence villagers have attacked the peacekeepers.[52]

The reactions of the population to the engagements of the Civil Affairs Department with the community reveal that UNIFIL is frequently confronted with Hizbullah's hegemony in southern Lebanon. Because of the long-term Israeli occupation of southern Lebanon, Hizbullah has become a respected and entrenched authority in the south. The reality is that there is little distinction between Hizbullah and the community: Hizbullah is part of the community and not an alien force that can be simply pushed out. In the bigger picture, UNIFIL's ostensible attempt to supplant Hizbullah seems quixotic. Inevitably, UNIFIL's attempt to secure the Blue Line rubs against the aspirations of the residents in towns like Kheir, where there are claims to land and water that are on the Israeli side of the line. The southern Lebanese population's view of the programs of UNIFIL is colored by their own aspirations for their land and water, which appear to be obstructed by UNIFIL's mandate.

Performing UNIFIL's Politics

After every successfully fulfilled QIP, UNIFIL organizes an inauguration ceremony in cooperation with the concerned municipalities.[53] James C. Scott explains how official rituals—such as inaugurations, parades, and ceremonies—can reveal how their organizers think, see the world, and wish to present themselves to others.[54] Using Scott's framework, we can read such rituals as events in which UNIFIL attempts to legitimize their role in the eyes of the populace. In turn, we can likewise observe how the population reacts to UNIFIL's claims to authority.

According to the former mayor of Kheir, UNIFIL requires municipalities to hold inaugurations in order to publicize their work.[55] Indeed, the rituals themselves are of higher importance to UNIFIL than to the citizens of the villages, as they are always very richly documented by the UNIFIL staff but are often not well attended by the villagers. They function as an attempted justification for UNIFIL locally and internationally—as advertisements for the beneficial projects UNIFIL has conducted in southern Lebanon.

During an inauguration of a newly furnished community room in the village center of Kheir, I observed a local teacher give a speech that was very critical of the political situation under the aegis of UNIFIL. For him, what made UNIFIL's presence and development initiatives in the south necessary was recurring Israeli aggression.[56] The teacher elucidated his frustration about the suffering that the Lebanese population had to bear and how many killings had happened and kept happening in this area. He also appealed to the international community, which in his opinion allowed Israeli violations to happen: "We were born in this country suffering and we are facing a lot of fear and despair because the Israeli enemy is regularly violating our lands and killing our children under an international and an American cover where we are blamed and the Israelis are innocent. My brothers, we are here for peace, not war. We want to live, not die. But our fate is to face the net, as it was imposed on us. And we have to face the enemy for its violations."[57] The teacher emphasized that the reasons for the military buildup in southern Lebanon were Israel's violations that prevented villagers from living a dignified life. Despite his critical assessment of the situation and his emotional speech, his words were not given any further attention during the inauguration. After the event, the Civil Affairs officer emphasized to me that political comments such as the teacher's were not welcome at these kinds of events. She said, "What you heard is unique, the comments about Israel.... We rather don't want them to say that on events like this."[58]

In line with Scott's theory, this incident at the inauguration was highly emblematic of UNIFIL's position and role in southern Lebanon. The inauguration itself was intended to present UNIFIL's authority in the area. The teacher's intervention, however, revealed that UNIFIL's perceived aim for southern Lebanon, on which it based its legitimacy (i.e., the enforcement of peace and the delegitimization of any resistance to Israel) was not shared by the population. The intervention of the teacher questioned UNIFIL's legitimacy, which was why it was purposely ignored. Instead of addressing the political situation and engaging with the locals' views about the conflict, UNIFIL's Civil Affairs Department attempts to impose its own model of improving relations. Conflict resolution paradigms of funding, inaugurating, and documenting humanitarian projects can be understood as attempts to compete with Hizbullah's own humanitarian and social activities in the region.[59] Despite the pretense of objectivity, UNIFIL has its own narrative of the conflict in which it holds Hizbullah accountable, and any alternative to this narrative is considered highly politicized and therefore far from neutral and impartial.[60] In this way, UNIFIL's rhetoric of "impartiality" obscures what is otherwise obviously a pro-Israeli position on the nature of the Arab-Israeli conflict.[61] The people of the towns and villages of southern Lebanon are acutely aware of this imbalance. To preserve a climate of what UNIFIL regards as "impartiality," the work of Civil Affairs avoids or shuts down discussions of actual or potential Israeli culpability in the making of present-day southern Lebanon. The former mayor of Kheir, for one, connects UNIFIL's attitude of preventing discussion about Israel when interacting with the population with the interests of Western powers and Israel itself.[62]

The Blue Line around the olive groves and water well shows an attempt to create a "neutral" buffer zone, administered by UNIFIL: the successful demarcation of the Blue Line could potentially create a space in which UNIFIL's influence counts.[63] However, just as can be observed with the inauguration ritual, the local population purposely rejects UNIFIL's demarcation line, and with it UNIFIL's authority. UNIFIL has further funded several QIPs in Kheir in order to improve the water situation of the village, which again could help support the Blue Line demarcation. The biggest project that was funded in Kheir was a water tank for the entire village that cost US$75,000, an amount that exceeded UNIFIL's usual limit for each QIP of US$25,000 by three times.[64] As I learned from the deputy head of Civil Affairs, the project was funded to make up for the well, which is not accessible for the villagers anymore.[65] Yet the villagers were not satisfied with UNIFIL's proposed consolation prize and kept going to the well and crossing the Blue Line. Cutting off the access to the well was perceived, not as a step toward making this area more secure, but as a continuing appropriation of people's land, an appropriation that had begun with the establishment of Israel in 1948. Since UNIFIL is perceived to hold a pro-Israeli position, local people are often unwilling to grant it authority over the demarcation of Lebanon's—or even the village's—borders. Such widespread resistance prevents UNIFIL from defining a meaningful field of influence for itself.

The teacher's reaction during the inauguration and the conflicts over the well and the Blue Line show that the villagers ultimately link UNIFIL's existence to the wider Arab-Israeli conflict, and not to the presence of arms outside an otherwise trusted state authority. Villagers and mayors use their interactions with UNIFIL to bring up unresolved issues of the conflict and to underline and defend their political position of resisting Israel. Naturally, they link UNIFIL's existence to Israeli actions, which since its creation has changed their lives dramatically. However, neither UNIFIL's mission under Security Council Resolution 1701 nor its previous mandate under Security Council Resolution 425 (1978) addresses the Palestinian question or clarifies the relation of UNIFIL's mission to the Arab-Israeli conflict. The absence of the Arab-Israeli conflict in the work of Civil Affairs leads to political disagreements with the local population, who are an important party to this conflict. The villagers feel threatened as UNIFIL deliberately avoids addressing the history of this region and takes a pro-Western, pro-Israeli stance on the conflict, thereby severely limiting its influence and legitimacy in its area of operations.[66]

GEOPOLITICAL CONFLICT IN A LOCALIZED ARENA: UNIFIL'S LACK OF PARITY

One of the most persistent challenges UNIFIL faces in its relations with the local population is the obvious lack of balance in treating the populations on either side of the border. The mayor of Beshara asked me a simple question: "Are they doing the same things in Israel they are doing here?"[67] The answer is no. There is no parity in UNIFIL's operations on the Israeli and Lebanese side of the border; and there could never be, since UN peacekeeping troops are stationed only on the Lebanese side. The absence of the mission's presence on the Israeli side was even a central point in the strategic review of UNIFIL, which was pursued at the end of 2011. The review underlines that the establishment of a UNIFIL office in Tel Aviv "remains of critical importance for UNIFIL, to enhance the current level of liaison and allow for a strategic dialogue with the Israel Defense Forces and other Israeli authorities on UNIFIL-related issues." According to the report, the government of Israel had agreed in February 2007 to the establishment of an office, but there has been no mention of why this has not occurred yet.[68] The southern Lebanese population often feels threatened by UNIFIL's practices that are aimed to contain their movements and political activities in the area while no similar restraint is placed upon Israel. UNIFIL clearly aims to prevent any kind of attack on Israel from southern Lebanon, but there is no comparable mission on the Israeli side of the border, from which the most devastating violence has been launched.[69]

The lack of parity in UNIFIL's mission design can be seen as a result of US hegemony in international organizations, chief among them the UN Security Council. The United States and members of the European Union such as France list the entirety of Hizbullah as a terrorist organization, and the EU lists at least Hizbullah's military wing as terrorist. Such designations work to limit the peacekeepers' range of options. Since the European nations, especially France, Italy, and Spain, are the main countries funding the QIPs, they have more authority in the interactions with the local population than non-European missions have. Many of the larger QIPs require funding outside the UN budget, so it is mostly the Spanish, Italian, and French battalions who decide which of the proposed projects will be funded by their governments. Hence, this is where tensions may occur, as the individual battalions have the authority over which projects they would like to support. Such decisions are dependent on the local context and the relationships with the local municipalities. Sometimes such a relationship can be fragile, especially because of disputes over UNIFIL's actions and politics. Some of UNIFIL's actions that have not been tolerated have been instances when it tried to enter and search buildings without authorization by the local municipalities or without the presence of the LAF. The position of these key donor countries toward Hizbullah clashes with many of the local municipalities that are in support of the party's stance on Israel. Sometimes this can lead to the discontinuation of QIPs in such areas as the relationships between these key donor countries and the local municipality sour. The following two examples illustrate this fragile relationship.

The relationship between the UNIFIL troops and the municipalities changes depending on the overall relations with UNIFIL in the south. In June 2010 UNIFIL carried out conspicuous training exercises in Bohsasa, a Lebanese village, without the participation of the LAF, which sparked a major upheaval against UNIFIL by the local population. As UNIFIL's senior Political Affairs officer told me, such training would be needed in case there were strong indications that rockets would be launched from this area into Israel. Already in 2009 a larger incident had occurred in Bohsasa due to an explosion that UNIFIL assumed came from a major Hizbullah arms cache. When UNIFIL tried to further investigate this occurrence, the people hindered its personnel from entering the village by throwing stones at them and burning tires.[70] UNIFIL's deployment exercise did not just cause a bad relationship with the inhabitants of Bohsasa but also affected UNIFIL's relationship with the municipality in Beshara, as I learned in a meeting between Spanish CIMIC officers and the mayor of that town in October 2010. As the CIMIC officer told me, a planned QIP, the installation of solar lamps, was not executed because of the mayor's reluctance to communicate with UNIFIL during the summer.[71] According to the mayor of Beshara, UNIFIL's engagements in Bohsasa and elsewhere at that time had not encouraged a trustful relationship, and consequently a rift had developed.

In another incident that I was able to witness more recently, in December 2014, UNIFIL's French CIMIC unit withdrew a project from the village of Baraka after the mayor of the village refused to allow peacekeepers to teach French at a local school. The peacekeepers had an official permit from the Ministry of Education, but the mayor of Ibn el Balad, who was responsible for the governorate of Baraka, disputed the validity of the permit from the ministry. According to him, the local authorities should have the final word, and UNIFIL could not perform any work without their permission. This incident reflects long-standing tensions between the central government and provincial authorities as much as tensions between the municipalities and UNIFIL. When the mayor of Baraka refused to cooperate, the French CIMIC contingent decided to withdraw funding for a recently approved electricity generator for the village.

Both cases show how UNIFIL's political activities in southern Lebanon, especially the ones that are aimed against Hizbullah, can worsen the relationship with the local population and representatives. Both parties, the municipalities and UNIFIL, can choose to withdraw from a QIP for political reasons. The cases also show that the local population often perceives UNIFIL's political stances against Hizbullah more as a threat than as a welcomed intervention.

A Civil Affairs officer whom I interviewed emphasized how, "unlike in western Europe," grassroots organizations in southern Lebanon were not "a strong stronghold of civil society," but organizations that were politically affiliated and therefore weakened by local politics and the resistance.[72] For the vast majority of the population of southern Lebanon, the invalidation of Hizbullah's role in the area is unreasonable. Regardless of American, European, and Israeli views, Hizbullah is recognized locally as a democratically elected party that plays an official role in the present coalition government. In UNIFIL's area of operation, Hizbullah and its allies earn upwards of 70 percent of votes, and in many areas they win upward of 90 percent of votes.[73] Clearly, UNIFIL faces an uphill battle in altering the power structure of southern Lebanon.

On a national level, the overall Lebanese population is more evenly divided on the question of Hizbullah's arms and political role. The legitimacy of Hizbullah's military operations as a resistance army is ambiguous. At the end of the Lebanese civil war, in the Taif Agreement, Hizbullah was the only party that was not disarmed. This was because they were recognized across the board by Lebanese politicians as an organization whose primary function was to resist the Israeli occupation of Lebanese territory. Again, in the present period, the government's latest ministerial statement, issued on March 14, 2014, explicitly affirms "the right of Lebanese citizens to resist Israel, repulse its attacks and recover occupied territory."[74] This reveals that Hizbullah's political project has widespread, though contested, legitimacy in the Lebanese political arena. Therefore utilizing UNIFIL to counter Hizbullah constitutes a significant intervention into the Lebanese domestic arena and not only into international conflict. This further adds to the challenges UNIFIL faces in achieving the goals of its mission.

UNIFIL's Quick Impact Projects aim to create and strengthen cooperative networks between UNIFIL and individuals, groups, and organizations or municipalities not affiliated with Hizbullah. This outreach to a nascent clientele represents UNIFIL's attempt to slowly construct a rival authority and influence in southern Lebanon—an attempt to subvert and perhaps even to replace Hizbullah. At the same time, through the QIPs, UNIFIL is able to maintain interaction with the entire local population so as not to be rejected, and this forces them to collaborate as well with local authorities they know are politically affiliated with Hizbullah. UNIFIL's efforts in southern Lebanon contribute to a positive and supportive climate for its mission, largely because of their provision of employment and investment opportunities, as well as their provision of QIPs. UNIFIL's efforts further guard the safety of its troops against a local upheaval, and help legitimate its presence in South Lebanon. Yet UNIFIL's overall operations, such as the demarcation of the Blue Line and invasive searches in villages, are deemed illegitimate by a large part of the population. These oppositional tendencies lead to a complex dynamic and a weak tolerance of UNIFIL's ongoing presence. This dynamic is further circumscribed by the lack of parity in UNIFIL's deployment, which favors one side of the conflict—Israel—while subjecting southern Lebanon to an international mission highly reminiscent of colonial supervision.

The population's acceptance of UNIFIL's financial support but rejection of its political activities leaves even the more robust peacekeeping mission after 2006 effectively powerless to implement its agenda.[75] Without a political solution for the wider Arab-Israeli conflict, any peacekeeping mission will be able only to survive but not to solve the root issue of the conflict, namely the Israeli occupation and the Palestinian refugee question. UNIFIL's Blue Line initiatives and other activities signify the emphasis on a security approach, which is limited to its own established boundaries. Fifteen years after the end of Israeli occupation, and a decade after the war of 2006, southern Lebanon remains a stronghold of social, political, and military support for Hizbullah. Little else could more clearly indicate the frustration—even failure—of UNIFIL's mission, or more precisely that of its main Western Security Council sponsors, in the aftermath of the 2006 war.

NOTES

1. Stanley Meisler, *United Nations: The First Fifty Years* (New York: Atlantic Monthly Press, 1995), 286.

2. See ibid.; UN Peacekeeping, "Financing Peacekeeping," n.d., accessed April 1, 2016, www.un.org/en/peacekeeping/operations/financing.shtml.

3. UN General Assembly, "General Assembly Adopts UN Budget for 2016–17," n.d., accessed April 1, 2016, www.un.org/pga/70/2015/12/23/general-assembly-adopts-un-budget-for-2016–17/.

4. Boutros Boutros-Ghali, "An Agenda for Peace, Preventive Diplomacy, Peacemaking and Peace-Keeping," Report of the Secretary-General, June 1992, A/47/277—S/24111, www.cfr.org/peacekeeping/report-un-secretary-general-agenda-peace/p23439.

5. See David Chandler et al., *A Liberal Peace? The Problems and Practices of Peacebuilding* (London: Zed Books, 2011).

6. Mark Duffield, *Global Governance and New Wars* (London: Zed Books, 2001), 37; Mahmood Mamdani, "Responsibility to Protect or Right to Punish?," *Journal of Intervention and Statebuilding* 4, no. 1 (March 2010): 53–67; Amy Bartholomew, *Empire's Law: The American Imperial Poject and the "War to Remake the World"* (London: Pluto Press, 2006).

7. See Duffield, *Global Governance*, 2.

8. Mamdani, "Responsibility to Protect," 55; Amitav Ghosh, "The Global Reservation: Notes toward an Ethnography of International Peacekeeping," *Cultural Anthropology* 9, no. 3 (1994): 412–22; Kristín Loftsdóttir and Helga

Björnsdóttir, "The 'Jeep-Gangsters' from Iceland: Local Development Assistance in a Global Perspective," *Critique of Anthropology* 30 (2010): 26; Sherene Razack, *Dark Threats and White Knights: The Somalia Affair, Peacekeeping, and the New Imperialism* (Toronto: University of Toronto Press, 2004), 11–12; Sherene Razack, "From the 'Clean Snows of Petawana': The Violence of Canadian Peacekeepers in Somalia," *Cultural Anthropology* 15, no. 1 (2000): 129.

9. Shalini Randeria and Andreas Eckert, *Vom Imperialismus zum Empire* (Frankfurt: Suhrkamp, 2009); Ghosh, "Global Reservation"; Odd Arne Westad, *The Global Cold War* (Cambridge: Cambridge University Press, 2007).

10. See, e.g., Duffield, *Global Governance;* Mamdani, "Responsibility to Protect'"; Loftsdóttir and Björnsdóttir, "'Jeep-Gangsters'"; Razack, *Dark Threats.*

11. UNIFIL Deployment, Map No. 4144, Rev. 35, June 2015, http://reliefweb .int/sites/reliefweb.int/files/resources/unifil_june2015.pdf.

12. According to the NATO "Allied Joint Doctrine for Civil Military Cooperation," CIMIC serves to assist the local population in multiple ways, such as the provision of infrastructure, capacity building, security, and expertise, in order to strengthen the support of the local population for the military. For this it also cooperates with locally present civilian agencies.

13. Prior to the invasion, in 1976 Israel had set up and supported a proxy militia, the South Lebanese Army, in order to fight the local Palestinian and Lebanese resistances. James A. Reilly, "Israel in Lebanon, 1975–1982," *MERIP Reports,* no. 108 /109 (1982): 14. See also Karim Makdisi, "Reconsidering the Struggle over UNIFIL in Southern Lebanon," *Journal of Palestine Studies* 43, no. 2 (Winter 2014): 24–41.

14. UN Security Council Resolution 425, S/RES/425, March 19, 1978, and Resolution 426, S/RES/426, March 19, 1978, both at www.securitycouncilreport .org/atf/cf/%7B65BFCF9B-6D27–4E9C-8CD3-CF6E4FF96FF9%7D/IP%20 SRES%20425.pdf.

15. Until 2000 the mandate was renewed every six months. After 2000 this has changed to a yearly mandate renewal. Karim Makdisi, Timur Göksel, Hans Bastian Hauck, and Stuart Reigeluth, "UNIFIL II: Emerging and Evolving European Engagement in Lebanon and the Middle East," EuroMesco Paper No. 76, January 2009, 5, www.aub.edu.lb/ifi/Documents/images/paper76eng.pdf.

16. The Blue Line is based on slightly adapted versions of the 1920 French and English boundary descriptions of modern Lebanon that were never fully enforced. Lebanon does not recognize the state of Israel as legitimate, which means it also doesn't endorse the idea of having a "border" with Israel. Israel does not regard the border with Lebanon as a final border either. For further information, see Asher Kaufman, *Contested Frontiers in the Syria-Lebanon-Israel Region: Cartography, Sovereignty, and Conflict* (Washington, DC: Woodrow Wilson Center Press, 2013).

17. For more information on the 2006 Lebanon war, see Nubar Hovsepian, *The War on Lebanon* (Northampton, MA: Olive Branch Press, 2008); Gilbert Achcar and Michel Warschawski, *The 33-Day War: Israel's War on Hezbollah in Lebanon*

and Its Consequences (Boulder, CO: Paradigm, 2007); Karim Makdisi, "Israel's 2006 War on Lebanon: Reflections on the International Law of Force," *MIT Electronic Journal of Middle East Studies* 6 (2006): 9–26.

18. UN Security Council Resolution 1701, S/Res/1701, August 11, 2006, www .unsco.org/Documents/Resolutions/S_RES_%201701(2006).pdf.

19. Ibid., 2–3.

20. Ibid.; Karim Makdisi, "Constructing Security Council Resolution 1701 for Lebanon in the Shadow of the 'War on Terror,'" *International Peacekeeping* 18, no. 1 (February 2011): 4–20. For more on this, see Makdisi's chapter in this volume.

21. Makdisi et al., "UNIFIL II," 25–26.

22. Ibid.

23. Makdisi, "Constructing Security Council Resolution 1701," 19–20. Makdisi writes: "Moreover, a new government of national unity was formed in November 2009 with a clear mandate to implement the non-controversial elements of UNSCR 1701, that is shorn of the remnants of UNSCR 1559, and asserting Lebanon's right to resist Israel's occupation and threats." The international conflict of 2006 was now fought on a national level, having the US-backed March 14 government, which "den[ied] the claims of an armed resistance," and the Iran- and Syria-backed March 8 coalition as its main players. This rivalry erupted violently during the clashes of May 2008, which ended with the Doha Agreement that according to Makdisi implied a victory for Hezbollah's interpretation of UN Security Council Resolution 1701.

24. I have changed the names of places and informants.

25. Daniel Meier, "The South Border: Drawing the Line in Shifting (Political) Sands," *Mediterranean Politics* 18, no. 3 (2013): 364.

26. "Israel Releases Two Kidnapped Lebanese Farmers," *Now.Lebanon,* December 20, 2008, https://now.mmedia.me/lb/en/nownews/israel_releases_ two_kidnapped_lebanese_farmers.

27. Deputy mayor of Kheir Municipality, interview by author, Beirut, September 2, 2014, 1; mayor of Kheir, conversation with author, field notes, May 10, 2014, 1.

28. Deputy mayor of Kheir, interview by author, Beirut, September 2, 2014, 1.

29. "Israel Releases Two Kidnapped Lebanese Farmers."

30. Field notes, Kheir, September 3, 2014.

31. See Mamdani, "Responsibility to Protect"; Loftsdóttir and Björnsdóttir, "'Jeep-Gangsters' from Iceland," 26; Duffield, *Global Governance*, 37; and, more generally, Mark Duffield and Vernon Hewitt, *Empire, Development and Colonialism: The Past in the Present* (Suffolk: James Currey, 2009).

32. UN Department of Peacekeeping Operations, "Policy: Quick Impact Projects (QIPs)," Ref. 2012.21, January 21, 2013, 3, https://docs.unocha.org/sites /dms/documents/dpko_dfs_revised_qips_2013.pdf; Spanish Civil Military Coordination (CIMIC) Unit, interview by author, Ain al-Qamar, September 28, 2010; UNIFIL, "UNIFIL Civil Interaction," n.d., accessed December 30, 2013, http://unifil.unmissions.org/Default.aspx?tabid=11581&language=en-US.

33. UN General Assembly, "General Assembly Adopts UN Budget."

34. The Spanish battalion, for example, funds at least one project per village in the area under its commando, UNIFIL's "Sector East." Spanish CIMIC Unit, interview by author, Ain al-Qamar, September 28, 2010, 6.

35. Civil Affairs officer II, interview by author, Ras al-Bahr, Lebanon, June 17, 2015.

36. Italian CIMIC officer, conversation with author, in field notes, Daou, March 13, 2015, 3.

37. UNIFIL, "UNIFIL Civil Interaction"; UN Department of Peacekeeping Operations, "Policy: Quick Impact Projects," 3.

38. UN Department of Peacekeeping Operations, "Policy: Quick Impact Projects," 3.

39. Ibid.

40. Head of Civil Affairs Department at UNIFIL, interview by author, Ras al-Bahr, May 8, 2009, 3.

41. Foreign forces continuously face the problem of legitimation in the eyes of skeptical locals. The challenge of "winning hearts and minds" is often invoked in such situations; for further reference, see Sir Robert Sandeman quoted in Thomas Henry Thornton, *Colonel Sir Robert Sandeman: His Life and Work on Our Indian Frontier* (London: John Murray, 1895), i; Jeremy Joseph, "Mediation in War: Winning Hearts and Minds Using Mediated Condolence Payments," *Negotiation Journal* 23, no. 3 (July 2007): 219–48. For critical studies, see Tina Wallace, "NGO Dilemmas: Trojan Horses for Global Neoliberalism?," in *The New Imperial Challenge*, ed. Leo Panitch and Colin Leys (London: Merlin Press, 2003), 203–19.

42. Spanish CIMIC Unit, interview by author, Ain al-Qamar, September 28, 2010, 5.

43. Ibid.

44. Civil Affairs officer, interview by author, Kheir, southern Lebanon, May 24, 2009, 2.

45. Ibid.

46. Spanish CIMIC Unit, interview by author, Ain al-Qamar, September 28, 2010, 5; field notes, Kheir, October 23, 2014, 1.

47. Senior political affairs officer at UNIFIL, interview by author, Beirut, September 14, 2010, 6. For various UNIFIL media outlets, see UNIFIL webpage "Communication," http://unifil.unmissions.org.

48. Mamdani, "Responsibility to Protect," 55; See in general Ghosh, "Global Reservation."

49. Deputy mayor of Kheir Municipality, interview by author, Beirut, September 2, 2014, 1.

50. Ibid.

51. Ibid.

52. Ibid.

53. For further discussion of rituals and their place in society, see James C. Scott, *Domination and the Arts of Resistance: Hidden Transcripts* (New Haven, CT: Yale University Press, 1990), 58–61.

54. Ibid., 59.

55. Mayor of Kheir, interview by author, Kheir, May 24, 2009, 2.

56. "Ritual Kheir," field notes, May 21, 2009, 3.

57. Ibid., 6.

58. Ibid., 1.

59. For works on Hezbollah's social programs, see Melani C. Cammett, *Compassionate Communalism: Welfare and Sectarianism in Lebanon* (Ithaca, NY: Cornell University Press, 2014).

60. Ibid.; Civil Affairs officer I, interview by author, Kheir, southern Lebanon, May 24, 2009, 2.

61. "Ritual Kheir," 1; Civil Affairs officer I, interview by author, Kheir, southern Lebanon, May 24, 2009, 2.

62. Mayor of Kheir, interview by author, Kheir, May 24, 2009, 4; mayor of Beshara, interview by Author, Beshara, October 2010, 8.

63. See in general Meier, "South Border."

64. UNIFIL, "Civil Interaction," n.d., accessed November 8, 2011, http://unifil.unmissions.org/Default.aspx?tabid=1520.

65. Deputy head of Civil Affairs, conversation with author, Ras al-Bahr, December 5, 2014.

66. Ray Murphy, "Peacekeeping in Lebanon and Civilian Protection," *Journal of Conflict and Security Law* 17 (2012): 379.

67. Mayor of Beshara, interview by author, Beshara, October 2010, 3.

68. UN Security Council, "Letter Dated 12 March 2012 from the Secretary-General Addressed to the President of the Security Council," S/2012/151, March 12, 2012, 3, https://documents-dds-ny.un.org/doc/UNDOC/GEN/N12/257/96/PDF/N1225796.pdf?OpenElement.

69. Based on Security Council Resolution 1701; senior Political Affairs officer at UNIFIL, interview by author, Beirut, September 14, 2010, 8.

70. "Hizbullah Kept Arms Cache in Violation of Resolution 1701," *Daily Star Lebanon,* July 25, 2009, www.dailystar.com.lb/News/Lebanon-News/2009/Jul-25/53647-hizbullah-kept-arms-cache-in-violation-of-resolution-1701-un.ashx#sthash.jz9WS1iR.dpuf.

71. Field notes, Kheir/Beshara, June 5, 2009, 2.

72. Civil Affairs officer I, interview by author, Kheir, southern Lebanon, May 24, 2009, 2.

73. Richard Chambers, "Lebanon's 7 June Elections: The Results," International Foundation for Electoral Systems, June 9, 2009.

74. "Lebanon's Cabinet Approves Policy Statement," *Daily Star Lebanon,* March 14, 2014, www.dailystar.com.lb/News/Lebanon-News/2014/Mar-14/250322-lebanons-cabinet-to-approve-policy-statement.ashx#ixzz2x2No5PuO.

75. See also Murphy, "Peacekeeping in Lebanon," 402.

TWENTY-THREE

The Protective Shields

CIVIL SOCIETY ORGANIZATIONS AND THE UN IN THE ARAB REGION

Kinda Mohamadieh

IN RECENT HISTORY, SINCE THE POSTCOLONIAL and statebuilding period, civil society organizations (CSOs) in various Arab countries have faced various complex political, social, and economic contexts. Yet they share a persistent attempt by their political regimes to clamp down on the independent spaces available for civil society's contribution.

Generally, human rights organizations in the Arab region have focused their attention on defending civil and political rights. This can be partly explained by the dominance of a context that has posed challenges to CSOs' mere existence and their right to operate. Within that context, the relationship between CSOs and the United Nations with regard to development in the Arab region has taken various forms, which have sometimes been beneficial and have sometimes also created tensions, as discussed below.

To a certain extent, we need to separate the discussion of CSOs' engagements with UN processes at the international level, especially the UN-led development conferences, from their engagements at the regional and national levels. The latter takes various forms, including operational partnerships and cooperation, policy discussions, and advocacy work.

This chapter discusses various roles undertaken by CSOs in the Arab region and their implications for UN-CSO collaboration. Although it touches on the role of welfare- and charity-focused groups, organizations focused on policy and legislative change, think tanks and research centers, and unions, it focuses primarily on the role of CSOs in policy debates and the human rights movement. Tracing the history of CSO-UN interactions in the Arab region, it explores the new challenges and possibilities raised during the period of the Arab uprisings.

CSOs in the Arab region, mainly those working on policy and legislative issues, have been engaged with UN-led processes and conferences since the

1992 Earth Summit, and including the 1995 Summit on Social Development and the 2000 Millennium Summit. They have developed operational cooperation with various UN agencies, such as the UN High Commission for Refugees (UNHCR), the UN Children's Emergency Fund, the UN Development Programme (UNDP), and the UN Educational, Scientific and Cultural Organization. UN agencies have sometimes played a significant role in providing a platform for CSOs to have a say in policy making. This is especially significant when the relationship between CSOs and state actors is complicated by governments' attempts to dominate CSOs, as has been the case in the Arab region.

Operational cooperation between CSOs and UN agencies on specific programs has enabled CSOs' links with and understanding of community specifics to be combined with the expertise of UN agencies at thematic and sectoral levels. However, as some UN agencies, driven by a quest for funding, have moved into programmatic interventions, tensions have sometimes emerged between CSOs and UN agencies when some UN agencies have ended up potentially competing with CSOs for funding or crowding out the space available for CSOs.

This essay attempts to explore some of these dynamics and related questions, drawing in part on the experience of the Arab NGO Network for Development (ANND). ANND is a platform of CSOs working in twelve Arab countries on economic and social rights and policies. Its experience sheds light on some aspects of the dynamic and changing relationship between CSOs and the UN in the Arab region. I discuss selected examples of cooperation between UN agencies and CSOs, and the way this interface has provided a platform for CSOs to influence the development discussion in the Arab region.

The terms *CSOs* and *nongovernmental organizations (NGOs)* are used interchangeably in this text to refer to organized public interest nonprofit entities that are engaged in the sphere differentiated from the state, the family, and the market.

GLOBAL AND REGIONAL TRENDS IN CSO-UN
INTERACTIONS

Interactions between CSOs and the UN evolved to unprecedented levels during the 1990s, when the UN embarked on a series of development-focused international conferences on issues of the environment and development, population and development, human rights, women's rights, and social development, among other policy areas.[1] Before that period, engagement was confined to a formal interface mostly involving international nongovernmental organizations of different varieties, including professional and business associations that were granted formal consultative relations with the UN, specifically the UN Economic and Social Council.[2] This form of relation between civil society and the UN applied as well to the situation in the Arab region. In the latter, the limitations of the interface could also be explained by the limited active civil society dynamics in various Arab countries, most of which were still struggling with nation-building dynamics.

During the 1990s, the involvement of NGOs with the UN system became much more widespread and political. It reflected an attempt by NGOs to be involved in institutional and governance matters related to the UN and in agenda shaping inside the UN.[3] The involvement expanded to include national, regional, and international NGOs, networks, and coalitions.

ANND was the result of an initiative by a number of CSOs from different Arab countries, mainly Lebanon, Tunisia, and Egypt, to organize their voices and enhance their impact within the UN processes and conferences organized during the 1990s. The decision to organize the networking process among these groups was taken in light of the 1995 World Summit for Social Development held in Copenhagen. Subsequently, the regional secretariat of ANND was established in Beirut in the year 2000. ANND's mandate focused on enhancing networking and coordination among civil society groups from across the Arab region with a view toward strengthening their voice in international policy forums, such as the UN summits. Consequently, ANND's role expanded across the Arab region and in 2014 it included members working in twelve Arab countries. Moreover, ANND's mandate was broadened to include coalition building and research for policy advocacy objectives, with a focus on economic and social policies and rights, in addition to peace and security issues.

ANND has consistently taken part in UN processes on development issues, trying to expand the space for civil society groups from the Arab region. It also contributed to organizing several of the civil society forums associated with UN summits, such as the civil society forum at the International Conference on Financing for Development held in Doha, Qatar, in 2008, and the civil society forum at the quadrennial conference of the UN Conference on Trade and Development (UNCTAD XIII) held as well in Doha in 2012 (See more on this conference under the section below on UNCTAD.)[4]

ANND engaged with UN processes and partnered with several UN agencies on different occasions, including the UN Economic and Social Commission for West Asia, the UNDP, the UN Non-governmental Liaison Service, and UNCTAD. Yet ANND has been careful to distinguish its narrative on various development issues from that of the UN. It has often been in a position of critique of UN-led agendas, such as the Millennium Development Goals (MDGs; discussed below).

Civil society's engagement with UN agencies in the Arab region has evolved along lines similar to those of the global trends. Yet the civil society dynamics of the region shapes much of the breadth and depth of this relation. Besides that, differences emerge out of the way the UN agencies operate in the Arab region and the availability of mechanisms dedicated for enhancing the CSOs' engagement with the UN.

Civil society's role in the Arab region stretches across a diverse spectrum of functions. Most of civil society groups in the region operate within welfare- and charity-focused frameworks and are primarily involved in service provision and social assistance.[5] These types of groups are less prone to pressures by the ruling regime, given that they are often not engaged in direct policy advocacy. Many such groups are funded by donations from wealthy elites of other Arab countries, especially Gulf countries. Groups receiving such funding can become at odds with the ruling regime, especially when funding is driven by political motivations and not merely religious ones.

Civil society groups focused on policy or legislative change in the Arab region, including human rights organizations, have often had tense relations with their government. It is such groups that mostly engage with the UN in the Arab countries. The majority of CSOs in this category rely on foreign funding to maintain their operations and programs. Governments have often used such funding as pretext to tighten the spaces available to these groups and to accuse them of being a threat to national security. Groups focused on capacity development and trainings also rely on foreign funding. These groups have had less tension with the ruling regimes. Capacity building and training are often functions undertaken by policy advocacy and human rights groups.

Think tanks, research centers, and publishing houses, such as the Center for Arab Unity Studies based in Lebanon and the Al-Ahram Center for Strategic Studies based in Egypt, have also played a significant role throughout the history of the region by promoting research, policy analysis, documentation, and collective dialogue on pertinent issues such as economic relations, political parties, the Israeli occupation, democracy, social challenges, water, and civil society. However, they have not come into direct conflict with the government. This can be attributed in part to the way these centers have been managed and to the success of their founders and leading intellectuals in keeping a balanced relation with the governments. In some cases, this can be attributed to the choice of city of establishment. For example, incorporating in Beirut, where more freedom of association and expression are allowed than in other Arab cities, represents a conscious decision with the objective of avoiding pressures from the ruling regime. Some of these groups have received funding from certain ruling elites in the region. In many instances, their work has been marginalized by the government.[6]

While such groups have not been abundant in the region, the functions of a think tank are increasingly integrated in the operations of traditional policy-focused civil society groups in the region. Moreover, universities are increasingly hosting think tanks, such as the Issam Fares Institute for Public Policy and International Affairs at the American University of Beirut and the Center for Migration and Refugee Studies at the American University of Cairo.[7] Furthermore, international think tanks are establishing offices in the region, such as the Carnegie Endowment Middle East office in Beirut.

Unions have had varying experiences across the Arab region. Overall, the ruling regimes have often actively weakened organized labor movements and unions. This backlash has sometimes included imprisoning union leaders or sowing division among unionists. The labor movement in Tunisia survived the days of the dictatorship and played a major role in establishing the grounds that led to the popular revolution at the end of 2010. In other countries, such as Egypt and Lebanon, the unions were divided because of infiltration of their ranks by affiliates of the government. Organized and independent labor movements have unevenly regained momentum in the region after the revolutions and popular uprisings starting in 2010/2011.

The broad categorization reflected above does not represent an exhaustive mapping of the roles and functions of civil society groups in the region. Moreover, the classification of these groups is not clean cut, and overlaps exist.

In some instances, the UN has served as a platform for like-minded coalition building among governments and CSOs (as in the case of the International Criminal Court and the Landmine Convention). Also, various forms of multistakeholder, public-private public policy networks and partnerships have emerged, such as the Global Compact and partnership agreements that resulted from the 2002 World Summit on Sustainable Development in Johannesburg.[8]

Yet these new forms of partnerships have raised many critical questions concerning the role of the UN as a broker of partnerships. Advocacy NGOs closely following and engaged with the UN agenda are skeptical of such trends, which are promoted under the rationale of enhancing multistakeholder processes. This is especially the case given the expanding role and influence of private sector actors in shaping the UN agenda.[9] These trends are seen as undermining transparent multilateralism, weakening democratic public institutions, and reflecting worrying conflicts of interest.

CHALLENGES SPECIFIC TO THE ARAB REGION

Several challenges specific to the Arab region have left a mark on the history of interactions between CSOs from the region, their counterparts from other regions, and the UN.

During the period of nation building, the newly independent Arab states played a significant role in shaping discussions at the global level, such as the discourse behind the "New International Economic Order,"[10] and in addressing the struggle of Palestine and the Israeli occupation. Yet organized civil society groups from the Arab region, especially those concerned with policy change, did not play a role till later.

Not long after the independence period, tensions between civic activism and newly established regimes started to arise. As previously noted, CSOs involved in advocacy for rights-based policy change have faced the greatest obstacles compared to other groups, including charities, philanthropy groups, and service providers. The majority of Arab countries have been led by military regimes or monarchies and have often been ruled by martial law. In most countries of the region, constitutional laws have been violated, and the notions of citizenship and participation have been marginalized. The legal framework addressing the role of CSOs in these countries has often imposed significant restrictions on the role of civil society groups.

However, one cannot generalize too broadly about the context in which civil society groups operated in Arab countries before the popular revolutions and mobilizations of 2010/2011. For example, in Egypt the intensity of confrontation with the regime was higher than in Tunisia, although the repression that civil society groups faced in Tunisia did not allow CSOs to take as active a role as in Egypt.

It is worth noting that the Arab Human Development Report (AHDR) of 2002) stressed that the lack of freedom and democracy in the Arab region was one of the main reasons for the failure of developmental efforts. The report notes, "There are significant deficits in Arab countries with respect to key elements of human well-being, civil and political freedoms, the status of women in society and access to knowledge."[11] The report cites a need for governance reform that is "designed to improve the enabling environment for human development. . . . The twin pillars of governance reform are a competent state and an active civil society."[12] The AHDR also cites two reform priorities that are crucial for enlivening civil society in Arab countries: "First, legal and administrative obstacles hampering the establishment and effective functioning of civil-society institutions need to be removed. . . . Second, civil associations themselves need to be transformed into a widespread popular movement, undertaking sustainable collective action."[13] With regard to reinvigorating civil action, the report points out, "The first reform consists of reducing the burden of domination by the state. . . . The second reform has to do with financing. It will be important to expand domestic financing of Arab civil-society organizations and thus to break the pattern of dependence on foreign (or public authority) resources."[14]

Over the years following the nation-building era, the space for constructive engagement between CSOs and the state in its various roles shrank, while tensions emerged in a variety of forms. Governments in Arab countries often perceived CSOs as agents of the West. Such perceptions and accusations were often easy to construct in the popular sphere given the reliance of many CSOs on Western funding. These accusations were utilized to undermine the role of CSOs.

The majority of CSOs in Arab countries, as in other regions of the developing world, depend on foreign funding, especially since national governments do not usually allocate budgets to support civil society dynamics. Civil society groups that are part of the Islamist movements in the region did not face these constraints, given that much of their funding came from community-level fund-raising through the Zakat.[15] Foreign funding sometimes comes from autonomous foundations and other times comes from international cooperation agencies that are part of the foreign affairs machinery of Western governments. Funding associated with the US government, particularly that coming through the US Agency for International Development, was seen most suspiciously. Ironically, this contentious relation took place in countries where governments themselves received substantial amounts of foreign aid, often making major parts of the governmental machinery dependent on such foreign funding.

The context of foreign funding was often complicated by the role of certain Western funders vis-à-vis the recipient organizations. As part of their institutional mechanisms, some funding agencies were involved in an attempt to brand recipients. This could take place visually, through a requirement to produce funded publications or meetings or other programmatic work using the logo of the funder, or through funders' attempts to influence the narrative of the recipient groups by adding dimensions to the narrative that did not necessarily emerge from the local context—a practice that could further alienate recipient groups from local communities and dynamics, embedding them in a conduct foreign to their locality. Moreover, some international funders defined their funding priorities in an overprescriptive way. Major issues within the domestic context ended up being marginalized.

Furthermore, the Arab region witnessed consistent threats to security and numerous eruptions of conflicts, with the main one being the Israeli occupation and violation of the rights of the Palestinian people. This situation kept security and peace concerns, including the humanitarian aid dimension, at the top of civil society's agenda. To a significant extent, it also shaped the narratives of civil society groups and alliance building among them.

Often, the reality reflected through the factors discussed above had the effect of focusing CSOs' priorities away from socioeconomic questions facing the region, and more toward civil and political rights. A study analyzing data from the first and second cycle of the Universal Periodic Review (UPR), which is undertaken under the auspices of the UN Human Rights Council, noted that "in situations of political tensions, where repressive policies and severe restrictions on civic life are in practice, NGOs highlight civil and political rights. . . . Conversely, in situations of relative stability, opportunities arise for CSOs to engage the government on fine-tuning its human rights practice, and their concerns are spread more evenly across the spectrum of human rights issues. . . . It may be that if a country is relatively stable and not facing significant political crises, everyone—States and civil society—can be free to pursue the necessary agenda of development and focus more on important economic and social issues facing the country."[16]

Yet global policies and policy making have created new spaces for civil society groups to work together more effectively. Linking up with global channels of mobilization and international solidarity movements has often provided alternative channels of influence that could affect national governments. Yet generally CSOs in the Arab region have not participated as much in global campaigns and movements as CSOs from other regions.[17] This is partly because CSOs in the Arab region often find themselves overwhelmed by domestic and local agendas, limiting their interest and capacities to participate in regional and global processes. Moreover, CSOs from the Arab region often see no potential to change this system. They are also concerned about international laws and institutions reflecting double standards, unbalanced representation, and being exploited as a tool for dominance. Given this context, CSOs in the Arab region have approached engagement with the UN by focusing on advocacy vis-à-vis the UN bodies. They attempt to find a role in agenda setting inside the UN and in holding the UN agencies and processes accountable to their development mandate.

Often civil society spokespeople are cautious about the development narrative developed inside the UN, considering it to be the result of compromises between governments, from both the North and the South, and the result of influence from multiple stakeholders, including corporate actors. CSOs are often expected to present an alternative narrative to that of the UN, or at least a complementary one. But for this to happen, UN instruments need to serve as a platform for CSOs to engage in dialogue with governments, particularly in the human rights milieu. The UN's role with regard to human rights has become especially prominent in the Arab region given the limited role that the League of Arab States has played in this regard, and the barriers for effective engagement between the League of Arab States and CSOs.

THE EFFECT OF ARAB POPULAR REVOLUTIONS AND UPRISINGS ON CSO-UN RELATIONS

Civil society dynamics in various Arab countries have been systematically undermined by the political regimes in power through restrictions and violations with regard to CSOs' freedom of association, expression, and action. This has been part of regimes' efforts to prevent the emergence of effective opposition movements.

The developments in the region since the year 2011 have reinforced that civil society and social movements are key stakeholders in enriching and preserving the continuous struggle for democracy, freedom, and alternative thinking about political, social, and economic conditions and policies. Yet this opening quickly met with a backlash in several Arab countries. The popular uprisings, revolutions, and continuous mobilizations witnessed in various shapes and forms, including the reemergence of labor unions in Tunisia, Egypt, Morocco, Lebanon, and Jordan, among other countries, have signaled a new era for the role of CSOs and their standing in relation to political power and public policy making in general.

Nevertheless, since 2011 several Arab countries have attempted to suppress these movements, by tightening the legal framework.[18] Moreover, Western funding has remained a controversial issue and has been used as a pretext for crackdowns on foreign-funded NGOs. The most dramatic case has been the crackdown by the Egyptian government in December 2011 that led to the closure of eight NGOs.

On another front, this period of massive political change that several Arab countries have witnessed since 2011 has brought to the forefront the issue of how socioeconomic development in the region is connected with democratization. It has highlighted CSOs' necessary role of attending to this question and exploring new avenues of influence to shape policy: downward connections to grassroots groups, communities, and noninstitutional forms of mobilization emerging in several Arab countries and upward connections with actors leading public policy making.

CSOs face the challenge of shifting from a defensive position to the more proactive and public role of elaborating and promoting alternatives on all fronts, political, social, and economic. They are also closer to the processes of policy making than before. They have a major role in ensuring that reforms integrate concepts of justice, human rights, nondiscrimination, and equality.

At this point, UN agencies recognize more clearly the need to connect more with civil society dynamics in the region, which have been central to the development of the Arab uprisings. For example, the UNDP launched a new strategy for working in countries of the region, one that is geared to engaging diverse stakeholders including CSOs and community-based organizations. CSOs, according to the UNDP's statement, are "crucial partners in bringing about concrete, sustainable, and nationally-owned change at all levels of society."[19]

Thus for both the UN and CSOs, similar questions have arisen from this period of change, including how to understand these dynamics and what kind of internal changes need to be made to respond to what has been witnessed on the streets of multiple Arab cities.

The interface between CSOs and the UN in the Arab region has been primarily shaped by CSOs' quest to protect their right to association and participation from the practices of repressive regimes. This was reflected through their active engagement with the UN human rights arms. Driven by the need to respond to repressive governmental measures, the human rights movement has been more mature in the region than other civil society groups and has taken a greater role across the region.

CSOs from the Arab region have been less engaged with UN processes and agencies on development issues than on political and civil rights issues. This is so for several reasons, including CSOs' limited attention to social and economic questions, especially before the revolutions and popular mobilizations in 2010/2011. Another reason is the disenchantment among some CSOs with the role of the UN and the development narrative and agenda it promotes. As for the International Labour Organization, the tripartite dialogue (between the governments, employers' groups, and unions) has languished in the Arab countries for a while, given the backlash against organized labor movements and unions.

The following section explores different dimensions of CSO-UN relationships by presenting four cases of CSO-UN engagement in the Arab region: CSOs' involvement in the MDGs and the post-2015 development framework discussions;[20] their use of UN human rights mechanisms; their defense of UNCTAD; and their engagement with the AHDRs.

The Millennium Development Goals

The MDGs were launched in the year 2000, with the commitment of all world leaders to achieving them by the year 2015. They came out of global development conferences that the UN led throughout the 1990s and were a practical reflection of the Millennium Declaration (2000). All Arab countries were among the 189 states that committed to the Millennium Declaration and to the achievement of the eight MDGs by the year 2015. Arab countries have participated in the preparation of national reports on the MDGs.

Yet there has been a broad consensus, especially after a decade of the MDGs' implementation, that they represent a watered-down development agenda. The MDGs have overlooked core systemic development questions in the quest to build a targeted, quantifiable, and easily monitored agenda.

Besides ignoring systemic issues, the MDGs have focused on the responsibilities of developing countries in terms of achieving national development goals. The agenda does not effectively address the shared responsibility of the developed countries and their role in contributing an enabling environment for sustainable development. Furthermore, the MDGs do not cover employment and job creation. In 2008, a partial target on employment was added to the MDGs. Consequently, many civil society groups have perceived the MDGs as an agenda that propagates aid dependency among developing countries and does not provide a balance in addressing the responsibilities of developing and developed countries.

Discussion on MDGs in the Arab region was primarily led by UN agencies, which tried to get CSOs on board. Several meetings involving UN agencies and CSOs were held in the region, such as regional meetings organized by ANND, starting in the year 2005. In a report to the Social Watch in 2005, ANND noted, "When looking at the MDGs as an agenda for development in the Arab region, one should consider that development policies are not a priority for most Arab States, and it is often overshadowed by the complex political dynamics that the region faces."[21] This statement still reflects a significant part of what makes engagement between civil society, the UN, and governments in the Arab region problematic.

In the case of the MDGs, the UN agencies were not able to create a space for deeper dialogue between governments and CSOs on development priorities in the Arab region. At the same time, the MDGs agenda did not mobilize CSOs' widespread and consistent engagement, since many were skeptical about its efficacy. This was partly because they perceived an imbalance in the interests that shaped the agenda. For example, it lacked a human rights framework and thus alienated much of the human rights movement. It also did not tackle systemic issues at the heart of the interests of CSOs working on development policies.

Addressing systemic issues has been a central priority for CSOs tackling development challenges in the Arab region and globally. For example, a statement issued by CSOs from the Arab region participating in the 1995 World Summit on Sustainable Development noted that the summit did not address the real reasons and responsibilities behind poverty, marginalization, unemployment, and other social ills. The statement stressed the need to consider national social problems within the global context and to look at the impact of structural adjustment policies, financial policies, and the global trading system on development trends. The statement also addressed the need for debt cancellation as a right for developing countries, the importance of reforming the basics of free trade and open markets in the world, and the quest to balance employment needs and unjustifiable restrictions on movement of labor.[22]

The weakness of institutional structures and the lack of transparency of policy making in the Arab region limit CSOs' opportunities for effective monitoring and engagement in the policy-making process. Overall in the MDGs-related processes, CSOs from the Arab region exhibited caution regarding the UN discourse on the goals, which they often perceived as a UN agenda and not a nationally owned one.

The discussions on the post-2015 development agenda and Sustainable Development Goals represent the current global platform for the debate that will construct the future narrative on development. Unlike the MDGs, this agenda will be the result of negotiations among UN member states. It also incorporates some lessons learned from the MDG experience, specifically the need to address the systemic issues emerging out of the global economic and financial policies as well as trade and investment regimes.

CSOs from the Arab region have been actively participating in this process.[23] Two issues are problematic. One is the expanding role of corporate actors in shaping this agenda, especially through the increasing role of private finance inside the UN.[24] The other is the vested interest of certain UN development agencies in a fund-generating agenda, similar to that of the MDGs, that they could lead. These factors are causing significant tension between UN agencies and CSOs that are calling for an inclusive representative process. They are also impeding cooperation between the UN and CSOs in this process.

The Universal Periodic Review

In a tradition of engagement with UN human rights mechanisms, CSOs from the Arab region have been utilizing the Universal Periodic Review (UPR) mechanism, established in 2006,[25] to hold states accountable to their human rights obligations. Fateh Azzam—previously head of the Middle East Regional office of the High Commissioner for Human Rights (OHCHR)—noted that the UPR brings "the traditional methods of 'naming and shaming' into new perspective . . . and represents an important 'social accountability' mechanism."[26]

Research commissioned by the OHCHR Middle East Regional Office found that between 2004 and 2009 national NGOs within the Arab region made sixty-six submissions to nine treaty bodies, more than a third of which were to the CEDAW (Convention on the Elimination of Discrimination against Women) and CRC (Convention on the Right of the Child) committees.[27] In comparison, national NGOs offered 192 UPR submissions through its first cycle of four years.[28] Their engagement with the UPR is an extension of the engagement over decades with human rights treaty bodies through submission of shadow reports and engagement with mandate holders appointed by the Human Rights Council (previously the Commission on Human Rights).

The interactions with human rights bodies have generally involved more cooperation and less tension between CSOs and UN bodies than interactions around the MDGs agenda, perhaps partly because the benchmark for reference, the international human rights conventions and governments' obligations in this regard, is a well-established human rights framework. Thus UN agencies active in this space are considered neutral arbiters that focus only on the human rights–based approach and framework and do not otherwise play a role in shaping the debate or policy, as is the case in the broader development issues.[29]

Furthermore, the UPR provided a cooperative framework and opportunity for CSOs at the national and regional levels to be part of formal discussions of human rights conditions in their countries. It also gave them an opportunity to engage in more discussion with governments on how to further human rights in their countries. In the Arab region, the cooperation between civil society groups and the regional office of the High Commissioner for Human Rights played a major role in facilitating and enhancing the role of CSOs in this area. This experience reflects the importance of outreach mechanisms at the UN that are dedicated to engaging CSOs and facilitating their participation in UN processes.

The UPR reviews spurred several initiatives for collaborative work among CSOs in the Arab region. Groups worked together across multiple fields of expertise to present collective reports on the status of human rights in their countries. For example, in 2010, more than twenty groups in Lebanon came together to submit a joint report on economic and social rights to the UPR process of Lebanon.[30] The coalition included groups working in various areas of specialization including women's rights, rights of people with disabilities, labor rights, and the right to education. Similarly, coalitions worked together on joint submissions for the UPR reviews of Yemen, Egypt, Tunisia, Sudan, Jordan, Syria, and Bahrain.

Moreover, the work of CSOs on human rights education and capacity building—such as the work of the Arab Institute for Human Rights based in Tunisia—presents a successful model for spreading human rights education and advocacy across the Arab region. It reflects the importance of specialized capacity-building interventions among CSOs, especially those that enable CSOs to benefit more from UN mechanisms and processes.

United Nations Conference on Trade and Development

Globally, CSOs have considered UNCTAD as an alternative voice in global governance. UNCTAD was established in 1964 to offer analysis and advice to UN member states on development issues related to trade, finance, and technology. It focused on supporting developing countries to strengthen their position in international economic affairs and to design national development strategies. The importance of UNCTAD's work was highlighted during the period of the global financial and economic crisis. While the Bretton Woods institutions had been consistently promoting policies of liberalization and deregulation of markets and finance, which produced the crisis, UNCTAD's analysis consistently pointed out the dangers of these policies, especially through its flagship *Trade and Development Report*.

At the thirteenth conference of UNCTAD (UNCTAD XIII) held in Doha, Qatar, in April 2012, UNCTAD's mandate came under attack from a group of developed countries.[31] Some Northern governments did not agree to "reaffirm" the mandate given to UNCTAD at its previous session that had been held in Accra in 2008.[32] The key contested paragraph in the negotiations called for UNCTAD to "continue, as a contribution to the work of the UN, research and analysis on the prospects of, and impact on, developing countries in matters of trade and development, in light of the global economic and financial crisis."[33] What happened in Doha was a more intense pushback against UNCTAD's alternative voice and role in considering key issues of interest to developing countries, although this trend had been ongoing for a long time.

The UNCTAD XIII Civil Society Forum opened on April 17 in Doha against the background of these worrying developments within the official negotiating process. CSOs mobilized across the corridors of the conference center in Doha and together with their peers in capitals to bring attention to the fierce attack launched on UNCTAD's mandate. Civil society groups extended their support to the Group of 77 and China, a group of over one hundred developing countries, in their pushback against this attack. They also put pressure on negotiators of countries leading the attack on UNCTAD's mandate by arranging one-on-one meetings with these negotiators and informing the media of the ongoing negotiations and sharing their insights about the fights taking place at the negotiations level. Together they held several press conferences and issued almost daily press releases.

The CSOs called for UNCTAD XIII's reaffirmation of the Accra Accord. They demanded that UNCTAD's crucial research and analytical work, especially on the global financial crisis and other development challenges, including those arising from globalization, be continued.[34] The CSOs' press release stated, "UNCTAD serves as an important countervailing forum where the interests of developing countries can be paramount when trade, development and interrelated issues are being discussed. This value and its proven track record is why the attack on UNCTAD's mandate has to be resisted."

Some groups, seeking to strengthen certain aspects of the final declaration, such as the language on debt sustainability, raised specific thematic issues for the negotiators to consider. Groups also provided analysis of various thematic areas key to UNCTAD's agenda and the conference's theme of inclusive and sustainable development, such as issues of investment, financial regulation, the World Trade Organization, debt, tax policy, food security, and the social protection floor.

The engagement of CSOs from the Arab region with UNCTAD more generally has been limited, perhaps partly because CSOs from the Arab region have not focused much on international economic governance issues, such as international trade, investment, and finance policies, and partly because the Arab region has had limited exposure to UNCTAD's work and analysis. Even so, during UNCTAD's XIII session that was held in Doha, CSOs from the Arab region joined CSOs from various regions of the world in the mobilizations to defend UNCTAD's mandate.[35]

The significant effort invested by CSOs from the Arab region, as part of broader civil society mobilization to preserve UNCTAD's mandate as an organization that addresses macroeconomic policies, finance, trade, and investment from a development perspective, has reflected the value that these groups placed on such a role within the United Nations. Indeed, it attests to the importance that CSOs from the Arab region give to the role of the UN as an alternative voice in global economic governance, especially at a time when the region is facing major questions on economic, social, and political fronts.

In the aftermath of the UNCTAD XIII conference, engagement between civil society groups and the UNCTAD secretariat increased. This was driven by the deeper realization by UNCTAD's leadership and secretariat that CSOs were essential allies in defending the mandate of the organization.

Arab Human Development Reports

The process of preparing and releasing the four AHDRs has been yet another UN arena in which CSOs of the Arab region have been actively engaged. The UNDP's Regional Bureau for Arab States published a series of the AHDRs starting with a report entitled *Creating Opportunities for Future Generations* in 2002, followed by three reports entitled *Building a Knowledge Society* (2003), *Towards Freedom in Arab Society* (2004), and *Empowerment of Arab Women* (2005). A fifth report, entitled *Challenges to Human Security in Arab Countries*, was published in 2009.[36]

The AHDRs define development as the increase of human freedom through enlargement of the choices available to people.[37] The third AHDR, released in 2004, tackles the central issue of freedom and outlines several deficiencies in the Arab region, including curtailment of freedom of expression and association, government threats to individuals' lives, abuse of minorities, discrimination against women, malnutrition, and poor education.[38]

The reports were broadly supported among CSOs in the Arab region because they presented an important tool for advocacy, especially at the national and regional levels. With their authoritative UN backing for some bold opinions on the situation of democratic practice and development challenges in the Arab region, the reports could be used by CSOs to advance positions they had been calling for in such areas as the right to information and women's rights. According to Michael Fakhri, "The 'reports' greatest strength is that their tone and substance helps empower individuals to overcome defeatism and encourages the criticism of entrenched autocracies and international powers."[39]

While the AHDR initiative was well received among CSOs in the Arab region, the UN agencies fell short of capitalizing on the dynamic created by the reports to spur a constructive policy dialogue inside the UN system among Arab-region governments, intergovernmental agencies such as the League of Arab States, and CSOs. The Arab governments seemed to adopt "a strategy of almost completely ignoring the AHDRs," which held them responsible for the deteriorating situation in Arab countries.[40] As one of the authors of the AHDRs noted, Arab governments avoided lending credence to the reports and instead reacted to them with "disregard, evasion, negligence, and occasionally casting doubts." The author added, however, that the reports were intended not only for governments but for the Arab people in general.[41]

Yet overall the experience with the reports again attested to the importance that CSOs in the Arab region place on the UN's role as a platform for policy dialogue. CSOs that are active at the policy level used the reports to assert the centrality of democratization for development processes in the Arab region. The reports' central message that no development is possible without democracy, which includes an active role by civil society and fulfillment of women's rights, recaptured the focus on freedom, democracy, and development in the research and policy discussions in the region.[42]

CHALLENGES FACING THE REGION

This essay attempts to demonstrate that the relationship between CSOs and the UN in the context of development in the Arab region is shaped by two major dimensions: by the subjective nature of CSOs' role and the priorities they set, and by the thematic area of engagement and the nature of operations of the involved UN agencies. CSOs' engagements with the UN in the Arab region have reflected their quest to find at the UN a platform for policy dialogue with governments and for an alternative development narrative. This has been demonstrated through their engagements with the MDGs agenda, UNCTAD, and the AHDRs.

CSOs' engagements with the UN in the Arab region have also reflected their quest for ways to hold their governments accountable and for *protective shields* from the backlash against CSOs' role at the national levels. This has been demonstrated in the various forms of engagement with the UN human rights mechanisms.

A major challenge facing CSOs is to insist on effective and transparent monitoring, reporting, and accountability mechanisms in the UN with regard to corporate influences and corporate benefit from official development aid. The changing nature of influence exerted by corporate actors and private finance in the agenda setting of the UN is a defining factor for the future of the whole UN system and its role.

Platforms for dialogue on development policies have been important areas for engagement between CSOs and the UN in the Arab region. Such platforms should effectively engage the relevant executive bodies from Arab countries, global UN agencies advancing alternative development thinking, such as UNCTAD, and regional bodies such as the League of Arab States.

The effectiveness of such interventions depends on UN agencies' ability to avoid competition among the mandates of various agencies, to nurture consistency in agency processes, and to avoid the duplicative work that sometimes results from one-time conferences that are detached from a longer-term vision.

Moreover, the success of such processes depends on the ability of the UN and CSOs to build a narrative based on the needs and specifics of the region and to avoid blanket importation of narratives from global mainstream approaches. Furthermore, there is a need to increase and improve the tools for engagement between CSOs and the UN in the Arab region.

NOTES

I thank Ziad Abdel Samad, executive director of the Arab NGO Network for Development, for his input, and Vijay Prashad for his input and suggestions on multiple drafts. The responsibility for the content of the essay, and any errors in it, are fully my own.

1. Resolution 1996/31 presented the formal legal framework for relations between the UN and nongovernmental organization (NGO) relations and replaced Resolution 1296 (XLIV) of 1968, advancing on it by explicitly opening up UN consultative status to national NGOs. Resolution 1296 had established for consultative status of NGOs with the UN, laying down the principles governing the nature of the consultative arrangement and separately addressing consultations with the Economic and Social Council, with commissions and other subsidiary organs of the Council, with ad hoc committees of the Council, and with international conferences called by the Council. The resolution provides that an NGO "shall undertake to support the work of the United Nations and to promote knowledge of its principles and activities, in accordance with its own aims and purposes and the nature and scope of its competence and activities." UN Economic and Social Council, ECOSOC Resolution 1296 (XLIV), May 23, 1968, https://www.globalpolicy.org/component/content/article/177/31832.html.

2. Tony Hill, "Three Generations of UN-Civil Society Relations: A Quick Sketch," UN Communications Group, UNCG/2006/12, June 2006, www.cinu.org.mx/comgroup/regional2006/docs/NGLS-12.doc. There were some exceptions to this, in particular the Stockholm Conference on the Human Environment in 1972

and the work of International Coalition for Development Action and others that engaged in the North-South Dialogue for a New International Economic Order (under UNCTAD's auspices) through the 1970s and early 1980s.

3. Ibid. In 1993, partly in response to the experience of NGO participation in the Rio Conference of 1992, a working group established by the UN Economic and Social Council began a review and evaluation of relations with NGOs. In 1996, Resolution 1996/31 was adopted as the formal, legal framework for UN-NGO relations, explicitly opening up UN consultative status to national NGOs. It replaced Resolution 1296 of May 1968. Article 71 of the UN Charter provides that the Economic and Social Council "may make suitable arrangements for consultation with non-governmental organizations which are concerned with matters within its competence." UN Economic and Social Council, ECOSOC Resolution 1996/31, July 25, 1996, www.un.org/esa/coordination/ngo/Resolution_1996_31/.

4. ANND also took an active role in the discussions around the reform of the UN, which built up toward and followed up on the "Cardoso Report" (UN General Assembly, Panel of Eminent Persons on United Nations–Civil Society Relations, "We the Peoples: Civil Society, the United Nations and Global Governance," A58/817, June 11, 2004, https://www.globalpolicy.org/images/pdfs/0611report.pdf). The report was prepared by a twelve-member panel of eminent persons that was appointed by the UN secretary-general in February 2003. Its mandate included a review of existing practices involving civil society at the UN with a view to identifying new and better ways for the UN system to interact, in particular with developing-country NGOs and CSOs. The report was criticized by CSOs, some of which claimed that the report "carries all the dangers of creating a bureaucracy within a bureaucracy. Its major drawback is that, in its approach to global governance, it fails to take account of the imbalances and injustices in the UN's own Security Council as well as global trade and financial institutions" (see Third World Network, "The Cardoso Report on UN-Civil Society Relations: A Third World Network Analysis," August 2004, www.un-ngls.org/orf/o8twn.pdf) and that the changes proposed by the report "could weaken the role of NGOs and even undermine the UN's legislative function in favor of ill defined 'multi-constituency dialogues'" (see Global Policy Forum, "Panel of Eminent Persons on United Nations–Civil Society Relations (Cardoso Panel), 2002–2004)," n.d., accessed March 17, 2016, https://www.globalpolicy.org/empire/32340-panel-of-eminent-persons-on-united-nations-civil-society-relations-cardoso-panel.html).

5. Ziad Abdel Samad, "Civil Society in the Arab Region: Its Necessary Role and the Obstacles to Fulfillment," *International Journal of Not-for-Profit Law* 9, no. 2 (April 2007), www.icnl.org/research/journal/vol9iss2/special_1.htm.

6. See Moataz Abdel Fattah, "Impact of the Arab Human Development Reports," September 9, 2009, Carnegie Endowment website, http://carnegieendowment.org/2009/09/09/impact-of-arab-human-development-reports/fih9.

7. For more on think tanks in the Arab region, see UN Development Programme (hereafter UNDP) and Foundation for the Future, "Arab Think Tanks Directory: Policy-Oriented Research Centers amid Transitions," n.d., accessed November 14,

2014, www.foundationforfuture.org/en/Portals/0/Conferences/Think%20
Tank%20Forum/Directory%20of%20Arab%20Think%20Tanks.pdf.

8. Hill, "Three Generations."

9. See Barbara Adams and Gretchen Luchsinger, "Fit for Whose Purpose?," July 2015, Global Policy Forum, Global Policy Watch #8, www.globalpolicywatch.org /wp-content/uploads/2015/07/GPW8_2015_07_27.pdf.

10. Omari H. Kokole, "African and Arab States and the Call for a New International Economic Order," *Issue: A Journal of Opinion* 13 (1984): 14–19.

11. UNDP and Arab Fund for Economic and Social Development, *Arab Human Development Report 2002: Creating Opportunities for Future Generations* (New York: UNDP, 2002), 31, www.arab-hdr.org/publications/other/ahdr/ahdr2002e.pdf.

12. Ibid., 114.

13. Ibid., 117.

14. Ibid., 118.

15. *Zakat* is one of the five pillars of Islam and is expected to be paid by all practicing Muslims who have the financial means.

16. Fateh Azzam, *Arab States and UN Human Rights Mechanisms*, Research Report (Beirut: Issam Fares Institute for Public Policy and International Affairs, July 2013), 35, https://www.aub.edu.lb/ifi/public_policy/rapp/Documents/20130710ifi_ RAPP_rr_Arab_States_and_UN_Human_Rights_Mechanisms.pdf.

17. Ziad Abdel Samad and Kinda Mohamadieh, "The Arab NGO Network for Development: A Case Study on Interaction between Emerging Regional Networking and Global Civil Society," in *Critical Mass: The Emergence of Global Civil Society,* ed. James Walker and Andrew Thompson (Waterloo, Ont.: Wilfred Laurier University Press, 2008), 111–28; Ziad Abdel Samad and Kinda Mohamadieh, "The Role of CSOs in the Arab Region at the International Level: The Potential Rise of New International Solidarity Movements," 2010, CSR-DAR resource portal, http://csrdar.org/sites /default/files/RoleCSOs_ArabRegion_InternationalLevel.pdf.

18. The Cairo Institute for Human Rights documents how human rights defenders and the organizations with which they work have been subjected to serious attacks in the Arab region, particularly in Bahrain, Saudi Arabia, Egypt, and Algeria, where repressive legal frameworks are employed to prevent organizations from becoming legally registered or to criminalize rights activities and refer those involved in them to trial. See Cairo Institute for Human Rights Studies, "In Post-revolutionary Arab States, Rights Situation Dire," May 21, 2013, Ifex, https://www .ifex.org/middle_east_north_africa/2013/05/21/delivering_democracy/; Ziad Abdel Samad and Kinda Mohamadieh, "The Revolutions of the Arab Region: Socio-Economic Questions at the Heart of Successful Ways Forward," *Perspectives: Political Analysis and Commentary from the Middle East,* no. 2, April 2011, https:// ps.boell.org/sites/default/files/downloads/Perspectives_02–17_Ziad_Abdel_ Samad_and_Kinda_Mohamadieh3.pdf.

19. UNDP, "Civil Society and Civic Engagement in the Arab States Region," February 2013, www.undp.org/content/dam/undp/library/corporate/results /english/Results-CSO-ArabStates_E-7Feb2013.pdf.

20. The post-2015 development agenda encompasses the debate on what will replace the MDGs after they expire in 2015. The new agenda will reflect new development challenges and is linked to the outcome of "Rio + 20"—that is, the UN Conference on Sustainable Development—that took place in June 2012 in Rio de Janeiro, Brazil. These discussions cover the debate about a set of new global development goals, referred to as the Sustainable Development Goals, and the wider discussions on a post-2015 development framework. For more information, see UN Department of Public Information, "Beyond the Millennium Development Goals: The Post-2015 Sustainable Development Agenda," September 2013, www.un.org /millenniumgoals/pdf/EN_MDG_backgrounder.pdf.

21. Arab NGO Network for Development, "The Millennium Development Goals in the Arab Region: Review of a Five Year Period," Social Watch Report 2005, http://csrdar.org/sites/default/files/From%20ANND,%20report%20on%20 the%20MDGs.pdf.

22. Ziad Abdel Samad and Kinda Mohamadieh, "MDGs in the Arab Region: A Tool and a Challenge," Arab NGO Network for Development and the Social Watch, 2005, www.socialwatch.org/sites/default/files/pdf/en/mdgsarab2005_eng .pdf.

23. Declaration of Civil Society Organizations from the Arab Region on the Post-2015 Framework, March 14, 2013, Beirut, regional consultation on the Post-2015 Development Agenda, organized by the Arab NGO Network for Development and the UN Economic and Social Commission for West Asia, www.socialwatch .org/sites/default/files/Post2015-ArabRegion-CSODeclaration0313.pdf.

24. See, on this topic, the webcast of the event, "The Privatization of the Post-2015 Development Agenda?," April 2014, www.ustream.tv/channel/the-privatization-of-the-post-2015-development-agenda-issues-and-challenges-in-part-nerships-with-the-private-sector.

25. The UPR was created through UN General Assembly Resolution 60/251, adopted on March 15, 2006, which established the Human Rights Council itself. It is a cooperative process, which, as of October 2011, had reviewed the human rights records of all 193 UN member states. For more information, see OHCHR, "Universal Periodic Review," n.d., accessed November 10, 2014, www.ohchr.org/en /hrbodies/upr/pages/uprmain.aspx.

26. Fateh Azzam, *Arab States*, 35, and Azzam's chapter in this book.

27. Joseph Schechla, "The Use of Human Rights Mechanisms by Human Rights Defenders in the Middle East, 2004–2009," OHCHR Middle East Regional Office, June 2010.

28. Azzam, *Arab States*, 37.

29. Ibid.

30. Coalition of Civil Society Groups Active in Lebanon, "Joint UPR Submission on Economic and Social Rights, Lebanon," December 2010, www.annd .org/data/item/pdf/291.pdf.

31. Vijay Prashad, "UNCTAD: The South Stands Up to the North," *Third World Resurgence,* no. 260 (April 2012): 9–12.

32. Martin Khor, "Battle to Save UNCTAD's Mandate," *Star,* April 16, 2012.

33. Deborah James, "Victory at UNCTAD XIII—A Civil Society Perspective," *Third World Resurgence,* no. 260 (April 2012): 13–15.

34. The CSOs mobilizing in Doha were concerned that the JUSSCKANZ group of countries (Japan, the United States, Switzerland, Canada, South Korea, Australia, New Zealand) and the EU were so opposed to UNCTAD's vital analytical and advisory work on finance and responses to the crisis that they were refusing to even reaffirm UNCTAD's mandate as agreed upon in Accra. Third World Network, "Civil Society Says 'No' to Moves to Weaken UNCTAD's Mandate," reproduced from *South-North Development Monitor,* no. 7353 (April 19, 2012), and *Third World Resurgence,* no. 260 (April 2012): 23.

35. Our World Is Not for Sale, "Global Civil Society Calls on Governments to Strengthen, Not Weaken, UNCTAD's Role in Global Governance," sign-on letter delivered to negotiators at UNCTAD XIII in Doha, 2012, http://ourworldisnot forsale.org/it/node/24216.

36. UNDP, *Arab Human Development Report 2009: Challenges to Human Security in the Arab Countries* (New York: UNDP, 2009), www.arab-hdr.org /contents/index.aspx?rid=5.

37. Michael Fakhri, "Images of the Arab World and Middle East: Debates about Development and Regional Integration," *Wisconsin International Law Journal* 28, no. 3 (2011): 391–429.

38. Ibid.

39. Ibid.

40. Moataz Abdel Fattah, "Impact of the Arab Human Development Reports," Carnegie Endowment, September 2009, http://carnegieendowment.org/2009 /09/09/impact-of-arab-human-development-reports/fih9.

41. Nader Fergany, interview by Al Jazeera television, 2002, quoted in ibid.

42. Ziad Abdel Samad, executive director of ANND (see website at www.annd .org), interview, August 10, 2014.

CONTRIBUTORS

CAROLINE ABU SA'DA is Director of the Research Unit of Médecins Sans Frontières (MSF) Switzerland; Honorary Lecturer at the Humanitarian and Conflict Response Institute, University of Manchester; and Senior Research Associate and module convenor at the School of Advanced Studies, University of London. She has worked on food security, agriculture, and health issues and has coordinated programs in the Middle East for Oxfam GB, the United Nations, and MSF Switzerland. She has written several articles, reports, and books about humanitarian issues and has just recently finished a documentary, *Non-assistance*, that debuted at the International Film Festival and Forum on Human Rights in Geneva in March 2016.

LORI ALLEN is Senior Lecturer in Anthropology at the School of African and Oriental Studies (SOAS), University of London. She is the author of *The Rise and Fall of Human Rights: Cynicism and Politics in Occupied Palestine* (Stanford University Press, 2013).

FATEH AZZAM was Founding Director of the Asfari Institute for Civil Society and Citizenship at the American University of Beirut. Previously he was Regional Representative of the UN High Commissioner for Human Rights and held a number of other posts at the American University in Cairo, the Ford Foundation, the Palestinian human rights organization Al-Haq, and elsewhere. He led the process of establishing the Arab Human Rights Fund, the first Arab philanthropic organization focused on support for human rights activities, serving as its first chair for five years. He is currently a member of the Independent Commission for Human Rights, the Palestinian national human rights institution. He has authored numerous articles and studies in Arabic and English on human rights, the right to development, civil and political rights in Arab constitutions, the Responsibility to Protect, and other topics. He holds an LLM in international human rights law from the University of Essex.

JEFF BACHMAN is a Professorial Lecturer in Human Rights and Co-director of the Ethics, Peace, and Global Affairs MA Program at American University's School of International Service.

ASLI BÂLI is Professor of Law at the University of California, Los Angeles (UCLA) School of Law and Director of the UCLA Center for Near Eastern Studies. She teaches subjects in international law as well as the comparative law of the Middle East. She is the author of numerous articles, including "Troubling the Turkish 'Model' after the Uprisings" (2016), "Negotiating Non-proliferation" (2014), and "Pax Arabica: Provisional Sovereignty and Intervention in the Arab Uprisings" (with her coauthor, Aziz Rana; 2012). She also currently serves as a Turkey page editor for the e-zine *Jadaliyya* and as chair of the Advisory Committee for Human Rights Watch–Middle East.

POORVI CHITALKAR is a Senior Program Officer at the Global Centre for Pluralism (Ottawa, Canada). Prior to this, she worked at the International Development Research Centre and the Office of the Ontario Ombudsman and practiced law at the Bombay High Court. She holds an LLB from Symbiosis University (India) and an LLM from the University of Toronto (Canada).

OMAR DAHI is an Associate Professor of Economics at Hampshire College (USA). His publications have appeared in outlets such as the *Journal of Development Economics, Applied Economics, Forced Migration Review,* and *Southern Economic Journal.* From 2014 to 2016, he was a consultant for the National Agenda for the Future of Syria Program at the United Nations Economic and Social Commission for Western Asia (ESCWA).

NOURA ERAKAT is an Assistant Professor at George Mason University (GMU), where she teaches in the legal studies, international studies, and human rights/social justice studies concentrations. Her scholarly interests include humanitarian law, human rights law, refugee law, and national security law. She earned her BA and JD from Berkeley Law School and her LLM in national security from the Georgetown University Law Center. She is a cofounder and editor of *Jadaliyya* e-zine. Prior to beginning her appointment at GMU, she was a Freedman Teaching Fellow at Temple Law School, and she has taught international human rights law and the Middle East at Georgetown University since 2009.

RICHARD FALK is Albert G. Milbank Professor Emeritus of International Law at Princeton University and Research Fellow of the Orfalea Center of Global Studies at the University of California, Santa Barbara. His most recent books are *Humanitarian Intervention and Legitimacy Wars* (Routledge, 2014); *Palestine: The Legitimacy of Hope* (Just World Books, 2014); and *Chaos and Counterrevolution: After the Arab Spring* (Zed Books, 2015). Between 2008 and 2014 Falk served as UN Special Rapporteur on Human Rights in Occupied Palestine.

ANDREW GILMOUR has been the Director for Political, Peacekeeping, Humanitarian and Human Rights Affairs in the Office of the UN Secretary-General since 2012. Over a period of more than twenty-five years he has served four UN secretaries-general in Afghanistan, Lebanon, Jerusalem, Gaza, the Balkans, West Africa, Iraq, and South Sudan, as well as covering Middle East affairs in the office of Kofi Annan when he was secretary-general. He has master's degrees in modern history from Oxford University and in politics from the London School of

Economics. He was an Adjunct Fellow at the Center for Strategic and International Studies in Washington, D.C., and has contributed articles to a wide range of publications, including the *Times,* the *Spectator, Newsweek,* the *Nation,* the *Journal of Palestine Studies, Ethics and International Affairs, Christian Science Monitor,* and the *Chicago Tribune.*

FILIPPO GRANDI has been the United Nations High Commissioner for Refugees since January 1, 2016. Prior to that he was the Commissioner General of UNRWA, the UN Agency for Palestinians, from 2010 to 2014, after being its Deputy Commissioner-General for four years. He has worked in the area of international cooperation for thirty years, twenty-eight of them as a United Nations official. He has an honorary doctorate from the University of Coventry and was an Issam Fares Institute Senior Research Fellow in UN and International Affairs at the American University in Beirut, and an Honorary Associate of the Department of International Development of the University of Oxford.

WALID HAMDAN's career at the International Labour Organisation (ILO) ranged from the regional office in Beirut to the central office in Geneva, and from the post of Desk Officer for the Arab region desk of the ILO's Bureau for Workers' Activities (ILO-ACTRA) to that of Senior Labour Specialist.

CORALIE PISON HINDAWI is Assistant Professor of International Relations and International Law at the American University of Beirut. She is the author of the book *Vingt ans dans l'ombre du Chapitre VII* (Twenty years in the shadow of Chapter VII; L'Harmattan, 2013). She has been recently working on the doctrine of the Responsibility to Protect and has coauthored (with Karim Makdisi) *Creative Diplomacy amidst a Brutal Conflict: Analyzing the OPCW-UN Joint Mission for the Elimination of the Syrian Chemical Weapons Program* (Issam Fares Institute for Public Policy and International Affairs, 2016).

JALAL AL HUSSEINI is an Associate Research Fellow in political sociology at the French Institute for the Near East (IFPO) and a freelance consultant for numerous United Nations and international cooperation agencies. Based in Amman since 1997, he has specialized in refugee assistance issues and more broadly in the socio-economic and political development of the Middle East. Holder of a PhD obtained at the Graduate Institute of International Studies (Geneva), with a doctoral dissertation on the political dimensions of the mandate of the Relief and Works Agency for Palestine Refugees in the Near East (UNRWA), Al Husseini is the author of *Les Palestiniens entre État et diaspora* (Karthala, 2012).

ARAFAT JAMAL is a United Nations official with over twenty years of international experience focused on leadership in emergencies, operations management, interagency coordination, humanitarian diplomacy, refugee resettlement, multilateral negotiation, and the formulation and evaluation of policy. He currently heads the Inter-Agency Coordination Service of the Office of the United Nations High Commissioner for Refugees (UNHCR). His Middle East/North Africa experience includes serving as UNHCR's Team Leader Libya (2011), Deputy Representative Jordan (2008–12) and Regional Resettlement Head Lebanon (2005–8); he has also served in western Asia, Africa, and Geneva. He has authored several papers focusing on topics such as minimum standards and essential needs, the practical meaning of refugee protection, and emergency response. He has a master's in forced migration (Oxon) and a BA in history and BSc in urban and regional studies (Cornell).

SUSANN KASSEM is a PhD candidate in anthropology and sociology at the Graduate Institute of International and Development Studies in Geneva. She holds an MA in Middle Eastern studies from the American University of Beirut and a BA in European ethnology from Humboldt University of Berlin. She is researching the intersection of UN peacekeeping, development initiatives, and political containment in southern Lebanon.

RAJA KHALIDI is a development economist educated at the Universities of Oxford and London who has researched and published since 1981 on Palestinian economic conditions in Lebanon, Israel, and the Occupied Territory. He served with the United Nations Conference on Trade and Development (UNCTAD) from 1985 to 2013, including as its Coordinator of Assistance to the Palestinian people. He currently lives in Palestine and works as a Senior Economist with the Palestine Economic Policy Research Institute (MAS).

SHADEN KHALLAF is Senior Policy Officer for the United Nations High Commissioner for Refugees' Middle East and North Africa Bureau and has been working on displacement issues in the region for seventeen years. Her areas of experience have included refugee status determination, repatriation and postconflict transitions, refugee women and child protection, advocacy and communications, strategic partnerships with regional organizations, goodwill ambassador management, and public affairs. She has also lectured at the Department of Law and Center for Migration and Refugee Studies in the School of Global Affairs and Public Policy at the American University in Cairo (AUC). She is a member of the AUC President's Advisory Council and is a fellow at the Graduate Institute for International and Development Studies, and she has published numerous papers on displacement in the Middle East/North Africa.

KARIM MAKDISI is Associate Professor of International Politics and Director of the Program in Public Policy and International Affairs at the American University of Beirut (AUB). He is the Research Director of the UN in the Arab World program at the Issam Fares Institute for Public Policy and International Affairs at the AUB and has previously worked at the UN Economic and Social Commission for West Asia (ESCWA). Makdisi is, most recently, the coeditor of *Interventions in Conflict: International Peacekeeping in the Middle East* (Palgrave-Macmillan, 2016), and *Creative Diplomacy amidst a Brutal Conflict: Analyzing the OPCW-UN Joint Mission for the Elimination of the Syrian Chemical Weapons Program* (coauthor with Coralie Pison Hindawi, Issam Fares Institute for Public Policy and International Affairs, 2016).

DAVID M. MALONE has been the Rector of the UN University since 2003. Prior to that he served as President of Canada's International Development Research

Centre; Canada's Representative to the UN Economic and Social Council; and Ambassador to the United Nations. Malone has also published extensively, most recently *The UN Security Council in the 21st Century* (coeditor, 2015, Lynne Rienner Publishers); *The Oxford Handbook of Indian Foreign Policy* (coeditor, 2015, Oxford University Press); and *Law and Practice of the United Nations* (coauthor, 2016, Oxford University Press).

ZACHARIAH MAMPILLY is Director of the Program in Africana Studies and Associate Professor of Political Science at Vassar College. He is the author of *Rebel Rulers: Insurgent Governance and Civilian Life during War* (Cornell University Press, 2011) and, with Adam Branch, *Africa Uprising: Popular Protest and Political Change* (Zed Books, 2015).

KINDA MOHAMADIEH is Research Associate at the South Centre, where her work pertains to trade law, investment agreements, and corporate liability in the area of human rights. She previously worked as Policy Advisor at the Arab NGO Network for Development, addressing development and economic policies in the Arab region. Kinda holds an LLM. in International and European Economic Law from the University of Lausanne and a master's degree in public affairs and international development from the University of California, Los Angeles.

VIJAY PRASHAD is Professor of International Studies at Trinity College and Senior Non-Resident Fellow at the Issam Fares Institute for Public Policy and International Affairs at the American University of Beirut. His most recent book is *The Death of a Nation and the Future of the Arab Revolution* (University of California Press and LeftWord Books, 2016). He is a columnist for *Frontline*, *BirGün*, and *Alternet*, as well as a frequent contributor for the *Hindu*. He is the Chief Editor at LeftWord Books (New Delhi).

AZIZ RANA is a Professor of Law and member of the fields of government, history, and peace studies at Cornell University. He is the author of *The Two Faces of American Freedom* (Harvard University Press, 2010) and is currently writing a book on the rise of constitutional veneration in twentieth-century American politics.

HANS-CHRISTOF VON SPONECK was UN Assistant Secretary-General in Baghdad (1998–2000) as well as UN Resident Coordinator (Gaborone, Islamabad, and New Delhi) and is currently a Fellow at the Conflict Research Centre of the University of Marburg (Germany).

MANDY TURNER is the Director of the Kenyon Institute (Council for British Research in the Levant) in East Jerusalem, occupied Palestine, and a Visiting Fellow at the Middle East Centre, London School of Economics. Her research focuses thematically on the political economy of conflict and peace, particularly Western donor-led peacebuilding interventions. Her most recent publications include *The Politics of International Intervention: the Tyranny of Peace* (coedited with Florian Kuhn; Routledge, 2016) and *Decolonizing Palestinian Political Economy: De-development and Beyond* (coedited with Omar Shweiki; Palgrave Macmillan, 2015).

INDEX

Abbas, Mahmoud, 106
Abdallah, King of Saudi Arabia, 42
Abdullah, King of Jordan, 361–62
Abuzayd, Karen, 326
Academic Council on the United Nations
    System, 12–13
Accra Accord, 496, 503n34
Action Group for Syria, 122
Afghanistan, 126, 139n11, 182, 240, 356n8,
    384n1; Soviet invasion of, 171
Africa-India Forum Summit, 245
African Union, 213, 238, 245
Afro-Asian-Latin American group, 61,
    70n70
Agency for International Development,
    487
Ahmed, Ismail Ould Cheikh, 44
Ahmedinejad, Mahmoud, 125
Ahwazi, 348
Al-Ahram Center for Strategic Studies,
    484
Albright, Madeleine, 176, 209n26, 300n47
Algeria, 47, 153, 356n8, 394–95, 501n18
Ali Pasha, Muhammad, 402
Al Jazeera, 103
Allawi, Iyad, 181
Al-Nusra Front, 183
Al Qaeda, 151, 165n18, 181; September 11,
    2001, attacks by, 77, 79, 150, 177, 197, 431
Amal, 467–48
American University of Beirut, 17, 485
American University of Cairo, 485
Amnesty International, 225

Amorim, Celso, 291–92, 299n35
Amos, Valerie, 380
Anbari, Abdul, 297n13
Angola, 235
Annan, Kofi, 34–40, 48–50, 51n1,
    54nn42,43, 55n46, 57nn72,74, 187; Iraq
    sanctions policies of, 283, 288, 290, 292,
    296, 297n15; during Israel-Lebanon
    War, 157, 158; personal envoy to Quartet
    of, 55n46; special representative
    appointed to UNAMI by, 179; Syrian
    mediation attempts of, 7, 121–24,
    126–27, 135, 139n7
Annexation Wall, 103, 109
anticolonialism, 68, 71–72n12, 104, 393
anti-Semitism, accusations of, 33, 54n39,
    54n40, 76, 80, 86–87
apartheid, 61–62, 87, 89, 99, 107–8
Arab Charter on Human Rights, 267
Arab Human Development Reports
    (AHDRs), 487, 491, 497–98
Arab Institute for Human Rights, 494
Arab-Israeli wars, 5, 9, 15, 28–29. *See also*
    Israel-Lebanon War; Six Day War; of
    1948, 1, 51n1, 85, 314n1, 320, 355n
Arab Labour Organization, 456
Arab League, 58, 139n11, 349, 489, 497, 499;
    during Libyan crisis, 213, 214; ratifica-
    tion of human rights treaties by mem-
    bers of, 256; United Nations collabora-
    tive peace efforts in Syria with, 121–23,
    126, 128, 137; UNRWA and, 323, 332
Arab Nationalist Movement, 393, 402, 404

Arab NGO Network for Development
(ANND), 482–84, 492, 500n4
Arab Spring, 7, 11, 42, 48, 399
Arafat, Yasser, 30, 36, 86, 98, 101, 418, 421,
440, 441
Armistice Line, 107
Assad, Bashar al-, 37, 40, 44, 115–28, 130,
185, 382
association, freedom of, 139n5, 263, 485,
489; workers' rights for, 273n35, 449,
451, 452, 454–57, 458n2
Assyrians, 349
asylum, 336, 337, 340–46, 351, 362, 364
Atassi, Jamal, 393
Athisaari, Martti, 278, 297n4
atrocities. See war crimes
Australia, 79, 128, 140n17
Aziz, Tariq, 282
Azzam, Fateh, 484

Baath Party, 181, 348, 393
Bahais, 181, 349
Bahrain, 27–28, 257, 258, 400, 449,
454–44, 458n4; human rights practices
in, 262–64, 268, 495, 501n18
Baker, James, 101, 173
Balad party, 104
Balfour Declaration, 85
Bandaranaike, Sirimavo, 62
Bandung Conference (1955), 61
Bangladesh, 234, 235, 237
Ban Ki-moon, 39–49, 51n1, 55n56,
56nn57,62,64, 79, 212; during Syrian
crisis by, 121, 125, 126, 140n13
Baradei, Mohammad El, 178
Barak, Ehud, 35–36
Barnard, Anne, 140n13
Bashir, Omar al-, 240
Bayat, Asef, 397
Bedjaoui, Mohammaed, 394
Ben Ali, Zine El Abidine, 120
Benghazi massacre, 215
Ben-Gurion, David, 23–24, 52n15
Benomar, Jamal, 43
Bernadotte, Count Folke, 2, 22–23, 52n6
Berthoud, Paul, 400
Bir Zeit University, 420
Black, Ian, 140n17

Blair, Tony, 287
Blix, Hans, 178
Blue Line, 36, 38, 156, 462–65, 468–69, 471,
475, 476, 477n16
Bokova, Irina, 220
Bolton, John, 76
Bosnia, 34, 56n62, 215
Boston Globe, 214–15
Boston Marathon bombing, 79
Bothe, Michael, 379
Bouckaert, Peter, 224, 225
Boutros-Ghali, Boutros, 30, 32–34, 50, 51n1,
54nn39,42, 57nn66,67; Agenda for Peace
report of, 431, 460; independence of
office asserted by, 49, 57n72; Oil-for-
Food program initiated by, 54n42, 282
Bowles, Samuel, 396
Boycott, Divestment, and Sanctions (BDS)
campaign, 89–90, 107
boycotts, 58, 59, 124, 172, 195, 204, 440;
against Israel, 89–90, 107, 404
Brahimi, Lakhdar, 7, 124–27, 129,
139n11, 180
Brazil, 153, 214, 235, 245, 299n35, 349.
See also BRICS
Bremer, Paul, 180
Bretton Woods institutions of (BWIs),
410, 414, 417–20, 423, 495
Bretton Woods system, 393, 394. See also
International Monetary Fund, World
Bank
BRICS, 244, 245, 323
Britain. See also United Kingdom;
Palestine Mandate of, 1, 21, 46, 85,
96, 477n16
British Empire, 10, 231–32, 234
Brown, Gordon, 189
Buddhism, 53n20
Bunche, Ralph, 2, 22–23, 26–28, 52n8
Burke, Roland, 70n12
Bush, George H. W., 5, 31, 173–75,
200–201, 205
Bush, George W., 36, 39, 163, 165n18, 240,
418; human rights violations during
presidency of, 75; Middle East reconfig-
ured by policies of, 104, 150–52, 184;
National Security Strategy of, 177–78
Butler, Richard, 186

Cairo Declaration on Human Rights in Islam, 267

Cairo Institute for Human Rights, 501n18

Cameron, David, 141n31, 224

Camp David Accords, 36, 102, 171, 329, 418

Canada, 79, 92n2, 181, 323

Cardoso Report, 500n4

Carnegie Endowment, 485

Castle, Stephen, 141n31

Center for Arab Unity Studies, 484

Center for Migration and Refugee Studies, 485

Center for United Nations Peacekeeping (New Delhi), 236

Central African Republic, 377

Central Intelligence Agency (CIA), 175

Ceylon, 62

Chaldeans, 349

Chandler, David, 158

chemical weapons, 7–9, 46, 124, 129–32, 136, 178, 184

Chesterman, Simon, 173, 214

Chile, 343, 349

China, 171, 185, 226, 235, 343, 440, 495. See also BRICS, P5; in Action Group for Syria, 122; Responsibility to Protect misused by, 6, 190; Security Council interventions opposed by, 128, 129, 153, 205, 213

Chirac, Jacques, 166n34

Christians, Iraqi, 42, 181, 348–50

Churchill, Winston, 21–22, 232

Civilian Military Coordination (CIMIC), 461, 467, 474, 477n12

civil society, 43, 75, 89–91, 255, 264–70. See also nongovernmental organizations; Lebanese, 467, 474; Palestinian, 103, 111

Clapp, Gordon R., 392

Clinton, Bill, 33, 36, 155–56, 209–10n31, 287, 297n11

Clinton, Hillary, 40, 140n12, 224

Cluster Approach, 384–85n1

coalition building, 485

Coalition Provisional Authority (CPA), 180–82

Cold War, 6, 31, 32, 177, 186, 233, 302. See also post-Cold War period; anti-imperialism during, 10, 393, 398; Arab-Israeli wars during, 1, 5, 27; peacekeeping efforts during, 196, 235, 243

Cole, Juan, 215

colonialism, 61–62, 85, 87, 461, 468; Israeli settler, 89, 102, 103, 110–11

colonization, Israeli, of Palestine, 59, 69, 98–99, 434, 436, 439, 443

Commission on Human Rights, 3, 35, 69. See also Human Rights Council

Committee on Inalienable Rights of the Palestinian People, 71n21, 98–100, 414

Committee to Protect Journalists, 221

communism, 302, 305. See also Cold War, Soviet Union

Comoros, 256

Compensation Commission, 198–99, 289, 299n33

Conference on Grade and Development (1964), 10

Conference on Law of the Sea, 414

Conference on Sustainable Development, 502n20

Congo, 5, 215, 235–37, 247

Consolidated Appeal Processes, 377

Convention on the Elimination of Discrimination Against Women the (CEDAW), 256, 257, 494; Committee on, 262, 264, 265

Convention Relating to Status of Refugees, 311, 337–39, 356n9

Convention on the Rights of the Child (CRC), 256, 257, 494; Committee on, 262, 264, 265

Convention against Torture (CAT), 256–58; Committee of, 263, 264

Copts, 32

Corm, George, 394

Correll, Hans, 297n13

Council of Europe, Committee on Migration, Refugees and Displaced Persons, 223

Council on Foreign Relations, 418

Council for Namibia, 99

counterterrorism, 128, 131, 132, 154, 266, 412, 441. See also war on terror

Coutts, Adam, 382

Crimea, 170, 186, 189

Crocker, Ryan, 345

Cuba, 297n10
Cuban missile crisis, 53n20
Cyprus, 291, 400

Da'esh. *See* Islamic State
Daily Zaman, 76
Da'na, Seif, 106
Darfur, 48, 215, 238, 348
D'Argent, Pierre, 198
Dayton Forces, 105
Decent Work concept, 451–52
Declaration for the Establishment of a New
    International Economic Order, 10
Declaration on Granting Independence to
    Colonial Countries and Peoples, 61
Declaration on the Right to Development,
    269
decolonization, 1, 61, 102
Delaunay, Sophie, 384n1
Democratic Republic of Congo. *See* Congo
Department of Peacekeeping Operations,
    236
Diamond, Larry, 184–85
Dinka people, 239
Disengagement Observer Force, 2, 29
displacement, 6, 383, 399, 434. *See also*
    resettlement; of Iraqis, 335–36, 342; of
    Palestinians, 96, 112n14, 312, 334; of
    Syrians, 359–63, 368
divestment, 89–91, 100, 107
Division for Palestinian Rights, 98
Doctors without Borders, *see* Médecins
    Sans Frontières (MSF)
Doha Agreement, 150, 162–64, 191
double-tap strikes, 218
Doucet, Lyse, 318
Douste-Blazy, Philippe, 161
Dubai, 306
Duffield, Mark, 460
Dugard, John, 76, 77, 86, 87, 91
Dutch Disease, 395

Earth Summit (1992), 482
East Timor, 240–41, 438
Eban, Abba, 27, 52n18
Eckel, Jan, 71n17
Economic Commission for Africa, 401
Economic Commission for Europe, 401

Economic Commission for Latin America
    and the Caribbean, 401
economic development, 4, 10, 185, 238, 390,
    415, 450, 490. *See also* Economic and
    Social Commission for West Asia;
    peacebuilding and peacekeeping and,
    440–42, 460–61
Economic and Social Commission for Asia
    and the Pacific, 401
Economic and Social Commission for West
    Africa, 269
Economic and Social Commission for
    West Asia (ESCWA), 17, 389–90,
    399–405, 413, 484; *Arab Integration*
    report, 392, 399, 401–5, 419
Economic and Social Council, 99, 255, 259,
    411, 413, 483, 499n1, 500n3; Committee
    on, 262
Ecuador, 297n10
education, 95, 133, 160, 292, 474 *See also*
    United Nations Educational, Scientific
    and Cultural Organization, United
    Nations Relief and Works Agency;
    development and, 390, 395, 398, 401,
    402; nongovernmental and civil society
    organizations' role in, 262, 264, 266,
    494–95, 497; refugee crises concerns
    about, 350–51, 354, 361–62, 365–66
Egypt, 79, 88, 185, 224, 235, 389, 425. *See*
    also Suez Crisis; civil society organiza-
    tions in, 483–84, 486, 495; coup of 2013
    in, 88, 404; human rights violations in,
    263, 268, 501n18; Israeli peace treaty
    with, 171; labor unions in, 396, 485,
    490; Palestinian refugees in, 302, 332,
    338; secretaries general and, 23–29, 32,
    33, 36, 42, 43; social and economic
    development in, 392–94, 396, 400, 402;
    during Syrian crisis, 360, 361, 365;
    United States alliance with, 104–5, 173
Einsiedel, Sebastian von, 173
Eisenhower, Dwight D., 24, 50
Eitel, Tono, 287
Elaraby, Nabil, 121
Epstein, Charlotte, 148
Erdoğan, Recep Ayyip, 183
Eritrea, 232
Erlanger, Steven, 141n31

Ethiopia, 232, 238
ethnic cleansing, 89, 109, 212, 328
European Commission, 323, 358n28, 437
European Community Parliament, 404
European Union (EU), 189, 330, 402, 436–38, 473, 503n34. *See also* Quartet; during Lebanon Civil War, 153, 158, 160; in Middle East peace process, 36, 37, 415, 417; Syria crisis response of, 115, 122, 128, 130
Evans, Gareth, 214
expression, freedom of, 497

Fakhri, Michael, 497
Falk, Richard, 3, 7, 14, 15, 18n8, 92n9, 93n16, 94n24,n27,n29, 164n1
Fatah, 103, 104, 108, 421
Fayyad, Ali, 163
Fayyad, Salam, 419, 421, 437
Feldman, Ilana, 2
First Gulf War. *See* Gulf War
Foley, James, 344
Food and Agricultural Organization, 291
"Forensic Oceanography" report, 222–23
Fouad, Fouad, 382
France, 97, 122, 171, 232, 243, 374, 438, 477n16. *See also* P5; Iraq no-fly zone air strikes by, 205, 210n38, 287; during Lebanon civil war, 153, 154, 160, 162, 166n34; Libya opposition supported by, 224; in Suez Crisis, 24, 231; United Nations Interim Force in Lebanon role of, 462, 466, 468, 473
Fréchette, Louise, 281, 290, 292
Freedom Flotilla, 89
Free Officers Revolution, 393
Free Syrian Army (FSA), 121
free trade, 402, 511
Friedman, Thomas, 399

Gaddafi, Muammar. *See* Qaddafi, Muammar
Gaza, 2–3, 16, 59, 61, 97, 101–5, 440–42; Israeli "disengagement" from, 85, 93n14, 103, 435; obstacles to economic growth in, 4, 436, 440–42; Palestinian refugees deported from, 33, 112n14; secretaries general and, 24, 36, 40–42, 51n1, 56n57;

United Nations Relief and Works Agency in, 301, 305–307, 309, 315n9, 319, 321, 324, 328, 331, 334, 337, 348, 412, 413; war crimes and human rights violations in, 14, 76–79, 84–88, 103, 105, 109–10, 171
G-8 Summit, 157
Geiss, Robin, 220
General Agreement on Tariffs and Trade, 393
General Assembly, 2, 8, 15, 60, 355n2, 415, 500n4, 502n25; delegates of Arab states to, 58, 269; development program role of, 400, 411, 417, 425; Human Rights Council special rapporteur and, 83, 89, 90; Occupied Palestinian Territories concerns of, 61–62, 65, 71n21, 97–102, 112n14; Palestine as nonmember participant in, 84, 95, 98, 108, 413; Palestinian refugee resolutions of, 302–4, 308–9, 313, 320; partition of Palestine approved by, 1, 22, 85–86; peacekeeping missions and, 242, 243, 246, 466; secretaries general and, 25–27, 33, 35, 44, 53n18, 54n43; during Syrian crisis, 122, 125
General Union of Palestinian Students, 104
Geneva Communiqué, 123–24, 139n8, 143n42
Geneva Conventions, 63, 98, 107, 113n30, 217, 218, 220, 222
geopolitics, 5–7, 10, 84, 231, 233, 247, 472–75. *See also* hegemony; Israeli impunity from, 90, 91, 160; post-Cold War, 194, 207; United Nations constrained by, 6, 7, 74, 87, 92n1, 302, 411; of United Nations Relief and Works Agency funding, 302, 324
George VI, King of England, 232
Germany, 28, 160, 214, 244, 438; Nazi, 77, 87
Ghoga, Abdelhafed, 224
Global Compact, 485
Global Government, 12–13
globalization, 10, 409, 416–17, 421, 436, 496
Global Security, 210n40
Global South, 391, 393
Golan Heights, 29, 30, 61, 64, 85, 112n14
Goldstein, Baruch, 33

Goldstone Commission, 14, 59, 86–87, 107
Goodman, Peter S., 138n1
Gorbachev, Mikhail, 172, 201
Gordon, Michael R., 140n13
Goulding, M., 316n25
Gowan, Richard, 243
Grandi, Filippo, 362
Greater Middle East Initiative, 398
Great Recession, 391
Greece, 364
Green Line, 103
Greenstock, Jeremy, 182
Grieger, Wolfgang, 100, 114n36
Griffin, David Ray, 77
Group of 77 (G77), 10, 71n17, 394, 496
Guardian, 224
Gulf Cooperation Council (GCC), 101, 115, 137, 256, 456, 457; Human Rights Declaration of, 267–68
Gulf War, 51n1, 173–74, 179, 280. *See also* Kuwait, Iraqi invasion of; Security Council resolutions related to, 195–200; United States-led coalition in, 5, 101, 149, 170, 188, 196
Guterres, António, 342, 359

Habib, Philip, 29–30
Habitat International Coalition, Housing and Land Rights Network, 99
Haddad, Major Saad, 29
Hadi, Abd Rabbuh Mansur, 43
Hafiz, Yasin al-, 393
Hague Special Ad Hoc International Tribunal for the Former Yugoslavia, 86
Hain, Peter, 289
Haiti, 139n11, 298n21
Halliday, Denis, 278, 100n42
Ham, General Carter F., 215
Hamas, 41, 86, 89, 108, 151, 157, 441; Annan's position on, 37, 40, 55n46; in Gaza, 36, 85, 103–5; United Nations Works and Relief Agency's dealings with, 325–26
Hammarskjöld, Dag, 2, 23–25, 32, 48–51, 51n1, 52nn8,9,15, 57n74
Hariri, Rafiq, 37, 39, 152–55, 166n34, 169n85
Harman, Chris, 441
Harper, Stephen, 323

hasbara, 100, 426
Hashemite Kingdom of Jordan, 302
Hasmy, Dato Agam, 296
Hayek, Reem Al-, 364
health care systems, 103, 133, 343, 350, 385n9, 452. *See also* United Nations Relief and Works Agency; in development programs, 390, 395; during Syrian crisis, 381–83, 385n16
Heath, General Lewis, 232
Hebrew University, 86
Hebron massacre, 33
hegemony, 16, 61, 71n17, 234, 469; United States, 74, 101, 102, 147–49, 207, 396, 473
Helton, John, 141n31
Hersh, Seymour, 175
Hezbollah. *See* Hizbullah
High Level Group on Syria, 380
Hilterman, Joost, 182
Hirst, David, 150
Hitler, Adolph, 87, 212
Hizbullah, 31, 34, 36, 39, 104, 149, 151–64; in Israel-Lebanon War, 4, 37, 147–49, 155–59, 161, 163, 331, 461; UNIFIL and, 461–63, 467–69, 471; war on terror discourse on, 151–61, 163–64, 165n18, 473–76
Hofman, Michiel, 384n1
Holocaust, 87
Hoo, Victor, 2
Houthis, 43
human development, 269, 390–91, 395–98, 401, 404, 487; United Nations Relief and Works Agency framework of, 301, 308, 313, 314, 329–31
Human Development Index, 395, 397–98
human rights, 8, 3, 35, 69, 253–55, 259. *See also* Office of the High Commissioner for Human Rights, Human Rights Council; Arab initiatives for, 256, 267–68, 494; in Occupied Palestinian Territories, 62, 74–94, 260; Universal Declaration of, 60, 61, 259, 267; violations of, 43, 75–76, 85, 218, 219, 262–64, 268–70, 291, 413, 501n18
Human Rights Council (HRC), 2, 3, 74–94, 107, 271n7, 413, 494; accused

of bias against Israel, 74–81, 90–91; Commission of Inquiry on Libya report to, 225–26; engagement with Special Procedures of, 258; Ministerial Conferences and Summits, 411; in Occupied Palestinian Territory, 84–90; role and office of special rapporteur of, 81–84; Universal Periodic Review by, 255, 259–61, 263–69, 488, 493, 495, 502n25

Human Rights Watch (HRW), 80–81, 215, 217–19, 224–25

Hungary, 343, 393

IBSA, 245

identity politics, 59

imperialism, 52n15, 59, 61, 66, 150, 394, 402, 461

Independent International Commission on Kosovo, 86

India, 6, 94n24, 214, 231–49, 393. *See also* BRICS

Indo-Chinese "boat people," 344

Indonesia, 61, 240, 466

Indyk, Martin, 108

infrastructure, 390, 404, 415, 418, 436, 450; destruction of, 41, 119, 157, 160, 196, 197, 219, 279, 441; development of, 438, 440, 467, 477n12; for refugee camps and resettlement, 307, 310, 316n26, 324, 345, 353, 361–62, 365

interactive dialogue, 79, 83, 260

Inter-Agency Standing Committee, 337

International Atomic Energy Agency (IAEA), 175, 178, 199–200, 414

International Coalition for Development Action, 500n2

International Commission of Inquiry on Libya, 225–26

International Committee of the Red Cross (ICRC), 217, 220, 340, 354, 374, 376, 378–80

International Compact for Iraq, 182

International Confederation of Arab Trade Unions, 454, 459n17

International Conference on Financing for Development (2008), 483. *See also* Doha Agreement

International Convention on Elimination of Racial Discrimination (ICERD), 257

International Convention for Protection of All Persons from Enforced Disappearance (ICPPED), 257

International Convention on the Protection of the Rights of All Migrant Workers and Members of Their Families (ICRMW), 256, 257

International Court of Justice, 2, 47, 85, 95, 100, 107

International Covenant on Civil and Political Rights (ICCPR), 256, 257

International Covenant on Economic, Social and Cultural Rights (ICESCR), 256–58

International Criminal Court (ICC), 46, 80, 84, 110, 116, 119–20, 122, 128, 215, 220, 255, 485

International Crisis Group, 182

international financial institutions (IFIs), 410, 415–16, 421. *See also* Bretton Woods system

International Forum on Assistance to the Palestinian People, 419

international humanitarian law (IHL), 216–21, 224, 226, 379

internationalism, 235, 353

International Labor Organization (ILO), 9, 269, 274n35, 415, 448–59, 491; Bureau for Workers' Activities (ACTRAV), 454–57, 459n17; Constitution of, 458n3; Conventions of, 449, 457; Decent Work Country Programs of, 451

international law, 7, 69, 129–30, 147, 194, 198, 201, 254, 308; in Arab world, 394, 489; humanitarian (IHL), 216–21, 224, 226, 379; in Occupied Palestinian Territories, 84, 87, 88, 90, 91, 93n14, 99–102, 328; secretaries general and, 38, 40, 50

International Monetary Fund (IMF), 4, 416, 418, 433, 437, 438. *See also* Bretton Woods institutions; International Labor Organization and, 450–51; negative role in Global South of, 390, 393; on Palestinian economy, 419, 421

International Organization for Migration, 354

International Peace Conference on the Question of Palestine, 99

International Relief and Development, 364

International Road Transport Union, 414

International Syrian Support Group (ISSG), 39, 45–46, 143n42

International Trade Union Confederation, 454–56

Internet, 263, 398, 403

intifada, 31, 36, 67, 101, 309, 313, 317n30; second, 103, 329–30, 410, 417–19, 422, 435, 438, 440–41

Iran, 28, 30, 80, 104, 285, 298n21, 348, 404. *See also* Iran-Iraq War, Iraq War; Hizbullah linked to Syria and, 147, 149, 151, 153, 157, 162, 478n23; human rights violations in, 85; regional influence of, 12, 116; during Syrian crisis, 118, 122, 124–25, 139nn7,14; United States nuclear negotiations with, 136

Iran-Iraq War, 31–32, 51n1, 170–72, 186, 396

Iraq, 10, 126, 139n11, 170–211, 270, 299n31, 360, 375, 404. *See also* Gulf War, Iran-Iraq War, Iraq War; in Action Group for Syria, 122; economic and human development in, 395, 399, 400; human rights violations in, 263; Islamic State in, 42, 48, 119, 131, 170–71, 183–84; Kuwait invaded by, 31, 35, 42, 170, 172–73, 175, 186, 194–200, 202, 205, 278, 280, 289, 295, 306; no-fly-zones in, 204–5; peacebuilding in, 181–83; refugees from, 335–58; sanctions against, 175–76, 202–4, 206, 278–300; secretaries general and, 24, 30, 34, 48; Syrian refugees in, 133, 361, 372; weapons inspections in, 175, 178, 200–203; workers' rights in, 458n4

Iraqi Governing Council, 180, 181

Iraq War, 5–7, 12, 16, 118, 120, 157, 166n34, 178–81, 188, 207; aftermath of, 7, 129, 151; Bush administration unilateralism in, 178–79, 184, 240; sanctions preceding, 278, 280–81, 295; secretaries general during, 38–39, 50, 51n1;

Security Council members opposed to, 155n34, 178–79, 189, 202

Islam, 267–68, 456, 501n15. *See also* Muslims

Islamic State (ISIS/ISIL), 5, 12, 43, 131, 183; in Iraq, 42, 48, 119, 131, 170–71, 183–84; in Syria, 116, 118, 119, 126–28, 134, 136, 142–43n40

Islamism, 118, 150, 305, 309, 404, 487

Ismail, Ali and Mohammad, 464

Israel, 25, 99, 185, 260, 314, 396, 412, 420–27. *See also* Arab-Israeli wars, Israel-Lebanon War, Occupied Palestinian Territory; Arab development impeded by, 402–4, 414–15; borders of, 2, 119, 389, 477n16; boycotts against, 89–90, 107, 404; Oslo Accords bilateral framework for Palestine and, 416, 417, 421; Palestinian citizens of, 104; partition of Palestine and creation of, 10, 22–23, 58, 85, 96, 231, 390, 392; propaganda of, 24, 100, 426–27; secretaries general and, 22–28, 31–42, 50–51, 53nn18,26, 54n43, 57n74; United Nations Interim Force in Lebanon and, 462, 464, 469–76; United Nations Relief and Works Agency criticized by, 301, 305, 316n24, 328; war crimes and human rights violations allegations against, 14, 76–79, 84–88, 103, 105, 109–10, 171

Israel-Lebanon War, 3–4, 37, 147–69, 331, 461

Issa, Perla, 357n21

Issam Fares Institute for Public Policy and International Affairs, 485

Italy, 160, 224, 232, 462, 466, 468, 473

Jadid, Salah, 393

Jamālī, Muhammad Fādil al-, 58

Japan, 128, 323

Jayadev, Arjun, 396

Jerusalem, 22, 53n20, 77, 85, 107, 413, 414, 417; East, 61, 84, 93n14, 104, 109, 314

Jewish National Fund, 109

Jews, 349; accused of anti-Semitism, 80, 86–87; national homeland for. *See* Israel; Nazi persecution of, 77, 87

Jihad, Abu, 101

Jordan, 5, 12, 79, 109, 177, 303, 347; human
rights violations in, 262; Iraqi refugees
in, 181, 339–42, 345, 372; Israeli peace
treaty with, 171; Palestinian refugees in,
97, 301, 302, 306, 307, 315nn9,18, 319,
320, 322, 326, 332, 337, 348; secretaries
general and, 23–25, 28; in Six-Day War,
85; social and economic development in,
399, 400; during Syrian crisis, 119, 133,
134, 352–53, 360, 361, 364–67, 375;
United States alliance with, 104;
workers' rights in, 449, 454–55,
458n4, 459n14, 490

Jordanian Labour Watch, 459n15

July 14th Revolution, 393

Kadafi, Muammar. See Qaddafi, Muammar

Kakais, 349

Kashmir, 94n24

Kennedy, John F., 53n20

Kenya, 234

Keren, Battle of, 232

Kerry, John, 40, 94n26, 108, 124, 130,
140n12, 438

Khadafy, Muammar. See Qaddafi,
Muammar

Khalidi, Rashid, 438

Khallaf, Shaden, 377–78

Khan, Sadruddin Aga, 297

Khomeini, Ayatollah Ruhollah, 171

Khouri, Rami, 376

Kiir, Salva, 239, 240

King, Martin Luther, Jr., 234

Kirkpatrick, David, 215

Kissinger, Henry, 29

Kobler, Martin, 43

Korean War, 5, 196

Kosovo, 86, 188, 439

Kostyshak, Scott, 395, 398

Krishna, S.M., 245

Krugman, Paul, 442

Kuperman, Alan, 214–16

Kurdistan Regional Government, 42, 342

Kurds, 180, 182, 284, 287, 293–95, 338–40;
Islamic State resistance of, 183; no-fly-
zone established in reaction to repression of, 204; Oil-for-Food program for,

285, 295; post-Desert Storm rebellion
of, 174; resettlement of, 348; in Syria,
118, 126

Kuwait, 46, 122, 210n38, 262, 324, 400,
458n4; Iraqi invasion of, 31, 35, 42, 101,
170, 172–73, 175, 186, 194–200, 202,
205, 278, 280, 289, 295, 306. See also
Gulf War

labor movements, 453, 454, 485, 491

Lahoud, Emile, 152, 153, 155

Landmine Convention, 485

Lao refugees, 342

Latti al Obedi, Abdal al, 245

Lavrov, Sergey, 124, 300n47

League of Arab Peoples, 404

League of Arab States. See Arab League

League of Nations, 1, 10, 21, 85; Permanent
Mandates Commission of, 59, 96

Lebanese Armed Forces (LAF), 463–65,
473

Lebanon, 12, 16, 97, 126, 139n11, 171. See
also United Nations Interim Force in
Lebanon, Israel-Lebanon War; during
Bush administration, 104; civil society
organizations in, 483–85, 494; civil war
in, 180, 462; Economic and Social
Commission for West Asia in, 399, 400,
413–14; Iraqi refugees in, 339, 341, 342,
345, 347; Palestinian refugees in, 152,
301–4, 307, 311, 312, 315nn9,20, 319–20,
326, 331–34, 337, 348, 462; secretaries
general and, 24–25, 31, 33–35, 36–39, 48,
51n1, 57n74; during Syrian crisis, 119,
133, 353, 360, 361, 365, 372, 375; workers'
rights in, 262, 449, 458n4, 490

Levant, 393, 404, 450. See also modern
nations historically included in

Liberia, 298n21

Libya, 16, 42, 170, 186, 189, 212–30, 400;
collapse of Qaddafi regime in, 43, 120;
human rights violations in, 263, 270;
NATO intervention in, 6–7, 80,
214–26, 244–45; Responsibility to
Protect in, 6, 246; Security Council
resolutions on, 212–14; United Nations
mission in, 12, 15

Libyan Arab Jamahiriya, 213, 220, 221

Lie, Trygve, 21–23, 48, 50, 51, 51n1
London Conference (1946), 58
Lugar, Richard, 398

Machar, Riek, 239
Madrid Peace Conference (1991), 31, 101, 410, 415, 417
Makdisi, Karim, 18n8, 164n1, 167n54, 169n78, 477n13,n15, 478n17,n20,n21,n22,n23
Malaya, 234
Malaysia, 296, 297n10, 465
Maliki, Nouri al-, 42
Malloch Brown, Lord Mark, 189–90
Mandeans, 349, 350
Mann, Michael, 150
Maoism, 246
Marr, Phebe, 185
Marton, Kati, 52n6
Marxism, 394
Mauritania, 257
Mavromatis, Andreas, 291
Mazower, Mark, 10, 13, 18n10, 70n7,n8, 71n15
Médecins Sans Frontières (MSF), 12, 225, 372–83, 385n16
Mehlis, Detlev, 154
Meir, Gideon, 157
Meir, Golda, 28, 157
Millennium Declaration (2000), 491
Millennium Development Goals (MDGs), 484, 491–94, 498, 502n20
Millennium Summit (2000), 482; Outcome Document of, 269
Mission for the Referendum in Western Sahara (MINURSO), 46–47
Mistura, Staffan de, 7, 126–27, 141n42, 299n35
Mitchell effort, 40
Mitri, Tarek, 15
Mkandawire, Thandika, 396
Mladenov, Nickolay, 40
Monde, Le, 380
Monitoring, Verification and Inspections Commission, 299n33
Morocco, 46–47, 258, 400, 484
Morsi, Mohamed, 43
Mozambique, 235

Mubarak, Hosni, 42, 104, 105
multilateralism, 342, 390, 413, 415, 427, 486; in peacebuilding, 431, 436–39
Muslims, 62, 150, 188, 231, 349, 356n8, 397, 501n15

Nakba, 4, 306, 392–93, 409, 437, 409
Namibia, 99
Nasrallah, Hassan, 154
Nasser, Gamal Abdel, 24–27, 52n15, 393, 402
National Democratic Institute, 181
nationalism, 83, 305, 393; Arab, 52n15, 67, 394, 404, 421–22
Nehru, Jawaharlal, 235
neoconservatives, 152, 154, 157, 163, 398
neoliberalism, 391, 396, 404, 411, 420–23, 451; in peacebuilding, 430, 432–33, 437, 440, 442
Nepal, 466
Nesirky, Martin, 139n7
Netanyahu, Benjamin, 41
Neuer, Hillel, 79
neutrality, 49, 58, 127, 152, 172, 375, 383; of United Nations Relief and Works Agency, 321, 325–27, 333
New International Economic Order (NIEO), 394, 401, 500n2
New York Times, The, 41, 78, 215, 218
NGO Monitor, 92n2
Nobel Peace Prize, 2, 23, 35, 412
no-fly zones, 115, 128, 174, 204, 210n38, 214–15, 244, 287
No Lost Generation, 366
Nonaligned Movement (NAM), 10, 62, 235, 241–47, 393, 402
nonconventional warfare, 147, 199–200, 203. See also chemical weapons, weapons of mass destruction
Non-governmental Liaison Service, 484
nongovernmental organizations (NGOs), 11, 75, 259, 268–69, 481–503; Arab countries' restrictions on, 264, 398, 481; humanitarian, 373–80; human rights and, 74–76, 254, 255, 263–66; in peace process, 99–100, 103; pro-Israeli, 75, 76, 79–81, 85–86, 90, 92nn2,11; refugee program partnerships of, 310, 366–67

North Atlantic Treaty Organization
(NATO), 15, 159, 160, 188, 212–29,
299n41, 477n12; Libya intervention of,
6–7, 80, 214–26, 244–45
North Korea, 40
Norway, 323
Nuer people, 233, 239

Obama, Barack, 75, 88, 129–30, 141n31, 163,
179, 216, 218, 224
Occupied Palestinian Territory (OPT),
61–62, 404, 410, 447n53, 484, 486,
488. *See also* Gaza; West Bank;
human rights concerns in, 62, 74–94,
260; Oslo peace process and, 98,
101–6, 409; Palestinian refugees in,
309–14, 317n30, 320; peacebuilding in,
430–31, 433–43; Special Committee
on, 62–69
O'Connell, Mary Ellen, 216
Office for Coordination of Humanitarian
Affairs (OCHA), 133, 282, 291, 297n14,
299n35, 418–19, 426; Syria crisis
response of, 378–81, 383, 384n9
Office of the High Commissioner for
Human Rights (OHCHR), 75–79,
81–83, 92n1, 257, 269, 493–94
Office of Iraq Program (OIP), 282, 288,
291–93, 295, 297nn14,15, 299n35
Office for Political Peace-Keeping, Human-
itarian and Human Rights, 8
Ogata, Sadako, 354
Oil-for-Food (OFF) program, 6, 176–77,
285, 286, 299n40, 335; creation of,
54n42, 176, 204; mismanagement of,
38–39, 186–88, 282–83, 288–96, 298
Olmert, Ehud, 37, 40, 156
Oman, 256, 264, 400; workers' rights in,
449, 458n4
Operation Brother's Keeper, 435
Operation Cast Lead, 78, 86, 107, 324
Operation Defensive Shield, 435
Operation Desert Fox, 175, 205, 287–88
Operation Desert Storm. *See* Gulf War
Operation Iraqi Freedom. *See* Iraq War
Operation Protective Edge, 105
Operation Provide Comfort, 338–39
Oral History Project, 15

Organization for Economic Cooperation
and Development (OECD), 414
Organization of the Islamic Conference, 213
Organization of Islamic Cooperation, 267
Organization of the Petroleum Exporting
Countries (OPEC), 172
Organization for the Prohibition of Chem-
ical Weapons (OPCW), 7–8, 131
Oslo Accords (1993), 36, 88, 96, 99–110, 427,
434–47; Committee on the Exercise of
the Inalienable Rights of the Palestinian
People condemnation of, 99–100; frame-
work of, 434–36; Palestinian participa-
tion, 101–6, 109, 415–17, 421–24, 434;
Palestinian refugee issue in, 208, 315n11,
329, 331, 431; peacebuilding in Occupied
Palestinian Territory after signing of,
426–43; secretaries general and, 32;
United Nations support of, 409, 410;
United States domination of, 3, 86, 438
Ottoman Empire, 183

Pakistan, 94n24, 232, 234, 235, 237
Palestine, 1–4, 12, 32, 136, 375, 400, 409–29,
458n4, 472. *See also* Occupied Palestinian Territory, Palestinian Authority,
Palestinian refugees; British mandate
over, 1, 21, 46, 85, 96; development in,
409–20; human rights violations in,
75–76; intifadas in, 31, 36, 67, 309, 417,
418; partition of, 10, 22–23, 58, 85, 96, 231,
390; peacebuilding in, 430–47; secretaries general and, 32, 33, 38, 40, 48, 50, 51,
54n43, 55n56, 57n74; statebuilding and
reform as survival tactics in, 420–23;
United Nations commissions' engagement with, 58–59; United Nations status
of, 8, 95–114, 270–71n10
Palestine Liberation Organization (PLO),
30, 306, 311, 411, 425, 431, 438; financial
policies of, 418, 420; General Assembly
observer status of, 97–98; mandated to
represent all Palestinians, 321, 409; Oslo
process participation of, 101–106, 109,
415–17, 421–24, 434; social and economic development pursued by, 410,
413–14; United Nations statehood bid
of, 95–96, 106–8

Palestine Papers, 103–4
Palestinian Authority (PA), 41, 84–85,
    94n26, 322, 422, 425–26, 437–43;
    Hamas and, 37, 89, 103; Higher Com-
    mission on Investment and Finance,
    418; Oslo Accord participation of, 100,
    102–6, 417, 424, 434; refugee policies
    of, 349; statehood preparedness of, 411,
    418–21; United Nations statehood bid
    of, 2, 95–96, 103–4, 106–9
Palestinian National Council, 104
Palestinian refugees, 25, 98, 112n14, 372. *See
    also* United Nations Relief and Works
    Agency; in Iraq, 348–49, 357n21; in
    Jordan, 12, 262, 301, 302, 306, 307,
    315nn9,18, 319, 320, 322, 326, 332, 337,
    348; in Lebanon, 12, 16, 152, 301–4, 307,
    311, 312, 315nn9,20, 319–20, 326, 331–34,
    337, 348, 462
Palme, Olaf, 30, 172
Pan-Arabism, 402
Paris Economic Protocol (PEP), 417, 421,
    435, 440
Paris terrorist attacks, 131–32
Pattison, James, 214
peacebuilding, 4, 147, 179, 418, 430; in
    Palestine, 316n24, 430–47
Peacebuilding Commission, 432, 433
Peacekeeping Operations, UN Department
    of, 466
peacemaking, 2, 16, 430, 434, 460. *See also*
    peacebuilding
peace process, 2, 4, 14, 98, 115, 155, 240, 420,
    467. *See also* Camp David Accords,
    Oslo Accords; secretaries general and,
    31–32, 35, 41; United Nations Relief and
    Works Agency and, 301, 311, 315n11,
    317n30, 331
Peres, Shimon, 34
Perez de Cuellar, Javier, 30–32, 46, 48, 49,
    51n1, 57nn66,67, 172, 290, 297n4
Picco, Giandomenico, 31
P5, 9–10, 12, 43, 74, 177, 188–89, 296,
    297nn10,12; divisions in, 172, 175–78,
    186–87, 280; Islamic State condemned
    by, 170–71, 183–84; in peacekeeping
    operations, 235, 242; veto power of, 8,
    15, 97, 98, 128, 129, 177, 188, 226

Pickering, Thomas, 173
Pillay, Navi, 80, 81
Polisario Front, 46, 47
political prisoners, 110, 121
Pol Pot, 212
Population Fund, 413
post-Cold War period, 2, 8, 158, 201, 430,
    460; response to Iraqi aggression in,
    172–73, 194, 205; terrorism in, 150,
    431–32; United States hegemony in, 101,
    110, 396
Power, Samantha, 79
Prashad, Vijay, 17n7, 18n11, 70n7,n8, 71n15,
    113n26, 114n36, 215, 216
Prebisch, Raul, 401
Prendergast, Kieran, 293
Program for Development of the Palestin-
    ian National Economy (PDP), 421
Program for Reform, 253
propaganda, 215, 219, 220, 288, 319; Israeli,
    24, 100, 426
Puri, Hardeep Singh, 245
Puri, Manjeev Singh, 246

Qaddafi, Muammar, 42, 80, 212, 214–16,
    222, 226, 245; collapse of regime of,
    43, 120, 216; human rights abuses
    committed by, 218, 219
Qasim, Abdel Karim, 393
Qatar, 122, 161, 163, 224, 256, 264, 267,
    400; worker's rights in, 449, 456, 457,
    458n4
Quartet, 36–37, 40, 55n46, 417, 438
Quick Impact Projects (QIPs), 461–63,
    466–69, 471, 473–75
Qurie, Ahmad, 421

Rabin, Yitzhak, 33, 54n39, 86
racism, 33, 66, 98
Rafsanjani, Akbar Hashemi, 31
Rajagopal, Balakrishnan, 394
Ram, Richhpal, 232
Ramlawi, Nabil, 424
Rauch, James, 395, 398
realpolitik, 60, 100, 103, 186
Red Crescent, 375, 379
Red Cross. *See* International Committee of
    the Red Cross

Regional Refugee and Resilience Plan
(3RP), 354, 362, 363, 365
Republican Party, 141n31
resettlement, 342–43, 349–50, 356n8,
357nn20; of Iraqi refugees, 336, 339,
341–48, 350–51, 357n23; of Palestinian
refugees, 97, 303, 305, 348–49, 392; of
Syrian refugees, 352–55, 362, 366–67
Respect for Implementation of Human
Rights in Occupied Territories, Resolu-
tion on, 62
Responsibility to Protect (R2P) doctrine, 6,
15, 244–46
Rhodesia, 5
Rice, Condoleezza, 40, 159–60
Rice, Susan, 79
Roadmap for Peace, 36–37, 438, 440–42
Roed-Larsen, Terje, 35, 154, 163, 410
Rome Statute, 110, 220
Roosevelt, Franklin D., 60
Roth, Ken, 81
Rouhani, Hassan, 125
Rovera, Donatella, 225
Rowswell, Ben, 181
Rubin, James, 32
Rudd, Kevin, 140n17
Russia, 6, 185, 205, 237, 286. See also BRICS
P5, Quartet, Soviet Union; interference
in internal matters of state opposed by,
153, 190, 213; during Syria crisis, 7–8, 45,
116, 118, 119, 122, 124, 125, 128–30, 132
Rwanda, 32, 133, 215
Ryngaert, Cédric, 379

Sadat, Anwar, 32
Saddam Hussein, 141n31, 172, 185, 210n31,
279, 287, 293; invasion of Kuwait by, 101,
278; Oil-for-Food program and, 54n42,
283, 285, 296; overthrow of, 120, 177,
188, 203, 207; refugees from regime of,
340, 345; weapons inspections
obstructed by, 35, 175, 202
Sahrawi refugees, 37, 38
Salam, Nawaf, 15
Saleh, Ali Abdullah, 43
Samed, 421
sanctions, 5, 55n46, 212–13, 266, 298n21, 335,
340; on Iraq, 5–6, 170, 172–73, 175–77,

182, 186–89, 199–204, 206–7,
209nn25,31, 278–96, 300n44; on
Israel, 52n6, 89, 100, 107; on Syria, 123,
128–29, 135
Sangqu, Baso, 219
Sangwan, Subahdar Dharmesh, 233
Sarkozy, Nicolas, 224
Saudi Arabia, 44, 152, 210n38, 256, 258, 324;
human development in, 399, 400;
human rights violations in, 263, 501n18;
regional influence of, 12, 42, 88; during
Syria crisis, 45, 118–20, 122, 127; work-
ers' rights in, 449, 456, 457, 458n4
Sauerbrey, Ellen, 345
Save the Children, 366
Schabas, William, 87
Schechla, Joseph, 99
Scott, James C., 469
Second World War. See World War II
Secretariat, 16, 31, 174, 287, 288, 411, 425–
26. See also names of individual secretaries general; Department of Economic
and Social Affairs, 400; Department of
Political Affairs Division of Palestinian
Rights, 414; India's role expanded by,
244; during Iraq War, 6; Oil-for-Food
program mismanagement by, 38–39,
186–88, 282, 288–91, 296; tensions
within and between Security Council
and, 279–81; voluntary contributions
appeals of, 279
Security Council, 1–3, 10, 147–92, 287,
297n15, 298nn26,27, 389, 478n23,
500n4; during Gulf War, 173, 196–99;
humanitarian and human rights concerns of, 69, 98, 99, 174, 298n16, 379–81,
386n26; International Tribunal for
Former Yugoslavia established by, 86;
during Iran-Iraq war, 171–72, 186;
during Iraq War, 177–85, 189; during
NATO attacks on Libya, 15, 212–15,
219–24, 226; occupation of territory
acquired by force declared illegal by, 62,
85; Oil-for-Food program and, 282, 286,
287, 289–92, 294–96, 300n44; Palestine statehood bid and, 95, 102, 108–10,
113n30; Palestinian development programs supported by, 411, 413, 415;

Security Council (*continued*)
peacekeepers deployed by, 233, 235,
238–40, 244–46, 462–63, 472, 476;
permanent members of. *See* P5; refugee
concerns addressed by, 309–10, 338–39,
354; sanctions imposed by, 172–73, 195,
200–207, 209n29, 278–81, 284, 298n21;
secretaries general and, 22, 23, 27–38,
40, 41, 45–47, 50, 56n62; during Syrian
crisis, 117, 122, 124, 127–32, 134, 137,
142nn33,37, 379–81; use of force authorized by, 5, 7, 157–58, 173; weapons
inspections required by, 175–77,
199–200
self-determination, Palestinian, 3, 59, 67,
88, 95, 105–8; inalienable right to,
85–86, 96, 98; Oslo Accords as detri-
ment to, 100, 102, 105
Senegal, 71n21
September 11, 2001, terrorist attacks (9/11),
77, 79, 150, 177, 197, 431
Serbia, 188
Serry, Robert, 40, 420
Sevan, Benon, 288, 299n35
Seynes, Philippe de, 400
Shabaks, 181
Shalgam, Abdel Rahman, 212
Shapiro, Adam, 357n21
Shariah, 267–68
Sharm el-Sheikh summit, 36
Shiites, 42, 180, 287, 341, 463, 467
Shlaim, Avi, 434
Sierra Leone, 235
Simon, Joel, 221
Sinai Peninsula, 24, 26, 30, 112n14, 303
Singh, Subahdar Kanwar Pal, 233
Singh, Sushant, 243
Siniora, Fouad, 157, 160, 163
Sisi, Abdel Fattah al-, 43, 104, 404
Sistani, Grand Ayatollah, 42
Six-Day War (1967), 26, 27, 112n14, 355n4,
400
661 Sanctions Committee, 172–73, 187–88
Social Development Summit (1995), 482
social safety nets, 279, 307, 451, 452
Social Watch, 492
Solana, Javier, 36
Solomon, Erika, 138n1

Somalia, 32, 34, 62, 71n21, 235, 256, 356n8,
384n1
Soto, Alvaro de, 55n46, 420
South Africa, 62, 76–78, 87, 99, 139n11, 219,
244–46. *See also* BRICS
South Korea, 39, 40, 128
South Sudan, 231–33, 235–41, 377
Soviet Union, 23, 28, 29, 49, 52n15, 395. *See
also* Cold War; collapse of, 5, 416–17,
432
Spain, 160, 162, 223, 462, 463, 466, 468,
473, 479n34
Special Committee on Apartheid, 99
Special Committee to Investigate Israeli
Practices Affecting the Human Rights
of the Population of Occupied Territo-
ries, 62–69, 99
Special Procedures, 255, 258, 268–69
Sri Lanka, 62
steadfastness (*sumud*), 87, 333–34, 419, 420
Steinhauser, Paul, 141n31
Stockholm Conference on the Human
Environment, 499n2
Stokes, Christopher, 225
Strik, Tineke, 223
Sudan, 9, 48, 231–33, 235, 247, 256, 349,
358n8, 400, 494
Sudan People's Liberation Movement/
Army (SPLM/A), 238–40
Suez Crisis, 2, 15, 24, 52n15, 231, 393
Sunnis, 42, 118–19, 127, 131, 181
Sustainable Development Goals, 493,
502n20
Sweden, 323
Switzerland, 323
Sykes-Picot Agreement, 184
Syria, 7, 16, 173, 177, 185, 263, 449, 478n23.
See also Golan Heights, Syrian refugees;
Arab nationalism in, 393–95, 404;
chemical weapons in, 7–9, 129, 141n33,
184; civil society organizations in,
494–95; civil war in, 39, 44–46, 48, 50,
56n64, 115–43, 270, 183, 331, 335, 372, 373,
376–83, 389; human rights violations in,
262–64; Iraqi refugees in, 181, 340, 341,
345, 347, 352; during Israel-Lebanon
War, 147, 149, 151–55, 157, 160, 162,
166n34; Palestinian refugees in, 97,

301–4, 312, 318–21, 325, 330, 334, 337, 348, 412; secretaries general and, 23, 25, 28, 29, 36, 37, 41; Security Council discord over, 170, 186, 189; United States policy toward, 104, 179

Syria Accountability and Lebanese Sovereignty Restoration Act (2003), 151

Syrian National Coalition, Aid Coordination Unit (ACU) of, 382

Syrian National Council, 121

Syrian refugees, 11, 12, 336, 353–55, 358n28, 359–72, 378

Taif Agreement, 180, 475

Taithe, Bernard, 376

TEAM International, 413–14

Tennessee Valley Authority, 392

terrorism, 29, 105, 180, 189, 240, 399. *See also* Al Qaeda, counterterrorism, Islamic State; Hizbullah identified by Western states with, 149, 151, 152, 161, 473; secretary generals' responses to, 36, 42, 44, 50–51, 56n64; United Nations Relief and Works Agency accused of supporting, 309, 325

Thant, U, 25–28, 30, 49, 51n1, 53nn18,20

Third World, 9, 68, 150, 233, 401, 405. *See also* Nonaligned Movement; identity politics of, 59–61, 66, 71n17

Third World Coalition, 394

Time magazine, 398

torture, 44, 60, 63–65, 121, 258, 260, 347, 454; nongovernmental organizations concerned with, 224–25, 254, 264

Transitional Administrative Law (2004), 180–81

Traub, James, 184

tripartism, 448–49, 452, 457, 491

Tripartite Aggression. *See* Suez Crisis

troop contributing countries (TCCs), 231, 463, 466, 468

Truce Supervision Organization, 2

Truman, Harry S., 392

Tueini, Ghassan, 15

Tunisia, 42, 120, 391, 400, 483, 485, 486

Turkey, 80, 97, 183, 339, 210n38, 395; Oil-for-Food program and, 177, 285; during Syrian crisis, 116, 118, 119, 121, 122, 126, 129, 381; Syrian refugees in, 133, 353, 360–62, 372

Turkmen, 42

two-state solution, 22, 36, 40, 41, 48, 88, 108, 420

Uganda, 343

Ukraine, 50, 246

unilateralism, 40–41, 47, 158, 181, 202, 206, 221; Israeli, 88–89, 103, 159, 321, 409, 435; of United States-led, 129, 136, 174, 175, 177, 184, 188

Union of Soviet Socialist Republics (USSR). *See* Soviet Union

United Arab Emirates (UAE), 256, 258, 263, 375, 400; workers' rights in, 449, 456, 457, 458n4

United Arab Republic, 25, 27, 393

United Kingdom (UK), 177, 213, 299nn35,41, 323, 359, 393, 438. *See also* P5; India and, 237, 243; during Iran-Iraq War, 171; in Iraq War coalition with United States. *See* Iraq War; Libyan opposition supported by, 224; in military operations against Iraq during 1990s, 175, 204–5, 210n38, 287–88, 298nn27,29; relaxation of sanctions opposed by, 284–89, 294; secretaries general and, 24–25, 27–28, 37; during Syrian crisis, 122, 130, 141n31

United Nations Assistance Mission for Afghanistan (UNAMA), 182

United Nations Assistance Mission for Iraq (UNAMI), 179–83

United Nations Charter, 2, 99, 157, 185, 190, 242, 290, 500n3; fundamental principles of, 279, 287n26, 375; human rights system mechanisms established under, 255; objectives contained in, 16; secretaries general and, 48–50; Security Council's powers set out in Chapter VII of, 42, 161, 172, 183, 191n14, 194–211, 214; universal human values invoked in, 60; unlawful use of aggressive force in violation of, 216

United Nations Children's Emergency Fund (UNICEF) 9, 11, 281, 289, 291, 366, 413, 582

United Nations Conciliation Commission on Palestine (UNCCP), 97, 314n6

United Nations Conference on Trade and Development (UNCTAD), 390–91, 483, 484, 491, 495–99, 503n34; in Palestinine, 413–15, 417–20, 424–26; Third World and Nonaligned movements and, 391, 393–94

United Nations Development Program (UNDP), 291, 390, 391, 415, 433, 455, 497; Arab Human Development Reports commissioned by, 14–15, 253, 392, 397–99, 402; civil society organization operational cooperation with, 482, 484, 490; in Palestine, 410, 413–15, 417, 418, 426, 437; Syrian crisis response of, 354, 363

United Nations Economic and Social Office in Beirut (UNESOB), 400

United Nations Economic Survey Mission for the Middle East (Survey Mission Report, 1949), 392, 399, 406n9

United Nations Educational, Scientific and Cultural Organization (UNESCO), 9, 220, 281, 291, 413, 415; human rights concerns of, 263, 269; operational cooperation of civil society organizations and, 282

United Nations Emergency Force (UNEF), 2, 15, 24, 26, 29, 53n18

United Nations High Commissioner for Refugees (UNHCR), 3, 97, 143n44, 222, 383, 390, 482; Comprehensive Plan of Action of, 342; Iraq refugee operation and, 335–58; in Jordan, 5, 134; registration of refugees with, 133; Statute of, 311, 337, 355n2; during Syrian crisis, 360–63, 366, 367, 378

United Nations Hybrid Operation in Darfur (UNAMID), 238

United Nations Industrial Development Organization (UNIDO), 413, 417

United Nations Interim Force in Lebanon (UNIFIL), 2, 4, 29, 37, 39, 156, 160, 162, 389, 460–80. See also Blue Line, Quick Impact Projects

United Nations Interim Security Force for Abyei (UNISFA), 237, 238

United Nations Mission in South Sudan (UNMISS), 233, 237–38

United Nations Mission in Sudan (UNMIS), 238

United Nations Monitoring and Verification Commission (UNMOVIC), 178, 186

United Nations Office on Drugs and Crime, 269

United Nations Office of Humanitarian Coordinator for Iraq (UNOHCI), 283, 291, 299n33

United Nations Relief and Works Agency (UNRWA), 2, 3, 301–34, 392, 419, 426, 437; community participation in, 308–11; criticism of, 327–29; educational system of, 305–6, 326; funding of, 321–25; human development practices of, 329–31; Infrastructure and Camp Improvement Program (ICIP), 316n26; institutional and operational development of, 303–53; interaction of Office of High Commissioner for Refugees and, 337–38; levels of dependency on, 306–8; mandate of, 97, 112n14, 302–3, 330, 348, 359, 412; in Occupied Palestinian Territory, 325–27, 410, 413–14; protection of refugees by, 311–13; secretaries general and, 25, 33; sustainability of, 331–33; in Syria, 142n37, 318–20, 325, 331, 334, 412

United Nations Special Commission (UNSCOM), 175–76, 186, 187, 199–200, 205, 299n33

United Nations Special Committee on Palestine (UNSCOP), 58, 59

United Nations Special Coordinator Office for the Middle East Peace Process, 410, 437

United States, 7–9, 98, 111, 240, 243, 393, 401, 474. See also Cold War, Gulf War, Iraq War, Oslo Accords, P5, Quartet; on Conciliation Committee on Palestine, 97; development programs and, 402, 414, 425; hegemony of, 74, 101, 102, 147–49, 207, 396, 473; Human Rights Council special rapporteur opposed by, 74–75, 79–81, 86, 87, 89,

91, 92n2; during Iran-Iraq War, 171; Iran nuclear negotiations with, 136; Iraq sanctions supported by, 175–77, 203–4, 286, 289, 298n23, 299n35; during Israel-Lebanon War, 150–54, 157, 159, 161–63; Libya intervention participation of, 213, 216, 224; National Security Strategy (NSS) of, 151, 177–78; no-fly zones enforced by, 204–5, 210n38, 287–88, 298nn27,29; Palestinian statehood bid opposed by, 95–96, 106–9; peacebuilding activities of, 434, 436–38, 440; peacekeeping mission involvement of, 231, 237, 461; refugee programs supported by, 302, 304, 309, 323, 325, 356, 358, 365; resettlement of refugees in, 344–46, 350–52, 356n14, 415; secretaries general and, 22–25, 29–34, 36–42, 45, 49; during Syrian crisis, 118, 119, 122, 124, 125, 128–30, 132, 136–37, 140n13, 141n31, 184; terrorist attacks on, 77, 79, 150, 177, 197, 431

Uniting for Peace resolution, 15

Universal Declaration of Human Rights (UDHR), 60, 61, 259, 267; Committee on, 263

Universal Postal Union, 414

UN Watch, 75, 79–81, 92nn2,11

Urquhart, Brian, 26, 27, 29, 53n18,n19

use of force, 64, 177–78, 195, 205, 235, 460. See also specific interventions and wars; Security Council resolutions authorizing, 5, 7, 157–58, 173

van der Stoel, Max, 290–91, 299n34

Veolia Environment S.A., 107

Versailles Treaty, 402

Vieira de Mello, Sergio, 6, 52n9, 179–81, 297n14, 299n35

Vietnamese refugees, 342

Volcker, Paul, 39

Volcker Report, 186

Waldheim, Kurt, 28–30, 49, 50, 51n1, 57n66, 172

war crimes, 14, 107, 120, 122, 212, 220. See also torture

war on terror, 3, 6, 15, 147–52, 155–63, 396

Washington Consensus, 11, 390, 433

weapons of mass destruction (WMDs), 129, 136, 150–52, 175, 177–78, 184, 269. See also chemical weapons

Weiss, Thomas G., 13

West Bank, 41–42, 66, 93n14, 97, 101–5, 112n14, 423, 435 ; Annexation Wall constructed in, 89, 103, 107, 109; Human Rights Commission special rapporteur denied entry to, 77–78; human rights violations in, 84–85; intifadas in, 101, 103, 309; Israeli attacks on, 110; Israeli settlements in, 102; obstacles to economic growth in, 4, 102, 326, 440–42; Palestinians deported to Lebanon from, 33; political economy of, 436; United Nations opposition to occupation of, 61; United Nations Relief and Works Agency in, 305–7, 315n18, 319, 322, 337, 348, 412, 413

Westphalian sovereignty, 148, 158, 161, 162

Whitehead, Alfred North, 77

Wiesenthal Center, 80, 92n10

Wilkinson, Rorden, 13

Williams, Daniel, 225

workers' rights. See International Labor Organization

World Bank, 4, 182, 253, 361, 365, 398, 409, 416. See also Bretton Woods institutions; International Labour Organisation and, 450–52; negative role in global South of, 390, 393; on Palestinian economy, 409, 415, 418–20; in peacebuilding process, 433, 436–38

World Conference on Human Rights (Vienna, 1993), 253

World Food Program (WFP), 133, 134, 281, 284, 291

World Health Organization (WHO), 285, 297n3, 378, 381–82, 415

World Heritage Sites, 109

World Humanitarian Summit, 370n17

World Summit (2005), 212

World Summit for Social Development (1995), 482

World Summit on Sustainable Development (2002), 485, 492–93

World Trade Organization, 10, 417, 496

World War II, 1, 28, 232, 234; aftermath of, 21, 231, 338

Yau Yau, David, 239, 240

Yemen, 136, 297n10, 338, 349, 400, 458n4; civil war in, 12, 43–44, 270; human rights in, 263, 494

Yezidis, 349

Yom Kippur War, 28–29

Yugoslavia, 62, 71n21, 393; breakup of, 32, 57n67, 328

Zakat, 487, 501n15

Zionists, 33, 58, 81, 85, 86, 96, 98

Zoabi, Haneen, 104

Zucchino, David, 223–24

Zuckerman, Mortimer, 54n40